D1290199

Behavioral Assessment in Schools

Behavioral Assessment in Schools
Conceptual Foundations and Practical Applications

Edited by

EDWARD S. SHAPIRO, PH.D.
Lehigh University

THOMAS R. KRATOCHWILL, PH.D.
University of Wisconsin–Madison

THE GUILFORD PRESS
New York   London

© 1988 The Guilford Press
A Division of Guilford Publications, Inc.
72 Spring Street, New York, NY 10012

Printed in the United States of America

Last digit is print number: 9 8 7 6 5 4 3 2 1

Library of Congress Cataloging-in-Publication Data

Behavioral assessment in schools.

   Includes bibliographies and index.
   1. Behavioral assessment of children. I. Shapiro,
Edward S. (Edward Steven).
II. Kratochwill, Thomas R. [DNLM: 1. Child Behavior.
2. Child Behavior Disorders—diagnosis. WS 350.6 B4177]
LB1124.B43   1988   370.15′3   87-11966
ISBN 0-89862-711-7

To our families
Sally, Daniel, and Jay (E.S.S.)
Carol and Tyler (T.R.K.)

Preface

Over the past ten years, significant attention has been given to the process of behavioral assessment. This is evidenced by the growing number of books and professional publications devoted to the topic. Indeed, many graduate training programs in schools and other applied areas of psychology now offer courses in behavioral assessment.

Despite the extensive advances that have been made in the use of behavioral assessment, careful examination of the literature suggests that a significant portion of assessment strategies were developed to meet the requirements of practitioners and researchers in out-patient and in-patient clinical settings. Applications of behavioral assessment to educational settings were made by assuming that the differences between those settings should not significantly affect the assessment methodology. Unfortunately, educational settings often present problems not typically encountered in clinical settings, and introduce the need to assess variables not commonly considered in behavioral assessment.

For example, although diagnostic decisions in clinical settings may revolve around the appropriate choice of DSM-III-R classifications, such discriminations may not be as relevant in schools. The essential diagnostic discrimination here is whether the child is eligible for special education services and if so, under which category (Learning Disabled, Behavior Disordered, and so on). In addition, while academic skills are rarely a concern of practitioners in clinical settings, they make up the largest proportion of reasons for referral to school psychologists.

In growing recognition of this need, increasing attention has been given recently to the application of behavioral assessment in school settings, with the appearance of new books and professional publications on this topic. Although many of these publications offer practical and valuable descriptions of the process of conducting behavioral assessment in schools, what has so far been lacking is a comprehensive conceptual and research base for the techniques. The present volume has been prepared to fill this void.

The purpose of this text is to offer a comprehensive review of the strategies of behavioral assessment. Each chapter is designed to offer extensive discussion of the conceptual and research base for the procedure, as well as to share descriptions of the practical applications of the technique. In particular, the chapters were written with the intended audience of professionals working in educational settings. Specifically, the book is valuable for school psychologists, child clinical psychologists, educational consultants, counselors, and other mental health and educational professionals who work in school settings.

The development of any writing project always requires the collaboration and cooperation of many individuals. First, our thanks are extended to the many contributors who obviously took special efforts to meet the sometimes difficult demands of the editors. We would also like to thank John Cone, Bill Jensen, Steve Elliott, and Craig Edelbrock for their part as reviewers of sections of the manuscript. A special thanks is extended to Sharon Panulla, Senior Editor at Guilford Press, for her ongoing support as the book developed. Sincere appreciation is also expressed to Sharon Yaszewski at Lehigh University and Karen Kraemer at the University of Wisconsin–Madison, our secretaries, who continue to make our jobs easier. Finally, a loving thank you is extended to our families for their continuing understanding when our professional dedication temporarily reduces our time with them.

Edward S. Shapiro
Thomas R. Kratochwill

ABOUT THE EDITORS

Edward S. Shapiro, Ph.D., earned his doctorate in Educational Psychology (school psychology major) at the University of Pittsburgh. He is currently Associate Professor and Director, School Psychology Program, in the Department of Counseling Psychology, School Psychology, and Special Education at Lehigh University. A 1987 recipient of the Lightner Witmer award, Dr. Shapiro has published over fifty journal articles and book chapters. His primary areas of research are the use of behavioral assessment in educational settings, interventions for academic problems, and self-management skills with handicapped students. Dr. Shapiro is also associate editor of *School Psychology Review*, official journal of the National Association of School Psychologists.

Thomas R. Kratochwill, Ph.D., is Professor of Educational Psychology, Director of the School Psychology Program and Psychoeducational Clinic, University of Wisconsin–Madison. Dr. Kratochwill received his doctoral degree in Educational Psychology (school psychology major) from the University of Wisconsin–Madison. The 1977 recipient of the Lightner Witmer award, Dr. Kratochwill has written and edited several books including the *Advances in School Psychology* series, and *The Practice of Child Therapy* (with R. Morris). He is currently editor of *Professional School Psychology*, the journal of the Division of School Psychology of the American Psychological Association.

ABOUT THE CONTRIBUTORS

Galen Alessi, Ph.D., is a member of the Clinical and School Psychology graduate faculty in the department of Psychology, Western Michigan University, and directed the program from 1974 to 1982. He has practiced as a certified school psychologist in Maryland and is an approved special education hearing officer in Michigan. Dr. Alessi has received the Presidential Recognition Award from the Michigan Association of School Psychologists, and the Excellence in University Teaching Award from the Association for Direct Instruction.

Frank Andrasik, Ph.D., received his doctorate in clinical psychology from Ohio University in 1979. Upon completing his internship at the University of Pittsburgh School of Medicine, he served on the faculty in the Department of Psychology at the State University of New York–Albany. He is now Professor and Director of Graduate Studies in the department of Psychology at the University of West Florida. His current research interests include the assessment and treatment of pain and stress disorders, with a special focus on psychophysiological processes.

Dudley D. Blake, M.A., is a doctoral student in clinical psychology at the State University of New York–Albany and is currently completing his internship at the

Boston VA Medical Center. Receiving a Master's Degree in Applied Behavior Analysis at the University of the Pacific in 1981, Mr. Blake has several years of experience with behavioral and biobehavioral assessment and treatment of children. Mr. Blake's interests include biofeedback applications with children and adults, parent training, and group and individual psychotherapy.

Diane M. Browder, Ph.D., is Associate Professor of Special Education at Lehigh University. She directs a program for adults with severe handicaps and consults in a Lehigh-affiliated school for children with severe emotional disturbance. Her current research interests include using data to make instructional decisions, teacher behavior change, and issues in the transfer of stimulus control.

Michael P. Carey is a doctoral candidate in clinical child psychology at Louisiana State University. His primary research interests include assessment and treatment of affective and anxiety disorders of children and adolescents.

Timothy A. Cavell is a doctoral candidate in clinical child psychology at Louisiana State University. His current interests include assessment of social competency and cognitive distortions among adolescents and behavioral/family therapy.

Christine L. Cole, Ph.D., teaches in the department of Rehabilitation Psychology and Special Education, University of Wisconsin–Madison, and serves on the research staff of the Rehabilitation Research and Training Center in Mental Retardation. She is also director of Psychological Services in a facility serving the developmentally disabled. Dr. Cole's research and clinical practice focuses on teaching self-management skills to behaviorally disordered persons with developmental disabilities.

Cecilia J. Davis is a graduate student in clinical psychology at Louisiana State University. Her current research interests focus on eating disorders in adolescents and adults.

Craig Edelbrock, Ph.D., received his doctorate in child development from Oregon State University in 1976. He then completed a three-year postdoctoral fellowship at NIMH. Dr. Edelbrock is currently Associate Professor and Research Director in the department of Psychiatry and Behavioral Sciences at the University of Massachusetts Medical School.

Susan M. Ferber is a school psychologist with the Schalmont (N.Y.) Central Schools. She previously served on the faculties of the State University of New York–Albany and James Madison University, and has professional experience in school, residential treatment, child development, and special education settings. She completed graduate work in developmental disabilities at the University of Wisconsin–Madison and in school psychology at James Madison University.

Steven R. Forness, Ed.D., is currently Professor of Psychiatry and Biobehavioral Sciences, director of the Mental Retardation and Developmental Disabilities Interdisciplinary Training Program, Principal of the Neuropsychiatric Hospital School, and Chief of Educational Psychology Services in the Child Psychiatry Outpatient Clinic, all at the University of California–Los Angeles. Dr. Forness received his doctorate from UCLA in 1968 and has authored or co-authored more than one hundred journal articles, chapters, and books in special education. He is a fellow of both the American Association on Mental Deficiency and the International Association for Research on Learning Disabilities, and is president of the Council for Children with Behavioral Disorders of International Council for Exceptional Children.

William I. Gardner, Ph.D., is a professor in the department of Rehabilitation Psychology and Special Education at the University of Wisconsin–Madison. Dr. Gardner serves as faculty advisor for graduate students in both special education and rehabilitation psychology. His current research activities include the study of self-management in the developmentally disabled.

Maribeth Gettinger, Ph.D., is Associate Professor in the School Psychology Program of the department of Educational Psychology at the University of Wisconsin–Madison. She received her doctorate in school psychology from Teachers College, Columbia University in 1978. Her current teaching and research interests include academic and behavioral assessment and remediation for children with learning disabilities, academic engaged time, and mastery learning theory and practice.

Frank M. Gresham, Ph.D., is Professor of Psychology in the department of Psychology at Louisiana State University. He received his doctorate from the University of South Carolina in 1979 and taught at Iowa State University from 1979 to 1981 before joining the faculty at Louisiana State University. His major research interests are social skills assessment and training, behavioral consultation, and behavior disorders of children and adolescents.

Robert W. Heffer is a doctoral student in clinical child psychology at Louisiana State University. His interests include treatment acceptability and pediatric psychology.

Francis E. (Ed) Lentz, Jr., Ph.D., is Assistant Professor in the department of School Psychology and Counseling at the University of Cincinnati. Formerly on the faculty of Lehigh University, Dr. Lentz has also served as a consultant for Project Behavior Analysis Follow-Through at the University of Kansas. Dr. Lentz is also on the editorial boards of *School Psychology Review* and *Professional School Psychology*. His research interests focus on the areas of behavioral assessment and intervention for academic problems.

Brian K. Martens, Ph.D., is Assistant Professor of Psychology and Education at Syracuse University. He earned his doctorate in school psychology at the University of Nebraska. His current research interests include multivariate approaches to applied behavior analysis, consultation with parents and teachers, and acceptability of school-based interventions.

H. Thompson Prout, Ph.D., is Associate Professor with the school psychology training program at the State University of New York–Albany. He previously served on the faculties of James Madison University and the University of Wisconsin–Madison, and has professional experience in school, medical, child development, mental health, and developmental disabilities settings. He received his doctorate in school psychology from Indiana University in 1976.

Esther Sinclair, Ph.D., is currently Associate Professor of Psychiatry and Biobehavioral Sciences, and an educational psychologist in the Child Outpatient Department, University of California–Los Angeles Neuropsychiatric Institute. She received her doctorate from the University of Southern California in 1979 and has published more than two dozen articles on diagnosis and classification of children with learning disabilities, mental retardation, and emotional disorders. She is a clinical consultant to Headstart and a consulting editor on two journals in the area of behavior disorders.

Martha E. Snell, Ph.D., is an Associate Professor of Special Education at the University of Virginia where she has taught since 1973. Her primary role is to train teachers of students with severe handicaps. In addition, she is directing a three-year research project on the topic of data-based decisions. Marti currently serves as president-elect for The Association of Persons with Severe Handicaps.

Joseph C. Witt, Ph.D., is Associate Professor of Psychology at Louisiana State University and director of the school psychology program. His primary interests include ecological behavior analysis, teacher and parent resistance to the implementation of interventions, and the quantification of consultative interactions.

Contents

Behavioral Assessment
in Schools

CHAPTER 1

Introduction: Conceptual Foundations of Behavioral Assessment in Schools

THOMAS R. KRATOCHWILL
University of Wisconsin–Madison
EDWARD S. SHAPIRO
Lehigh University

INTRODUCTION

The field of behavioral assessment continues to grow rapidly in the areas of research, theory, and practice. Developments in behavioral assessment of children in clinical and applied psychology have important implications for the application of these procedures in educational settings. To begin with, behavioral assessment has been offered as an alternative to (and sometimes a replacement for) traditional academic and social assessments conducted in applied fields. Many questions have been raised over the norms, reliability, validity, and even utility of traditional assessment devices and procedures (e.g., projective tests, intellectual, and psychoeducational tests; see Salvia & Ysseldyke, 1985). Finally, behavioral assessment has frequently been considered as an alternative to traditional testing because there often have been no solutions to the psychometric and conceptual problems of these traditional procedures and devices. In this chapter we provide a brief review of some of the more salient issues in behavioral assessment.

Aside from the more general contribution to child assessment, behavioral assessment techniques and procedures have much to recommend them in the area of nondiscriminatory or nonbiased assessment. Many behavioral procedures have been linked with the area referred to as criterion-referenced or curriculum-based assessment; and so, enthusiasm has been high for their adoption as alternatives to traditional testing procedures where concerns of bias in testing have been prominent. Increasingly, it has been recognized that behavioral assessment techniques offer conceptual and methodological advances in the area of nonbiased assessment (Kratochwill, Alper, & Cancelli, 1980; Kratochwill & Cancelli, in preparation; Reschly, 1981).

Major interest in behavioral assessment has also occurred as a result of the development of specific measures in outcome research on child behavior disorders. Behavioral assessment has offered researchers a wide range of outcome measures that attest to the efficacy of treatment programs. For example, behavioral assessment measures such as direct observation, psychophysiological recordings, and self-monitoring have advanced knowledge of what treatments are effective with what disorders, and what components of various treatments are active in certain therapeutic programs (Kazdin, 1980). In particular, behavioral outcome measures have provided alternatives to established outcome measures used in past research that are influenced by various sources of artifact and bias (e.g., self-report, global ratings). There have been many developments in behavioral assessment with advances in single-subject or time-series research methodology used in clinical research. In partnership with various designs, assessment schemes have helped document behavior change of great practical and social significance (Barlow & Hersen, 1984; Kratochwill, 1978).

A prominent feature of behavioral assessment that has attracted a great deal of interest in applied fields is the conceptual and practical linking of assessment with treatment. The role that assessment plays in designing an intervention program has been considered a concern with "treatment validity" (Nelson & Hayes, 1979). Recently, Nelson, Hayes, and Jarett (1986) have provided an extensive discussion of methodologies to evaluate treatment validity, along with a review of the studies that have examined some of these dimensions. Few applications of treatment validity, however, have appeared in child behavior assessment. Often psychologists practicing in educational settings have found that assessment techniques had little or no relation to establishing and monitoring an intervention program. Psychologists might engage in testing practices that have been aimed at classification or diagnosis, but information related to designing a treatment procedure has been frequently unavailable in such assessments. For example, after reviewing nearly a decade of research on the McCarthy scales, Kaufman (1982) concluded that there is little information related to how this measure of children's abilities can be used for designing intervention programs and monitoring these programs.

In behavioral assessment, the assessment and treatment procedures can be linked in three ways: (1) designing the intervention program to be specific to the client's problem; (2) linking the assessment to environmental conditions of the individual's behavior; and (3) making assessment continuous throughout the treatment process so that decisions can be made to modify treatments if necessary. Although behavioral assessment may have been oversold on these dimensions of contribution, there is clear evidence that it has led to the development and monitoring of treatment programs across many diverse childhood disorders and problems (Mash & Terdal, 1981a).

These areas of growing interest in behavioral assessment of children convey something of the flavor of the strong enthusiasm in using these techniques in educational settings. Yet, many unresolved issues prevail in the field of behavioral assessment generally, and child behavior assessment in particular.

ISSUES IN CHILD BEHAVIORAL ASSESSMENT

Although a phenomenal amount of writing exists in the area of behavioral assessment generally, relatively little of this work has focused on theory, research, and practice in the child behavior assessment. Recently, however, a number of books have been published that provide a discussion of issues relevant to the assessment of children (for example, Ciminero, Calhoun, & Adams, 1977; 1986; Cone & Hawkins, 1977; Hersen & Bellack, 1981; Shapiro, 1987) and a growing number of chapters have appeared that focus exclusively on assessment of children (for example Ciminero & Drabman, 1977; Evans & Nelson, 1977, 1986; Kratochwill, 1982). Marsh and Terdal (1981b) provided a comprehensive overview of behavioral assessment in a text organized around specific types of childhood disorders.

A major issue in the field of child behavioral assessment is defining exactly what one means by "behavioral assessment." Anyone familiar with the recent literature on behavioral assessment will appreciate its remarkable variety, and that it is becoming even more diverse in a number of areas. In practice, behavioral assessors embrace a wide range of measures. A primary reason is that behavioral assessment is part of the larger domain of behavior therapy, or modification, known to be extraordinarily diverse in theoretical approaches, research methods, and therapy techniques (Kazdin, 1979). Behavioral assessment has always been linked closely with the development of behavior therapy (Kratochwill, 1982; Mash & Terdal, 1981b). Currently, behavior therapy consists of certain subdomains, including applied behavior analysis, neomediational S–R approaches, social learning theory, and cognitive behavior modification (Kazdin & Wilson, 1978; Wilson & Franks, 1982). It is beyond the scope of this brief introductory chapter to provide an overview of these areas and the reader should consult original writings for a review of some of the unique contributions of these areas to child behavioral assessment (see Chapters 5, 6, 7, and 8 in Wilson & Franks, 1982, for a review of conceptual foundations of the approaches).

Each of these major areas of behavior therapy has tended to include its own assessment techniques and procedures reflective of the theoretical position advanced. For example, individuals affiliated with applied behavior analysis have used the most restrictive conceptualization of behavior as compared, for example, with their cognitive behavior counterparts. In applied behavior analysis, cognitive states or internal covert activities are generally not considered part of the assessment focus in applied work (see Kratochwill & Bijou, in press). Thus, assessment involves, almost entirely, direct observational measures of specific behaviors in analogue or naturalistic settings. In contrast, cognitive behavior therapists consider internal states or cognitions not only the proper focus for assessment and therapy, but as playing a major role in directing behavior (Kendall & Braswell, 1985; Meichenbaum, 1977). Thus, assessors use measures that tap cognitions and so a heavy reliance on self-report is characteristic. It is therefore apparent that fundamental differences in assessment strategies have occurred across diverse theoretical approaches within the field of behavior therapy.

A related issue concerns the actual techniques that are considered part of behavioral assessment. Keeping in mind these variations in theoretical approaches within behavior therapy, the number of different techniques and procedures subsumed under the rubric of behavioral assessment is growing extremely large. Defining what behavioral assessment is now and what it will be in the future will likely be determined by expanding theoretical perspectives rather than through some conceptual approach that maps specific techniques and procedures. Behavioral assessment is generally regarded as a hypothesis testing process about the nature of problems, causes of problems, and evaluation of treatment programs (Mash & Terdal, 1981b). This concept allows many techniques and methods of assessment. In this hypothesis-testing process of behavioral assessment, the assumptions, implications, uses of data, levels of inference, method, timing, and scope of assessment are said to differ from more traditional approaches used in educational settings (Hartmann, Roper, & Bradford, 1979). Table 1-1 provides an overview of the differences between traditional and behavioral assessment. Nevertheless, evolving theoretical conceptions of what is to be included within the domain of behavior therapy make the area of behavioral assessment difficult to define, even when comparisons are made with so-called traditional techniques.

Generally, the traditional assessment models that involve norm-referenced psychoeducational and intellectual testing consider intraorganistic variables as essential in explaining the academic and behavioral performance of children. In traditional models, overt performance, either in the social or academic domain, is usually regarded as symptomatic of underlying dysfunction of psychic disturbance. In this regard, the assessor assumes that something more fundamental than the overt behavioral performance of the client is an issue to be measured and assessed. One of the clearest examples of this is in the personality assessment domain where objective testing might be employed to reveal unconscious factors or personality traits potentially related to client performance. In the assessment of academic performance processing dysfunctions, minimal cerebral dysfunction might be a focus and assessment would be implemented to measure these aspects of hypothesized functioning. More important, traditional assessors typically de-emphasize situational or environmental factors during the assessment process and in interpretation of the data.

It is generally assumed among behavioral assessors that measurement must focus on a sample of overt behavior (or covert, depending on the theoretical

TABLE 1-1 Differences Between Behavioral and Traditional Approaches to Assessment

	Behavioral	Traditional
I. Assumptions		
1. Conception of personality	Personality constructs mainly employed to summarize specific behavior patterns, if at all	Personality as a reflection of enduring underlying states or traits
2. Causes of behavior	Maintaining conditions sought in current environment	Intrapsychic or within the individual
II. Implications		
1. Role of behavior	Important as a sample of person's repertoire in specific situation	Behavior assumes importance only insofar as it indexes underlying causes
2. Role of history	Relatively unimportant, except, for example, to provide a retrospective baseline	Crucial in that present conditions seen as a product of the past
3. Consistency of behavior	Behavior thought to be specific to the situation	Behavior expected to be consistent across time and settings
III. Uses of data	To describe target behaviors and maintaining conditions	To describe personality functioning and etiology
	To select the appropriate treatment	To diagnose or classify
	To evaluate and revise treatment	To make prognosis; to predict
IV. Other characteristics		
1. Level of inferences	Low	Medium to high
2. Comparisons	More emphasis on intraindividual or idiographic	More emphasis on interindividual or nomothetic
3. Methods of assessment	More emphasis on direct methods (e.g., observations of behavior in natural environment)	More emphasis on indirect methods (e.g., interviews and self-report)
4. Timing of assessment	More ongoing; prior, during, and after treatment	Pre- and perhaps posttreatment, or strictly to diagnose
5. Scope of assessment	Specific measures and of more variables (e.g., of target behviors in various situations, of side effects, context, strengths as well as deficiencies)	More global measures (e.g., of cure, or improvement) but only of the individual

Source: D. P. Hartmann, B. L. Roper, & D. C. Bradford. Source relationships between behavioral and traditional assessment. *Journal of Behavioral Assessment,* 1979, *1*, 3–21. Reproduced by permission of the author and publisher.

orientation) in a variety of situations. In addition, assessors emphasize that the individual-environmental factors are assessed in multiple settings because environmental factors are said to influence performance in and across settings. Moreover, empirical data have often shown that an assessment of the functional relations between behavior and environment will identify factors that control subject performance. The important issue is that the focus on individual and environmental factors in behavioral assessment is usually made without a reliance on underlying processes or hypothetical constructs (Goldfried, 1986).

The conceptual approach to behavioral assessment may provide some consistency in defining the field, but expands considerably the range of possible techniques and procedures that can be included in child behavior assessment. Behavior assessment has usually been characterized as consisting of some general domains of assessment including the interview, self-report, checklist and rating scales, self-monitoring, analogue assessment, and direct observational measures (see Cone, 1978). In this regard, behavioral assessment is conceptualized based on the contents assessed, the methods used to assess the contents, and the types of generalizability for scores on the measures that can be classified on the Behavioral Assessment Grid (Cone, 1978, 1979). The consideration of these three dimensions is presented in Figure 1-1. A tripartite response system (or content area) typically guides the behavioral assessment process, namely along the motor, cognitive, and physiological domains. Thus, a learning or academic problem would involve conceptualizing assessment along the lines of the three response systems insofar as they might contribute to the understanding and design of a treatment program for the child. For example, specific motor activities may be assessed, such as time spent working. In addition, cognitive components (positive or negative self-statements, rehearsal of specific skills) may be assessed as they relate to the solution of academic problems. Moreover, physiological arousal could be monitored to understand further the child's reactions to the conditions of learning. When the three response systems are monitored, it is not assumed that they are highly correlated (Cone, 1979; Evans & Nelson, 1986).

Behavioral assessment methods mentioned above are usually presented along a continuum of directness/indirectness representing the extent to which they (1) measure the behavior of clinical relevance, and (2) measure it at the time and place of its natural occurrence (Cone, 1978). Thus, interviews, self-report, and

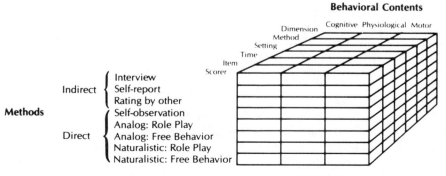

FIGURE 1-1 The Behavioral Assessment Grid (BAG)

Source: Reprinted from J. D. Cone, "The Behavioral Assessment Grid (BAG): A Conceptual Framework and a Taxonomy," *Behavior Therapy*, 1978, 9, 882–888. Copyright © 1978 by the Association for Advancement of Behavior Therapy. Reprinted by permission of the publisher and the author.

ratings by others are considered *indirect* assessment strategies. For example, in the case of the interview and self-report measures, the behavior observed represents a verbal representation of activities taking place at some other time and place relative to the assessment occasion. When ratings are completed by other individuals (teachers, parents), the sample of behavior is considered a retrospective description that may or may not involve the clinical behavior of interest. The direct assessment category includes self-monitoring, analogue assessment, and naturalistic observation. These methods are direct in that assessment takes place on some clinically significant target behavior at the time of its natural occurrence.

Clearly, the expanding conceptualizations of child behavioral assessment within the context of the hypothesis testing approach and the conceptual framework for assessment allow many and diverse techniques to be considered as parts of the assessment scheme of the clinician. It is now conceded that behavioral assessors embrace a wide range of idiographic and nomothetic measures (Cone, 1986, in press). For example, even traditional projective formats might be used to provide information on a client's cognitions or reinforcer preferences (see Chapter 9 this volume). Moreover, traditional tests could often be conceptualized as a format to provide standardized measures of skill performance, such as in the area of IQ testing (e.g., Nelson, 1980) or achievement and perceptual motor tests (e.g., Mash & Terdal, 1981b), and neurological assessment (Goldstein, 1979). However, these nomothetic-trait measures are regarded as inappropriate for practitioners interested in single case treatment within the idiographic-behavior framework (Cone, in press).

A related issue that has its source of activity in the field of child behavioral assessment and remains to be resolved pertains to the psychometric features of assessment. As Goldfried has often pointed out (Goldfried, 1979, 1986), behavioral assessors run the risk of making the same type of mistakes that have often been made in traditional assessment, especially as reflected in the proliferation of techniques. Possibly due to a rejection of the traditional assessment approaches and their associated measurement guidelines, and especially conceptual models embraced by traditional assessors, many of the psychometric features of child behavior assessment such as norming, reliability, validity, and generalizability have not been addressed adequately (Hartmann *et al.*, 1979; Mash & Terdal, 1981b). For example, in the area of norming, concerns have been raised regarding the rather ambiguous meaning of many assessments conducted with children without concrete reference to either a carefully defined population or the ecology environment in which they are assessed. This raises concerns regarding the appropriate use of data from child behavior assessment in classification and in establishing special goals for intervention programs (Evans & Nelson, 1986; Kratochwill, 1984). In addition, there are still relatively few investigations examining the reliability of childhood behavioral observation techniques. Behavioral assessors have been concerned primarily with establishing agreement measures, but have traditionally tended not to establish the reliability and validity of many assessment techniques with conventional psychometric criteria. Although behavior assessors have focused on such areas as content validity, the process through which this has been accomplished has often been informal, inadequate, and incomplete (Hartmann *et al.,* 1979). Generalizability theory has been proposed as an option, to address psychometric properties of behavioral assessment. However, little work has occurred in this area. To complicate matters even further, there has been a great deal of controversy regarding the appropriateness of traditional psychometric concepts (Cone, 1981, 1986, in press; Strosahl & Linehan, 1986). For example, Cone (1981) argued that furture work in the behavioral assessment field must focus on a paradigm radically different from the traditional nomothetic-trait psychometric model now used for establishing the reliability, validity, and generalizability of tests. More recently Cone (in press) argued that since behavioral assessment procedures are based on a different conceptual model of individual variability than traditional approaches (idiographic-behavior), the traditional psychometric features vary widely in appropriateness depending on the type of reliability and validity being considered. As an alternative, Cone proposed that accuracy be the primary method for establishing psychometric dimensions of behavioral assessment strategies as applied to the single case. Nevertheless, it remains somewhat unclear as to what psychometric strategies might be employed for behavioral assessment techniques and how the field will deal with various devices and procedures that have embraced traditional psychometric criteria.

An important concern based on the above analysis in the behavioral assessment field relates to feedback that practitioners have provided regarding the actual practices of child behavior assessment in applied settings (Anderson, Cancelli, & Kratochwill, 1984; Swan & MacDonald, 1978; Wade, Baker & Hartmann, 1979). A consistent finding has been that behavioral assessors have used a great number of traditional assessment devices. For example, Wade *et al.* (1979) found that nearly half of their respondents who are members of the Association for the Advancement of Behavior Therapy used traditional interviews and a large number of projective and objective tests. Such factors as agency requirements for prescribed test use, requirements for testing involving labeling and classification, and a reported difficulty implementing behavioral assessment in applied settings were offered as possible reasons for failure.

The results of Wade *et al.* (1979) correspond to reported practices of school psychologists presented in an investigation by Anderson *et al.* (1984) who found that select behaviorally oriented members of the American Psychological Association, Division 16, and the National Association of School Psychologists employ traditional testing procedures and devices. Thus, use of a wide range of traditional assessment techniques may be cause for concern in light of the lack of adequate psychometric support and the failure to address the idiographic behavioral analyses. One of the major issues in the field relates to the future development of effective and standardized behavioral assessment procedures that embrace the accuracy psychometrics proposed by Cone (in press).

The issues raised in the preceding paragraph convey something of the concerns that are being addressed currently in child behavioral assessment, and behavioral assessment generally. The issues raised here reflect only some of the more general concerns that have emerged, but by no means do they represent a comprehensive overview. Each of the authors in this text addresses a broad spectrum of issues raised in this chapter. The authors in the current text have provided a comprehensive overview of their own areas, taking into account diverse methods, techniques, and conceptual formats for practice.

OVERVIEW OF CHAPTERS

The chapters in this text have been arranged along the direct–indirect continuum suggested by Cone (1978). Those chapters that either describe direct observation procedures or use techniques that involve the assessment of behavior under naturally occurring situations come first.

Chapters that use or describe direct observation procedures under analogue, or more indirect conditions, follow. Authors of these chapters describe the use of self-monitoring, the assessment of academic problems, emotional and behavioral problems, and the use of more traditional personality measures within behavioral assessment.

In the next set of chapters, authors describe the more indirect procedures of interviewing and informant report. In the final chapter the authors discuss issues of assessment practices related to educational classifications and diagnosis.

Chapter 2, on direct observation, emphasizes the conceptual process of conducting behavioral observation rather than an extensive description of the methods alone. In particular, Alessi provides extensive discussion of the importance of a functional analysis in conducting direct observation. His discussion goes beyond the identification of antecedent and consequence relations, and examines other variables contributing to functional analysis: situational factors, response hierarchies, sequential analysis, and pathognomonic contingencies. Recognizing the importance of family interrelationships in understanding child behavior, Alessi also discusses what he terms "systemic functional analysis" or the evaluation of more than dyadically focused functional analysis.

Alessi then offers a systematic methodology for conducting direct observations that link the functional analysis of behavior and its measurement. Case illustrations are also provided.

In Chapter 3, Lentz examines the use of direct observation procedures in the assessment of academic behavior. In this chapter, critical issues are raised with traditional methods of observing academic skills, but more importantly, Lentz examines in detail the conceptual development of the direct assessment of academic skills. Lentz also points out research questions that need to be addressed related to the recent development of the use of behavioral assessment for evaluating academic skills. Like Alessi, Lentz notes the critical nature of conducting a functional analysis of the academic environment as an often neglected component of the assessment process.

In Chapter 4 Browder and Snell provide a discussion of the current issues in the assessment of individuals with severe handicaps. Psychologists called upon to assess these individuals often rely on traditional, norm-referenced measures not typically sensitive to the critical areas of assessment population. The primary methodology advocated by these authors requires direct observation of behavior under naturally occurring conditions and offers strong linkages from assessment to intervention. They provide a case study illustrating the procedures.

An often neglected area of behavioral assessment with children is the use of physiological measures in assessing educational problems. In Chapter 5 Blake and Andrasik discuss the types of physiological variables measured and how these measures may be related to assessing academic learning problems. They provide a discussion of the physiological monitoring of children's activity. This chapter provides a blend of practical applications and research issues related to the use of these measures. A case illustrating the use of physiological measures in behavioral assessment with a school-based problem is also provided.

In Chapter 6 Gardner and Cole discuss the use of self-monitoring procedures in behavioral assessment. Their chapter offers a detailed description of the methodology and related research issues. They note the differences in using self-monitoring as an intervention and assessment procedure with extended discussion of the variables that affect self-monitoring. The authors also provide a case illustration of the use of these procedures.

The use of analogue measures play a large role in behavioral assessment activities. These measures involve data collection under conditions that approximate the natural conditions under which behavior occurs. Three chapters address this type of assessment process.

In Chapter 7 Gettinger provides an extensive discussion regarding the use and conceptualization of analogue assessment for academic problems. She examines a number of different types of analogue assessment procedures and how they can be applied across different academic skill areas. Directions for future research as well as a case illustration are provided.

In Chapter 8 Shapiro and Kratochwill discuss the various analogue methods used to assess emotional and behavioral problems of children and adolescents. Included in their discussion are the assessment of avoidance problems, compliance, social skills, and problem-solving and other cognitive variables. Assessment strategies used for many of these measures include role-play or contrived situational assessments as well as paper-and-pencil analogues.

One of the more controversial issues in behavioral assessment is the degree to which one should or could use within a behavioral assessment context measures typically considered as traditional personality measures. Prout and Ferber discuss the potential use of projective assessment within behavioral assessment. After providing a rationale for how projective measures may be used in this way, the authors review a number of instruments that meet their criteria. Finally, a case study describing the potential use of these measures is included.

A very common method of behavioral assessment involves the use of rating scales and checklists completed by knowledgeable informants. Parents and teachers often provide data that assists in understanding the child's behavior in a unique way. Edelbrock provides an overview of the development of rating scales and checklists. He specifically discusses in detail the use of three commonly employed instruments as well as discussing briefly several others. Finally, he offers guidelines for selecting a measure and provides a case example where the Child Behavior Checklist was used.

Witt, Cavell, Heffer, Carey, and Martens offer a discussion of the use of self-report measures in behavioral assessment. After providing a rationale and discussion of the limitations for this method of data collection, Witt *et al.* offer a set of practical suggestions for addressing some of these limitations. Additionally, a review of structured and unstructured interviewing techniques is provided.

Despite the importance of direct observation in behavioral assessment, the use of interviewing still remains a primary strategy for data collection. Gresham and Davis discuss the conceptual foundations of interviews from a behavioral perspective. They then offer an extended discussion of behavioral interviewing within a consultative framework. Much of Gresham and Davis's writing is based upon the behavioral consultation model of Bergan (1977), who has developed one of the most systematic procedures for conducting the behavioral consultation process. Finally, Gresham and Davis examine psychometric issues related to behavioral interviewing.

The final chapter, by Sinclair and Forness, provides an overview of issues related to special education classifications. Special attention is given to the relation of the educational classification of seriously emotionally disturbed/behavior disorders and psychiatric diagnoses based on the DSM-III.

References

Anderson, T., Cancelli, A. A., & Kratochwill, T. R. (1984). Self-reported assessment practices of school psychologists. *Journal of School Psychology, 22,* 17–29.

Barlow, D. H., & Hersen, M. (1984). *Single case experimental designs: Strategies for studying behavior change* (2d ed.). Elmsford, N.Y.: Pergamon.

Barrios, B., & Hartmann, D. P. (1986). The contributions of traditional assessment: Concepts, issues, and methodologies. In R. O. Nelson & S. C. Hayes (Eds.), *Conceptual foundations of behavioral assessment* (pp. 81–110). New York: Guilford Press.

Bergan, J. R. (1977). *Behavioral consultation.* Columbus, Ohio: Charles E. Merrill.

Ciminero, A. R. (1986). Behavioral assessment: An overview. In A. R. Ciminero, K. S. Calhoun, & H. E. Adams (Eds.), *Handbook of behavioral assessment* (2d ed., pp. 3–11). New York: John Wiley & Sons.

Ciminero, A. R., Calhoun, K. S., & Adams, H. E. (Eds.). (1977). *Handbook of behavioral assessment.* New York: John Wiley & Sons.

Ciminero, D. R., Calhoun, K. W., & Adams, H. E. (Eds.). (1986). *Handbook of behavioral assessment* (2d ed.). New York: John Wiley & Sons.

Ciminero, A. R., & Drabman, R. S. (Eds.). (1977). Current developments in the behavioral assessment of children. In B. B. Lahey & A. E. Kazdin (Eds.), *Advances in clinical child psychology* (Vol. 1, pp. 47–82). New York: Plenum Press.

Cone, J. D. (1978). The behavioral assessment grid (BAG): A conceptual framework and a taxonomy. *Behavior Therapy, 9*, 882–888.

Cone, J. D. (1979). Confounded comparisons in triple response mode assessment research. *Behavioral Assessment, 1*, 85–95.

Cone, J. D. (1981). Psychometric considerations. In M. Hersen & A. S. Bellack (Eds.), *Handbook of behavioral assessment* (2d ed., pp. 38–68). Elmsford, N.Y.: Pergamon Press.

Cone, J. D. (1986). Idiographic, nomothetic, and other perspectives in behavioral assessment. In R. O. Nelson & S. C. Hayes (Eds.), *Conceptual foundations of behavioral assessment* (pp. 111–128). New York: Guilford.

Cone, J. D. (in press). Psychometric considerations and the multiple models of behavioral assessment. In M. Hersen & A. S. Bellack (Eds.), *Behavioral assessment: A practical handbook* (3d ed.). Elmsford, N.Y.: Pergamon Press.

Cone, J. D. & Hawkins, R. (1977). *Behavioral assessment: New directions in clinical psychology.* New York: Brunner/Mazel.

Evans, I. M., & Nelson, R. O. (1977). Assessment of child behavior problems. In A. R. Ciminero, K. S. Calhoun, & H. E. Adams (Eds.), *Handbook of behavioral assessment* (pp. 603–681). New York: John Wiley & Sons.

Evans, I. M., & Nelson, R. O. (1986). Assessment of children. In A. R. Ciminero, K. S. Calhoun, & H. E. Adams (Eds.), *Handbook of behavioral assessment* (2d ed., pp. 601–630). New York: John Wiley & Sons.

Goldfried, M. R. (1979). Behavioral assessment: Where do we go from here? *Behavioral Assessment, 1*, 19–22.

Goldfried, M. R. (1986). Behavioral assessment: An overview. In A. R. Ciminero, K. S. Calhoun, & H. E. Adams (Eds.), *Handbook of behavioral assessment* (2d ed., pp. 81–107). New York: John Wiley & Sons.

Goldstein, G. (1979). Methodological and theoretical issues in neuropsychological assessment. *Journal of Behavioral Assessment, 1*, 23–41.

Gresham, F. M., & Reschly, D. J. (in press). Issues in the conceptualization, classification, and assessment of social skills in the mildly handicapped. In T. R. Kratochwill (Ed.), *Advances in school psychology* (Vol. 6). Hillsdale, N.J.: Lawrence Erlbaum Associates.

Hartmann, D. P., Roper, B. L., & Bradford, D. C. (1979). Some relationships between behavioral and traditional assessment. *Journal of Behavioral Assessment, 1*, 3–21.

Hersen, M., & Bellack, A. S. (Eds.). (1981). *Behavioral assessment: A practical handbook* (2d ed.). Elmsford, N.Y.: Pergamon Press.

Kaufman, A. S. (1982). An integrated review of almost a decade of research on the McCarthy Scales. In T. R. Kratochwill (Ed.), *Advanced in school psychology* (Vol. 2, pp. 119–169). Hillsdale, N.J.: Lawrence Erlbaum Associates.

Kazdin, A. E. (1978). *History of behavior modification: Experimental foundations of contemporary research.* Baltimore, Md.: University Park Press.

Kazdin, A. E. (1979). Fictions, factions, and functions of behavior therapy. *Behavior Therapy, 10*, 629–654.

Kazdin. A. E. (1980). *Research design in clinical psychology.* New York: Harper & Row.

Kazdin, A. E., & Wilson, G. T. (1978). *Evaluation of behavior therapy: Issues, evidence, and research strategies.* Cambridge, Mass.: Ballinger.

Kendall, P. C., & Braswell, L. (1985). *Cognitive-behavioral therapy for impulsive children.* New York: Guilford Press.

Kratochwill, T. R. (1978). *Single subject research: Strategies for evaluating change.* New York: Academic Press.

Kratochwill, T. R. (1982). Advances in behavioral assessment. In C. R. Reynolds & R. B. Gutkin (Eds.), *Handbook of school psychology* (pp. 314–355). New York: John Wiley & Sons.

Kratochwill, T. R. (1984). Selection of target behaviors: Issues and directions. *Behavioral Assessment, 7*, 3–5.

Kratochwill, T. R., Alper, S., & Cancelli, A. A. (1980). Nondiscriminatory assessment: Perspectives in psychology and special education. In L. Mann & D. A. Sabatino (Eds.), *Fourth review of special education* (pp. 229–286). New York: Grune & Stratton.

Kratochwill, T. R., & Bijou, S. W. (in press). The impact of behaviorism on educational psychology. In J. A. Glover & R. R. Rouning (Eds.), *A history of educational psychology.* New York: Plenum Press.

Kratochwill, R. R., & Cancelli, A. A. (in preparation). *Nonbiased assessment and treatment in psychology and education.* New York: Plenum Press.

Mash, E., & Terdal, L. (Eds.). (1981a). *Behavioral assessment of childhood disorders.* New York: Guilford Press.

Mash, E. J., & Terdal, L. G. (1981b). Behavioral assessment of childhood disturbance. In E. J. Mash & L. G. Terdal (Eds.), *Behavioral assessment of childhood disorders* (pp. 3–76). New York: Guilford Press.

Meichenbaum, D. (1977). *Cognitive behavior modification.* New York: Plenum Press.

Mischel, W. (1968). *Personality and assessment.* New York: John Wiley & Sons.

Mischel, W. (1971). *Introduction to personality.* New York: Holt, Rinehart, & Winston.

Nelson, R. O. (1980). The use of intelligence tests within behavioral assessment. *Behavioral Assessment, 2,* 417–423.

Nelson, R. O. (1981). Realistic dependent measures for clinical use. *Journal of Consulting and Clinical Psychology, 49,* 168–182.

Nelson, R. O., & Hayes, S. C. (1979). Some current dimensions of behavioral assessment. *Behavioral Assessment, 1,* 1–16.

Nelson, R. O., Hayes, S. C., & Jarrett, R. B. (1986). Evaluating the quality of behavioral assessment. In R. O. Nelson & S. C. Hayes (Eds.), *Conceptual foundations of behavioral assessment* (pp. 463–503). New York: Guilford Press.

Reschly, D. J. (1981). Psychological testing in educational classification and placement. *American Psychologist, 36,* 1094–1102.

Salvia, J., & Ysseldyke, J. E. (1985). *Assessment in special and remedial education* (3d ed.). Boston: Houghton Mifflin.

Shapiro, E. S. (1987). *Behavioral assessment in school psychology.* Hillsdale, N.J.: Lawrence Erlbaum Associates.

Strosahl, K. D., & Linehan, M. M. (1986). Basic issues in behavioral assessment. In A. R. Ciminero, K. S. Calhoun, & H. E. Adams (Eds.), *Handbook of behavioral assessment* (2d ed., pp. 12–46). New York: John Wiley & Sons.

Swan, G. E., & MacDonald, M. L. (1978). Behavior therapy in practice: A national survey of behavior therapists. *Behavior Therapy, 9,* 799–807.

Wade, T. C., Baker, T. B., & Hartmann, D. P. (1979). Behavior therapists' self-reported views and practices. *The Behavior Therapist, 2,* 3–6.

Wilson, G. T., & Franks, C. M. (Eds.). (1982). *Contemporary behavior therapy: Conceptual and empirical foundations.* New York: Guilford Press.

CHAPTER 2

Direct Observation Methods for Emotional/Behavior Problems

GALEN ALESSI
Western Michigan University

INTRODUCTION

Behavioral assessment has grown rapidly during the past decade. More than twenty books have been published on the topic. At first, general texts appeared (Ciminero, Calhoun, & Adams, 1977, 1986; Cone & Hawkins, 1977; Haynes, 1978; Haynes & Wilson, 1979; Hersen & Bellack, 1976, 1981, 1988; Keefe, Kopel, & Gordon, 1978). Later works focused on special client problems such as adult disorders (Barlow, 1981); childhood disorders (Mash & Terdal, 1981, 1987; Ollendick & Hersen, 1984); behavioral medicine (Keefe & Blumenthal, 1982; Tryon, 1985); behavior therapy (Mash & Terdal, 1976); marriage (Filsinger & Lewis, 1981); child custody (Marafiote, 1985); school psychology (Alessi & Kaye, 1983; Shapiro, 1987); mental retardation (Sackett, 1978); severe developmental disabilities (Powers & Handleman, 1984); and traumatic brain damage (Edelstein & Couture, 1984). Texts also focused on specialized topics such as adaptive behavior (Coulter & Morrow, 1978); cognitive-behavior therapy (Kendall & Hollon, 1981); measurement of children (Glow, 1984, 1985); conceptual issues (Nelson & Hayes, 1986); methodology (Bakeman & Gottman, 1986; Meister, 1985); and program evaluation (Deno & Mirkin, 1977). Two journals have been founded that are devoted to behavioral assessment. Although many recently edited texts on behavioral topics include chapters on behavioral assessment (Bornstein & van den Pol, 1985; Evans & Wilson, 1983; Goldfried, 1982; Hartman & Wood, 1982; Katz, Varni, & Jay, 1984), chapters are also appearing regularly in edited texts with more general titles in psychological assessment (Haynes, 1984); clinical psychology (Haynes, 1983); clinical child psychology (Ciminero & Drabman, 1977; Wasik, 1984) school psychology (Kratochwill, 1982;

Sackett, Landesman-Dwyer, & Morin, 1981); and mental retardation (Rojahn & Schroeder, 1983).

Federal as well as many state laws and rules now require behavioral assessment data as part of diagnostic evaluations determining eligibility of children for various special education and mental health services. A major report, based on a two-year study by the National Academy of Sciences, concluded that systematic behavioral observation data should be obtained when evaluating children for possible identification as educationally handicapped (Heller, Holtzman, & Messick, 1982). Clearly, behavioral observation and assessment are well established in the overall assessment area.

This chapter will review issues in applying behavior observation and assessment methods to the evaluation and treatment of emotional and behavioral problems. It will focus on such questions as: Why are direct observations important when reports about behavior can be obtained more readily by interviews or checklists? What is a functional analysis of behavior, and what is a systemic functional analysis? How do settings relate to assessment of behavior problems? Why is it important to assess interpersonal sequences of behavioral interaction? How do microcontingencies differ from macrocontingencies, and why are both important for assessment? What role do metacontingencies play in resolving behavior problems? What are micronorms, and how are they used in behavioral assessment? How can the design of behavior observation methods lead to distorted results? What reliability and validity issues pertain to direct observation measures?

OBSERVATION AND VERBAL REPORTS

Why Not Rely on Interviews and Behavioral Checklists?

Systematic, direct observations take time and resources. Behavioral checklists, interviews, and teacher and parent questionnaires are less costly to administer. Why not use these methods to assess emotional and behavior problems?

Verbal reports often do not concur with measures of behavior obtained by systematic, direct observation. Few published behavior rating scales include validation data on the relationship between what others report that the child does and what the child does when directly observed.

The assumption that verbal reports about behavior should agree with the occurrences of reported behaviors is fostered by a *rational* model of human behavior. By contrast, a *behavior analysis* model (Skinner, 1957) makes no such assumptions. This model assumes that reporting about and actually engaging in those behaviors are two functionally different kinds of responses, that is, under the control of, or a function of, different sets of behavioral contingencies. When the two sets of contingencies overlap sufficiently, the verbal report and the behavior to which it refers may more closely agree. But when contingencies function differently, sometimes even incompatibly, the verbal report would not be expected to agree closely with observed behaviors. As a result, direct observation and the verbal report often measure different behaviors, although they purport to measure the same behaviors.

Verbal Reports on Child Behavior

Shapiro, Lentz, and Sofman (1985) evaluated agreement between teacher report and direct observation of classroom outbursts and agressiveness. They concluded: "Overall, the results indicate that indirect paper-and-pencil measures and direct observation measures attempting to assess the same behavior may to some extent assess different behaviors. The important question is obviously which behaviors these instruments may be measuring" (p. 76). When direct observations differ from teacher (or parent) spoken or paper-and-pencil reports—interview, checklist, questionnaire—on the same behaviors, which measures should hold greater weight both in making diagnoses and in developing educational plans?

Patterson (1982) concluded that there is little support for the validity of parents' global judgments about child-rearing patterns. He stated that: "different interviewers obtain different information from parents, and that the same interviewers receive different information from parents from one interview to the next" (p. 43). Low levels of agreement have been found between parent report and reports from the child, school records, and systematic observations. Low levels of agreement are also found between a mother's and a father's global rating of the same child. Parent recollection of past events in a child's life has been found unreliable.

Patterson further concluded that such findings "raise doubts about the utility of intensive efforts to get developmental histories using traditional child guidance interview procedures" (p. 43). In sum, verbal reports about children's behaviors are influenced by factors other than the occurrences of those behaviors as observed.

Verbal Reports on Treatment Effects

In evaluating therapy change, Eyberg and Johnson (1974) found that parents' estimates of child improvement in treatment increased even when no improvements were noted on objective measures. Schnelle (1974) found little congruence between parents' judgments of improved school attendance by their children after treatment for this problem and actual school attendance records. He concluded: "The results are clear in illustrating the potential for the total invalidity of questionnaires as representative of behavioral change, even when the questionnaire is very specific and does not ask for subjective statements from the client" (p. 343). Patterson's (1982) review of this issue concluded:

> The bias is a relatively consistent tendency on the part of parents of disturbed children to report improvement in the behavior of the child when in fact no real changes have occurred. . . . Roughly two-thirds of such parents will report improvements when asked for global judgments. This means that even if the therapy *isn't working*, the therapist

will receive supportive comments from the *majority* of the families with which he works. . . . (p. 43)

The rate of improvement (60%) obtained with global verbal reports when no observable change has been detected parallels research findings on placebo effects. Further, when both global verbal reports and specific measures were employed in the same study, Frank (1973) found immediate positive effects as measured by global report (at times even *before* the first therapy session), whereas positive gains using more specific measures were not detected until completion of several treatment sessions. Howard, Kopta, Krause, and Orlinsky (1986) present data that can be interpreted similarly, and Sulzbacher (1972) reported similar results in a review of the effects of medication on classroom behavior.

Verbal Reports on Compliance, Physiological Responses, and Historical Events

Patient verbal reports of compliance with medical regimes do not match compliance estimates obtained with more objective measures, such as urine or blood serum assays (cf. Haynes, Taylor, and Sackett, 1979). Masek (1982) concluded: "When compared with the results of objective measures of compliance, there exists little experimental evidence to indicate that patient self-report is a reliable measure of compliance" (p. 530). Patients tend to *overestimate* their levels of compliance by about 30% to 40%. Smokers tend to *underestimate* their use of cigarettes by about one-third. Similar problems may exist for self-report data used in treating drinking and eating disorders. Apparently, verbal reports on personal behavior are distorted by factors other than the objectively measured behaviors themselves.

In a review of literature on the accuracy of reporting physiological events such as heart rate, palmar sweat, and muscle tension, Pennebacker (1984) found low levels of agreement between verbal report and physiological assessment results within each of these areas. He also found that socially isolated people report more medical symptoms, and that people in boring jobs report more physical symptoms, take more aspirin, and report more days of restricted activity due to poor health than do people with more interesting jobs. In sum, verbal reports about physiological events can be influenced more by external, ecological factors than objective reports can be. These findings are relevant to training and treatment using biofeedback techniques. The findings are pertinent to treatment for any condition defined by subjective, verbal report, for example, chronic pain, depression, anxiety, fear.

Mood states may distort what is noticed or what is recalled. Fogarty and Hemsley (1983) found that depressed persons often distort recent life events by emphasizing unfavorable aspects, which leads to confusion about whether recalled negative events are the cause, or effect, of the depression. Nelson and Craighead (1977) reported that depressed spouses recall more negative and fewer positive experiences. McMahon, Forehand, and Griest (1982) report on a series of studies suggesting that mothers' personal adjustment (depression and anxiety), rather than the children's observed deviant and noncompliant behavior, was the significant factor affecting ratings of the children on behavior checklists. Changes in rater mood may affect changes in behavior ratings without observed behavior change.

Little congruence has been found between verbal recall of child-rearing patterns by parents and established historical records (see studies reviewed by Patterson, 1982). Loftus (1979) has demonstrated that reports of past events are easily influenced and distorted by cues supplied by the interviewer (cf. Kantor, 1963, pp. 5–9). Spence (1982) presents a review of evidence and persuasive argument that verbal reports about the past are collaborative constructions made within the current interview situation. Such constructions not only shape our view of the past, but also are creations of the present which actually *become* our past. In sum, verbal reports about historical events also can be distorted readily by current, external factors unrelated to the documented historical events.

Implications for School Psychologists

When indirect measures of behavior fail to correspond with direct observations, the sources of such disagreement must be determined before making diagnoses and starting treatment. A note of caution, however, is due here. As will be seen later, the accuracy of direct observation data often will be as questionable as that from indirect, verbal sources. The evaluation team must be prepared to estimate the accuracy of both kinds of measures. The implications for school psychologists include, but are not limited, to the following:

1. Manuals for published checklists and questionnaires should include validity data on the agreement between the results obtained from that tool and from direct, systematic observations. Local school system data should be collected to compare with publisher data. More research is needed on how verbal estimates of behavior compare with occurrences of those behaviors, and which variables enhance or undermine concurrence.

2. Systematic, direct observation data are needed to compare with obtained global reports. Global reports about behavior (cf. symptoms) could be considered inferences or conclusions about, rather than measures of, behavior occurrences (cf. signs). Psychologists carefully distinguish between measures of behavior as it occurs, and opinions and inferences drawn about that behavior. Facts about behavior must be collected before proper inferences can be drawn. When inferences are given without accompanying facts, psychologists must backtrack to obtain the factual basis from which the inferences purportedly were drawn.

3. Even when there are disagreements, verbal report data would be considered relevant as *estimates* or *opinions* of others significant in the child's life. Disagreements among measures call for different interventions. The child whose behavior does *not* improve on Ritalin, but for whom others report improvement, requires a different approach (e.g., placebo medication) from the child whose behavior improves on Ritalin. The child who engages in adaptive behavior, but for

whom others report little adaptive behavior, requires a different treatment plan from a child who engages in little adaptive behavior. The child referred for being overly disruptive in class, but who is no more disruptive than classmates, needs a different treatment plan from the child who is more disruptive than peers.

4. The diagnostic impression of the child gained in an interview may depend less on the child's behavior than on who interviewed the teacher or parent, or which parent or teacher was seen, or on which day the interview was taken.

5. Almost any treatment designed for the child might be evaluated as effective by global verbal report, when in fact no objectively measured improvement is found. This may lead to proliferation of "pop" therapies that remain in force for the child, regardless of their effect, thus preempting delivery of effective services. Patterson (1982) has argued that the lack of overall progress in psychological treatment during the past half century (cf. Rachman & Wilson, 1980; Strupp, Hadley, & Gomes-Schwartz, 1977) may be due in large part to the fact that therapists receive noncontingent positive verbal evaluations from clients, whether or not treatments have worked. Testimonials about treatment success must not be confused with results from experimentally controlled studies.

6. Much of the time, energy and costs involved in taking long and involved social histories may be not only unnecessary, but at times iatrogenic. Such methods allow ample opportunity for many biases of both the interviewee and interviewer to become woven into the fabric that later will be presented as the child's "social" or "psychiatric history."

Yet, this opportunity could be used by a skilled therapist to benefit the child. When the history presented appears dismal, the therapist could help the parent or teacher construct a history that would be more helpful therapeutically. Thus, the child's history, as remembered and reported, can be shaped and *reframed*, (cf. Minuchin & Fishman, 1981; Watzlawick, Weakland, & Fisch, 1974). Once believed, history as remembered and reported can become either an obstacle or a bridge to therapeutic change, depending on the tiny sliver of history highlighted.

FUNCTIONAL ANALYSIS OF BEHAVIOR

Given that behavior observations will be made, school psychologists need a conceptual guide for collecting and analyzing such data. As with research, the value of data depends largely on how the collection process was initially designed and executed. Principles of experimental design provide a framework for collecting useful data in research (Kazdin, 1982). Principles of a functional analysis of behavior provide this structure for obtaining useful observational data when analyzing behavior problems (cf. Ferster, Nurnberger, & Levitt, 1962).

The way we define problems may prevent us from solving them (Watzlawick *et al.*, 1974). Defining and analyzing behavior problems from a functional analysis model sets the occasion for developing constructive, positive, and elegant solutions to a variety of behavior problems (cf. Goldiamond, 1974; Schwartz & Goldiamond,

1975). This section will examine the principles and perspectives needed to guide the collection and analysis of data when assessing behavior problems. Later sections will address the details of carrying out these analyses.

From an interbehavioral systems perspective, the child's behavior "is viewed as a behavioral system operating within a nested hierarchy of ever-encompassing behavioral systems" (Wahler, Berland, & Coe, 1979, p. 57). The behavior of interest is nested between functional *antecedents* and *consequences*. Each "antecedent-behavior-consequent" (A-B-C) operant event is nested within a *functional response class hierarchy*, as well as within functional *sequences* of events, within different *settings*. These larger behavioral structures are nested within complex social interaction patterns involving families, schools, workplace, and various community agencies. Each level of the system is affected by the dynamics of the levels above and below it. The following sections will only suggest factors to be considered when assessing each level of the behavioral system. We will begin with the basic three-term (A-B-C) behavioral contingency, and move up through more complex arrangements. School psychologists would assess behavior problems in the same order, going to the next level only when problems could not be resolved using data from the basic levels. The direction will be from basic functional analyses of behavior toward systemic functional analyses.

Functional analyses identify factors influencing or controlling the behavior being assessed. The analysis requires careful examination across different situations of the interdependencies among three behavioral terms: (1) the functional *antecedents* that occur just before the behavior; (2) the *behavior* itself; and (3) the functional *consequences* that occur just after the behavior. Inattention to any one of these terms, or to changes in functional relationships among them across settings or time, will lead to a distorted interpretation of the behavior being assessed (cf. Bijou, Peterson, & Ault, 1968).

Functional Antecedents

Of the many antecedents occurring prior to a behavior, *discriminative stimuli* are directly relevant to the functional analysis of behavior problems. In a given situation, different responses in one's repertoire will come to strength depending on the presence or absence of different discriminative stimuli. They occur almost immediately before responses, and in their presence the effectiveness of selected responses in a given situation is either increased or decreased (Michael, 1980). For example, a teacher's turned back while writing on the board may function as a stimulus, in the presence of which a student can more successfully pass a note to a neighbor. A child walking past another's desk may function as a stimulus, in the presence of which the sitting student can more effectively trip the walker by extending a leg. The classroom lights flicked off and on by the teacher may function as a stimulus, in the presence of which talking out will be more effectively noticed and punished. A child's raised hand may function as a stimulus, in the presence of which the teacher is more likely to call on that pupil.

Relevant aspects of antecedents usually involve their *function* rather than form or structure. Thus, although for one teacher flicking the lights off and on might be a condition in which talking out is more likely to be punished, for another teacher it may not. In one classroom, a raised hand might be a condition in which a child is more likely to be called upon, whereas in another class it may be a condition under which that possibility is reduced. Psychologists need to assess the idiosyncratic function of any antecedent for each pupil.

Functional Response Classes

Behavior has both topography (structure or form) and function. For example, a man is running. Is he running for a train, or training for a run? The form tells little about the function of the behavior. Function can be determined only by analyzing *contextual factors*. Funtional analyses identify contextual factors of which the behavior is a function.

Whereas topographical analyses group behaviors by form, regardless of differences in function, functional analyses group behaviors by function, regardless of differences in form. Functional analyses thus often seem counterintuitive. The same response forms may function quite differently depending on context, and thus be placed into separate *functional response classes*, while different forms may function similarly in a given context, and thus be grouped in the same functional response class. Teacher attention can be obtained by different response forms:

1. Completing all work accurately.
2. Raising a hand and waiting quietly.
3. Doing extra tasks and assignments.
4. Calling out.
5. Talking to and disturbing classmates.
6. Leaving the seat.
7. Pushing all materials off the desk, or doing many other things.

Rather than consider these as different behaviors (by form), they could be grouped together according to the same controlling functional variables involving child requests or demands for teacher attention.

Hierarchy

Behaviors may be arranged hierarchically according to strength within a functional response class. One pupil may complete all assignments as a first step in obtaining teacher attention. When this fails he moves to a second step, which might be leaving his seat, or dropping pencils on the floor. Another pupil may call out first to obtain teacher attention. When this fails, she may go to her second step, completing all assignments, or raising her hand and waiting quietly. Identifying relative hierarchical strengths of responses within a functional response class for a given child in a given situation may lead to more effective interventions.

Functional Consequences

Of the many postcedents occurring after a behavior, functional consequences are most relevant to assessing behavior problems. Such consequences occur *immediately* after a behavior and function to increase, or decrease, the likelihood that similar behaviors will occur in similar situations in the future. This is a kind of natural selection of behavior: In time, behaviors more effective in obtaining reinforcement in a given situation are added to the repertoire, as less effective ones are discarded. Functional consequences can be said either to strengthen or to weaken the behaviors they follow (Michael, 1973). In everyday language, they strengthen behavior because of some *gain* to the pupil (reward, praise, attention, accomplishment, relief, escape, avoidance, task termination), or weaken behavior because of some *loss* to the pupil (punishment, ridicule, failure, overwhelming effort, frustration, loss of opportunity to be reinforced, interruption of reinforcing activity).

In functional analyses, consequences (like antecedents and behaviors) are defined by *function* rather than form. Thus, candy and praise may function to strengthen one child's behavior, but weaken another's. Criticism and ridicule may weaken one child's behavior, but strengthen another's. Interruption of recess may weaken one child's behavior, but strengthen another's. Forms become "red herrings" when analyzing antecedents, behaviors, or consequences. Functional analyses factor forms to highlight controlling functions.

Functional Situational Factors

Functional antecedents, behaviors, and consequences change dynamically across situations. Situational factors may moderate the strength of any or all three terms in the basic A-B-C contingency. As a result, a child may misbehave in one room, but not another; in one academic subject, but not another; with one teacher, but not another; in large groups, but not small ones; during independent seatwork, but not in teacher led instruction; at the beginning of a period, but not near the end, and so forth. By carefully assessing which situational factors strengthen or weaken which basic A-B-C contingencies for a given child, psychologists can develop *strategic* intervention plans (plans that yield maximum therapeutic change with minimum intervention).

When behavior problems occur in one situation but not another, four broad areas can be probed.

1. Does the child have a repertoire appropriate for that situation?
2. Is appropriate behavior being prompted and strengthened (reinforced), or weakened (punished) in that situation?
3. Does the child have a competing inappropriate repertoire?
4. Is competing inappropriate behavior being prompted and strengthened (reinforced), or weakened (punished) in that situation?

The first and third questions focus on the middle or *behavior* component of the basic A-B-C contingency. Answers to these questions distinguish between what teachers often call "can't do" versus "won't do" problems. A child not working because he can't do the task requires a different intervention than the child not working because he won't do it (cf. Mager & Pipe, 1970, p. 3).

Appropriate and inappropriate repertoires are assessed by observing the child's patterns of correct and incorrect responses during class, from recently completed workbook pages and tests, by informal inventories (Alessi, 1978a; Ashlock, 1986; Carnine & Silbert, 1979; Johnson & Kress, 1964; Silbert, Carnine, & Stein, 1981), and by administering criterion referenced academic assessment tests. Standardized achievement tests are less helpful, because they usually are linked too loosely to the scope and sequence of the school's curriculum to give valid estimates of the match between the pupil's skills and the prerequisites needed to perform adequately at that stage of the curriculum (Jenkins & Pany, 1978; Leinhardt & Seewald, 1981). Because other authors (Shapiro & Lentz, 1985), and chapters by Gettinger and Lentz in this volume focus on assessing appropriate academic repertoires, this section will address the last three questions listed above. But the first question must be answered in order to put the others into proper perspective.

Note, however, that all four of these areas interact in subtle ways. For example, a child may have an adequate repertoire for reading class, but not for mathematics. This may result in enough reinforcement to keep the child on-task in reading, but not in mathematics. On the other hand, a child with a strong repertoire in math may misbehave because math class peers or the teacher prompt and strengthen his competing inappropriate behavior. Another child may have an adequate repertoire in math, but a superior one in reading. The reinforcement available in math class, although quite adequate to maintain other pupils' behavior, may be insufficient for this child, in contrast with much higher levels of reinforcement available in reading. Relationships among skill repertoires and classroom settings must be assessed before interventions are planned.

The second and fourth questions focus on the two terms bracketing behavior in the basic A-B-C contingency (the functional antecedents and consequences). Some situational factors have greater impact than others on strengthening or weakening these components. A partial list of factors to consider when assessing these areas includes:

1. Grouping arrangement. (Is it large group, small group, or individual instruction? Are low performers in smallest group, and high performers in largest group?)
2. Grouping levels. (Are pupils placed in the curriculum so that they are answering correctly at least 80% of the time? Are groupings flexible so that pupils can be moved to another group as relative skill levels change?)
3. Seating arrangement. (Are students arranged so that inappropriate behavior is less likely to be strengthened by peers, and more likely to be noticed and weakened by teacher? Is small instruction group facing the corner so

that teacher can face the group but still see the rest of the class? Are low performers and behavior problem pupils seated front and center?)

4. Teacher directed or student directed activity. (Is the teacher leading a large or small group or are pupils assigned independent large or small group seat work activity? Is the teacher pace fast enough to keep pupils on task?)

5. Instructional format. (Is the lesson in progress focusing on initial teaching, corrective teaching, generalization, discrimination, skill integration, application, expansion, cumulative review, or practice and drill?)

6. Subject area—reading, math, spelling, art, science, music, gym. (Is the subject area one in which the child's available repertoire is more, or less, likely to be reinforced?)

7. Physical arrangement and organization of classroom. (Can each pupil see the teacher's demonstrations? Are pupils consequated for having all necessary materials and being ready when class begins? Are teacher materials prepared before class and distributed efficiently?)

8. Transition routines between subjects and classes. (Are there rules for putting away materials for one class and getting out materials for the next, or coming in from recess to begin class, or moving down the hall from one activity to another? Is transition out of academic classes determined by completing work to criteria or merely by passing time? Are transition routines structured so that inappropriate behavior is less likely to be strengthened by peers, and more likely to be weakened by teacher, and so that appropriate behavior is more likely to be strengthened by teacher or peers?)

9. Schedule for daily classes. (Is schedule posted so all pupils know what is to be done when? Is schedule followed? Are assignments clearly stated, with precise objective criteria for adequate completion? Are the criteria enforced? Is additional academic adjustment time planned for pupils who do not meet criteria during class (for example, during recess, lunch, before or after school, on Saturday)? Are hard subjects taught in morning, easier subjects in afternoon; low performer groups taught first, high performer groups taught last?)

10. Choices. (Are pupils given alternatives and choices for when, how or to what criteria assignments may be completed? Are they taught responsibility by being made to accept the consequences of their choices or agreements, or taught to be irresponsible by being allowed to slip out from under them?)

Any of these situational factors, or combinations of them, may weaken or strengthen basic A-B-C contingencies crucial for appropriate behavior in that classroom. Extended discussion of these factors can be found in the literature (Becker, 1986; Becker, Engelmann, & Thomas, 1975; Brookover *et al.*, 1982; Canter, 1976; Paine, Radicchi, Rosellini, Deutchman, & Darch, 1983; Sprick, 1981, 1985).

Checklists have been developed for assessing these classoom factors (Alessi, 1978b; Monteiro & Heiry, 1983). Situational factors affecting behavior in home settings have also been discussed widely in recent literature (Burgess & Richardson, 1984; Lutzker, 1984; Patterson, 1982; Wahler, 1980; Wahler & Dumas, 1984; Wahler & Graves, 1983).

Functional Analysis of Sequences

Basic A-B-C contingent events are linked into sequences (cf. Bateson, 1972, p. 317; Kantor, 1974, p. 7). The same events can be linked together to yield quite different functional behavioral outcomes. Such outcomes cannot be identified from an isolated behavioral event, or from a single sequence of events. When a series of sequences are studied, functional outcomes become apparent. For example, in the following interpersonal sequence (adapted from Atkinson & Forehand, 1981, pp. 188–89), a child engages in several problem behaviors in response to requests by his mother.

> Child is watching TV. Mother makes request→Child ignores→Mother repeats→Child whines→Mother insists→Child Screams→Mother says, "OK, I'll do it myself." Child quiets down, watching TV.

In this situation, the mother's request in the sequence has no effect on the child's compliance. The child's ignoring then functions as an antecedent in the presence of which the mother repeats the request. The repeated request functions as an antecedent in the presence of which the child emits an escape response: whine. The child's whine evokes the mother's insistence on compliance with the request. The mother's insistence evokes the child's escalation of escape behavior: screaming. The child's screaming sets the occasion for the mother to give in and say, "Ok, I'll do it myself."

Consequences are also operating in the same sequence. The child's disregard of the mother's request is not only an antecedent setting the occasion for the mother to repeat the request, but is also a consequence for her original requesting behavior. In everyday language, one might say the child's disregard functions to weaken the mother's requesting behavior. The mother's repeating the request functions to weaken the child's ignoring. The child's whining then weakens the mother's behavior of repeating requests. The mother's insisting (perhaps changing voice tone and raising volume) weakens the child's whining behavior. The child's screaming then weakens the mother's behavior of insistence. The mother gives in. The child then strengthens the mother's yielding by ceasing to scream and throw a tantrum.

In this sequence, the child's functional response class of *escape* behaviors is strengthened by the mother giving in to it. Furthermore, the hierarchical strength of later escape responses within the class has been increased (seen as child persistence and escalation), whereas the mother's functional response class of requesting behaviors, and the hierarchical strength of later responses within this class, has been weakened by the child's behavior (seen as the mother's lack of follow-through).

Not only can behaviors act as stimuli in behavioral sequences, but such stimuli can also take on as many as three different functions. A child's whine may function to weaken the parent's initial request, as a discriminative stimulus evoking louder repetition of the request, and as a conditioned (or unconditioned) stimulus eliciting conditioned (or unconditioned) emotional responses from the parent (cf. Staats, 1975, Chapter 4). The reciprocal *respondent* eliciting effects of such behavioral interchanges (acting in concert with the above operant contingencies) may contribute to a pattern of escalation from verbal abuse to physical punishment, and finally to abusive assault (Reid, Patterson, & Loeber, 1981; Vasta, 1982). A high ratio of such aversive to pleasant interactions between parent and child may result in each becoming a generalized, conditioned aversive stimulus for the other. Each would tend to avoid being in the other's presence, and the mere presence of one may set the occasion for the other to initiate aversive behavior without provocation.

The following interpersonal sequence, with response forms very similar to the one above, is functionally quite different. It ends with the mother physically guiding the child to complete the task, and the child reluctantly complying. In this sequence, the mother's string of requests is strengthened by the child's completion of the task requested. Furthermore, the mother's persistence and escalation of firmness have been strengthened by the child giving in, whereas the child's string of escape behaviors, and escalation in aversiveness, has been weakened by the mother's responses.

> Child is watching TV. Mother makes request→Child ignores→Mother repeats→Child whines→Mother insists→Child Screams→Mother takes child by arm and guides toward task→Child reluctantly completes task→Mother says, "Now you can go back to watching TV." Child quiets down, watching TV.

Two points are made by comparing these episodes. First, although the forms of behavior are quite similar, the functional outcomes are very different. One link can change the functional impact of a sequence. Merely counting behaviors and sorting them into separate A-B-C bins would miss this functional linkage and would yield similar data for both sequences. When A-B-C events are linked together into interpersonal sequences, however, functionally different episodes appear.

Second, although the child engages in different forms of behavior (ignore, whine, scream), these all can be grouped into the functional response class of escape behaviors. Although the mother engages in different forms of behavior (repeat louder, insist, take arm and guide), these all can be grouped into the functional class of responses that induce the child's compliance with a request.

Contingent linkages among behaviors can be noted only by analyzing sequences of interactions. The underlying methodology for assessing such sequences is presented clearly in both Bakeman & Gottman (1986) and Patterson (1982). An alternate analytical approach would include state-diagramed behavioral sequences (Snapper, Kadden, & Inglis, 1982).

Pathogonomic Contingencies

School psychologists assessing behavior problems at home or in the classroom often face these kinds of functional interpersonal chains involving *compliance*. The antecedents usually involve a task being assigned, or behavior being requested, followed with noncompliance by the child. Noncompliance often follows a predictable hierarchy from simple *avoidance* by being off-task passively, escalating to *escape* by verbal off-task, then motor off-task, and finally ending with escape by terminating the task situation itself.

As an example, the child might first ignore the teacher's request (passive off-task). If the teacher notices and repeats the request, the child may escalate to verbal off-task, saying, "I don't want to," or "I can't do it," or "I'm not feeling well." If the teacher insists on task work, the child might escalate to motor off-task responses, turning around in his seat, sliding to the floor, or leaving his seat. If the teacher persists, the child might resort to various task termination behaviors: breaking pencils, tearing papers, turning over the desk, or hitting others.

A variant of the above scenario occurs when the child initiates the request (or demand) and the teacher or parent refuses to comply. The same sequence of aversive behaviors, persistence, and escalation follows, leading to functionally different outcomes, again depending only on one or two links in the interpersonal chain.

With persistent teachers, a child sometimes will learn to truncate the sequence, escalating directly to termination behaviors. Thus, when the teacher makes a request, the child begins breaking pencils and tearing papers. If this instant escalation tactic had been developed with a parent or previous teacher, the current teacher may be puzzled by the apparent over-reaction, and consider the child "crazy" or emotionally impaired. When we talk about children in these terms, most likely we are not privy to the history of interaction that has shaped the current response pattern.

When we understand the functional antecedents, operating contingencies, and history for such behavior, it seems more predictable, less crazy, and more amenable to change. Functional analyses usually provide this kind of hopeful, therapeutic information.

The *demand* interpersonal scenario, and the complementary avoidance-escape-termination scenario, may account for the majority of behavior problems encountered by school psychologists. Consistent with Patterson's data (1982), these two modes of interpersonal contingencies may be core etiological factors (pathogonomic signs) responsible for a variety of conduct and oppositional behavior problems seen by psychologists (disruption, destruction, hitting, biting, kicking, self-injurious behavior, stealing, lying, and so on). Effective programs have been developed which focus on just such compliance issues (Engelmann & Colvin, 1983; Forehand & McMahon, 1981).

SYSTEMIC FUNCTIONAL ANALYSES

Dyadically focused functional analyses can miss crucial factors affecting basic A-B-C contingencies. This can be avoided by adopting a systemic perspective. Systemic factors strengthen or weaken the operation of clusters of related basic A-B-C contingencies. Whereas dyadic functional analyses study factors influencing the child's behavior, systemic functional analyses build upon this by studying factors influencing individuals who affect the child. It is done ideally by performing additional functional analyses on the behaviors of others that may need to be changed to change the child's behavior. It seeks answers to the question: Why do people act in ways that shape or maintain the child's problem behaviors?

Sequential analyses mark the transition from basic to systemic perspectives. Focus is placed on *triadic* (or more complex) social interactions, *macro* (molar) functions of the behavior problem within the larger social context, and *metacontingencies* (contingencies on who can set contingencies, how, on which behaviors).

These terms, and systemic analysis itself, do not imply that any new principles of behavior are involved, but instead are used to mark important dimensions along which basic contingencies may be influenced. Systemic analyses are described in differing ways by Burgess and Richardson (1984), Fisch, Weakland, and Segal (1982), Goldiamond (1984), Haley (1963, 1976, 1980), Harris (1982), Minuchin (1974), Wahler (1976), Wahler, Berland, and Coe (1979), Wahler and Dumas (1984), Watzlawick, Weakland, and Fisch (1974), and Wells and Forehand (1981). Similar issues have been addressed on a more abstract, theoretical level by J. R. Kantor (1959) and Kantor and Smith (1975).

Dyadic versus Triadic Sequences

Systemic analyses focus on triadic rather than dyadic interactions (cf. Wahler, 1976, p. 517; Wahler, Berland, & Coe, 1979, p. 58; Wahler & Hann, 1986, p. 157). Basic A-B-C contingencies for two people can be radically altered by involvement of a third, or fourth, person. For example, in the two mother-child sequences presented above, very different outcomes occurred based on the change in one link in each sequence. A systemic functional analysis asks, "Why did mother act one way in the first sequence, and another way in the second?" Perhaps during these episodes the father was in the other room relaxing after work, reading the paper. In the first sequence, as the interaction between mother and child escalated, the father screamed at the mother, "Keep that child quiet so I can relax and get some peace of mind," so the mother gave in to the child. In the second sequence, as the interaction escalated, the father may have shouted to the child, "If you don't do as your mother asks, you won't watch TV tonight," so the child gave in and completed the task. The father's reaction in turn may vary depending on problems at work, or economic, family, personal, or marital problems. Thus, several persons may directly and indirectly influence the functional outcome of the sequence for the child. Sometimes the triangulating force involves teachers, therapists, professionals from social agencies, the police, bill collectors, or other coercive forces from the community (cf. Burgess & Richardson, 1984; Wahler, 1980; Wahler & Graves, 1983).

Several problem triadic interactions may operate consecutively or concurrently within a family (cf. Haley, 1981). The grandmother may form a coalition with grandchild undermining the mother. The grandmother may form a coalition with daughter (wife) undermining husband. The mother might form a coalition with another child undermining the father. Each of these coalition patterns can serve to change the functional outcome of any dyadic sequence of interaction in the family. Of course, family members do not enter coalitions to cause trouble, but often to *protect* the child or another family member. Psychologists understanding this position will design treatment plans incorporating these protective concerns.

Similar triangulating patterns operate in schools, with coalitions formed unwittingly between principal and child, undermining teacher; or between school psychologist (or social worker) and child, undermining teacher; or between one teacher and child, undermining another teacher; or between parent and child, undermining teacher.

Systemic functional analyses lead to intervention plans that incorporate the resources and skills of all relevant family members or school staff. The likelihood that plans will be implemented as designed, and supported rather than undermined by others, is increased. The likelihood that gains will maintain over time, and transfer across settings, tasks, and other behaviors, may likewise be increased.

Macro- and Microcontingencies

Systemic functional analyses also distinguish between immediate and remote postcedents. Within *micro*contingencies, postcedents immediately following a behavior affect that behavior (are functional consequences). Within *macro*contingencies, postcedents only remotely linked to the behavior appear to affect that behavior. It is not clear how these could function effectively as behavioral consequences. But somehow macrocontingencies apparently strengthen or weaken clusters of related basic A-B-C microcontingencies.

Often molecular microcontingent A-B-C events are embedded as molar units within macrocontingencies. For example, a girl may have a skin infection that itches. She scratches the area to relieve itching, but scratching further damages the skin, leading to more itching. The cycle continues until the skin is so damaged that hospitalization is required.

At a *micro*contingency level the pattern can be explained by invoking the basic principle of negative reinforcement: scratching relieves itching. Effective treatment could be developed from this functional analysis. Although treatment at the microcontingency level works in the hospital, relapses might occur regularly upon discharge.

A *macro*contingency analysis might find that the itching-scratching-hospitalization molar (or fused) event allows the girl to avoid school. This *macro* may weaken effects of basic A-B-C microcontingency interventions, thus making treatment difficult, and leading to relapses and rehospitalization. Relapses might be prevented with intervention plans incorporating both micro- and macrocontingencies.

Microcontingency events can function as molar units in a larger context, not only for the same person but across persons in the social network. In the above example, macrocontingency analyses might further note that the girl's mother, having been out of work for ten years raising a family, dreads going back to work now that her last child is in school. The skin condition enables both to stay home. Macrocontingencies for both girl and mother thus may interact in a synergistic way, rendering ineffective any number of basic A-B-C microcontingencies designed to resolve the skin problem. Noncompliance with treatment plans might become the major obstacle to improvement.

As another example, a college woman's bulimic episodes could be a function of various basic A-B-C *micro*contingencies related to fasting and eating. However, the molar event (bulimic episode) might function in a *macro*contingency to allow the woman to avoid attending dreaded social activities or taking stressful exams. This macrocontingency may weaken the effect of various treatment plans aimed only at microcontingencies for binging and purging (cf. Goldiamond, 1984).

There are also community level macrocontingencies. Sometimes availability of disability income may weaken plans for treating chronic pain. Availability of hospitalization (respite care) may weaken home intervention plans for a disruptive child. Availability of special classrooms may weaken plans to resolve a child's problem in mainstream classrooms. Rather than *secondary* gain, such macrocontingencies could be said to yield *systemic* gain.

As with individual behaviors, only patterns of sequences among molar events can indicate whether a given behavior problem is functionally related to broader levels of social contingencies. The examination would include a systemic rather than a dyadic focus. First consider the following episode:

1. Child increasingly acts up, beyond level mom can control.
2. Dad (or therapist) steps in to help mom get child under control.
3. Child's behavior is controlled. Dad (or therapist) disengages as child acts normally.

This episode is punctuated in terms of a dyadic focus on child and parent. It appears that as the child acts up, dad steps in to restore order. Later the child might "relapse" after dad disengages. From a dyadic perspective this may suggest that dad is competent in handling the child, whereas mom is not. The solution may involve training mom in parenting skills. However, punctuating the same episode triadically, as in the following sequence (adapted from Haley, 1976, pp. 106–107), might lead to another interpretation.

1. Father is disengaged from family due to marital conflict.
2. As part of the marital conflict, mother continually nags father for his disregard of family.
3. Marital fighting escalates to level of extreme discomfort for all family members.
4. Child increasingly acts up, eventually beyond a level mom can handle alone.
5. Dad and mom temporarily suspend marital fighting to cooperate on crises involving child. Dad steps in to help mom get control of child.
6. Child's behavior problems become controlled, partially due to parents presenting united front to child, and partially due to reduced marital (and therefore family) stress.
7. Without child crises, marital conflict again comes to strength with mother criticizing how father disciplines child (he is too harsh, or too easy; too quick, or too slow; too rigid, or too wishy-washy; and so on).
8. Dad begins to disengage from family to previous position.
9. Mom increases nagging of dad for disregard for family.

This second episode is punctuated triadically to show how the child's problem behavior as well as the marital problem could function as molar units within the larger family context. The three steps in the first episode occur as steps four, five and eight in the second episode. Comparing the two episodes suggests that the dyadic interaction in the first example provides linkage in a more elaborate sequence involving other family members and issues. The second example also suggests that one type of problem is linked to another in a complementary fashion (Bateson, 1972, pp. 68–72; Haley, 1963, pp. 8–19). Furthermore, the last step in the second sequence leads back to the first, suggesting a continuous, circular pattern of interactions.

Whereas a psychologist with a dyadic focus might see an incompetent mother and a series of behavioral cures and relapses, one with a systemic focus might see the behavior problem as a *functional arc* (or linear segment) in a broader, *circular* social interaction pattern, with interlocking components rather than cures and relapses. Either analysis could lead to quite different treatment strategies. The psychologist with a systemic focus would devise treatment plans that anticipated potential functional relationships between the child's behavior and the marital relationship, and the possible impact of a change in one on the other.

Without a systemic focus, a psychologist focusing on topography might consider as a curiosity the family in which she treated the daughter for school phobia two years ago, the mother for agoraphobia one year ago, and now the parents for marital difficulties. Psychologists with systemic perspectives might consider all these problems as different complex topographical expressions of the same family dynamics, and underlying functional social contingencies.

Behavior Analysis by Metaphor

Microcontingencies involve applications of basic behavioral principles of reinforcement and punishment. Macrocontingencies involve more subtle arrangements, because the postcedents are too remote to have a direct affect on the behaviors in question. Reinforcement and punishment processes (as currently understood) operate only within a narrow temporal conditioning window, usually measured in seconds. Although postcedents in macrocontingencies appear to be functional consequences, the events are too far removed from the behavior to be called properly either reinforcement or punishment. Macrocontingent postcedents may strengthen or weaken behavior only in a metaphorical sense: They function *as if* or *like* reinforcement or punishment, but may not in fact be such. How remote outcome postcedents affect behavior remains to be explained by the theoretical or experimental branches of behavior analysis (Michael, 1986; Minervini, 1985, 1986).

Metacontingencies

There are rules and contingencies controlling *who* can set contingencies on another's behavior, *how* and *when* those contingencies are to be set and enforced, and limits to *what* can be included. These could be called *"meta*contingencies" (Alessi, 1979; cf. Haley, 1963), and they can either strengthen and enable; or weaken, prevent, or interrupt the application of various micro- and macrocontingencies to the solution of behavior problems (cf. Skinner, 1978, 1986). Metacontingencies evolve through a process that Skinner (1981) terms the third level of selection by consequences: cultural selection.

Metacontingencies can be formal or informal. Formal metacontingencies include laws (cf. Martin, 1979), local school policy, professional ethical standards (APA Ethical Standards), or religious tenets. They function as a special type of rules the person can describe as well as apply when setting contingencies (cf. Skinner, 1968, Chapter 6). Informal metacontingencies include cultural norms, values, attitudes, beliefs, moral standards, or practices established through precedent in a family, group, community, or agency. They accurately describe someone's contingency setting behavior, but are not necessarily identified or used as such, and perhaps even denied, by that person.

Disagreement over metacontingencies may weaken clusters of micro- and macrocontingencies. Two parents may disagree on who should consequate which child behavior, or in what manner, or when. A parent and teacher may similarly disagree. Sometimes parents disagree because of differing child rearing attitudes, or differing approaches to handling a child with a chronic illness (Is the child "bad" or "mad" or "sick"?), or to more general marital conflicts.

Parents, teachers, principals, and school psychologists may disagree on meta-contingency issues related to classroom management. Such disagreements may involve issues of training and skills, role definition (Can school psychologists tell teachers how to run their classrooms?), or inept consultation skills.

Rules about who can tell whom what to do, when, and how, evolve in subtle ways. Compare the following statements. A teacher says to a pupil, "If you complete your work, you may go to recess early." A pupil says to a teacher, "If I complete my work, may I go to recess early?" The two statements include the same basic contingency, but different metacontingencies. The first explicitly states a contingency about recess upon completing work, while implying the metacontin-gency: Teachers set contingencies in this class. The second explicitly states the same contingency, but implies a different metacontingency: Pupils set contingen-cies in this class. A pattern of acceptance of such statements over time establishes which informal metacontingency describes a classroom or home situation.

A parent may try to get a child to eat peas, when the child wants carrots. The child may vigorously resist. On a basic level the outcome may be strictly a matter of behavioral consequences. On a metacontingency level, however, the struggle may be about establishing who can tell whom what to eat, or when or how to eat, or whether to eat anything at all. The same issues apply to school consultation. A teacher's rejection of the school psychologist's recommendation may be because it is not feasible, or may relate to the fact that accepting such advice shifts the nature of their relationship at a metacontingency level: School psychologists can now tell teachers how to teach.

A family may operate under a rule that children should not be rewarded merely for doing what they should do anyway, or that only "bad" parents need advice from professionals on how to raise their children. A teacher may operate under a rule that misbehaving pupils should not receive special attention and consideration, or that changing teaching practices to resolve behavior problems confirms that the problems were caused by faulty past teaching practices. When unaware of the informal metacontingencies under which others operate, we often say they have hidden agendas.

Restructuring metacontingencies with children may lead to rapid behavior changes, because broad clusters of micro- and macrocontingencies may be strengthened simultaneously. The same basic principles of behavior analysis are involved, but the focus is on establishing who can set and enforce basic contingen-cies. Recent behavioral research and treatment on *generalized compliance* is especially relevant to restructuring metacontingencies (Engelmann & Colvin, 1983; Forehand & McMahon, 1981; Neef, Shafer, Egel, Cataldo, & Parrish, 1983; Parrish, Cataldo, Kolko, Neef, & Egel, 1986; Patterson, 1982; Russo, Cataldo, & Cushing, 1981; Slifer, Ivancic, Parrish, Page, & Burgio, 1986; Wells, Forehand, & Griest,

1980). Some home and school programs also emphasize this level of intervention (Canter, 1976, 1985).

Systemic concepts also may apply. Often a coalition between a child and adult (e.g., other parent or grandparent) may change the child's relationship with the other parent at a metacontingency level. Some medical or psychological symptomatology (e.g., diabetes, hemophilia, anorexia, pyromania, selective mutism) may change or reverse the parent-child relationship at a metacontingency level. These sorts of complications make metacontingency restructuring substantially more difficult, but still feasible (Haley, 1963).

Restructuring metacontingencies for parents and teachers is more problematic. Persuasion by way of logic and research data usually fails, often alienating the parent or teacher from the school psychologist. Paradoxically, the harder one tries to change a firmly held belief about metacontingency issues, the more vigorously they are defended. Psychologists thus should search for and work within metacontingency frameworks on which both they and the teacher or parent can agree, and avoid those over which they disagree. For example, a parent might disagree that children should be rewarded for an accomplishment, but might agree that families should celebrate such accomplishments. A high school teacher might deny that discipline is part of his job, but accept teaching of responsibility as part of the job.

Metacontingencies can be identified in several ways. First, a pattern of struggles across a variety of micro- and macrocontingencies suggests a metacontingency conflict. A two-year-old child says she wants eggs for breakfast, but after eggs are prepared, she wants pancakes instead. When pancakes are prepared, she wants cereal instead. When cereal is presented, she wants toast instead. At one level we might say she doesn't know what she wants. At another level, she is establishing an informal metacontingency that her parents follow her directives, rather than the other way around. Psychologists focusing on the basic level may target behaviors such as scanning all options before choosing an item. This approach may or may not work, because it may address the wrong target.

Second, school psychologists sometimes can confirm metacontingency problems by presenting a *compliance routine* (Engelmann & Colvin, 1983). For example, suppose a child refuses to read a list of words in his reader. The teacher could ask him to complete a series of very simple tasks (touch your ear, stand up, raise your hand, touch the book), interspersing within the series a few requests to read the words. If the child readily responds to the simple tasks, but not the reading ones, the problem may be a lack of skill or faulty basic contingencies. Refusal to do any of the tasks, however, suggests that the issue is one of who can tell whom what to do.

A third approach to assessing metacontingencies is by noting the language people use. Metacontingencies are framed in the contexts of "shoulds" and "ought tos." A parent ought to do this. A teacher should do that. Note how directives are given and consequences stated. Look for frequencies of *alpha* versus *beta* commands (Forehand & McMahon, 1981, p. 34). An alpha command is clear, simple, do-able and usually requires a motoric response within a briefly defined time limit (e.g., "Sit down now at your desk and start your homework"). A beta command, by contrast, is vague, complex, not do-able, and has no time limit (e.g., "You'd better straighten out and get better grades"). Likewise, how practical and do-able are the consequences threatened? What is the ratio of threats to taking threatened action? A parent threatening to "ground her until she's eighteen years old" might sound tough, but is implicitly saying, "I won't do it." A parent threatening to "ground her for two weeks" may sound less tough, but is implicitly saying, "And I'll do it."

In families operating under metacontingencies that adults set contingencies, parents give alpha requests, state realistic consequences, monitor compliance, and warn, threaten or scold very little before following through. They are in charge and act like it. In families operating under metacontingencies that children set contingencies, parents give beta commands (to avoid challenging the authority of the child), don't monitor compliance (to avoid confronting the child), state patently absurd consequences (to let the child know they aren't really serious) and warn, threaten, whine, and scold rather than take corrective action. They are not in charge, and act like it (cf. Patterson & Bank, 1986).

Implications for School Psychologists

1. Comprehensive assessments of behavior problems cannot rely solely on observations of forms of behavior, but must note how these forms fit into context with antecedents and consequences, in differing situations, and within differing interpersonal sequences. A functional analysis of behavior sequences is needed. A single behavioral link in a complex sequence may change the functional outcome of the entire interaction.

2. Assessment should address why others do what they do to help maintain the problem. A systemic functional analysis may be needed. Is the behavior problem partially maintained by a coalition between the child and another adult, undermining the contingency setting ability of the person affected by the problem? Does the problem behavior itself function as a molar unit within a broader social context? Is the problem behavior partially maintained by its function for the child in another context, or for another person in this context? Assessment should consider how resolving this behavior problem might affect the interpersonal positions of those in the child's social network.

3. Although there is no symptom substitution, there may be topographical substitution within functional response classes. Likewise, there may be systemic problem migration within the functional social network. Although there is no secondary gain, there may be systemic gain.

4. Large problems (generalized noncompliance) may develop as the cumulative effect over time (cf. Maruyama, 1963) of a relatively minor dysfunctional behavior interaction pattern, such as a reversal of one or two links in a functional interpersonal sequence. Often the detail is small enough to go un-

noticed even by experienced psychologists, who then develop elaborate and complex diagnoses under the belief that big problems demand big explanations.

5. Large problems may be solved by making relatively minor changes in patterns of behavior interaction (cf. Maruyama, 1963). Big problems do not always demand big interventions. Sometimes change will occur quickly, but more often large changes will occur slowly as the small intervention works its cumulative effect throughout the system over time. Although psychologists may feel pressure to use standard, proven "off the shelf" programs to get dramatic short-term results, more durable changes may occur as a result of highly focused, specific interventions tailored to address the idiosyncratic functional variables of the given problem situation.

This broad conceptual model for understanding and evaluating behavior problems has been presented to ensure that psychologists see behavior not as a simple function of a limited set of factors. Assessing behavior problems also is not a simple, clear-cut process, although at times it may seem that way. The next section will explore how school psychologists can begin to assess various aspects of this complex interbehavioral system.

STRATEGIES OF BEHAVIOR OBSERVATION

This section describes strategies for obtaining behavior observation data in order to derive useful analyses and interpretations. Later sections will address issues and problems involving both reliability and validity of such data.

The strategy proposed here involves collecting the least amount of data necessary to functionally analyze and resolve the referral problem. The functional analysis model was presented to suggest the complexity of variables influencing any given behavior in a natural setting. Practicing school psychologists cannot be expected to assess all areas included in a complete functional analysis. Indeed, the technology has not been developed to assess all areas even if one had the time and energy. Some variables are difficult to assess because they are private or covert (cf. Alessi & Kaye, 1983, pp. 32–36). More importantly, many variables crucial to a complete analysis of a current behavior pattern are no longer available for assessment. These variables had their influence historically, and current behavior is the only trace of their existence.

Fortunately, complete functional analyses of antecedents, behaviors, consequences, situations, sequences, and systemic factors rarely are necessary to resolve most school behavior problems. Psychologists can develop effective interventions after analyzing only high priority antecedent and postcedent conditions across a carefully selected sample of situations. The approach advocated here begins with a focus on the referral problem and a basic analysis of that problem. Other dimensions would be added to this initial analysis only as needed.

Interviewing the Teacher or Parent

Success in school consultation hinges on the initial interview. For details involved in interviewing teachers, see Alessi and Kaye (1983) and Gresham (this volume). The initial interview must accomplish three tasks: obtaining a clear definition of the problem behavior and an estimate of how often, when, and where it occurs; probing for potential functional variables that may be influencing the behavior; and establishing a solid constructive foundation for future consultation.

Have the parent or teacher describe the problem in detail. Ask for examples of the least, and most, serious incidents. Describe the usual incident. Probe potential discriminative stimuli by asking for a description of what happens just before the incidents, in terms of activities, settings, and actions of others. Probe potential functional consequences by asking for a description of what happens just after the incident, in terms of changes in activities, settings, or actions of others. Probe possible hierarchical functional response classes by asking for other kinds of behavior the child might engage in were he unable to exhibit the described inappropriate behavior. Probe potential situational factors by asking when the problems occur most and least often. Note any differences across teachers, class-rooms, subjects, peer groups, days of week, activities, and so forth. Probe potential sequential linkage patterns by asking for two or three incidents: What happened next? What happened then? What next? After that? If feasible, trace out a dozen interactions before stopping.

Probe for potential systemic *macro*contingencies (cf. Tomm, 1987) by asking the parent, "Who in the family is most concerned about the child's problem? Who is least concerned?" Ask who is most adversely affected by it. Ask how the parent's (or teacher's) life would be different were the problem resolved. If the problem has been longstanding, ask why the referral was made at this time. Find out parent's (teacher's) estimate of how long it will take to resolve problem, if at all. Find out who is willing to invest the most in getting a resolution. Who the least?

Probe potential triadic involvements by asking which family adults interact with the child on a regular basis, and the nature of those interactions. Ask who is most protective and nurturant of the child. Ask who is the "heavy" in terms of discipline. Ask parents for their own theories on why the child has this problem. Ask parents what theories have been offered by grandparents, friends, and relatives to explain the child's problems, and whether they as parents agree or disagree, and why.

Probe potential *meta*contingency problems by asking for the kinds of things the parent (teacher) has done in the past for similar problems that have been at least partially successful. Ask them about the harshest discipline they give, and then ask how they feel when they have to do it. Ask for the different kinds of advice they have received from family and friends for resolving the problem behavior, and whether or not they agree with each kind, and why. Note their use of "shoulds" and "ought tos," in relation to discipline.

Selecting Target Behaviors

When consultation and intervention are based on narrowly defined constructs such as "off-task," "talking out," or "out of seat," school psychologists can feel comfortable using direct observations as the major assessment tool. Fortunately, most consultation will be aimed at just these kinds of narrowly defined targets. However, school psychologists should not feel as comfortable using direct observation on a limited number of discrete behaviors to assess such broadly defined constructs as "emotional impariment" or "autism." For these broader constructs, various other measures would be needed in addition to counting behaviors (cf. Nunnally, 1978).

Assuming you have assessed several more narrowly defined behavior problems, there are at least six criteria for selecting behavior problems for intervention. First, one could begin with the behavior problem that is most distressing to the parent or teacher (cf. Tharp & Wetzel, 1969). Obtain a rank ordering of the top three priority behaviors to change, and go down the list. Second, one could target the behavior problem that would be relatively easy to change, thus building up parent (teacher) skills and confidence for more difficult problems. Third, one could strategically select a target behavior that is a general prerequisite to a range of other problem behaviors. Generalized compliance would meet this criteria. Fourth, one could select a target behavior because it is deemed most important by the child, or might improve the child's life the most. Fifth, one could select a target behavior because it stands out too far from the norms for that age child in the problem situation. Sixth, a pair of behavior problems may be selected in cases in which one can be used to modify the other (Haley, 1976, p. 48). For example, if a child needs both to increase his exercise and to practice the piano, one might suggest that he complete so many exercises for each minute of piano practice missed, or vice versa. If a child needs both to practice addition and to stop interrupting class, one might suggest that she complete so many addition problems for each instance of disruption. In this way two target behaviors are selected and played against each other. Whatever the criteria for selecting target behaviors, agreement should be reached with the parent (or teacher) and, whenever possible, the child.

Collecting Observation Data

The details of collecting observation data by school psychologists have been described in depth in a manual by Alessi and Kaye (1983), Deno and Mirkin (1977), Kratochwill (1982), O'Leary, Romanczyk, Kass, Dietz, and Santogrossi (1979), and Sackett (1981). Coding systems for observation have been developed for school (Saudargas, 1982), and home settings (Patterson, Ray, Shaw, & Cobb, 1969; Reid, 1977; Wahler, House, & Stambaugh, 1976). Protocols for collecting behavior observation data in school settings and placing behavior within sequences between antecedents and consequences, are available in Alessi (1980), Alessi and Kaye (1983), Cobb and Ray (1972, 1976), Ray (1976), and Stuart (1974). The Alessi and

Kaye manual provides extensive appendices including several observation protocols, suggested formats for interviewing teachers or parents, and sample copies of school psychological reports based on direct observation data. A videotape for training school psychologists in observational techniques is also available (Alessi & Kaye, 1982), and is designed to complement the above manual. Readers not already familiar with details of obtaining direct observation data are urged to study some of these materials before attempting to collect such data.

Behavior observations can yield both inter- and intraindividual analyses, to answer different questions. *Inter*individual analyses compare the pupil's performance with those of other pupils. *Intra*individual analyses compare one area of the pupil's performance with other areas of her own performance (behavior in different settings, with different persons, in different subjects, doing different tasks). Behavioral assessment begins with an interindividual analysis, and proceeds to the intraindividual level only as indicated.

Stage 1: Interindividual Behavior Analyses

Interindividual behavior analysis is the initial stage of assessment, yielding data most relevant to making screening, identification, and placement decisions. For problem behavior referrals, school psychologists must first answer two questions: Does the child's observed behavior agree with the verbal report of the teacher (or parent), and is the child's behavior sufficiently deviant from that of peers to warrant intervention? If the answer to both questions is "no," usually the child need not be singled out for further scrutiny. If the answer is "yes," further analyses of the problem behavior are completed.

Comparison Pupils

Answering these questions requires observational data on the referred child and at the same time on other pupils in the same class and activity. Comparison pupils can be selected in several ways. First, the teacher could suggest pupils of the same sex who will be engaged in the same task during the observation sessions. Teachers are cautioned against suggesting only the "model" pupils. The psychologist then randomly selects one pupil as the comparison. Second, the psychologist could randomly select a comparison pupil from a classroom seating chart. Third, the psychologist could systematically observe all (or most) pupils in the group within which the referred pupil is working during the observation session. A time-sample method (Thompson, Holmberg, & Baer, 1974), which will be described later, can be used.

Scan-Checking

Brief samples of the entire classes' behavior can be taken to provide a broader perspective on classroom norms. These broader samples are obtained by a procedure called *scan-checking*, adapted by Alessi (1980) from PLA-CHEK procedures

(Cataldo & Risley, 1974; Risley, 1972). Every minute or two during the session, the observer looks up to scan the entire class to note how many pupils are behaving appropriately at these times. Data from scan-checks may be construed as norms of behavior accepted by the teacher and pupils in that class and activity.

Local Micronorms

The "referred pupil/comparison pupils" strategy (cf. Alessi, 1980; Alessi & Kaye, 1982, 1983; Deno & Mirkin, 1977; Patterson, Shaw, & Ebner, 1969; Ray, 1976; Stuart, 1974; and Walker & Hops, 1976) provides what Alessi (1980) has termed local *micronorms*, composed of the behavior of other pupils of the same sex in the same situation and task requirements, but who have not been identified as exhibiting behavior adjustment problems. Data on the referred pupil can then be compared with this local micronorm to decide whether further assessment is necessary. When differences are confirmed, the norms provide a basis for setting behavioral goals for the referred pupil.

Problems with Micronorms

The use of local micronorms for evaluating pupils' performances may be inappropriate. It is possible that the norm should be adjusted based on the level of behavior acceptable were the pupil to be transferred to another class where more tolerance or other norms would render the referral problem less deviant. These, however, are issues of school practice, procedure, and policy. School psychologists more often than not must accept and work within the norms as set by the teacher (and principal). The local micronorm approach is a practical way of working in schools with quite diverse norms and task requirements, to do what is in the best educational interest of the pupils.

However, pupils should not be considered well adjusted merely because behavior matches the micronorms of a particular class. Perhaps the behavior of the class is unacceptable within the norms of the local school building or school system. Classes as well as individuals may exhibit problem behavior. In these cases, the comparison units would be that class and other classes of the same grade and composition in that building or across the system. The assessment strategy would be the same as that applied to the individual, but entire classes would become the *referred* and *comparison* units, with scan-check data collected from similar classes in the system. Further details on doing such performance analyses can be found in Gilbert (1978).

Validity Issues with Interindividual Analyses

There are four threats to the validity of behavioral observation data often encountered when using the "referred pupil/comparison pupil" strategy. First, the psychologist may observe the pupils during a nonproblem part of the day, or on an unusually good day. Second, the comparison pupil also may be a classroom behavior problem, but not referred by the teacher . . . yet. Third, the critical behaviors may have been misidentified or poorly defined. Fourth, the referred pupil may not have as serious an adjustment problem as reported by teacher, with a possible hidden agenda behind the referral. Teachers are most likely to challenge validity of results when the data do not support their perceptions. Usually the challenge involves one or more of the above four possibilities. Careful preobservation planning can minimize, but not eliminate, each of these threats.

Use the initial teacher interview to determine the most opportune time and place to observe. Ask the teacher: "When do these behaviors occur most often? At what time? Which day? Which subject area? Which is the very best situation to observe to ensure that the behavior will be seen?" Then arrange your schedule to observe at this prime time. Whenever possible, plan to spread your observation time over three or four ten-minute sessions, rather than one thirty to forty minute session. Spread the shorter sessions over a week or so. If feasible, have the teacher switch activities from those of strength to weakness, or vice versa, during your observation session.

With proper scheduling, observations can be done on several cases the same day in the same building. In one hour, several ten-minute samples could be taken in different classes. By observing only when the behaviors are most likely to occur, and by taking several samples, the problem of missing the behavior is reduced considerably. If you observe many sessions and continue to miss the behavior, this may indicate that the behavior occurs so seldom it may not be as severe a problem as initially reported, or perhaps something else is the problem.

Invalid samples often are obtained because the teacher has trouble staying on schedule. At the agreed time, the planned activity may not be occurring and for various reasons the teacher cannot begin it while you are there. If this happens often, the teacher may be having classroom management problems. Such problems must be resolved before successful assessment or intervention is possible.

Alternately, the pupil just may not engage in the problem behaviors when you are present. In this case, reassure the teacher that this means that the problem is getting better already. If pupils inhibit inappropriate behavior merely in the presence of a stranger, that behavior is clearly under voluntary control. The solution lies in establishing a management system to help the pupil keep behavior under control when strangers are not present.

The second threat is that you have somehow selected a comparison pupil with similar behavior problems. To control for this, select different comparison pupils for each ten-minute observation session. This will expand your limited sample, allowing better representation of usual classroom behavior. Perform scan-checks every minute or so throughout each session. Scan-check data may indicate that most pupils engage in the problem behavior. Such data put into context other data that have been collected on a possibly biased comparison pupil.

Group scan-check data are helpful to refer to when someone says: "Yes, the data show no differences between the two pupils, but that's because the comparison pupil is just as bad as the other one." Evaluate this interpretation against the scan-check data.

The third possible threat to validity is that somehow you have misidentified or poorly defined the problem behavior. This issue relates to construct validity. For example, the teacher may be concerned about "talking out" in class. After assessment, you may intervene and successfully reduce the pupil's talking out by 90%, to levels below almost all other classmates.

In spite of your carefully implemented treatment, and evaluation data, the teacher may say that the problem is as bad as ever. You probably have been working with the wrong target behavior. Sit down with the teacher and review the definitions. Perhaps the teacher is not as concerned as much about the talking out as with the content of what is said. The 10% left of talking out may be laced with vulgarities. The teacher may have been too sensitive or shy to frankly offer the exact nature of the talking out problem. With this new information, you are in a better position to resolve the teacher's true concern.

When initial definitions do not isolate the precise concerns of the teacher or parent, you are setting yourself up for a "no win" situation: Even if you resolve the problems as identified, your program is considered unsuccessful. Good consultation and interviewing skills can help prevent this dilemma.

The fourth validity threat may be a hidden agenda behind the referral; the reported problem is not the issue of concern. This may be the most difficult threat to handle. Unless the hidden agenda can be flushed out tactfully, the real problem cannot be targeted, much less resolved.

Sometimes the hidden agenda is that the teacher wants the pupil removed to another room. Many teachers have at least some kinds of pupils with whom they do not feel comfortable. They may assume these feelings are rare among teachers, unprofessional, and not to be shared. One teacher may intensely dislike working with a pupil with personal hygiene problems. Another teacher may dislike working with pupils with certain kinds of physical deformities. The teacher might hope to have the pupil removed by submitting a referral for an ostensive behavior problem.

When no differences in behavior can be found between the referred and comparison pupils (or with the class scan-check), the psychologist might explore possible hidden agendas. Again, good consultation and interview skills can help resolve this issue. In the kindest manner possible, give permission for the teacher to disclose the hidden agenda. Sometimes brief self-disclosure of your own personal biases may give that permission. Sometimes teachers are not even aware of their own personal biases. The bias may only surface when the teacher is told that the pupil will not be removed to another class.

Stage 2: Intraindividual Behavior Analyses

After confirming that the referred pupil indeed engages in behaviors inappropriate for the class and teacher, *intra*individual analyses of behavior are needed to identify specific factors of which the problem behavior is a function. This analysis will lead directly to intervention plans that have the greatest possibilities of success with the least amount of time and energy expended by the teaching staff.

This second stage may take considerably more time than usually expected from traditional methods for diagnosing pupils as emotionally impaired or behaviorally disordered. Although more traditional methods take less time to reach a diagnosis, they seldom lead to effective intervention plans. As noted in the report from the National Academy of Sciences (Heller *et al.*, 1982), an assessment does not meet the intention of federal mandatory special education laws as "comprehensive" unless it identifies educational needs in a way that leads to effective intervention (see pp. 98–99). Behavioral assessment, by functionally analyzing the problem, meets the legal intent of assessment comprehensiveness.

Phase 1: Analysis Across Settings and Tasks within Settings

The first phase of intraindividual behavior analysis involves assessing situations or settings associated with increased problem behavior, and with decreased problem (and increased appropriate) behavior. More simply, what are the pupil's settings of relative strength and weakness? Does the pupil engage in problem behavior in reading, but not spelling? With one teacher, but not another? With one group of peers, but not others? Within the same class, does the pupil engage in problem behavior with some tasks (e.g., independent seat-work) but not others (e.g., small group teacher-led instruction)? Or with initial teaching activities, but not with review and practice? Use the list of situational factors presented earlier as a guide to possible variables to probe. Finding intraindividual variability is crucial for identifying factors that will be effective in changing the problem behaviors.

Data from settings of strength and weakness can be examined conjointly to identify how they differ in terms of the presence or absence of factors relating to effective teaching practices (Becker, 1986; Brookover *et al.*, 1982), classroom management (Becker, 1986; Becker, Engelmann, & Thomas, 1975; Paine *et al.*, 1983; Sprick, 1981, 1985), and curriculum (Carnine & Silbert, 1979; Engelmann & Carnine, 1982; Greer, 1980; Martin & Hrycaiko, 1983; Silbert, Carnine, & Stein, 1981). When discrepancies in problem behavior are found between different tasks within the same class, further examination may reveal differences in teaching practices for the different tasks.

Phase 2: Analysis of Sequences of Antecedents and Consequences

Within settings, focus is on examining the interdependencies among functional antecedents, behaviors, and consequences. What occurs just before and just after the problem behavior? Are there *avoidance, escape,* or *termination* behaviors by the pupil to requests or demands made by the teacher (or parent)? Is there an escalating pattern among these behaviors? Are there *demand* behaviors by the child for teacher, parent, or peer compliance? Is there an escalating pattern here, as teacher, parent, or peers try to avoid or escape these demands? What are the functional outcomes of these interpersonal sequences? If such factors are noted, do they occur more often in problem or nonproblem behavior settings?

Confirmation Probes. Finding differences is one thing. Finding out whether those differences make a difference is another. School psychologists do this by asking the teacher to change *only one thing* that is most likely to be related to the behavior discrepancy. If a reduction in behavior problems follows, this factor may be the only change the teacher need make. If problem behavior is unaffected, another change is *substituted* for the first. When behavior problems decrease, but not as much as desired, the teacher is asked to change *only a second* factor. If this results in acceptable reduction in problem behavior (or increase in appropriate behavior), no further assessment may be needed, and the case can be placed on follow-up and maintenance status.

In this way, the teacher's burden is diminished by asking for only the minimum necessary to change the pupil's behavior. By changing the environment in the "least restrictive" way to resolve the presenting problem, the pupil's civil rights are minimally threatened (Heller *et al.*, 1982; Martin, 1979), and the psychologist avoids a lengthy, traditional comprehensive assessment process that usually consumes more staff resources and time merely to diagnose a problem than it would take to resolve it using a *strategic* behavioral assessment approach.

Phase 3: Assessing Systemic Influences

When assessment reveals factors functionally related to the problem behavior, but one plan after another fails to resolve the situation, the school psychologist may look for systemic factors that may be working at cross-purposes to the agreed intervention plans. Likewise, when the intervention works repeatedly, but chronic relapses occur afterwards, systemic influences may be operating. If resolving the behavior problem can justify further time and resources, the psychologist may focus more closely on systemic factors.

Psychologists should be aware of systemic influences and note such possibilities from the beginning of consultation. When it is clear from the initial interview that systemic factors are involved, this stage may be entered before Phase 1. At times, these issues and problems must be resolved before focusing directly on the problem behavior (cf. Burgess, 1979; Burgess & Richardson, 1984; Lutzker, 1984; Reid, Taplin, & Lorber, 1981; Wahler, 1980; Wahler, Berland, & Coe, 1979; Wahler & Dumas, 1984; Wahler & Graves, 1983; Wells & Forehand, 1981). In this case, however, the psychologist reassures others that intervention plans ultimately are aimed at the presenting problem.

Directly observing systemic factors operating in home settings usually is not a practical option for school psychologists. Systemic data currently are gathered in analogue situations by interviewing families with *all* members present, and by observing how family members interact (agree or disagree, minimize or maximize, support or undermine, attack or protect, help or obstruct, praise or criticize, accept or deny responsibility) in this artificial situation when presented with certain questions, problems, classroom tasks, and homework assignments.

Systemic influences on teachers' classoom behaviors also often relate to factors operating outside the school setting (e.g., job stress, marital difficulties, family problems, depression), and are thus not directly observable by school psychologists. At this time the most feasible approach is to understand such influences and recognize signs of their possible operation. Most data are obtained through careful questioning, and study of patterns among sequences of molar behavioral events (cf. Alessi & Kaye, 1983; Haley, 1976; Madanes, 1981, 1984).

Clinical Examples

In 1962, Ferster *et al.* proposed, in a classic paper, that clinical problems be analyzed with a functional analysis of behavior. Mischel (1969) presented strong evidence that behavior disorders are influenced more by situational ("state") than dispositional ("trait") factors. Recent published reports include examples not only of how functional analyses identify these factors, but also data confirming the effectiveness and elegance of the approach.

For example, Carr, Newsom, and Binkoff (1980) functionally analyzed aggressive behavior of two retarded children. They found that aggressive behavior occurred more often when *requests* were made of the children, and also was strengthened when the aggression allowed *escape* from these requests or demands.

Iwata *et al.* (1982) functionally analyzed self-injury in nine developmentally delayed children. They assessed each child across four situations suspected of being related to self-injury—that is, during academic tasks, when alone, at play, and during social disapproval for self-injurious behavior. They found that self-injurious behavior was functionally different for the different children, in the following ways.

Two children engaged in the behavior more often in academic task situations, suggesting that escape or termination from such teacher demands functioned to strengthen such behaviors. Four other children engaged in self-injurious behavior mainly when alone, suggesting that for them the behavior might be maintained by its self-stimulatory function.

The final three children engaged in self-injurious behavior across all four situations, suggesting that their self-injurious behaviors, although formally (topographically) similar, were nonetheless functionally quite distinct. Self-injurious behavior for each child at one time might function as an *escape* response, at another time as *self-stimulation*, and at another as a *demand* for attention. These children might require multicomponent treatments designed to address each separate function. Treatment aimed at a single function might appear only partially successful overall, even though very effective with the particular function targeted.

Stereotypic behavior was functionally analyzed by Mace, Yankanich, and West (in press). Four situations suspected to be related functionally to stereotypic behaviors were evaluated (playtime quiet room no classmates, playtime classroom no music, playtime classroom music, and playtime classroom music with headphones). Stereotypic behavior occurred most often in the classroom with no music playing, substantially less often in the classroom with music playing, and very little either in the classroom listening to music through headphones, or in the quiet room without music or classmates. Thus, two factors associated with weakened stereotypic behavior were identified: presence of music, and absence of normal classroom noise.

Other studies by Mace, Page, Ivancic, and O'Brien (1986) and Slifer, Ivancic, Parrish, Page, and Burgio (1986) have also examined the relationship of demand and attention (social disapproval) to aggressive and disruptive behavior with developmentally delayed children and adolescents. In each study, different conditions were found to be related functionally to rates of behavior, thus suggesting different intervention strategies. More detail regarding the specific methodology used in performing these analyses and their applicability to school-based problems can be found in Mace, Yankanvich, and West (in press).

Behavioral Covariation

Slifer *et al.* (1986) also present interesting data on the *covariation* of compliance with all three inappropriate behaviors. Because aggression was related to escape from task demands, compliance training for task completion was chosen as the intervention. Not only did aggression decrease as task compliance increased, but disruptiveness and destruction likewise decreased, without direct intervention.

Behavioral covariation has been reviewed in depth by Wahler and Fox (1981). "It is assumed that the events of interest (this case, responses) become grouped into functional classes because they are controlled by common stimuli in the child's environment. Thus, predictable covariation across a number of a child's behaviors might be due to the fact that all share the same discriminative and/or reinforcing stimuli" (Wahler *et al.*, 1979, p. 40). Behavioral covariation across settings may, or may not, be observed, depending on possible influence of systemic factors (Wahler, 1969; Wahler & Hann, 1986). Topographical, but not functional, response covariation has been reported with some self-injurious children (Maag, Wolchik, Rutherford, & Bradford, 1986). Behavioral covariation has not been found in some studies (cf. McMahon, Forehand, & Griest, 1981, p. 223). Most of the studies in which covariation has been found apparently involve some form of compliance training. This may support the notion that these problem behaviors are functionally linked at a metacontingency level.

The demonstration of behavioral covariation in the Slifer *et al.* study and others (Cataldo, Ward, Russo, Riordan, & Bennett, 1986; Neef, Shafer, Egel, Cataldo, & Parrish, 1983; Parrish, Cataldo, Kolko, Neef, & Egel, 1986; Russo, Cataldo, & Cushing, 1981; Wells, Forehand, & Griest, 1980) has important implications for treatment of behavior problems. If one behavior can be changed indirectly by targeting another, then the therapist can focus on those covarying target behaviors most accessible and easy to treat. *If* problem behaviors are functionally linked at a metacontingency level, interventions aimed at restructuring metacontingencies (compliance training) may eliminate a broad range of untargeted undesired behaviors while strengthening an equal number of untargeted appropriate ones. Comprehensive programs are available to treat noncompliance (Engelmann & Colvin, 1983: Forehand & McMahon, 1981). As noted earlier, noncompliance may be a core etiological condition linked developmentally to a wide range of conduct disordered behavior (cf. Patterson, 1982: Patterson & Bank, 1986).

Behavioral covariation also raises ethical questions about unsuspected and unmonitored treatment side effects. Although the little research to date has identified mainly positive effects, the possibility of negative effects remains. Undesirable effects of covariation would be a kind of "behavioral pollution," in need of further scrutiny.

Structural Analyses of Behavior

Sometimes the important variables in assessing a behavior problem are not a matter of stimulus control or consequences. The problem instead may involve *response production* difficulties. Here, the topography or structure of the response itself may be the object of analysis (cf. Engelmann & Carnine, 1982, Chapter 23). Structural analyses produce antecedent stimuli (i.e., discriminative stimuli) in the presence of which therapists can more successfully modify topographical features of the child's response production repertoire. Iwata, Riordan, Wohl, and Finney (1982) structurally analyzed eating responses as part of a functional analysis of pediatric feeding disorders. Structural components assessed included open mouth for food acceptance, mouth closure, tongue thrust, and mouth empty. Breaking down the eating response into discrete components permitted an analysis of precise steps at which difficulties arose for different children. The identified components could then act as antecedent stimuli in the presence of which the therapist's shaping interventions would be more effective. Structural analyses usually are applied only to response production problems.

Summary. In the above examples, behavioral assessment identified factors functionally related to a variety of problem behaviors. The results were then confirmed by *probes* during which the teacher or parent changed the identified factor and noted the effect on the behavior. Later, interventions would be designed to incorporate these changes into the setting or daily routine of the pupil, or teacher, or parent. Using this strategy, each of the above behavior problems was measurably improved with relatively simple and nonintrusive procedures. Such analyses have been successfully applied to a wide range of behavior problems, including whining, verbal abuse, throwing a tantrum, noncompliance, aggression, disruption, destruction, self-injury, stereotypic behaviors, feeding problems, Pica, selective mutism, and others. The range covers the great majority of behavior problems referred to school psychologists. Interventions successful with one target behavior can affect several nontargeted covarying behaviors, leading to greater program flexibility and efficiency, but also to unresolved questions about the practicality of monitoring such broad band behavioral side effects.

The extra time invested in carefully assessing problems reduced time in treatment. With more precise analyses of critical factors influencing behavior problems, interventions can become specific, less complex, briefer, and more effective. Conversely, with less precise analyses of critical factors, interventions will remain general, more complex, longer-term, and less effective.

SELECTING A MEASUREMENT SYSTEM

Even when proper strategies are followed for functionally analyzing behavior, results can be distorted and weakened by several problems related to how observation data are collected. The following five methods of recording classroom behavior have been presented in detail elsewhere (Alessi, 1980; Alessi & Kaye, 1982, 1983). Brief descriptions are given here as a basis for the discussion to follow on issues that can distort the accuracy of direct observation data.

Interval Recording

Interval recording results in a measure of the *number of intervals* (time blocks) within which the behavior was observed to occur (e.g., Andrew was on-task during 9 of the 30 intervals observed). Interval length usually is set from six to a maximum of thirty seconds each. When several behaviors are being observed and recorded, the interval is broken down into two separate parts, one for observing and the other for recording. When only a few behaviors are observed, recording can be done while observing, without need for separation within each interval. Behavior may be recorded when it occurs for any portion of the interval (*partial* interval recording), or only when it continues during the entire interval (*whole* interval recording).

Note that this method results in the number of intervals in which the behavior was observed to occur, not the number of times or the amount of time the behavior occurred. Conclusions from interval records are carefully worded: "Cheswick was observed to be 'on-task' during 60% of the *intervals* assessed."

Time Sample Recording

Time sample recording results in the number of times the behavior was observed to occur at specified sampling points in time (at the end of every 10-second period, or at the end of every 10-minute period). The major difference between time sampling and interval recording is that with time sampling one observes the pupil momentarily and only at the prescribed times, whereas with interval recording one observes the pupil throughout the interval. The disadvantage of time sampling is that you get a much smaller sample of the observation time. The advantage is that one can do other things between samplings, such as observe other pupils.

Note that this method results in a measure of how many times the behavior occurred at the specified times, but not the number of the times the behavior occurred at other times, or the amount of time the behavior occurred during any session. Conclusions from time sampling records are carefully worded: "Sarah was observed to be on-task for 80% of the *times sampled.*"

Event Recording

Event recording results in a measure of the *number of occurrences* of the behavior during the entire observation session (e.g., Chelton spelled 18 words correctly in 15 minutes). Event recording is more difficult to use than interval or time sample methods because the definitions of behavior must be more precise. With interval and time sample methods you note whether or not the behavior is occurring during (or at) the times observed. For event methods, you must be able to note exactly when a behavior either starts or stops (Kunzelmann, Cohen, Hulten, Martin, and Mingo, 1970).

When the number of occurrences of the behavior are divided by the time of the observation session, the resulting measure is the rate or frequency of the behavior observed. As noted by Alessi (1980), rate of behavior is a universal measure, capable of incorporating all other aspects of behavior (duration, latency, intensity, topography, function, speed, or repetition) within the definition of the particular unit of behavior to be counted. Thus, one may count only behaviors of a given duration, intensity, latency, or topography. One may define several different categories merely by differences in latency, duration, or intensity of behaviors of the same topography. Rate data thus allows one to analyze structure or topography of behavior as it may relate to functional environmental variables.

Permanent Products

Event recording also is well suited for behaviors that result in *permanent products* (Hall, 1971; Webb, Campbell, Schwartz, & Sechrest, 1966). Behaviors that leave permanent products (number of problems completed on worksheets, number of words spelled in composition, answers written in workbooks) often are easy to measure, because the observer does not have to be present when the behavior occurs. The teacher (or parent) can collect the permanent products from the pupil and give them to the psychologist for later tabulation. With some experience and creativity, permanent product methods may be devised for a variety of school- and home-based behavior problems.

Duration Recording

Duration recording results in a measure of the length of time each behavior continued (e.g., Caitlin painted for 16 minutes). Duration is more difficult to measure because one has to identify exactly when the behavior both starts and stops. By comparison, event recording requires that one identify when the behavior either starts or stops. For this reason, duration measures are used only when elapsed time per se is the major concern for the teacher.

Latency Recording

Latency recording results in a record of the precise length of time between a specified classroom event and either the onset or completion of the defined behavior; the teacher asks Mary to stand, and ten seconds later Mary stands up. Latency recording is difficult to use because one needs to define exactly when the signaling event occurs *and* when the signaled behavior either starts or is completed. For this reason, latency recording is recommended only when elapsed time by itself is the major concern of the teacher or parent, and no other method can be found to measure the problem. Usually, latency records are used with compliance problems such as sitting down, beginning assignments, putting away objects when asked, or generally following directives.

Combinations

Combinations of methods sometimes can be selected to better measure a problem. For example, recording event data within an interval framework allows detection of changes in rate of behavior across intervals within a session (cf. Alessi, 1980, pp. 36–39). Marked changes in rate are usually caused by an environmental change of some kind. School psychologists would note any factor(s) preceding drops in rate of behavior within a session, and then systematically manipulate these factors to confirm a functional relationship to the problem behavior.

PSYCHOMETRIC CONSIDERATIONS

The above five recording methods, and combinations of them, cover the great majority of situations encountered both in applied research and field practice. With these definitions, discussion now can turn to psychometric characteristics pertinent to direct observation data, and especially to reliability and validity.

Stability versus Sensitivity

Traditional psychometric approaches to reliability and validity are not directly applicable to behavioral assessment using a functional analysis approach (Cone, 1981). For example, stability of measures over time is considered crucial in most psychometric methods. This might be reasonable when measuring phenomena that are relatively stable over time (e.g., height or achievement). Such concepts are inappropriate when judging a tool that measures something that changes within brief time periods, such as behavior across contexts. Assessment tools that are sensitive to changes in behavior as the environment changes may appear unstable or unreliable. However, stability is expected only when the contexts and behaviors measured do not change. When they do change, sensitivity is more important than stability.

Functionally Analyzing "Recording Behavior"

Observation protocols contain records made by psychologists while observing behavior. These records are permanent products of *responses* made by the observer at the time. Rather than apply traditional psychometric concepts blindly to behavior observation methods, a more useful approach might be to analyze functionally the behavior of the observer while recording observations. "Recording responses," as such, are influenced by the same kinds of factors as most other behaviors.

A functional analysis of observation behavior focuses on two issues. First, is the recording behavior exclusively under the stimulus control of the behavior observed? Second, do these records enhance success in dealing with the problem at hand? That is, are they functional antecedent stimuli for more effective behavior by those dealing with the situation (discriminative stimuli)?

Observation procedures are devised to ensure that recording responses are solely under the stimulus control of the ongoing behavior observed, and not influenced by factors that might distort this relationship. In terms of a functional analysis (Skinner, 1957, pp. 91–117), recording responses should qualify as *generic tact extensions* (i.e., under the control of the essential, and only the essential, features of the defined responses being recorded), as opposed to qualifying as *metaphorical tact extensions* (under the control of some, but not all, the essential features), or *metonymical tact extensions* (under the control only of irrelevant features that may have accompanied essential features in the past). Furthermore, recording responses should qualify as "pure" tacts (under exclusive control of discriminative stimuli), rather than "impure" tacts (distorted by functional consequences applied to the responses) (Skinner, 1957, pp. 149–152).

Records of behavior observations become discriminative stimuli, in the presence of which the school psychologist's behavior will be more, or less, effective in dealing with the referral problem (cf. Whaley, 1973, pp. 11–14). The validity of such data would be determined by the effect on the psychologist's subsequent behavior, as determined by analyses of such behavior under conditions with and without data, or with different kinds of data.

In everyday language, one might loosely say that the data act as "feedback" (discriminative stimuli and perhaps reinforcers) to guide the psychologist's behavior (cf. Peterson, 1982). The greater the increase in the effectiveness of therapist behavior compared with conditions without such data, the greater the functional quality of the data collected. Traditional psychometric methods would be applicable when they lead to increases in the quality of behavioral data, and less applicable when they do not.

Accuracy or sensitivity is usually a prerequisite for data to function effectively as discriminative stimuli. But many factors can distort the accuracy of data obtained, or confidence in such data. Factors that may distort recording responses include: demand conditions affecting the recorder, which may distort both how deviant behaviors are defined as well as how they are recorded using those definitions; fatigue and distractions; the method of recording (interval, time sample, event); the size of interval or sample cycle (10 versus 60 seconds); and many others. Procedures for recording and interpreting behavior should be designed to minimize these possible distortions, and increase confidence in results.

Interobserver Agreement

Interobserver agreement is an index of how well two independent observers agree on what did or did not occur while watching the same event. It is an estimate of objectivity. It implies that the recordings obtained are more a function of the behavior of the object observed than the behavior of the subject doing the observing. By contrast, subjectivity would imply that the recordings reflect more the behavior of the subject doing the observing than the object observed. We certainly imply in psychological reports that results reflect pupil characteristics rather than examiner idiosyncracies. Interobserver agreement methods enable the detection of such personal biases distorting observation records.

This requirement, however, creates other problems. For example, obtaining interobserver agreement indexes is very difficult using standard event recording methods. Thus, researchers were shaped into switching to either interval or time sample recording so that interobserver agreement estimates could be obtained more readily. Using interval and time sample methods in turn led to an emphasis on topography of behavior observed rather than *operant function*, and discrete behaviors rather than A-B-C operants.

Topography was rarely the focus in basic behavioral analysis research. A bar press was counted regardless of its form; it could have been pressed down with a right or left paw, or pulled down with either paw, or tail, head, shoulder or back. What was counted was not the response form, but the function of closing the electronic relay. All these behaviors, which differ in form, were counted in the same functional response class.

Identifying functional relationships was further impaired by the inability of interval or time sample methods to record precise A-B-C sequences as they occurred in relation to environmental stimuli. Instead, data usually were recorded in separate bins, defined by topography, and summarized as totals within bins, ignoring functional connections between events across bins. The result has been a change in the basic data structure underlying applied behavior analysis. Although the field was founded on laboratory research using mainly rate data on functional response classes, research now is conducted using mainly interval or time sample data on topographical response classes (Springer, Brown, & Duncan, 1981). The shift also introduced an additional set of probelms relating to how interobserver agreement indexes were to be obtained.

Problems Calculating Indexes of Agreement

Interobserver agreement indexes can be obtained in different ways. *Correlations* can be calculated on the data from two observers over a series of sessions, using scored interval or time sample data. Several factors can distort this index. If one observer is consistently more lenient than the other, correlations will be spuriously high. If there is a restriction in range of behavior exhibited during the sessions, correlations will be spuriously low. When correlation indexes are computed from overall agreement scores, high correlations may occur even when two observers fail to agree on any single behavior occurrence, because the approach does not require occurrence-by-occurrence agreement. For these and other reasons, correlation methods are rarely used today to calculate indexes of interobserver agreement.

Agreement indexes also have been calculated by counting the total number of intervals in which a behavior was scored by one observer, repeating the process for the second observer, and then dividing the smaller number obtained by the larger. This method, however, often led to highly inflated agreement scores, because it (like correlation methods) was not sensitive to whether two observers agreed on any given interval. For example, were one observer to score behavior occurrences only in each of the first ten of twenty intervals, while the second observed scored occurrences only in each of the last ten, both would still obtain indentical occurrence and nonoccurrence interval results (10 occurrence, 10 nonoccurrence), as well as perfect *overall* agreement on numbers of intervals scored with occurrences and nonoccurrences (10 each for both observers). Neither observer would have agreed on a single scored interval.

Interval-by-interval agreement methods correct this by counting as agreements only those intervals for which *both* observers agreed that the behavior either occurred or did not occur. In the above example, this method would have resulted in 0% agreement, because the two observers failed to agree on any single interval.

Interval-by-interval agreement indexes, however, are vulnerable to another kind of distortion whenever there is either a very high, or very low, portion of total intervals scored with behavior nonoccurrences. For example, when only a few intervals are scored with behavior occurrences (e.g., 20%), two observers can obtain overall interval-by-interval agreement indexes of 80% without agreement on a single interval in which a behavior occurrence had been scored.

Interobserver agreement on seeing no behavior is different than agreement on behavior occurring. Prevalence of phenomena affects false positive and false negative rates whether the subject is signal detection (cf. Egan, 1975), personnel selection (Arvey, 1979), clinical diagnosis (Baldessarini, Finkelstein, & Arana, 1983; Cebul & Beck, 1985), or behavior observation (Bijou, Peterson, & Ault, 1968).

Reporting separate *occurrence* and *nonoccurrence* indexes of agreement can correct this kind of distortion. Interval-by-interval agreement can be calculated separately for (1) intervals in which at least one observer recorded a behavior (scored occurrence agreement), and (2) for intervals in which at least one observer reported no behavior (scored nonoccurrence agreement). Sometimes the resulting indexes will differ considerably from each other, as well as from the composite interval-by-interval results. For proper confidence in interpreting such data, all three indexes of interval-by-interval agreement should be reported: composite agreement, occurrence agreement, and nonoccurrence agreement.

Problems with Interval Size

Large interval sizes can lead to inflated indexes of interobserver agreement. Two observers may disagree scoring each occurrence of behavior, yet obtain nearly identical overall scores as well as high levels of interobserver agreement. For example, consider the case where the behavior occurs in both the first and last half of each interval, and a twenty-second *partial interval* method is used. If one observer scored occurrences only in the first half, whereas the other scored occurrences only in the second half of each interval, both would obtain very similar overall scores, and nearly perfect interval-by-interval agreement indexes. However, observers would not have agreed on any single occurrence of behavior within any interval. This would have become obvious with a shorter interval (e.g., a 10-second rather than a twenty-second interval).

In general, the higher the rate of the behavior, and the briefer the behavior duration, the shorter the interval size applied. Interval size should be set ideally so that not more than one behavior will occur within the same interval. However, such a record would then become functionally equivalent to an event measure.

Problems with Event Records

As noted earlier, indexes of observer agreement are more difficult to obtain from *event* behavior records. First, two observers record occurrences on separate pieces of paper, both synchronized to the same time base. Second, the two records are compared to determine if both observers recorded events *at the same instant*. Such data can be obtained when both observers use hand-held (e.g., Hewlett-Packard HP-71 B) or lap-top (for example, Kaypro 2000 Plus; Toshiba 1100 Plus; Zenith 181 or 183) computers synchronized on a real time base. Agreements are scored when both observers record an event at the same time. Disagreements are scored when one observer notes an event, but the second observer either does not note it, or instead notes another event.

Computers can record not only *rate* of behaviors, but also *durations* and *latencies*, depending on how long the observers held down various recording keys. Computers can track and analyze *sequences* of events, as well as *trends* within and across sessions. They quickly can calculate indexes of interobserver agreement and even graph the resulting data. Lap-top computers also can perform the word processing tasks required to integrate the data into psychological reports or into larger databases. Although designed for Digital Equipment's PDP-11 minicomputer, the SKED-11 program (Snapper & Inglis, 1984) provides a sophisticated example of the capabilities of computer technology as applied to the analysis of behavioral data.

The requirement that two observers record behaviors at the same *instant* for interobserver agreement is a stringent one. With interval recording, agreement is counted even though one observer records the behavior as soon as it begins, whereas the other records when it ends, or even a few seconds after the interval is over. With computer recording devices, such records would not be counted as agreements, because both were not made at the same instant.

With paper and pencil recording, an observer can correct a mistake, or reconsider quickly and revise a previously marked interval. The real time clock base that allows two computers to be synchronized for checking agreements prevents such corrections, unless a special function, clear entry key can be dedicated to each category of behavior. Even this would not adjust for the discrepancies between the times both observers scored the behaviors, unless the corrections replaced the original record. With event records, and especially when using computers to record data, particular attention must be given to defining exactly when a given behavior starts (or stops) and then counting only those microevents (Kunzelmann *et al.*, 1970).

A less stringent but readily available strategy would be to record event data within rows of intervals and then calculate event agreement interval by interval. Two methods of calculating event-within-interval agreement indexes are *exact* agreement (Repp, Dietz, Boles, Dietz, & Repp, 1976), and *block-by-block* agreement (Bailey & Bostow, 1979). With exact agreement, both observers must have counted the same number of events in an interval for it to count as an agreement. For example, if one observer noted twenty events within an interval, but the other noted only eighteen, the entire interval would be scored as a nonagreement (0% agreement).

With block-by-block agreement, the smaller event count of the two observers is divided by the larger count for each interval. In the above example, eighteen would be divided by twenty, resulting in an agreement index of 90% for that interval. The mean of the resulting quotients for all intervals would be reported as the agreement index.

Exact agreement methods impose extremely stringent requirements on observer agreement, whereas block-by-block methods impose moderately stringent requirements. The more stringent or precise the criteria for agreement, the lower the resulting index. The precision capable with computers may lead to deflated agreement indexes, in the 0% to 10% range, when in fact the data are of higher quality. For event methods, in contrast to interval methods, the cost of greater precision in calculating agreement indexes is less clarity when interpreting results.

Future research with computer recording will determine which size block should be used when calculating event agreement indexes (1 second, 5 seconds, etc.).

In summary, for the same observation session, different levels of agreement can be obtained depending on which method is chosen to calculate observer agreement. For example, while composite interval-by-interval agreement might yield 90% agreement, a separate analysis for scored occurrences and nonoccurrences might yield indexes of 80% for nonoccurrences and 50% for occurrences. Had event records been obtained in the same intervals, block-by-block agreement methods might have yielded only 40% to 50% agreement. Applying exact agreement methods to the same data might have yielded only 20% agreement.

Clearly, the level of interobserver agreement can be inflated or deflated by the method used to record data and calculate the index. School psychologists should note in their reports the methods used to record the observations as well as the exact method used to calculate observer agreement.

Changes in Behavior during Sessions

Distortions in observation records can result from changes across sessions in the behavior either of the observer or the child observed. *Observer drift* refers to changes in the recording behavior of the observer across (or within) sessions, whereas *topographical drift* refers to changes in the target behavior exhibited by the child observed.

Topographical Drift Outside the Target Definition

Over a number of sessions, but especially during treatment phases, the topography of the targeted behavior may drift outside of the boundaries of the definitions used. For example, the behavior might be defined as self-injury by *face slapping*. When treatment begins, face slapping decreases, but *arm biting* increases. Treatment might be considered effective, when in fact it is not. The psychologist now is faced with a dilemma: Can arm biting be added to the behavior definition when it had not been counted before? How would this affect the validity of the resulting data? This problem points to the importance of assessing functional rather than topographical response classes.

Topographical Drift within Definition Boundaries

Sometimes lack of observer agreement is due to subtle differences in target behaviors between two children, or in the same child's behavior across sessions. For example, both children may be observed for very similar self-injurious behavior involving head and face slapping. Two observers may agree on occurrences for one child but not another, or on one child during some sessions, but not others.

The differences may relate to the fact that every time one child's hand moves above his shoulder line, he slaps his head, whereas the second child often raises his hand to scratch his cheek, rub his chin, or brush his hair. The examples of target behaviors differ more clearly from nonexamples for the first child, but more closely resemble nonexamples for the second child. Such changes also could occur for the same child across sessions, changing levels of agreement between the observers.

When behavior occurrences and nonoccurrences differ only minimally, observer agreement problems can be expected. From a functional analysis perspective (Skinner, 1957, pp. 107–114), the differences are derived from the fact that the observers' recording responses are not under the control of the specific subset of stimuli within the complex situation that exclusively relates to head slapping. Recording is influenced by such irrelevant factors as the gross location of the child's hand. Such recording response errors would be considered metaphorical or metonymical, rather than generic, tact extensions. As previously noted, for valid and reliable data, recording responses must meet the criteria for nondistorted *abstract tacts* (occur in the presence of the specific discriminative stimuli of the target behavior, and *only* those features, and not be under the control of any specific functional consequences).

Observer Drift. Observers may drift in their criteria for scoring a behavior, but in the same direction (*consensual drift*). Resulting scores thus agree, but are inaccurate estimates of the behaviors emitted. Observers need to be periodically assessed and *recalibrated* to prevent such drifting criteria. A standard set of videotapes can be used to calibrate behavior observers at various times during the year. In addition, new observers can be introduced at various times to probe for any drift from the original criteria by the primary observers (Kazdin, 1977).

VALIDITY AND AGREEMENT

Merely because two independent observers agree on behaviors recorded does not necessarily assure that the records accurately represent what occurred in the session. As already noted, two observers may drift consensually outside the definitional boundaries of behavior. Alternately, two observers may make similar misinterpretations of the same event. For example, many observers in the audience may agree that a magician flipped four aces off the top of a well-shuffled deck of cards. This does not ensure that the cards came from the top of the deck. Interobserver agreement, even among fifty observers, does not ensure accuracy. A single magician in the audience may report that the cards came from the bottom of the deck, or from the performer's sleeve. In this case, the accurate report is the one without interobserver agreement.

Although helpful, independent agreement among observers may not be essential to all purposes for which behavior observation data are used. As Skinner noted in his classic 1945 critique of operationalism:

> The public-private distinction emphasizes the arid philosophy of "truth by agreement." . . . The ultimate criterion for the goodness of a concept is not whether two people are brought into agreement but whether the scientist who uses the concept can

operate successfully upon his environment—all by himself if need be. What matters to Robinson Crusoe is not whether he is agreeing with himself but whether he is getting anywhere with his control over nature. . . . agreement alone means very little. Various epochs in the history of philosophy and psychology have seen whole-hearted agreement on the definition of psychological terms. This makes for contentment but not for progress. The agreement is likely to be shattered when someone discovers that a set of terms will not really work, perhaps in some hitherto neglected field, but this does not make agreement the key to workability. On the contrary, it is the other way round. . . . (Skinner, 1972, p. 383).

Workability usually requires that data adequately map recursive relationships between behavior and environment. This is related to, but not identical with, validity. Although interobserver agreement increases confidence that recording behavior has not been distorted in some way in the observation session, other factors can distort the relationship between data obtained and interbehavioral events that occurred. Such distortions may reduce the behavioral quality of the data as discriminative stimuli in comparison with data of greater accuracy or validity.

Summary

Distortions in recordings may account for the discrepancies found between global verbal reports about the pupil's behavior, and the results of direct observation. Bringing together issues covered in this chapter, such discrepancies may relate to the following possibilities:

1. The *definitions* of target behavior may not match the concerns of the teacher or parent reporting a problem. There may be inadequate definitions, observer drift in applying definitions, or behavior topography drift by the pupil within or outside the definitional boundaries. Sometimes problems may relate more to systemic issues than the reported specific problem behavior.

2. The observation samples may not adequately represent the behavior being observed. The referred pupil may be observed on unusually good days. The comparison pupil may have an unusually bad day, or also be a problem pupil. The class scan-checks may represent an unusually bad day, or be distorted by the timing of the brief samples.

3. The observation method may not record defined behaviors as they occur in session. Different recording procedures may give different results for the same defined events (Repp *et al.*, 1976; Springer, Brown, & Duncan, 1981).

For example, using interval recording, longer intervals may yield less sensitive and reliable data than shorter intervals for behaviors that occur frequently. Assume the event occurs steadily and on average six times per minute, and both ten- and sixty-second interval methods are applied. While the ten-second interval might yield five or six scored intervals per minute observed, the sixty-second interval would yield only one. If the behavior were then to decrease to one time per minute, no differences might be detected by the sixty-second interval method, while the ten-second interval method might show a drop from five or six to one scored interval. Event records, by comparison, would show the exact number of occurrences in either situation.

Time sampling methods may be less sensitive than interval or event methods for behaviors that occur very briefly. Assume that the behaviors in the above example lasted on average only three seconds. A ten-second time sample method might have detected only one or two behaviors when they were occurring at six times per minute, and none when the rate dropped to one per minute. Had the behaviors lasted on average eight seconds, the same time sample method might have detected five or six events when they were occuring at six times per minute, and perhaps one while the rate was once per minute.

Partial interval methods can overestimate the actual amount of time behaviors occur during a session, whereas whole interval methods can underestimate it. Assume the observed behaviors occur every thirty seconds, last only ten seconds each, are evenly distributed throughout the session, and a thirty-second interval method is applied. A partial interval method would result in all intervals being scored (since the behavior occurred during part of each interval), whereas a whole interval method would result in no intervals scored (because no behavior occurred for an entire interval).

Partial interval methods may be less sensitive than event records for behaviors that occur very frequently. Assume the behavior occurs twenty times per minute, and occurs steadily throughout the minute. Whereas an event method would record twenty discrete behaviors per minute, a sixty-second interval method would yield one scored occurrence in that same minute. A thirty-second interval method would yield two scored occurrences for the twenty behaviors, a fifteen-second interval four scored intervals, and a six-second interval ten scored occurrences.

Whole interval methods may be less accurate than duration methods in measuring the amount of time behaviors continued. Whereas the duration methods would yield the exact length of time the behaviors continued, the whole interval method would have missed all intervals for which the behavior did not occur during the entire interval, thus underestimating the actual duration of all behaviors.

Implications

Such distortions not only may explain part of the disagreement between verbal report and observed behavior, but also may lead to serious misinterpretations of data. For example, assume an intervention decreased a pupil's inappropriate behavior rate from fifteen to one per minute. Although an event method would have detected the large decrease, a sixty-second partial interval method would show no change, because only one occurrence would be scored whether one or fifteen behaviors occurred during the interval. The teacher might say the plan was effective. Although event data would have supported this view, interval data would not have.

Assume you receive one referral for high rates of inappropriate behaviors (talking out) and another for a less frequent but troublesome behavior (out of seat).

Using the whole interval method for talking out, you may detect no differences between the referred and comparison pupils. Had an event, or even partial interval method, been selected, clear differences may have been found. Although whole interval method data would not have supported the teacher's verbal report, partial interval data might have.

Using an event record for out-of-seat behavior may have detected no differences between referred and comparison pupils. However, a whole or partial interval method, or duration method, may have shown that while both pupils leave their seats the same number of times, the referred pupil remains out of her seat for much longer periods. Although event data would not have supported the teacher's verbal report, duration data would have.

Interobserver agreement also is integrally related to proper interpretations of observation data. As noted, different ways of calculating agreement can yield different estimates of agreement. For interval methods, this is especially influenced by the ratio of scored to unscored intervals.

For example, when performing interindividual analyses, referred and comparison pupils may be observed for a target behavior: disruption. Many intervals may be scored with disruptions for the referred pupil, while few are scored for the comparison. This seems to indicate a clear difference until one considers that the estimates of interobserver agreement may be different for the two pupils. Agreement estimates for the referred pupil are based mainly on occurrences, whereas those for the comparison pupil are based on nonoccurrences, of disruption. If the nonoccurrence agreement index is 90%, while the occurrence index 50%, the two pupils' data cannot be confidently compared. These concerns apply equally to interpretations of results from intraindividual analyses across settings of strength and weakness for the same pupil.

This issue applies to the interpretation of treatment evaluation data. Disruption may decrease from a pretreatment high rate to a posttreatment low rate. With low interobserver agreement on occurrence data, less confidence can be placed in this interpretation. Such differences could be due to recording errors.

For proper perspective, psychologists need to report results of interval data in either of two ways. First, composite agreement indexes could be reported, along with separate indexes for both occurrence and nonoccurrence data. Alternatively, composite agreement indexes could be reported separately for each phase of the assessment (baseline, treatment, etc.). If indexes of agreement are high within both baseline and treatment, but scored occurrences drop or rise markedly from baseline to treatment, one can *assume* high levels of agreement for both scored occurrences and nonoccurrences of the behavior measured.

Ethical Dilemmas

Parents (or teachers) refer children on the basis of global verbal report data. When results from direct observation do not concur with teacher (or parent) verbal report, what should be done? Should the child be treated only on the basis of global verbal data, when direct observations do not concur? Should the child be denied treatment because direct observations fail to concur with global estimates by parents or teachers?

On the other hand, direct observations may initially concur with global verbal report. After three weeks of therapy, the teacher (or parent) may report that the child has greatly improved, beyond the point where further therapy is deemed necessary. If direct observation data do not concur, should the child stay in therapy beyond the perceived needs of teachers and parents, or should the case be closed? Should this case be considered as a successful treatment (based on global verbal level), or as a failure (based on direct observation data)? If direct observation data show marked improvement, but global teacher or parent reports do not concur, should treatment be continued? Is this case a success? Considering that most children become involved in treatment on the basis of initial global verbal report, should they be dismissed from treatment based on similar reports, or held until additional direct observation data meet criteria set by the therapist?

Perhaps a greater likelihood of relapse is associated with case terminations in which direct observation and global verbal report data do not concur. Perhaps global verbal reports should be considred as symptoms, and direct observation data as signs. Perhaps global verbal reports relate more to systemic factors, whereas direct observation data relate more to basic A-B-C microcontingencies. Perhaps global verbal reports set the stage for *dispositional*, trait-based interpretations of behavior, whereas direct observations set the stage for *situational*, state-based interpretations. Perhaps global verbal reports more often represent distorted tacts, or metaphorical or metonymical tact extensions, whereas direct observation data more often represent generic, undistorted tact extensions. Perhaps none of these is true. Future research may tell.

CASE EXAMPLE

Name: Chelsea Seaton
Grade: 2
School: Erehwon
Teacher: Ms. Information
Psychologist: K.A.
Total case time for all services:
  14 hrs 40 min
Date of Birth: 1-10-78

Age: 8 yr 1 mo
Date of Referral: 2-6-86
Dates of Evaluation: 2-11; 1-13; 2-15;
2-18; 2-20.
Date Program Begun: 2-18-86
Date of Report: 2-25-86
Date of Follow-up: 4-17-86

Reason for Referral

Mother and teacher both report that Chelsea "just does not follow directions, throws tantrums, and is very aggressive when requested to do things." She is falling behind in school because of this, and disrupting both school and home life for others.

Assessment Methods

1. Review of school records.
2. Review of recent class workbooks, tests, worksheets, and informal academic skill assessment.
3. Structured teacher and parent interview.
4. Direct observation, using 10-second partial interval methods. Both inter- and intraindividual analyses were performed.

Results

Records Review

A review of school records indicates that Chelsea has been absent ten days and tardy eighteen times since September 1985. She passed her vision screening in the fall of 1985, but failed the hearing screen. The school social worker met with the mother and recommended that Chelsea be taken to the hearing clinic. Chelsea has moved three times since starting kindergarten in the fall of 1983, changing schools each time. The changes in schools also involved three changes in her basal reading and math programs. These programs are not well matched in scope and sequence, so she may be experiencing some confusion in how concepts have been presented. Previous teachers noted some behavior problems, but nothing as severe as indicated in the present referral.

Informal Academic Skills Assessment

A review of workbooks and worksheets showed that Chelsea does not understand some basic concepts in addition and subtraction; many of her error patterns involve regrouping and borrowing. She likely does not understand place value and face value distinctions. Worksheets with mixed addition and subtraction problems show that she does not attend closely to the operation sign before starting to solve a problem. Her errors in reading group suggest that she does not pay attention when others read in the group. Since children take turns according to seating order, she can anticipate when she will have to read, and cannot pay attention until the child next to her is reading. She does not know some letter sounds, has trouble blending sounds, and has a bad habit of looking at the ceiling, rather than at her book, when trying to decode an unfamiliar word.

Teacher and Parent Interview

The teacher reports that Chelsea engages in much more disruptive behavior than peers, and the disruptions sometimes are in the form of defiance. Chelsea apparently knows some concepts required in her reading and math curricula, but these appear to be mainly "splinter skills." The teacher has not noted any pattern to Chelsea's inappropriate behavior; it appears rather spontaneously, and is unpredictable. Chelsea does best when seated near the teacher, where she can be closely watched and prompted to stay on task. The teacher is not sure why Chelsea has missed so much school this year, but notes that there had been some medical problems involving ear infections.

Mother reports that Chelsea often does not want to go to school, has headaches and earaches often, and does not follow directions or obey at home very well. Mother cannot predict Chelsea's outbursts; they appear "out of the blue." Sometimes she "just gets a stubborn streak in her." Mother has tried reasoning with her, but Chelsea doesn't seem to listen. When her mother spanks her, she straightens up for a little while, but that doesn't last very long. Her mother doesn't know why Chelsea is like this.

Interindividual Analysis

Chelsea was observed along with another girl in similar activities. The behaviors of major concern defined in consultation with the teacher included "out of seat" and "noncompliance with teacher requests." Observations were made in Chelsea's areas of strength and weakness, as determined by the teacher. Data were collected across three ten-minute samples in a setting of strength, seated at end of small group in front of teacher, and doing structured activity under teacher's direction. A total of 180 intervals were observed.

	Out of Seat	Noncompliance
Chelsea	31	48
Comparison	0	2
% group of 6 (30 scans)	10% (3/30)	20% (6/30)

Oberservations were made during three ten-minute samples in a weak setting, at her own desk doing independent seat work (math computation for addition and subtraction, with regrouping), and with the teacher working with small groups. A total of 180 intervals were observed.

	Out of Seat	Noncompliance
Chelsea	123	156
Comparison	17	4
% group of 21 (30 scans)	10% (2/21)	0

The data suggest that Chelsea is out of seat and noncompliant considerably more than her peers. This is true for both her weak and strong settings, but she is much better behaved in her setting of strength. With these results, it was decided to continue with intraindividual analyses to try to identify which factors influence Chelsea's inappropriate behavior.

Intraindividual Analyses

From interview and previous classroom observations, it was decided to assess the following variables as possibly affecting Chelsea's inappropriate behavior: seating location in front of teacher and center, rather than at end of a small group; vary tasks that rely on verbal directions with those that rely only on modeling or demonstration; during seat work vary tasks Chelsea surely can do versus math tasks she is having trouble with; vary immediately following through with guided compliance when she is noncompliant with request versus only reminding her to do it. Probe calling on group members randomly rather than in seating order (with Chelsea running her finger under words read by other pupils so teacher can monitor her reading along silently) to see the effect on Chelsea paying attention and knowing her place when asked.

Results of observations during one five-minute sample in a small group, in each condition (30 intervals for each condition) were as follows:

	Out of Seat	Noncompliance
1. In middle group versus	0	5
at end of group	7	9
2. Verbal directives versus	—	22
modeled directives	—	2
3. Guided compliance versus	1	2
repeat or remind	10	16
(both at end of group)		

	Looking at Reader	Knows Place
4. Random finger point versus	24	3/3 calls
call in seating order	5	1/3 calls

The results of one five-minute sample in each condition in a large group, with independent seatwork (30 intervals each condition) were as follows:

	Out of Seat	Disruptive
1. Add and subtract, no regrouping	10	8
versus add and subtract with	19	15
regrouping		
2. Guided compliance versus	2	3
warn, scold, remind	18	19
(both with add and subtract with		
regrouping tasks)		
3. Demonstrates task versus	5	5
gives only verbal directives	11	10

The results indicate that in a small group, Chelsea spends considerably more time in her seat, and is much more compliant, when she sits in the center of the group, at arm's length in front of teacher, when the teacher follows through with guided compliance rather than warnings, and when required tasks can be understood from a model given rather than when she has to rely only on verbal directions. Chelsea also watches her book more, and knows her place when called on, when the teacher calls on children randomly rather than in order in the reading circle. In a large group, Chelsea is in her seat more and is less disruptive when assigned tasks she clearly has the skills to do, when assigned tasks the teacher demonstrates rather than just verbally describes them at her seat, and when the teacher immediately follows through with guided compliance, rather than giving reminders, warnings, or verbal scolding.

From the observations, it also appears that Chelsea may have hearing problems, at least in her left ear (she sits at the end of the reading circle on the teacher's left). In the middle she may hear a little better. She performs better on tasks demonstrated rather than verbally described to her. Her hearing should be checked further. Note that even if hearing is a problem, it does not explain why she behaves much better with immediate guided compliance, when tasks are given at her skill level, and when called on randomly.

In summary, it appears that Chelsea's major behavior problems could be reduced to acceptable levels within the regular classroom if certain changes are made in her educational program. It is recommended that she receive further hearing tests, and that the academic skills specialist assess her skills in reference to the three different curricula Chelsea has been placed in, and match her known and unknown skills to the curriculum scope and sequence. Remedial tutoring on a set of specific skills may be needed to prepare her to work independently. The school psychologist will help the teacher implement these recommendations, on request.

Follow-Up

Upon inquiry, Chelsea's mother said that Chelsea had a hearing loss in one ear, relating to a series of ear infections she has had since birth. She took Chelsea to the hearing clinic when the social worker requested it. Since Chelsea had a "nonlinear" hearing loss, the needed hearing aide would have to be made to prescription and would cost a few hundred dollars. Her mother couldn't afford it. The schools arranged to have the hearing aide purchased for Chelsea by the local chapter of the Optimist Club. After some probelms getting her to wear it, Chelsea now wears it regularly. This and the other changes made in Chelsea's educational program have resulted in her teacher reporting that, while she still has occasional problems, she is no longer so serious as to need special education services.

Follow-up data collected two months after the initial referral supports the teacher's view. Her mother also reports improved behavior at home, after implementing guided compliance procedures immediately upon any noncompliance.

Her mother also reports that Chelsea now likes to come to school, and her headaches are now seldom.

On April 17, 1986, three ten-minute samples were taken in a setting of weakness: doing seatwork in math computation. The teacher was working with a small group. Results of observations for the 180 intervals observed were as follows:

	Out of Seat	Noncompliance
Chelsea	19	7
Comparison	14	3

Although Chelsea engages in more inappropriate behavior than the comparison child, the levels are substantially reduced, and the teacher can easily tolerate the current levels. The case is closed. The psychologist will follow up in several months.

Total case time, for assessment and treatment: 14 hours 40 minutes.

CONCLUSIONS

The first stage of behavior observation focuses on *inter*individual analyses, to confirm the teacher report that the pupil's behavior indeed is deviant from that of classmates. After this has been confirmed, using comparison pupils, scan-checks, and resulting local micronorms, further observation shifts to a second stage focused on intraindividual analyses: functionally analyzing the behavior of concern.

Functional behavioral analyses are needed to detect factors influencing the problem behaviors reported. This involves observing behavior in the context of its functional antecedents and consequences, as well as across settings of relative strength and weakness. Sequences of behavioral events must be analyzed to isolate precise linkages that contribute to different interpersonal outcomes. Confirmation probes are then used to ensure that precise functional variables have been identified.

Strategic problem-solving treatment plans are then devised that are focused, specific, and tailored to the idiosyncratic functional variables identified for the problem situations. The treatment plans are designed to yield the maximum amount of therapeutic effect with the minimal amount of intervention, thus protecting the civil rights of the child, while imposing only minimal burdens on the teacher.

When teachers or parents do not comply with agreed plans, or when relapses consistently follow improvements, systemic functional analyses are performed. When the plans are followed, and the problem is resolved, the case is placed on maintenance and follow-up. There is no need to administer further assessment tools to determine whether the child is identifiable as emotionally impaired, because the problem behaviors no longer adversely affect the pupil's educational performance (a legal requirement for such an educational diagnosis).

Instead of insisting on traditional psychometric methods, the functional analysis of behavior model is applied to the behavior of recording in the same way it is applied to pupil behavior. When the analysis indicates that the data from the recording methods function well as discriminate stimuli for more effective psychologist behavior, the methods are considered valid from a behavioral perspective (cf. Whaley, 1973).

The model presented here focuses on changing ineffective educational situations to avoid labeling pupils rather than labeling pupils to avoid changing ineffective educational situations. A growing body of research is appearing that substantiates the effectiveness of this general approach.

Personal experiences with this approach, as well as that of many others, suggests that, conservatively speaking, 70% to 80% of behavior problem school referrals can be analyzed effectively and treated in regular education classrooms. Such analyses may take several hours of observation time, but overall do not take any more time than completing a comprehensive assessment and meeting the due process requirements needed to identify a pupil as emotionally impaired. The time saved in treatment and in the expense of the program will more than offset the extra time invested in assessment. The approach requires that psychologists have reasonable consultation skills, a working knowledge of classroom management, curriculum, and instructional principles, and backing by school administrators committed to creating effective schools. Functional analyses of behavior problems and emotional impairment are only part of what psychology has to offer education . . . now (Bijou, 1970).

Acknowledgments

Portions of this chapter have been reprinted from the following two sources, with the permission of the authors and publisher. Alessi, G. (1980). Behavioral observation for the school psychologist: Responsive-discrepancy model. *School Psychology Review, 9,* 31–45; and Alessi, G., & Kaye, J. (1983). *Behavioral assessment for the school psychologist.* Stratford, Conn.: NASP Publications.

Many of the ideas presented in this chapter resulted from teaching, supervising, and consulting with many practicing school psychologists associated with the program at Western Michigan University (1974–86). They attempted to put many of these theoretical concepts into practice. Much of what we learned in that process is contained herein. I appreciate their enthusiasm and collegial involvement. I would like to thank Jack Michael for constructive comments on a draft of the present paper, as well as for his guidance in developing some of the ideas presented.

References

Alessi, G. J. (1978a). *Informal reading inventory* and *Informal math inventory.* Unpublished protocols, Department of Psychology, Western Michigan University, Kalamazoo, Mich.

Alessi, G. J. (1978b). *Classroom behavior management checklist.* Unpublished protocol, Department of Psychology, Western Michigan University, Kalamazoo, Mich.

Alessi, G. J. (1979). Systems analysis vs. behavior analysis: Two sides of the same coin, or two hands clapping? Paper presented at the 5th Annual Conference. Association for Behavior Analysis, Dearborn, Mich.

Alessi, G. J. (1980). Behavioral observation for the school psychologist: Responsive-discrepancy model. *School Psychology Review, 9,* 31–45.

Alessi, G. J., & Kaye, J. H. (1982). *Behavior observation methods for the school psychologist.* Stratford, Conn.: NASP Publications (National Association of School Psychologists). A videotape training presentation.

Alessi, G. J., & Kaye, J. H. (1983). *Behavioral assessment for school psychologists.* Stratford, Conn.: NASP Publications (The National Association of School Psychologists).

Arvey, R. D. (1979). *Fairness in selecting employees.* Reading, Mass.: Addison-Wesley.

Ashlock, R. B. (1986). Error patterns in computation: A semi-progammed approach. 4th ed. Colombus, OH: Charles E. Merrill.

Atkinson, B. M., & Forehand, R. (1981). Conduct disorders. In E. J. Mash & L. G. Terdal (Eds.), *Behavioral assessment of childhood disorders* (pp. 185–220). New York: Guilford Press.

Bailey, J. S., & Bostow, D. (1979). *Research methods in applied behavior analysis.* Talahassee, Fla.: Copygrafix.

Bakeman, R., & Gottman, J. M. (1986). *Observing interatction: An introduction to sequential analysis.* Cambridge: Cambridge University Press.

Baldessarini, R. J., Finklestein, S., & Arana, G. W. (1983). The predictive power of diagnostic tests and the effect of prevalence of illness. *Archives of General Psychiatry, 40,* 569–573.

Barlow, D. H. (Ed.). (1981). *Behavioral assessment of adult disorders.* New York: Guilford Press.

Bateson, G. (1972). *Steps to an ecology of mind.* New York: Ballantine.

Becker, W. (1986). *Applied psychology for teachers: A behavioral-cognitive approach.* Chicago: Science Research Associates.

Becker, W., Engelmann, S., & Thomas, D. (1975). *Teaching 1: Classroom management.* Chicago: Science Research Associates.

Bijou, S. W. (1970). What psychology has to offer education—now. In P. Dews (Ed.), *Festschrift for B. F. Skinner* (pp. 401–407). New York: Irvington.

Bijou, S. W., Peterson, R. F., & Ault, M. H. (1968). A method to integrate descriptive and experimental field studies at the level of data and empirical concepts. *Journal of Applied Behavior Analysis, 1,* 175–191.

Bornstein, P. H., & van den Pol, R. A. (1985). Models of assessment and treatment in child behavior therapy. In P. H. Bornstein & A. E. Kazdin (Eds.), *Handbook of clinical behavior therapy with children* (pp. 44–74). Homewood, Ill.: Dorsey Press.

Brookover, W. B., Beamer, L., Efthim, H., Hathaway, D., Lezotte, L., Miller, S., Passalacqua, J., & Tornatzky, L. (1982). *Creating effective schools: An in-service program for enhancing school learning climate and achievement.* Holmes Beach, Fla.: Learning Publications.

Burgess, R. L. (1979). Child abuse: A social interactional analysis. In B. B. Lahey & A. E. Kazdin (Eds.), *Advances in clinical child psychology* (Vol. 2, pp. 141–172). New York: Academic Press.

Burgess, R. L., & Richardson, R. A. (1984). Coercive interpersonal contingencies as a determinant of child maltreatment: Implications for treatment and prevention. In R. F. Dangel & R. A. Polster (Eds.), *Parent training: Foundations of research and practice* (pp. 239–259). New York: Guilford Press.

Canter, L. (1976). *Assertive discipline: A take-charge approach for today's educator.* New York: Harper & Row.

Canter, L. (1985). *Lee Canter's assertive discipline for parents* (rev. ed.). New York: Harper & Row.

Carnine, D., & Silbert, J. (1979). *Direct instruction reading.* Columbus, Ohio: Charles E. Merrill.

Carr, E. G. (1977). The motivation of self-injurious behavior: A review of some hypotheses. *Psychological Bulletin, 84,* 800–816.

Carr, E. G., Newsom, C. D., & Binkoff, J. A. (1980). Escape as a factor in the aggressive behavior of two retarded children. *Journal of Applied Behavior Analysis, 13,* 101–117.

Cataldo, M., & Risley, T. (1974). Evaluation of living environments: The MANIFEST description of ward activities. In P. O. Davidson, F. Clark, & L. Hammerlynk (Eds.), *Evaluation of behavioral programs in community, residential and school settings* (pp. 201–222). Champaign, Ill.: Research Press.

Cataldo, M. F., Ward, E. M., Russo, D. C., Riordan, M. M., & Bennett, D. (1986). Compliance and correlated problem behavior in children: Effects of contingent and noncontingent reinforcement. *Analysis and Intervention in Developmental Disabilities, 6,* 265–282.

Cebul, R. D., & Beck, L. H. (Eds.). (1985). *Teaching clinical decision making.* New York: Praeger Scientific.

Ciminero, A. R., Calhoun, K. S., & Adams, H. (Eds.). (1977; 1986). *Handbook of behavioral assessment* (2d ed.). New York: Wiley Interscience.

Ciminero, A. R., & Drabman, R. S. (1977). Current developments in the behavioral assessment of children. In B. Lahey & A. Kazdin (Eds.), *Advances in clinical child psychology* (Vol. 1, pp. 47–82). New York: Plenum Press.

Cobb, J. A., & Ray, R. S. (1976). The classroom behavior observation code. In E. J. Mash & L. G. Terdal (Eds.), *Behavior therapy assessment: Diagnosis, design, and evaluation* (pp. 286–294). New York: Springer.

Cobb, J. A., & Ray, R. S. (1972). Manual for coding discrete behaviors in the school setting. In F. W. Clark, D. R. Evans, & L. A. Hammerlynk (Eds.), *Implementing behavioral programs in schools and clinics* (pp. 187–201). Proceedings of the Third Banff International Conference on Behavior Modification. Champaign, Ill.: Research Press.

Cone, J. D. (1981). Psychometric considerations. In M. Hersen & A. Bellack (Eds.), *Behavioral assessment: A practical handbook* (2d ed., pp. 38–68). Elmsford, N.Y.: Pergamon Press.

Cone, J. D., & Hawkins, R. P. (Eds.). (1977). *Behavioral assessment: New directions in clinical psychology.* New York: Brunner/Mazel.

Coulter, W. A., & Morrow, H. W. (Eds.). (1978). *Adaptive behavior: Concepts and measurements.* New York: Grune & Stratton.

Deno, S., & Mirkin, P. (1977). *Data-based program modification: A manual.* Reston, Va.: The Council for Exceptional Children.

Edelstein, B. A., & Couture, E. T. (Eds.). (1984). *Behavioral assessment and rehabilitation of the traumatically brain damaged.* New York: Plenum Press.

Egan, J. P. (1975). *Signal detection theory and ROC analysis.* New York: Academic Press.

Engelmann, S., & Carnine, D. (1983). *Theory of instruction: Principles and applications.* New York: Irvington.

Engelmann, S., & Colvin, G. (1983). *Generalized compliance training.* Austin, Tex.: Pro-Ed.

Evans, I. M., & Wilson, F. E. (1983). Behavioral assessment as decision-making: A theoretical analysis. In M. Rosenbaum, C. Franks, & Y. Jaffe (Eds.), *Perspectives on behavior therapy in the eighties* (pp. 35–53). New York: Springer.

Eyberg, S. M., & Johnson, S. M. (1974). Multiple assessment of behavior modification with families: Effects of contingency contracting and order of treated problems. *Journal of Consulting and Clinical Psychology, 42,* 594–606.

Ferster, C. B., Nurnberger, J. I., & Levitt, E. B. (1962). The control of eating. *The Journal of Mathetics, 1,* 87–109.

Filsinger, E. E., & Lewis, R. A. (Eds.). (1981). *Assessing marriages: New behavioral approaches.* Beverly Hills, Calif.: Sage.

Fisch, R., Weakland, J. H., & Segal, L. (1982). *The tactics of change: Doing therapy briefly.* San Francisco: Jossey-Bass.

Fogarty, S. J., & Hemsley, D. R. (1983). Depression and the accessibility of memories. *British Journal of Psychiatry, 142,* 232.

Forehand, R., & McMahon, R. (1981). *Helping the noncompliant child.* New York: Guilford Press.

Frank, J. (1973). *Persuasion and healing: A comparative study of psychotherapy.* Baltimore, Md.: The John Hopkins University Press.

Gilbert, T. (1978). *Human competence: Engineering worthy performance.* New York: McGraw-Hill.

Glow, R. A. (Ed.). (1984–85). *Advances in the behavioral measurement of children.* (Vols. 1 & 2). San Francisco: Jossey-Bass.

Goldfried, M. R. (1982). Behavioral assessment: An overview. In A. Bellack, M. Hersen, & A. Kazdin (Eds.), *International handbook of behavior modification and therapy.* (pp. 81–108). New York: Plenum Press.

Goldiamond, I. (1974). Toward a constructional approach to social problems. *Behaviorism, 2,* 1–84.

Goldiamond, I. (1984). Training parent trainers and ethicists in nonlinear analysis of behavior. In R. F. Dangel & R. A. Polster (Eds.), *Parent training: Foundations of research and practice* (pp. 504–546). New York: Guildford Press.

Greer, R. D. (1980). *Designs for music learning.* New York: Teacher's College Press.

Haley, J. (1963). *Strategies of psychotherapy.* New York: Grune & Stratton.

Haley, J. (1976). *Problem solving therapy.* San Francisco: Jossey-Bass.

Haley, J. (1980). *Leaving home: The therapy of disturbed young people.* New York: McGraw-Hill.

Haley, J. (1981). Toward a theory of pathological systems. In J. Haley (Ed.), *Reflections on therapy and other essays* (pp. 94–112). Washington, D.C.: The Family Therapy Institute.

Hall, R. V. (1971). *Behavior management series, part I: The measurement of behavior.* Lawrence, Kans: H & H Enterprises.

Harris, S. L. (1982). A family systems approach to behavioral training with parents of autistic children. *Child and Family Behavior Therapy, 4,* 21–35.

Hartman, D. P., & Wood, D. D. (1982). Observation methods. In A. Bellack, M. Hersen, & A. Kazdin (Eds.), *International handbook of behavior modification and therapy* (pp. 109–138). New York: Plenum Press.

Haynes, R. B., Taylor, D. W., & Sackett, D. L. (Eds.). (1979). *Compliance in health care.* Baltimore, Md.: The John Hopkins University Press.

Haynes, S. N. (1978). *Principles of behavioral assessment.* New York: Gardner Press.

Haynes, S. N. (1983). Behavioral assessment. In M. Hersen, A. Kazdin, & A. Bellack (Eds.), *The clinical psychology handbook* (pp. 397–454). Elmsford, N.Y.: Pergamon Press.

Haynes, S.N. (1984). Behavioral assessment of adults. In G. Goldstein & M. Hersen (Eds.), *Handbook of psychological assessment* (pp. 369–401). Elmsford, N.Y.: Pergamon Press.

Haynes, S. N., & Wilson, C. C. (1979). *Behavioral assessment: Recent advances in methods and concepts.* San Francisco: Jossey-Bass.

Heller, K. A., Holtzman, W. H., & Messick, S. (Eds.). (1982). *Placing children in special education: A strategy for equity.* Washington, D.C.: National Academy Press.

Hersen, M., & Bellack, A. S. (Eds.). (1976; 1981; 1988). *Behavioral assessment: A practical handbook* (3d ed.). Elmsford, N.Y.: Pergamon Press.

Howard, K. I., Kopta, M., Krause, M. S., & Orlinsky, D. E. (1986). The Dose-effect relationship in psychotherapy. *American Psychologist, 41,* 159–64.

Iwata, B. I., Dorsey, M. F., Slifer, K. J., Bauman, K. E., & Richman, G. S. (1982). Toward a functional analysis of self-injury. *Analysis and Intervention in Developmental Disabilities, 2,* 3–30.

Iwata, B. I., Riordan, M. M., Wohl, M. K., & Finney, J. W. (1982). Pediatric feeding disorders: Behavioral analysis and treatment. In P. J. Accardo (Ed.), *Failure to thrive in infancy and early childhood* (pp. 297–329). Baltimore, Md.: University Park Press.

Jenkins, J. R., & Pany, D. (1978). Standardized achievement tests: How useful for special education? *Exceptional Children, 44,* 448–453.

Johnson, M. S., & Kress, R. A. (1964). *Informal reading inventories.* Newark, Del.: The International Reading Association.

Kantor, J. R. (1959). *Interbehavioral psychology: A sample of scientific system construction.* Chicago: Principia Press.

Kantor, J. R. (1963). *The scientific evolution of psychology, vol. 1.* Chicago: Principia Press.

Kantor, J. R., & Smith, N. W. (1975). *The science of psychology: An interbehavioral survey.* Chicago: Principia Press.

Katz, E. R., Varni, J. W., & Jay, S. M. (1984). Behavioral assessment and management of pediatric pain. In M. Hersen, R. Eisler, & P. Miller (Eds.), *Progress in Behavior Modification* (pp. 163-193). New York: Academic Press.

Kazdin, A. (1977). Artifact, bias, and complexity of assessment: The ABC's of reliability. *Journal of Applied Behavior Analysis, 10,* 141-150.

Kazdin, A. (1982). *Single-case research designs: Methods for clinical and applied settings.* New York: Oxford University Press.

Keefe, F., & Blumenthal, J. (Eds.). (1982). *Assessment strategies in behavioral medicine.* New York: Grune & Stratton.

Keefe, F., Kopel, S., & Gordon, S. (1978). *A practical guide to behavioral assessment.* New York: Springer.

Kendall, P. C., & Hollon, S. D. (1981). *Assessment strategies for cognitive-behavior interventions.* New York: Academic Press.

Kratochwill, T. R. (1982). Advances in behavioral assessment. In C. R. Reynolds & T. B. Gutkin (Eds.), *The handbook of school psychology* (pp. 314-350). New York: John Wiley & Sons.

Kunzelmann, H. P., Cohen, M. A., Hulten, W. J., Martin, G. L., & Mingo, A. R. (1970). *Precision teaching: An initial teaching sequence.* Seattle, Wash.: Special Child Publications.

Leinhardt, G., & Seewald, A. (1981). Overlap: What's tested, what's taught. *Journal of Educational Measurement, 18,* 85-96.

Loftus, E. E. (1979). *Eyewitness testimony.* Cambridge, Mass.: Harvard University Press.

Lutzker, J. B. (1984). Project 12-ways: Treating child abuse and neglect from a ecobehavioral perspective. In R. Dangel & R. Polster (Eds.), *Parent training: Foundations of research and practice* (pp. 260-297). New York: Guilford Press.

Maag, J. W., Wolchik, A. A., Rutherford, R. B., & Bradford, T. P. (1986). Response covariation on self-stimulatory behavior during sensory extinction procedures. *Journal of Autism and Developmental Disorders, 16,* 119-132.

Mace, F. C., Page, T. J., Ivancic, M. T., & O'Brien, S. (1986). Analysis of environmental determinants of aggression and disruption in mentally retarded children. *Applied Research in Mental Retardation, 7,* 203-221.

Mace, F. C., Yankanich, M. A., & West, B. J. (in press). Toward a methodology of experimental analysis and treatment of aberrant behavior. *Special Services in the Schools.*

Madanes, C. (1981). *Strategic family therapy.* San Francisco: Jossey-Bass.

Madanes, C. (1984). *Behind the one-way mirror.* San Francisco: Jossey-Bass.

Mager, R., & Pipe, P. (1970). *Analyzing performance problems: You really oughta wanna.* Belmont, Calif.: Fearon.

Marafiote, R. A. (1985). *The custody of children: A behavioral assessment model.* New York: Plenum Press.

Martin, G. L., & Hrycaiko, D. (1983). *Behavior modification and coaching.* Springfield, Ill.: Charles C. Thomas.

Martin, R. (1979). *Educating handicapped children: The legal mandate.* Champaign, Ill.: Research Press.

Maruyama, M. (1963). The second cybernetics: Deviation amplyifying mutual causal processes. *American Scientist, 51,* 164-179.

Masek, B. J. (1982). Compliance and medicine. In D. M. Doleys, R. L. Meredith, & A. R. Ciminero (Eds.), *Behavioral medicine: Assessment and treatment strategies* (pp. 527-546). New York: Plenum Press.

Mash, E. J., & Terdal, L. G. (Eds.). (1976). *Behavior therapy assessment: Diagnosis, design, and evaluation.* New York: Springer.

Mash, E. J., & Terdal, L. G. (Eds.) (1981, 1987). *Behavioral assessment of childhood disorders.* (2nd ed.). New York: Guilford Press.

McFall, R. M. (1986). Theory and method in assessment: The vital link. *Behavioral Assessment, 8,* 3-10.

McMahon, R. J., Forehand, R., & Griest, D. L. (1982). Parent behavioral training to modify child noncompliance: Factors in generalization and maintenance. In R. B. Stuart (Ed.), *Adherence, compliance, and generalization in behavioral medicine* (pp. 213–238). New York: Brunner/ Mazel.

Meister, D. (1985). *Behavioral analysis and measurement methods.* New York: John Wiley & Sons.

Michael, J. (1973). Positive and negative reinforcement, a distinction that is no longer necessary; or a better way to talk about bad things. In E. Ramp & G. Semb (Eds.), *Behavior analysis: Areas of research and application* (pp. 31–44). Englewood Cliffs, N.J.: Prentice-Hall.

Michael, J. (1980). On terms: The discriminative stimulus or S.^{d} *The Behavior Analyst,* 3, 47–50.

Michael, J. (1986). Repertoire-altering effects of remote contingencies. *The Analysis of Verbal Behavior,* 4, 10–18.

Minervini, M. (1985). Metaphorical extensions in the analysis of human behavior. Paper presented at the 11th Annual Conference of the Association for Behavior Analysis, Columbus, Ohio.

Minervini, M. (1986). An analogy of a natural science. Kalamazoo, Mich.: Major review paper submitted in partial fulfilment of the requirements for the doctor of philosophy degree in psychology, Western Michigan University.

Minuchin, S. (1974). *Families and family therapy.* Cambridge, Mass.: Harvard University Press.

Minuchin, S., & Fishman, H. C. (1981). *Family therapy techniques.* Cambridge, Mass.: Harvard University Press.

Mischel, W. (1968). *Personality and assessment.* New York: John Wiley & Sons.

Monteiro, M. J., & Heiry, T. J. (1983). A direct instruction supervision model. *Direct Instruction News,* 2, 8–9. Eugene, Oreg.: Association for Direct Instruction.

Neef, N., Shafer, M. S., Egel, A. I., Cataldo, M. F., & Parrish, J. M. (1983). The class specific effects of compliance training with "do" and "don't" requests: Analogue analysis and classroom application. *Journal of Applied Behavior Analysis,* 16, 81–89.

Nelson, R. E., & Craighead, W. E. (1977). Selective recall of positive and negative feedback, self-control behaviors, and depression. *Journal of Abnormal Psychology,* 86, 379–388.

Nelson, R. O., & Hayes, S. C. (Eds.). (1986). *Conceptual foundations of behavioral assessment.* New York: Guilford Press.

Nunnally, J. (1978). *Psychometric theory* (2d ed.). New York: McGraw-Hill.

O'Leary, K. D., Romanczyk, R. G., Kass, R. E., Dietz, A., & Santogrossi, D. (1979). *Procedures for classroom observation of teachers and children.* Stony Brook, N.Y.: Psychology Department, SUNY at Stony Brook.

Ollendick, T. H., & Hersen, M. (Eds.). (1984). *Child behavioral assessment: Principles and procedures.* Elmsford, N.Y.: Pergamon Press.

Ollendick, T. H., & Meador, A. E. (1984). Behavioral assessment of children. In G. Goldstein & M. Hersen (Eds.). *The handbook of psychological assessment* (pp. 351–368). Elmsford, N.Y.: Pergamon Press.

Paine, S. C., Radicchi, J., Rosellini, L. C., Deutchman, L., & Darch, C. B. (1983). *Structuring your classroom for academic success.* Champaign, Ill.: Research Press.

Parrish, J. M., Cataldo, M. F., Kolko, D. J., Neef, N., & Egel, A. I. (1986). Experimental analysis of response covariation among compliant and inappropriate behaviors. *Journal of Applied Behavior Analysis,* 19, 241–254.

Patterson, G. R. (1982). *Coercive family processes.* Eugene, Oreg.: Castalia Press.

Patterson, G. R., & Bank, L. (1986). Bootstrapping your way in the nomological thicket. *Behavioral Assessment,* 8, 49–73.

Patterson, G. R., Cobb, J. A., & Ray, R. S. (1972). Direct intervention in the classroom: A set of procedures for the aggressive child. In F. W. Clark, D. R. Evans, & L. A. Hammerlynck (Eds.), *Implementing behavioral programs in schools and clinics,* (pp. 151–186). Proceedings of the Third Banff International Conference on Behavior Modification. Champaign, Ill.: Research Press.

Patterson, G. R., Ray, R. S., Shaw, D. A., & Cobb, J. A. (1969). *Manual for coding family interactions.* Document No. 01234, 6th revision. New York: ASIS National Auxiliary Publications Service.

Patterson, G. R., Shaw, D., & Ebner, M. (1969). Teachers, peers, and parents as agents of change in the classroom. In A. M. Benson (Ed.), *Modifying deviant social behaviors in various classroom settings*. Eugene, Oreg.: University of Oregon Press.

Pennebacker, J. (1984). Accuracy of symptom perception. In A. Baum, S. Taylor, & J. Singer (Eds.), *Social psychological aspects of health* (pp. 189–217). Hillsdale, N.J.: Lawrence Erlbaum Associates.

Peterson, L., Homer, A., & Wonderlich, S. (1982). The integrity of independent variables in behavior analysis. *Journal of Applied Behavior Analysis, 15*, 477–492.

Peterson, N. (1982). On terms: Feedback is not a new principle of behavior. *The Behavior Analyst, 5*, 101–102.

Powers, M. D. & Handleman, J. S. (1984). *Behavioral assessment of severe developmental disabilities.* Rockville, Md.: Aspen Systems.

Rachman, S. J., and Wilson, G. T. (1980). *The effects of psychological therapy,* (2nd ed.). Elmsford, N.Y.: Pergamon Press.

Ray, R. S. (1976). Naturalistic assessment in educational settings: The classroom behavior observation code. In E. J. Mash & L. G. Terdal (Eds.), *Behavior therapy assessment: Diagnosis, design, and evaluation* (pp. 279–285). New York: Springer.

Reid, J. B. (1977). *Observation in the home setting*. Eugene, Oreg.: Castalia Press.

Reid, J. B., Patterson, G. R., & Loeber, R. (1981). The abused child: Victim, instigator, or innocent bystander? In D. J. Bernstein (Ed.), *Response structure and organization,* (pp. 47–68). Nebraska Symposium on Motivation, Vol. 29. Lincoln, Neb. University of Nebraska Press.

Reid, J. B., Taplin, P. S., & Lorber, R. (1981). A social interactional approach to the treatment of abusive families. In R. B. Stuart (Ed.), *Violent behavior: Social learning approaches to prediction, management and treatment* (pp. 83–101). New York: Brunner/Mazel.

Repp, A. C., Dietz, D. E., Boles, S. M., Dietz, S. M., & Repp, C. F. (1976). Differences among common methods for assessing interobserver agreement. *Journal of Applied Behavior Analysis. 9*, 109–113.

Repp, A. C., Roberts, D., Slack, D., Repp, C. F., & Berkley, M. (1976). A comparison of frequency, interval and time-sampling methods of data collection. *Journal of Applied Behavior Analysis, 9*, 501–508.

Risley, T. (1972). Spontaneous language and the preschool environment. In J. C. Stanley (Ed.), *Preschool programs for the disadvantaged: Five experimental approaches to early childhood education* (pp. 92–110). Baltimore, Md.: The Johns Hopkins University Press.

Rojahn, J., & Schroeder, S. R. (1983). Behavioral assessment. In J. Matson & J. Mulick (Eds.), *Handbook of mental retardation* (pp. 227–244). Elmsford, N.Y.: Pergamon Press.

Russo, D. C., Cataldo, M. F., & Cushing, P. J. (1981). Compliance training and behavioral covariation in the treatment of multiple behavior problems. *Journal of Applied Behavior Analysis, 14*, 209–222.

Sackett, G. P. (Ed.). (1978). *Observing behavior: Data collection and analysis methods* (Vol. 2). Baltimore: Md. University Park Press.

Sackett, G. P., Landesman-Dwyer, S., & Morin, V. N. (1981). Naturalistic observation in design and evaluation of special education programs. In T. R. Kratochwill (Ed.), *Advances in school psychology* (Vol. 1, pp. 281–306). Hillsdale, N.J. Lawrence Erlbaum Associates.

Saudargas, R. A. (1982). *Student-teacher observation code*. Knoxville, Tenn.: University of Tennessee Press.

Schnelle, J. F. (1974). A brief report on invalidity of parent evaluations of behavior change. *Journal of Applied Behavior Analysis, 7*, 341–343.

Schwartz, A., & Goldiamond, I. (1975). *Social casework: A behavioral approach.* New York: Columbia University Press.

Shapiro, E. S. (1987). *Behavioral assessment in school psychology.* Hillsdale, N.J.: Lawrence Erlbaum Associates.

Shapiro, E. S., & Lentz, F. E. (1985). Assessing academic behavior: A behavioral approach. *School Psychology Review, 14*, 325–338.

Shapiro, E. S., Lentz, F. E., & Sofman, R. (1985). Validity of rating scales in assessing aggressive behavior in classroom settings. *Journal of School Psychology, 23*, 69–80.

Silbert, J., Carnine, D., & Stein, M. (1981). *Direct Instruction Mathematics.* Columbus, Ohio: Charles E. Merrill.

Skinner, B. F. (1945). The operational analysis of psychological terms. *Psychological Review.* Reprinted in: *Cumulative Record,* (3rd ed. pp. 270–77). (1972). Englewood Cliffs, N.J.: Prentice-Hall.

Skinner, B. F. (1957). *Verbal behavior.* Englewood Cliffs, N.J.: Prentice-Hall.

Skinner, B. F. (1969). *Contingencies of reinforcement: A theoretical analysis.* Englewood Cliffs, N.J.: Prentice-Hall.

Skinner, B. F. (1972). *Cumulative record* (3d ed.). Englewood Cliffs, N.J.: Prentice-Hall.

Skinner, B. F. (1978). The ethics of helping people. In B. F. Skinner (Ed.), *Reflections on behaviorism and society.* Englewood Cliffs, N.J.: Prentice-Hall.

Skinner, B. F. (1981). Selection by consequences. *Science, 213,* 501–504.

Skinner, B. F. (1986). What is wrong with daily life in the Western world? *American Psychologist, 41,* 568–574.

Slifer, K. J., Ivancic, M. I., Parrish, J. M., Page, T. J., & Burgio, L. D. (1986). Reducing aggression in a profoundly retarded adolescent: A systematic evaluation of required compliance. *Journal of Behavior Therapy and Experimental Psychiatry, 17,* 203–213.

Snapper, A., & Inglis, G. (1984). *SKED-11 manual.* Kalamazoo, Mich: State Systems.

Snapper, A., Kadden, R., & Inglis, G. (1982). Computer technology: State notation of behavioral procedures. *Behavior Research Methods and Instrumentation, 14,* 329–342.

Spence, D. P. (1982), *Narrative truth and historical truth.* New York: W. W. Norton.

Sprick, R. (1981). *The solution book: A guide to classroom discipline.* Chicago: Science Research Associates.

Sprick, R. (1985). *Discipline in the secondary classroom: A problem-by-proplem survival guide.* West Nyack, N.Y.: The Center for Applied Research in Education.

Springer, B., Brown, T., & Duncan, P. K. (1981). Current measurement in applied behavior analysis. *The Behavior Analyst, 4,* 29–32.

Staats, A. W. (1975). *Social behaviorism.* Homewood, Ill.: Dorsey Press.

Strupp, H. H., Hadley, S. W., & Gomes-Schwartz, B. (1977). *Psychotherapy for better or worse: The problem of negative effects.* New York: Jason Aronson.

Stuart, R. B. (1974). Behavior modification techniques for the educational technologist. In R. E. Ulrich, T. J. Stachnik, & J. Mabry (Eds.), *Control of human behavior: Behavior modification in education* (Vol. 3 pp. 18–39). Glenview, Ill. Scott, Foresman.

Sulzbacher, S. (1972). Behavior analysis of drug effects in the classroom. In G. Semb (Ed.), *Behavior analysis and education* (pp. 37–52). Lawrence, Kans.: University of Kansas Support and Development Center.

Tharp, R. G., & Wetzel, R. J. (1969). *Behavior modification in the natural environment.* New York: Academic Press.

Thompson, C., Holmberg, M., & Baer, D. (1974). A brief report on a comparison of time-sampling procedures. *Journal of Applied Behavior Analysis, 7,* 623–626.

Tomm, K. (1987). Interventive interviewing: Part II. Reflexive questioning as a means to enable self-healing. *Family Process, 26,* 167–183.

Tryon, W. W. (Ed.). (1985). *Behavioral assessment in behavioral medicine.* New York: Springer.

Vasta, R. (1983). Physical child abuse: A dual-component analysis. *Developmental Review, 2,* 125–149.

Wahler, R. G. (1969). Setting generality: Some specific and general effects of child behavior therapy. *Journal of Applied Behavior Analysis, 2,* 239–246.

Wahler, R. G. (1976). Deviant child behavior within the family: Developmental speculations and behavior change strategies. In H. Leitenberg (Ed.), *Handbook of behavior modification and behavior therapy* (pp. 516–546). Englewood Cliffs, N.J.: Prentice-Hall.

Wahler, R. G. (1980). The insular mother: Her problems in parent-child treatment. *Journal of Applied Behavior Analysis, 13,* 207–219.

Wahler, R. G., Berland, R. M., & Coe, T. D. (1979). Generalization processes in child behavior change.

In B. B. Lahey & A. E. Kazdin (Eds.), *Advances in clinical child psychology* (Vol. 2, pp. 35–69). New York: Plenum Press.

Wahler, R. G., & Dumas, J. E. (1984). Changing the observational coding styles of insular and noninsular mothers: A step toward maintenance of parent training effects. In R. F. Dangel & R. A. Polster (Eds.), *Parent training: Foundations of research and practice* (pp. 379–416). New York: Guilford Press.

Wahler, R. G. & Fox, J. J. (1981). Response structure in deviant child-parent relationships: Implications for family therapy. In D. J. Bernstein (Ed.) *Response structure and organization* (Vol. 29, pp. 1–46). Lincoln, Neb.: The University of Nebraska Press, The Nebraska Symposium on Motivation.

Wahler, R. G., & Graves, M. G. (1983). Setting events in social networks: Ally or enemy in child behavior therapy? *Behavior Therapy, 14,* 19–36.

Wahler, R. G., & Hann, D. M. (1986). A behavioral systems perspective in childhood psychopathology: Expanding the three-term operant contingency. In N. A. Krasnegor, J. D. Arasteh, & M. F. Cataldo (Eds.), *Child health behavior: A behavioral pediatrics perspective* (pp. 146–167). New York: John Wiley & Sons.

Wahler, R. G., House, A., & Stambaugh, E. (1976). *Ecological assessment of child problem behavior.* Elmsford, N.Y.: Pergamon Press.

Walker, H. & Hops, H. (1976). Use of normative peer data as a standard for evaluating classroom treatment efforts. *Journal of Applied Behavior Analysis, 9,* 159–168.

Wasik, B. H. (1984). Clinical Application of Direct Behavioral Observation. In B. Lahey & A. Kazdin (Eds.), *Advances in clinical child psychology* (Vol. 7 pp. 153–193). New York: Plenum Press.

Watzlawick, P., Weakland, J., and Fisch, R. (1974). *Change: Principles of problem formation and problem resolution.* New York: W. W. Norton.

Webb, E. J., Campbell, D. T., Schwartz, R. D., & Sechrest, L. (1966). *Unobtrusive measures: Nonreactive research in the social sciences.* Chicago: Rand McNally.

Wells, D. C., & Forehand, R. (1981). Childhood behavior problems in the home. In S. M. Turner, K. S. Calhoun, & H. E. Adams (Eds.), *Handbook of clinical behavior therapy* (pp. 527–567). New York: Wiley-Interscience.

Wells, K. C., Forehand, R., & Griest, D. L. (1980). Generality of treatment effects from treated to untreated behaviors resulting from a parent training program. *Journal of Clinical Child Psychology, 9,* 217–219.

Whaley, D. L. (1973). *Psychological testing and the philosophy of measurement.* Kalamazoo, Mich.: Behaviordelia.

CHAPTER 3

Direct Observation and Measurement of Academic Skills: A Conceptual Review

FRANCIS E. LENTZ, JR.
University of Cincinnati

INTRODUCTION

School psychologists have traditionally treated academic referrals as if the referred problem were totally within the locus of the child (low intelligence, deficit information processing, insufficient knowledge). According to the available literature, the assessment process has been largely indirect in relation to the student behaviors that elicited the referral, usually involving norm-based achievement tests and measures of hypothesized constructs or intervening variables (Lentz & Shapiro, 1985; Ysseldyke & Mirkin, 1982) and seldom involving direct observation and measurement of academic behavior in the classroom (Lentz & Shapiro, 1985). These indirect procedures are logically related to the notion that identification of the processes underlying direct academic performance is critical; either for remediation of the process deficits or so instructional remediation can be oriented around modality strengths (Lentz & Shapiro, 1985). The measures closest to actual academic performance (that are commonly used) are derived from norm-based achievement tests that are usually designed to represent a global skill construct (Anastasi, 1982).

Unfortunately for school psychologists, recent conclusions drawn from the empirical literature have failed to support either the uitility of process measures in planning for remediation of basic academic skills, or the utility of underlying constructs as targets in the remedial process (Arter & Jenkins, 1978; Ysseldyke & Mirkin, 1982). Similarly, the adequacy of traditional measures for the classification of exceptional children has often been questioned (Lentz & Shapiro, 1985). Even less process-oriented measures like norm-based achievement tests appear differentially related to various basic academic curricula (Jenkins & Pany, 1978; Leinhardt & Seewald, 1981), and have not proven very useful for planning specific academic remediations (Deno, 1985). Thus, indirect measures and indirect intervention procedures do not provide an effective linkage between assessment and treatment.

On the other hand, the evidence strongly suggests that a viable assessment and treatment linkage may result by combining more direct, possibly repeated, measures of the academic skills actually taught in the classroom with direct remediation of identified academic problems (Ysseldyke & Mirkin, 1982). For the purposes of this chapter, direct measurement refers both to procedures focusing on the repertoire of actual academic skills, especially those included in the student's curriculum, and to the measurement of related classroom behaviors.

On the assessment side of the direct linkage "coin," a number of "new" and more "direct" procedures have been recently introduced to school psychologists and special educators. These include criterion-referenced testing (e.g., Cancelli & Kratochwill, 1982), path-referenced assessment (Bergan, 1982), curriculum-based assessment or measurement (CBA or CBM) (e.g., Deno, 1985), precision teaching and measurement (e.g., White & Liberty, 1976), and ecobehavioral classroom assessment (Greenwood, Delquadri, Stanley, Terry, & Hall, 1985). These new measurement procedures all can be conceptualized, to some degree, as involving direct observation and measurement of academic behavior and more closely fitting the behavioral assessment model than the traditional trait-oriented model. Yet, there are tremendous differences between them in types of inferences intended to be made from data, settings where measurement occurs, conceptualizations about measurement, recognition of the importance of settings on assessment results, and the assumed relationship between measures and actual behavior in the natural environment.

Perhaps the most efficacious direct academic interventions have been those utilizing behavioral approaches (e.g., Baer & Bushell, 1981; Becker, Engelmann, Carnine, & Maggs, 1982; Lentz & Shapiro, 1985; Sulzer-Azaroff & Mayer, 1985). These interventions emphasize direct, repeated assessment of target behaviors, advocate direct observation and analysis of environmental variables related to the academic problem (Sulzer-Azaroff & Mayer, 1977), and employ interventions that directly target academic behavior. It would seem that the connection between assessment and intervention would be clear—but the relationship between the direct assessment procedures mentioned above, indirect measures (like interviews), and all aspects of behavioral interventions is far from obvious.

Although the relationship between all forms of the direct measurement of academic problems and successful academic interventions is not clear, there is a clear and current emphasis on school psychologists becoming involved in interventions with academic problems (Graden, Casey, & Christenson, 1985; Lentz & Shapiro, 1985; Tindal, Wesson, Deno, Germann, & Mirkin, 1985). There is a sore need for some integrative framework for conceptualizing direct measurement of academic behavior within an academic assessment model, and for understanding subsequent relationships to interventions. This is especially urgent if school psychologists are to act as consultants for academic problems in the classroom, rather than as psychometricians interested in the legal classification of children. Further, if school consultants are to be professionals and not technicians they must fully understand the rationale for judging and evaluating the utility of the various methods suggested for the direct measurement and assessment of academic problems.

The general purpose of this chapter is to provide an integrated review of the concepts, functions, and procedures related to direct observation and measurement of academic behavior within problem assessment. Two basic assumptions within the chapter are critical. First, direct measurement of academic behavior is essential to the resolution of academic problems in the classroom of origin, and in functional identification of the need for special placement (Lentz & Shapiro, 1985). Second, data derived from direct measurement require a nontraditional measurement model to be correctly interpreted and understood either for planning intervention or for verifying the need for special education. In particular, there are three related purposes:

1. The behavioral assessment model of measurement is reviewed as it relates to academic assessment. An overview is provided of what academic behaviors and related settings are relevant to understanding and evaluating the validity of direct measurement.
2. Specific procedures that can be classified as direct measurement within academic assessment are reviewed. These include direct classroom observation; the use of curriculum-based probes; and direct measurement of students' academic responses in natural classroom settings.
3. A functional assessment model, clearly related to the behavioral assessment model, is elucidated for the examination of the direct measurement procedures within academic assessment. This model provides for integration of the various methods for direct academic measurement, provides the usage framework for judging the validity of direct data, and delineates the relationship of direct to more indirect procedures.

CONCEPTUALIZING DIRECT MEASUREMENT IN ACADEMIC ASSESSMENT

Direct academic measurement procedures (as opposed to traditional, process-oriented procedures) have in fact been widely used in both behavioral research and within behaviorally oriented academic assessment. In the latter sense, several conceptually similar assessment models have been described.

One type of model is typified by the behavioral school psychology procedures suggested by Lentz and Shapiro (1985, 1986), and Shapiro and Lentz (1985). In this model, referrals for academic problems are assessed directly by school psychologists in regular classrooms, with the goal of designing interventions rather than simple eligibility evaluation. Teachers are first interviewed using a behavioral interviewing format (Bergan, 1977). Then, as needed, student skill repertoires are assessed with curriculum-based assessment (CBA) types of probes, student performance in the classroom environment is directly observed, and student academic products are examined. These data are used to analyze the problem, identify remedial targets (both student skill and environmental variables), and to design interventions. CBA probes may then be used to monitor intervention progress.

Deno (1985) describes a curriculum-based assessment model that seems primarily oriented to the determination of special education eligibility, setting individual education plan (IEP) goals, and monitoring progress. Using brief timed skill probes (see below) that are developed from the student's curriculum and that yield student rates of responding, one can screen referred students to determine if their performance is so different from expectancies that full special education assessment is warranted. If so, similar probes are used to place students with materials so they can be instructed or to identify more specific discrepancies. If performances remain below criteria, students are deemed eligible for special education, and curriculum-based IEP goals are set. Repeated CBA probes are then used to monitor the effects of interventions and to evaluate the special program. There appears to be little assessment of the student's actual classroom performance or of the classroom environment outside of observation of on-task rates within classroom settings (Tindal, Wesson, Germann, Deno, & Mirkin, 1985).

A direct assessment model similar to Deno's (1985) is described by Haring, Lovitt, Eaton, and Hansen (1978). It uses direct curriculum-based probes, but is oriented towards direct assessment of students already placed into a structured special education environment. Skill probes appear more specifically related to daily instructional goals than Deno's (1985), but there is still no direct assessment of the academic environment. This may be reasonable given that the environment is already specifically engineered for the special education program.

Although these models are generally well described within the sources above, there exists no clear analysis of precisely what measurement model is most amenable to direct measurement, or even what precisely constitutes direct versus less direct measurement procedures. These issues are critical to this chapter and, more importantly, to full understanding of current practices and future research needs.

A Rationale for Selecting Academic Assessment Procedures

Two general goals of academic assessment, whether direct or indirect, have been the measurement of both academic repertoires (skills) and the variables related to learning and performance of expected skills. Indirect measurement (traits, processes, global constructs) have failed to do this adequately for many reasons, two most applicable to this discussion are: a misoriented view of causal processes in instruction and learning, and a methodological framework that hampered proper conceptualization. In the latter sense, measurement procedures built on the distribution of individual differences have encouraged reification of descriptive terms to causal variables (e.g., Cone, 1981); and hampered direct examination of environmental settings and the observable instructional interactions that take place there. A different measurement model, not based quantitatively on individual differences, is needed to match the notions surrounding direct examination of precise academic skills and academic performance in the classroom.

A Behavioral View of Classroom Learning

Haring and Eaton (1978) provide a concise, behavioral view of the critical elements in classroom learning. Their conceptualizations appear very useful, and have provided a good empirical framework for examining the impact of academic interventions (Haring et al., 1978). Likewise, it is highly related to decisions about what to measure and what to choose as appropriate targets for intervention. In their view, schools arrange events so that students can "perform new skills in increasingly more complex situations." For any definable skill, the student must first acquire it (specific behaviors must come under appropriate stimulus control); then become fluent (increase rate of) in performance and maintain performance levels across time; and finally generalize and adapt the skill to new situations. (Note that mere presence of a response in a repertoire is not the end goal; fluency must also occur.) One set of skills to be developed includes strategies for students to employ in order to be more active learners. In order for these things to happen with the myriad skills that are taught in school, the student must be actively engaged in responding within a variety of academic activities, including instruction, practice, and drill (Greenwood, Delquadri, & Hall, 1984).

The academic curriculum provides a sequence for presentation and development of skills and partially provides opportunities for students to make the responses needed to progress both through the hierarchy described above and through the sequence of integrated skills. The teacher must arrange the classroom so that critical events occur (Lentz & Shapiro, 1986), including arranging: instruction for new responses, concepts, skills, and so on; frequent opportunities to respond in appropriate activities (Greenwood, Delquadri, & Hall, 1984); and contingencies adequate to support these activities (Lentz & Shapiro, 1986). (The reader is referred to Haring, et al. [1978], or Engelmann & Carnine [1982] for more complete discussions.)

What Should Be Measured during Problem Assessment

Within this conceptualization of school-based learning, there are three general classes of events that are important in terms of possible remediation, and therefore assessment (Lentz & Shapiro, 1986). The first class consists of those behaviors and changes in behavior that are conceptualized as the *academic skills* that are the goals of instruction. A wide variety of academic behaviors have been directly modified (Sulzer-Azaroff & Mayer, 1985). The second involves the behaviors of students as they are engaged in activities arranged to meet educational goals. These include active responses that may be considered academic (for example, answering questions, practicing, asking questions, and reading), orientation to academic materials or media, and other behaviors that may be considered critical to learning. Behavioral interventions have likewise modified a wide variety of these types of behavior (e.g., Baer & Bushell, 1981). The third class includes those environmental events related to instruction or to supporting student engagement.

From this conceptualization, there are several reasons that a child may be referred. First, the child might have deficits in skills. A teacher might perceive this because the child is unable to perform in several academic situations that require these skills; because classroom tests seem to indicate deficits; or both of these situations could be manifested. As will be seen, skills are conceptualized as clusters of different behaviors under control of topographically different stimuli. It may be that, for a particular child, some of the set of behaviors are present and under stimulus control while others are not. For example, a child could orally answer questions about a previously read passage, but be unable to write answers.

Secondly, a child might have a behavioral repertoire sufficient to meet classroom expectations, but not exhibit desirable performance in some academic situations. Not surprisingly, the student's behaviors that resulted in a referral made by the teacher may be identical to those above, although the "problem" is not the same. In the case of poor performance alone, the environmental events and their relationship to the child may be inadequate. It may be that the general behaviors for a particular activity (for example, sitting still and reading) are not under appropriate control, that reinforcement is inadequately arranged for the academic behavior including test performance, or that other competing behaviors have stronger contingencies. Note that inadequacy of environmental support is idiosyncratic.

Assessment of academic problems must derive from the identification of stimulus and behavior relationships that are considered the skills, or goals, of instruction. It must derive from a consideration of behavioral performance related both to behavioral repertoires and to the environmental situations where academic responding must occur. Finally, it must derive from the idea that assessment should directly identify the targets for remediation, both in terms of what skills should be developed, what environmental events must be changed, or both. The model of measurement must be conceptually adequate for these premises, incorporating the notions about behavior and environment relationships into measurement concepts and thus to the appropriate inferences that should be made from data.

The Behavioral Assessment Model

The behavioral assessment model has offered an alternative to the traditional trait-oriented model that once dominated psychology and education (e.g., Ciminero, Calhoun, & Adams, 1977; Hersen & Bellack, 1981). Although the behavioral assessment literature appears to have been generally applied to nonacademic behaviors, there are a number of academic assessment systems oriented towards direct measurement of academic "skills" that relate to this model in terms of assumptions about measurement and the functions of assessment (e.g., Deno, 1985; Haring *et al.*, 1978; White & Liberty, 1976). Also, direct observation procedures that are already conceptualized as behavioral assessment have been widely used in classroom research and assessment (e.g., Kazdin, 1984). Although more detailed discussions of behavioral assessment are found elsewhere in this volume, a brief discussion of critical characteristics of the behavioral assessment model is necessary so that direct academic measurement may be examined within it.

Briefly, the prime characteristics of behavioral assessment include a direct interest in behavior and its absolute measurement for an individual, with a low level of inference beyond the behavior itself; assessment conceptualized as involving samples of behavior rather than as a sign of some abstract construct; a consideration of behavior as being to some degree situationally specific; and a strong emphasis that both reliability and validity must be judged relative to actual behavior in natural settings (Cone, 1981).

Measurement procedures derived from a behavioral assessment model have several possible uses, including: a clinical function, selection of clients, and research (Goldfried & Linehan, 1977). The clinical function includes identification of target behaviors, delineation of controlling variables, selection of treatment procedures, monitoring of the effects of treatment, and evaluation of outcomes (Nelson & Hayes, 1981). Direct repeated measures of target behaviors in the environment(s) of interest are highly desirable. The functions for behavioral assessment clearly match the idea of linkage between academic assessment and direct interventions.

Reliability and Validity in Behavioral Assessment

Within the behavioral assessment model, like the traditional psychometric model, data qualities are judged based on the use of the data. However, there are notable differences that are specifically related to direct observation and measurement of behavior (academic in this case). The first critical quality of data derived from direct observation of behavior is accuracy (Cone, 1981). Whatever the rules for measuring behavior while observing (frequency counts, time sampling, etc.), the recorded data must accurately reflect the actual occurrence of behavior. Accuracy goes beyond the notion of interscorer reliability (Cone, 1978), although if two scorers are both accurate they will agree (the converse is not necessarily true, however; see Johnson & Bolstad, 1973). More "conservative" researchers would require each recorded occurrence to be accurate (Johnston & Pennypacker, 1980), while others would require across session observation count to be accurate (Johnson & Bolstad, 1973).

Traditional reliability concepts such as internal consistency or test-retest stability have been used by behavioral assessors (Cone, 1981). However, the importance of the internal consistency of a measurement instrument is not critical when the behavior observed is the precise target, accuracy of the recording is the standard, and the behavior will vary across time and places depending on the environmental conditions. Test-retest reliability is also less applicable when the measure is not intended to represent a stable trait (Cone, 1981). The concept of a somewhat stable capacity, or capability, or presence of a behavior in a repertoire, however, is of interest to academic assessors, and has been targeted for measurement within some systems using direct skill probes such as the curriculum-based measurement discussed by Deno (1985).

Several types of validity for behavioral assessment will be examined when the functions of direct academic assessment are discussed below. For any of these, however, there must be an explicit examination of the set of behaviors that are to be assessed, their interrelationships, and the stimulus situations under which they are to be exhibited. The requirement for such an explicit examination is critical when the inferences that are validly made from behavioral measures are evaluated. It will also be critical to this discussion.

Academic Assessment and the Behavioral Assessment Model

Educational measurement of such constructs as intelligence and mental processes is clearly in contrast to the characteristics of the behavioral assessment model. Even when the behavior of the examinee during such testing is considered, inferences about global tendencies (persistence, patterns of impulsivity) are typically made (Sattler, 1982).

Less trait-oriented educational measurement procedures such as norm-referenced achievement tests still relate to global constructs of academic skills, and depend on the relative nature of individual differences to derive their meaning (Anastasi, 1982). Norm-based achievement tests have been highly criticized in several aspects that are related to the differences between traditional and behavioral assessment models. For example, they do not offer absolute measures of academic behavior; rather, the meaning of derived measures comes from a student's relative standing in a norm group. They are also difficult to use in a frequent, repeated fashion and are thus not useful for progress monitoring. The lack of direct relationship between achievement tests and what is actually taught to children has also been highly criticized (Deno, 1985; Deno & Mirkin, 1977; Jenkins & Pany, 1978). Finally, norm-referenced achievement tests do not appear to be sensitive to short-term changes resulting from a specific intervention (Deno, 1985).

Some types of criterion-referenced tests (Livingston, 1977), at least in terms of their content and their focus on samples of behavior, may be more similar to behavioral assessment procedures. Linehan (1980) also considers behavioral assessment similar to criterion-referenced tests. It is less clear than it may first seem to be how performance on a criterion-referenced test is directly related to required classroom responses, although criterion-referenced tests could certainly be considered analogue measures (see below). Examination of even some curriculum-derived, criterion-referenced tests has indicated variable quality (Tindal, Fuchs, Fuchs, Shinn, Deno, & Germann, in press).

Academic assessment and intervention systems such as curriculum-based assessment (e.g., Deno, 1985), precision teaching (White & Liberty, 1976), or data-based instruction (Haring *et al.*, 1978) have been developed to measure academic skills and to overcome problems with norm-based achievement tests (Deno, 1985). To some extent, all of these systems employ direct observation and measurement procedures. These procedures target academic skills that are taught within the classroom and often use stimulus materials taken directly from student's curricula (Deno, 1985; Deno & Mirkin, 1977). They involve brief, timed probes of specifically defined academic behavior, and are used in a repeated fashion, differentiating them from other criterion-referenced tests. Although the measurement stimuli are natural, situations and conditions for assessment may or may not be, and it appears that the data have been used to make inferences about more global constructs (e.g., Deno, 1985; Magnusson & Marston, 1985), as well as being interpreted directly as the behavior of interest (White & Liberty, 1976). These distinctions are important in understanding the concept of direct observation of academic skills.

Measurement systems designed to measure important behaviors of students during academic situations have also been developed (Greenwood *et al.*, 1985; Lentz & Shapiro, 1986). Rather than specific skills, the student's behavior during academic instruction, academic engagement with materials, and concurrent environmental events are the focus (Lentz & Shapiro, 1986). Behavioral observation has long been analyzed within the framework of behavioral assessment.

Direct Measurement: Analogue or Naturalistic?

Measures within a behavioral assessment model must be related ultimately and directly to behaviors in natural environments. However, there are both indirect and direct procedures contained under the rubric of behavioral assessment (Cone, 1978). Although both types focus on behavior, indirect methods (interviews, self-report) do not involve concurrent observation of the target behavior. Direct measurement procedures may be conceptualized as either analogue or naturalistic (Cone, 1978). In both cases, behavior is directly observed, but in the former the setting for assessment is not the real time natural one. Typically, stimulus events are arranged in an attempt to elicit the target behavior in order to observe it (Cone, 1978). Perhaps the most common analogue procedures involve role-playing tests.

Although the difference between analogue and naturalistic observation would appear reasonably clear for such constructs as social skills, it is not so clear for academic behavior. In typical classrooms, stimuli are frequently arranged solely for the purpose of assessing academic responses. For example, an academic behavior like oral reading (a typical direct academic measure) that occurs directly in the natural environment (classroom) could be measured in several ways, differing along different dimensions. Oral reading rates could be directly measured during the regular reading group, by the teacher, under typical instructional conditions. On the other hand, oral reading could be measured using probes taken from natural stimulus materials (the child's basal reader) under regular instructional conditions, but in a nonnatural setting by a stranger (the school psychologist in his office). Likewise, the teacher could use such oral reading probes in the classroom but under different instructions and outside the reading group (the natural time and place for oral reading). If teachers are increasing their use of procedures like oral reading probes as a natural part of the classroom environment (e.g., Germann & Tindal, 1985), then what determines whether a direct academic measurement should be classified as analogue or naturalistic?

Regardless of the precise distinction between analogue and natural observation, and unless a behavior is measured continuously in all settings where it may occur, some type of generalization or inference from the direct measure must occur. Inferences could involve generalizing across unobserved situations, unobserved times, other assessors, other assessment methods, or dimensions of behavior (Cone, 1978). Thus, in order to judge the content validity of a direct measure of academic behavior or to understand the legitimate inferences that may be made, the dimensions of these generalizations must be specified clearly (Linehan, 1980). This is made particularly complex by the previously discussed assumption that behavior is situationally specific, and this is a very critical point to this chapter.

Kazdin (1979) has referred to situational specificity as a "two-edged sword" for behavioral assessment; if one assumes that behavior is naturally specific to a situation, then generalizations from the assessment situation to natural settings can be a conceptual problem. Traditionally, measures of academic skills or achievement have assumed a cross—situational validity of global skill constructs (reading comprehension or written expression skills), with less consideration of the many classroom behaviors subsumed under any academic skill—reading, for example. Further, the impact of the immediate assessment environment is downplayed in the interpretation of these test results (Fuchs & Fuchs, 1986).

ACADEMIC BEHAVIOR IN THE NATURAL SETTING

Prior to the examination of specific measurement systems within an assessment framework, a final task remains—explicitly describing what are academic behaviors, settings where they occur, controlling stimuli and related environmental variables, and interrelationships among these. As has been discussed, without such an explicit examination, the nature of inferences allowed from various data and the actual quality of the data themselves cannot be examined. It should be noted that although research provides strong evidence about what variables affect behavior in the classroom (Lentz & Shapiro, 1986), the nature of the specific ecological settings is not yet fully understood (Greenwood *et al*; 1985). Also, this discussion is not intended to serve as a conclusive review; rather, it is to ensure that the necessary ingredients are available to use in the evaluation of direct academic measures.

In the following section, the variables that combine to produce different settings, and that may be expected to result in different behaviors, will be described from "the response up." First, specific classroom academic behaviors that have been directly observed, measured, and often empirically modified are discussed. Next, the specific stimuli (antecedent and consequent to responses), that control academic behavior and academically related behavior are examined. Finally, more molar physical setting variables are delineated. The "finished product" will be a concept about academic behaviors and the important stimulus variables that form natural settings. Remember, it is observable events, usually in one or several of these settings, that bring teachers to refer students for academic problems. Further, it is in the natural settings that remediation must be successful (Trieber & Lahey, 1983).

This chapter generally focuses on externally observable and measureable behaviors. Internal behaviors like thinking are certainly critical in any educational setting and fall well within the realm of behavioral assessment and intervention. Likewise, such behaviors are and should be a prime educational target. The possible scope of this chapter, coupled with the overlapping content of other chapters in the present volume, precludes the investigation of this topic. Finally, even if thinking or cognitive events are targeted within interventions, the eventual impact on external behavior and student performance must still be measured.

Although ultimately important, the discussion of the important dimensions of classroom settings will (because of space limitations) ignore the premise that the ultimate goals and behaviors targeted by schools do not occur in schools, or even concurrently with the schooling process. The purpose of this section is to delineate educationally important phenomena within the school environment that relate to variability of student responding in the classroom and that affect measurement inferences.

Student Academic Behaviors

Academic behaviors, for the purpose of this discussion, are classified along three dimensions. The first dimension is orientation of the child during an academic activity (defined as one where instructional activities are occurring) to relevant academic materials or events (media, teacher lectures). Second are the motor activities exhibited by the child as he or she interacts with materials or people during academic activities (writing, answering questions). Finally, there are permanent products resulting from such interactions. This section will discuss the various academic behaviors separately even if it is somewhat difficult to discuss them without consideration of the stimuli with which the child is interacting.

Orientation of Students to Materials or Events

Rather widely investigated within the behavioral literature as "on-task" behavior (e.g., Lentz & Shapiro, 1986), the orientation of students during academic activities appears related to various measures of achievement, and to more specific measures of academic performance (percentage correct on assignments, performance on weekly tests, etc.). Student orientation to task is a logically relevant behavior to consider when discussing academic behavior since students cannot appropriately be engaged in academic activities unless they are to some degree oriented towards them. However, research also indicates that academic performance and on-task behavior can at times be independent behaviors (e.g., Hay, Hay, & Nelson, 1977).

A second reason orientation to events or materials may be relevant for direct observation and measurement is that students appear to learn through observation within classroom settings (Hanley-Maxwell, Silcox, & Heal, 1982; McCurdy, Cundari, & Lentz, in review). It is judged that the combined evidence and logic is sufficient to consider orientation within the framework of academic behavior.

Motor Activities

Greenwood *et al.* (1985) define general classes of academically related motor behaviors that are exhibited within academic settings, including: writing, reading aloud, reading silently, asking questions, answering questions, academic talk, and academic game play. These behaviors were selected because they represent active response classes that are exhibited across many classroom situations and activities, and because they are varieties of academic responses arranged during activities that are considered crucial in both student acquisition of new behaviors, and in drill or practice. Certain of these behaviors are critical for in- and out-of-class assessment measures, for example oral reading and answering questions.

Other investigators have observed more molecular behaviors exhibited during academic activities, such as eye movements (e.g., Lahey, Vosk, & Habif, 1981; Roberts, 1981). This type of behavior, however, is very difficult to observe except in situations contrived outside the classroom and would seem to be more clearly related to direct but analogue measurement.

Permanent Products

Written permanent products have been a mainstay of both behavioral assessment and intervention in the classroom. Although not responses in themselves, permanent products may be observed and measured directly; they occur within definable situations, to specifiable discriminative stimuli; and they represent the outcome of a specific response (writing) to a veritable plethora of potential eliciting stimuli. For example, writing responses are controlled by teacher verbalizations (i.e., spelling), written questions in reading, math, or content textbooks, and written or oral tests. Perhaps most importantly, it is likely that some form of written permanent product is strongly related to the reasons teachers refer children in the first place.

To emphasize further the importance of written products, they are naturally used within the classroom environment to assess student competences in such skills as reading, math, and language arts. The dimensions of written products that are observed depends clearly on the purpose of assessment. The mechanics of hand-writing might be observed, for example (Hopkins, Schutte, & Garton, 1971). Words or letter sequences might be the units of analysis if "spelling" skills were being assessed (Starlin, 1982). At the most molar level, sentence or paragraph semantical features, or even "creativity," could be observed directly (Campbell & Willis, 1978). Clearly, written products are critical in the direct observation and measurement of academic behavior.

Stimuli Directly Controlling Academic Responding

School is not a "free operant" setting in terms of academic behavior. The variety of academic responses are elicited or signaled by an equally wide variety of antecedent stimuli, ranging from teacher questions, written problems, or text material, to verbal directions for students to exhibit classes of responses, to stimuli that act as conditional discriminative stimuli (in whose presence a particular response is controlled by another stimulus).

Research from various theoretical orientations has strongly supported the idea that academic achievement cannot occur unless students are engaged in making appropriate academic responses (e.g., Greenwood *et al.*, 1984; Lentz & Shapiro, 1986). Students must make responses when acquiring new skills, when practicing to develop proficiency or to maintain performance, or when learning to generalize previous skills (Haring & Eaton, 1978). These opportunities to respond (Greenwood *et al.*, 1985) are provided by a wide variety of antecedent task stimuli that are arranged within instuctional activities in the classroom.

Thus, one critical feature of an academic setting is the set of stimuli that "control" or set the stage for the wide variety of student academic responses. The behavior analysis literature overwhelmingly supports the notion that different arrangements of classroom stimuli and contingent reinforcers will drastically affect the quality of student responses (e.g., Sulzer-Azaroff & Mayer, 1985). Therefore, the ecological arrangements of both discriminative stimuli and contingent reinforcement should be carefully analyzed in any discussion about classroom situations and the effects on student responses. This discussion is divided into four sections: stimuli that set the stage for other stimuli to provide specific opportunities to respond; specific academic task stimuli; stimulus events contingent on responses; and stimuli during the instruction of new skills. Once these stimuli are described and related to the academic responses discussed earlier, the core of concepts about academic skills, and functional academic settings, will be present.

Antecedents for Response Classes

The relevant controlling, or discriminative academic stimuli include those intended to control classes of response, such as directions to respond orally, begin work, read questions and write answers (Becker, Engelmann, & Thomas, 1976). These signals are more or less effective depending on the consistency of contingent reinforcement patterns when they are presented. The physical dimensions of such discriminative stimuli include written (instructions within a textbook, or instructions on a board); verbal (teacher given directions before an activity); or they can even become inherent within the overall setting (during certain activities, certain responses are always expected).

Interestingly, setting variables such as teachers' telling students that they are being timed during an activity, both in the presence of contingency systems and not, can increase the rate of student responding (Ayllon, Garber, & Pisor, 1976; Rainwater & Ayllon, 1976). This has serious implications for use of timed probes in direct academic assessment (see below).

A related class of discriminative stimuli are those Becker *et al.* (1976) call "attention signals." these are intended to control student attention (orientation) to a task stimulus, or even to the teacher ("Look at me"; "Listen to me"). Bringing student behavior under control of this type of stimuli appears important in managing effective group lessons.

Other stimuli within specific classroom settings can come to control patterns of responses unintentionally, for example teacher proximity may serve as a discriminative stimulus for "working" for individual students. Likewise, instructional arrangements, such as lecturing at the front of the room, may exercise only incomplete stimulus control of student orientation to the lecturer (e.g., Greenwood, Dinwiddie, Terry, Wade, Stanley, Thibadeau, & Delquadri, 1984). The interactive effects of the almost infinite arrangement patterns for all of these stimuli is increasingly being realized by behavioral researchers (e.g., Greenwood *et al.*, 1985). The relevant research indicates that there are specific arrangements of environmental stimuli that produce predictable changes in student behavior during periods when they should be engaged in academic activity (Greenwood *et al.*, 1984; Greenwood *et al.*, 1985). Further, these behavioral changes are functionally related to other academic behaviors, such as success on classroom tests (Greenwood, *et al.*, 1984).

Task Stimuli

At a more molecular level of stimulus control of student responses are the specific task stimuli (like items in student workbooks or specific teacher questions) to which students are expected to make specific responses (usually written or oral). The important issue here is that different forms of task stimuli can significantly alter the correctness of student responses, even when the responses might be considered equivalent indicators of skill. For example, Decorte and Savickas (1985) altered word arrangement in math word problems while retaining identical characters, elements, and operations to solve, and they demonstrated significant changes in student solution accuracy.

The equivalence of student response accuracy to the same stimulus material after different intervening student behavior may also be questionable. For example, the research concerning students' answering questions from the same textual material read silently or orally is mixed (Miller & Smith, 1985). However, the greater the difference of the stimuli or responses within any larger skill class, reading for example, the greater the potential for independence of responses. Lovitt, Eaton, Kirkwood, and Perlander (1971) demonstrated that changes produced in oral reading rates (the reinforcement target) were not always accompanied by changes in student accuracy in answering questions based on reading comprehension. Others have demonstrated that while related, oral reading rate and comprehension can be changed separately (Roberts & Smith, 1980). Unfortunately, task stimuli for wide focus skills such as comprehension vary. Use of different stimuli may result in different conclusions about various relationships among task stimuli, responses, and intervention effects.

The number of stimuli that have been used to occasion responding in such areas as "reading comprehension" is quite large (Guthrie & Tyler, 1976), and subsequently, making operational what is meant by such categories is difficult. Complicating the situation is the apparent fact that features in task stimuli that might not be considered critical to the academic issue might control responding. Several researchers (Vargas, 1984) have demonstrated that extraneous (to the comprehension of the text) features of items supposedly eliciting comprehension responses actually control student responses.

Instructional Prompts

Recently, data on the importance of teacher-arranged prompts during instruction of new skills and behaviors have accumulated (e.g., Etzel & LeBlanc, 1979). These include prompts to produce behavior in the presence of task stimuli (Schoen, 1986); prompts to attend to relevant dimensions of task stimuli (Engelmann *et al.*, 1976); models of correct responses (Hendrickson & Gable, 1981); and procedures to fade these prompts (Etzel & LeBlanc, 1979). These events can and have been directly observed and measured (Stowitschek, Stowitschek, Hendrickson, & Day, 1984), and certainly could differ in efficacy across different academic situations, thus affecting student acquisition of new behaviors.

Consequences

The literature on the effects of contingent events on academic behavior is overwhelming (e.g., Lentz & Shapiro, 1986; Sulzer-Azaroff & Mayer, 1985). There should be little doubt that contingent reinforcement is operable within the entire range of behaviors discussed above. Further, reinforcement enhances instruction of new skills and can drastically affect the performance of academic behaviors that are *already* in student repertoires. Lentz and Shapiro (1986) discuss several classes of potentially potent contingencies, including contingencies *immediately* impinging on student academic responses, like teacher praise, teacher feedback about accuracy, tangible events, and so on, and postwork contingencies for work accuracy and completion.

Although the experimental literature makes the effects of reinforcement very clear, investigations into natural rates of such possible reinforcers as praise indicate that they may be low rate and variable (White, 1975). Further, some types of contingent stimuli may not serve as reinforcers for some children. It is also unclear if various contingencies are consistent across situations; if not, it certainly could account for variability in student performance across different activities. What is clear is that performance and acquisition of academic behaviors are strongly affected by contingent events.

The Relevant Physical Settings

The physical structure of the classroom (aside from events within the environment that interact dynamically with the behaving student) has to some degree been ignored in the behavioral literature (although not ignored elsewhere; see Weinstein, 1979). It includes such things as desk arrangements, size of the classroom, objects in the classroom, temperature, lighting, and so forth. There are also subsettings within the classroom that could functionally be related to academic behavior; for example, the arrangement of desks or students during group lessons, or the relationship between the target student's desk and other parts of the classroom.

Winett, Battersby, and Edwards, (1975) examined the effects of desk arrangement on academic performance of fifth-grade students. Although not conclusive, their data seem to indicate that rearrangement of desks improved the performance of some groups of students in two different curriculum areas. Other investigators have demonstrated the effects of desk arrangement (e.g., Axelrod, Hall, & Tams, 1976; Paine, Radicchi, Rosellini, Deutchman, & Darch, 1983) on student performance. These data are hypothesized to have resulted because rearrangement facilitated behaviors related to academic success (peer help).

The relevant physical environment certainly ought to include environmental arrangements that appear to affect student behavior, for example, sequence of activities. Krantz and Risley (1977), demonstrated that the sequence of activities in a preschool affected behaviors related to instruction. The potency of access to desirable activities contingent on participation in less desirable activities, for example, also has been demonstrated (e.g., Hopkins *et al.*, 1971).

Although there may eventually be evidence concerning the probability of physical setting variables being potent variables across students, it must be remembered that it is the idiosyncratic effects that are critical. The physical environment can also be conceptualized in relation to other ecological variables such as instructional format, interactions, and so on. In either case, it is a setting variable that should be considered in examination of generalization from direct observation and measurement of behavior.

The Importance of Directly Measuring
Classroom Responses

It appears that one goal of education is to inculcate general capabilities in various academic areas so that students will exhibit appropriate responses in a wide range of tasks, supposedly related to a specific skill. This requires both acquisition of increasingly complex behaviors, and practice for fluency and proficiency. From a behavioral perspective, tasks or skills involve arrangements of setting stimuli, task stimuli, responses and contingencies within physical settings. This assumption also means that a student may "have" a response under certain conditions, but not exhibit the response in other required settings. In essence, this delineates the performance or skill question for academic assessors. The previous discussion has, if nothing else, demonstrated the extremely complex nature of academic skills and setttings in terms of dimensions of generalization for measurement.

The behavioral assessment model clearly conceptualizes that inferences from measurements must be evaluated along such dimensions as scorer, task stimuli, situations, time, and behaviors (Cone, 1981). Thus, although it may appear simple to observe behavior directly, or to give a direct academic skill probe, desirable inferences may not be simple at all. There are very few situations involving direct observation and measurement of academic behavior when inferences *beyond* the immediate assessment setting are not desirable. Likewise, the purpose of assessment dictates the types of measurement inferences that should be supported.

Selecting the "correct" behaviors to be assessed and understanding their relationship to environmental settings is a critical aspect in the development of any behavioral measurement system (Linehan, 1980). Traditional assessment of academic skills has conceptualized skills as some general performance capacity of the student that is generalized beyond the particular stimulus characteristics of the assessment materials and setting. That assumption has been heavily criticized. Behaviorally oriented assessors and behavioral academic researchers (e.g., Deno, 1985; White & Liberty, 1976) likewise appear interested in the assessment of skill capacities or capabilities, but must not repeat the errors of traditional assessment. It must also be remembered that the teacher has seen something that resulted in a referral. Unless that "Something" is logically divorced from the academic setting, then the problem in the classroom must be examined.

An example of a behaviorally defined "skill" may be illuminating—for example, reading comprehension. The first problem is that reading comprehension is not in practically any sense a skill that is similar across different types of texts or for different developmental levels (across, for example, a basal reader and a text on cosmology for graduate students when discussing fourth-grade students). This observation by no means blithely suggests an easily quantifiable continuum; however, for the purposes of this example, assume the examination of reading comprehension is for fourth- and fifth-grade students.

A skill is considered a cluster of responses under specifiable conditions. In this case, it may include a set of discrete topographical student behaviors under control of a definable set of task stimuli. This could include: student oral answers to teacher questions after another student read a passage, the teacher read a passage, or the student read a passage; student written responses to questions after a basal reader story, reading a chapter of social studies, science or health; student written responses on a curriculum-based mastery test; student written responses to a word problem in math; student motor responses to written instructions in any textbook; student oral responses to a request to tell about a story or book. Would these be separate "skills" or would students be expected to have generalized some "comprehension" skill?

To complicate the issue further, any of these behaviors could be elicited under conditions of reinforcement or not; at home or at school; in the classroom or in the psychologist's office. In sum, reading comprehension may be defined as a set of behaviors, under the control of a set of stimuli, under varying contingencies. Is there a generalizable comprehension skill for every child? Would every child be able to perform under all of these conditions, only some, or none? Would a child have to exhibit none of these behaviors before it was decided he did not have a skill? Might referred children's topographically dissimilar behaviors not be under control of the entire set of skills-relevant stimuli? Is it more efficacious for in-class interventions to assess, in some respect, an individual child's particular repertoire? In fact, there does not appear to be any empirically based answer, although Engelmann and Carnine (1982) have developed a coherent instructional theory around the expanded notion of a concept or skill. Yet, academic assessments must be made if interventions are to be planned.

It is conceded that for some academic areas, math for instance, there is likely to be some sort of hierarchy of behaviors under definable requisite relationships (Bergan, 1982; Resnick, Wang, & Kagan, 1973). In those subjects, assessment of capacity is likely to be more straightforward, although the conditions under which behaviors are expected to be exhibited must still be carefully considered.

Nonetheless, if assessment data are to be linked effectively to intervention in classrooms, then the functional units of academic behavior *in the classroom* must ultimately be measured and changed (Trieber & Lahey, 1983). Functionality must be defined from an analysis of what behaviors or permanent products should be exhibited within daily academic settings. Certainly, assessment of the adequacy of particular behavioral repertoires (skills) is critical to the selection of interventions (for example, deciding to teach new behaviors or to rearrange contingencies for common practice conditions). Such an assessment may not be divorced from classroom settings if intervention is to be planned. Finally, the critical environmental variables affecting these functional behaviors must be directly measured *if* intervention is to be planned in the classroom setting.

Thus, the bottom line for judging the ultimate utility of an academic measure, from a direct behavioral perspective, is the relationship between the measure and both functional academic behavior and the environmental events affecting it. This appears to be an unusual perspective on academic assessment for several reasons. First, behavioral intervention programs for academic problems have often occurred in special classrooms (Epstein & Cullinan, 1980; Haring *et al*; 1978), or in special programs where the entire environment is structured (e.g., Bushell, 1978). In these cases, assessment requirements are not the same as for a consultant in a regular classroom, a classroom that may have very idiosyncratic features. Secondly, even recently developed systems such as the curriculum-based assessment of Deno and his colleagues (Deno, 1985, 1986) seem virtually to ignore actual classroom behavior, treating skill probes as some sort of traditional or, at best, analogue behavioral measure. Unfortunately, there appear to be very limited data bearing directly on the total assessment issues surrounding attempted interventions in regular classrooms.

TYPICAL DIRECT MEASUREMENT PROCEDURES

Extending from the previous discussions, academic measurement procedures are direct to the extent that they focus on concurrent measurement of relevant behaviors within the settings of interest. Direct measurement procedures fall within the behavioral assessment model and, for the purposes of this chapter, are important during assessment that leads to intervention planning and subsequent monitoring of intervention effects. Further, it is not so much the student response topography that defines a direct measurement, as it is the relationship between the conditions of measurement and the behavior(s) in the natural environment. For example, having a student read aloud during academic assessment is part of some standardized reading tests and curriculum-based assessment. Yet, the interpretation of student responses and relationships to natural materials and conditions are different, and would be judged differently within a traditional versus a behavioral assessment model.

Four measurement strategies are of particular interest here: behavioral interviewing, direct observation in natural settings, use of curriculum-based skill probes or progress monitoring units, and direct measurement of student responding in the classroom. Table 3-1 illustrates how the variables previously defined as academic behaviors or critical environmental events may relate to these direct measurement procedures.

Behavioral interviewing (Bergan, 1977) is an indirect behavioral assessment procedure heavily utilized in behavioral consultation. When focused on behavioral and related environmental events, interviews play a critical role in an assessment of student academic problems (Bergan, 1977; Lentz & Shapiro, 1985; Lentz & Shapiro, 1986; Shapiro & Lentz, 1986). Thus, if complete behavioral assessment of a referral problem leading to intervention planning is the goal, both indirect and direct procedures are used. Behavioral research, on the other hand, could employ only direct measurement procedures.

Shapiro and Lentz (1986) and Lentz and Shapiro (1986) provide a good overview of the employment of direct measurement of the academic environment and student skill repertoires during school-based problem assessment. Other assessment models have focused heavily on skill repertoires, with less emphasis on the environment (Deno, 1985; Haring *et al.*, 1978). Following a closer examination of the three direct measurement procedures, use of direct measurement within a general behavioral assessment model will be discussed.

TABLE 3-1 Measurement Procedures for Academic Behavior and Environment

Variable	Type of Related Measurement Procedure			
	Interview	Direct Observation	Permanent Product	Skill Probes Assessment
A. Student academic behaviors				
1. Orientation to materials and events	a			
2. Academic responses	a	b,c	b,c	b,c
writing				
reading aloud				
reading silently				
oral answers				
academic talk				
3. Permanent products	a			
class/homework			b,c	
worksheets/books			b,c	b,c
tests			b,c	b,c
B. Skill repertoires	a		b,c	b,c
C. Critical events				
1. Antecedent stimuli	a	b		
work directions				
verbal				
written				
2. Task stimuli	a	b		
task material				
oral questions				
3. Instruction methods	a	b		
4. Consequent stimuli	a	b		
praise/disapproval				
contingencies for performance				
D. Physical setting variables	a	b		
grouping/desks				
teacher position				
activity sequence				
alloted time				

a = indirect, focus on natural behaviors/settings; b = direct, in setting of interest; c = direct, arranged task stimuli outside of setting

Direct Observation

A wide range of standardized systems have been developed to measure classroom behavior through observation and related environmental events, going from those measuring single behaviors such as on-task (e.g., Hay *et al.*, 1977), to those concurrently measuring numerous behaviors of target students and other persons who interact with them (Greenwood *et al.*, 1985; Saudargas & Lentz, 1986; Wahler, House, & Stambaugh, 1976). The least comprehensive have been employed in an empirical examination of interventions with student on-task such as that of Hay *et al.* (1977), while the most comprehensive have been used to examine academic ecologies or to help analyze academic problems (Shapiro & Lentz, 1985). For example, Greenwood *et al.* (1985) employed a direct observation code measuring several types of active student academic respondings, teacher behaviors, and types of activities. Direct observation is most appropriate for measuring student behavior during academic activities (performance measurement), related impinging environmental variables, and the physical setting.

A variety of behavioral measures may be derived from direct observation, including frequency, latency, duration, and intensity (Saudargas & Lentz, 1985). In addition, behavior may also be sampled across observational sessions, yielding data that is intended to relate to the real time measures (although the relationship is different across the time sampling schemes, and various combinations of real time parameters [Saudargas & Lentz, 1985]).

Accuracy, defined as the accurate transduction of observed behavior to numbers (Johnson & Pennypacker, 1980), is perhaps the prerequisite psychometric characteristic for judging the suitability of direct observational measures (Cone, 1978), although seldom directly assessed (Johnson & Bolstad, 1973). Related measures such as interobserver agreement, on the other hand, are frequently examined.

Content validity is the most crucial quality in judging suitability of direct observation systems for various assessment purposes (Linehan, 1980), with content referring to the adequacy of sampling of behaviors and settings. Although the variables discussed in the above section on the natural academic environment form the pool for judging content validity, it is not entirely clear exactly which variables are critical to which assessment functions (Lentz & Shapiro, 1986). As will be seen, direct observation and the other two direct procedures are closely interrelated within a behavioral model of academic assessment, and they all may serve different purposes within the various functions of academic assessment.

Direct observational measures are typically "low inference" in the sense that the behaviors of interest are measured directly in the settings of interest. Even so there are a number of inferences that may be needed, such as inferring levels of the subject's unobserved behavior in the same or different settings at the same or different time periods. Other inferences have to do with who makes the measurements. For example, if different observers are equally accurate across different subjects and settings, then observational measures may be generalized across the dimensions of observer, subjects, and settings. However, this assumption is best made from an empirical standpoint. Further, since most observational codes define even similar behaviors in different ways, generalization across codes, measuring similarly named behaviors, may not be warranted. Thus, even with highly direct measures there are often troublesome inferences that must be made.

Skill Probes and Progress Monitoring

Basic to a number of behavioral intervention systems (Haring *et al.*, 1978; White & Liberty, 1976) and performance or progress monitoring systems (Deno, 1985; Deno & Mirkin, 1977) have been curriculum-based skill probes or progress monitoring units. These measures have been typically employed to assess academic competences (repertoires, capacities, etc.).

Curriculum-based Probes

Academic assessment probes derived directly from curriculum materials or skill sequences are usually considered performance measures of a closely defined academic skill (Deno & Mirkin, 1977). Typically, probes are brief (1 to 2 minutes), curriculum-derived samples of student behavior. (See Deno, 1985; Germann & Tindal, 1985; Haring *et al.*, 1978; Idol-Maestas, 1983; and White & Liberty, 1976 for more complete accounts.) Use of these probes may be considered more or less direct measurement depending on their relationship to actual curriculum-based materials or classroom task stimuli, their relationship to operational definitions of the skills that are actual targets of instruction, and where and by whom they are administered (see above).

For reading assessment, probes consisting of 100- to 300-word samples from basal texts are read aloud by a child yielding the rate of correct and incorrect words per minute (Deno, 1985). The emphasis on rate is deemed quite important since it reflects both accuracy and fluency (Hendrickson, Gable, & Stowitschek, 1985). Comprehension may be assessed by a variety of brief procedures, including asking questions about a passage, or having a child tell everything he remembers about a passage (Starlin, 1982). Lists of isolated words, also taken from basal texts, have been used in a similar fashion (Deno, Mirkin, & Chiang, 1983).

Words from spelling texts have been dictated (Germann & Tindal, 1985), or passages dictated at steady rates (Starlin, 1982), with the rate of words or letter sequences correct per minute as a measure of spelling. In arithmetic, specific types of computational problems, in the form of a worksheet, are worked for 1 to 2 minutes, yielding digits correct and incorrect per minute. "Story starters" are used to elicit brief written expression samples (3 minutes) (Germann & Tindal, 1985). Finally, letters, words, or paragraphs may be copied (or dictated) to assess handwriting (Starlin, 1982).

Recently, a large amount of research into the qualities of academic probes has been conducted at the University of Minnesota (e.g., Deno *et al.*, 1984; Deno, Marston, Shinn, & Tindal, 1983; Deno, Mirkin, & Chiang, 1982; Fuchs, Deno & Marston, 1983; Fuchs, Fuchs, & Deno, 1982; Fuchs, Tindall, & Deno, 1984; Germann, & Tindall, 1985; Marston, & Deno, 1981; Shinn & Marston, 1985; Tindal & Deno, 1981). Researchers were primarily interested in developing a measurement system with the qualities necessary in a system of setting and monitoring academic goals so that instruction could be guided empirically and outcomes easily evaluated.

The psychometric research out of Minnesota seems to have been conducted from a traditional measurement model. For example, oral reading rates, data from probes for written expression, and spelling probe data correlate highly with standardized achievement tests (Deno, 1985), thus exhibiting traditional concurrent validity. Likewise, reading and written expression probes demonstrate adequate internal consistency, and test-retest validity (at least for short periods) (Fuchs, 1982; Marston & Deno, 1981). Finally, probe data discriminate between students already classified, receiving Chapter One services, and in regular education (Deno, 1985). In summary, probe data are as psychometrically sound as standardized achievement tests, are much simpler to administer, and are much less expensive. In addition they are repeatable and thus may serve a monitoring function for the efficacy of instruction (Deno, 1985). Additional research will be discussed in the sections below.

General versus specific probes as direct measurement. Deno (1985) describes performance probes as "vital signs" of academic progress and seems to indicate that they may not be appropriate targets for direct remediation. Performance probes in this sense are high inference measures (compared with academic behavior in the classroom) that are often administered by nonclassroom personnel, in nonclassroom settings. Interestingly, Deno and Mirkin (1977) discuss performance probes as useful both as related to direct instructional targets and as more general monitoring data.

As has been discussed, however, a behavioral assessment view of skill constructs includes specification of task stimuli, a range of response topographies, and setting variables (see also Engelmann & Carnine, 1982). It is often unclear if performance probes should be appropriately classified as indirect, analogue, or direct behavioral assessment procedures. Probes are, of course, samples of behavior to more or less natural stimuli. It is the conditions of assessment and the degree of relationship that may vary widely. Nevertheless, they are one of the most prevalent procedures touted as direct measurement of specific academic skills, and those who conduct academic assessments have a critical interest in behavioral repertoires or capacities (Linehan, 1980).

Other researchers (e.g., Haring *et al.*, 1978; White & Liberty, 1976), have used the same probe data as direct targets for specific interventions. Typically, performance probes were established and used by teachers as part of normal classroom instruction; few inferences beyond the actual data were made. In fact, oral reading rates have often been targeted as the goal of instruction (Haring *et al.*, 1978), not merely as a "vital sign" (Deno, 1985). Likewise, phonic skills and sight words have been directly instructed, with direct probes used to determine when new words have been acquired, rather than as a "sign" of reading ability (Idol-Maestas, 1983; Lahey & Drabman, 1973). When used as an intervention target, not as an inference about more general skills, performance probes more clearly fit the behavioral assessment model, and can more surely be labeled as direct measures of academic behavior. The differences in inferences and purposes clearly mark the different measurement models for the use of topographically identical procedures.

It is useful to categorize direct performance probes into two types—general (the Minnesota variety) and specific (the variety associated with direct or precision instruction). The general probes are meant to represent overall ability in a curriculum, and the content is selected accordingly. For example, in math a set of general fifth-grade computational skills is selected, perhaps division and multiplication facts (see Marston & Magnusson, 1985), and a whole set of probes is constructed to monitor overall student progress, decide eligibility, or set goals. Specific probes, used more directly in instruction, are constructed to reflect more narrow goals of instruction. For example, if multiplication facts up to five were instructed, those types of facts would be the only ones on the probe sheets. The "story starters" of Marston and Magnusson (1985) are clearly a general probe meant to reflect some general ability in written expression.

For some academic areas, the form of the probes may exactly coincide—in reading, for example, when general probes are selected from the fifth-grade book to monitor general, cross-year progress of a student, and when specific probes are taken from the fifth-grade book because that is where instruction is occurring. However, in the latter example, if instruction was no longer in the fifth-grade book, additional specific probes would be constructed from the current instructional book; general probes would not change. In fact a fifth-grade book may never be the instructional book (see Deno, 1985; Deno, Mirkin, & Wesson, 1984; or Germann & Tindal, 1985). This distinction is important to an examination of direct measurement of academic behavior.

Progress Monitoring

Progress monitoring involves the creation of curriculum units (pages, chapters, skill units) so that a child's progress can be monitored (Deno & Mirkin, 1977). Although quite different from the performance probes, progress monitoring has been suggested as an alternative to the use of performance probes (Fuchs, 1982; Germann & Tindal, 1985) but has not received the published coverage. While not representing as uniform a behavioral measure as performance probes, in some ways progress units are more direct measures, since they more directly represent daily curriculum-based behavior in the classroom.

Several standardized educational programs have used progress monitoring to determine individual student progress (Jackson, 1976; Peterson, Heistad, Peterson, & Reynolds, 1985; Weis, 1976). Peterson *et al.* (1985) used skill units, each with a domain-referenced mastery test, to measure progress. Normative data on time taken to complete particular units were collected and used to set short-term goals for individual students. Units were sequential and cross year progress could be measured; students not progressing through the units beyond a criterion norm-based rate (20th percentile) could be referred. Data indicated that this type of screening discriminated between students receiving and students not receiving special services for academic problems.

Jackson (1976) and Weis (1976) report use of pages completed per day as the unit of progress in basic skill areas within the Behavior Analysis Follow-Through model. Curriculum-based mastery tests provided checks, and data were used to determine adequate progress towards idiosyncratic goals. Since daily assignments were in terms of pages, this progress measure is a very direct, classroom-related performance measure, and would appear to be one type of functional academic behavior unit (Trieber & Lahey, 1983). Lentz and Eakins (1980) report high correlations between curriculum placement and standardized achievement test data. Jackson (1976) reports utilization of progress data in instructional model validation.

Since Peterson *et al.* (1985), Jackson (1976), and Weis (1976) report use of these data in programs with standardized instructional and management procedures, these data are closely involved in actual classroom procedures, and related to functional units of academic behavior. In fact, an instructional ecology including on-task, oral performance, contingencies, and antecedent prompts was directly observed, measured, and related to progress units in Jackson (1976). Thus, progress monitoring can clearly be conceptualized as a direct measure of academic behavior.

Directly Measuring Academic Responding in the Classroom

A mainstay of behavioral intervention research has been student performance on daily written assignments, classroom tests, or in oral responding during instruction (Shapiro & Lentz, 1985). Such measures as quality, creativity, and structure of written stories (Campbell & Willis, 1978), spelling tests (Delquadri, Greenwood, Stretton, & Hall, 1983), handwriting (Kosiewicz, Hallahan, & Lloyd, 1981), and daily math practice sheets (Kirby & Shields, 1972) that are part of the regular academic setting have been used as measures of change in student behavior. These measures can be considered functional units of academic behavior (Trieber & Lahey, 1983) and are very direct measures of behaviors that may be clustered into skill constructs.

Examination of research data reveals that the level and stability of such measures is under the control of antecedent or consequent events (e.g., Haring *et al.*, 1978). Variability is not assumed to result from measurement error, although given different tasks from day to day, performance may vary as a function of task stimuli. Accuracy in scoring these measures is the typical reliability measure reported. Thus, daily performance in the classroom is clearly within the behavioral measurement model, both conceptually and practically.

One of the most serious validity questions raised about this type of direct measure has to do with the validity of target variables beyond the immediate intervention (Bailey & Lessen, 1984). In other words, if discrete academic behaviors can be modified, what is their utility to overall student progress in a particular curriculum area? This is, in essence, a question of the valid scope of the content of specific measurements, as related to the associated critical behavioral dimensions. As such, it is very important in the assessment of the validity of direct academic measures.

Summary

Three classes of direct academic measures may be identified. Collectively, they allow assessment of both skill repertoires and functional academic behavior in the natural classroom environment. The content validity of any of these measures must be judged in relation to academic behavior in natural environments. However, at least in terms of measuring repertoires, both analogue (general probes) and more direct (specific probes) procedures have been used. Although such a distinction is conceptually possible, discriminating between analogue and natural direct measures is not always easy. Yet a discrimination is critical when evaluating the types and degree of inferences that may need to be drawn from measurements.

DIRECT MEASUREMENT OF ACADEMIC BEHAVIOR WITHIN A FUNCTIONAL ACADEMIC ASSESSMENT MODEL

In this final section, the use of direct measurement procedures within academic assessment is explored in the context of a comprehensive clinical assessment model. It is argued that academic assessment employing more direct measurement procedures may avoid some of the pitfalls of traditional assessment (see above), and allow a functional connection between assessment data and intervention planning (Deno, 1985; Shapiro & Lentz, 1985). However, there are a number of different but related functions within academic assessment that direct measurement may serve. There are also differing requirements for demonstrating that direct measurement procedures are valid for these different functions. Certainly, any measure is not blanketly valid; rather, it is valid or not valid for some particular purpose. This basic measurement doctrine is often ignored by both practitioners and researchers, and is likely to have contributed to much of the controversy surrounding applied psychological and educational measurement.

Hawkins (1979) provides an excellent discussion of the functions of assessment that is applicable for examining the utility of direct academic measurement. He likens assessment for individual problems to a funnel that initially provides wide scope, becoming gradually more narrowly focused on individual problems. This leads to intervention planning and evaluation. Five, phases are delineated: screening and general disposition; definition and general quantification of the presenting problem; specific problem identification and design of an intervention; monitoring of progress; and follow-up. Although these phases are basically similar to other such conceptualizations (including the process for behavioral consultation [Bergan, 1977], and data-based program modification [Deno & Mirkin, 1977]), Hawkins's (1979) structure provides an excellent framework for discussion of the use of direct measurement procedures during school-based assessment for academic problems.

Screening

Screening and general disposition of a referred case are the purposes at the wide end of Hawkins's (1979) funnel model. In general, direct measurement procedures will not be widely used in screening, although curriculum-based probes have been used to begin screening for special education eligibility. However, it is believed that approaching screening from a behavioral assessment model is highly appropriate and that direct measurement may be necessary to validate indirect behavioral procedures.

Purposes of Screening

There are at least four possible overlapping assessment functions identified as being served during screening: (1) whether or not the referral is likely to be appropriate (for example, for the school psychologist to process); (2) to provide a guide that allows subsequent assessment procedures to be as efficient as possible; (3) if a case is not deemed appropriate for continuance, to recommend appropriate disposition; (4) to serve the function of filtering children who may be eligible for special services. Children "passed" through the screening filter would then be provided additional eligibility evaluation. Certainly, any of the first three functions may also lead to eligibility evaluation, however, traditional screening has often served this sole purpose.

Regardless of which function screening assessment is to serve, screening will be a wide-ranging, gross process that begins the narrowing of assessment efforts. Screening procedures should be inexpensive. Finally, for any referral, some sort of screening, whether implicit or explicit, always occurs.

There are two distinct channels of assessment that follow screening. The first is a channel dedicated to the determination of eligibility. The traditional psychoeducational assessment model follows this channel (Lentz & Shapiro, 1985), as do many preschool screening programs, and newly developed programs using curriculum-based assessment probes (Deno, 1985; Marston & Magnusson, 1985). Deno (1986) has recently suggested the use of direct curriculum-based assessment by the school psychologist to screen referrals. However, it is unclear what the disposition of cases *not* meeting screening criteria would be. The second channel is primarily concerned with collecting information that allows remediation of a referred problem where special education eligibility is not the immediate assessment question.

Eligibility Screening and
Curriculum-based Probes

Marston and Magnusson (1985) report the use of CBA probes in screening academic referrals for special education eligibility. If a student's performance on academic skill probes was less than 50% of the district norms, he or she was then more extensively evaluated for special education. Little mention is made, however, of the disposition of the case if these criteria were not met. Further, if the reported norming sample data are distributed normally, the percentage of children that could be passed through the screening filter decreases across grade levels. The only logic offered is that the screening program should identify those children who are significantly different from their peers and need special attention (Marston & Magnusson, 1985). Further, the purpose of screening is clearly actuarial across a generally conceived skill dimension. This is bothersome when interventions into behaviors like oral reading rates are examined, and the sometimes rapid changes in rate are noted (Hansen & Eaton, 1978). Would this mean that a brief in-classroom intervention could quickly raise many children's rates above the screening criteria?

It appears that the conceptualization of CBA in this instance more closely fits a traditional measurement model, and that measurement of some generalized academic skill is being attempted. Children are either "passed" through the screen or not based on their relative position in a norming distribution. The validity data that are reported are those discussed above, with the concurrent relationship to standardized achievement tests given heavy weight. No consideration is made of the relationship of direct academic measures to actual classroom behavior or of the future of similar children who are not "passed". For example, a student may have oral reading rates that exceed the criteria for passing through screening, but never exceed 25% accuracy in any classwork (the converse of the example cited above). In this usage, then, these curriculum-based measures do not fit a behavioral model very well, especially a direct measurement model.

Graden, Casey, and Christensen (1985) report implementation of a prereferral intervention system that also employed CBM. Screening was employed differently in different schools, with some schools having screening committees that routinely recommended interventions in the classroom first, before any evaluation for special education. Interestingly, rates of actual placement in special education were reduced. How do these data relate to the outcomes of systems adopting a straight probe criteria for determining eligibility for additional evaluation or for special education? Unfortunately, the answer is unclear.

Perhaps determining possible eligibility for special education should not be a function for the screening phase, rather should come only after remedial efforts in the regular classroom have failed (see also the discussion about the next assessment phase). The notion of using an empirical demonstration of an intervention failure in a regular classroom to determine the need for eligibility evaluation is an important point in a number of ways. Lentz and Shapiro (1985) have criticized the traditional model for not providing services to students or teachers unless a student is considered eligible for special education. Likewise, several states have recently enacted legislation mandating that some preclassification intervention be attempted within the regular classroom (Coulter, 1985).

The Role of Direct Measurement in Screening

The function of screening academic problems from a direct behavioral assessment standpoint is to increase the efficiency of subsequent assessment functions.

From this perspective, it is asserted that the prime screening procedures would be behavioral but indirect to a large extent. A behaviorally oriented checklist or a behavioral interview, focusing on the academic behaviors and environments discussed above, would be the prime vehicle to ascertain that, for some set of these behaviors in the classroom there is a problem, and to guide the assessment process. The only direct data that are both useful and inexpensive during screening would derive from a direct examination of permanent products. To the extent that this begins to focus on the nature of the child's problem in terms of performance during regular classroom tasks, their examination may prove very fruitful for the efficacy of the overall assessment (Lentz & Shapiro, 1986).

The prime function of direct academic measurement for the function of screening is to establish the content validity of an indirect interview or checklist. The question is, what indirect procedures produce data most closely related to actual student academic behavior in the classroom? For example, Bolstad and Johnson (1972) found that teachers' ranking of estimated student on-task behaviors correlated highly with direct observation. However, teachers' estimates of on-task levels for low achieving students were lower than actual levels, often by 30% to 40%. From a traditional view of validity, the concurrent validity was good. However, from a behavioral view, the level for an individual student is critical, and validity would not be good.

This study provides an ideal example of the difference in the assumptions inherent in different measurement models. For a classroom consultant, it is the idiosyncratic relationship between an indirect measure and natural classroom behavior that is critical. It is not, as it is in traditional measurement, a group relationship. There is not to say that traditional measures may not be useful for some purposes. It is to say that they may not be useful for identifying what functional academic behaviors are problematic under what conditions. The eventual goal of a behavioral assessment of academic problems is to collect data leading to an effective design of interventions; screening should ideally serve the function of focusing and enhancing the impact of subsequent measurement procedures. Research, using direct measurement procedures, into the validity of indirect behavioral measures during screening is badly needed.

Definition and General Quantification

The second assessment phase described by Hawkins (1979) serves the related functions of: (1) more closely identifying the skill areas where there are problems; (2) providing a general quantification of the problem; and (3) making a decision about where remediation may be most efficient in terms of placement in a curriculum or setting for beginning intervention. Note that appropriate curriculum placement may not specifically identify particular instructional or other targets; that is a function served in the next phase.

CBA probes have been used to place students in appropriate curriculum levels or materials. Placement is a general quantification function because it allows the identification of the discrepancies between actual (based on skills) and expected placement (Deno & Mirkin, 1977). This quantified discrepancy between actual (according to general skill level) and expected placement provides more narrow guidance for beginning to identify possible targets for intervention. The discrepancy has also been used to set criteria for special education eligibility decisions (Deno, 1985).

Curriculum Placement: General Problem Identification and Quantification

Placement of a student with curriculum materials that are most appropriate for beginning remedial instruction is best achieved by using measures derived directly from the curriculum materials (Deno, 1985) that are to be used for remediation. Lovitt and Hansen (1976) report on the use of oral reading data for placing children into basic reading texts, as do Deno (1985), and Marston and Magnusson (1985). In each case, rate criteria for oral reading performance on curriculum-based text samples are established for placement within a curriculum series. For example, in reading, the highest basal text in which a student can read at an established "instructional" rate is considered his or her placement level. For both math (Deno & Mirkin, 1977) and language arts (Starlin, 1982), probes sampling across a range of skills in a curriculum sequence have been used to place children in the appropriate level within the sequence.

Both Marston and Magnusson (1985) and Germann and Tindal (1985) developed reading rate criteria levels from norms taken across a district. Initial student placement in a reading book for either remedial planning or eligibility decisions was based on logically selected rate (on CBA probes) criteria. Program goals were then oriented toward a student's reaching normative rates in materials appropriate for his or her grade. Deno (1985, 1986) persuasively argues that curriculum-based rate goals are the most useful for continuous evaluation of special programs. Certainly, if the goal is to alter a student's academic behavior in a manner related to classroom expectancies, then use of curriculum materials requires the smallest inference.

Direct Measurement and Curriculum Placement

It is assumed that one major goal of placement in a sequenced curriculum is to facilitate selection of individual teaching objectives (the next, more narrowly defined assessment phase). However, a second important goal is to use measurement data to decide if an intervention in a particular setting, given that particular curriculum placement, has a chance of being successful.

Both goals are to some extent concerned with the repertoire of the student as related to skills required for success in a particular curriculum. In some areas, math for example, it appears that various skills are related in a hierarchal fashion (Bergan, 1977; Resnick, Wang, & Kagen, 1973). In these cases, some skills are dependent on the previous acquisition of others. Such procedures as path-referenced assessment (Bergan, 1982) or criterion-referenced assessment (Cancelli & Kratochwill, 1982) may then be quite useful in determining which skills are present in a repertoire and thus at what level a student should begin.

Predicting success of interventions. School psychologists who choose to follow an intervention-oriented model would of course benefit from information predicting whether a regular classroom intervention is possible or whether special education placement is where remediation should occur. Data directly bearing on this question of prediction are apparently not available if the question is rephrased: What data predict success in a setting *if* a well constructed academic intervention is planned or implemented? Unfortunately, that is the exact question that would have the most bearing on the linkage of assessment data to intervention.

Several researchers have demonstrated that, if a student is assigned work that is too difficult, the rate of undesirable or off-task behavior increases (Center, Deitz, & Kaufman, 1982; Gickling & Thompson, 1985). Although these studies partially address the validity questions posed, they provide no parametric information concerning: placement in regular curricula; prediction of the likelihood of success of regular classroom placement; identification of student skill clusters that are absolutely critical for regular classroom success; and relationship of probe data, such as oral reading rates and actual academic behavior, in the natural classroom environment.

Fuchs *et al.* (1984) and Marston and Magnusson (1985) report an examination of the validity of initial student placement in different reading curriculum levels in terms of the subsequent "slope" of change in performance on oral reading probes. Unfortunately, these studies are seriously confounded by a lack of knowledge of particular intervention procedures, the relationship of initial placement to progress in reaching the expected text placement, or of differing classroom conditions across students.

It seems clear that CBA probe data cannot be used unilaterally to predict success of interventions. This is basic since they do not address the critical natural setting and its idiosyncratic effects. Certainly there may be identifiable criteria for CBA probes that would rule out successful interventions. However, direct measurement of both student behavior *and* the academic environment would seem a necessary accomplishment for prediction. At any rate, validation of predictions based on CBA will require direct measurement of student changes in performance on both CBA probes and on functional natural tasks. Thus, as in screening, direct measurement is critical in validating the use of less direct measures (probes).

The use of skill probe data for student placement in curriculum materials (from a behavioral perspective) allows a general quantification of skill deficits and leads to the next assessment phase—identification of specific remedial targets. The functions served at this point cannot be considered unidimensionally, that is, just from the perspective of identifying general skill in academic areas. If only general probes are given for the purpose of curriculum placement in regular classrooms, then unwarranted assumptions about problems may occur. All academic referrals are not a result of skill deficits alone—they are often related to performance problems with regular classroom tasks. Collecting data bearing on the distinction between skill and performance at this level may require direct observation of the student in the natural setting and examination of permanent products.

One approach to discriminating between skill and performance problems may involve arranging to observe and measure student behavior in different materials and under different contingencies in order to place students in materials in the regular class that will lead to efficacious remediation. For example, the teacher might audiotape student oral reading during group (for later measurement) under different explicit contingencies for accuracy or rate. Likewise, students could be placed in a different group (with a different text) in another classroom for a day, under reinforcement, and observed by the psychologist. Another illustration is the assessment of handwriting, a behavior that seems particularly variable across different demand conditions (Graham, 1986). An assessor might compare handwriting across different natural situations and performance contingencies. Such a comparison would be useful in clearly identifying both the nature of a student's repertoire from a behavioral assessment perspective, and possibly discriminating skill from performance problems.

The roles for direct observation and measurement within the functions of this phase need to be researched if a clear understanding of the assessment needs for interventions in the regular classroom are to be fully understood. Empirical data bearing on student performance criteria identifying the level of placement in curricular material that is most likely to meet educational goals is badly needed.

Pinpointing and Design of Intervention

This phase involves clear identification of remedial targets and an analysis of environmental conditions maintaining problem performance or possibly impeding intervention success. This is clearly an assessment phase in which use of direct measurement procedures is critical if the goal of assessment is to design an intervention within class. It is the assessment phase that has been most neglected in traditional academic assessment (Hawkins, 1979). Perhaps the neglect has to do with the fact that special education eligibility is often decided at the previous assessment stage. If the child is deemed not eligible, then the referral is typically dropped (Lentz & Shapiro, 1985); if the child is eligible, a drastic change in environments is usually sought and any remedial planning would then occur in the new setting.

From a direct measurement perspective, this phase requires precise decisions about academic behaviors that need to be acquired by the student, and about environmental conditions that must be changed. To accomplish these two objectives, both specific direct skill probes (for defining immediate targets for instruction), and direct observational measurement of the student's behavior and the related environment conditions are the methods of choice. Thus, direct measurement procedures are critical in this phase and provide data for several purposes: (1) selection of target behaviors for instruction—direct and narrowly defined skill probes seem ideal for indentifying instructional targets; (2) the selection and measurement of important environmental variables (Lentz & Shapiro, 1986) including how opportunities for responding are provided that may need modification; (3) the establishment of the expected conditions and expected student performance in the classroom; (4) development of an intervention that matches the problems analysis; and (5) assessment of the resources needed for implementation.

Identification of Academic Targets

Although the behavioral assessment model provides for direct measurement of problems in their environment, there often appears to be little agreement among behavioral practitioners when it comes to the selection of specific target variables that must be changed during an intervention. For academic assessment, the problem is compounded because both instructional targets and environmental modification targets must be identified. The CBA systems developed in Minnesota have not been oriented toward this phase; in essence, general probe data have been examined for use in the previous phase and in the next phase—progress monitoring.

Specific skill probes, however, have been used extensively in special education programs for the purpose of identifying instructional target variables, although not necessarily for identifying potent environmental variables (Haring *et al.*, 1978). Strangely, Deno (1985) appears to be critical of the use of probes in a specific as opposed to a more general manner. This is peculiar since the two types of probes have distinctly different purposes. The latter are considered general "vital signs" for the purpose of general program monitoring, while the very narrow, specific probes have been used to identify specific behaviors for instruction.

In terms of identifying specific instructional targets, Idol-Maestas (1983) reports the use of oral reading probes designed to measure fluency in the specific phonic skills that are instructed within a particular basal reader. All of the specific phonic skills in a basal reader are identified, placed in lists on a sheet, and the child then reads the list aloud. Instruction is tied directly to the measured variables, measures are taken repeatedly, and rate goals may be set. The use of such probes would seem to relate nicely to the previous use of general oral reading probes to place a child in a particular reader. Once a child is placed in a reader, the phonics probes identify specific instructional targets. There are also data (Hansen & Eaton, 1978) that indicate that direct practice with phonics, accompanied by repeated measures of phonic fluency, is associated with improvements in oral reading rates in associated basal readers. Such data goes a long way toward the validation of target behavior selection.

Other direct skill probes, taken from particular levels in a curriculum, may be useful in identifying specific behaviors that should be instructed. For example, lists of basal words have been used to measure general progress in reading. If these words were the words targeted for instruction, then such lists would also constitute probes to identify targets for instruction. Probes in math have also been used to pinpoint particular deficits in curricular skills (Haring *et al.*, 1978), as have repeated probes of handwriting.

Finally, it may well be that rather than target new skills to be taught, child performance on regularly scheduled classroom tasks may be targeted. Such targets may be chosen if it is determined that the student has an adequate repertoire to accomplish regular tasks but does not perform adequately. Performance targets have frequently been illustrated in research into behavioral interventions in the classroom, and involves direct measurement of completion and accuracy on these assignments (e.g., Johnston & McLaughlin, 1982; Redd, Ullmann, Stelle, & Roesch, 1979; Terry, Deck, Huelecki & Santogrossi, 1978). This type of direct measurement is highly "natural" and most closely relates to what has been called "functional academic behaviors" (Trieber & Lahey, 1983).

Identification of Environmental Targets

The student's behavior in the natural context must be assessed in order to identify the environmental conditions contributing to the referred problem, and needing alteration during a classroom intervention. Lentz and Shapiro (1986) have tentatively outlined a "potent academic ecology" containing environmental variables that should be assessed during this phase. They also identified several direct observational systems that appear to measure many of these variables. Direct measurement is through direct observation of the student in the classroom during periods when the child is involved with the academic problem area (Lentz & Shapiro, 1986). Content validity is the key to the composition of observation systems for this phase, and valid content would sample across the dimensions of the environment that have an impact on student academic performance and progress. It must likewise be clear to those using direct observation that inferences will inevitably be made from the times and settings actually observed about unobserved times and settings because the assessor desires a "typical" picture of the academic behavior in natural settings.

The number and duration of observations leading to a typical "picture" is unclear and may be quite idiosyncratic (Lentz & Shapiro, 1986). From a behavioral standpoint, if contingencies or antecedent stimuli vary widely across different activities or the same activity from day to day, the student behavior will then be more variable. The key to direct measurement must be the use of appropriate questions during structured behavioral interviews of classroom staff so that a guide to potential variability problems may be found (Lentz & Shapiro, 1986). Again, indirect and direct behavioral methods must be effectively combined.

Use of Data in Planning Interventions

Deno (1985) indicates that consultants never know what combination of inverventions may be effective for a particular child, and that once placement in materials occurs, intervention planning is to a large extent educated guessing. A qualification of this view might be more appropriate. First, variables targeted for instruction should be chosen from the selected curricula at the identified placement level. These target variables should be directly related to required responses and task stimuli used in a particular classroom. Although skill targets can be identified, particular, topographically different activities that provide opportunities for responding and reinforcement may take many forms and may be differentially effective across children and, likewise, for the nature of specific contingencies for performance.

Second, remediation should include contingencies for student performance and there must be frequent opportunities for responding (Greenwood *et al.*, 1984) to selected task stimuli (directly related to classroom curricula). Direct classroom observation can identify what current practices in the classroom may need to change. Until there is empirical evidence concerning the relative efficacy of particular types of student activities for academic progress, then matching activities for improving skill deficits, and targeting changes in environmental events requires direct measurement of repertoires and the environment. Once the required direct measurement data on existing environmental conditions are at hand, then, perhaps, "educated guessing" is required.

The debate about the selection of target variables for instruction takes a somewhat different twist when decisions about whether to remediate specific skills, to teach children specific strategies, or to combine both are considered (Lloyd, 1980). Although there are positive data on the efficacy of strategy training, there do not appear to be generalized conclusions. One conclusion is that students must have the requisite component skills in order to apply most strategies. The issue of strategy versus specific skill training points to the difficulty in determining which instructional targets are valid for which problems or students.

Finally, at the risk of being repetitious, any use of skill probes or other procedures to select instructional and environmental targets, whether highly direct or not, must eventually be related to day-to-day academic behavior. For example, assume that a teacher is using daily oral reading probes to assess any improvement in reading resulting from an intervention. Changes in probe behavior levels that are not accompanied by improvement in the child's reading during reading group or performance on other classroom tasks may not appear valid to the teacher. If such an event occurred, it may well indicate that appropriate environmental variables were not targeted, even though appropriate instructional targets were selected. This scenario does not appear unlikely in regular classrooms in which contingencies for academic improvement or performance may not be routinely programmed (as they may be in a structured special education class). However, the author has assessed children whose oral reading rates would be considered low (Deno, 1985) but not in need of placement and whose classroom performance was nearly at a zero level. Surely, unless classroom behavior were directly modified together with any particular academic repertoire, this child would still be considered a problem.

Progress Monitoring

In this phase, still a relatively narrow part of the assessment funnel, the performance of students on target measures during intervention should be repeatedly assessed so that interventions may be modified if needed (Hawkins, 1979). Several approaches related to the direct measurement of academic behavior are feasible, including monitoring of performance in daily classroom tasks, monitoring of progress through the curriculum (see the discussion above), use of specific performance probes closely related to narrow teaching objectives, use of more general skill probes, or some combination of the above. All approaches advocate frequent, repeated measures of some sort that are used to judge progress against some expected rate of change in student behavior. There are a reasonably impressive set of data indicating that continuous progress monitoring of some sort improves the outcome of remediation efforts (Fuchs & Fuchs, in press).

The most direct measurement procedures for progress monitoring involve repeated measurement of regular classroom behaviors and permanent products, and is typical of behavioral single case research. In these cases, the repeated measure is usually the intervention target (although not always). Inferences about what behaviors are changing in these cases are very low. Conversely, inferences about the overall impact of student progress within a curriculum may be quite high. Haring *et al.* (1978) provide many examples of specific skill probes being used to monitor progress with particular remedial efforts. In reading, for example, oral rates from textbook passages in which the child is being instructed are taken repeatedly to monitor progress. Oral reading appears to be accepted as a valuable target in and of itself. If readers change during treatment, oral probes are taken from the new reader. Rate goals can be established in each reader for the short-term, with long-term goals including progressing through different readers.

In contrast, Deno (1985) and Marston and Magnusson (1985) argue for selecting one particular level of a reader (usually the level representing the ultimate goal of intervention) to use to take more general repeated probes during intervention, even if the reader in which the child is being instructed is different or changes during intervention. The argument here is that the probe data represent a general sign of the impact of an intervention on a more general skill, and that this provides sufficient information to evaluate program effectiveness formatively and additively.

Certainly the former approach involves a more direct behavioral measure because the target for intervention in the natural setting is always selected for direct measurement. Deno (1985) provides a discussion of data, however, that would indicate that the more general impact measure, or vital sign, is sufficient to monitor interventions and to judge when they should be modified. Taken in sum, however, the existing research seems to indicate that the more closely the repeated measure is related to the actual intervention target, the more sensitive in terms of reflecting change in behavior it is. For example, Fuchs (1982) summarizes research in reading indicating that the more closely lists of isolated words correspond to words being instructed, the more sensitive repeated measure data series are to change. Likewise, Lovitt *et al.* (1971) found that oral reading data on passages from the book in which instruction occurred showed greater change than passages from a matched level reader from another series.

Fuchs (1982) argues that during progress monitoring, preferable time series created from repeated CBA probes are those that exhibit steeper slopes, and more apparent effects. From this logic, students should then initially be placed into a curriculum level that will yield data with these characteristics. She also discusses data variability around slopes as an inherent characteristic, rather than a reflection of actual variation in behavior levels. This is illogical from a behavioral assessment model. Logically, time series data that are the most accurate in transducing behavior in the natural setting to numbers are the preferable ones. Slope ought not be inherent in data unless there are actual changes in behavior. It is the selection of behavioral measures directly related to tasks in instruction that will be the most sensitive if student behavior changes during instruction. If there is no change in behavior, why should there be a steep slope even in sensitive measures? Again, there appear to be clear differences in viewing the same data when behavioral or traditional models are used for interpretation.

Validity of measures in this phase must be judged along several dimensions. For example, it is important to know what type of progress monitoring systems, under similar intervention strategies, allow the most efficient and effective modification of intervention procedures. There are well-developed decision rules using specific skill probes and frequent measurement for when to change interventions (Eaton, 1978). It would be useful to know if identical decision rules were effective for both general and specific probes; currently this is unknown. Effectiveness ought to be judged against some criterion of performance indicating success in regular classroom activities. If this assumption is correct, then direct measurement of classroom behavior may periodically need to be a part of progress monitoring; it is the prime tool in assessing validity. Finally, continued direct observation of the student during regular classroom activities serves the function of verifying planned changes in the academic environment. This type of direct measurement may be expensive in terms of consultant time, but important in the determination of whether planned treatments were implemented and thus need change.

Follow-up

Postintervention follow-up is the phase of assessment most ignored by practitioners of any persuasion. At this point in the assessment funnel, the scope again widens, economy is an important issue, and more general effects of treatment may need to be assessed. Although the durability of change of functional academic behavior is the bottom line, assessment measures may be more indirect and "wide scoped". At this point the argument about specificity in skill probes might seem to be resolved on the side of more general impact or vital sign measures. If such probes are taken periodically, and brief behavioral interviews or checklists concerning the actual classroom behavior were combined, enough data to judge the necessity for additional intervention should be present. The most valid measure (or combination) ought to be those that meet the purpose at hand, program evaluation, or even a back end sort of screening.

Summary

Behavioral assessment of an academic problem begins with a wide focus. Subsequent assessment methods become more direct until specific behaviors are selected for treatment, and an analysis of the environment allows selection of environmental variables for modification. Deno (1985) also outlines a funnel type of assessment for eligibility and subsequent program planning that uses general probes and that narrows its focus by altering the rate criteria on the probes and increasing the number of probes used. In this system, there are few procedures for identifying instructional or environmental targets, and the connection between assessment and intervention planning is not made. The general probe funnel literally skips that phase and goes to progress monitoring.

It is strongly believed that the use of direct measurement of functional academic behavior in the natural environment must accompany the use of any skill probes if the problems with more traditional assessment are to be avoided and regular class interventions are to be planned. It is clear, however, that empirical evidence for the efficacy of various assessment procedures is still not complete for the link between assessment data and intervention planning. Evidence, on the other hand, exists that once interventions are implemented, repeated academic measures, either general or specific, are efficacious in enhancing positive effects (Fuchs, Deno, & Mirkin, 1984; Fuschs & Fuchs, in press). Finally, any academic assessment procedure must ultimately be validated by direct measures of behavior in the classroom in both a general sense of producing knowledge for professionals and in idiosyncratic interventions with specific students.

CONCLUSIONS

It has been argued throughout this chapter that direct measurement of behavior in the natural classroom setting, and the measurement of related environmental events are, at the least, the standards against which less direct measures are judged. It is acknowledged that some direct measurement procedures, direct observation for example, are quite expensive in terms of time and effort. Also, from the standpoint of a behavioral assessment model, judging the validity of a procedure in general is conceptually difficult. This situation exists because it is assumed that the target of assessment is both behavior and the relationship between behavior and different settings and conditions. Such relationships may be highly idosyncratic. Does this assumption lead to the notion that any sort of validity of measurement (both direct and indirect) must be assessed for each individual? This author does not think that this is entirely the case and that perhaps the question is rather, to what extent must functional behavior of an individual student be measured to validate any individual assessment?

First, any academic measure—indirect, analogue, or direct—must exhibit content validity. That is, there must be a relationship between the behaviors sampled and important behaviors exhibited in the natural environment. The notion of functional units of academic behavior derived from this assumption is, for this purpose, important. Content validity, therefore, is not idiosyncratic. Second, any academic measure must be accurate in the sense that real behavior is accurately transduced to numbers within a clearly defined set of rules. For direct observation, the rules most often involve some form of count, either continuous or sampled (Saudargas & Lentz, 1986). Accuracy is a constant issue; however, it can be evaluated for a particular system to yield the standard set of procedures for using a system to generally produce accurate numbers. Whether any particular use is then standard does remain an empirical question.

Third, the relationship between indirect or analogue measures of academic behavior (interviews or probes used as analogues) and natural, functional academic behavior is essentially unknown. Given this assumption, it is asserted that success in interventions must be demonstrated in data taken in the *classroom* setting, not just in probe data. Thus, the next research issue for CBA should be derived from the behavioral assessment model if the role of CBA for classroom consultants who desire to link assessment data to planning interventions is to be validated.

A final, extremely relevant issue is whether detailed behavioral assessment is necessary in the planning of interventions even in the natural setting. Trieber and Lahey (1983) point out that very molar interventions have often been quite effective in remediating classroom academic problems. Does this mean that a more efficient funnel for assessment might be to reduce the assessment effort on the part of the consultant, rely more on the indirect assessment within a behavioral consultation model (Bergan, 1977), and use packaged interventions to funnel referrals to the need for more intense assessments?

To answer any questions posed in this chapter, and there were many unanswered ones, will require research into the process of making decisions during attempted academic interventions in regular classrooms. This is extremely difficult research and consequently little appears to exist. Academic behavior can be modified directly—there is a very adequate knowledge base in this area (e.g., Baer & Bushnell, 1982; Lentz & Shapiro, 1986). Not enough is known about the parameters of decision making and data use under natural conditions of consultation. It is strongly believed, however, that the correct perspective from which to address such a broad issue is from a behavioral assessment model, not a traditional one. It is time to focus more intensively on the relationship between data and on what teachers see and generally base referrals—the interactions between students' behavior and the classroom environment.

References

Anastasi, A. (1982). *Psychological testing.* New York: Macmillan.

Arter, J., & Jenkins, J. (1978). *Differential diagnosis—prescriptive teaching: A critical appraisal.* (Technical Report No. 80). Champaign, Ill.: University of Illinois at Champaign-Urbana, Center for the Study of Reading.

Axelrod, S., Hall, R., & Tams, A. (1976). A comparison of two common seating arrangements. *Academic Therapy, 15,* 29–36.

Ayllon, T., Garber, S., & Pisor, K. (1976). Reducing time limits: A means to increase behavior of retardates. *Journal of Applied Behavior Analysis, 9,* 247–252.

Baer, D., & Bushell, D. (1982). The future of behavior analysis in the schools? Consider its recent past and then ask a different question. *School Psychology Review, 10,* 259–270.

Bailey, S., & Lessen, E. (1984). An analysis of target behaviors in education: Applied but how useful? In W. Heward, T. Heron, D. Hill, & J. Trap-Porter (Eds.), *Focus on behavior analysis in education* (pp. 162–176). Columbus, Ohio: Charles E. Merrill.

Becker, W., Engelmann, S., Carnine, D., & Maggs, A. (1982). Direct instruction technology—making learning happen. In P. Karoly & J. Steffen (Eds.), *Advances in child behavior analysis and therapy* (pp. 151–206). New York: Gardner Press.

Becker, W., Engelmann, S., & Thomas, D. (1975). *Teaching 2: Cognitive learning and instruction.* Chicago: SRA.

Bergan, J. (1977). *Behavioral consultation.* Columbus, Ohio: Charles E. Merrill.

Bergan. J. (1982). Path referenced assessment in school psychology. In T. Kratochwill (Ed.), *Advances in school psychology* (Vol. 1, pp. 225–280). Hillsdale, N.J.: Lawrence Erlbaum Associates.

Bolstad, O., & Johnson, S. (1972). The relationship between teacher's assessment of students and the students' actual behavior in the classroom. *Child Development, 48,* 570–578.

Bushell, D. (1978). An engineering approach to the elementary classroom: The Behavior Analysis Follow-Through Project. In C. Catania & T. Brigham (Eds.), *Handbook of applied behavior analysis: Social and instructional processes* (pp. 525–561). New York: Irvington.

Campbell, J., & Willis, J. (1978). Modifying components of "creative behavior" in the natural environment. *Behavior Modification, 2,* 549–564.

Cancelli, A., & Kratochowill, T. (1982). Advances in criterion-referenced assessment. In T. Kratochowill (Ed.), *Advances in school psychology,* (Vol. 1, pp. 213–254). Hillsdale, N.J.: Lawrence Erlbaum Associates.

Center, D., Deitz, S., & Kaufman, M. (1982). Student ability, task difficulty, and inappropriate classroom behavior. *Behavior Modification, 6,* 355–374.

Ciminero, A., Calhoun, K., & Adams, H. (1977). *Handbook of behavioral assessment.* New York: John Wiley & Sons.

Cone, J. (1978). The behavioral assessment grid (BAG): A conceptual framework and a taxonomy. *Behavior Therapy, 9,* 882–888.

Cone, J. (1981). Psychometric considerations. In M. Hersen & A. Bellack, (Eds.), *Behavioral assessment: A practical handbook* (pp. 38–70). Elmsford, N.Y.: Pergamon Press.

Coulter, A. (1985). Implementing curriculum-based assessment: Considerations for pupil appraisal professionals. *Exceptional Children, 52,* 277–281.

Decorte, E., & Savickas, M. (1985). Influence of rewarding verbal problems on children's problem representations and solutions. *Journal of Educational Psychology, 77,* 460–470.

Delquadri, J., Greenwood, C., Stretton, K., & Hall, R. (1983). The peer tutoring spelling game: A classroom procedure for increasing opportunity to respond and spelling performance. *Education and Treatment of Children, 6,* 225–239.

Deno, S. (1985). Curriculum-based measurement: The emerging alternative. *Exceptional Children, 52,* 219–232.

Deno, S. (1986). Formative evaluation of individual student programs: A new role for school psychologists. *School Psychology Review, 15,* 358–374.

Deno, S., Marston, D., Shinn, M., & Tindal, G. (1983). Oral reading fluency: A simple datum for scaling reading disability. *Topics in Learning and Learning Disabilities, 2,* 53–59.

Deno, S., & Mirkin, P. (1977). *Data-based program modification: A manual.* Reston, Va.: The Council for Exceptional Children.

Deno, S., Mirkin, P., & Chiang, B. (1982). Identifying valid measures of reading, *Exceptional Children, 49,* 36–45.

Deno, S., Mirkin, P., & Wesson, C. (1984). How to write effective data-based IEPs. *Teaching Exceptional Children, 16,* 99–104.

Eaton, M. (1978). Data decisions and evaluation. In N. Haring, T. Lovitt, M. Eaton, & C. Hansen (Eds.), *The fourth R: Research in the classroom* (pp. 167–190). Columbus, Ohio: Charles E. Merrill.

Engelmann, S., & Carnine, D. (1982). *Theory of instruction.* New York: Irvington.

Epstein, M., & Cullinan, D. (1980). An educational application of the social comparison method. *Child Behavior Therapy, 2,* 69–71.

Etzel, B. & LeBlanc, J. (1979). The simplest treatment alternative: The law of parsimony applied to choosing appropriate instructional control and errorless-learning procedures for the difficult-to-teach child. *Journal of Autism and Developmental Disorders, 9,* 361–381.

Fuchs, D., & Fuchs, L. (1986). Test procedure bias: a meta-analysis of examiner familiarity effects. *Review of Educational Research, 56,* 243–26.

Fuchs, L. (1982). Reading. In P. Mirkin, L. Fuchs, & S. Deno (Eds.), *Considerations for designing a continuous evaluation system: An integrative review* (Monograph No. 20) (pp. 29–76). Minneapolis, Minn.: University of Minnesota, Institute for Research on Learning Disabilities (ERIC Document No. 226 042).

Fuchs, L., Deno, S., & Marston, D. (1983). Improving the reliability of curriculum-based measures of academic skills for psychoeducational decision making. *Diagnostique, 8,* 135–149.

Fuchs, L., Deno, S., & Mirkin, P. (1984). The effects of frequent curriculum-based measurement and evaluation of pedagogy, student achievement, and student awareness of learning. *American Educational Research Journal, 21,* 449–460.

Fuchs, L., & Fuchs, D. (in press). Effects of systematic formative evaluation: a meta-analysis. *Exceptional Children*

Fuchs, L., Fuchs, D., & Deno, S. (1982). Reliability and validity of curriculum-based informal reading inventories. *Reading Research Quarterly, 18,* 6–26.

Fuchs, L., Fuchs, D., & Deno, S. (1984). Inaccuracy among readability formulas: Implications for the measurement of reading proficiency and selection of instructional material. *Diagnostique, 9,* 86–95.

Fuchs, L., Tindal, G., & Deno, S. (1984). Methodological issues in curriculum-based reading assessment. *Diagnostique, 9,* 191–207.

Germann, G., & Tindal, G. (1985). An application of curriculum-based assessment: The use of direct and repeated measurement. *Exceptional Children, 52,* 244–265.

Gickling, E., & Thompson, V. (1985). A personal view of curriculum-based assessment. *Exceptional Children, 52,* 205–219.

Goldfried, M., & Linehan, M. (1977). Basic issues in behavioral assessment. In A. Ciminero, K. Calhoun, & H. Adams (Eds.), *Handbook of behavioral assessment.* New York: John Wiley & Sons.

Graden, J., Casey, A., & Bonstrom, O. (1985). Implementing a prereferral intervention system, part II: The data. *Exceptional Children, 51,* 487–497.

Graden, J., Casey, A., & Christenson, S. (1985). Implementing a prereferral intervention system, part I: The model. *Exceptional Children, 51,* 377–387.

Graham, S. (1986). A review of handwriting scales and factors that contribute to variability in handwriting scores. *Journal of School Psychology, 24,* 62–71.

Greenwood, C., Delquadri, J., & Hall, R. (1984). Opportunity to respond and student academic performance. In W. Heward, T. Heron, D. Hill, & J. Trap-Porter (Eds.) *Focus on behavior analysis in education* (pp. 58–89). Columbus, Ohio: Charles E. Merrill.

Greenwood, C., Delquadri, J., Stanley, S., Terry, B., & Hall, R. (1985). Assessment of eco-behavioral interaction in school settings. *Behavioral Assessment, 7*, 331–347.

Greenwood, C., Dinwiddie, G., Terry, B., Wade, L., Stanley, S., Thibadeau, S., & Delquadri, J. (1984). Teacher- versus peer-mediated instruction: An ecobehavioral analysis of achievement outcomes. *Journal of Applied Behavior Analysis, 17*, 521–538.

Guthrie, J., & Tyler, J. (1976). Operational definitions of reading. In T. Brigham, R. Hawkins, J. Scott, & T. McLaughlin (Eds.), *Behavioral analysis in education: Self control and reading* (pp. 174–182). Dubuque, Iowa: Kendall/Hunt.

Hanley-Maxwell, C., Silcox, B., & Heal, L. (1982). A comparison of vocabulary learning by moderately retarded students under direct instruction and incidental presentation. *Education and Training of the Mentally Retarded, 17*, 214–221.

Hansen, C., & Eaton, M. (1978). Reading. In N. Haring, T. Lovitt, M. Eaton (Eds.), *The fourth R: Research in the classroom* (pp. 41–92). Columbus, Ohio: Charles E. Merrill.

Haring, N., & Eaton, M. (1978). Systematic instructional procedures: An instructional hierarchy. In N. Haring, T. Lovitt, M. Eaton, & C. Hansen (Eds.), *The fourth R: Research in the classroom* (pp. 23–41). Columbus, Ohio: Charles E. Merrill.

Haring, N., Lovitt, T., Eaton, M., & Hansen, C. (1978). *The fourth R: Research in the classroom.* Columbus, Ohio: Charles E. Merrill.

Hawkins, R. (1979). The functions of assessment: Implications for selection and development of devices for assessing repertoires in clinical, educational, and other settings. *Journal of Applied Behavior Analysis, 12*, 501–516.

Hay, W., Hay, L., & Nelson, R. (1977). Direct and collateral changes in on-task and academic behavior resulting from on-task versus academic continences. *Behavior Therapy, 8*, 431–441.

Hendrickson, J., & Gable, R. (1981). The use of modeling tactics to promote academic skill development of exceptional learners. *Journal of Special Education Technology, 4*, 20–28.

Hendrickson, J., Gable, R., & Stowitschek, J. (1985). Rate as a measure of academic success for mildly handicapped students. *Special Services in the Schools, 1*, 1–15.

Hersen, M., & Bellack, A. (Eds.). (1981). *Behavioral assessment: A practical handbook.* Elmsford, N.Y.: Pergamon Press.

Hopkins, W., Schutte, R., & Garton, K. (1971). The effects of access to a playroom on the rate and quality of printing and writing of first- and second-grade students. *Journal of Applied Behavior Analysis, 4*, 77–87.

Idol-Maestas, L. (1983). *Special educator's consultation handbook.* Rockville, Md.: Aspen.

Jackson, D. (1976). Behavior analysis certification: A plan for quality control. In T. Brigham, R. Hawkins, J. Scott, T. McLaughlin (Eds.), *Behavioral analysis in education: Self control and reading* (pp. 7–15). Dubuque, Iowa: Kendall/Hunt.

Jenkins, F., & Pany, D. (1978). Standardized achievement tests: How useful for special education? *Exceptional Children, 44*, 448–453.

Johnson, S., & Bolstad, O. (1973). Methodological issues in naturalistic observation. In L. Hamerlynck, L. Handy, & E. Mash (Eds.), *Behavior change: Methodology, concept, and practice* (pp. 7–67). Champaign, Ill.: Research Press.

Johnston, J. & Pennypacker, H. (1980). *Strategies and tactics of human behavioral research.* Hillsdale, N.J.: Lawrence Erlbaum Associates.

Johnston, R., & McLaughlin, T. (1982). The effects of free time on assignment completion and accuracy in arithmetic: A case study. *Education and Treatment of Children, 5*, 33–40.

Kazdin, A. (1979). Situational specificity: The two-edged sword of behavioral assessment. *Behavioral Assessment, 1*, 57–75.

Kazdin, A. (1984). *Behavior modification in applied settings.* Homewood, Ill.: Dorsey Press.

Kirby, F., & Shields, F. (1972). Modification of arithmetic response rate and attending behavior in a seventh-grade student. *Journal of Applied Behavior Analysis, 5*, 79–84.

Kosiewicz, M., Hallahan, D., & Lloyd, J. (1981). The effects of an LD student's treatment choice on handwriting performance. *Learning Disabilities Quarterly, 4*, 281–286.

Krantz, P., & Risley, T. (1977). Behavioral ecology in the classroom. In S. O'Leary & K. O'Leary (Eds.), *Classroom management: The successful use of behavior modification*. Elmsford, N.Y.: Pergamon Press.

Kratochwill, T. (1982). Advances in behavioral assessment. In C. Reynolds & T. Gutkin (Eds.), *The handbook of school psychology* (pp. 314–350). New York: John Wiley & Sons.

Lahey, B., & Drabman, R. (1973). Facilitation of the acquisition and retention of sight word vocabulary through token reinforcement. *Journal of Applied Behavior Analysis, 6*, 475–480.

Lahey, B., Vosk, B., & Habif, V. (1981). Behavioral assessment of learning disabled children: A rationale and strategy. *Behavioral Assessment, 3*, 3–14.

Leinhardt, G., & Seewald, A. (1981). Overlap: What's tested, what's taught. *Journal of Educational Measurement, 18*, 85–96.

Lentz, F., & Eakins, D. (1980). *The relationship of curriculum placement, math and reading achievement for the Trenton Follow-Through Project*. Unpublished memorandum, Behavior Analysis Follow-Through Project, Dept. of Human Development, University of Kansas.

Lentz, F., & Shapiro, E. (1985). Behavioral school psychology: A conceptual model for the delivery of psychological services. In T. Kratchowill (Ed.), *Advances in school psychology*, (Vol. 4, pp. 191–222). Hillsdale, N.J.: Lawrence Erlbaum Associates.

Lentz, F., & Shapiro, E. (1986). Functional assessment of the academic environment. *School Psychology Review, 15*, 346–357.

Linehan, M. (1980). Content validity: Its relevance to behavioral assessment. *Behavioral Assessment, 2*, 147–159.

Livingston, S. (1977). Psychometric techniques for criterion-referenced testing and behavioral assessment. In J. Cone & R. Hawkins (Eds.), *Behavioral assessment: New directions in clinical psychology*. New York: Brunner/Mazel.

Lloyd, J. (1980). Academic instruction and cognitive behavior modification: the need for attack strategy training. *Exceptional Education Quarterly, 1*, 53–63.

Lovitt, T., Eaton, M., Kirkwood, M., & Perlander, J. (1971). Effects of various reinforcement contingencies on oral reading rate. In E. Ramp & B. Hopkins (Eds.), *A new direction for education: Behavior analysis*. (pp. 54–71). Lawrence, Kans.: University Press.

Lovitt, T., & Hansen, C. (1976). Round one—placing the child in the right reader. *Journal of Learning Disabilities, 9*, 18–24.

Marston, D., & Deno, S. (1981). *The reliability of simple, direct measures of written expression*. (Research Report No. 50). Minneapolis, Minn.: University of Minnesota, Institute for Research on Learning Disabilities (ERIC DOcument No. 212 663).

Marston, D., & Magnusson, D. (1985). Implementing curriculum-based measurement in special and regular education settings. *Exceptional Children, 52*, 266–276.

McCurdy, B., Cundari, L., & Lentz, F. (in review). Enhancing instructional efficiency: an examination of time delay and the opportunity to observe instruction.

Miller, S., & Smith, D. (1985). Differences in literal and inferential comprehension after reading orally and silently. *Journal of Educational Psychology, 77*, 341–348.

Nelson, R., & Hayes, S. (1981). Nature of behavioral assessment. In M. Hersen & A. Bellack (Eds.), *Behavioral assessment: A practical handbook* (2d ed., pp. 3–37). Elmsford, N.Y.: Pergamon Press.

Paine, S., Radicchi, J., Rosellini, L., Deutchman, L., & Darch, C. (1983). *Structuring your classroom for academic success*. Champaign, Ill.: Research Press.

Peterson, J., Heistad, D., Peterson, D. & Reynolds, M. (1985). Montevideo individualized prescriptive instructional management system. *Exceptional Children, 52*, 239–243.

Rainwater, N., & Ayllon, R. (1976). Increasing academic performance by using a timer as an antecedent stimulus: A study of four cases. *Behavior Therapy, 7*, 672–677.

Redd, W., Ullmann, R., Stelle, C., & Roesch, P. (1979). A classroom incentive program instituted by tutors after school. *Education and Treatment of Children, 2*, 169–176.

Resnick, L., Wang, M., & Kagan, J. (1973). Task analysis in curriculum design: A hierarchically sequenced introductory mathematics curriculum. *Journal of Applied Behavior Analysis, 7,* 679–710.

Roberts, M., & Smith, D. (1980). The relationship among correct and error oral reading rates and comprehension. *Learning Disability Quarterly, 3,* 54–64.

Roberts, R. (1981). Naturalistic assessment for classroom intervention: Speech and motor behavior as predictors of academic competence. *Behavioral Assessment, 3,* 15–30.

Sattler, J. (1982). *Assessment of children's intelligence and special abilities* (2d ed.). Boston: Allyn & Bacon.

Saudargas, R., & Lentz, F. (1986). Estimating percent of time and rate via direct observation: A suggested observational procedure and format. *School Psychology Review, 15,* 36–48.

Schoen, S. (1986). Assistance procedures to facilitate the transfer of stimulus control: Review and analysis. *Education and Training of the Mentally Retarded. 21(1),* 62–74.

Shapiro, E., & Lentz, F. (1985). Assessing academic behavior: A behavioral approach. *School Psychology Review, 14,* 325–338.

Shinn, M., & Marston, D. (1985). Differentiating mildly handicapped, low-achieving, and regular education students: A curriculum-based approach. *Remedial and Special Education, 6,* 31–38.

Starlin, C. (1982). *Iowa monograph on reading and writing.* Des Moines, Iowa: State Department of Public Instruction.

Stowitschek, C., Lewis, B., Shores, R., & Ezzell, D. (1981). Procedures for analyzing student performance data to generate hypothesis for the purpose of educational decision making. *Behavior Disorders, 5,* 136–150.

Stowitschek, J., Stowitschek, C., Hendrickson, J., & Day, R. (1984). *Direct teaching tactics for exceptional children: A practice and supervision guide.* Rockville, Md.: Aspen.

Sulzer-Azaroff, B., & Mayer, G. (1977). *Applying behavior analysis procedures with children and youth.* New York: Holt, Rinehart, & Winston.

Sulzer-Azaroff, B., & Mayer, G. (1985). *Achieving educational excellence: Using behavioral strategies.* New York: Holt, Rinehart, & Winston.

Terry, M., Deck, D., & Huelecki, M., & Santogrossi, D. (1978). Increasing arithmetic output of a fourth-grade student. *Education and Treatment of Children, 1,* 25–29.

Tindal, G. (1985). Investigating the effectiveness of special education: An analysis of methodology. *Jounral of Learning Disablties, 18,* 101–112.

Tindal, G., & Deno, S. (1981). *Daily measurement of reading: Effects of varying the size of the item pool* (Research Report No. 55). Minneapolis, Minn.: University of Minnesota, Institute for Research on Learning Disabilities (ERIC Document No. ED 211 605).

Tindal, G., Fuchs, L., Fuchs, D., Shinn, M., Deno, S., & Germann, G. (in press). Empirical validation of criterion-referenced tests. *Journal of Educational Research.*

Tindal, G., Wesson, C., Germann, G., Deno, S., & Mirkin, P. (1985). The Pine County Model for special education delivery: A data-based system. In T. Kratchowill (Ed.), *Advances in school psychology,* (Vol. 4, pp. 223–250). Hillsdale, N.J.: Lawrence Erlbaum Associates.

Trieber, F., & Lahey, B. (1983). Toward a behavioral model of academic remediation with learning disabled children. *Journal of Learning Disabilities, 16,* 111–116.

Vargas, J. (1984). What are your exercises teaching? An analysis of stimulus control in instructional materials. In W. Heward, W. T. Heron, D. Hill, & J. Trap-Porter (Eds.), *Focus on behavior analysis in education* (pp. 126–144). Columbus, Ohio: Charles E. Merrill.

Wahler, R., House, A., & Stambaugh, E. (1976). *Ecological assessment of child problem behavior: A clinical package for home, school, and institutional settings.* Elmsford, N.Y.: Pergamon Press.

Weinstein, C. (1979). The physical environment of the school. *Review of Educational Research, 14,* 577–610.

Weis, L. (1976). The Behavior Analysis National Communication System: A continuous progress assessment strategy. In T. Brigham, R. Hawkins, J. Scott, & T. McLaughlin (Eds.), *Behavioral analysis in education: Self control and reading.* Dubuque, Iowa: Kendall/Hunt.

White, M. (1975). Natural rates of teacher approval and disapproval in the classroom. *Journal of Applied Behavior Analysis, 8,* 367–372.

White, O., & Liberty, K. (1976). Behavioral assessment and precise educational measurement. In N. Haring & R. Schiefelbusch (Eds.), *Teaching special children* (pp. 31–69). New York: McGraw-Hill.

Winett, R., Battersby, C., & Edwards, S. (1975). The effects of architectural change, individualized instruction, and group contingencies on the academic performance and social behavior of sixth graders. *Journal of School Psychology, 13,* 28–40.

Ysseldyke, J., & Mirkin, P. (1982). Assessment information to plan instructional interventions. A review of the research. In C. Reynolds & T. Gutkin (Eds.), *The handbook of school psychology* (pp. 395–409). New York: John Wiley & Sons.

CHAPTER 4

Assessment of Individuals with Severe Handicaps

DIANE M. BROWDER
Lehigh University

MARTHA E. SNELL
University of Virginia

INTRODUCTION

In the last decade, services for individuals with severe handicaps have expanded greatly. Not only have such services increased, they have become more integrated in the mainstream of the community and public schools. Although the extent of deinstitutionalization and public school integration varies across states, legislation (e.g., P. L. 94-142) and litigation (e.g., *Fialkowski* v. *Shapp,* 1975; *Halderman* v. *Pennhurst State School and Hospital,* 1977) have supported this trend.

To help students develop the skills needed to function in community living arrangements, public school settings, and integrated work sites, Brown and colleagues encouraged educators to forget readiness activities and to concentrate on the direct instruction of skills needed in daily life (Brown, Branston-McLean, Baumgart, Vincent, Falvey, & Schroeder, 1979; Brown, Branston, Hamre-Nietupski, Pumpian, Certo, & Gruenewald, 1979). During the late seventies, some public school programs for students with severe handicaps began to reflect this priority. Teachers began to concentrate solely on *functional* skills (skills required in daily living) and to discard activities that required considerable generalization to be useful (e.g., peg boards, bead stringing). Many of these discarded activities were borrowed from infant and preschool curricula "adapted" for individuals with severe handicaps. However, many educators realized that such an approach did not lead to adult independence, since their students progressed at such a slow rate that the numerous "prerequisites" were never wholly acquired.

Donnellan (1984) summed up this educational trend towards community-integrated instruction as one that follows the "criterion of the least dangerous assumption." That is, it is probably less dangerous to assume that the direct instruction of life skills will enhance community independence than to assume that students will generalize unrelated activities. Virtually no research exists that supports the long-term benefits of using developmental psychology to design curricula for this population. Furthermore, a growing body of research demonstrates the ability of students with severe handicaps to learn community living skills. Therefore, it seems most logical to design curricula for school-age students and adults with severe handicaps that are related closely to skills needed to live and work in the community.

Resources on the education of students with severe handicaps that have emerged since the midseventies describe in detail methods to design and implement a community-integrated instructional approach (e.g., Falvey, 1986; Gaylord-Ross & Holvoet, 1985; Sailor & Guess, 1983; Snell, 1987; Wehman, Renzaglia, & Bates, 1985; Wilcox & Bellamy, 1982). Common themes for characteristics of educational programs are set forth in these resources.

1. Classrooms for students with severe handicaps should be integrated in schools with nonhandicapped students. If students with severe handicaps are to have opportunities to learn and develop social skills appropriate to age, they need the experience of attending school with their peers. Preferably, their classroom is in their neighborhood school so friendships can be enjoyed at school and home.
2. The school day should include planned interaction with nonhandicapped peers. When a student has severe social skill deficiencies, interaction with nonhandicapped peers needs to be fostered through special integration opportunities and direct instruction in social skills. For example, Gaylord-Ross, Haring, Brien, and Pitts-Conway (1984) taught adolescents with autism to engage in a simple dialogue and use materials that attracted nonhandicapped peers to interact with them (e.g., tape player, chewing gum, portable video game).
3. The curriculum should reflect instruction in real activities of daily living. To determine what skills are required for a student to function in the community, the educator conducts an "ecological inventory." For example, the teacher may interview the student's parents and visit a potential group home to learn what domestic skills are required in these least restrictive living environments. Potential employers may be interviewed to determine skills that would be needed at work. The student's own age group of peers may be observed during leisure time to discover potential targets for recreation skills. While some school districts have written a core curriculum for life skills, this inventory process is still necessary to ensure that the skills selected for an individual student's IEP are those that are needed in a given student's current and future environments.
4. Students need to be taught skills for and in community environments. To ensure that students will use the skills taught at the appropriate time

and place, teachers must assess skill generalization. Often, the activities cannot be simulated in a classroom and must be taught at the time and place they would typically occur (e.g., lunchtime at a fast-food restaurant). Most life skills programs for students with severe handicaps will target skills required for functioning in the community and will teach these skills in community settings. Some researchers have addressed ways to promote skill generalization when instruction occurs either in the classroom alone or in both the community and the classroom (for a review, see Snell & Browder, 1986). However difficult logistically it may be for the teacher, it appears that community-based instruction is the best means to obtain realistic skill performance by students with severe handicaps. With no easy or effective substitute for teaching in the community, programs need to have the flexibility and resources to include this important service.

5. Students need learning environments and activities that are similar to their own age group of peers. The application of a developmental program model rests on the concept that students with severe handicaps have the mental age of infants and preschool children. The result of this conceptualization has been the use of materials and environments similar to preschool classrooms for older students and even adults. If students with severe handicaps are to achieve their highest level of independence, they need to learn skills to interact with their peers. They also deserve the dignity of a learning environment similar to their nonhandicapped peers.

6. Applied behavior analysis is the foundation for instruction and assessment. To enhance students' development of useful skills similar in appearance to their own age group of peers, applied behavior analysis procedures are used to define these skills and to develop instructional methods. Gaylord-Ross and Holvoet (1985), Sailor and Guess (1983), Snell (1987), and Wilcox and Bellamy (1982) have summarized the application of these procedures to individuals with severe handicaps.

BEHAVIORAL LIFE SKILLS ASSESSMENT

The six preceding characteristics have implications for both assessment and intervention in programs for students with severe handicaps. Two principles guide the design of life skills assessment and intervention. The first principle is normalization, which provides a basis for *what* to assess and instruct.

The second principle is applied behavior analysis, which provides guidelines for *how* to assess and instruct. Normalization is the premise that the goals and opportunities for living typical of people without handicaps are also appropriate for people with handicaps (Wolfensberger, 1972). Most people in American society expect to develop a vocation, form their own family, and own or rent a home where they have considerable freedom in planning their leisure. Traditionally, people with handicaps have had limited access to these opportunities. For students with severe handicaps, denial of these opportunities can be attributed both to societal discrimination and to the failure of educational programs to teach individuals to function at their highest levels of independence in integrated settings. Often, an attitude of overprotection, while intended to be benevolent, robs the individual with severe handicaps of the dignity of taking risks and making choices. The second principle is applied behavior analysis, which focuses on observable, measurable behavior and the antecedents and consequences of that behavior (Bijou & Baer, 1961). Applied behavior analysis grew out of Skinner's work (1969) and has developed into a technology for measuring and influencing a wide range of behaviors. In following the ideals of normalization, the educator sets goals for an enriched life in the community for all students. Through the application of behavior analysis, progress towards these goals can be defined, measured, and enhanced.

If the ultimate criteria for service quality is a normalized, community-integrated experience, assessment must identify skills needed to improve functioning in community settings. The assessor using this approach will first identify the skills required by the community environments in which the student currently functions and those for which the student is preparing to enter (e.g., future job or group home) and second will assess the student's strengths and needs on the indentified skills. Thus, life skills assessment provides an evaluation of what the community requires of the student to function like his or her peers and what the student needs to learn.

An important consideration in the application of life skills selection and assessment is to recognize students' preferences. Community requirements for adult living often allow a range of acceptable behavior which permits many options for choice: clothing styles, eating preferences, job selection, and so on. Some students may not have learned to make choices or they may not yet have the communication skills to express them. Preferences still can be assessed by observing the student when exposed to various materials and experiences. Parents' preferences will also be important to consider, since many of the skills to be taught require making judgments about the student's family lifestyle. For example, the teacher will need to determine if the family has certain values regarding eating habits that would influence choices for food preparation instruction (e.g., vegetarianism; preference for convenience foods).

APPLICATIONS TO SCHOOL SETTINGS

The application of life skills assessment to school programs has implications for initial evaluation, comprehensive educational assessment, and ongoing evaluation. A flow chart of the interrelationship between these assessment purposes is shown in Figure 4-1. As the table indicates, the initial evaluation for identification and placement will begin the assessment of the student's skills, preferences, and community skill needs (Step 1). A comprehensive educational evaluation (Step 2), to be

FIGURE 4-1 Model for Behavioral Life Skills Assessment for Students with Severe Handicaps

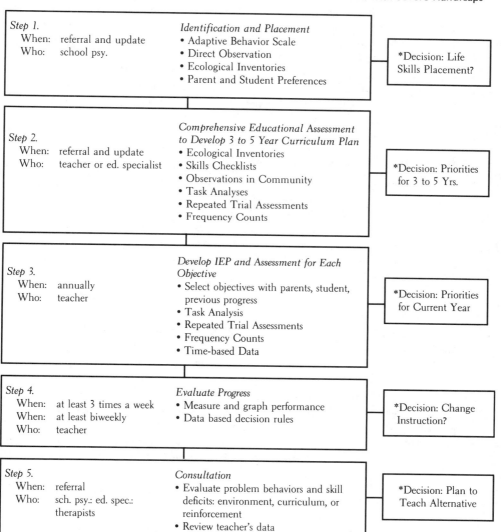

repeated every three to five years, can provide an individualized curriculum for the student's upcoming Individualized Educational Plan. Annual review of progress, preferences, and the curriculum leads (Step 3) to the development of a one-year plan—the Individualized Educational Plan. Ongoing assessment and evaluation (Step 4) provides the measurement necessary to ensure that instruction is effective. In conducting consultation (Step 5), a learning specialist, school psychologist, or therapist (e.g., speech, OT, PT) can utilize this ongoing review to help the teacher improve instructional effectiveness. Each of these assessment purposes is described in the following sections.

Evaluation for Identification and Placement

Several problems complicate the goal of assessing individuals with severe handicaps to determine eligibility for services. The school psychologist or other educator may be challenged by: (1) definitional issues, (2) limitations of the student to be tested, (3) limitations of current instruments, and (4) the absence of a well-defined curriculum. These difficulties sometimes lead the professional to conclude that a student is "untestable." Such conclusions yield little benefit to the student or the receiving teacher.

Definitional Issues

To place students in services, state guidelines for placement usually must be followed. Before considering how states have defined this population, it may be useful to consider how professionals have conceptualized this diverse group of students. The trend in the field of severe handicaps is to deemphasize labels and to concentrate instead on service needs, rather than trying to define a permanent trait of the individual. The definition suggested by Bellamy (1985) for adult services is an example of defining severe handicaps by service needs. Bellamy (1985) proposed this definition to resolve the discrepancy across agencies' conceptualization of the population considered to have severe handicaps. He defined them as

> those adults who require ongoing support in several major life areas in order to participate in the mainstream of community life, and who are expected to require such support throughout life. (p. 6)

While written to define an adult service population, this definition is easily applicable to students across the age span. The advantages Bellamy (1985) attributes to this definition also would be applicable to its use for school-age students. He notes that this definition: (1) acknowledges the diversity of people who will need the defined service; (2) allows communication about a group of people without reference to psychological tests of dubious validity; and (3) focuses on the need for ongoing services. The definition also avoids assignment of a permanent trait that would preclude movement to less intensive service. The need for lifelong, intensive support is "expected," but expectations can change with student progress.

Guess and Mulligan (1982) use the term functional retardation rather than mental retardation to describe skill deficiencies of individuals with severe handicaps. Functional retardation, unlike mental retardation, does not assume either a permanent trait or, necessarily, skill deficiencies due primarily to intellectual deficiencies. Prior to intensive educational efforts and technological adaptations to overcome physical limitations, it is unclear how far most students with severe handicaps will progress. What *is* clear with students who will be classified as having severe handicaps is that their current deficiencies in daily living skills are significant. These deficiencies may be a result of a retardation of social, physical, or sensory development. When the severe delay in the development of life skills occurs without sensory, social, or physical deficiencies, a general cognitive deficiency is typically assumed. Traditional labels for such deficiencies include mental retardation, autism, cerebral palsy, deafness and blindness, and so on. The term *severe handicaps* becomes appropriate when ongoing intensive support and instruction are needed in several areas of daily living. The term would not necessarily be appropriate for students with multiple or severe physical handicaps if such students communicate well and manage their daily living needs. While the population of people with severe handicaps is quite diverse, their number is low (less than 1% of the general population) and their learning needs are similar. Thus, it is often unnecessary to create subcategories of people with severe handicaps for the purpose of service delivery (e.g., severe retardation with cerebral palsy, profound mental retardation, severe autism).

In response to the public school services for this population, many states have developed definitions for classification. Geiger and Justen (1983) reviewed state definitions for public school services and found that thirty-five states had definitions pertaining to students with severe handicaps. Of these, nineteen had *categorical* definitions, while the remainder had *generic* definitions. Categorical definitions made explicit reference to a category, such as autism or severe mental retardation. Generic definitions referred to commonalities of educational need for this diverse population. When categorical definitions exist, school psychologists face the difficult task of gathering evidence to distinguish between students with similar service needs. Sometimes these categorical definitions give defined IQ ranges. (The problems of IQ testing with this population will be discussed in a later section.) As mentioned earlier, when a student has severe skill deficiencies and multiple handicaps, determination of whether or not the student has severely impaired intellectual functioning is often impossible. A definition that requires such a diagnosis presents the school psychologist with the dilemma of providing a fair evaluation for a very difficult-to-test student. Generic definitions can avoid both the need to obtain an IQ score and the need to distinguish between types of students with severe handicaps, who in reality have similar service needs.

However, generic definitions are not without their problems. Sometimes a decision is still needed to distinguish between skill levels. Such a decision would not be used to exclude students from preparation for the full opportunities of adult living. For example, students with severe handicaps can obtain jobs in the community with appropriate instruction and ongoing support. However, the route to achieve these opportunities will be different for the student who begins with no formal communication of care of self, in contrast with the student who has basic self-care, a small vocabulary, and emerging skills in housekeeping. In a small school district, the assignment of students with severe handicaps may be simple because of the low incidence of students in the district who need the life skills programs. For example, if numbers only justify three or four classes, the best way to assign students with severe handicaps would be by chronological age. Such an assignment makes it more feasible for the teacher to plan an age-appropriate learning environment. In larger school districts, once age-appropriate assignments have been made, enough students may be available to have more than one class at each level. In this case, the district must define current service needs by some other criteria. Assigning students by their distance from the school supports the priority of instruction in skills related to the student's own home community. In the rare district (e.g., large urban area) where still further distinctions can be made due to large numbers of students, the district will need to develop criteria related to current skill levels. By contrast, the small district may not have enough students to have one class at each age level for students with severe handicaps. Such districts may combine services for students with moderate mental retardation and for students with severe handicaps to provide chronological age-appropriate classes. The distinction between routes to achieve community integration will be defined by the teacher in planning the curriculum for the diversity of students typical in classes for students with severe handicaps.

Even if identification of service needs is simplified with a generic definition, documentation that a student qualifies for the life skill services specified for students with severe handicaps is essential. Definitional problems are not the only ones that make this documentation a difficult process. Limitations of the student, of available tests, and of existing curriculum also complicate this identification and placement.

Student Limitations

Most school psychologists have had the experience of trying to test a student with severe handicaps. The student may be blind and/or deaf, may have severe physical impairments that limit hand and arm use and head control, and may have intermittent seizures. Others may have no sensory or physical handicaps, but may instead lack "test behaviors." Such students may refuse to sit for the duration of the test or may engage in high rates of stereotypic behavior. Another student may use an alternative form of communication, such as manual signing or a communication board, and, if so, with a small vocabulary that does not permit making the responses required by the test. These characteristics can make traditional testing unfeasible. In fact, to use traditional test procedures with students who cannot make the responses because of sensory and physical impairments is discriminatory (Duncan, Sbardellati, Maheady, & Sainato, 1981). Furthermore, students with severe handicaps may need to be positioned properly to have a full range of motion in their arms. A student who is blind may require specialized escorting to walk safely to a novel setting. Students with severe behavior problems may require special motivational procedures and may not react well to strange people, tasks, and settings. To become skilled in such management procedures requires extensive training that often is not available to related services school staff. However, the school psychologist must devise methods to conduct a fair evaluation of students who require intensive care and supervision. Such methods will need to include the participation of the teacher, therapists, parents, and others who provide information based on their ongoing knowledge of the student. However, direct assessment with a standardized test probably will not be the way this information will be obtained, even by those familiar with the student, because of the limitations of the instruments as well as of the student.

Limitations of Instruments

Historically, identification and placement for special services has relied heavily on intelligence testing. This practice is especially inappropriate for students with severe handicaps, since the student may not be able to make the physical responses required on the test. Often, IQ tests have weak reliability at the lowest end of the scale. Sometimes the school psychologist is only able to administer one or two items because the student can not perform the simplest item. In files of students with severe handicaps, it is not unusual to find IQ scores on the WISC or Stanford-Binet of 7 or 13 and distinctions made in reports between people being "severely" or "profoundly" retarded. The practice of downward extrapolation of IQ scores below minus three standard deviations promotes a false sense of test accuracy.

Furthermore, to extrapolate extremely low scores and to define people as having *severe* versus *profound* retardation provides little information on educational needs. Instead, such a practice may present a bleak picture of educational potential. One alternative approach has been to use infant developmental assessments. On such assessments, many more items may be applicable to the student with severe handicaps. However, this approach still has little relevance to educational needs if the student will be taught age-appropriate skills. Instead it may present a damaging and invalid view of the student as being comparable to an infant in "mental age."

Since the early sixties, consideration of adaptive behavior has also been discussed as being important for identification and placement of students with mental retardation (Grossman, 1977). Unlike intelligence testing, most adaptive behavior scales rely on indirect assessment (e.g., interviews). Many adaptive behavior scales yield profiles rather than single scores, making interpretation more complex. However, adaptive behavior scales are more likely to contain information relevant for educational planning in a life skills program.

Absence of a Well-Defined Curriculum

An important new trend in psychological evaluations is the use of curriculum-based assessment (Tucker, 1985). In this approach, the school's curriculum is used as a basis for evaluation of an individual student. Combined with other behavioral assessment (e.g., for social behavior), such an approach avoids some of the problems inherent in intelligence testing or other trait assessment. For students with severe handicaps, a similar approach is needed. However, schools often do not have a well-defined life skills curriculum. By contrast, the trend for curriculum development for students with severe handicaps is to design individualized curricula based on inventories of the skills needed to function in community environments. Typically, the evaluation for placement precedes the comprehensive educational assessment needed to develop such a curriculum. How then does the school psychologist design a curriculum-based assessment when the curriculum is not yet defined for a student?

Life Skills Approach

While many problems face the school psychologist or other professional who must classify a student for services, they are not insurmountable. If the approach suggested in Figure 4-1 is followed, the school psychologist provides more global educational information. The teacher uses this information to design more detailed assessments. Adaptive behavior scales will constitute the major portion of the school psychologist's evaluation for several reasons. It would not be feasible for the school psychologist to create assessment tools for each student assessed. Of the existing instruments, the adaptive behavior scales provide the most educationally relevant information for a life skills orientation. Also, the additional expenditure for the intensive programs typical for students with severe handicaps often must be justified through norm-referenced, comparison data. Many adaptive behavior scales provide this comparison, which can be an acceptable substitute for an intelligence test for students with severe handicaps. Adaptive behavior scales avoid the issue of functional versus mental retardation. If a student has severe deficiencies in adaptive behavior, an intensive life skills program is probably appropriate. The avoidance of permanent labels will allow the few students who progress quickly enough to be considered for a more traditional academic placement to obtain these services. The indirect approach of the adaptive behavior scale also may be a benefit for the psychologist and student, since it avoids setting up difficult testing situations. The reliability of information collected through the interview may be evaluated by conducting observations of the student at school, in the community, or at home with the teacher or parents.

Adaptive behavior scales with more items and categories of items related to life skills are best suited to evaluate students with severe handicaps. If a category is missing, the school psychologist may need to develop observation items to supply this information (e.g., on community mobility). If too few items are supplied for each category, a student with partial mastery of a skill may not receive credit. In Table 4-1, several adaptive behavior scales are evaluated by life skill categories and number of responses per category, allowing easy selection of a scale with sufficient breadth for assessment of a given student. Table 4-2 delineates other measurement characteristics of adaptive behavior scales relevant to this population. While many of the existing scales have numerous responses related to life skills, most scales still are lacking these other considerations.

To compensate for missing items on a scale or for a lack of items adapted for physical and sensory impairments, the school psychologist may want to design some supplementary assessment tools. These tools might include a skills checklist to be completed by the teacher or parent, or an observational assessment. For example, Table 4-3 shows a checklist to assess shopping skills.

Sometimes the school psychologist may wish to go a step further and begin to identify skills needed by the student in specific environments. The evaluation of skills needed for specific environments is called an *ecological inventory*. Table 4-4 shows an ecological inventory conducted in a home environment. To collect the information for an ecological inventory, the school psychologist may interview individuals in that environment (e.g., potential employers, parents, store manager) or observe nonhandicapped peers in that environment. The inventory shown in Table 4-4 is based on a parent interview and observation of the home. The purpose of such an inventory is to make educational recommendations specific to an individual student's life needs. Note that this particular inventory also provides a mechanism to consider the student's and parents' preferences.

Comprehensive Educational Evaluation

Once a student's educational placement has been identified as a life skills program, the next step is to develop an individualized curriculum, based on a comprehensive educational evaluation. This assessment typically will be conducted every three to five years by the teacher, or by a master teacher or educational diagnostician. Once such a plan is developed, it can guide the development of IEPs for several years. Some school districts have simplified this step of the assessment plan by developing a comprehensive life skills curriculum for the particular area (Philadelphia School District, 1985). When such a curriculum exists, the assessment data will describe current skill competencies and deficiencies, but only in areas of importance to a student. In the absence of such a curriculum assessment data will describe tools that must be developed to include skill requirements for a given community and family across several life domains.

The comprehensive educational evaluation is organized by life domains rather than by the traditional subject areas of reading, fine motor, language, and so

TABLE 4-1 Skills Assessed by Adaptive Behavior Scales

Life Skills	Scales and Number of Response Per Skill Area							
	AAMD ABS	Balthazar[a]	Callier-Azusa[b]	Camelot	CTAB	Pyramid	SIBS	Vineland
Domestic								
Toileting	*	**	***	*	**	***	**	**
Hygiene/Grooming	***	N	****	**	**	***	**	***
Dressing	**	****	****	**	****	***	**	***
Eating	**	****	****	**	***	***	**	***
Food Preparation	N	N	****	**	****	**	**	**
Housekeeping	N	N	****	***	****	**	**	**
Clothing Care	**	N	*	**	**	**	*	*
Lawn/Vehicle Care	N	N	N	**	**	*	N	N
Health Care	*	N	N	*	**	N	*	*
Home Leisure	*	N	N	**	**	**	N	***
Community								
Pedestrian	*	N	N	*	**	N	*	*
Travel/Bus	*	N	N	**	**	N	**	*
Shopping	**	N	N	*	**	N	*	*
Restaurant Use	*	N	N	N	*	N	*	*
Self-Identification	**	N	*	*	**	N	*	*
Telephone Use	*	N	N	**	**	N	*	**
Banking/Money	**	N	N	**	**	***	***	**
Job Specific Skills	*	N	N	**	N	*	*	N
Job Related Skills	**	N	N	**	**	**	**	*
General Skills[c]								
Language—vocal	**	N	****	**	***	****	****	****
Language—nonvocal	*	N	**	*	*	*	*	*
Ambulation—walk, sit	*	N	*	*	**	**	*	**
Ambulation—wheelchair	N	N	N	N	N	N	N	N
Social interaction	**	***	****	**	**	***	**	****
Problem behaviors	****	***	N	N	N	N	****	****
Academics	**	N	**	***	****	****	***	****

Note. N No responses; * 1–5 responses; ** 6–24 responses; *** 25–50 responses; **** more than 50 responses. Some items had several responses per item. Each response was counted, rather than each item.

[a]Designed for individuals with severe handicaps.

[b]Designed for individuals who are deaf or blind.

[c]Expressive and receptive communication.

This figure was typeset by Paul H. Brookes for *Assessment of individuals with severe handicaps*, p. 36–37, w/permission from Guilford Press.

TABLE 4-2 Results Reported by Adaptive Behavior Scales

Types of Results	AAMD	Balthazer	Callier-Azusa	Camelot	CTAB/NABC	Pyramid	SIBS	Vineland
Comparisons								
1. Standardized comparison to nonhandicapped peers	*				*		*	*
2. Intraindividual comparison	*	*	*	*	*	*	*	*
Scores								
1. Norm-referenced	*		*		*		*	*
2. Criterion-referenced	*	*		*	*			
3. Single score	*				*		*	*
4. Profile summary	*	*	*	*	*	*	*	*
Type of Assessment								
1. Test student		*			*			
2. Observe student		*	*	*		*		
3. Interview caregiver	*					*	*	*
4. Interview teacher	*						*	
5. Checklist by caregiver				*	*	*		
6. Checklist by teacher	*		*	*	*	*	*	*
7. Interview student							*	

TABLE 4-3 Checklist to Assess Shopping Skills

Student: _____John_____ Date: ____8-20-88____

Person Completing Checklist: ____James Nicholas____

Relationship to Student: ____Father____

Approximately how many times have you seen the student try these skills? __numerous__ . When was the last time you observed the student trying these skills? __last month__

Check how often the student performs the stated skill without instructional prompts:

	Never	Sometimes	Most of the Time	Don't Know
1. Enters/exits doors— push-pull type		X		
2. Enters/exits doors— automatic			X	
3. Manipulates cart	X			
4. Chooses items	?		Grabs	
5. Selects items on list	X			
6. Grasps, releases item		X		
7. Waits in line		X		
8. Uses wallet, purse	X			
9. Pays for item	X			
10. Uses restrooms	X			
11. Interacts courteously		X smiles		

on. Many different options exist for the definition of these domains. Brown *et al.* (1979) suggest that skills be arranged in vocational, recreational, domestic, and community skills domains. While this organization provides a broad framework for life skills, it sometimes underrepresents the communication, social, and motor skills needed to support specific daily living skills. Brown, Evans, and Weed (1983) suggest using the domains of personal management, vocational and school skills, and leisure. For each of these domains, they consider daily and episodic activities, core skills (e.g., essential steps in doing the laundry), and extension skills (e.g., discussing the laundry, planning when to do laundry). All activities are viewed in the context of *routines,* which are large chunks of behavior required to complete an entire activity (e.g., dressing, eating, getting items ready for school, and so forth). Another simple organization is to consider skills needed in the home and skills needed in the community. For both of these domains, related skills (communication, motor skills, academics) and problem behaviors can be considered.

To decide exactly what to assess in each domain, the teacher conducts ecological inventories as a first step to this educational assessment. That is, the teacher identifies the specific home and community environments in which the student currently functions and those to be used in the near future. For each of

TABLE 4-4 Example of an Ecological Inventory Conducted in a Home Environment

Student's Name:	John	Source:	Observation, Interview
Date:	August 15, 1985	Place:	John's family home
Age:	13		

1. Describe the characteristics of the environment that are relevant to the student's instruction:
   Large kitchen with lots of counter work space.
   Few decorations or materials are present due to John's pica (eating nonedibles).
2. What activities are typical of nonhandicapped peers of the same age in this environment?
   John's 16-year-old sister plays records, talks on the phone, makes cookies, reads, and makes crafts in her free time. She is responsible for vacuuming the house, doing the dishes, and keeping her room clean.
3. What are the student's current skills in this environment?
   John performs no chores and has no leisure skills. He likes his dad to wrestle with him. Typically, John walks from room to room chewing on his hand.
4. What problem behaviors limit the student's participation in this environment?
   John eats nonedible objects.
5. What are the family's preferences and customs for activities in this environment? What are the student's preferences?
   The parents would like both children to share in household chores. They also read, make crafts, and watch television. They are concerned that John has no creative way to occupy his time.
   John frequently approached and touched bright objects in the environment (e.g., a colorful lamp). He likes physical activity (i.e., his dad's horseplay).
6. What skills appear needed?
   Simple crafts: teach to braid rug as an alternative to mouthing or ingesting it; use bright colors.
   Chores: wipe table to help sister with dishes, throw clothes in hamper, dust.

these environments, the teacher gathers information on skills needed to function well in each environment. The ecological inventory shown in Table 4-4 can be repeated for each environment selected (e.g., grocery store, shopping mall, physician's office). These places would become the environments for instruction when the IEP is written.

For each activity considered, the teacher might use one of several approaches to assess a student's performance of the activity. One simple procedure is to use a *skills checklist,* which is similar to adaptive behavior scales, though probably more detailed. This teacher-made checklist will typically have more specific responses so that participation can be planned for students with minimal independent responses. For example, Table 4-5 presents a skill checklist on the use of recreational facilities. This checklist may be filled out by a teacher or parent based on their memories of observed behaviors.

For some priority skills that the student has not had the opportunity to perform, it may be worthwhile to observe the student directly engage in the activity. Table 4-5 presents a summary of a checklist assessment made during an observation. Obviously, due to time requirements, such observations must be carefully selected to obtain information that cannot be obtained from prior records or interviews with parents.

Another approach that may be used is the *task analysis.* In the assessment of individuals with severe handicaps, the task analysis typically specifies the chain of behaviors required to perform an activity. Because task analytic assessment is time-consuming and provides assessment data on a narrowly defined skill, its use is limited to those skills shown to be of importance by the ecological inventory. To use a task analysis for assessment, the teacher gives the student an opportunity to perform the task and scores each step as correctly or incorrectly performed. If the assessment is conducted during instruction of the task, the teacher may score the level of prompt needed to perform the step. To assess some skills, the teacher provides *multiple opportunities* to complete the chain of responses. Following each omitted or incorrectly performed step, the teacher records it as incorrect and completes the step without comment. The student's performance of the next step is then observed. At other times, a *single opportunity* is given to perform the entire chain of responses. Since performance is stopped after the first error or omission, the single opportunity task analytic assessment approach is faster but gives a more conservative view of the student's ability to perform the task uninterrupted. Snell and Grigg (1987) describe task analytic assessment in further detail. Table 4-6 provides an example of a task analytic assessment.

Repeated Trial Assessment is useful for measuring discreet behaviors less suitable to task analysis. Examples of discreet behaviors include many communication skills (signing, pointing to pictures), social skills (sharing toys, shaking hands), some motor skills (steps taken without falling, repetitions during exercises), and maladaptive behavior (biting, yelling, stereotypic behavior). To observe these behaviors, the teacher either observes naturally occurring opportunities to respond or presents opportunities to respond across the day. For example, use of the manual

TABLE 4-5 Example of Checklist for Recreational Facility

Student's Name: John   Source: Observation _X_   Interview _____

Date: August 24, 1988   Environment: YMCA

Age: 13   Person Interviewed: NA

Evaluator: Teacher, Ms. Callahan

Doors	Check If Typical or Observed	List Alternative Behavior That Is Typical or Observed
1. Push door open	X	
2. Pull door open	—	Pounded door when unable to
3. Open door knob	X	open it.
4. Walk in automatic door	—	
Tickets/Reception		
1. Use purse; wallet	—	
2. Show identification	—	Wandered and chewed on
3. Give money	NA	hand.
4. Pocket money; ID	—	
Mobility		
1. Walk alone	X	
2. Locate room	—	Walked with me.
Activity		
1. State preference	—	
2. Watch quietly	—	Wandered, chewed hand,
3. Use equipment	—	tried to put magazine in
4. Participate with group	—	mouth.
Personal		
1. Locate restroom	—	
2. Use toilet alone	—	Waited to be helped.
3. Wash hands	—	
Refreshments		
1. Locate stand	X	
2. Express preference	X	Walked to vending machine
3. Use wallet; purse	—	and touched soda sign. Spilled
4. Pay	—	his drink.
5. Eat and drink	—	
Other		
1. Initiates interaction with companion	—	Made no response to my com-
2. Discusses event	X	ments about the YMCA.
3. Avoids strangers		

TABLE 4-6 Example of Task Analytic Assessment Conducted for John's Table Clearing Task

Student's Name: John   Task: Clearing Table

Teacher: Ms. Callahan   Date: September 1, 1988

Directions: Response latency: 3 sec .   Instructional cue: none
Location, conditions: Dining area: visibly dirty table

Scoring: I   Independent; performed without help
G Performed with Gesture
V Performed with Verbal Direction
M Performed with Model
P Performed with Physical Guidance
— Step not performed or incorrect during test

Student Performance

Steps Dates:	Instructional Data 10/4	Test Data Multiple Opportunity 10/4
1. Get tray	I	I
2. Pick up trash (napkins, etc)	M	—
3. Put trash on tray	P	—
4. Throw trash in trashcan	V	—
5. Scrape and stack plates	M	—
6. Put silverware on tray	I	—
7. Put glasses on tray	M	—
8. Carry tray to counter	P	—
9. Wipe tray with sponge	V	—
10. Replace tray	I	I
Number Independent Correct: Percentage Correct:	3 30%	2 20%

sign for "more" might be assessed by presenting opportunities for requesting more of something ten times in a day. *Frequency counts* may also be used for spontaneous behaviors that the teacher may wish to accelerate or decelerate (e.g., approaching peers, biting). *Time-based measures,* such as interval recording or measures of latency or duration, provide useful information but can be difficult for the teacher to implement.

An example of a curriculum chart that was developed with ecological inventories and direct assessment of the student is shown in Table 4-7. As the chart indicates, core skills have been chosen which will enable performance of activities in the four domains. The specific skills to be listed on the first year's IEP for this plan are starred. The selection of the specific skills to be listed on the curriculum chart and IEP requires setting priorities for the next few years of instruction. Some of the variables to consider in setting these priorities are: (1) the frequency of use of the skill, (2) the importance of a skill across environments, (3) the student's preferences, d) parental preferences, and (4) the long-term usefulness of the skill.

Developing the IEP and Assessment Procedure

The development of an individualized curriculum plan, discussed in the previous section, is a process that will be repeated every three to five years (e.g., when a student progresses from elementary school to junior high school or moves to a new school district). Each interim year, the chart is reviewed to select the objectives for the upcoming year. These might include: (1) skills partially mastered the previous year to be continued for mastery; (2) skills mastered the previous year to be targeted for further generalization or fluent performance; and (3) new skills from the three to five year curriculum plan. Contact with the parents and student is also needed to ensure that the chart is still a relevant reflection of their priorities and preferences.

Once the IEP is written in observable, measurable objectives, an assessment method is needed for each objective (see Table 4-8). Assessment methods will be similar to those listed for the comprehensive plan, though the procedures most frequently used in data-based classrooms for students with severe handicaps are task analytic assessment (see Table 4-6) and repeated trial or observational assessment. Sometimes the repeated trial assessment includes a cycle of several different responses that are repeated across activities. This latter approach has been called the "individualized curriculum sequencing approach" (Guess, Horner, Utley, Holvoet, Maxon, Tucker, & Warren, 1978). Whichever approach is used, it must be "portable." Teachers of students with severe handicaps typically conduct assessment while teaching or immediately before or after instruction. Since this instruction often takes place outside the classroom (e.g., shopping instruction in the store, pedestrian skills in the community), the assessment procedures need to be easily portable. For example, taking frequency counts with a wrist counter is feasible for data collection in community settings, while interval recording with a cassette tape cue is not. Task analytic assessment sometimes must be adapted from 8 × 10 inch pages on clipboards to small sheets carried in small spiral notebooks or on pocket-size index cards. Data collected is then graphed for evaluation of student progress.

Evaluation of Progress

The next, and most critical, point associated with the process of ongoing assessment, regardless of the manner in which it is accomplished, is that this data be

TABLE 4-7 An Example of a Curriculum Chart Developed for a 13-Year-Old Boy—John

Domain: DOMESTIC

Current Environment: Family's Home   *Future Environment*: Group Home
  Subenvironment: Kitchen

Activities	Skills
Meals and Snacks	Select snack*
	Communicate hunger*
	Pour drink
	Eat with spoon*
	Drink without spilling*
	Prepare simple snacks
	Set table
Clean Up	Clear table*
	Wipe table*
	Sweep
	Put dishes away

  Subenvironment: Bedroom

Activities	Skills
Dressing	Undress alone*
	Put on pants
	Put on shirt
	Put on socks; velcro shoes
Clean Up	Put laundry in hamper*
	Strip sheets
	Hang up coat
	Make bed

  Subenvironment: Bathroom

Activities	Skills
Grooming	Brush teeth
	Wash hands*
	Wash face*
	Comb hair
	Shave
Toileting	Eliminate accidents*
	Use toilet paper*
Cleaning	Clean sink
	Clean toilet

  Subenvironment: Living Room

Activities	Skills
Cleaning	Dust
	Run vacuum

Domain: RECREATION

Current Environment: Family's Home   *Future Environment*: Group Home
  Subenvironment: Living Room

Activities	Skills
Group	Adapted card game
Conversation	Instant camera*
Alone	Video game*
	Photo album*
	Cassette player*
	Rug braiding
	Exercise bike*
	Eliminate pica*

cont'd.

TABLE 4-7   *(Continued)*

Domain: RECREATION

Subenvironment: Outdoors
   Activities   *Skills*
   Sports   Neighborhood Football
Current Environment: School   *Current and Future*: YMCA
  Subenvironment: Gym
   Activities   *Skills*
   Fitness   Jogging*
                                      Basketball
                                      Football
                                      Stationary bike*
                                      Communicate choice*
                                      Social greetings

  Subenvironment: Locker Room
   Activities   *Skills*
   Dressing   Same as home and locker id.
   Toileting   Same as home*

Domain: COMMUNITY

Current and Future Environment: Shopping Plaza
  Subenvironment: Grocery Store
   Activities   *Skills*
   Small purchases   Select item
                                      Put item in cart*
                                      Push cart*
                                      Wait in line*
                                      Pay
                                      No pica*

  Subenvironment: Drug Store
   Activities   *Skills*
   Fill prescription   Communicate w/pharmacist
                                      Pay
                                      Wait

Current and Future Environment: Physician's Office
  Subenvironment: Waiting Room
   Activities   *Skills*
   Wait to be called   Give name
                                      View magazine
                                      Go when called

  Subenvironment: Examining Room
   Examination   Communicate hurt*
                                      Participate in exam
                                      Shirt on/off (off*)
                                      No pica*

Domain: VOCATIONAL

Current Environment: School   *Future Environment*: Supported Work (Bench-
                                    work packaging or custodial in industry)
  Subenvironment: Work Bench
   Activities   *Skills*
   Packaging   Package*
                                      No pica*
                                      Productivity
                                      Work until bell

cont'd.

TABLE 4-7   (*Continued*)

Domain: VOCATIONAL	
Subenvironment: Break Area	
Activities	*Skills*
Socialize	Conversation
	Social greeting
Snacks	Use vending machine
	Drink soda*
	Open packages
Lunch	Open containers*
	Drink without spilling*

*IEP objectives.

used to maximize student learning. The purpose of the collection of accurate performance data within classroom settings is to make instructional decisions to improve or maintain student progress. While most teacher training programs emphasize the importance of making program modifications based upon student performance, this is not necessarily common practice. For example, Adams (1982) noted that a survey conducted by The Association for Persons with Severe Handicaps indicated that less than half of the teacher respondents used data to make program modifications. Obviously, teachers must obtain ongoing data in order to be able to make data-based decisions. Some teachers may believe that they can judge progress without ongoing data collection. Halvoet, O'Neil, Chazdon, Carr, &

TABLE 4-8   Sample Objectives from John's IEP and Method of Assessment for Each

1. When given a glass half full at meals or snacktime, John will drink its contents without spilling on three out of three observations across two days.

   Assessment: Task Analytic-Single Opportunity Probe.

2. When shown two snacks at snacktime, John will point to the snack of his choice at least three times out of five opportunities in a week.

   Assessment: Repeated Trials presented by the teacher across days.

3. During independent leisure or work time, John will have no incidents of attempting to eat nonedible objects (pica) for five out of five consecutive days.

   Assessment: Frequency Count.

4. When given the opportunity to ride a stationary bike at home or school, John will pedal the bike for ten minutes on five days out of the week for a month.

   Assessment: Duration Recording by adaptive PE teacher and by parents at home.

5. When given the opportunity to use a cassette tape player, John will use the recorder to play both sides of a tape on three out of three observations in a week.

   Assessment: Task Analytic-Multiple Opportunity Probe.

6. Duration leisure time at school or home, John will select a leisure material from a closet and then sit and interact with the material for twenty minutes.

   Assessment: Repeated Trials as they naturally occur for selection of material without prompting; duration recording for length of time sitting with material.

Warner (1983) found, by contrast, that teacher judgments were better when data collection was used.

Two other prerequisites to data-based instructional decisions are the accurate summary of the performance data and utilization of decision rules. One method of evaluating performance is visual inspection of graphs, similar to applied behavioral research procedure (Tawney & Gast, 1984). However, applied behavioral researchers usually include preintervention baselines and replications to help guide their judgments regarding the effectiveness of intervention. Teachers may not use either. Furthermore, when visual inspection is used to evaluate a data trend, poor reliability may result whether the data is evaluated by teachers (Liberty, 1972), graduate students (Wampold & Furlong, 1981) or experts (DeProspero & Cohen, 1979). By contrast, using a standard method to summarize the level and trend of the data can improve the reliability of the data summary (Bailey, 1984; White, 1972).

Haring, Liberty, and White (1980) developed and evaluated guidelines for making data-based instructional decisions that include instructions for both the data summary and the type of decision appropriate for different data patterns. Using their method, a teacher draws standard quarter intersect lines and then follows a set of empirically derived rules to make decisions about instructional changes. While their work was based on standard precision teaching charts that use rate data graphed on semilogarithmic scales, the effectiveness of the use of these rules was replicated by Browder, Liberty, Heller, and D'Huyvetters (1986) with nonstandard grid graphs in a program for students with severe behavior disorders and multiple handicaps. Table 4-9 lists the rules used by Browder *et al.* (1986) and illustrates one data-based instructional decision. Note that before making the decision, the teacher evaluates the trend in the graphed data using the standard quarter intersect method for trend estimation. To do this, the teacher locates the midday and midpoint of the first three data points of the period of evaluation and the midday and midpoint of the last three data points of the period of evaluation. These intersections are connected to show the line of progress as illustrated in Table 4-9. From this estimation of trend, the teacher can then consider the "rules" for instructional decisions shown in Table 4-9. Thus, instructional changes are selected by considering the data pattern.

Consultation

When learning does not occur or severe behavior problems arise, assessment also provides an objective data base for the teacher, parents, and educational consultants. Typically, the school psychologist or an outside consultant is called in when severe behavior problems arise. However, when students have few adaptive behaviors, simply decelerating the problem behavior is often inappropriate. Students with high rates of stereotypic behaviors, for example, may have *no* alternative adaptive behaviors to fill long, unstructured hours. If the stereotypic behavior

TABLE 4-9 Example of Evaluation of Data to Make Instructional Decisions

This example shows three biweekly reviews for John's table clearing task and utilizes a combination data collection and graphing form. The teacher scores the steps from the bottom up and uses multiple opportunity task analytic assessment. The number of independent corrects (slashes) are counted and that number is filled in to indicate that day's performance.

Steps	Student Performance																	Mastery
Replace tray	10	10	10̸	10̸	10̸	10̸	10̸	10̸	10̸	10̸	10̸	10̸	10̸	10̸	10̸	10̸	●	●
Wipe tray	9	9	9	9	9	9	9	9	9̸	9	9̸	9̸	9̸	9̸	9̸	●	9̸	9̸
Carry tray	8	8	8	8	8	8	8	8	8	8	8	8	8	●	8	8̸	8̸	8̸
Glasses on tray	7	7	7	7	7	7	7	7	7	7	●	7	●	7̸	●	7̸	7̸	7̸
Silverware	6	6	6	6	6	6	6	6	6	6	6̸	6̸	6	6	6	6	6̸	6̸
Scrape/Stack	5	5	5	5	5	5	5	5	5	5	5	●	5	5̸	5	5̸	5̸	5̸
Trash in can	4	4	4	4	4	4	4	4̸	●	4̸	4̸	4̸	4̸	4̸	4̸	4̸	4̸	4̸
Trash on tray	3	3	3	3	3	3	3	●	3	●	3̸	3	3	3̸	3̸	3̸	3̸	3̸
Pick up trash	2	2	●	●	●	●	●	2	2	2	2	2	2̸	2̸	2̸	2̸	2̸	2̸
Get tray	●	●	✗	✗	✗	✗	✗	✗	✗	✗	✗	✗	✗	✗	✗	✗	✗	✗
	0	0	0	0	0	0	0	0	0	0	0	0	0	0	0	0	0	0
Dates	5	6	7	8	9	12	13	14	15	16	19	20	21	22	23	24	26	27

September

Date of Decisions

	Trend	Decision Rule
9/27/85	__X__ Met criteria	__X__ Move on to next skill
9/20/85	__X__ Acceleration is adequate	__X__ No changes
9/12/85	__X__ Acceleration: very slow	__X__ Improve prompts
	_____ Flat: No progress since program began	_____ Task analyze
	_____ Flat: After progress	_____ Improve consequences *or*
		_____ Remediate difficult skill
	_____ Deceleration or Highly Variable	_____ Move on to next skill *or*
		_____ Improve consequences *or*
		_____ Vary activity

creates social problems because of its high rate or unusual topography, the goal may be to teach alternative leisure skills and social interaction. Thus, the consultant who is called to address a student's severe behavior problem will need to address that student's skill deficiencies as well as the problem behavior itself.

Several models have been proposed to evaluate problem behaviors and identify alternative behaviors for instruction (e.g., Evans & Meyer, 1985; Gaylord-Ross, 1980). Gaylord-Ross (1980) suggested that the following steps be followed:

1. Assessment. First, the consultant works with the teacher to collect baseline data that enables the assessment of whether a problem actually exists. The consultant and teacher will also want to identify the rationale for changing the behavior (e.g., is it creating physical harm?). They will want to discuss medical problems that might influence the behavior and seek medical treatment if appropriate (e.g., check for ear infection if ear slapping or head banging is observed). If the problem is serious and cannot be corrected with medical treatment but is verified with baseline data, the consultant will consider the next step.

2. Reinforcement procedures. The simplest intervention is to provide contingent social attention for alternative behaviors and to withhold attention of the problem behavior. This often constitutes the consultant's first action in resolving the problem while curricular changes are being planned. Sometimes the teacher's use of attention may resolve the problem without further effort. Many times, however, the problem relates to a skill deficiency that is not being addressed in the curriculum, or to problems in the general environment.

3. Ecological component. Another, often simple solution to the problem may lie in the teaching environment. Frequently, students with severe handicaps have no way to express discomfort or boredom except with behaviors that create a disturbance in the teacher's routine. The consultant may want to examine the teaching environments used by the teacher. Do the environments have comfortable furniture, temperature levels, and adequate lighting? Does the student have adequate space? Are leisure materials accessible that the student likes and knows how to use during free time? Does a student with health problems have the opportunity to rest? Does the daily schedule provide varied activities? Is "dead" or noninstructional time kept to a minimum? If the environment is comfortable and includes adequate activities and materials for the student to be actively engaged most of the day, curriculum changes, the next component, may be warranted.

4. Curriculum component. Often, the problem behavior reflects skill deficiencies. The student may have few leisure skills or appropriate social behavior. Communication may be extremely limited. The teacher and consultant may conduct what is called a discrepancy analysis to identify the deficient skills (Evans & Meyer, 1985). In this analysis, rather than just looking at the behavior, the educator considers the environments in which the maladaptive behavior occurred and alternative skills needed to function successfully in these settings. Table 4-10 presents an example of a discrepancy analysis for problem behavior during independent work or leisure time. Problem behaviors often occur in clusters and may intensify as the student tries alternative responses to get the desired effect (e.g., peer or teacher attention).

The consultant also may wish to consider the quality of instruction. Is the teacher providing adequate prompts and reinforcement during instruc-

TABLE 4-10 Example of a Discrepancy Analysis

Student's Name: John		Environment:	Classroom during individual work or leisure
Date: September 20, 1985		Source:	Observation

Activities of Nonhandicapped Peers	Activities of this Student	Discrepant Skills
Sit at table	Run	Locate own table
Obtain materials	Grab materials close by	Select materials, communicate need for materials
Work or play	Put objects in mouth	Play, work skills
Talk with peers	Scream, laugh	Communicate with peers

tion? If the consultant is a physical or occupational therapist, positioning problems, motor, or sensory deficiencies may be assessed. This may be a good time to review graphs of the IEP objectives. Is the student making progress? Can the student perform enough correct responses during instruction to receive an adequate schedule of reinforcement? At times the curriculum component is reviewed repeatedly in order to find additional reasons for the problem behavior.

5. Consequences for the problem behavior component. Punishment is too often overused in programs for students with severe handicaps. Gaylord-Ross (1980) lists prerequisites for the consideration of its use that include extensive efforts to eliminate the problem with less intrusive procedures. Too often punishment is selected before these extensive efforts have been made. Another consideration in avoiding the use of punishment is that the procedures used with people with severe handicaps typically are not used with people who have not been classified as handicapped. For example, many school districts do not allow teachers to use corporal punishment. The application of noxious substances and the use of physical restraint could be considered forms of corporal punishment. If a consequence is selected to decelerate behavior, consideration should be given to procedures that are accepted for people without handicaps that do not place the student at risk for physical harm and that do not infringe on the student's right to receive instruction. For example, reprimands, nonexclusionary time-out, and response cost are all used in the mainstream of public schools and can be effective with students with severe handicaps. (Some people would not use the term "punishment" for procedures like time-out and reprimands. However, each provides mildly aversive consequences to decelerate a behavior and thus, should not be used until other procedures have been tried.) If the choice is made to use consequences for engaging in

the target problem behavior after implementing several less intrusive procedures, reinforcement for alternative behavior should still be used. Also,
careful review of the data should reveal that the procedures selected
actually decelerate the behavior.

Any consequences for problem behavior can potentially serve as reinforcers. For example, escape from a lesson can function as reinforcement
for problem behaviors such as self-abuse (Iwata, Dorsey, Slifer, Bauman, &
Richman, 1982). To use time-out when a student's behavior is maintained
by the termination of a lesson will probably accelerate the problem behavior. Similarly, the use of reprimands for attention-seeking behavior may
serve as reinforcement to accelerate or maintain this behavior. Thus,
because of ethical considerations and the risk that any consequence for the
problem behavior could serve as reinforcement, this component should be
the last considered in planning for problem behavior and should always be
paired with positive procedures when used.

Whichever intervention is used to resolve a behavior problem, ongoing review
of data will help the teacher and consultant evaluate its effectiveness. Despite the
absence of decision rules to evaluate deceleration of behavior, the educator should
monitor both the acceleration of alternative behaviors and the typical pattern of
deceleration for the intervention used (e.g., punishment usually results in quick
deceleration; withdrawing social attention to extinguish a behavior may result in
an increase in behavior prior to a gradual, steady decrease).

RESEARCH ON BEHAVIORAL LIFE SKILLS ASSESSMENT

While use of behavioral life skills assessment for students with severe handicaps is a
popular practice, few resources exist to describe the overall development of this
model for assessment. Several current resources describe models similar to the one
in this chapter (Browder, 1987; Brown, 1987; Brown, Evans, & Weed, 1985; Powers
& Handleman, 1984; Snell & Grigg, 1987). However, many research questions need
to be addressed concerning the feasibility and quality of this model's application.
Some of the specific, unanswered issues are: (1) classification of students with
severe handicaps, (2) the design of task analyses, (3) the reliability and validity of
ecological inventories, and (4) the validity of using rules for instructional decisions.

Classification of Students with Severe Handicaps

When a student is referred for evaluation for special services, assessment is usually
designed to determine the nature of the problem, the severity of the problem, and
the appropriate service to remedy the problem. Usually, students with severe
handicaps have severe developmental delay, and may have obvious physical
problems. Most typically for this population, the physician is the professional who

will make the initial diagnosis of the child. Sometimes this initial diagnosis is made at birth. However, it is often difficult for the physician to predict how a child with neurological impairment and other physical anomalies will respond to treatment. A survey of 215 families by Abramson, Gravink, Abramson, and Sommers (1977) of families with preschool children who had been classified as mentally retarded exemplifies this initial diagnosis and the parents' reaction to it. Of the families surveyed, 94% sought a diagnosis and advice from a physician first. Unfortunately, only 18% thought the advice they received was either sympathetic or informative, and a small percentage (9%) received a bleak prognosis and misinformation (e.g., that all children who are mentally retarded should be institutionalized).

Once a student reaches school-age, parents are often well aware that their child is handicapped when the handicaps are severe or multiple. However, parents may not agree with the label for the handicap that school professionals provide. Since many students receive as many as three different diagnostic labels in separate evaluations it is not surprising that parents lose confidence in the ability of professionals to discriminate between types of handicaps. If parents move from one state to another, the chances of their child receiving new labels increases. For example, one student known to the authors of this chapter was classified as autistic in one state, severely handicapped in a second, mentally retarded in a third, and severely emotionally disturbed in a fourth.

Educators who expend efforts to discriminate between such labels probably do not contribute anything to the life of the child because there is little evidence that these specific classifications have significantly different service needs. Rather, a classification system is needed that distinguishes between the types, amounts, and durations of special services a student needs. Standardized intelligence and achievement testing have not assisted the process of identifying service needs for students with severe handicaps. In a comprehensive assessment project called Molly Stark, Bricker and Campbell (1980) used a battery of standardized assessments to identify the educational needs of students with severe handicaps who had never received public school services. Some of the instruments used were the Columbia Mental Maturity Test, the Peabody Picture Vocabulary Test, the Bayley Scales of Infant Development, and the Denver Developmental Screening Test. Some behavioral checklists were also used, such as the Pennsylvania Training Model (Somerton & Turner, 1975) and the Behavior Characteristics Profile (Vort Corporation, 1973). The estimated cost of the total process of assessment by project and medical staff was estimated at $1500 per student. From this multidisciplinary evaluation, nearly 400 recommendations were made for treatment and further evaluation. Of these, only 29% were evaluated to be appropriate (e.g., a recommendation to teach a blind student to use a picture communication board was inappropriate). Only 11% of the recommendations were actually implemented in the year that followed. Bricker and Campbell (1980) concluded:

> The results were confused and confusing due to the confounding of motivational problems and interference of learned forms of institutional, stereotyped behavior. The

effort directed toward deriving meaningful assessment results may have been better spent in teaching and training the students rather than in such extensive and ultimately meaningless testing. One is hard pressed to advocate substantial financial resources for services that yield such limited results. (p. 11)

The catch-22 for educators is that state guidelines typically require special prescriptions to be based on a reliable, valid comparison of a student with the norm reference group. As mentioned earlier, adaptive behavior scales offer an alternative to intelligence tests. Some of the recent adaptive behavior scales have reflected careful standardization (e.g., Comprehensive Test of Adaptive Behavior, Scales of Independent Behavior). As noted earlier, these scales also more closely approximate the life skills curriculum into which a student will be placed. However, future research must determine whether adaptive behavior scales discriminate between students who need a life skills approach to curriculum development rather than the more academic approach found in programs for students with milder handicaps. Can the use of adaptive behavior scales, combined with direct observation and parent or teacher interviews, enable the school psychologist to discriminate levels of life skills service needs? For example, students traditionally classified as trainable mentally retarded often benefit from some academic instruction, but will need substantial life skills instruction as well. How would such students be classified in contrast to a student who has no communication or self care?

If adaptive behavior scales can discriminate between students with handicaps who have different service needs, then a more meaningful classification system might employ levels of adaptive behavior rather than IQ scores. An alternative might be to define entry and exit criteria for different levels of service. These entry and exit criteria would be behavioral descriptors. This latter approach is flexible and allows a student to "graduate" from a classification. Graduation to a class with certain entry skill requirements (e.g., independent toileting; street crossing) would be more logical than having a student progress from profound to severe mental retardation—labels that are supposed to be permanent traits. Parents might also find it more reasonable to have a student's placement based on defined behaviors used as entry criteria rather than based on labels. Unfortunately, the field has not developed such entry or exit criteria. If they were developed, the low incidence of students with severe handicaps in many school districts would not permit developing levels of classes at each age level. As mentioned previously, the best current practice for assigning students with severe handicaps to classrooms is to further chronological age and geographic location. Further research is needed to define criteria for levels of service and evaluate their effect on students' promotion to less restrictive placements.

The Design of Task Analyses

Task analysis evolved from the applied behavior analysis tradition and has played a role in many studies on teaching life skills (e.g., Cronin & Cuvo, 1979; Cuvo, Leaf,

& Borakove, 1978; Spears, Rusch, York, & Lilly, 1981). When applied to the instruction of life skills, task analysis is usually a defined chain of behavior required to execute a task. Research using task analyses for assessment and instruction has reported good to excellent interobservor reliability. What is less certain is the validity of talk analyses. Several people may write a task analysis and have completely different steps in the chain. This may be due to idiosyncracies in performing life skills (e.g., ways people comb their hair) and to differences in how specific responses are defined in the chain.

Cronin and Cuvo (1979) describe an elaborate procedure for validating a task analysis through consultation with experts and observation. This approach will produce a task analysis that is either judged by a daily living expert (e.g., home economist) to be efficient and effective, or typical of most nonhandicapped people. Whether either or both of these procedures is adequate in producing a valid task analysis is unknown. White (1980) raises another issue that has implications for the validity of task analyses. White (1980) proposes that it is not *how* the task is performed, but the critical effect of performance. Thus, the validity of a task analysis might also be judged by the outcome of its performance by a person with severe handicaps. Others (Brown, Evans, & Weed, 1985) have viewed the analysis of tasks more broadly and noted that most tasks or routines consist of several components: core components—exceptional steps such as usually included in most task analyses (initiate, prepare, solve problems, monitor quality and tempo, and terminate task); and enrichment components or nonessential elements of a task, such as related communication, social skills, and choice. Finally, some evidence exists that the specificity of the responses defined as steps of the task analysis may influence outcome (Crist, Walls, & Haught, 1984). More research on the development of task analyses would reduce the guesswork by educators who use this important measurement approach.

Ecological Inventories

Since students with severe handicaps often learn slowly and fail to generalize skills unless taught directly to do so, it is crucial that skills selected for instruction relate directly to the community environments in which they live. To identify the skills needed for an individual student, the teacher might conduct an ecological inventory that consists of obtaining information about the activities of nonhandicapped peers in environments proposed for the student. Although this process has been illustrated and described, there is no research to validate or define this process. Several approaches for conducting ecological inventories have been taken. Wilcox and Bellamy (1982) suggest cataloging in community's opportunities for vocational, leisure, and domestic activities. This approach would be time-consuming, but relevant for quite a while. Holvoet, Guess, Mulligan, and Brown (1980) recommend that clusters of behaviors frequently needed by an individual student be identified. Freagon, Wheeler, Hill, Brankin, Costello, and Peters (1983) use a checklist of domestic routines that is developed for a specific geographic region.

Renzaglia, Aveno, and Hutchins (1984) interviewed the parents, the next teacher, and the community staff to generate a list of skills to be taught.

Because the ecological inventory does not follow a well-defined method of assessment and has not been evaluated in research, it is uncertain whether two people who would conduct the same inventory with the same sources of information would obtain the same results. Yet the procedure is an important new trend in prioritizing skills for instruction. Early development of research in using more defined ecological inventory procedures is found in a study by Rusch, Schutz, and Agran (1982), who verified the critical survival skills required by employers. More research of this type is needed to define and evaluate methodologies for the indentification of normalized behaviors that will be selected for students with severe handicaps.

Data-Based Instructional Decisions

While some existing evidence supports the premise that teachers make better instructional decisions when they collect data (Holvoet *et al.*, 1983), it is not clear how often data must be collected to make these decisions. Also, without specific training in the visual analysis of data to make instructional decisions, teachers may not make accurate conclusions about either the data trend or whether or not to change instructional procedures (Liberty, 1972; White, 1972). Haring, Liberty, and White (1981), and Browder *et al.* (1986) found that teachers were more successful (i.e., more student progress occurred) when teachers followed the decisions rules similar to those listed earlier in this chapter and in Table 4-9. Browder *et al.* (1986) also found that self-management enhanced teachers' maintenance of the data evaluation procedures. While these two studies favor the application of a standard method of data inspection and use of a set of rules to make data-based decisions with students with moderate and severe handicaps, replications of the predictive validity of the rules and the reliability with which the teachers apply the rules are needed.

CASE STUDY

The five steps of assessment for students with severe handicaps can be illustrated in the case study of John (a fictitious person based on composites of students known to the authors). John's family moved to a small Pennsylvania town during the summer that John turned thirteen. One of their reasons for moving was to find a school district that would provide good services for both John and their sixteen-year-old daughter, Pamela. (Pamela was an above-average student who would continue her college-bound studies at the local high school.) In August, the multidisciplinary team conducted their evaluation of John for identification of the appropriate educational service.

In John's previous placement, a school psychologist had attempted to test

John's IQ on several occasions. His written report stated that John could not be tested with conventional intelligence tests because of his inability to sit during testing. The previous school psychologist had used an infant developmental checklist since IQ testing was unsuccessful. This evaluation had yielded an infant level mental age. Adaptive behavior assessment had not been used. The previous school psychologist had kept a data log of John's attempted consumptions of nonedible objects (pica) and of the teacher's frequent referrals for help in John's overall management. John's educational program had used an infant development model, so his previous individualized plan listed goals in cognitive and motor skills similar to those expected of a two-year-old. John had received speech thereapy that focused on "readiness" to communicate and did not teach communication per se. In their first communication with the director of special education for their new school district, the parents expressed their disappointment with John's educational program to date and requested that his new IEP reflect "useful" skills.

The school psychologist began John's psychological evaluation by giving John's parents the parent form of the Comprehensive Test of Adaptive Behavior (CTAB). He attached a letter to the form inviting the parents to write to him about John's interests and preferences. The parents returned the form with a letter noting John's interests. The school psychologist then scheduled a home observation of John with the parents. During this home observation, the school psychologist had five primary goals: (1) to complete the Normative Adaptive Behavior Checklist (NABC) by reviewing items from the parent's survey, (2) to conduct an ecological inventory of skills John needed in his home environment, (3) to note any preferences indicated by John as activities were presented, (4) to obtain information on John's performance of a public activity (shopping) by interviewing the parents, and (5) to observe the extent of John's problem behaviors. To achieve these goals without a home visit would have been difficult, since many of the activities to be observed required materials only readily available in the home. The observation lasted about two hours. From the NABC, the school psychologist obtained a raw score of 10 on the NABC and 22 on the CTAB for John. (The NABC uses a subset of items on the CTAB and can be used for comparison with nonhandicapped students.) This raw score gave John a standard score below 67 and a percentile rank below the first percentile in comparison with nonhandicapped students (the lowest obtainable in this comparison) on the NABC. In comparison with CTAB scores of mentally retarded students in public school settings, John's raw score placed him in the second percentile. Since Pennsylvania requires categorical classification based on intellectual functioning, this normative comparison was used to support the recommended placement for John in the program for students with severe and profound mental retardation. Some of the specific skill deficiencies noted were:

1. Daytime bladder control (I, A-5).
2. Washing face (I, B-2).
3. Putting on underpants (I, C-12).
4. Using a spoon (I, D-6).

5. Dusting furniture (II, A-18).
6. Clearing table (II, C-2).
7. Putting clothes in hamper (II, D-5).
8. Using vending machine (III, E-4).
9. Working alone (III, F-5).
10. Communicating hello and good-bye (IV, B-3).
11. Walking up stairs with handrails (V,-29).

The school psychologist's report also included a description of John's many attempts to place household objects in his mouth during the home observation. When the parents talked with the school psychologist, John wandered from room to room picking up objects. His sister had followed him and reprimanded him for each object he picked up by saying, "Don't eat that!" When John was presented with a specific assessment activity, he stayed in the proximity of the activity but attempted to place each object related to the activity in his mouth. From this observation, the school psychologist concluded that John would need constant, close supervision in his initial classroom placement and that a plan to decelerate John's pica was needed.

The initial assessment for identification and placement also included evaluations by a family physician, physical therapist, occupational therapist, speech therapist, adaptive physical education teacher, and curriculum consultant. The curriculum consultant's evaluation will be presented next since it yielded John's three-year curriculum plan. The other evaluations are beyond the scope of this chapter but information relevant to his educational program will be described briefly. The occupational and physical therapist did not recommend ongoing therapy but did note that special attention should be given to John's development of more mature prehension patterns (grasp). The adaptive physical education teacher noted that, while John showed an interest in rough and vigorous activity, he had no organized game or leisure skills. Fitness testing also revealed the need for an exercise program to improve John's cardiovascular fitness. The speech therapist noted that, while John had no formal system of communication, he had idiosyncratic responses that were successful in communicating to others in several ways, but that could be improved and perhaps expanded. For example, John vocalized and looked at an object when he wanted it. He also smiled and nodded when greeting familiar people. When others laughed, John also laughed and made eye contact with them. When John did not want an object or activity, he screamed loudly and moved away from it.

Once the decision for a life skills placement was made, the curriculum development was begun. The multidisciplinary evaluation provided input for this curriculum. This school district had a person, the curriculum consultant, who conducted comprehensive educational evaluations of individual students and was responsible for the development of the district's special education curricula. The curriculum consultant conducted further ecological inventories to obtain information on skills John would need in future vocational, community, and recreational placements to supplement the home inventory completed by the school psychologist. The specific environments chosen with the parents and John's next teacher were: an area adult-supported work program, a nearby shopping plaza, the YMCA, and the physician's office. (See Table 4-5.) To streamline this process, the teacher made a checklist of skills that might be important in each environment. She then called or visited employees in each environment to check the importance of each skill on the lists. From the skills recommended by employees as important, the consultant then asked the parents which skills John had. The parents were also asked to circle any skill deficiencies on the list that were priorities to them. The consultant also wanted to make one observation of John in public since his next placement would include frequent instruction in the community. She chose the shopping plaza and the activity of purchasing a snack to make this observation. John's father was asked to accompany them and to purchase the family's groceries as usual to provide a natural context for the trip and the observation. She found that John traveled quietly and crossed streets and parking lots when cued by her. However, in the store he grabbed and tried to consume many objects (edible and nonedible). She noted in her report that John's initial community instruction might require the assignment of an aid or volunteer to assist the teacher since John would require direct instruction and close supervision.

The consultant developed a curriculum plan for John based on these inventories and skill assessments. She shared the plan with John's parents to obtain their suggestions for revisions. This three-year plan is shown in Table 4-6. The plan also incorporates the recommendations of the adaptive physical education teacher and the speech therapist whose services John would also receive.

The third step in John's assessment was the selection of skills for the first year's IEP and the development of procedures to measure progress on each objective. In this school district, this step was performed by the professional responsible for providing instruction. John's special education teacher wrote the IEP and developed the assessment for each objective in all skills except the active recreation objectives written by the adaptive PE teacher and the communication objectives written by the speech therapist. Table 4-8 shows some of these first-year objectives and the method of ongoing assessment that would be used for each.

The fourth step of John's assessment began in late September when the teachers and therapist conducted their first biweekly review of John's progress. To illustrate how this evaluation was conducted for each objective, John's cleanup program can be reviewed. John's performance in the cleanup program was evaluated through an analytic assessment of a single opportunity to clean up the trash from an entire table. This was followed by instruction in cleaning each table in the cafeteria (about ten instructional trials). However, the first "test" trial was the data graphed and used for evaluation. An example of this assessment is shown in Table 4-8. As the table indicates, the teacher noted the correct number of responses for each step of the task analysis. Table 4-9 shows the graph of each day's performance. The teacher connected each day's data point. During the biweekly review, the teacher also used the standard quarter intersect method (described earlier in this chapter) to estimate the trend. Using this trend estimation and the level of performance, the teacher reviewed the appropriate instructional decision. In the first review, the data pattern was slow acceleration. The teacher decided to modify the prompting system to try to enhance John's rate of acquisition of this skill. In the second review, the pattern was clear acceleration, so the teacher decided to maintain the instructional procedure until the next biweekly review. In the third review, John had mastered the cleaning task for tables. The teacher decided to teach the next skill, which was production and generalization of cleaning. The graph also shows data on John's clearing of a table at a fast-food restaurant, which was taught once a week. The teacher noted this generalization in evaluating mastery for this objective. In the next assessment, the teacher would measure John's rate for cleaning all the tables in an area of the cafeteria.

The fifth step of John's assessment also began in late September. The teacher contacted the school psychologist and curriculum consultant because John's pica had not decreased. The teacher had counted John's attempts to consume nonedible items throughout the day by counting the frequency of occurrence and recording it on a wrist counter. While daily fluctuations occurred, the range of frequency was twenty to fifty incidents a day. Although the teacher had been able to block his consumption of the objects, she noted the physician's precaution that if John succeeded in one of these attempts, the result could be life threatening. The teacher also noted that the high frequency of pica disrupted the entire teaching schedule for all students in the program because she stopped instruction to take objects from John.

The school psychologist and curriculum consultant noted that the teacher had submitted excellent baseline data and rationale for intervention for this urgent behavior. The teacher's only management strategy to date had been to prevent John's pica by "guarding" him and praising him for the many alternative responses he was prompted to make during instruction. In following the decision model described earlier, the consultants noted that the teacher was using reinforcement for alternative behaviors and that some simple environmental changes could be made to make John's management easier until he acquired more alternative skills. They recommended that he have access to leisure materials too large to consume when not engaged in instruction and that he be seated by the teacher during classroom instruction. The teacher did accompany John closely in public with the assistance of an aid who accompanied and instructed the other students. Two weeks after the introduction of these simple environmental changes, John's pica had decreased to fifteen to thirty incidents per day but stabilized at this still high rate. The curriculum consultant then carefully reviewed the IEP and the teacher's instructional plan to highlight the specific alternative behaviors John needed. She conducted a discrepancy analysis of one of his most difficult times—independent leisure or work time. This discrepancy analysis is shown in Table 4-10. From this analysis, the consultant recommended that John receive further instruction in the use of varied leisure materials. The consultant recommended that the teacher use more group instruction to minimize John's independent work times until his skills improved. Also, until his skills improved, the teacher needed to give John an independent activity that he could do without help and that had little "risk," so that the overall schedule could be maintained. The consultant noted that John's objective to learn to open his lunch containers might lend itself to trial and error learning. During independent work times, John was given a large plastic container with a snack inside and allowed to open the container to obtain the snack through trial and error. This took John about twenty minutes initially. Two weeks of data after these curriculum changes were made revealed slight decreases in his pica, which stabilized at about eighteen a day.

The curriculum consultant then asked the school psychologist to consider further intervention. The school psychologist decided to cycle through the decision model again rather than to consider punishment. The school psychologist took data on the teacher's use of attention for alternative behaviors and to interrupt pica. While the teacher seemed to give frequent praise and attention for alternative behaviors, when John was not close to the teacher attention for pica far exceeded reinforcement for alternative responses. Also, during these times the teacher and aid often were busy with other students (e.g., toileting; assisting with putting coats on). When John obtained an object and began to put it in his mouth, the teacher would run across the room exclaiming loudly, "No. Don't eat it." The teacher and the school psychologist designed a DRO (differential reinforcement of other behavior) program for John that would include instructions to self-reinforce. When the teacher needed to move into activities that were on a high-risk level for John's pica (typically management of other students), she played a tape with chimes at two-minute intervals. If John had not attempted to eat objects, the teacher praised him from wherever she was standing and prompted him to go to a closet to turn on some music or select a leisure material. The long-term plan was for the teacher to fade her praise and prompts and for John to select materials when cued by the chime. Eventually the chime would be faded. When the teacher finished her work with another student and if John had not engaged in pica, she would race over to him and make enthusiastic comments about whatever he was doing. If he did attempt to eat an object, she would remove it without comment or eye contact and give a leisure material from the closet to the student with whom she was working. This procedure was shared with the parents who also implemented it at home during leisure hours. The parents found the chime tape especially helpful in cuing them to attend to John when he was not attempting to eat objects. The next biweekly review showed a gradual but steady deceleration in John's attempts to eat nonedibles, so the program was continued.

For the rest of John's year, the teacher's biweekly reviews of John's progress continued with instructional changes made as necessary. The school psychologist and curriculum consultant made a few phone calls and visits during the year to check on John's overall progress. When the school's report cards were issued, the teacher sent the parents copies of the biweekly reviews with an explanation. Their concerns were noted and used appropriately to revise instruction (e.g., to teach generalization across materials and settings when generalization was not noted at home).

SUMMARY

In order for educational assessment of students with severe handicaps to be meaningful, the traditional assessment approach requires extensive modification. These students are characterized by slow acquisition of skills, poor retention when skills are not used, and minimal skill generalization beyond the stimulus conditions under which a skill is acquired. Given these characteristics, the curricula for such students must be carefully chosen to reflect the skills predicted to be useful to a particular student now and in the future. The ecological inventory process has become the method to identify these skills, while norm-referenced developmental assessment will not provide this information. Furthermore, the psychologist's role in the identification and placement can complement the teacher's efforts to identify these needed skills, particularly when initial psychological assessment replaces intelligence testing with more meaningful assessment, including adaptive behavior measurement, direct observation of the student, assessment of parent and student preferences and initial ecological inventories. Also, assessment for the purpose of identifying students with severe handicaps has more recently leaned toward a focus on service needs, rather than defining intellectual characteristics.

Once placed, a student with severe handicaps requires at least four other general types of educational assessment: (1) comprehensive educational assessment to develop a three- to five-year curriculum plan, (2) annual assessment to develop an IEP and assessment procedures for each objective, (3) ongoing, regular evaluation of progress (e.g., biweekly), and (4) consultation assessment to solve educational problems. Assessment strategies include both indentification of the specific skills needed in the student's environments and evaluation of the student's current repertoire of these skills. Standardized testing has far less value to educational planning for these students than indirect (e.g., parent interviews) and direct assessment made by the teacher (e.g., observations, task analytic assessment) of the student's educational needs.

References

Abramson, P., Gravink, M., Abramson, L., & Sommers, D. (1977). Early diagnosis and intervention of retardation. A survey of parental reactions concerning the quality of services rendered. *Mental Retardation, 15*, 28–31.

Adams, G. L. (1982). Curriculum development and implementation. In L. Sternberg & G. L. Adams (Eds.), *Educating severely and profoundly handicapped students* (pp. 135–162). Rockville, Md.: Aspen.

Bailey, D. B. (1984). Effects on lines of progress and semilogarithmic charts on ratings of charted data. *Journal of Applied Behavior Analysis, 17*, 359–365.

Bellamy, T. (1985). Severe disability in adulthood. *Newsletter of the Association for Persons with Severe Handicaps, 11*, 1, 6.

Bijou, S. W., & Baer, D. M. (1961). *Child development II: Universal state of infancy.* New York: Appleton-Century-Crofts.

Bricker, W., & Campbell, P. H. (1980). Interdisciplinary programming. In W. Sailor, L. Brown, & B. Wilcox (Eds.), *Methods of instruction for teaching the severely handicapped* (pp. 3–45). Baltimore, Md.: Paul H. Brookes.

Browder, D. (1987). *Assessment of individuals with severe handicaps.* Baltimore, Md.: Paul H. Brookes.

Browder, D., Liberty, K., Heller, M., & D'Huyvetters, K. (1986). Self-management by teachers: Improving instructional decision making. *Professional School Psychology, 1*, 165–175.

Brown, F. (1987). Meaningful assessment of persons with severe and profound handicaps. In M. E. Snell (Ed.), *Assessment of individuals with severe handicaps.* Columbus, Ohio: Charles E. Merrill.

Brown, F. A., Evans, I. M., & Weed, K. A. (1985). *A component model of functional life routines* (Tech. Rep. No. 6). Binghamton, N.Y.: University Center at Binghamton.

Brown, F., Holvoet, J., Guess, D., & Mulligan, M. (1980). The individualized curriculum sequencing model (III): Small group instruction. *Journal of the Association for the Severely Handicapped, 5,* 352–367.

Brown, L., Branston, M. B., Hamre-Nietupski, S., Pumpian, I., Certo, N., & Gruenewald, L. (1979). A strategy for developing chronological age-appropriate and functional curricular content to severely handicapped adolescents and young adults. *Journal of Special Education, 13*, 81–90.

Brown, L., Branston-McLean, M. B., Baumgart, D., Vincent, L., Falvey, M., & Schroeder, J. (1979). Utilizing the characteristics of current and subsequent least restrictive environments in the development of curricular content for severely handicapped students. *AAESPH Review, 4*, 407–424.

Crist, K., Walls, R. T., & Haught, P. (1984). Degree of specificity in task analysis. *American Journal of Mental Deficiency, 89*, 67–74.

Cronin, K. A., & Cuvo, A. J. (1979). Teaching mending skills to retarded adolescents. *Journal of Applied Behavior Analysis, 12*, 401–406.

Cuvo, A. J. (1979). Multiple baseline design in instructional research: Pitfalls of measurement and procedural advantages. *American Journal of Mental Deficiency, 84*, 219–228.

Cuvo, A. J., Leaf, R. B., & Borakove, L. S. (1978). Teaching janitorial skills to the mentally retarded: Acquisition, generalization, and maintenance. *Journal of Applied Behavior Analysis, 11*, 345–355.

DeProspero, A., & Cohen, S. (1979). Inconsistent visual analysis of intrasubject data. *Journal of Applied Behavior Analysis, 12*, 573–579.

Donnellan, A. M. (1984). The criterion of the least dangerous assumptions. *Behavioral Disorders: Journal of the Council for Children with Behavioral Disorders, 9*, 141–150.

Duncan, D., Sbardellati, E., Maheady, L., & Sainato, D. (1981). Nondiscriminatory assessment of severely physically handicapped individuals. *The Journal of the Association for People with Severe Handicaps, 6*, 17–22.

Evans, I. M., & Meyer, L. H. (1985). *An educative approach to behavior problems.* Baltimore, Md.: Paul H. Brookes.

Falvey, M. A. (1986). *Community-based curriculum: Instructional strategies for students with severe handicaps.* Baltimore, Md.: Paul H. Brookes.

Fialkowski v. Shapp, 405 F. Supp. 946 (E.D. Pa. 1975).

Freagon, S., Wheeler, J., Hill, L., Brankin, G., Costello, D., & Peters, W. H. (1983). A domestic training environment for students who are severely handicapped. *The Journal of the Association for Persons with Severe Handicaps.* 8, 49–61.

Gaylord-Ross, R. (1980). A decision model for the treatment of aberrant behavior in applied settings. In W. Sailor, B. Wilcox, & L. Brown (Eds.), *Methods of instruction for severely handicapped students* (pp. 135–158). Baltimore, Md.: Paul H. Brookes.

Gaylord-Ross, R. J., Haring, T. G., Brien, C., & Pitts-Conway, V. (1984). The training and generalization of social interaction skills with autistic youth. *Journal of Applied Behavior Analysis, 17*, 229–247.

Gaylord-Ross, R., & Holvoet, J. (1985). *Strategies for educating students with severe handicaps.* Boston: Little, Brown.

Geiger, W. L., & Justen, J. E. (1983). Definitions of severely handicapped and requirements for teacher certification: A survey of state departments of education. *The Journal of the Association for the Severely Handicapped, 8,* 25–29.

Grossman, H. J. (Ed.). (1977). *Manual on terminology and classification in mental retardation.* Washington, D. C.: American Association on Mental Deficiency.

Guess, D., Horner, D., Utley, B., Holvoet, D., Maxon, D., Tucker, D., & Warren, S. (1978). A functional curriculum sequencing model for teaching the severely handicapped. *AAESPH Review, 8,* 202–215.

Guess, D., & Mulligan, M. (1982). The severely and profoundly handicapped. In E. L. Meyer (Ed.), *Exceptional children and youth: An introduction* (2d ed.). Denver: Love.

Halderman v. Pennhurst State School and Hospital, 446 F. Supp. 1295 (E.D. Pa. 1977).

Haring, N., Liberty, K., & White, O. (1980). Rules for data-based strategy decisions in instructional programs: Current research and instructional implications. In W. Sailor, B. Wilcox, & L. Brown (Eds.), *Methods of instruction for severely handicapped learners* (pp. 157–192). Baltimore, Md.: Paul H. Brookes.

Haring, N., Liberty, K., & White, O. (1981). *An investigation of phases of learning and facilitating instructional events for the severely/profoundly handicapped.* Final project report. Seattle, Wash. University of Washington.

Holvoet, J., Guess, D., Mulligan, M., & Brown, F. (1980). The Individualized Curriculum Sequencing Model (II): A teaching strategy for severly handicapped students. *The Journal of the Association for the Severely Handicapped, 5,* 337–35.

Holvoet, J., O'Neil, C., Chazdon, L., Carr, D., & Warner, J. (1983). Hey, do we really have to take data? *Journal of the Association for the Severely Handicapped, 8,* 56–70.

Iwata, B. A., Dorsey, M. F., Slifer, K. J., Bauman, K. E., & Richman, G. S. (1982). Toward a functional analysis of self-injury. *Analysis and Intervention in Developmental Disabilities, 3,* 3–20.

Liberty, K. A. (1972). *Data decision rules.* Unpublished manuscript. Eugene, Oreg.: University of Oregon, Regional Resource Center.

Powers, M. D., & Handleman, J. S. (1984). *Behavioral assessment of severe developmental disabilities.* Rockville, Md.: Aspen.

Renzaglia, A., Aveno, A., & Hutchins, M. (1984). *Curriculum development procedures for learners with severe handicaps.* Charlottesville, Va.: University of Virginia, Department of Special Education.

Rhodes, L. E., & Valenta, L. (1985). Industry based supported employment: An enclave approach. *The Journal of the Association for Persons with Severe Handicaps, 10,* 12–20.

Rusch, F. R., Schutz, R. P., & Agran, M. (1982). Validating entry-level survival skills for several occupations: Implications for curriculum development. *The Journal of the Association for the Severely Handicapped, 8,* 32–41.

Sailor, W., & Guess, D. (1983). *Severely handicapped students: An instructional design* (pp. 137–145). Boston: Houghton Mifflin.

Skinner, B. F. (1969). *Contingencies of reinforcement: A theoretical analysis.* Englewood Cliffs, N.J.: Prentice-Hall.

Snell, M. E. (1987). Systematic instruction of people with severe handicaps (3d ed.). Columbus, Ohio: Charles E. Merrill.

Snell, M. E., & Browder, D. M. (1986). Community-referenced instruction: Research and issues. *The Journal of the Association for Persons with Severe Handicaps, 11,* 1–11.

Snell, M. E., & Grigg, N. C. (1987). Instructional assessment. In M. E. Snell (Ed.), *Systematic instruction of people with severe handicaps* (3d ed.). Columbus, Ohio: Charles E. Merrill.

Somerton, E., & Turner, L. (1975). *Pennsylvania training model.* Harrisburg, Pa.: Pennsylvania Department of Education.

Spears, D. L., Rusch, F. R., York, R., & Lilly, M. S. (1981). Training independent arrival behaviors to a severely mentally retarded child. *Journal of the Association for the Severely Handicapped, 6,* 40–45.

Tawney, J. W., & Gast, D. L. (1984). *Single subject research in special education.* Columbus, Ohio: Charles E. Merrill.

Tucker, J. A. (1985). Curriculum-based assessment: An introduction. *Exceptional Children, 52,* 199–204.

Vort Corporation. (1973). *Behavioral characteristics progression.* Palo Alto, Calif.: Vort Corporation.

Wampold, B. E., & Furlong, N. J. (1981). The heuristics of visual inference. *Behavioral Assessment, 3,* 79–82.

Wehman, P., & Krugel, J. (1985). A supported work approach to competitive employment of individuals with moderate and severe handicaps. *The Journal of the Association for Persons with Severe Handicaps, 10,* 3–11.

Wehman, P., Renzagila, A., & Bates, P. (1985). *Functional living skills for moderately and severely handicapped learners.* Baltimore, Md.: Paul H. Brookes.

White, O. R. (1972). *A manual for the calculation and use of the median slope—A technique of progress estimation and prediction in single case.* Eugene, Oreg.: University of Oregon Regional Resource Center.

White, O. R. (1980). Adaptive performance objectives: Form versus function. In W. Sailor, B. Wilcox, & L. Brown (Eds.), *Methods of instruction for severely handicapped students.* Baltimore, Md.: Paul H. Brookes.

Wilcox, B., & Bellamy, T. (1982). Design of high school programs for severely handicapped students. Baltimore, Md.: Paul H. Brookes.

Wolfensberger, W. (1972). *The principle of normalization in human services.* Toronto: National Institute of Mental Retardation.

Appendix: Adaptive Behavior Scales

Balthazar Scales of Adaptive Behavior

Earl E. Balthazar 1976
Consulting Psychologist Press, Inc.
577 College Avenue
Palo Alto, California 94306

AAMD Adaptive Behavior Scale

Nadine Lambert, Myra Windmiller,
Deborah Tharinger, Linda Cole 1981

Publishers Test Service
CTB/McGraw-Hill
Del Monte Research Park
Monterey, California 93940

The Callier-Azusa Scale

Robert Stillman (Editor) 1978
The University of Texas at Dallas
Callier Center for Communication
  Disorders
1966 Inwood Road
Dallas, Texas 75235

Camelot Behavioral Checklist

Ray W. Foster 1974
Camelot Behavioral Systems
P.O. Box 3447
Lawrence, Kansas 66044

*Comprehensive Test of Adaptive Behavior
and NABC*

Gary L. Adams 1984
Charles E. Merrill
Columbus, Ohio 43216

The Pyramid Scales

John D. Cove 1984
Pro-Ed
5341 Industrial Oaks Blvd.
Austin, Texas 78735

*Scales of Independent Behavior
Woodcock-Johnson Psychoeducational
  Battery: Part Four*

Robert H. Bruiminks, Richard W. Woodcock, Richard F. Weatherman, & Brad-
  ley K. Hill 1984
Developmental Learning Materials
Allen, Texas 75002

Vineland-Adaptive Behavior Scales

Sara S. Sparrow, David A. Balls, & Do-
  menic V. Cicchetti 1985
American Guidance Service
Circle Pines, Minnesota 55014-1796

CHAPTER 5

Physiological and Activity Measures with Educational Problems

DUDLEY DAVID BLAKE
State University of New York at Albany

FRANK ANDRASIK
University of West Florida

INTRODUCTION

Physiological measures offer a viable yet neglected approach for the assessment of educational problems. Physiological measures can play a part in assessing gross or specific learning dysfunction and so may be valuable in curriculum planning and in placement decisions. Alternatively, these measures can be used to identify and ameliorate physical concomitants of educational problems, as can be seen in biofeedback and activity feedback applications. However, for the purposes of both assessment and treatment, physiological measures have typically been overlooked or underutilized in educational settings.

The notion of measuring physiological parameters with children has a relatively long history, one that, in fact, can be traced to the early days of the field of psychology. Over a half century ago, Duffy (1930) used handgrip strength as an overall index of tension in nursery school children. Tension was calculated by averaging gross recordings of each child's free handgrip pressure on a rubber tension bulb measured under neutral, noxious, and pleasant stimulus conditions. Tension was found to be highly correlated with parental ratings of childrens' excitability, and the most excitable children were found to tense their fists to the greatest extent under noxious stimulation (provided by randomly sounding a loud Klaxon horn).

To substantiate these findings further, Duffy conducted a second study with a group of eighteen nursery school children using visual discrimination and hand-tapping exercises (Duffy, 1932). Again, tension levels corresponded with individual differences in "emotional tendencies." Children who were rated as being excitable by their parents and judged as poorly adjusted to nursery school showed the greatest amount of tension. Thus, results from this simple "physiological assessment" paralleled differences noted by parents and others. Duffy also found that handgrip pressure varied with increasing task demand, which points to the potential of this simple physiological measure as a barometer for task difficulty.

Other early researchers showed similar interest in the physiological assessment of children. For example, Jost (1941) compared galvanic skin responses, blood pressure, electroencephalograms, and other physiological indexes of "emotionally stable" and "emotionally unstable" children. The group of unstable children was comprised of individuals with diagnoses of schizophrenia, neuroses, and behavior problems, whereas the stable group was comprised of children from a local elementary school. Results of the study showed marked differences between the groups on ten of fifty-two indexes. The unstable group showed a more labile physiology during rest periods, a greater physiological reaction pattern to laboratory stressors, and a slower return to prestressor levels. Thus, at a physiological level, Jost found that the concept of "emotional stability" appears to distinguish accurately between normal and problem children. Despite the absence of certain important design features (i.e., subjects were not matched for age or other potential contaminating variables), this early study represents an impressive attempt to examine physiological differences between child populations.

In more recent times, physiological measures have gained in popularity, partly as a result of their use in behavioral assessment and behavioral medicine (Blanchard, 1981; Haynes, 1978; Ray & Raczynski, 1981), and partly from the critical role played by these measures in biofeedback applications with adults (see various chapters in Hatch, Fisher, & Rugh, 1987). As an inevitable result of this increased popularity, the use of physiological measures has generalized to other populations; once again, their utility with children is being recognized (Andrasik & Attanasio, 1985; Cobb & Evans, 1981; Finley, 1983; Gresham & Evans, 1979; Linkenhoker, 1983; Prout, 1977; Walden & Thompson, 1981). Relatedly, this increased popularity has been paralleled by growing numbers of reports of physical activity measures (Eaton, 1983; Nishikido, Kashiwazaki, & Suzuki, 1982; Schulman, Stevens, Suran, Kupst, & Naughton, 1978; Williamson, Calpin, DiLorenzo, Garris, & Petti, 1981), which are not "physiological" measures per se, but are much in the same spirit of earlier investigations (e.g., Duffy, 1930, 1932).

Physiological and activity measurements can play an important role in optimizing a student's educational adjustment and achievement. First, this form of measurement may help to identify less obvious educational problems, such as inefficient attention, reading, or writing skills, or excessive physiological arousal and physical activity during classroom tasks. Once identified, these problems can be handled in many ways although subject to the availability of resources at the school. The most immediate and less intensive way to manage an identified problem is to make adjustments in the student's curriculum. A less demanding, more individualized educational plan may go far to place the student on the right track. Alternatively, a classroom environment with more or less structure and stimulation may be indicated. Another option might be to change the physiological component of the identified problem. For instance, in the case of excessive muscle activity, relaxation or EMG feedback may successfully reduce the elevated tension levels. In some cases, however, this may not get at the "real" problem; for example, in the case in which a particular curriculum is well beyond the student's current ability, the "treatment" may be simply postponing an eventual failure experience. This possibility points to the value of maintaining a multifaceted or holistic approach in educational assessment. Finally, physiological and activity data may lend support for placing a student in a classroom environment where more individualized resources are available.

Physiological and activity measurements can be conducted in a variety of ways, which vary in level of technical sophistication. They can be done informally through observation and direct monitoring of physical activity or various physiological indexes (e.g., checking a student's pulse or respiration), or with more formal and mechanical means (e.g., measuring the level of one's muscle tension using electromyography). Formal physiological measures generally involve three components: (1) response-specific measurement sensors (electrodes) and couplers, with many measures, for example, EEG, EMG, plethysmography, requiring a conductive medium in the form of electrode gel or cream, (2) preamplifier and amplifier units for enhancing the magnitude of the measured activity while at the same time filtering out extraneous artifact, and (3) a polygraph strip chart, or other instrumentation for recording or displaying the product of the measurement. Recent advances in physiological measurement instrumentation have resulted in a viable technology for classroom use. For example, modern measurement apparatuses usually include a microcomputer and specially designed data acquisition devices, as shown in Figure 5-1. This measurement equipment has the added advantage of being readily modifiable so that physiological data can be fed back to the student, in an attempt to remediate classroom problems or their physiological concomitants (to be discussed later in this chapter). Activity measures, however, have not evolved to such a high degree of technical sophistication. These measures typically involve some form of mechanical balance or circuitry that is activated when distinct motions are made by the person in contact with the device.

The purpose of this chapter is to acquaint the reader with several formal measurement approaches as they can be applied to educational problems. In later sections, each application will be detailed as space permits; for more information on physiological measures, the reader is advised to review the texts (Greenfield & Sternbach, 1972; Hassett, 1978; Stern, Ray, & Davis, 1980) and chapters (Kallman & Feuerstein, 1977; Ray & Raczynski, 1981) on physiological assessment. Before

FIGURE 5-1 Modern Physiological Measurement Instrumentation with Microcomputer and Data Acquisition Unit

describing the educational applications of physiological and activity measurement, one general issue merits discussion. This issue involves the practical interrelationship between these measurement strategies and treatment interventions, a point that distinguishes physiological and activity measures from most other forms of assessment.

Assessment and Treatment Interrelationship

More than with any other measurement approach, physiological and activity measures have played a prominent role in *treating* the variable they were developed to measure. These applications primarily consist of feeding measurement data, with instructions and incentives to change, back to the person who is being assessed. From this basic framework, the field of *biofeedback* has evolved. This distinction from other approaches becomes clear if one imagines using more traditional measures in the same manner: for example, informing the testee about his or her performance on the Rorschach or WISC-R so that alterations in the desired direction can be achieved. Clearly such a notion is inconsistent with how traditional tests were designed. These tests are thought to "get at" some dispositional characteristic, underlying dynamic, or perceptual or cognitive style. Efforts to change seldom include informing the individual about what the assessment specifically revealed. In contrast, physiological and activity assessments are integrally linked to treatment, and when one employs these measures, a treatment approach is implied in the process.

As much as possible, treatment aspects are not emphasized in this chapter. However, due to the close link between assessment and treatment in physiological and activity measurement, some overlap is unavoidable. Further, this chapter is written with the belief that, at a practical level, keeping the two aspects separate is not as important as is providing the educator with a broader context by which to understand more fully the utility of these measures.

This chapter summarizes the uses of physiological and physical activity measures with children in educational settings. Reliability and validity issues will be highlighted and discussed throughout. In most cases these applications are directly relevant to the educational setting (e.g., monitoring the rates of in-seat behavior of overactive students), while in others cases the relationship may not be so clear (e.g., monitoring peripheral skin temperature with learning disabled children). However, the utility of each application should become clear as the chapter progresses. The applications to be described in greatest detail include *electromyographic, activity, electroencephalographic,* and *skin temperature* measures.

ELECTROMYOGRAPHIC (EMG) MEASURES

Electromyography (EMG) is perhaps the most widely used physiological measure employed with classroom-related problems. This approach involves the use of surface electrodes or sensors to detect electrical discharges that result from muscle activity (constriction). These bioelectric potentials are typically measured in microvolt units, and generally range between 0 to 100 microvolts in children. Figure 5-2 shows a battery-operated portable device for measuring muscle activity.

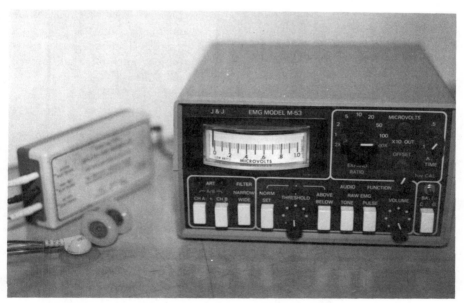

FIGURE 5-2 Portable Electromyographic (EMG) Measurement Instrument

Since a child's muscle tension can vary across tasks and task demands, EMG equipment may need to be recalibrated at various times in order to measure fully the range of muscle activity expected, for example, between 0 and 40 microvolts. In conducting EMG assessments, a balance must be reached between measurement precision and generality. The more narrow the range measured the less generality across contexts and children and, conversely, the broader the range the less precise are the measurements.

For treatment purposes, the amplified EMG signals are used as feedback to aid the individual in gaining control over muscle activity. This feedback is usually provided in the form of lights, tones, or digital readouts (Attanasio, Andrasik, Burke, Blake, Kabela, & McCarran, 1985; Linkenhoker, 1983). EMG measurement can play a prominent role in cases where elevated muscle activity is associated with identified classroom problems. For illustration, the difficulty a student encounters while learning to write may be coincident with and aggravated by excessive neck and forearm tension. Once identified, excess or extraneous muscle tension can be reduced through EMG feedback or relaxation training.

Unfortunately, many reported applications of EMG measurement have not been conducted with such a data-based approach. That is, many of the EMG uses have involved employing these measures exclusively for treatment and not for assessment. Hyperactive children, stutterers, child headache sufferers, and so on, apparently have received EMG feedback training solely because of the intuitive logic of the tactic. Some of these children have evidenced improvement with their respective problems, while others have not. To advance understanding of muscle tension involvement in educational problems, normative data and idiographic information must be obtained. In addition to this problem, EMG measures share with all other forms of psychophysiological assessment psychometric (reliability and validity) issues that are distinct from other measures. Therefore, these issues will be detailed here so that the educator can be aware of potential pitfalls as well as the strengths of EMG and other physiological measures.

Psychometric Issues

Other chapters in this volume have admirably outlined and described validity and reliability work relevant to the respective measurement approach discussed. With physiological measures, mechanical apparatuses are typically employed and the complexity these "psychometric" issues changes accordingly; in fact, reliability and validity are often implicitly assigned a lesser status or neglected altogether. Reliability and validity are nevertheless important issues in physiological measurement. Many variables can affect the reliability of physiological recordings. Kallman and Feuerstein (1977) delineate two broad classes of these variables: artifacts and psychobiologically relevant stimuli. The former include factors such as movement, electrode placement, and electrical interference. The latter variables refer to factors that may predispose an organism to a particular physiological response pattern.

Any shifts that occur between subject and physiological sensor are liable to introduce artifact into the recordings. As a result, it is often best to conduct recordings while the subject is relatively inactive. This presents a potential drawback in cases where the educator finds it especially important to measure physiological phenomena in situ. As an alternative, the educator can note and consider concomitant movements when interpreting the measurement record.

Failure to use a conductive gel or paste, or using conductive mediums that are excessively dry, moist, or of unsuitable quality (i.e., not specifically designed for use with electrode placements) with some measures may also serve to maximize artifact. Here is a case where one should attend to the details of the measurement, as they may have a substantial effect on the clarity and general usefulness of the measurement data. Appropriate conductive mediums usually are available from the distributors of the physiological recording equipment.

Nonsystematic and careless electrode placement will result in markedly different readings between measurements or lead to avoidable artifacts within a measurement occasion. For example, some plethysmography devices for assessing blood volume pulse require that the electrode be placed directly over a targeted artery; failure to do so may result in a poor signal and may render the recording useless. Several publications detail standardized electrode placements (Basmajian & Blumenstein, 1980; Jasper, 1958) and it behooves the researcher, clinician, and educator alike to refer to these sources before conducting physiological measurements.

Electrical interference from power surges, outages, and other anomalies present another potential source of artifact and may result in damage to expensive and sensitive equipment. If used, it is generally good practice to shield one's hardware electrically from the AC power source (i.e., 120-volt wall outlet); many units have factory-installed isolators or surge protectors. Otherwise, it may be good insurance to purchase them separately. If measurements are conducted near flourescent light fixtures or other electrical equipment, artifact again may be introduced, particularly with those measurements that involve bioelectric currents (EEG, EKG, EMG). Since even small, stray electrical activity can produce artifact, steps should be taken to minimize these other sources of interference. If the physiological equipment operates from an AC power source, other potential problems are created. First, the subject being assessed runs some risk of shock unless shielded from the instrumentation. This can be done physically with walls or partitions, but is usually done by using preamplifier isolation devices that regulate the amount of voltage permitted at the electrode level.

As Kallman and Feuerstein (1977) note, psychobiologically relevant stimuli can also affect physiological recordings. In brief, subjects evidence idiosyncratic physiological arousal patterns when exposed to novel stimuli, but with time, they habituate and return to preexposure physiological levels. Generally, greater arousal is seen with certain stimuli, typically those that are psychobiologically relevant or have survival value to the subject (e.g., exposure to menacing-looking snakes or vermin). To overcome measurement problems due to this phenomenon, some investigators suggest conducting recordings over repeated sessions (Kallman, 1975, as cited in Kallman & Feuerstein, 1977). Others recommend using a sustained "adaptation" period at the start of each assessment (Andrasik, Blanchard, Arena, Saunders, & Barron, 1982; Lichstein, Sallis, Hill, & Young, 1981; Taub & School, 1978). In classroom settings it is sufficient to warn that habituation effects occur so that the educator will not confuse these phenomena with diagnostic information or with the changes anticipated from planned change efforts.

Organismic variables have also been found to affect physiological recordings. Gender (Buck, Miller, & Caul, 1974; Cohen, Kircher, Emmerson, & Dustman, 1985; Friedman, Brown, Vaughan, Cornblatt, & Erlenmeyer-Kimling, 1984) and age (Arena, Blanchard, Andrasik, & Myers, 1983; Bryan, 1982; Cohen, *et al.*, 1985; Ginter, Hollandsworth, & Intrieri, 1986) reliably affect these measurements and must be considered when relying on physiological measures. For example, comparing a group of predominately female children with one that is predominately male may lead to inaccurate conclusions based on physiological differences due to gender rather than to the grouping factor of concern. Similarly, students thought to show gains based on comparisons between measurements conducted at the beginning and end of a school year may simply be evidencing maturational change. Thus, it is important to consider both age and gender of the student when conducting and interpreting physiological recordings.

Validity is another important factor in physiological measurement. As with other forms of assessment, validity depends on the reliability of the measure. Once confidence in the reliability of the measurement is achieved, validity issues can be assessed from several standpoints. First, *construct validity* can be assessed; this concept pertains to the certainty with which one uses and interprets the measure, that is, do physiological indexes measure the constructs for which they are intended? In answer, it is essential to ascertain the constructs one intends to measure. On one hand, physiological measures can be considered to be reflections of some physiological process, such as heart rate, muscle tension, and so on (for an excellent discussion on this point, see Kallman & Feuerstein, 1977). On the other hand, it is doubtful whether these measures can provide direct access to more general and encompassing abstractions, such as emotions, anxiety, or cognitive processes. Thus, construct validity can be assessed only after the construct to be measured is determined and made operational, criteria that are not always met in psychophysiological assessment.

The question of validity can also be addressed by comparing measurement results with a criterion believed to represent the construct under study. For example, heart rate as an index for anxiety may be given *criterion validity* if it closely parallels an individual's subjective distress, for example, ongoing Subjective Units of Discomfort (SUDS) ratings. Similarly, *treatment validity* is approximated by noting expected changes resulting from a given successful treatment. For example, hand temperature measures as an index of vascular instability or sympathetic arousal and headache pathophysiology are supported when an individual shows reduced headaches coincident with gained control over his or her peripheral skin temperature.

While electromyography can measure most muscle activity, the region that is most commonly examined is the forehead, or frontal region, an area selected primarily because it is thought to be an indicant of general arousal (Stoyva & Budzynski, 1975). (However, whether it represents a valid measure of overall arousal remains equivocal; Thompson, Haber, & Tearnan, 1981.) A second, but less commonly used area is the forearm, typically with flexor and less so with extensor muscles, both of which are critical for writing and other academic tasks. Finally, laryngeal and other neck muscles have been examined because of their importance in subvocal speech and in stuttering.

Frontal EMG Measurement

As shown in Figure 5-3, frontal EMG is typically measured with three surface electrodes: two "active" electrodes placed directly above each of the child's eyebrows, and the "ground" electrode placed in between. Excessive levels of forehead tension have been associated with children who are hyperactive (Braud, 1978; Hughes, Henry, & Hughes, 1980) and learning disabled (Carter & Russell, 1979). Feeding this information back to the children has been shown to help in the remediation of these difficulties.

Two factors appear to play a significant role in the success of EMG feedback. First, both tonic (resting) and phasic (reactive) muscle relaxation are promoted; relaxation is incompatible with muscle activity so the child is less physiologically prepared to exhibit hyperactive behavior. Second, EMG feedback may encourage self-awareness and self-regulation. Children who have gained a heightened sensitivity to and control over their physiology and overt behavior are more apt to display self-regulatory behavior. Perhaps the most substantive work with EMG measures in the classroom has been in treatment research with hyperactive children. In these cases the value of EMG met a twofold purpose of assessment and treatment.

Hyperactivity

Although muscle tension does not appear to be a formally recognized associated feature of hyperactivity,[1] relaxation-based frontal EMG feedback treatment has been found successful in reducing hyperactive behavior (Anchor & Johnson, 1977). Eleven published studies in which EMG feedback was employed with hyperactive children are summarized in Table 5-1.

All of the studies report positive results with EMG feedback treatment of hyperactivity. Since our focus is not on treatment, the articles in Table 5-1 are summarized with attention paid to the use of EMG in assessment. Accordingly, the studies are described with regard to whether: (1) nonhyperactive controls were studied, to determine if aberrant physiology could be implicated in the experimental children's hyperactive behavior; and (2) physiological indexes were employed as dependent variables to verify that success was associated with changes in EMG-measured muscle tension. Before describing this summary information, several factors shown in the other columns of Table 5-1 deserve mention.

As is apparent, the group of studies represents a number of good, large *n* studies, particularly those conducted by Omizo and colleagues. This type of research enhances statistical power, but, as with much group research, a degree of idiographic information is lost (Barlow, Hayes, & Nelson, 1983). Typically, subjects were described in a single paragraph. Because of the failure to provide specific details, it is unclear which children will benefit from the treatment and which will

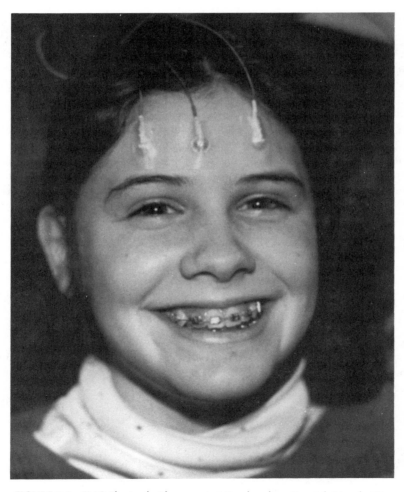

FIGURE 5-3   EMG Electrode Placement at Forehead, or *Frontal*, Muscle Site

not. In addition, group studies lack the descriptive flavor that makes them amenable to use by psychological practitioners and educational specialists.

The child populations studied have been largely comprised of males, except for studies by Braud (1978), Hampstead (1979) and Hughes, Henry, and Hughes (1980). The latter two studies do not involve a large n and hence do not benefit from the accompanying statistical power and ability to identify gender as a source of variance. While hyperactive children in general are male (American Psychiatric Association, 1987; Sandoval, 1977), differential results of the physiological measurements and in treatment effects may be present which necessitate taking this potential confound into account. Failure to do so also limits the generalizability of the findings.

Many of the studies included control groups at one level or another. However, in only one case (Braud, 1978) was a *nonhyperactive* control group employed. This is particularly critical in determining to what extent muscle tension contributes to hyperactive behavior. Hyperactive students who benefit from EMG feedback presumably will evidence elevated muscle tension to a greater degree than nonhyperactive students. Braud found his sample of hyperactive children to possess significantly higher frontal EMG levels than their nonhyperactive counterparts ($p < .002$; from their text, approximate M = 150 microvolts versus 70 microvolts). Furthermore, the hyperactive children's muscle tension levels decreased to and then went below that of the controls following the treatment. Muscle tension reductions covaried with decreases in hyperactivity, distractibility, irritability, explosiveness, aggressivity, impulsivity, and emotionality. However, these findings must be qualified by noting that the ratio of males to females between hyperactive and nonhyperactive samples was substantially disproportionate (12:3 versus 6:9, respectively), thus a gender confound may be present.

One would like to believe that the students who experience the greatest benefit from these treatments are those who evidence the highest levels of EMG-measured forehead tension prior to intervention. Such a straightforward result would support the use of EMG measurement as a particularly valuable option for classroom application. Students identified as hyperactive or having problems in the classroom could be routinely assessed for excessive muscle tension. Rather than exercising disciplinary action, engaging in efforts to have the child placed in a more intensive classroom setting, or referring the student for medication treatment, he or she might benefit from the treatment suggested from the measurement (i.e., EMG feedback and relaxation training). Furthermore, from the standpoint of the locus of control, the student will potentially play an active role in ameliorating his or her own educational problems rather than relying on an external agent.

Most but not all of the studies in Table 5-1 used frontal EMG as the dependent variable (exceptions are Denkowski & Denkowski [1984], Omizo [1980a], and Omizo & Michael [1982]). These data are a must in this type of work to examine treatment validity and for conducting process analyses. Furthermore, it is imperative to include EMG data to demonstrate how reduced muscle tension covaries with problem remediation. Eight of eleven studies reviewed showed

TABLE 5-1 Published Studies in Which EMG Feedback Was Employed in the Treatment of Hyperactive Children

Study	Subject group	n	Nonhyper Controls used	Dependent Measures	Dependent Variable Changes
Braud (1978)	Hyperactive children and controls (boys and girls)	15 15	yes	(1) frontal EMG activity (2) finger and forehead skin temperatures (3) parent behavioral ratings (4) Psychological tests (Bender-Gestalt, ITPA, WISC subtests)	Hyperactive Ss had greater EMG; reduced EMG and behavioral rating improvement and psychological test gains following treatment
Braud, Lupin, & Braud (1975)	Hyperactive boy	1	no	(1) frontal EMG activity (2) muscle activity ratings (3) emotionality rating (4) Psychological tests (5) observations by teachers, parents, investigators	Reduced EMG tension; behavioral and emotional rating improvements and psychological test gains following treatment
Denkowski & Denkowski (1984)	Hyperactive 3d, 4th, & 5th graders (gender not specified)	45	no	(1) Nowicki-Strickland Locus of Control (LOC) Scale (2) Connor's Teacher ratings (3) Gates-MacGinities Reading Tests	Increased internal LOC in relaxation groups; improved behavior and academic gains following treatment
Dunn & Howell (1982)	Hyperactive boys	10	no	(1) frontal EMG activity (2) Bender-Gestalt subscale (3) WISC-R subscales (4) Parent ratings (5) Behavioral observations	Reduced EMG tension; parent rating and behavioral improvements; psychological test gains following treatment

Study	Population	N	Control	Measures	Results
Hampstead (1979)	Hyperactive boys (5) and girl (1)	6 6	yes (only for psychological testing)	(1) frontal EMG activity (2) parent and teacher behavior ratings (Hyperkinesis index)	Reduced EMG tension; behavioral rating improvements following treatment
Hughes, Henry, & Hughes (1980)	Hyperactive boy (1) and girls (2)	3	no (selves as control)	(1) frontal EMG activity (2) time on task (math) (3) actometer readings (4) home behavior ratings	Reduced EMG tension; time on task gains and actometer reading decreases and improved home ratings following teatment
Omizo (1980a)	Hyperactive adolescent boys	56	no	(1) Nowicki-Strickland Locus of Control (LOC) Scale (2) Dimension of Self-Concept Scale (DOSC)	Shift to internal LOC and gains on DOSC scale following treatment
Omizo (1980b)	Hyperactive boys	52	no	(1) frontal EMG activity (2) DOSC	Reduced EMG tension; gains on 3 DOSC scales following treatment
Omizo & Williams (1981)	Hyperactive boys	3	no	Parent and teacher report of child cooperative and disruptive behavior	Reduced EMG tension; improved behavioral reports following treatment
Omizo & Williams (1982)	Hyperactive boys	32	no	(1) frontal EMG activity (2) Matching Familiar Figures Test (errors and latency) (3) Nowicki-Strickland LOC scale	Reduced EMG tension; decrease in MFFT errors and increased latency following treatment
Rivera & Omizo (1980)	Hyperactive boys	36	no	(1) frontal EMG activity (2) MFFT (errors and latency)	Reduced EMG tension; decrease in MFFT errors and increased latency following teatment

frontal EMG reductions that paralleled positive changes in behavior and academic performance. These data are particularly important in justifying the use of EMG measurement with this common educational problem; it also suggests that elevated muscle tension is a significant factor to assess when looking at the hyperactive student. Data of this type point to tension as a general source of learning-related problems. Information in this regard is reviewed next.

Reading and Writing

Children who are experiencing academic difficulties may also be frustrated, anxious, and unhappy. These students may have accompanying muscle tension and other physiological activity that impairs their ability to attend to or complete basic academic tasks such as reading and writing. Alternatively, existing learning problems may be compounded by promoting errors of repetition, substitution, hesitation, and omission. In any case, the identification of aberrant physiological arousal may be a key in addressing the critical needs of certain students.

In an uncontrolled treatment study, Hughes, Jackson, Dubois, and Erwin (1979) identified four females and five males from a fourth-grade regular classroom as poor writers. These children then participated in nine sessions in which they received frontal EMG feedback, first while lying down and then while sitting in a school chair. At posttest the children were found to have significantly lower forehead tension, a reduction that was accompanied by significant improvements in four of five writing characteristics: uniformity of letters, formation of letters, spacing, and general excellence. Unfortunately, since no control group was used, it is not known whether the children's poor writing was directly associated with above-normal levels of forehead tension. The fact that EMG levels decreased as the children's writing improved, however, suggests that this may be the case. Adding to this suggestion is a study by Carter and Synolds (1974) using relaxation training with hyperactive children. In this study, the writing samples of thirty-two boys in the experimental group were compared with those of a nonhyperactive age-matched control group. The controls were found to have better handwriting on all six categories rated. Following relaxation training, the handwriting of the boys in the experimental group improved in every category, suggesting that excessive muscle tension indeed was functionally related to poor handwriting. These findings are largely suggestive and controlled study is required to elucidate more fully the utility of forehead EMG measures on handwriting assessment and instruction.

Omizo and Williams (1982) conducted an investigation of frontal EMG feedback with thirty-two children classified as learning disabled. Half of the children received three biofeedback-assisted relaxation training sessions while the remaining subjects attended simultaneous sessions in which they listened to audiotapes of a neutral story. As training progressed, the experimental subjects learned increasingly to reduce their muscle tension, while no reductions were seen with the control children. Of importance here is the finding that reduced muscle tension in the experimental group was associated with posttest improvements in attention to task and impulsivity, both of which are critical correlates of academic success. This finding suggests that EMG physiological measures and biofeedback may be an asset to the educational curricula of learning disabled children.

Unfortunately, since Omizo and Williams did not study a control group of nonlearning disabled children, it is left unclear whether the children were selected for treatment on the basis of their high muscle tension levels or if EMG feedback was selected for these children because it seemed logical and appropriate. One implication is that normal children may also show significant benefits from biofeedback but are not targeted because they fail to show an obvious need. To ascertain which children will optimally benefit from EMG biofeedback and why, further study is needed.

Other Learning-Related Problems

Asthma is one psychosomatic problem that may interfere with a student's benefiting from classroom instruction. Asthma has been defined as an intermittent, variable, and reversible obstruction of the airway (Creer, 1982). While its exact etiology is unknown, this clinical phenomenon may result from an interplay between psychological and physiological factors. Children who experience asthma may derive substantial benefit from receiving EMG frontal biofeedback (e.g., Davis, Saunders, Creer, & Chai, 1973; Kotses, Glaus, Bricel, Edwards, & Crawford, 1978; Kotses, Glaus, Crawford, Edwards, & Scherr, 1976). From this work, suggestive evidence has been reported linking excessive frontal muscle tension to pulmonary function. As an assessment strategy, EMG measures appear to be of use in isolating excessive muscle tension in response to stressors as a source of bronchial blockage; unfortunately, the extent to which the study of excessive muscle tension has been a focus with child asthmatics does not lend itself to an encompassing review. Interested readers are referred to reviews by Andrasik and Attanasio (1985) and Kotses and Glaus (1981).

EMG feedback has also been employed with children who suffer recurrent headache. Most of these applications occur in clinical settings, and as such do not immediately apply to the classroom. However, headaches and other pain disorders clearly have a negative impact on children's academic success. For instance, Bille (1962) found that children who experience chronic headache miss significantly more days from school than their nonheadache counterparts. Further, Egermark-Eriksson (1982) found that nearly 70% of a sample of 400 children who missed four or more days of school suffered from recurrent headache. These findings point to a serious academic cost to children, in terms of the educational achievements they might otherwise attain.

One common type of headache, muscle contraction, is thought to be a consequence of the sustained contraction of muscles containing or adjacent to pain receptors. As a result of the muscle contraction, ischemia sets in and pain is further enhanced (Haynes, 1980).[2] Identifying excessive muscle tension in students with recurrent headache may lead to appropriate ameliorative efforts (e.g., relaxation or biofeedback treatments, exposing student to less demanding curricula, etc.).

Frontal EMG measures have been used in treating children who experience both migraine and muscle contraction headache. For example, Diamond and Franklin (1975) successfully treated thirty-two child migraineurs using EMG frontal biofeedback. Twenty-six of these children evidenced notable decreases in frequency and severity of headache, as indicated from anecdotal data. More recently, Andrasik, Blanchard, Edlund, and Attanasio (1983) used frontal EMG biofeedback in the treatment of an eleven-year-old female suffering from muscle contraction headaches. After twelve biofeedback sessions after which she demonstrated "moderate" success in self-regulating frontalis muscle tension, the subject showed a more than 75% reduction in headache frequency, intensity, and duration. This study is particularly important because it suggests a role for decreased EMG activity in relief of headache symptoms. Treatments such as these may also be useful if provided in the context of the classroom or other school settings. Support for the viability of school-based interventions with students who experience chronic headache can be seen in the successful relaxation treatment program reported by Larsson and Melin (1986).

Since the intent of this chapter is not to extol the use of physiological measures in *treating* education-related problems, other work in child headache will not be reviewed. Readers interested in learning about biofeedback treatments with child headache sufferers are referred to Andrasik, Blake, and McCarran (1986), Hoelscher and Lichstein (1983), and McGrath (1983).

Forearm EMG Measurement

Other investigators have reported promising findings in using forearm EMG measures in the assessment and treatment of both reading and writing problems (Carter & Russell, 1979, 1980). Figure 5-4 shows an electrode placement at the forearm site, on the skin surface above the extensor muscle. Active electrodes are placed several centimeters apart (depending on the degree of specificity wanted in the measurement). The ground electrode (dark) is typically placed directly either between the two active ones or off to the side. Flexor muscle placements are similarly aligned, but are affixed to the inside of the forearm.

Carter and Russell (1979) studied the forearm flexor EMG levels in a group of eleven boys with reading disabilities. The children showed progressively higher levels of tension when asked to read three paragraphs of increasing difficulty. In addition, EMG levels during baseline and reading were markedly lower for three boys who had previously undergone biofeedback training. These boys had made noteworthy gains in reading, spelling, and handwriting quality following biofeedback. Therefore, these findings suggest that elevated forearm muscle tension may play a significant role in reading problems and, upon identification of these aberrant levels, their reduction through EMG feedback or relaxation procedures may pave the way to a more successful educational experience.

More recently, Carter and Russell (1980) provided forearm EMG biofeedback with handwriting training to four boys who were learning disabled. Each boy

FIGURE 5-4 EMG Electrode Placement at Forearm *Extensor* Muscle Site

participated in weekly sessions in which he was instructed to relax his arm during ten minutes of visual EMG biofeedback followed by fifty minutes of handwriting practice. All boys showed impressive reductions in resting forearm EMG level (pretest M = 8.4 microvolts and posttest M = 3.1 microvolts, a decrease of 63%), which was accompanied by consistent gains in reading, spelling, and arithmetic. These striking results are further corroborated by the comments from the boys' mothers and teachers, that they showed

> . . . greater self-control, less impulsivity and distractibility, fewer careless errors, and a greater degree of conscientiousness in school work. One mother proudly reported that her son had spontaneously begun to write short stories. She further reported that this was unheard of only two months earlier; it was a real chore to get him to write anything. Another child made such dramatic change in school behavior that his teacher called and asked the investigator how he was effecting such dramatic change. (p. 485)

Findings such as these are quite impressive and highlight the need for more rigorous, controlled research in the area. For example, while significant reductions in forearm EMG occurred as a result of treatment, it is not known whether these children showed nonnormative EMG levels in the first place. While logic dictates that high baseline EMG values will indicate potential benefit from biofeedback training, definitive conclusions of the subject await further empirical study. In the meantime, educators have nothing to lose and everything to gain by including forearm EMG measurement in their assessments of educational problems.

Vocal (Laryngeal) EMG Measurement

Reading and Writing

Reading skills are learned gradually and are continually improved upon as a child proceeds through his or her school years. A milestone believed to occur in the development of efficient reading skills is the transition from overt and vocalized to covert and silent reading. Between these two developmental end points, some individuals may rely on lip movement and subvocal speech (primarily muscle activity in the larynx region). However, in the long run these speech patterns reflect inefficient reading, and subvocal speech in particular has been measured by vocal muscle activity and found to occur to an inordinate degree with poor readers (Esfeldt, 1960).

EMG sensors affixed to the throat near the child's laryngeal muscles provide one useful means for detecting and treating subvocal speech patterns (Hardyck & Petrinovich, 1969). To measure speech muscle activity while reading, the active electrodes are typically placed on both sides of the Adam's apple (thyroid carti-lage). As shown in Figure 5-5, the ground electrode (dark) is placed on the side of the child's neck.

To determine the occurrence of subvocal speech, artifact from movement, swallowing, and so on, needs to be ruled out. Hardyck and Petrinovich (1969) describe a clever method for verifying the presence of subvocal speech. This approach involves first having the child read *silently* for a few minutes, at which time he or she is given instructions to stop reading, but is told to maintain his or her current position. The child is then instructed to start reading once again, and this cycle is repeated for several trials. The EMG record is marked after each instruction so that changes accompanying each instruction can be noted. In this manner, subvocal speech is indicated by visible increases in EMG activity over the level seen during nonreading intervals.

Using this method, Hardyck and Petrinovich identified subvocal speech patterns and, by providing auditory feedback and relaxation instruction to the child(ren), helped them to reduce their subvocal speech. The investigators report that, while they did not see immediate increases in reading speed, the majority of treated individuals (from a college student sample) reported significant reductions in fatigue from reading.

However the picture with regard to subvocal speech may not be as clear as that. Some individuals who do not exhibit excessive laryngeal muscle activity when reading material of light to medium difficulty begin to show this subvocal speech

FIGURE 5-5 EMG Electrode Placement at Vocal, or *Laryngeal*, Muscle Site

pattern when difficult material is encountered (Hardyck & Petrinovich, 1970). Furthermore, if these individuals receive feedback to eliminate their subvocalizations, comprehension of the material drops. Hardyck and Petrinovich (1970) suggest that subvocal speech may serve an important function for more difficult reading. They analogize subvocal speech with the low gear of an automobile; the lower gear (subvocal speech) is indispensible for overcoming rough terrain, but driving in that gear at all times is dysfunctional and inefficient. Relatedly, McGuigan and Bailey (1969) conducted chin and lip EMG measurements with children assessed two and three years earlier. Marked reductions in covert oral behavior during silent reading occurred since the initial assessment, suggesting that this pattern diminishes with age. However, in cases where this tendency does not subside, EMG measurement may be useful in helping to identify subvocal speech and in the remediation of any reading difficulty which may be a result.

Using a college student sample, Riley and Lowe (1981) were unable to find a clear-cut relationship between subvocal speech and reading rate or comprehension of the material read. Subjects trained to alter their subvocalizations evidenced increases in reading speed but this was in the absence of actual change in EMG activity. These findings cloud the more parsimonious view of subvocal speech implied above. However, it is not clear whether age might account for the less clear-cut findings of Riley and Lowe, since young adults and not children were studied. Further study is needed to clarify the work on this area.

Stuttering

Educational potential may be hampered if a student is handicapped in his or her ability to communicate expressively with teachers and peers. Stuttering represents a complex communication disorder whose etiology is not well understood. Also known as stammering, stuttering is characterized by "... frequent repetitions or prolongations of sounds or syllables" (p. 86, American Psychiatric Association, 1987). Elevated tension in laryngeal and other speech muscles has been documented with adult stutterers (Kalotkin, Manschreck, & O'Brien, 1979; Shapiro, 1980); with children, this association is supported by findings from EMG treatment research. St. Louis, Clausell, Thompson, and Rife (1982) assessed the potential of biofeedback-assisted relaxation in reducing stuttering. These investigators report some success in helping a four-and-a-half-year-old boy reduce levels of muscle tension in the laryngeal area. Small reductions in the frequency of stuttering were also noted. In assessing these findings, several issues are important to consider. First, the report was a case study and suffers from numerous threats to internal validity (history, maturation, etc.), and the findings should be interpreted in that light. Second, a preschool child served as the subject, which, due to maturational and developmental factors, may severely limit the generalizability of the study's results. For example, EMG biofeedback may work better with older subjects and may explain why the youngster learned to reduce laryngeal tension "but not without some difficulty" (p. 195). Finally, no evidence is presented that elevated muscle tension was a presenting problem for the child. That is, for this child stuttering may have been brought on by factors other than muscle tension. Clearly, more rigorous research may address many of these methodological concerns.

More recently, the facial EMG (*orbicularis oris* muscles) tension levels of three boys who stuttered were measured in a study conducted by Craig and Cleary (1983). During speech, the boys showed higher tension levels when stuttering than when verbalizing nonstuttered words. Following EMG feedback all of the boys significantly reduced their EMG levels, an impovement which was accompanied by a 60% to 80% reduction in speech dysfluency. As this study indicates, EMG measures may be useful in identifying maladaptive muscle tautness involved in stuttering.

Summary of EMG Measurement

EMG measurement appears to hold substantial promise in a wide variety of educational contexts. This measurement approach may help identify excessive muscle tension in problems as diverse as hyperactivity, headache, and poor handwriting. Across these problems lies the same basic characteristic: students may approach educational demands with contracted or hyperreactive musculature and identifying this characteristic may be the first step toward eliminating the problem.

The research literature has largely provided only indirect support for justifying the use of EMG assessment in the classroom: students given *treatment* to reduce EMG levels evidence consistent improvement in learning-related areas. We have reviewed reports showing that learning disabled children evidence significant academic gains following forearm EMG feedback training. Does this finding mean that the problem involved forearm tension levels which were greater than that of nonLD children? In answer, we are reminded of the story sometimes used to illustrate the complexity of causality: Since aspirin works in ridding a headache, does this necessarily mean that the headache was a result of an "aspirin deficiency"? Clearly, the answer to this query is "no." To determine more adequately if elevated muscle tension is functionally involved in various educational problems, normative data with child populations are needed. These data could be obtained through large n assessment studies in which one or more student populations, balanced according to age, gender, and even SES and race, were studied. Of particular value would be information about EMG levels across resting, activity and stressor conditions. In treatment work, base rate information could be collected by assessing nonproblem-identified (control) students, and/or by carefully noting and recording pre- versus posttreatment EMG levels.

A question related to the issue of the involvement of excessive muscle tension with educational problems regards whether relaxation-based procedures, EMG feedback included, can indeed effect gains in academic achievement and potential. At present, the data are fairly supportive (e.g., see studies shown in Table 5-1); however, the methodological concerns noted earlier weaken the confidence one may have in these findings and indeed others (e.g., Kuna & Gariulo, 1979) have advised caution in determining the value of EMG feedback applications. While many have advocated the use of relaxation-based procedures (e.g., Anchor & Johnson, 1977; Omizo, Loffredo, & Hammett, 1982; Wood & Frith, 1984; Zenker, 1984), more systematic study is required to fully elucidate the value of these interventions in the classroom. This information will have clear benefit for present and future educational specialists.

Muscle tension also appears to be a useful indicant for measuring the degree of difficulty a child is having with a task. Whether it be pressure exerted on a tension bulb, subvocal speech, or forearm tension, individuals show increased muscle tension with greater task demand. Once it is determined that a child is having difficulty, this information can lead to direct remedial efforts aimed at helping him or her master the challenging task, to decrease tension levels so that they do not interfere with learning, or to consider alternative classroom placements that do not produce excessive arousal (e.g., self-contained classrooms).

How is the educator to use EMG in his or her assessment arsenal? Several options are available. First, EMG measurement instrumentation can now be obtained that is portable, inexpensive, and relatively easy to operate, which lends itself to general use by the educator him or herself. Alternatively the educator might use EMG measurement in consultation with trained school psychologists or certified biofeedback practitioners. These choices may be appropriate if sophisticated and exacting information is not required or if in situ data is desired. Otherwise, the educator is advised to refer this assessment to professionals in the community who have expertise in physiological measurement. Under any of these options EMG measurement can be a valuable asset in assessing educational problems.

The following section contains a case example to show how EMG measures can and have been used to help students improve their handwriting, a common educational focus.

Case Example of EMG Measurement Application

Hiram was known to have the "worst" handwriting in his first-grade class. Hiram's teacher, Ms. J, noted that he did not write legibly, with alphabet characters poorly developed, particularly those lowercase letters that require rounded strokes. Hiram completed many sentences with a hurried scribble; his parents kidded that he might make a fine doctor! Unfortunately, Hiram's poor writing was a source of embarrassment for him, and his writing seemed to get worse rather than better with increased effort.

Having taught writing skills for nearly ten years, Ms. J regarded this as a critical time to intervene and correct Hiram's poor writing skills. From her experience, Ms. J felt that Hiram's writing problems had their basis in his performance anxiety and concern about completing tasks quickly, issues that were reflected in his tendency to exert too much pressure on his writing hand.

Ms. J began a reeducative plan in consultation with a practicing biofeedback clinician by using the portable electromyographic (EMG) equipment available at the school to promote Hiram's relaxation and awareness of excessive muscle tension while he was writing. Hiram was explained the concept of EMG measurement, that it assesses muscle tension, and that the measure may help him to improve his handwriting. Ms. J then recruited one of Hiram's classmates as an exemplar. Affixing electrodes to the boy's forearm and neck muscles, Ms. J and Hiram were able to monitor the boy's EMG activity while at rest and while copying a passage from a book. Forearm EMG readings for the respective conditions were 4.3 and 18.8 microvolts, and for neck EMG, 5.4 and 9.3 microvolts.

Later, in a separate room, Hiram was similarly measured; the average readings during rest and while writing were 5.2 and 24.2 microvolts for his forearm and 7.1 and 15.4 for his neck. These EMG data were then compared with those of the other student; this comparison proved to be particularly enlightening for Hiram. He was able to see that he kept his muscles more taut than necessary and that, when writing, he tensed his forearm and neck muscles more than is required for the task.

Following a relaxation training program, Hiram evidenced marked reductions in muscle tension at forearm and neck areas, especially in levels measured during resting conditions. Hiram's parents noted that his writing had improved substantially and Ms. J observed that Hiram had slowed down and was more careful in his writing.

ACTIVITY MEASURES

Activity measures do not directly fall under the realm of "physiological measures." However, since physical activity is very much related to physiological change (e.g., neuromuscular and skeletomuscular activity accompanying movement), this assessment approach will be summarized here. Activity measures are mechanical instruments designed to provide an objective measure of human movement. In classroom settings, particularly those in which the educator is significantly outnumbered by his or her students, activity measurement provides an efficient and inexpensive means by which to assess the level of activity in a classroom or of targeted students.

Activity measures generally take one of two forms: those that are attached to classroom fixtures or furniture, and those considered to be free-ranging devices worn by the student. The most common apparatuses employed in these measurements are *stabilimetric* and *actometer* devices. Both are discussed briefly here.

Stabilimetric Devices

Sprague and Toppe (1966) used a stabilimetric chair device to assess thirty trainable mentally retarded children. This device involved pressure switches affixed to the leg of a platform-mounted chair. When the chair was tilted more than about one quarter of an inch, a microswitch and attached counters were activated. The children were assessed while waiting to receive edible reinforcers for correct response in a discrimination task. Activity level was found to vary inversely with task performance; that is, greater movement was related to lower performance and vice versa. One implication of this finding is clear: excessive classroom physical activity may preclude these (mentally retarded) children from receiving maximal benefit from educational programming. Stabilimetric devices may provide a vehicle for quantifying disruptive and overactive classroom behavior.

Stabilimetric measures have also been used in providing feedback to children about their classroom motoric behavior. Specific examples of this can be seen with the use of the stabilimetric cushion for measuring out-of-seat behavior (Christensen & Sprague, 1974; Edelson & Sprague, 1974). By and large these applications have been made in conjunction with classroom behavior management programs, such as a token economy or reinforcement programs designed to effect reductions or increases in monitored activity.

Christensen and Sprague (1974) placed stabilimetric cushions on the classroom chairs of twelve "socially maladjusted and conduct problem children." Seat movement was measured with four microswitches set into each student's chair cushion. Movement greater than 1.6 mm closed a circuit that activated an electronic counter. The stabilimeteric device was attached to a transmitter that emitted an FM signal when activated; this unit was linked to modular programming equipment in a room adjacent to the classroom. Increased activity was indicated when a red light on the box flashed, while stability and activity reductions were indicated by white lights. The latter also signaled that the child had earned two cents. Using this arrangement, the investigators found both contingent reinforcement and reinforcement plus methylphenidate (ritalin) to be successful in the treatment of hyperactivity.

Stabilimetric activity measures and feedback were employed in Edelson and Sprague's (1974) treatment of sixteen highly active, educable mentally retarded preadolescent male students. When the students exhibited a decrease in movement, they were provided "reinforcement," through feedback in the form of a flashing red light attached to their desks. The intervention proved successful in altering the students' in-seat behavior, and points to the utility of this relatively simple, inexpensive mechanical device for measuring classroom activity. In addition, this instrumentation is readily adaptable for promoting appropriate classroom behavior for the benefit of teachers and students alike.

Actometer Devices

Bell (1968) describes the modification of hand-wound wristwatches for recording physical activity, similar to one described by Schulman and Reisman (1959) and Maccoby, Dowley, Hagen, and Degerman (1965). This device has been referred to as the *actometer* (Figure 5-6) (Johnson, 1971). Briefly, the balance and hairspring assembly are removed from the watch and a small weight is attached to the fork end of the watch's pallet lever. This configuration results in a delicate balance whereby each time a separate and distinct movement is made in the plane of the watch's 3:00 to 9:00 axis, inertia forces the pallet to rotate on its pivot and advance the escape wheel (and second hand). Rapid movements are recorded as one full second, while slow movements are seen as one fifth of a second. To record

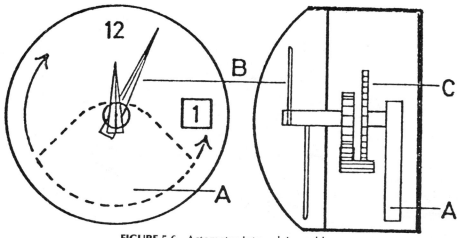

FIGURE 5-6 Actometer Internal Assemblage

Source: Reproduced with permission from Johnson, C. F. (1971). Hyperactivity and the machine: The actometer. *Child Development, 42,* 2105–2110. New York: Academic Press.

movement in more than one dimensional plane, additional watch units are needed. For example, three watch devices, placed in corresponding position, are needed to simultaneously record up-and-down, sideways, and back-and-forth motion (see Figure 5-7). The watch(es) are packaged in a leather packet and can be worn by the child on the feet, wrist, jacket, or wherever needed.

Bell (1968) conducted assessment trials on thirty-seven preschool girls and reported tridimensional activity norms for devices worn on the jacket and foot. In addition, the actometers were found to have high test-retest reliability (foot-worn $r = .55$, jacket-worn $r = .56$). This early study points to the viability of using actometer devices for monitoring activity in young children.

Halverson and Waldrop (1973) used jacket-worn activity recorders to monitor fifty-eight nursery school children while playing outdoors. Results showed the levels derived from these devices to be consistently related to indexes from behavioral observations and with teacher paper-and-pencil summary ratings (males M $r = .51$; females M $r = .44$). The authors conclude that the devices ". . . provide a simple, reliable, and valid method of obtaining a measure of how busy and motorically active young preschoolers are in free-play settings" (p. 67).

Stevens, Kupst, Suran, and Schulman (1978) used actometers worn on the ankle and wrists to measure the situational specificity of activity with thirteen preadolescent boys in four educational settings. The resulting readings were compared with behavioral ratings made by their mothers (Werry, 1968) and by six clinical staff members. The results of the study generally fulfilled the investigator's expectations, with the mothers' ratings significantly correlating with overall actometer levels and with activity measured in less structured settings. Ratings from

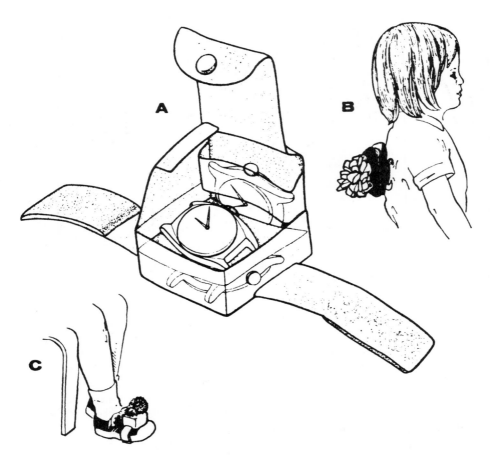

FIGURE 5-7 Modified Wristwatch Activity Measure: (a) jacket, (b) tridimensional, wrist, and (c) foot-worn units

Source: Reproduced with permission from Bell, R. Q. (1968). Adaptation of small wristwatches for mechanical recording of activity in infants and children. *Journal of Experimental Child Psychology, 6,* 302–305.

all six staff members were highly correlated with classroom activity levels. As a whole, the considerable agreement found between observer ratings and the mechanically derived measures lend support to the validity of activity level measurement devices.

Eaton (1983) examined the reliability and validity of actometers with nursery school children. Using fourteen different, commercially available actometers (Timex Model 108 Motion Recorders), the author arranged to have each of twentyseven children wear a different wrist device on that many (14) different twenty-one-minute assessments. In contrast to Bell's (1968) early study, Eaton found the test-retest reliability for a single actometer to be only about .33. With the addition of other actometers, however, reliability increased sharply (to .50 with two devices, .60 with three, and so on). Furthermore, composite (multiple) actometer readings were highly correlated with staff and parent behavior ratings of the children.

Consistent with past findings (Johnson, 1971), the author also found the wrist-worn devices to be related to child forearm length, as well as to age and gender. These three variables may be interrelated; males generally have longer forearms than females, as do older versus younger individuals, and males, older children, and children with longer forearms show higher activity level readings. As a whole, these findings lend support for the classroom use of the actometer to determine current activity levels and to assess treatment effects, particularly if the user employs multiple devices and takes into account the age and gender (and forearm length when using hand-worn units) of the child(ren) monitored.

Schulman, Stevens, and Kupst (1977) describe two experiments in which they assessed the reliability and validity of the *biomotometer*, an instrument for measuring movement, like the actometer, but which also is capable of providing sensory feedback to the wearer. The biomotometer consists of a small, lightweight box that can be affixed to a cloth belt typically worn at the waist. Activity is detected by three mercury-wetted microswitches that are mounted horizontally (i.e., parallel to the ground when the child is standing), and in directions 120° from one another. In this way, movement in any direction will displace the mercury in at least one of the microswitches. The device is capable of: (1) tabulating total activity counts, (2) tabulating the number of times the wearer exceeds a preset activity criterion for a given time interval, and (3) providing auditory feedback (via a removable crystal earphone) with each instance of overactivity, i.e., counts indicated by (2).

In an assessment with five emotionally disturbed male children, the biomotometer was found to be highly reliable ($r = .84$) across four measurements conducted in the classroom. In a second study with twenty children, the waist biomotometer readings were correlated with those obtained simultaneously from ankle and wrist *actometers*, and in five different situations. While only six of ten specific situational comparisons were significant, combined ankle and wrist actometer readings significantly correlated with biomotometer readings across all situations. Similar to Eaton's (1983) findings, Schulman *et al.* (1977) found that aggregated measurement information from several devices provides the most representative sample of classroom activity. The authors conclude that their findings show the biomotometer to possess criterion validity, that is, relative to the actometer.

As with stabilimetric activity measures, actometer and biomotometer devices have been used in altering classroom behavior. Using activity feedback, Ball and Irwin (1976) successfully increased the in-seat behavior and reduced the chair tilting of a twelve-year-old "overactive and distractible" boy. A portable automated device, designed with a mercury switch sensor for detecting postural change, was attached to the boy's pant leg while he sat at his desk in the classroom. When sitting with relatively little physical movement, the mercury switch circuit stayed open and a timer was activated. If the timer remained on for two minutes the boy received reinforcement; if the boy's posture changed abruptly or significantly and the circuit was closed, the timer automatically reset to zero. Results of the activity feedback were dramatic, with maximum performance achieved for in-seat behavior and chair tilting immediately after the device was put to use. These gains were maintained at a forty-six day follow-up after fading procedures had been invoked and when no timing device was used.

Schulman et al. (1978) employed a biomotometer in providing activity feedback to an eleven-year-old highly active boy, who was reported to have a "short attention span." The boy received rewards for reduced biomotometer-measured activity. Across five conditioning trials, the boy's activity decreased by nearly 50% and his teachers commented favorably about his improved classroom behavior. In a second experiment, the authors used the biomotometer in *increasing* the activity level of a ten-year-old boy who exhibited hypoactivity. In this case candy and toy reinforcement was given for increased activity, and resulted in nearly double the level seen prior to treatment. Unfortunately, the child's activity returned to pretreatment levels in the "extinction period" following the ten feedback trials provided. This failure to maintain training effects called for further systematic study. Partially meeting this need, Schulman, Suran, Stevens, and Kupst (1979) successfully used the biomotometer in the assessment and reduction of disruptive behavior shown by eleven overactive emotionally disturbed children. Unlike the previous study, these effects did not dissipate after the contingencies were removed. As a whole, the above studies illustrate the utility of the biomotometer in assessing activity changes that may result from classroom behavior management efforts.

More recently Williamson et al. (1981) treated a nine-year-old hyperactive boy with dexedrine and activity feedback. Large scale integrated activity monitors (Foster, McPartland, & Kupfer, 1978), equipped with integrated circuitry, a small mercury switch, and a digital display, were worn by the child on his wrist and ankle. These units recorded activity, with the wrist-worn device also providing feedback to the child when his behavior exceeded a predetermined criterion. Data collected before treatment revealed that the boy displayed over twice as much arm and leg movement as that observed in a group of nonhyperactive children ($n = 12$). While dexedrine administration was found to result in marked increases in on-task behavior and decreases in gross motor behavior, activity feedback was required to reduce the other important aspects of the hyperactive syndrome, excessive arm and leg movement. Thus, the activity measures were useful in identifying specific motoric components of hyperactivity as well as in effecting reductions in order to optimize the child's educational potential.

Other similarly developed activity measures have been employed in classroom situations and have more clearly illustrated some drawbacks to relying on activity measurements. Nishikido et al. (1982) compared observational data and parent and teacher rating of kindergarten children with simultaneous *pedometry* recordings. The mechanical recording devices were fitted to the clothing near each child's hip to count each of his or her steps. Teacher and parent ratings of children at each of two kindergarten classes were significantly related but inconsistencies were found between these ratings and measures taken from the behavioral observations and pedometry. This latter finding points to the possibility of a systematic bias with one or all forms of measurement or suggests that they may be measuring different phenomena. The pedometer recordings were most highly related to behavioral observations of the children when they were running and increasingly less so with observations during walking, standing, and sitting. Thus, this instrument was found to be reliable at least when used in situations where children were expected to be particularly active. These findings call for caution in interpreting activity measurement information and point to a need for further study in the area. Despite the tenuous validity and reliability grounds, educators can derive substantial benefit from using these measures as seen in the treatments described above.

Summary of Activity Measures

Mechanical activity recorders may provide important assessment information in the classroom. These devices may be helpful in making placement and treatment decisions, and avoid the stigma of labeling that may follow from the use of other assessment approaches, for example, "Sean is displaying high rates of out-of-seat behavior," versus "Sean scored above the cutoff for hyperactivity on the X scale." Furthermore, like the physiological measures discussed previously, stabilimetric and actometer devices are especially amenable to subsequent intervention efforts.

Activity measures may also serve as useful barometers for changes resulting from classroom interventions. For example, Hughes *et al.* (1980) provided frontal EMG biofeedback to three children identified as having problems with overactivity. An index of time on task was calculated from actometer readings and served as one of the primary dependent measures. As shown in decreases in the actometer readings, the biofeedback intervention was highly successful in effecting desired changes; this change was related to concomitant decreases in frontal EMG and improvements in parental behavior ratings. Thus, actometer ratings were found to correspond to other objective and subjective measures of hyperactivity (i.e., criterion validity). The Hughes *et al.* (1980) study also illustrates how activity and physiological measures can be used together in assessing and effecting change in the classroom.

Two issues merit consideration regarding activity measures. First, how much activity is too much (or too little)? This question highlights the need for base rate activity information. Of value would be data on various child populations and on children in various activities and settings. Another issue is the reliability and validity of activity measures, particularly actometers. For example, some investigators report that a single actometer may not possess acceptable reliability (e.g., Johnson, 1971). This appears to be a hardware problem that will ultimately be surmounted with applications of greater technical sophistication. With regard to validity, several investigators have reported that actometers do not possess significant correspondence with other measures, such as global paper-and-pencil ratings of behavior. However, data has been reported suggesting that more is better, in that multiple simultaneous measurements in different dimensional planes will greatly increase the criterion validity of that measure.

Other measurement applications that involve technology similar to that of activity measures were deliberately omitted from this section. These applications include advanced telemetry instrumentation fitted to free-ranging activity measures (Grunewald-Zuberbier, Grunewald, & Rasche, 1972; Herron & Ramsden, 1967) and vocal recorders (Fields & Ashmore, 1982; Gardner, 1973). Telemetry equipment represents an untapped dimension for educational assessment and we anticipate that were this chapter written ten years from today, a significant proportion would be devoted to the applications of that technology. Another application not described here concerns the body to head position and joint training devices recently developed for individuals with neuromuscular disorders. These devices may also be valuable for use in the classroom; however, they were not detailed here since at present they are used predominately in treatment applications, that is, muscle retraining. Interested readers are referred to Fernando and Basmajian (1978) and Milner (1983).

The following section contains a case example to show how activity level measures can and have been used with hyperactive behavior, a frequently seen educational problem.

Case Example of Activity Measurement Application

Jerry is an eight-and-a-half-year-old third grader whose teacher, Ms. B, describes him as being "a handful . . . no, two handfuls!" During structured in-seat activities, Jerry is consistently getting out of his seat or rocking his desk, raising his voice in an apparent effort to gain his teacher's attention, and, rather than attending to the assigned task, is often seen engaging in several activities in rapid succession.

In conferences with the boy's parents, the frustrated Ms. B suggested that Jerry might benefit from antihyperactivity medications, since he appears to be "truly hyperactive." Reluctantly, the parents conceded that Jerry may need medications, after which the family pediatrician started Jerry on a regimen of methylphenidate (ritalin). Within weeks, Jerry's disruptive behavior decreased markedly and his academic performance improved slightly.

Jerry's parents later contacted Ms. B to see if there might be an alternative way to calm their child and simultaneously effect greater improvement in his school work. They noticed that he was experiencing side effects from the medication, such as sleeplessness, dry mouth, periodic nighttime enuresis, and so on; the parents were becoming increasingly concerned about the wisdom of their choice. Ms. B, sensitive to the concerns of Jerry's parents, later discussed the issue with the school district's psychologist, who had received training in behavioral classroom management. With school funding, the psychologist had previously purchased an inexpensive actometer device and felt that it might provide a means to replace Jerry's medication with self-regulation. With the teacher's help and the cooperation of the parents and pediatrician, the psychologist devised a plan whereby Jerry would receive daily activity rewards for reductions in activity as indicated by the actometer. To determine criteria for successful responding, classroom norms were determined by having two other male students in the class wear the device for three one-hour periods each, at intervals distributed across the school day. The mean total activity readings for the morning (prelunch) was 52.4/hr, and for the afternoon, 59.3/hr. Baseline for Jerry was also obtained over four one-hour periods in which he wore the actometer; his mean activity levels, while on medication, were 48.7/hr and 62.1/hr, respectively.

The treatment plan had three phases. First, Jerry was given feedback on his activity level and rewarded for maintaining a level below that recorded during the baseline week; he graduated to the next phase after one errorless week of meeting this criterion. During the second and third phases, Jerry continued with the same activity-reward contingency plan, but his medication dosage was halved and then discontinued altogether (in consultation with his pediatrician). Three months after the treatment, Jerry was assessed once again with the biomotometer. His activity recordings showed that he had maintained his gains, with mean activity recordings of 51.3/hr and 53.2/hr in morning and afternoon recording times, respectively. Furthermore, Jerry's grades showed gradual improvement, particularly in arithmetic, where he was having the most problems prior to his medication. Ms. B attributed Jerry's improvement to the use of the actometer—he was now able to attend to a single task for a sustained period of time, which she believed resulted from his continued in-seat behavior.

OTHER MEASURES—FUTURE DIRECTIONS

Thus far we have touched on only a sample of the many physiological and activity measures available for classroom use. One reason for this is the fact that most other physiological and activity measures are not sufficiently developed and tested to be of clear value with educational problems. However, some measurement approaches should be described, not because of their current utility, but because in the not-to-distant future their classroom use may become widespread. One approach with particular promise for educational assessment and diagnosis is electroencephalography.

Electroencephalographic (EEG) Measures

The continuous measurement of brain wave activity, or electroencephalography (EEG), has an extensive history with school-age children (Gresham & Evans, 1979; Lewis & Freeman, 1977; Lubar & Deering, 1981). This physiological measure involves recording electrical activity, in the form of bioelectric potentials, at points on the scalp above preselected regions of the cortex (see Jasper, 1958). The usual recording of EEG activity entails affixing eight or more electrodes or electrode pairs on the scalp according to standard placement configurations (e.g., the International Federation ten twenty electrode system). Thus bioelectric potentials can be sampled simultaneously on numerous areas above the cortex, such as above and between temporal, occipital, and parietal regions.

The specific nature of EEG activity is unknown, but it is believed to be produced from postsynaptic potentials in the dendrites of cortical neurons (Kiloh, McGomas, & Osselton, 1972; as described in Lewis & Freeman, 1977). This activity is amplified extensively so that it can be recorded, using filters to reduce artifact, on continuously moving polygraph strip chart or converted for ongoing visual or auditory feedback. Diagnostic information is derived from frequency (Hertz or cycles per second) and amplitude (power) indexes of the EEG record. EEG patterns typically occur in sinusoid curve shapes, with the predominant frequencies showing the most marked change from environmental perturbance or organismic change (states of consciousness, medications, etc.). EEG activity is usually characterized by several distinct patterns and with regard to their amplitude (Hz). These brain wave patterns (i.e., frequencies) have been labeled by the letters of the Greek alphabet: alpha (7–13 Hz), beta (13–28 or 28–40 Hz), delta (0.5–3 Hz), theta (3.5–6.5 Hz).

At present, interpreting the EEG record presents a complicated task. For example, each brain wave can vary in terms of at least seven characteristics: (1) abundance, (2) specific frequency, (3) amplitude, (4) variability, (5) location, (6) propagation or conduction time to the different recording sites, and (7) circumstances of appearance (Brown, 1977). Since EEG recordings are complicated to use and interpret, most teachers cannot employ them as part of their assessment arsenal. In light of the technical advances that have occurred in the recent computer revolution, these current barriers should also be surmounted in the not-too-distant future.

It is important to note that the EEG picture is not completely clear at this point in time due to some conflicting reports, a phenomenon that might stem from the preliminary nature of EEG research. In addition, EEG recordings are known to be significantly affected by movement artifact. Problem-identified children often exhibit excessive movement, which may introduce artifact and obscure true differences between normal and nonnormal children. Related to this is the question of causality; upon the verification of EEG abnormalities for a given child population, it is uncertain whether these abnormalities are of etiological significance to the presenting problem or are a result of the "symptoms." Controlled treatment studies may help to partition the critical factors involved. To elucidate the value of brain wave assessments, further research is needed.

As with the EMG measurements, the value of EEG measurements for classroom use would be enhanced with the establishment of normative data. Fortunately, norms for children are now being established. Brown (1977) includes an appendix in which normal EEG patterns are illustrated; Westmoreland and Stockard (1977) describe normative patterns for infants and children; Friedman *et al.* (1984) provide data on the ERPs of a large sample of adolescents; and Coble,

Kupfer, Taska, and Kane (1984) have recently reported sleep EEG data for normal healthy children. Data of this type will certainly enhance the value of electro-encephalography with educational problems.

By and large, the chief utility of EEG assessment has been in supplementing available diagnostic information, but other uses have been explored (e.g., determining drug responsiveness). At present, EEG technology is complex, expensive, and cumbersome. The educational utility of EEG hinges on greater portability and simplicity of use. At the present time, EEG measurement is also relatively costly and prohibitively complex, both in conducting and interpreting the recordings. The educator needs to defer this task to specialists trained in EEG measurement.

Brain wave information may be an important aspect of the classroom assessment and diagnostic process in the future. In anticipation of the "EEG revolution," educators are advised to learn about this measurement approach. Even today EEG measurement has diagnostic value for certain educational problems and hence, there is a need to acquaint educational personnel with the potential uses of EEG so that they can decide when a referral to a qualified specialist is indicated. Alternatively, the educational specialist might deem the EEG as the appropriate means by which to test and corroborate diagnostic and prognostic impressions.

Brain Wave Patterns

EEG measurement has been used in assessing children thought to suffer Minimal Brain Dysfunction (MBD) and Hyperkinetic syndromes (Lubar & Deering, 1981, pp. 126–134). One type of assessment used in these cases involves a standard EEG examination, usually performed by a pediatric or general neurologist. A variety of educational problems have been associated with generalized, multifocal, and localized abnormalities in brain wave activity. Gross differences in electrical activity between normal and clinical populations sometimes correspond to evidence of central nervous system dysfunction. Specific abnormalities, such as positive spikes, slow wave activity, amplitude asymmetries, and dysrhythmias, have been found substantially more often with MBD and hyperactive children than with normal children (Lesny, Provaznik, Jirasek, & Komarek, 1977; Lubar & Deering, 1981; also see Hastings & Barkley [1978] for a review). This feature clearly has value for making diagnostic and placement decisions.

Certain brain wave activity has been related to alertness and visual attention (Mulholland, 1972, 1974; Mulholland & Gascon, 1972). Specifically, the synchrony of alpha activity is disrupted when an individual is exposed to a distinct visual stimulus; at this point a reduction in alpha activity can be seen, whereas alpha is more abundant when the stimulus is removed. Alternatively, alpha activity is enhanced with prolonged exposure just as attentional processes gradually diminish during habituation to stimuli. Furthermore, alpha is also suppressed when individuals are actively peering about while in a darkened room (Bryan, 1982; Mulholland, 1974). Thus, it may be the *process* of paying attention that is important, rather than only the characteristics of the stimulus being observed. Another finding of interest is that during the presentation of a visual stimulus less alpha is seen with adults and older children than with younger children (Bryan, 1982; Mulholland, 1974; Mulholland & Gascon, 1972). This finding suggests that attentional processes are developed and refined with maturation. The implication is that deficiencies in visual attentiveness may be a significant factor in the learning problems of some children. Once identified, efforts can then be started to ameliorate the problems through attention enhancement exercises, or directly with EEG feedback training (Boudrot, Mulholland, & Runnels, 1976; Brolund & Schallow, 1976; Brown, 1977; Gracenin & Cook, 1977; Mulholland & Goodman, 1982; O'Malley & Conners, 1972). However, other data on EEG feedback treatment indicate that alpha wave control is quite difficult to attain. In fact, some individuals given numerous training sessions have been found to have no greater control over their alpha waves than they did during baseline (for a review see Rockstroh, Birbaumer, Elbert, & Lutzenberger, 1984).

Recently attention has shifted to study on Sensorimotor Rhythm (SMR) a wave form between 12 Hz and 14 Hz in the absence of 4 Hz to 7 Hz activity, recorded over the sensorimotor cortex. This brain wave has also been found to correspond to attentional processes but has proven to be much more amenable to volitional regulation. Early work by Lubar and colleagues has shown that SRM-feedback training is effective in reducing children's epileptic seizures (Lubar & Bahler, 1976; Seifert & Lubar, 1975), but more recent work has shown that hyperactive behavior can be affected (Lubar & Lubar, 1984; Lubar & Shouse, 1976; Shouse & Lubar, 1979; Tansey & Bruner, 1983). This area may hold the most promise for classroom application; however, more empirical data will be needed to illuminate its value.

Event-Related Potentials

Another recording approach, which also holds promise for isolating differences between child populations, involves recording electrical potentials that occur following the presentation of selected stimuli (*Event-Related Potentials, ERP*). An arithmetic average is calculated across a number of stimuli to obtain a representative sample of the subject's evoked potentiality (e.g., 50 stimulus presentations). The nature of the stimuli can vary but most typically they are visual or auditory.

Recently, visually evoked responses have been used with some degree of precision in discriminating normal from disabled readers (Conners, 1971; Preston, Guthrie, & Childs, 1974), normal from retarded (Glidden, Busk, & Galbraith, 1971), and normal from dyslexic children (Sobotka & May, 1977). The visual ERP has also been shown to predict adequately the clinical response to methylphenidate of children diagnosed as hyperactive (Halliday, Callaway, & Rosenthal, 1984; Satterfield, Cantwell, Saul, Lesser, & Podosin, 1973; for a review, see Barkley, 1976).

Promising work has also been conducted with brain wave slow potentials. Aspects of this phenomenon have been related to information processing (for a more detailed account of this promising area, the reader is referred to Rockstroh, Birbaumer, Elbert, & Lutzenberger, 1984).

Skin Temperature Measures

Another type of physiological measurement that appears to hold promise for classroom application is skin temperature measurement and feedback. Skin temperature measurement typically involves affixing thermistor probes to the skin surface at selected sites. Like other forms of physiological measurement, these thermistors are attached to response-specific couplers and preamplifiers, and are fed into a physiological unit which can produce signals to provide written records of ongoing skin surface temperature and allows for visual or audio feedback. Inexpensive and portable temperature monitoring devices are currently available and present a viable option for classroom use, as can be seen with the device shown in Figure 5-8. Changes in temperature roughly correspond to changes in peripheral blood flow; warmer skin indicates greater flow of 98.6° F blood to the extremities. Most commonly, this is measured at fingertip and less frequently, forehead, sites. Figure 5-9 shows a fingertip thermistor placement. Peripheral blood flow (skin temperature) is thought to be under the control of the sympathetic branch of the autonomic nervous system.

Increased peripheral blood flow (i.e., warmer skin temperature) has been found to promote relaxation (Sargent, Walters, & Green, 1973) and, conversely, anxiety states and hyperactivity are presumably reflected in decreased peripheral blood flow. There is some evidence that measuring skin surface temperature may provide a viable means by which to assess and treat these conditions with children (Hersey, 1983; Hunter, Russell, Russell, & Zimmerman, 1976). For example, Hersey (1983) successfully taught three hyperactive boys to elevate their fingertip tempera-

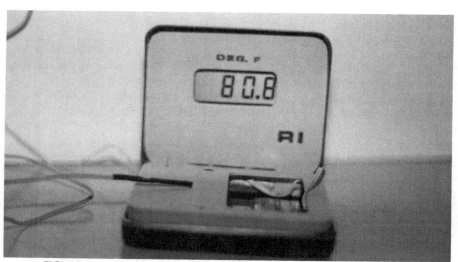

FIGURE 5-8   Portable Temperature Monitoring Device, with Digital Display

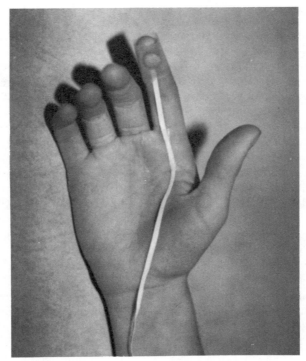

FIGURE 5-9 Skin Temperature Measure Taken at Fingertip Site

ture. Achieving mastery in skin temperature regulation corresponded with marked improvements in the boys' behavior and schoolwork.

Skin temperature measures may be especially useful for classroom application in light of the availability of portable units and their ease of use (e.g., they do not require electrode gel). However, as with the measures described already, establishing a basis of normative data is essential for understanding and using skin temperature measurement with education problems. Unfortunately, little skin temperature normative data exists (one exception is the migraineur norms reported by Boudewyns, 1985, and Boudewyns & Cornish, 1978). The types of data that would be of particular value include descriptive information on absolute temperature, lability, and response to various stimuli (akin to the ERPs measured in electroencephalography). This information may be of inestimable value for classroom application, for example in attempts to assess and reduce labile vascular activity in overanxious students. Along with this paucity of normative skin temperature data is a lack of treatment research on the skin temperature regulation for educational use. Those investigators who have studied the viability of this approach (e.g., Hersey, 1983) have been rewarded with encouraging, albeit tentative, findings.

OVERALL CONCLUSIONS

As this chapter has revealed, physiological and activity measures have substantial potential for educational problems. These measures may be of value for use in diagnostic and placement decisions, as well as in indexing treatment effects. Providing students with feedback about aberrant physiology can also serve as an important vehicle in remediation efforts, as shown in the biofeedback applications described above. Physiological and activity measures can be instrumental in classroom behavior change when converted as feedback to the student.

It is important to note that we did not attempt to review all of the physiological measures of potential utility with educational problems. To do so would require a volume or more, so instead we chose to describe the more common or available measures with greater detail. A sample of the measures not discussed include heart rate (see Figure 5-10), skin conductance, respiration, blood volume pulse, and blood pressure monitoring equipment. Substantial potential exists with these measures as well, although their use appears to be primarily for research purposes at this point.

One issue only indirectly addressed in the foregoing is that of testing qualifications. As with most of the measures described in this volume, to make appropriate use of and to obtain valid data from physiological measures, the assessor should have a reasonable degree of familiarity and formal experience with the instrumentation and its use. The variety of available physiological monitoring and

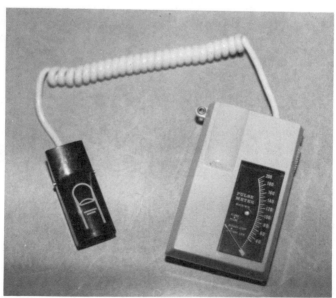

FIGURE 5-10 Portable Heart Rate (Pulse Meter) Monitoring Device, with Finger Attachment

biofeedback equipment can be overwhelming to the professional. This precludes our discussing the relative merits of specific instruments.[3] Familiarity can be gained by perusal of the many books and chapters on psychophysiological assessment. Novices may find it helpful to contact the two professional biofeedback societies to learn about educational offerings, credentialing procedures, selection of equipment, and other professional matters of interest.[4] Experience is gained through practice, preferably of the supervised kind, with the instrumentation. A "reasonable degree of familiarity and formal exposure" is admittedly an arbitrarily determined criterion. This issue, however, may not be as critical as it seems in light of the amazing simplification in use and interpretation seen with physiological and activity measures. Suffice it to say that, within a short period of deliberate and systematic practice, an educator can acquire sufficient expertise for functional use of most physiological and activity measures. While some argue for certification of those who use physiological measurement and biofeedback instruments, that issue will not be debated here.

One problem apparent in nearly all of the physiological measurements reviewed is the absence of normative data. The utility of these measurements with educational problems greatly depends upon having some basis by which to compare the data obtained in the classroom. In the meantime educators can still use these measurement approaches from a single case framework (Barlow, Hayes, & Nelson, 1983; Barlow & Hersen, 1984). In this manner, physiological measures conducted on a child can be compared with measurements from an earlier (preintervention) time. As noted previously, educators who use this approach should be cautioned about habituation effects and may want to include a series of measurements or an extended adaptation period. Similarly, if repeated measurements are conducted at extended intervals apart from one another, educators should be aware of age effects: as a child becomes older, his or her physiology also changes.

Physiological measures provide an assessment technology with immediate value in the classroom. One advantage is the short distance one needs to travel from assessment to treatment application; merely by feeding this measurement information back to the student reactive effects may produce substantial gains in remedying the problem. Relatedly, the feedback is frequently in a form (digital, counters, lights) that is particularly amenable to more traditional classroom behavior change approaches, such as individual incentive systems, token economies, and the like.

In light of the immense potential for physiological measures in the classroom, one unrealized possibility may be in their use with nonproblem-identified children. That is, these measures may serve as general educational aids, providing substantial benefit to all children in the classroom setting. For instance, Hughes, Jackson, Dubois, and Erwin (1979) used frontal EMG biofeedback in the successful treatment of the handwriting problems of "normal" children. Helping students to be aware of their physiology and physical activity when learning new skills may provide a firm basis on which to maximize the level of aptitude they ultimately attain. Although this suggestion is largely speculative, it raises the intriguing possibility that these measures can play a significant role in mainstream educational practice. Clearly, this possibility merits consideration.

While the current usefulness of physiological and activity measures is obvious, the future holds even greater promise. As is seen with computerization, greater portability and user friendly measurement instrumentation can be expected. Measures, which several decades ago could only be conducted in research or clinical laboratories, can now be used in school and home settings. Electroencephalography is one area which may see the most startling changes with regard to increased portability and simplicity. Telemetry may also be a key in extending the general utility of the various measurement tools.

Today is a fast-moving time with advances and change with every passing day. Physiological and activity measures ride at the forefront of this change and may someday revolutionize educational assessment and planning. The authors look ahead with excitement at the propsects and promise of physiological and activity measurement.

Notes

1. The latest version of the American Psychiatric Association's (1987) *Diagnostic and Statistical Manual-Revised (DSM-III-R*, pp. 50–53) categorizes this child syndrome under Attention-deficit Hyperactivity Disorder. Essential features are "developmentally inappropriate degrees of inattention, impulsiveness, and hyperactivity" (p. 50).

2. This explanation has been criticized, however, as being too simplistic and possibly even incorrect (Anderson & Franks, 1981; Haynes, Cuevas, & Gannon, 1982; Philips, 1978; Philips & Hunter, 1982; Pickoff, 1984).

3. Andrasik and Blanchard (1983) briefly discuss various approaches to instrumentation and summarize their advantages, disadvantages, and costs.

4. American Association of Biofeedback Clinicians
2424 Dempster Avenue
Des Plaines, Illinois 60016

Biofeedback Society of America
10200 West 44th Avenue, Suite 304
Wheat Ridge, Colorado 80033

Acknowledgment

Preparation of this chapter was supported by Research Career Development Award 1 K01 NS00818 from the National Institute of Neurological Communicative Disorders and Stroke, awarded to the second author.

References

American Psychiatric Association (1987). *Diagnostic and Statistical Manual of Mental Disorders* (3d ed.) *Revised.* Washington, D.C.: Author.

Anchor, K. N., & Johnson, L. G. (1977). The efficacy of EMG biofeedback in the treatment of hyperactivity. *Behavioral Engineering, 4,* 39–43.

Anderson, C. D., & Franks, R. D. (1981). Migraine and muscle contraction headaches: Is there a physiological difference? *Headache, 21,* 63–71.

Andrasik, F., & Attanasio, V. (1985). Biofeedback in pediatrics: Current status and appraisal. In N. L. Wolraich & D. K. Ruth (Eds.), *Advances in developmental and behavioral pediatrics* (Vol. 6, pp. 241–286). Greenwich, Conn.: JAI Press.

Andrasik, F., Blake, D. D., & McCarran, M. S. (1986). A biobehavioral analysis of pediatric headache. In N. A. Krasnegor, M. F. Cataldo, & J. D. Arasteh (Eds.), *Child health behavior:* Research and priorities in behavioral pediatrics (pp. 394–434). New York: John Wiley & Sons.

Andrasik, F., & Blanchard, E. B. (1983). Applications of biofeedback to therapy. In C. E. Walker (Ed.), *The handbook of clinical psychology: Theory, research, and practice.* (Vol. II, pp. 1123–1164). Homewood, Ill.: Dow Jones-Irwin.

Andrasik, F., Blanchard, E. B., Arena, J. G., Saunders, N. L., & Barron, K. D. (1982). Psychophysiology of recurrent headache: Methodological issues and new empirical findings. *Behavior Therapy, 13,* 407–429.

Andrasik, F., Blanchard, E. B., Edlund, R. S., & Attanasio, V. (1983). EMG biofeedback treatment of a child with muscle contraction headache. *American Journal of Clinical Biofeedback, 6,* 96–102.

Arena, J. G., Blanchard, E. B., Andrasik, F., & Myers, P. E. (1983). Psychophysiological responding as a function of age: The importance of matching. *Journal of Behavioral Assessment, 5,* 131–141.

Attanasio, V., Andrasik, F., Burke, E. J., Blake, D. D., Kabela, E., & McCarran, M. S. (1985). Clinical Issues in utilizing biofeedback with children. *Clinical Biofeedback and Health, 8,* 134–141.

Ball, T. S., & Irwin, A. E. (1976). A portable, automated device applied to training a hyperactive child. *Journal of Behavior Therapy and Experimental Psychiatry, 7,* 185–188.

Barkley, R. A. (1976). Predicting the response of hyperkinetic children to stimulant drugs: A review. *Journal of Abnormal Child Psychology, 4,* 327–348.

Barlow, D. H., Hayes, S. C., & Nelson, R. O. (1983). *The scientist-practitioner: Research and accountability in clinical and educational settings.* Elmsford, N.Y.: Pergamon Press.

Barlow, D. H., & Hersen, M. (1984). *Single case experimental designs: Strategies for studying behavior change* (2d ed.). Elmsford, N.Y.: Pergamon Press.

Basmajian, J. V., & Blumenstein, R. (1980). *Electrode placement in EMG biofeedback.* Baltimore, Md.: Williams & Wilkins.

Bell, R. Q. (1968). Adaptation of small wristwatches for mechanical recording of activity in infants and children. *Journal of Experimental Child Psychology, 6,* 302–305.

Bille, B. (1962). Migraine in school children. *Acta Paediatrica Scandinavica, 51,* 1–151.

Blanchard, E. B. (1981). Behavioral assessment of psychophysiologic disorders. In D. H. Barlow (Ed.), *Behavioral assessment of adult disorders.* New York: Guilford Press.

Boudewyns, P. A. (1985). Evaluating finger temperature data. *Journal of Behavioral Medicine, 8,* 301–307.

Boudewyns, P. A., & Cornish, R. D. (1978). Finger temperature norms of migraine headache sufferers. *Behavior Therapy, 9,* 689.

Boudrot, R., Mulholland, T., & Runnels, S. (1976). A clinical feedback EEG system. *American Journal of EEG Technology, 16,* 117–127.

Braud, L. W. (1978). The effects of frontal EMG biofeedback and progressive relaxation upon hyperactivity and its behavioral concomitants. *Biofeedback and Self-Regulation, 3,* 69–89.

Braud, L. W., Lupin, M. N., & Braud, W. G. (1975). The use of electromyographic biofeedback in the control of hyperactivity. *Journal of Learning Disabilities, 8,* 21–26.

Brolund, J. W., & Schallow, J. R. (1976). The effects of reward on occipital alpha facilitation by biofeedback. *Psychophysiology, 13,* 236–241.

Brown, B. B. (1977). *Stress and the art of biofeedback.* New York: Holt, Rinehart, & Winston.

Bryan, J. W. (1982). Note on the EEG orienting response with children. *Perceptual and Motor Skills, 54,* 675–677.

Buck, R. W., Miller, R. E., & Caul, W. F. (1974). Sex, personality, and physiological variables in the communication of emotion via facial expression. *Journal of Personality and Social Psychology, 30,* 587–596.

Carter, J. L., & Russell, H. (1979). Biofeedback and academic attainment of LD children. *Academic Therapy, 15,* 483–486.

Carter, J. L., & Russell, H. (1980). Relationship between reading frustration and muscle tension in children with reading disabilities. *American Journal of Clinical Biofeedback, 2,* 60–62.

Carter, J. L., & Synolds, D. (1974). Effects of relaxation training upon handwriting quality. *Journal of Learning Disabilities, 7,* 53–55.

Christensen, D. E., & Sprague, R. L. (1974). Reduction of hyperactive behavior by conditioning procedures and combined with methylphenidate. *Behavior Research and Therapy, 11,* 331–334.

Cobb, D. E., & Evans, J. R. (1981). The use of biofeedback techniques with school-aged children exhibiting behavioral and/or learning problems. *Journal of Abnormal Child Psychology, 9,* 251–281.

Coble, P. A., Kupfer, D. J., Taska, L. S., & Kane, J. (1984). EEG sleep of normal healthy children: I. Findings using standard measurement methods. *Sleep, 7,* 289–303.

Cohen, N. B., Kircher, J., Emmerson, R. Y., & Dustman, R. E. (1985). Pattern reversal evoked potentials: Age, sex, and hemispheric asymmetry. *Electroencephalography and Clinical Neurophysiology, 62,* 397–405.

Conners, C. F. (1971). Cortical visual evoked response in children with learning disorders. *Psychophysiology, 7,* 418–428.

Craig, A. R., & Cleary, P. J. (1983). Reduction of stuttering by a young male stutterer using EMG feedback. *Biofeedback and Self-Regulation, 7,* 241–255.

Creer, T. L. (1982). Asthma. *Journal of Consulting and Clinical Psychology, 6,* 912–921.

Davis, M., Saunders, D., Creer, T. L., & Chai, H. (1973). Relaxation training facilitated by biofeedback apparatus as a supplemental treatment in bronchial asthma. *Journal of Psychosomatic Research, 17,* 121–128.

Denkowski, K. M., & Denkowski, G. C. (1984). Is group progressive relaxation as effective with hyperactive children as individual EMG biofeedback treatment? *Biofeedback and Self-Regulation, 9,* 353–364.

Diamond, S., & Franklin, M. (1975). Biofeedback—choice of treatment in childhood migraine. In W. Luthe & F. Antonelli (Eds.), *Therapy in psychosomatic medicine* (Vol. 4). Rome: Autogenic Therapy.

Duffy, E. (1930). Tensions and emotional factors in reactions. *Genetic Psychology Monographs, 7,* 1–79.

Duffy, E. (1932). The measurement of muscular tension as a technique for the study of emotional tendencies. *American Journal of Psychology, 44,* 146–162.

Dunn, F. M., & Howell, R. J. (1982). Relaxation training and its relationship to hyperactivity in boys. *Journal of Clinical Psychology, 38,* 92–100.

Eaton, W. O. (1983). Measuring activity level with actometers: Reliability, validity, and arm length. *Child Development, 54,* 720–726.

Edelson, R. I., & Sprague, R. L. (1974). Conditioning of activity level in a classroom with institutionalized retarded boys. *American Journal of Mental Deficiency, 78,* 384–388.

Egermark-Eriksson, I. (1982). Prevalence of headache in Swedish school-children. *Acta Paediatrica Scandinavica, 71,* 135–140.

Esfeldt, A. W. (1960). *Silent speech and silent reading.* Chicago: University of Chicago Press.

Evans, J. R. (1977). A configuration of cortical coupling differentiating good from poor readers. *International Journal of Neuroscience, 7,* 211–216.

Fernando, C. K., & Basmajian, J. V. (1978). Biofeedback in physical medicine and rehabilitation. *Biofeedback and Self-Regulation, 3,* 435–455.

Fields, T. A., & Ashmore, L. (1982). Use of radiotelemetry to obtain expressive language samples. *Journal of Communicative Disorders, 15,* 1–19.

Finley, W. W. (1983). Biofeedback with children. In C. E. Walker & M. C. Roberts (Eds.), *Handbook of clinical child psychology.* New York: John Wiley & Sons.

Foster, F. G., McPartland, R. J., & Kupfer, D. J. (1978). Motion sensors in medicine, Part I. A report on reliability and validity. *Journal of Inter-American Medicine, 3,* 4–8.

Friedman, D., Brown, C., Vaughan, H. G., Jr., Cornblatt, B., & Erlenmeyer-Kimling, L. (1984). Cognitive brain potentials in adolescents. *Psychophysiology, 21,* 83–96.

Gardner, J. O. (1973). Evaluation of preschool children through radiotelemetry. *Journal of Speech and Hearing Disorders, 38,* 359–361.

Ginter, G. G., Hollandsworth, J. G., & Intrieri, R. C. (1986). Age difference in cardiovascular reactivity under active coping conditions. *Psychophysiology, 23,* 113–120.

Glidden, J. B., Busk, J., & Galbraith, G. C. (1971). Visual evoked responses to emotional stimuli in the mentally retarded. *Psychophysiology, 8,* 576–580.

Gracenin, C. T., & Cook, J. E. (1977). Alpha biofeedback and LD children. *Academic Therapy, 12,* 275–279.

Greenfield, N. S., & Sternbach, L. A. (1972). *Handbook of psychophysiology.* New York: Holt, Rinehart, & Winston.

Gresham, F., & Evans, J. R. (1979). Recent developments in electrophysiological measurement: Implications for school psychology. *Psychology in the Schools, 16,* 315–321.

Grunewald-Zuberbier, E., Grunewald, G., & Rasche, A. (1972). Telemetric measurement of motor activity in maladjusted children under different experimental conditions. *Psychiatria, Neurologia, Neurochirurgia 75,* 371–378.

Halliday, R., Callaway, E., & Rosenthal, J. H. (1984). The visual ERP predicts clinical response to methylphenidate in hyperactive children. *Psychophysiology, 21,* 114–121.

Halverson, C. F., Jr., & Waldrop, M. F. (1973). The relations of mechanically recorded activity level to varieties of preschool play behavior. *Child Development, 44,* 678–681.

Hampstead, W. J. (1979). The effects of EMG-assisted relaxation training with hyperkinetic children: A behavioral alternative. *Biofeedback and Self-Regulation, 4,* 113–125.

Hardyck, C., & Petrinovich, L. F. (1969). Treatment of subvocal speech during reading. *Journal of Reading, 12,* 361–368; 419–422.

Hardyck, C., & Petrinovich, L. F. (1970). Subvocal speech and comprehension level as a function of the difficulty level of reading material. *Journal of Verbal Learning and Verbal Behavior, 9,* 647–652.

Hassett, J. (1978). *A primer of psychophysiology.* San Francisco: W. H. Freeman.

Hastings, J. E., & Barkley, R. A. (1978). A review of psychophysiological research with hyperkinetic children. *Journal of Abnormal Child Psychology, 6,* 413–447.

Hatch, J. P., Fisher, J. G., & Rugh, J. D. (Eds.). (1987). *Biofeedback: Studies in clinical efficacy.* New York: Plenum Press.

Haynes, S. N. (1978). Psychophysiological measurement in behavioral assessment. In S. N. Haynes, *Principles of behavioral assessment.* New York: Gardner Press.

Haynes, S. N. (1980). Muscle contraction headache: A psychophysiological perspective of etiology and treatment. In S. N. Haynes & L. R. Gannon (Eds.), *Psychosomatic disorders: A psychophysiological approach to etiology and treatment.* New York: Gardner Press.

Haynes, S. N., Cuevas, J., & Gannon, L. R. (1982). The psychophysiology of muscle-contraction headache. *Headache, 22,* 122–132.

Hersey, M. (1983). Warm fingers, cool behavior. *Academic Therapy, 18,* 593–597.

Herron, R. E., & Ramsden, R. W. (1967). Continuous monitoring of overt human body movement by radiotelemetry: A brief review. *Perceptual and Motor Skills, 24,* 1303–1308.

Hoelscher, T. J., & Lichstein, K. L. (1983). Behavioral assessment and treatment of child migraine: Implications for clinical research and practice. *Headache, 24,* 94–103.

Hughes, H., Henry, D., & Hughes, A. (1980). The effect of frontal EMG biofeedback training on the behavior of children with activity-level problems. *Biofeedback and Self-Regulation, 5,* 207–219.

Hughes, H., Jackson, K., Dubois, E., & Erwin, R. (1979). Treatment of handwriting problems utilizing biofeedback training. *Perceptual and Motor Skills, 48,* 603–606.

Hunter, S. H., Russell, H. L., Russell, E. D., & Zimmerman, R. L. (1976). Control of fingertip temperature increases via biofeedback in learning-disabled and normal children. *Perceptual and Motor Skills, 43,* 743–755.

Jasper, H. H. (1958). The ten twenty electrode system of the International Federation. *Journal of Electroencephalography and Clinical Neurophysiology, 10,* 371–375.

Johnson, C. F. (1971). Hyperactivity and the machine: The actometer. *Child Development, 42,* 2105–2110.

Jost, H. (1941). Some physiological changes during frustration. *Child Development, 12,* 9–15.

Kallman, W. M. (1975). *Physiological and behavioral responses to altered sensory levels and stress.* Ph.D. diss., University of Georgia.

Kallman, W. M., & Feuerstein, M. (1977). Psychophysiological procedures. In A. R. Ciminero, K. S. Calhoun, & H. E. Adams (Eds.), *Handbook of behavioral assessment* (pp. 329–364). New York: John Wiley & Sons.

Kalotkin, M., Manschreck, T., & O'Brien, D. (1979). Electromyographic tension levels in stutterers and normal speakers. *Perceptual and Motor Skills, 49,* 109–110.

Kiloh, L. G., McComas, A. J., & Osselton, J. W. (1972). *Clinical electroencephalography* (3d Ed., p. 22). London: Butterworth.

Kotses, H., & Glaus, K. D. (1981). Applications of biofeedback to the treatment of asthma: A critical review. *Biofeedback and Self-Regulation, 6,* 573–593.

Kotses, H., Glaus, K. D., Bricel, S. K., Edwards, J. E., & Crawford, P. L. (1978). Operant muscular relaxation and peak respiratory flow rate in asthmatic children. *Journal of Psychosomatic Research, 22,* 17–23.

Kotses, H., Glaus, K. D., Crawford, P. L., Edwards, J. E., & Scherr, M. S. (1976). Operant reduction of frontalis EMG activity in the treatment of asthma in children. *Journal of Psychosomatic Research, 20,* 453–459.

Kuna, D. J., & Gargiulo, R. M. (1979). Hyperkinetic children and biofeedback: A cautionary note. *American Journal of Clinical Biofeedback, 2,* 40–41.

Larsson, B., & Melin, L. (1986). Chronic headaches in adolescents: Treatment in a school setting with relaxation training as compared with information-contact and self-registration. *Pain, 25,* 325–336.

Lesny, L., Provasnik, K., Jirasek, J., & Komarek, L. (1977). The value of EEG, especially hyperventilation test in learning disabilities. *Activas Nervosa Superior* (Praha), *19,* 263–264.

Lewis, D. V., & Freeman, J. M. (1977). The electroencephalogram in pediatric practice: Its use and abuse. *Pediatrics, 60,* 324–330.

Lichstein, K. L., Sallis, J. F., Hill, D., & Young, M. L. (1981). Psychophysiological adaptation: An investigation of multiple parameters. *Journal of Behavioral Assessment, 3,* 111–121.

Linkenhoker, D. (1983). Tools of behavioral medicine: Applications of biofeedback treatment for children and adolescents. *Developmental and Behavioral Pediatrics, 4,* 16–20.

Lubar, J. F., & Bahler, W. W. (1976). Behavioral management of epileptic seizures following EEG biofeedback training of the sensorimotor rhythm. *Biofeedback and Self-Regulation, 1,* 293–306.

Lubar, J. F., & Deering, W. E. (1981). Applications of behavioral medicine for minimal brain dysfunction syndrome: Hyperkinesis and specific learning dysabilities. In J. F. Lubar & W. E. Deering, *Behavioral approaches to neurology.* New York: Academic Press.

Lubar, J. O., & Lubar, J. F. (1984). Electroencephalographic biofeedback of SMR and beta for treatment of attention deficit disorders in a clinical setting. *Biofeedback and Self-Regulation, 9,* 1–23.

Lubar, J. F., & Shouse, M. N. (1976). EEG and behavioral changes in a hyperkinetic child concurrent with training of the sensorimotor rhythm (SMR): A preliminary report. *Biofeedback and Self-Regulation, 1,* 293–306.

Maccoby, E. E., Dowley, E. M., Hagen, J. W., & Degerman, R. (1965). Activity level and intellectual functioning in normal preschool children. *Child Development, 36,* 761–770.

McGrath, P. J. (1983). Migraine headaches in children and adolescents. In P. Firestone, P. J. McGrath, & W. Feldman (Eds.), *Advances in behavioral medicine for children and adolescents* (pp. 39–57). Hillsdale, N.J.: Lawrence Erlbaum Associates.

McGuigan, F. J., & Bailey, S. C. (1969). Longitudinal study of covert oral behavior during silent reading. *Perceptual and Motor Skills, 28,* 170.

Milner, M. (1983). Technology to aid and abet biofeedback approaches. In P. Firestone, P. J. McGrath,

& W. Feldman (Eds.), *Advances in behavioral medicine for children and adolescents* (pp. 131–160). Hillsdale, N.J.: Lawrence Erlbaum Associates.

Mulholland, T. (1972). Objective EEG methods for studying covert shifts of visual attention. In F. J. McGuigan & J. Schoonover (Eds.), *Psychology of thinking*. New York: Academic Press.

Mulholland, T. B. (1974). Training visual attention. *Academic Therapy, 10*, 5–17.

Mulholland, T., & Gascon, G. (1972). A quantitative EEG index of the orienting response in children. *Electroencephalography and Clinical Neurophysiology, 33*, 295–301.

Mulholland, T., & Goodman, G. (1982). Reduction in variability of EEG occipital, parietal, and central alpha rhythms by visual feedback stimulation. *Biofeedback and Self-Regulation, 7*, 269–282.

Nishikido, N., Kashiwazaki, H., & Suzuki, T. (1982). Preschool children's daily activities: Direct observation, pedometry or questionnaire. *Journal of Human Ergology, 11*, 214–218.

O'Brien, N. D. (1971). Cerebral blood flow changes in migraine headache. *Headache, 10*, 139–143.

O'Malley, J. E., & Conners, C. K. (1972). The effect of unilateral alpha training on visual evoked response in a dyslexic adolescent. *Psychophysiology, 9*, 467–470.

Omizo, M. M. (1980a). The effects of biofeedback-induced relaxation training in hyperactive adolescent boys. *Journal of Psychology, 105*, 131–138.

Omizo, M. M. (1980b). The effects of relaxation and biofeedback training on Dimensions of Self-Concept (DOSC) among hyperactive male children. *Educational Research Quarterly, 5*, 22–30.

Omizo, M. M., Loffredo, D. A., & Hammett, V. L. (1982). Relaxation exercises for the LD and family. *Academic Therapy, 17*, 603–608.

Omizo, M. M., & Michael, W. B. (1982). Biofeedback-induced relaxation training and impulsivity, attention to task, and locus of control among hyperactive boys. *Journal of Learning Disabilities, 15*, 414–416.

Omizo, M. M., & Williams, R. E. (1981). Biofeedback can calm the hyperactive child. *Academic Therapy, 17*, 43–46.

Omizo, M. M., & Williams, R. E. (1982). Biofeedback-induced relaxation training as an alternative for the elementary school learning-disabled child. *Biofeedback and Self-Regulation, 7*, 139–148.

Philips, C. (1978). Tension headaches: Theoretical problems. *Behavior Research and Therapy, 16*, 249–261.

Philips, C., & Hunter, M. (1982). A psychophysiological investigation of tension headache. *Headache, 22*, 173–179.

Pickoff, H. (1984). Is the muscular model of headache still viable? A review of conflicting data. *Headache, 24*, 186–198.

Preston, M. S., Guthrie, J. T., & Childs, B. (1974). Visual evoked responses (VERs) in normal and disabled readers. *Psychophysiology, 11*, 452–457.

Prout, H. T. (1977). Behavioral intervention with hyperactive children: A review. *Journal of Learning Disabilities, 10*, 141–146.

Ray, W. J., & Raczynski, J. M. (1981). Psychophysiological assessment. In M. Hersen & A. S. Bellack (Eds.), *Behavioral assessment*. Elmsford, N.Y.: Pergamon Press.

Riley, J. A., & Lowe, J. D., Jr. (1981). A study of enhancing vs. reducing subvocal speech during reading. *Journal of Reading, 24*, 7–13.

Rivera, E., & Omizo, M. M. (1980). The effects of relaxation and biofeedback on attention to task and impulsivity among male hyperactive children. *The Exceptional Child, 27*, 41–51.

Rockstroh, B., Birbaumer, N., Elbert, T., & Lutzenberger, W. (1984). Operant control of EEG and event related and slow wave brain potentials. *Biofeedback and Self-Regulation, 9*, 139–160.

St. Louis, K. O., Clausell, P. L., Thompson, J. N., & Rife, C. C. (1982). Preliminary investigation of EMG biofeedback induced relaxation with a preschool aged stutterer. *Perceptual and Motor Skills, 55*, 195–199.

Sandoval, J. (1977). The measurement of the hyperactive syndrome in children. *Review of Educational Research, 47*, 293–318.

Sargent, J. D., Walters, E. D., & Green, E. E. (1973). Psychosomatic regulation of migraine headaches. *Seminars in Psychiatry, 5*, 415–428.

Satterfield, J. H., Cantwell, D. P., Saul, R. E., Lesser, L. I., & Podosin, R. L. (1973). Response to stimulant drug treatment in hyperactive children: Prediction from EEG and neurological findings. *Journal of Autism and Childhood Schizophrenia, 3,* 36–48.

Schulman, J. L., & Reisman, J. M. (1959). An objective measure of hyperactivity. *American Journal of Mental Deficiency, 64,* 455–456.

Schulman, J. L., Stevens, T. M., & Kupst, M. J. (1977). The biomotometer: A new device for the measurement and remediation of hyperactivity. *Child Development, 48,* 1152–1154.

Schulman, J. L., Stevens, T. M., Suran, B. G., Kupst, M. J., & Naughton, M. J. (1978). Modification of activity level through biofeedback and operant conditioning. *Journal of Applied Behavior Analysis, 11,* 145–152.

Schulman, J. L., Suran, B. G., Stevens, T. M., & Kupst, M. J. (1979). Instructions, feedback, and reinforcement in reducing activity levels in the classroom. *Journal of Applied Behavior Analysis, 12,* 441–447.

Seifert, A. R., & Lubar, J. F. (1975). Reduction of epileptic seizures through EEG biofeedback training. *Biological Psychology, 3,* 157–184.

Shapiro, A. I. (1980). An electromyographic analysis of the fluent and dysfluent utterences of several types of stutterers. *Journal of Fluency Disorders, 5,* 203–231.

Shouse, M. N., & Lubar, J. F. (1979). Operant conditioning of EEG rhythms and ritalin in the treatment of hyperkinesis. *Biofeedback and Self-Regulation, 4,* 299–312.

Sobotka, K. R., & May, J. G. (1977). Visual evoked potentials and reaction time in normal and dyslexic children. *Psychophysiology, 14,* 19–24.

Sprague, R. L., & Toppe, L. K. (1966). Relationship between activity level and delay of reinforcement in the retarded. *Journal of Experimental Child Psychology, 3,* 390–397.

Stern, R. M., Ray, W. J., & Davis, C. M. (1980). *Psychophysiological recording.* New York: Oxford University Press.

Stevens, T. M., Kupst, M. J., Suran, B. G., & Schulman, J. L. (1978). Activity level: A comparison between actometer scores and observer ratings. *Journal of Abnormal Child Psychology, 6,* 163–173.

Stoyva, J., & Budzynski, T. (1975). Cultivated low arousal—an antistress response? In L. V. Dicara (Ed.), *Limbic and autonomic nervous system research* (pp. 370–394). New York: Plenum Press.

Tansey, M. A., & Bruner, R. L. (1983). EMG and EEG biofeedback training in the treatment of a 10-year-old hyperactive boy with a developmental reading disorder. *Biofeedback and Self-Regulation, 8,* 25–37.

Taub, E., & School, P. J. (1978). Some methodological considerations in thermal biofeedback training. *Behavioral Research Methods and Instrumentation, 10,* 617–622.

Thompson, J. K., Haber, J. D., Tearnan, B. H. (1981). Generalization of frontalis electromyographic feedback to adjacent muscle groups: A critical review. *Psychosomatic Medicine, 42,* 19–24.

Walden, E. L., & Thompson, S. A. (1981). A review of some alternative approaches to drug management of hyperactivity in children. *Journal of Learning Disabilities, 14,* 213–217; 238.

Werry, J. S. (1968). Developmental hyperactivity. *Pediatric Clinics of North America, 15,* 581–599.

Westmoreland, B. F., & Stockard, J. E. (1977). The EEG in infant and children: Normal patterns. *American Journal of EEG Technology, 17,* 187–206.

Williamson, D. A., Calpin, J. P., DiLorenzo, T. M., Garris, R. P., & Petti, T. A. (1981). Treating hyperactivity with dexedrine and activity feedback. *Behavior Modification, 5,* 399–416.

Wood, J. W., & Frith, G. H. (1984). Drug therapy? Let's take a closer look. *Academic Therapy, 20,* 149–157.

Zenker, E. R. (1984). In the dark about teaching spelling? Just relax! *Academic Therapy, 20,* 231–234.

CHAPTER 6

Self-Monitoring Procedures

WILLIAM I. GARDNER
CHRISTINE L. COLE
University of Wisconsin–Madison

INTRODUCTION

Self-monitoring, also termed self-observation, self-assessment, and self-recording (O'Leary & Dubey, 1979; Shapiro, 1984), offers a valuable assessment procedure for those working with children and adolescents in school settings. In self-monitoring, children are instructed to observe specific aspects of their own behavior and to provide an objective recording of these observations. Thus, self-monitoring involves the two processes of self-observation and self-recording. A child in a classroom may be asked to notice each time he or she talks to a peer during a silent reading period. Following this self-observation, the child makes a record of the observed behavior, for example, by placing a check mark on a card taped to the desktop.

Self-recording, in addition to providing frequency data, may reflect other measures of behavior strength such as the duration, latency, or intensity of the target behavior. Although self-monitoring most often involves discrete behaviors, a few studies describe the use of global ratings of the quality of the observer's behavior. As examples, Santogrossi, O'Leary, Romanczyk, and Kaufman (1973) and Turkewitz, O'Leary, and Ironsmith (1975) instructed disruptive children to make global ratings of their social behavior in the classroom following specified periods of time.

Children, in addition to providing data on the strength of their target behaviors, may be directed to record stimulus events that precede or follow specific actions. These behavior analysis data would be useful in developing hunches about events that may influence specific child behaviors and in selecting intervention procedures to change these targets.

The use of self-monitoring as an assessment procedure in school settings has considerable practical usefulness as child-collected data are more convenient to obtain than data collected by other observers. Also, the behavior may be of a covert nature, available only through self-observation. The self-monitoring of covert events is illustrated by Gottman and McFall (1972) who instructed students in a class for potential high school dropouts to monitor their failure to participate orally in class discussions even though they covertly wished to do so. In other instances, self-monitoring may be the only source of data regarding a child's or adolescent's behavior in the natural environment such as when information is needed about how a behavior is distributed across a wide range of times or settings. This was illustrated in a study by McConnell, Biglan, and Severson (1984) of smoking behavior among adolescents. Participants were asked to record both the number of cigarettes smoked throughout the day and the situations in which smoking occurred during a daily "intensive check" period.

In summary, the purpose of self-monitoring as an *assessment* procedure is to obtain data on specific student behaviors, either as an aspect of pretreatment behavior analysis to determine appropriate target behaviors and treatment strategies, or as a means of evaluating the effects of an intervention procedure or program. As noted below, however, certain characteristics of self-monitoring impose limitations on its routine use as a data collection procedure.

Self-monitoring, in addition to being used for assessment purposes, may be a useful means of *behavior change*. Numerous studies have demonstrated that the activity of focusing attention on one's own behavior and the subsequent self-recording of these observations may result in reactive effects, or changes in the strength of the behavior being monitored (Nelson, 1977; Shapiro, 1984). While reactivity does not always result from self-monitoring (Howell, Rueda, & Rutherford, 1983; Santogrossi *et al.*, 1973: Turkewitz *et al.*, 1975), the effect has been observed with sufficient regularity to support its potential as a clinically useful tool. In fact, the most frequent current use of self-monitoring in clinical, including classroom, settings is as a therapeutic or behavior change procedure. When reactive effects are observed following the initiation of data collection on one's own behavior, most typically positively valenced behaviors increase in strength, while negatively valenced targets show a decrease. These reactive effects, even though a positive feature of self-monitoring, create difficulties when the procedure is used for assessment purposes. The significance of the data obtained through self-monitoring is reduced as it is difficult to isolate the presence or magnitude of the reactive effects (Fleece & Jolly, 1983; Nelson, 1977). This problem is discussed in a later section.

To facilitate clinical applications of self-monitoring in school-based settings, a case study is described. In addition frequent illustrations of specific components of self-monitoring procedures are provided. While not comprehensive, the illustrations and related empirical studies are representative of the procedural, conceptual, and practical concerns relating to self-monitoring. For more detail, the interested reader is encouraged to refer to studies cited in this chapter and to critical and descriptive reviews by Armstrong and Frith (1984), Ciminero, Nelson, and Lipinski (1977), McFall (1977), Nelson (1977), and Shapiro (1984).

METHODOLOGY OF SELF-MONITORING

Types of Behaviors Self-Monitored

The types of behaviors that can be self-monitored by children and adolescents range from those objective behaviors that are readily observable by oneself or others (e.g., presence or absence of on-task behaviors, number of math assignments completed) to those personal features that are subjective and thus observable only to the person him- or herself (e.g., negative thoughts, urges to talk during class discussion). Behavioral targets of self-monitoring may include such activities as nervous ticks (Ollendick, 1981), story writing (Ballard & Glynn, 1975), hyperactivity (Heins, Lloyd, & Hallahan, 1986), on-task behavior (Sagotsky, Patterson, & Lepper, 1978), work behaviors (Seymour & Stokes, 1976), academic performance (Roberts & Nelson, 1981), classroom behavior (O'Leary & Dubey, 1979), disruptive behavior (Turkewitz et al., 1975), and oral class participation (Gottman & McFall, 1972).

Behaviors that may be self-recorded for assessment purposes vary along a number of different dimensions. These include:

1. Objectivity. As illustrated above, behaviors recorded may range from objectively defined and readily observable by oneself and others to highly subjective behaviors available only to the person who is self-monitoring.
2. Complexity. Behaviors observed and recorded may range from simple behaviors, such as the number of tasks completed correctly (e.g., Roberts & Nelson, 1981), to complex situational analyses in which the student is asked to identify specific antecedents or consequences that may be influencing occurrence and maintenance of the target behavior (e.g., McConnel et al., 1984).
3. Number of Behaviors. Behaviors that are self-monitored may range from a single one, such as the number of times talking out occurs in class, to recording multiple behaviors or related data, such as the number of problems completed, number of correctly spelled words, or the time required to complete a reading assignment. Christie, Hiss, and Lozanoff (1984) provide an illustration of self-monitoring of multiple behaviors. Third- and fourth-grade boys were trained to self-monitor eight categories of their behavior and to record which of these was occurring at the time of a teacher signal. These included such categories as emotional outburst, disruptive noise, talking, on-task, and attentiveness.
4. Timing of Recording. The child may record immediately following each occurrence of behavior, such as following completion of assignments (e.g., Piersel, 1985), or after a delay, such as after class or at the end of the school day (e.g., Schunk, 1982).

5. Schedule of Recording. The target behavior may be recorded following each occurrence (e.g., Ollendick, 1981) or on a less frequent time sampling basis (e.g., Sugai & Rowe, 1984).

Characteristics of Children Who Can Self-Monitor

The empirical literature has demonstrated the feasibility of self-monitoring procedures with children and adolescents presenting a variety of individual differences. Students in regular and special education classes, schools, or residential settings who present a range of behavioral, social, and academic difficulties have successfully provided assessment data through self-monitoring. These include students with such diagnoses as mental retardation (Howell *et al.*, 1983), learning disabilities (Kneedler & Hallahan, 1981), behavior disorders (McLaughlin, 1984), hyperactivity (Christie *et al.*, 1984), psychiatric impairment (Santogrossi *et al.*, 1973), and juvenile offenses (Wood & Flynn, 1978), as well as students with no exceptionality designation attending regular nursery (Workman, Helton, & Watson, 1982), kindergarten (Studwell & Moxley, 1984), elementary (Sagotsky *et al.*, 1978), and secondary (Broden, Hall, & Mitts, 1971) school programs. Although the type, number, and complexity of behaviors that could be self-monitored vary among children and adolescents differing in characteristics such as age, cognitive level, and emotional status, it is evident that the procedure may have utility with the entire range of children served within school settings.

Self-Monitoring by Individuals and Groups

Self-monitoring may be used by an individual child to assess and record target behaviors that occur in one or more settings. This was illustrated by Piersel (1985), who described a third grader who self-recorded completion of academic assignments and by Ollendick (1981), who instructed boys to self-record each occurrence of individually defined nervous tics in their respective school and home settings.

In addition to being valuable in providing assessment data for an individual, self-monitoring procedures have been used successfully with groups of students attending both special and regular education classes. Hallahan, Marshall, and Lloyd (1981) obtained data from a group of learning disabled children attending a self-contained class. A tape recorder, emitting tones on an average of every forty-five seconds, was placed on the side of the classroom. Each child, trained as a group by the classroom teacher, asked himself or herself, "Was I paying attention?" at the sound of each tone. Every member of the class then self-recorded their own assessment by checking a box for yes or no on a self-recording sheet placed on the child's desk. In a study using the same self-recording procedure, Rooney, Hallahan, and Lloyd (1984) obtained self-monitored data from an entire regular class of fourteen second graders in a small city school. The children self-monitored their attention during academic work.

In other variations, Howell *et al.* (1983) demonstrated the feasibility of using self-monitoring procedures with a group of moderately mentally retarded adolescents (CA range 10 to 13 years old; Binet IQ range 30 to 44) attending a public school self-contained class. Students self-monitored idiosyncratic target behaviors (off-task, tongue protrusion, stereotypic behavior) during a daily one-hour structured work situation. Self-monitoring by each student was completed following a teacher prompt. As the prompt (a tap on the shoulder) was individual in nature, other class members were not distracted from their work activities. Finally, Sagotsky *et al.* (1978) obtained data from groups of students attending fifth and sixth grades. Each child was instructed to note from time to time whether or not they were working on their math units and to mark their observation on a recording sheet.

In summary, self-monitoring procedures are adaptable for use with individual members of a group, with multiple members of a group, or with an entire group. The relatively unobtrusive nature of self-monitoring contributes to its potential for use as an assessment procedure in school settings.

Procedures of Self-Monitoring

In selecting a procedure for self-monitoring behaviors, several factors should be considered to ensure that students will, in fact, self-record behavior and that this recording will be done in an accurate manner. Initially, a procedure should be selected that is appropriate for the behaviors being recorded and is relatively easy to follow. For example, a time sampling procedure would be favored over continuous recording for high-rate behaviors. To be feasible for use in a school setting, the procedure should be inexpensive and relatively unobtrusive. Even though, as discussed in a subsequent section of this chapter, an obtrusive recording device may serve as a cue for self-monitoring and thus potentially enhance accuracy of recording, a balance is needed between the obtrusiveness of the device and one that is feasible and acceptable to the child and teacher.

Types of Data Collected

In most instances of self-monitoring in school settings, specific occurrences of a target behavior are recorded. These recordings may reflect (1) total frequency of the behavior within a designated period of time (e.g., every occurrence of out-of-seat behavior during a one-hour academic class), or (2) occurrences based on a time sampling procedure (e.g., presence or absence of on-task at the moment a signal is presented).

Frequency Counts. A data collection procedure commonly used in empirical studies reporting self-monitoring with children and adolescents involves recording each occurrence of the target behavior(s), usually at the time of occurrence. This procedure is most useful when frequency of the target behavior is relatively low, when the occurrence is of short duration, and when the behavior is discrete. Piersel

(1985), for example, instructed an adolescent to record on a prepared form the completion of academic assignments as he placed them in the work completion box on the teacher's desk. Ollendick (1981) trained two boys (CA 9 and 11) to use a wrist counter to record each occurrence of nervous tics. Data may be reported as total frequency or as rate of occurrence. Behavior rate is calculated by dividing the total number of occurrences by the total observation time.

Time Sampling. A second frequently used procedure in school settings is time sampling. Sugai and Rowe (1984) used a time sampling procedure to obtain self-monitoring data from a fifteen-year-old, mildly retarded male. At the end of ten-minute intervals, the adolescent was signaled by a kitchen timer to self-assess whether he had remained in his seat for the entire ten-minute period and to record an "I" or "O" dependent upon this assessment.

A popular variation of time sampling is that of spot-checking or momentary time sampling (e.g., Barton & Ascione, 1984; Kubany & Sloggett, 1973). In using this procedure, the child is provided with a signal on a fixed or variable interval schedule. On the occurrence of the signal, usually an auditory one, the child self-monitors the target behavior, decides on its occurrence, and then records this observation. Data typically are summarized as percentage measures calculated by dividing the number of occurrences recorded at the time of the signal by the total number of times the signal was given. This time sampling procedure was illustrated by Rooney *et al.* (1984). Learning disabled children attending regular classrooms were trained, upon hearing a tone delivered by a tape recorder on the average of every forty-five seconds, to decide if they were paying attention and to record their observations. As a second example, Howell *et al.* (1983) signaled self-monitoring in moderately mentally retarded children by randomly tapping them lightly on the shoulder 10 times during a one-hour period. A less precise time sampling procedure reported by Broden *et al.* (1971), McLaughlin (1984), Sagotsky *et al.* (1978), and others involves self-recording target behaviors from time to time, whenever the child thinks about it. McLaughlin (1984) and Sagotsky *et al.* (1978) illustrated this procedure in which students were instructed to mark a "+" when they felt they were studying and a "−" when they were not.

Narrative Descriptions. Self-monitoring may be useful in the initial stages of selecting a target behavior and in developing hunches about factors involved in its occurrence. These preliminary clinical data may be provided by a child or adolescent in the form of narrative descriptions in a behavioral diary. The data may be structured or unstructured. The child may be requested to record occurrences of a specified behavior and the circumstances involved. These observations may include only the setting or situation in which the behavior occurred (e.g., classroom, restroom), or may include antecedents and consequences. Kunzelmann's (1970) *countoon* provides an example of a structured diary for children. A pictorial sequence is provided to prompt the child to record instances of the target behavior as well as its consequences.

Devices Used in Data Collection

A variety of devices are available as aids in the collection of self-monitoring data. The most popular in school settings are paper-and-pencil procedures and mechanical counting devices used in frequency and interval recording, and timing devices used in collecting duration data. A number of considerations have been suggested as guidelines in selection of a specific recording device (Ciminero *et al.*, 1977; Watson & Tharp, 1972). First, to increase the accuracy of self-monitoring, the device should be available for recording the target behavior as it occurs. To ensure its availability when self-monitoring is to occur in more than one location (e.g., home and school, in different classes), the recording device should be portable. Second, the recording device should be easy to use and not distracting. For example, if the child continues to manipulate or attend to the device following recording, other task requirements, such as completion of math problems, may not be met.

The obtrusiveness of the device represents another selection consideration. The child should be sufficiently aware of the device to ensure that recording will occur. If excessively conspicuous, however, it may attract attention from others. This social feedback may, depending upon its positive or negative nature, interfere with the self-monitoring process and thus lead to inaccurate data. A final consideration in selecting a recording device is its cost. Wrist counters, for example, may be ideal to use with a large class of students because this device is portable and sufficiently obtrusive to serve as a reminder for recording. However, the cost to the school or child of this recording device may be prohibitive.

Paper-and-Pencil Procedures. Paper-and-pencil recording forms may vary, from a card or slip of paper on which the child makes a tally mark for each occurrence of the target behavior to more detailed and structured data forms (see Figure 6-1 for examples of these forms). McLaughlin, Burgess, and Sackville-West (1982) used a dittoed data sheet composed of fifty small squares. The child marked a "+" when the target behavior was occurring and a "−" if the behavior was not occurring at a designated time. Schunk (1982) provided a prepared data form containing the child's name and space to record the number of pages of math problems completed during the study period. In addition to information about the academic work completed, Sagotsky *et al.* (1978) used a data sheet that contained a grid of empty boxes for making a periodic record of whether the child was working or not. The recording form may be taped on the child's desk (e.g., Piersel, 1985), placed on the wall next to the child's desk (e.g., Workman *et al.*, 1982), included in the child's packet of work materials (e.g., Schunk, 1982), or carried by the adolescent throughout the day (e.g., McConnell *et al.*, 1984)

Mechanical Devices. Nelson, Lipinski, and Boykin (1978) described the use of both hand-held and belt-worn *counters* with mentally retarded adolescents to self-record appropriate verbalizations in a classroom setting. In another example, wrist

YES	NO

TALKING	NO TALKING

STUDY RECORD

Name: _____ Date: _____
Record a "+" if you were studying.
Record a "-" if you were not studying.

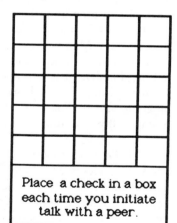

Place a check in a box
each time you initiate
talk with a peer.

FIGURE 6-1 Examples of Self-Monitoring Recording Forms

counters were used by boys to count their nervous tics (Ollendick, 1981). The boys were instructed to count each nervous tic on the wrist counter and to record the frequency on an index card at periodic intervals. The counters were used in both school and home settings.

A *timing device* such as a stopwatch or runner's wristwatch is useful in obtaining duration data. For example, a student may accumulate the total time spent in studying during a specified period by using either of these timing devices.

Nature of Prompts to Self-Monitor

During a designated self-monitoring period, the student may be prompted by an external signal to observe and record a specific target behavior, or may self-prompt this assessment and recording activity.

External Prompts. External prompts may involve verbal or nonverbal prompts delivered by another person or by a mechanical device. Howell *et al.* (1983) illustrated the use of staff-provided prompts. As noted earlier, self-monitoring of idiosyncratic behaviors by moderately mentally retarded students in a classroom was signaled whenever the teacher tapped them on the shoulder. As a second example, Christie *et al.* (1984) used verbal or nonverbal gestures to signal boys in third- and fourth-grade classrooms to record their target behaviors. Examples of prompting by a mechanical device are provided by Rooney *et al.* (1984), Lloyd, Hallahan, Kosiewicz, and Kneedler (1982), and Hallahan, Lloyd, Kneedler, and Marshall (1982) who used tape-recorded audio tones as a signal for self-monitoring task attention by children in self-contained and regular classroom settings. Finally, a kitchen timer was used by Workman *et al.* (1982) to signal the self-monitoring of study behavior in a four-year-old child attending a preschool program, and by Sugai and Rowe (1984) with a mildly retarded adolescent to prompt self-monitoring of in-seat behavior in the classroom.

Self-Prompts. Sagotsky *et al.* (1978) instructed boys and girls, enrolled in fifth and sixth grades in which an individualized mathematics instruction program was used, to note from time to time during the daily fifty-minute math period whether or not they were actually working on their math units. This self-prompted observation was then recorded on a data sheet containing a grid of twelve empty boxes. A similar procedure was reported by Broden *et al.* (1971) who instructed a junior high school student with study habit difficulties to self-record, whenever she happened to think about it, whether or not she was engaged in appropriate study behavior. Her evaluation was recorded on a slip provided each day by the school counselor.

Methods of Training Self-Monitoring

The specific methods used in training children to self-monitor their behavior are related to the complexity of the data collected and of the self-monitoring procedure itself, as well as to such subject characteristics as age, cognitive level, and presence of competing behaviors. The training procedures selected may range from simple verbal instructions to detailed training programs involving instructions, modeling, guided practice, performance feedback, independent practice, and reinforcement. Direct instruction combined with behavior rehearsal of simulated scenes or with videotaped scenes of actual behaviors and situations may be used. Training may occur in vivo or in a separate training location. Finally, training may involve the specific target behaviors selected for self-monitoring, or may involve other behaviors simulated to teach the self-monitoring process.

The specific training procedures selected should ensure that the child understands what is expected and has the skills to implement the self-monitoring process. Frith and Armstrong (1985) recommended that programs designed to train accurate self-monitoring among children and adolescents include: (1) explicit definition of the target behavior, (2) simplified behavior counting and recording procedures, (3) specific and relatively short time periods in which self-monitoring occurs, (4) teacher reliability checks and student feedback, and (5) sufficient practice to ensure that fluency in self-monitoring is attained. These writers offer sample plans for teaching self-monitoring skills and should be consulted by the interested reader.

Verbal Instructions

In most instances of discrete behaviors that are self-recorded on a prepared data sheet, training is simply a matter of brief verbal instructions. This training procedure was used by McLaughlin (1984) with a group of behaviorally disordered elementary school children attending a self-contained special education class. Each child was provided a dittoed sheet composed of fifty small squares and instructed to mark a "+" when they felt they were studying and a "−" when they were not.

Verbal Instructions, Modeling, and Feedback

Rooney *et al.* (1984) used a more elaborate training procedure involving instructions, teacher modeling, and feedback in training second-grade students in a regular class to self-record their attending behavior whenever signaled by a tone from a tape recorder. The teacher modeled both on-task and off-task behavior for the class and prompted the children to label and record their observations on a self-recording sheet. This training was followed by a brief session the next day to ensure that the students returned to work on their assignments after recording rather than waiting for the next tone.

Modeling, Guided Rehearsal, and Independent Practice

A four-year-old boy attending a preschool program and demonstrating a low rate of appropriate work behavior during task periods was trained in a self-monitoring procedure that involved making a mark on a sheet of paper if working on a teacher-assigned task when a kitchen timer rang. Training consisted of modeling the procedure on five trials; five trials of guided practice by the child; and ten trials of independent practice, during which feedback was provided for accurate recording (Workman *et al.*, 1982).

Use of Videotapes

Christie *et al.* (1984) used videotapes to teach self-monitoring skills to three third- and fourth-grade boys who were diagnosed as hyperactive and who were attending regular classes. The videotapes represented actual classroom behaviors that previously had been filmed through a one-way mirror. During six one-hour training sessions, each child was trained to use behavior observation recording sheets to classify his videotaped behaviors. A momentary time sampling procedure was used to assess and record eight mutually exclusive behaviors. Following training, the boys self-monitored these same behaviors in the classroom when signaled by the teacher to do so. The authors suggested that, in view of the rapid rate with which the children learned to record their behavior accurately, neither the many training sessions nor the videotape of the child's actual behavior were necessary. An alternative was suggested of having children view a vignette of any child who exhibited inappropriate classroom behavior. It would then be feasible for the teacher to view the videotape with the child and together they could learn the criteria for various behavior categories.

Multiple Phase Training

Howell *et al.* (1983) used a multiple phase training program to teach self-recording skills to five moderately mentally retarded students. Training took place outside the classroom and consisted of direct group instruction in self-recording through the use of *countoons*. This recording device consisted of drawings of stick figures either standing or sitting. Three training phases were used, during which overt cues to self-record were gradually faded. All daily training, carried out in the context of a musical chairs game, lasted for approximately thirty minutes. On signal from the trainer, students were taught to record on the countoon sheet whether they were standing or sitting. During Phase A, the trainer said aloud, "Am I standing or sitting?" and tapped one student on the shoulder. Each student then repeated the question aloud and recorded his behavior. The boys were praised for accurate recording.

During Phase B, which began on the sixth day of training, each student was tapped lightly on the shoulder and instructed to ask aloud, "Am I standing or sitting?" and then to mark the answer on the countoon. Repeated cuing was provided to ensure that each student asked the question and students were verbally praised following accurate verbalization and recording. All students were correctly following the procedure after three days of training.

In Phase C, students were trained to verbalize the question covertly and to record their assessment. This phase was completed in nine days. During the final phase, students self-recorded idiosyncratic target behaviors during a daily structured in-class work session. This phase required generalization of the self-recording skills across behaviors and settings. Each student was given new countoons of his or her own target behaviors and instructed to record these when signaled by the teacher. These countoons consisted of drawings of Snoopy, the well-known cartoon character, either engaging in the target behavior or not engaging in the behavior. Mean rater agreement between the student and trainer during the training phases ranged from .78 to .99 and was maintained during the self-recording phase (.76 to .90).

SELF-MONITORING AS AN ASSESSMENT PROCEDURE

Self-monitoring may be used as an assessment procedure to determine appropriate target behaviors and treatment procedures, or to measure the strength of a target behavior during baseline and intervention. Its usefulness as an assessment procedure is dependent upon both the accuracy with which students are able to monitor their behavior and the degree to which reactivity occurs.

Methodological Issues

Procedures for Determining Accuracy

Nelson (1977) described three procedures for determining accuracy of self-monitored data. The most commonly used procedure is to compare self-recordings with those made simultaneously by an external observer. The extent to which a student is able to match an observer's recordings of a particular behavior will determine the accuracy of self-monitored data. For example, McLaughlin (1984) determined the accuracy of student recordings of studying behavior by comparing these with simultaneous observations made by the teacher.

A variation of this procedure has been suggested by Shapiro (1984) in which self-recorded data are compared with a specific criterion that can be directly verified, such as a permanent product measure. In one study with a third-grade boy, the accuracy of self-monitoring of the completion of assignments was determined by comparing self-monitored data with teacher records (Piersel, 1985). Shapiro and Ackerman (1983) also demonstrated the use of this procedure with mentally retarded clients in a vocational setting. Accuracy of self-monitoring was assessed by comparing the self-recorded number of units completed with a count of the actual completed products. The advantage of this variation is that agreement with the criterion variable can be easily and objectively assessed.

A second procedure for determining accuracy is to compare self-recordings with those made simultaneously by a mechanical recording device. For example, Mahoney, Moore, Wade, and Moura (1973) determined accuracy by comparing student answers that were automatically recorded by a teaching machine with the students' own self-recordings. A final procedure for determining accuracy is to compare self-recordings with measures of a behavior believed to be related to the self-monitored behavior. A student's test scores, for example, may be used as an indication of the accuracy of his or her self-monitored study time.

Accuracy versus Interobserver Agreement

A distinction is typically made between observer accuracy and observer agreement (Johnson & Bolstad, 1973; Nelson, 1977). *Observer accuracy* is determined by comparing self-recordings with a previously established criterion or standard. The Mahoney *et al.* (1973) study, in which self-monitored data were compared with mechanical recordings, is an illustration of an observer accuracy measure. In contrast, *observer agreement* involves comparing self-recordings with simultaneous recordings made by an independent observer. A major limitation of this procedure is that individuals may agree with each other, yet both may be inaccurate.

Interobserver agreement has been assessed more frequently than interobserver accuracy of self-monitored data, although the term accuracy will be used in this chapter to refer to both. In most studies, data obtained from external observers (e.g., teachers, parents) is the standard against which self-recordings are compared. Although logic would suggest that adult observers' recordings are more accurate than children's self-recordings and thus should be used as the standard of comparison, there currently are insufficient data to support this assumption.

Accuracy of Self-Monitored Data

Numerous studies demonstrate that children and adolescents, varying widely in cognitive, social, emotional, and behavioral characteristics, are capable of accurately self-monitoring a variety of target behaviors (e.g., Howell *et al.*, 1983; Litrownik, Freitas, & Franzini, 1978; McLaughlin, 1984; Ollendick, 1981; Piersel, 1985; Santogrossi *et al.*, 1973). Many of these studies have reported child-observer agreement levels of at least .80, the generally established cutoff for acceptable levels of agreement. As examples, Santogrossi *et al.* obtained .95 agreement between ratings of independent observers and those of disruptive students who were instructed to make global ratings of their behavior. Ollendick (1981) found the accuracy of self-monitoring of nervous tics by two boys, (CA 9 and 11), to be .88 in school and .89 at home. Piersel (1985) reported .80 to 1.00 agreement between a third-grade student and his teacher when completion of his assignments was monitored. Finally in a study by Christie *et al.* (1984), third- and fourth-grade boys identified as hyperactive were able, with eight categories of behavior, to obtain a high level of agreement (greater than .90) during training with an independent observer. Although agreement levels were not as high during self-monitoring in the classroom (.84, .72, and .76 for the three boys), this study does demonstrate that children can be trained as reliable data collectors even with multiple behavior categories.

Although children's accuracy has been found to be acceptable in most instances, some studies have reported low or inconsistent accuracy. In two of the experiments reported by Nelson, Hay, Devany, and Koslow-Green (1980), elementary students' accuracy was moderate (range .51 to .79), and in a third experiment it was even lower (.07 to .20). Nelson, Lipinski, and Black (1976) and Zegiob, Klukas, and Junginger (1978) also reported moderate to low accuracy of self-recording by mentally retarded individuals. Broden *et al.* (1971) found an acceptable overall level of agreement between observers and students in the regular classroom, but found large day-to-day discrepancies in these recordings of study behavior. Other studies have found large discrepancies in levels of accuracy between individual subjects (e.g., Howell *et al.*, 1983; Shapiro, McGonigle, & Ollendick, 1980).

Kazdin (1974) suggested that children in general may be less accurate self-recorders than adults. Fixsen, Phillips, and Wolf (1972) investigated the accuracy of boys' reports of their own behavior and the behavior of their peers. Results indicated that, although there was .76 agreement between boys' self-reports on the cleanliness of their rooms and peer reports, there was only .50 agreement with adult observers' reports. This discrepancy, however, may reflect inaccurate self-monitoring by children or may merely suggest differences in the criteria used by adult and child observers.

In summary, results concerning the accuracy of children's self-monitoring have been equivocal. Accuracy is reported to be high in many studies and low in others. A number of factors that may account for this variability in accuracy of self-monitoring by students are discussed in the following section.

Variables Affecting the Accuracy of Self-Monitoring

Variables that may influence the accuracy of self-monitoring in children and adolescents include (1) students' awareness of accuracy assessment, (2) reinforcement for accurate self-monitoring, (3) training in accurate self-monitoring, (4) the valence of the target behavior, (5) the nature of the recording device, (6) the nature of the target behavior, (7) concurrent response requirements, and (8) the timing of self-monitoring.

Awareness of Accuracy Assessment

One variable that may influence the accuracy of self-monitoring is awareness of accuracy checks. When students are aware that their self-monitoring is being checked by others, self-monitoring is more likely to be accurate than when accuracy is checked covertly. This was illustrated by Nelson, Lipinski, and Black (1975) who reported a substantial increase in accuracy of self-monitored face touching (from .55 to .81) when college students became aware that their self-monitoring was being checked for accuracy. In a second example, with children, Santogrossi (1974) reported that initial low accuracy of students' self-monitoring correct reading responses was increased after children were informed that either a teacher or a peer was also monitoring their behavior. Comparable increases in accuracy were obtained with both peer and teacher checkers.

Reinforcement for Accurate Self-Monitoring

A number of studies have demonstrated that children's initial low levels of accuracy can be improved with contingent reinforcement for accurate self-monitoring. Fixsen et al. (1972) enhanced the level of agreement between peer reports and self-reports of room cleanliness (from .76 to .86) with contingent reinforcement for accuracy. A second study found an increased accuracy of self-monitoring arithmetic performance in seventeen male adolescents in a special education class following contingent reinforcement for accuracy (Hundert & Bucher, 1978). In another example, inaccurate self-assessment of the academic achievement of a sixth-grade girl was eliminated by providing contingent reinforcement for the accurate self-grading of her daily assignments (Flowers, 1972). Finally, McLaughlin and Trulicka (1983) found with behaviorally disordered elementary students that those who were reinforced for accurate self-monitoring of study behavior were more accurate than those who were not reinforced for accuracy. These studies demonstrate that children's accuracy can be improved with contingent reinforcement for accurate self-monitoring.

A related issue is whether high accuracy levels obtained with contingent reinforcement can be maintained when reinforcement schedules are thinned. Accuracy has been maintained in some cases (Hundert & Bucher, 1978; Robertson, Simon, Pachman, & Drabman, 1979; Wood & Flynn, 1978) and not in others. Drabman, Spitalnik, and O'Leary (1973) and Turkewitz et al. (1975), for example, found decreases in accuracy as the number of students checked and reinforced was decreased. However, in the Drabman et al. (1973) study, when all accuracy checks and reinforcement for accuracy were eliminated during a final self-evaluation phase, the accuracy of self-monitoring returned to the level attained when the children were receiving reinforcement for matching teacher ratings.

Training in Accurate Self-Monitoring

One procedure used in a number of studies to ensure high levels of self-monitoring accuracy is that of reinforcing students for closely matching simultaneous recordings made by an external observer, and penalizing them for inaccurate matching (e.g., Drabman et al., 1973; Robertson et al., 1979; Turkewitz et al., 1975). In the Robertson et al. (1979) study, for example, matching was introduced to a special education class of disruptive mentally retarded children following experience with an externally managed token system. During the matching phase, successful matching with the teacher's ratings resulted in the delivery of the number of points agreed upon and a bonus of an M & M candy. Failure to match resulted in no M & M candy and a point penalty. A series of fading phases then were introduced in which the number of children who "got to match" was systematically reduced until, finally, all students rated their own behavior and received the number of points they awarded themselves. Levels of agreement between student and teacher ratings increased from .69 during the initial matching phase to 1.00 following the fading phases.

Other training procedures have also been found to improve the accuracy of self-monitoring in children. Nelson, *et al.* (1978) provided four mentally retarded adolescents with practice in self-recording their appropriate classroom verbalizations both from videotape and in the regular classroom setting, with feedback from the trainer about correct and incorrect self-recording. Those who were trained in these procedures self-monitored more accurately than those provided only one session of minimal instructions in self-monitoring. Shapiro *et al.* (1980) found substantial improvements in accuracy among mildly and moderatedly mentally retarded, behaviorally disturbed children, who had been initially provided only instructions in general self-management procedures, when they were trained specifically in self-observation and self-recording procedures. This suggests that specific training in self-observation and self-recording, with feedback for correct and incorrect responses, may be necessary to increase the accuracy of self-monitoring in some students, especially those with cognitive limitations.

Valence of the Target Behavior

Kanfer (1977) proposed that accuracy of self-monitoring may be influenced by the valence of the behavior being recorded. More specifically, he suggested that negatively valenced behaviors may be self-monitored less accurately than positively valenced behaviors. He speculated that self-monitoring an undesirable behavior may result in covert negative self-evaluation and that, to avoid this, the person may not attend to or record occurrences of that behavior, thus producing inaccurate data. This notion was supported by Nelson, Hay, Hay, and Carstens (1977) in a study with teachers who were instructed to self-record their classroom verbalizations. They found that teachers' accuracy was greater for positive verbalizations than for negative verbalizations. In a study involving children, it was also found that appropriate classroom verbalizations were self-recorded more accurately than were their inappropriate verbalizations (Nelson *et al.*, 1980).

In contrast, in a study with mentally retarded adolescents, no differences in accuracy were found between those self-recording positive or negative behaviors (Litrownik & Freitas, 1980). According to the Kanfer hypothesis, these results would suggest that the mentally retarded subjects did not spontaneously self-evaluate or did not differentially evaluate the positive or negative valence of the behaviors and, as a result, did not avoid recording occurrences of negatively valenced behaviors.

For these retarded adolescents, desirable and undesirable behaviors apparently had not acquired the associated positive or negative valence necessary for differential self-evaluation of these behaviors. Perhaps limited cognitive skills and limited experiential histories may prevent many mentally retarded children and adolescents from spontaneously acquiring such self-evaluation skills. These speculations would suggest that teachers of mentally retarded and other developmentally disabled individuals should provide direct training in the basic skills of self-management.

Nature of the Recording Device

As described earlier, a number of different types of self-monitoring devices are available for use in school settings. Some of these self-monitoring methods, because of particular characteristics, may result in more accurate data collection than others. For example, devices that simplify self-monitoring and are less dependent on the child's memory may produce more accurate data (McFall, 1977). In addition, Nelson et al. (1978) investigated the interaction between accuracy and the obtrusiveness of the recording device with mentally retarded adolescents. They found that hand-held counters resulted in slightly more accurate self-monitoring than belt-worn counters. Thus, more obtrusive self-monitoring methods may, in some cases, result in more accurate data collection. The preliminary nature of these results, however, suggests that further investigation is needed before drawing definite conclusions about the nature of the recording device.

Other Variables

Several other variables have been demonstrated to influence the accuracy of self-monitoring in adults. One of these is the nature of the target behavior being self-monitored. It has been suggested that verbal behavior may be more difficult to self-record accurately than motoric behavior. This has been supported by a number of adult studies (e.g., Cavior & Marabotto, 1976; Hayes & Cavior, 1977; Lipinski & Nelson, 1974; Peterson, House, & Alford, 1975). Although studies with children are not available in which this aspect of the target behavior has been varied, it is interesting to note that a low level of accuracy (.07 to .79) was obtained in the Nelson et al. (1980) study in which children self-monitored appropriate and inappropriate verbal behavior. Thus, preliminary indications suggest that the selection of nonverbal target behaviors (e.g., in-seat behavior, attending to teacher, completion of assignments) may result in more accurate self-monitoring than verbal targets (e.g., talking out in class, participating in class discussions).

Another variable found to be related to accuracy of self-monitoring in adults is concurrent response requirements. Studies have demonstrated that adults are more accurate when they engage in self-monitoring alone than when they are required to perform a concurrent task. (Epstein, Miller, & Webster, 1976; Epstein, Webster, & Miller, 1975). The extension of these results to children in the classroom suggest that self-monitoring may be most accurate when children are able to focus on the target response with relatively few other task requirements to distract them.

Finally, the timing of self-monitoring has been shown to influence accuracy. Adults were found to be more accurate when they self-recorded each cigarette as it was smoked than when they recorded the number of cigarettes smoked at the end of each day or each week (Frederiksen, Epstein, & Kosevsky, 1975). This variable may also apply to children by using a procedure that is less dependent on memory: having children self-monitor soon after the target response has occurred is assumed to result in the most accurate data.

Summary

A number of variables may influence the accuracy of self-monitoring in children and adolescents. These should be considered when using self-monitoring procedures for assessment purposes to increase the likelihood of accurate data collection. The accuracy of self-monitored data obviously is crucial when such data are used as dependent measures in clinical or research situations. Thus, careful attention should be paid to the selection of target behaviors, as findings suggest that self-monitoring motor responses and positively valenced behaviors may result in higher levels of accuracy than monitoring other types of behaviors. The self-monitoring method selected should be uncomplicated, highly visible to the student, and should involve recording immediately following each occurrence of the target response. Before the implementation of self-monitoring, students should be thoroughly trained in the self-observation and self-recording procedure. Accuracy may also be enhanced if students are asked to self-record when they are not overly busy with other tasks, if the teacher occasionally checks students' accuracy, and if students are reinforced for accurate self-monitoring (Ciminero et al., 1977; Shapiro, 1984).

SELF-MONITORING AS A TREATMENT PROCEDURE

As noted previously, in addition to being a valuable assessment procedure, self-monitoring may also be used as a treatment procedure to facilitate positive behavior change (i.e., increase desired behaviors or decrease undesired behaviors). In fact, in some instances, self-monitoring has been successful as a therapeutic procedure after other external contingency programs have failed to produce positive results (Seymour & Stokes, 1976). In other cases, self-monitoring has been demonstrated to enhance a maintenance of behaviors initially strengthened through externally managed contingency programs. Because of the relative simplicity of this procedure, classroom staff and other school personnel are likely to be cooperative and even enthusiastic about its implementation. The nature of self-monitoring may be more acceptable philosophically to school and family than behavioral procedures based on teacher- or parent-controlled contingencies.

Demonstrations of Reactivity

A majority of the studies of self-monitoring with children and adolescents have investigated the reactive effects of this procedure. Although reactivity is not always present when self-monitoring is used as the only treatment procedure (e.g., Ballard & Glynn, 1975; Howell et al., 1983; Turkewitz et al., 1975), a range of behaviors have shown positive reactive effects when self-monitored in school settings. These include such targets as on-task behavior (Broden et al., 1971; McLaughlin, 1984; Rooney et al., 1984; Sagotsky et al., 1978; Workman et al., 1982), completion of assignments (Holman & Baer, 1979; Piersel, 1985; Schunk, 1982), correctness of assignments completed (Piersel & Kratochwill, 1979), disruptive behavior (Kunzelmann, 1970; Santogrossi et al., 1973), out-of-seat behavior (Sugai & Rowe, 1984), progress in academic tasks (Studwell & Moxley, 1984), nervous tics (Ollendick, 1981), and appropriate classroom conversation (Nelson et al., 1978).

Although many of these results reflect positive reactive effects in academically related behaviors, self-monitoring has not necessarily resulted in corresponding improvements in academic achievement. Some studies have reported increases in academic achievement when students self-monitored skill attainment or related academic behaviors (e.g., Sagotsky et al., 1978; Schunk, 1982). In contrast, Roberts and Nelson (1981), for example, found that the self-monitoring of on-task behavior and the accuracy of completed arithmetic problems by three third-grade boys increased on-task behavior and academic response rate, but did not increase their academic response accuracy. In other studies with learning disabled students who self-monitored on-task behavior, reactivity was most likely to occur in those who already possessed the skills necessary for task completion (Hallahan, Lloyd, Kosiewicz, Kauffman, & Graves, 1979). It appears that self-monitoring may be most valuable in altering behaviors that are already established in the student's repertoire, such as increasing attention to tasks for which he or she has demonstrated proficiency. Thus, if positive reactive effects are desired, target behaviors should be selected that are already in the student's repertoire or that involve tasks consistent with the student's existing skill level (Keogh & Hall, 1984; Roberts & Nelson, 1981). Tables 6-1, 6-2, 6-3, and 6-4 summarize the results of a number of studies with children and adolescents that present a range of learning, emotional, and behavioral difficulties.

Maintenance of Positive Behavior Change

Self-monitoring has been demonstrated to enhance the maintenance of behaviors initially strengthened through externally managed contingency programs. Bolstad and Johnson (1972), Knapczyk and Livingston (1973), and Turkewitz et al. (1975) demonstrated that the positive behavior changes resulting from token programs were maintained with self-monitoring alone. O'Leary and Dubey (1979) suggested that this maintenance effect may be due to the child's increased motivation (resulting from the token program) to exhibit appropriate behavior, or to an increased likelihood that self-monitoring prompted covert self-reinforcing statements.

There is also some evidence that self-monitoring facilitates behavior maintenance following withdrawal of both self-monitoring and external contingencies. For example, McLaughlin and Truhlicka (1983) and McLaughlin (1984), in groups of nine- to twelve-year-old behaviorally disordered students, demonstrated maintenance of therapeutic effects on academic performance six months following termination of self-monitoring procedures. Students who had been reinforced for matching teacher recordings showed greater maintenance effects than those who self-monitored without reinforcement for accuracy. Further, Wood and Flynn (1978) found that adolescents maintained room-cleaning habits following the withdrawal of program components better when they had previous experience with self-monitoring than when provided with only a token system. Maintenance of behavior gains was also found with a fifteen-year-old EMR student when the intervals between his self-recording in-seat or out-of-seat behavior were increased (Sugai & Rowe, 1984).

As a final example, Heins, Lloyd, and Hallahan (1986) reported the persistence of self-recording effects (increased attention to task and arithmetic productivity) over a two-and-a-half-month period following the termination of self-recording by learning disabled boys. These writers emphasized the importance of previous noncued self-recording experiences in promoting maintenance.

In contrast to these positive results, Workman *et al.* (1982) found no maintenance of on-task behavior in a four-year-old boy when self-monitoring was withdrawn. This suggests that maintenance of positive reactive effects of self-monitoring may not spontaneously occur, and thus must be actively taught in young children and perhaps in other students who have not had previous experience with contingency management procedures.

Use of Self-Monitoring to Enhance Generalization

Self-monitoring also may be used as a procedure to facilitate generalization of previously acquired skills across settings. Kelly *et al.* (1983) trained four adolescents attending vocational classes for behaviorally disordered youth to respond appropriately to supervisor instructions. Following training, no generalization of the behavior changes beyond the intervention site was noted. The addition of self-monitoring of target behaviors in the generalization site did, however, result in transfer of training. In a second study with an adolescent with similar characteristics, generalization of previously acquired social skills was enhanced by providing reinforcement for self-monitoring in three additional settings (Kiburz, Miller, & Morrow, 1984). Generalization effects of self-monitoring also were reported by Schloss, Thompson, Gajar, and Schloss (1985). Conversational skills developed by two head trauma youths in a training setting were found to generalize to a nontraining setting through use of self-monitoring procedures. Similar results were obtained by Anderson-Inman, Paine, and Deutchman (1984) with children

TABLE 6-1 Self-Monitoring with Children: Minor Problems

Reference	Subjects	Monitored Behavior	Setting	Reactivity	Accuracy	Comments
Ballard & Glynn (1975)	fourteen 3rd graders	writing responses	classroom	no reactive effects noted	.21, .36, .84 for the 3 responses monitored	improved with addition of self-reinforcement
Broden, Hall, & Mitts (1971)	one 8th-grade girl	on-task	classroom	increased on-task	average .98 observer-student agreement	increased on-task with addition of praise
Flowers (1972)	one 8th-grade boy one 6th-grade girl	talking out scores on daily assignments	classroom classroom	decreased talking out better grades	increased accuracy in self-scoring	
Holman & Baer (1979)	3 normal & 3 problem children	number pages completed in handwriting & arithmetic	classroom	increased academic rate		
Nelson, Hay, Devany, & Koslow-Green (1980)	24 elementary school students	appropriate & inappropriate verbalizations	classroom	no consistent changes	.51 for inappropriate & .79 for appropriate verbalizations	
	8 elementary school students	appropriate & inappropriate verbalizations	classroom	no consistent changes	.07 for inappropriate & .20 for appropriate verbalizations	

Ollendick (1981)	2 boys (CA 9 & 10)	nervous tics	school & home	decreased nervous tics in both settings	average .88 teacher & mother-child agreement
Piersel (1985)	one 3rd-grade boy (CA 8)	completion of assignments	classroom	increased assignments completed	80–100% teacher-student agreement
Piersel & Kratochwill (1979)	one 2nd grader	teacher's scoring of workbook pages	classroom	increased accuracy of performance	
Roberts & Nelson (1981)	three 3rd-grade boys	on-task & accuracy of arithmetic problems	classroom	increased on-task & response rate (not response accuracy)	near 100%
Sagotsky, Patterson, & Lepper (1979)	seventeen normal 5th & 6th graders	on-task	classroom	increased on-task & correct problem solutions	no data
Schunk (1982)	ten normal 8- & 9-year-olds	# pages of subtraction problems completed	classroom	improved self-efficacy, accurate problem solutions, & persistence	no data
Studwell & Moxley (1984)	43 kindergarten students	progress in academic tasks	classroom	increased academic performance	100% teacher-student agreement
Workman, Helton, & Watson (1982)	4-year-old boy with low work behavior & compliance	on-task	classroom	increased sustained schoolwork & compliance	100% teacher-student agreement

TABLE 6-2 Self-Monitoring with Children: Emotionally Disturbed

Reference	Subjects	Monitored Behavior	Setting	Reactivity	Accuracy	Comments
Drabman, Spitalnik, & O'Leary (1973)	8 boys (CA 9-10) with academic & emotional problems	global ratings of academic & social behavior	classroom	decrease in disruptive behavior	.42-.72 teacher-student agreement	
Fixsen, Phillips, & Wolf (1972)	6 predelinquent boys (CA 12-16)	room cleaning	residential facility	small initial increase in number of tasks completed	poor child-observer agreement	
Kelly et al. (1983)	4 behaviorally disordered adolescents (Ca 15-17)	social skills	vocational setting in residential facility	increase in % appropriate responses to instructions	no data	self-monitoring followed role-playing training
Kiburz, Miller, & Morrow (1984)	18-year-old behaviorally disordered boy	social skills (greeting, thanking)	classroom & generalization settings	slight increases in social skills	no data	greatest reactivity with addition of reinforcement
McLaughlin (1984)	4 behaviorally disordered students	on-task	special education classroom	increased on-task & assignments completed	.70 & .90 teacher-student agreement	
McLaughlin, Burgess, & Sackville-West (1982)	6 behaviorally disordered students	on-task	special education classroom	increase in % correct responses in workbook assignments		
McLaughlin & Truhlicka (1983)	4 behaviorally disordered students (CA 9-11)	on-task	special education classroom	increased % correct responses	.65 teacher-student agreement	greater accuracy & reactivity with addition of matching
Peacock, Lyman, & Rickard (1978)	9 disturbed boys (Ca 12-14)	cabin-cleaning behaviors	therapeutic camp	increased easy tasks completed; no effects on difficult tasks	significant differences found between observers & self-reports	accuracy increased with matching contingency

Author (year)	Subjects	Target behavior	Setting	Results	Reliability	Comments
Santogrossi, O'Leary, Romanczyk, & Kaufman (1973)	9 adolescent boys	disruptive behavior	psychiatric hospital classroom	no changes in disruptive behavior	.95 teacher-student agreement	decrease in behavior when external token program implemented
Seymour & Stokes (1976)	4 adolescent girls (CA 14-18)	work behaviors	residential facility classroom, kitchen, & workshop	increases in work output	no data	tokens present throughout
Wood & Flynn (1978)	6 predelinquent males (CA 11-15)	room-cleaning behaviors	residential facility	increased room-cleaning behaviors	greater than .80 with matching contingencies	tokens present throughout

TABLE 6-3 Self-Monitoring with Children: Mentally Retarded

Reference	Subjects	Monitored Behavior	Setting	Reactivity	Accuracy	Comments
Horner & Brigham (1979)	2 mildly retarded boys (CA 10 & 13)	on-task	special education classroom	initial increase in on-task behavior	.80 & .87 observer-student agreement	further increase with addition of self-reinforcement
Howell, Rueda, & Rutherford (1983)	5 moderately & severely retarded students (CA 10-13)	off-task, tongue protrusion, & shaking behaviors	special education classroom	no reactive effects observed	average agreement range .76-90	
Knapczyk & Livingston (1973)	13 junior high students	correct reading responses	EMR classroom	incresed % accuracy on reading assignments	no data	token system present throughout
Litrownik & Freitas (1980)	40 mildly to severely retarded adolescents (CA 15-21)	positive, negative, & neutral aspects of bead stringing task	laboratory	increased productivity for subjects who monitored positive & neutral aspects of task	.94-1.00	
Litrownik, Freitas, & Franzini (1978)	10 moderately to severely retarded adolescents	matching & bowling tasks	training center			training increased # correct self-monitored responses
Nelson, Lipinski, & Boykin (1978)	4 mildly & moderately retarded students (Ca 15-17)	appropriate verbalizations	residential center classroom	increased appropriate verbalizations; hand-held better than belt-worn	.78-.91	compared hand-held & belt-worn devices

Study	Subjects	Target behavior	Setting	Results	Reliability	Comments
Robertson, Simon, Pachman, & Drabman (1979)	12 mildly & moderately retarded children	disruptive behavior	special education classroom	continued decrease in disruptive behavior	.69-1.00 teacher-student agreement	token system present throughout
Shapiro & Klein (1980)	4 retarded/emotionally disturbed children (CA 6-9)	on-task	psychiatric hospital classroom	increased on-task, task accuracy, & performance; decreased disruptive behavior	no data	token system present throughout
Shapiro, McGonigle, & Ollendick (1980)	5 mildly & moderately retarded/behavior disordered children (CA 7-12)	on-task	psychiatric hospital classroom	increased on-task & decreased disruptive behavior	.53-.98	token system present throughout
Sugai & Rowe (1984	15-year-old male EMR student	out-of-seat	classroom	decreased out-of-seat behavior	no data	
Zegiob, Klukas, & Junginger (1978)	2 mildly & moderately retarded adolescents (CA 17 & 18)	nose/mouth picking & head shaking	state training facility	decrease in each inappropriate behavior	.11-.35 observer-subject agreement	increased reactivity with addition of praise & feedback

TABLE 6-4 Self-Monitoring with Children: Learning Difficulties/Hyperactive

Reference	Subjects	Monitored Behavior	Setting	Reactivity	Accuracy	Comments
Anderson-Inman, Paine, & Deutchman (1984)	15 handicapped & disadvantaged low-performing students (CA 10-12)	neat paper skills	classroom	improvement in neat paper skills	no data	
Christie, Hiss, & Lazanoff (1984)	3 hyperactive children	8 classroom behaviors	regular classroom	decreased off-task & inappropriate behaviors & increased on-task	.72-.84 teacher-student agreement	
Hallahan, Lloyd, Kneedler & Marshall (1982)	1 learning disabled boy (CA 8)	on-task	classroom	increased on-task & number of problems completed correctly	nonsignificant difference in teacher & child assessments	
Heins, Lloyd, & Hallahan (1986)	4 learning disabled boys (CA 8-9)	on-task	classroom	increased on-task & arithmetic productivity	significant correlation in teacher & child assessments	cued self-recording superior to noncued self-recording
Hundert & Bucher (1978)	4 boys (average CA 10)	arithmetic performance	special education classroom	no reactive effects observed	children self-rated accurately	
Hundert & Bucher (1978)	17 boys (average CA 15)	arithmetic performance	special education classroom	no reactive effects observed	accuracy improved with checks and bonus/penalty contingency	very inaccurate during token reinforcement for scores
Rooney, Hallahan, & Lloyd (1984)	4 learning disabled boys (CA 8-9)	on-task	classroom	increased on-task	no data	

(CA 10-12) being served in a resource room. Direct instruction of neat paper skills (e.g., use of margins, starting on the front side of the paper, proper placement of the student's name) showed minimal transfer to written assignments produced in nontraining settings. Introduction of a self-monitoring in these nontraining settings, however, facilitated this transfer, resulting in pronounced improvement in the neatness of students' papers across settings.

Variables Affecting the Reactivity of Self-Monitoring

A number of variables that may influence the reactivity of self-monitoring in children and adolescents have been identified. These include (1) the valence of the target behavior, (2) the presence and nature of the recording device, (3) students' motivation for behavior change, (4) goals, reinforcement, and feedback, (5) the timing of self-monitoring, (6) reinforcement for accurate self-monitoring, and (7) training in accurate self-monitoring. The relationship between these specific variables and the presence and magnitude of reactivity is not an invariant one. In most instances, reactivity and the magnitude of its effects are a product of the interaction between characteristics of the individual student and one or more of these additional variables. The reader should keep this in mind as each variable is discussed. It will become evident that, if reactive effects are to be optimized, the clinician should program for as many of these variables as possible.

Valence of the Target Behavior

One variable that may influence the reactivity of self-monitoring is the valence of the target behavior. Self-monitoring typically increases the frequency of desirable behaviors and decreases the frequency of undesirable ones. As examples, self-recording increased the study behavior (positive valence) of an eighth-grade girl and decreased inappropriate talking out (negative valence) in an eighth-grade boy (Broden *et al.*, 1971). Gottman and McFall (1972) found that having students self-record their classroom participation (positive valence) increased participation, whereas self-recording unfulfilled urges to participate (negative valence) decreased this behavior. Finally, valence has been shown to influence the reactive effects obtained with mentally retarded students. Litrownik and Freitas (1980) found that moderately mentally retarded adolescents who self-monitored positively valenced behaviors outperformed those who self-recorded negatively valenced behaviors on a bead-stringing task.

Presence and Nature of the Recording Device

Reactivity may be affected by the mere presence of the recording device used to self-monitor. In one study, the physical presence of the sheet on which a third-grade boy self-recorded number of assignments completed was found to be the critical variable in obtaining reactive effects (Piersel, 1985).

The obtrusiveness of the recording device also may influence reactivity. In general, the more obtrusive the device, the more reactivity there will be (McFall, 1977). Results obtained by Nelson et al. (1978) with mentally retarded adolescents who self-monitored appropriate verbalizations support this notion. Although both hand-held and belt-worn counters resulted in increased appropriate verbalizations, the hand-held counters tended to produce more positive reactive effects than the belt-worn counters. Nelson (1977) suggested that perhaps the device itself may serve as a discriminative stimulus controlling the frequency of the self-monitored response.

Motivation for Behavior Change

Students who express a desire or committment to change their behavior may be more likely to show reactive effects of self-monitoring than those who are not motivated or are resistent to change. Piersel (1980), for example, found that self-monitoring by elementary school children was more reactive for those students who wanted to increase their rate of school work completion or decrease undesirable behavior than for those who did not. In another study with college students, self-monitoring increased verbal participation in group discussion sessions only for those who had expressed an interest in modifying this behavior (Komaki & Dore-Boyce, 1978). A number of studies of smoking behavior in adults also have found more reactive effects for those who report that they are motivated to stop smoking than for those who are not motivated to stop (Lipinski et al., 1975; McFall, 1970; McFall & Hammen, 1971). Thus, students who already demonstrate a clear motivation to improve their behavior may be more likely than their unmotivated peers to achieve positive reactive effects with self-monitoring.

Goals, Reinforcement, and Feedback

To enhance students' motivation and increase the likelihood of positive reactive effects, students may be provided with specific performance goals, reinforcement, or feedback. Spates and Kanfer (1977), for example, found significantly improved performance on an arithmetic task only in those first graders who had been trained in criterion setting, either alone or in conjunction with other procedures. In this study, training in self-monitoring alone did not produce significant positive reactive effects. In a second example, boys' self-recorded tent cleaning improved when cleanliness was reinforced with prompt access to breakfast (Lyman, Rickard, & Elder, 1975).

In contrast, Sagotsky et al. (1978) compared the effects of goal setting, self-monitoring, and the combination of these two procedures with fifth and sixth graders. Results indicated that self-monitoring alone improved performance on an arithmetic task (i.e., time on-task and rate of correct problem solving) significantly more than goal setting alone. Further, the combination of goal setting and self-monitoring did not result in additional reactivity. The writers speculated that the complex and heterogeneous mathematics materials involved in the study may have been inappropriate for the evaluation of goal setting procedures and suggest use of tasks with more consistent or predictable difficulty levels.

Timing of Self-Recording

Reactivity of self-monitoring may be influenced by the timing of self-recording in relation to the actual occurrence of the target behavior. Kanfer's (1970) suggestion that self-monitoring before rather than after the occurrence of an undesirable behavior would produce greater reactivity by breaking undesirable behavior chains has been supported in adult studies (Bellack, Rozensky, & Schwartz, 1974; Rozensky, 1974). In a study with elementary school students, however, self-recording prior to or after the occurrence of a classroom verbalization did not differentially affect the reactivity of either appropriate or inappropriate verbalizations. The writers speculated that, for these children, self-recording itself may have been such a sufficiently novel and difficult response to perform that the more subtle effects of the timing of self-monitoring were not apparent (Nelson *et al.*, 1980).

Reinforcement for Accuracy

There is some evidence that reinforcement for the accuracy of self-monitoring may enhance the reactive effects of this procedure. McLaughlin and colleagues demonstrated that behaviorally disordered students who were reinforced for matching an adult's recordings of on-task behavior not only were more accurate but also showed more positive reactive effects (McLaughlin, 1984; McLaughlin & Truhlicka, 1983). In related examples, Drabman *et al.* (1973) and Robertson *et al.* (1979) demonstrated positive reactive effects when disruptive students were reinforced for closely matching teacher ratings of their behavior. Santogrossi *et al.* (1973) found, when adolescent boys in a psychiatric facility discovered that reinforcement for their behavior was *not* contingent upon accurate self-monitoring, positive reactive effects were lost (i.e., there was a dramatic increase in disruptive behavior). Finally, Peacock, Lyman, & Rickard (1978) demonstrated that when adolescent boys were reinforced for accurately self-monitoring easy tasks, both accuracy and task performance was increased. In contrast, when reinforced for accurately self-monitoring difficult tasks, only accuracy improved. Thus, there is some suggestion either that reinforcement for accuracy influences reactivity only when the self-monitored task is an easy one, or that self-monitoring influences only easy tasks independent of accuracy.

Training in Accurate Self-Monitoring

Reactivity may also be influenced by providing students with training for accuracy in self-monitoring. Shapiro *et al.* (1980) found more reactive effects in mentally retarded children when they were provided with specific training in self-observation and self-recording than when initially provided with only verbal instructions in general self-management procedures. In contrast to this supportive evidence, Nelson *et al.* (1978) found that training mentally retarded adolescents enhanced the accuracy of self-monitoring, but did not influence its reactivity. Self-monitoring increased appropriate classroom verbalizations both for those students who were provided extensive training and for those given only minimal instructions in self-monitoring. Additional research evaluating the effects of training on the reactivity of self-monitoring obviously is needed.

Relationship Between Accuracy and Reactivity

Studies investigating the relationship between accuracy and reactivity have produced mixed results. Some demonstrated greater reactive effects when children were trained to be accurate self-recorders (e.g., McLaughlin, 1984; McLaughlin & Truhlicka, 1983). Other studies reported reactivity even when accuracy was low. As noted above, Nelson *et al.* (1978) found comparable reactive effects in mildly retarded adolescents who were both accurate and inaccurate when they self-monitored appropriate verbalizations. Zegiob *et al.* (1978) also reported that self-monitoring, even when inaccurate, resulted in decreased socially undesirable behavior in mentally retarded adolescents. Finally, high accuracy may be demonstrated in the absence of positive reactive effects. Santogrossi *et al.* (1973) found that self-evaluation, although correlating highly with teacher evaluations of disruptive behavior, produced no reduction in the target behavior. These conflicting findings raise questions about the crucial aspects of self-monitoring that are ultimately responsible for behavior change.

Summary

When using self-monitoring as a treatment procedure, the objective is to maximize its potential reactive effects. This may be accomplished first by selecting students who are motivated to change their behavior, or by increasing positive motivation in those students who initially are neutral or resistant to change. The target behavior selected should be one that is already established in the student's repertoire and the recording device used should be relatively obtrusive to facilitate cueing of self-monitoring. Finally, students should be provided training and reinforcement for accuracy, as well as specific performance goals, reinforcement, and feedback for self-monitoring responses.

EXPLANATION OF REACTIVITY OF SELF-MONITORING

As illustrated, the reactivity of self-monitoring has been well documented. Factors influencing the occurrence and magnitude of the reactivity effect have been identified. The specific processes or mechanisms underlying this effect, however, remain a matter of speculation. Two basic theoretical explanations, one emphasizing covert variables (Kanfer, 1970, 1977), and the other focusing on controlling variables of an external nature (Rachlin, 1974), have been offered. The latter position has been expanded by Nelson and Hayes (1981) to include a wider range of controlling influences.

Kanfer (1970, 1977) offers a three-stage mediational model of self-regulation, involving self-monitoring, self-evaluation, and self-reinforcement, to account for reactivity. During the initial stage, an individual first self-observes the occurrence of a specific behavior (e.g., tic, on-task, task completion) and then self-records the occurrence on a recording device (e.g., a counter, a mark on a chart). This self-monitoring prompts a second-stage process consisting of a self-evaluation of the recorded behavior in relation to a personal criterion or standard for that behavior. The final stage, a motivational one, follows this self-evaluation and consists of self-reinforcement of the behavior that meets the person's performance standard or self-punishment of the behavior that fails to meet the personal standard. The self-consequence may consist of covert positive or negative verbalizations or overt self-delivery of positive or negative events. This covert or overt self-consequence is presumed to have motivational properties that either increase or reduce the strength of the preceding self-recorded behavior.

In contrast to the mediational process model, Rachlin (1974) suggests that both the self-recording of a target behavior and the self-administration of contingent consequences serve primarily as cues to remind the person of the external consequences that control the strength of that self-recorded response (e.g., completion of assignment = teacher praise; off-task = teacher reprimand). Thus, the emphasis is on the cue rather than the motivational properties of self-consequence.

Nelson and Hayes (1981) have extended the Rachlin cueing position in suggesting that:

> the entire self-monitoring procedure (therapist instructions, training in self-monitoring, the self-recording device, feedback from others, the occurence of the target behavior, and the self-recording response, when the latter two occur), rather than only the self-monitored response, serves to cue the ultimate environmental consequences contingent on the target behavior. . . . This elaboration is necessary to provide an adequate explanation for the occurrence of reactivity despite inaccurate self-monitoring, low frequency behavior, and unused self-monitoring devices. (p. 11)

Although studies reporting findings supporting each of these positions are available (e.g., Mace & Kratochwill, 1985; Nelson & Hayes, 1981), there is an evident lack of consistency of results to favor any one model over the others. In fact, one could assume that both cognitive-mediational processes and operant-environmental influences interact to produce reactive effects, with the magnitude of the effect dependent upon a number of characteristics of the child. That is, young children and more severely mentally retarded individuals with limited cognitive skills and experiential histories supportive of the development of self-regulation mediational processes and consistent standards of behavior would be less likely to show reactivity to self-monitoring. As described previously, there is some evidence to support this. In other older and more cognitively advanced persons, both covert and environmentally based consequences may occur and may combine to influence reactivity. In conclusion, instead of an either/or explanation, both the mediational-motivational hypothesis and the cueing-environmental positions propose useful ideas about the processes that underlie reactivity. Obviously, additional research is needed to evaluate these theoretical positions.

ISSUES IN ASSESSMENT AND REACTIVITY OF SELF-MONITORING

When self-monitoring is used as a behavior change procedure in a clinical setting, assessment of the reactive effects may be completed by an external observer or by the child. If both preintervention and intervention data are obtained by an independent observer, the presence and magnitude of reactivity might be identified.

In other instances, issues of practicality or economics may favor the use of the child as the data collector. In this case, self-monitoring is used simultaneously as an assessment and intervention procedure. Because of potential reactivity, this use of self-monitoring as the only data collection procedure would not ensure the clinician of an actual baseline rate of the monitored behavior. The reactive effects would potentially begin at the initiation of self-recording and thus would confound data interpretation. However, if the clinician's primary interest is in positive behavior change, the use of the data collected by the child as a measure of this change may be acceptable, assuming, of course, the accuracy of the self-recorded information.

The reactivity of self-monitoring becomes a significant issue, however, when the procedure is used in research endeavors as a data collection procedure to assess the effects of other variables. For example, in research designed to evaluate the differential effects of self-monitoring in children who vary in age or type of problem, or to determine the potential differential reactivity of other specific variables (e.g., the intrusiveness of the self-recording device), the use of independent observers to collect both pretreatment and treatment data obviously would be needed. Independent data collection procedures also would be required when self-monitored data are used to assess the effects of other independent behavior change variables. For example, a study designed to evaluate the effects of different levels of academic task difficulty on the on-task behavior of children with learning disabilities may use self-monitoring as the data collection procedure. Any changes in on-task behavior following changes in levels of task difficulty, however, may reflect the joint or interactive effects of self-monitoring and task difficulty. The researcher thus would find it necessary to use data collection procedures that make use of independent observers or experimental designs that controlled for reactive effects. Fleece and Jolly (1983) and Nelson (1977) describe the usefulness of various experimental designs and should be consulted by the interested reader.

CASE ILLUSTRATION

The following is an illustration of the application of self-monitoring procedures in the school experience with an adolescent enrolled in a special education program. This case illustration is interesting because it demonstrates the usefulness of self-monitoring as an intervention procedure with a disruptive behavior problem that had not responded favorably to more traditional behavioral treatment approaches. It also demonstrates that the positive effects associated with self-monitoring may be observed in settings other than those in which the procedure was used as a formal treatment approach. Finally, the case illustrates other positive side effects following reactivity. Other disruptive behaviors not treated directly showed a significant decrease and classroom productivity was observed to increase.

Carol is a sixteen-year-old mildly mentally retarded student with chronic behavioral and emotional difficulties. During class periods, especially in those with activities that she does not like, she frequently engages in disruptive verbal behaviors that involve mumbling and talking aloud to herself in a disorganized, rambling manner (e.g., "My tongue is coated. It should be scraped off," "You should never be mad at the teacher," "I'm going to call the cops and have you arrested!"). This disruptive talking occurs out of context and, when attempts are made to label her behavior and redirect her, Carol often becomes increasingly upset. She occasionally accelerates into major outbursts that include screaming, crying, threatening, striking out, and tipping or throwing objects. At other times, Carol responds appropriately to actual events or situations in the school environment.

At the time of the initiation of the self-monitoring procedure, Carol's behavior was very much a problem in two classes, a prevocational skills training class and a practical math class. Both classes met daily for periods in the morning and again in the afternoon. Previous behavioral approaches used unsuccessfully by the special education teachers included verbal reprimand, redirection, reinforcement for periods of remaining quiet, brief time-out, and response cost. Although the programs resulted in minor changes, these improvements were typically lost soon after the removal of the therapy procedures.

Observations made in each classroom suggested a typical behavior chain of talking to herself that occasionally escalated into more severe verbal and physical aggression. Thus, talking to herself was selected as the target for a self-monitoring program with the assumption that reduction of this behavior would also serve to reduce the occurrence of more severe forms of aggression.

During baseline, treatment, and follow-up phases, talking to herself was measured by having Carol's teachers, teacher aids, or teaching interns record data during five randomly selected two-minute intervals each class period. Every fifteen seconds, the staff member looked at Carol and made a judgment about whether or not she was talking to herself. These ratings were summarized as a percentage of each class period that was devoted to talking to herself. In addition, during the treatment phase when Carol self-monitored her talking, the accuracy of Carol's recordings was measured by a comparison of these self-recorded responses with ratings made simultaneously by the classroom staff. Finally, episodes of aggression were counted for total number of incidences.

The teacher, in consultation with the school psychologist, selected a multiple baseline design across settings (prevocational and math class) to evaluate the possible reactive effects. Self-monitoring procedures were implemented in the morning class periods only, with the afternoon class periods used to determine if any treatment effects obtained would also be evident in other settings in which formal self-monitoring was not used.

During self-monitoring intervention, Carol was informed that about every ten minutes (range 7 to 13) a tone would sound on a small tape recorder placed on the side of her desk or work table. After the tone, Carol was taught to ask herself, "Was I talking or not talking?" She was instructed to check the correct response on the prepared recording sheet at her desk. The self-recording sheet was divided length-wise. One side depicted a face with its mouth open and the world TALKING, and the other side depicted a face with its mouth closed and the words NO TALKING. Each side of the recording sheet contained boxes numbered 1 through 10. (See Figure 6-1 presented earlier for illustrations of recording sheets similar to the form used by Carol.)

Results of the self-monitoring procedure are presented in Figure 6-2. Follow-ing the initiation of self-monitoring in the prevocational training class in the morning, talking to herself decreased. There also was a slight decrease in talking in the math classes prior to initiation of self-monitoring in these classes. After self-monitoring was implemented in the morning math class, significant decreases in talking also were evident there. In addition, talking decreased noticeably in the afternoon generalization periods when intervention was implemented in the morn-ing periods.

Episodes of verbal and physical aggression toward teachers, peers, and prop-erty decreased from a weekly average of 5.6 episodes during baseline periods to an infrequent occurrence during the last two weeks of self-monitoring. As implied earlier, removal of the stimulus event (talking to herself) that occurred early in the chain of events ending in aggression was successful in virtually eliminating these disruptive outbursts. Finally, teachers in the prevocational and practical math classes reported a significant increase in Carol's productivity. As talking to herself decreased, Carol's attention began to focus more on the classroom activities and she seemed pleased with the successes that she now was experiencing.

This case illustrates a number of features of the self-monitoring procedure. Other than the time required to obtain daily observations of Carol's talking to herself, the procedure required only minimal staff involvement. After the first day or so, Carol appeared to enjoy the responsibility of completing her sheet(s) each day. In addition to the significant reduction of talking to herself, the procedure also produced some favorable side effects. Positive generalization effects were obtained, disruptive aggressive outbursts were virtually eliminated, and classroom productiv-ity increased.

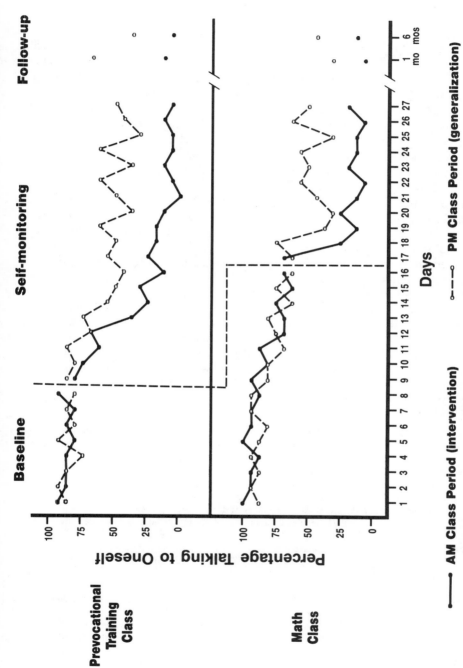

FIGURE 6-2 Percentage of Observation Intervals of Disruptive Talking to Oneself

● **AM Class Period (intervention)** ○---○ **PM Class Period (generalization)**

SUMMARY

Self-monitoring as an assessment and intervention strategy has enjoyed increased popularity in school settings during the last decade. Students varying in age (preschool to high school), cognitive level (mentally retarded to above average), setting (regular class, special class, institutional, home), type and degree of handicapping condition (e.g., mental retardation, learning disabilities, emotional disturbances, behavior disorders), and type of problem behaviors (e.g., nervous tics, academic performance, attention, aggression) have *all* successfully used self-monitoring procedures. In most instances of research, self-monitoring has served as an independent behavior change procedure. In most clinical instances, self-monitoring has been used simultaneously as an assessment and behavior change procedure. This is based on a growing body of evidence that self-monitoring can produce valuable and, in some instances, enduring positive therapeutic effects.

Even though research to date has improved upon the clinical utility of self-monitoring in school settings, several questions remain. The critical factors involved in both the accuracy and reactivity of self-monitoring have not been isolated. Although factors such as the child's motivation, the valence of the behavior monitored, and the nature of the self-monitoring procedure have been demonstrated to influence the accuracy and reactivity of self-monitoring, consistency of results are lacking in use with children with various problem characteristics. As a result, it is currently not possible to predict that particular self-monitoring procedures will have certain effects with children presenting specific problem characteristics. This is especially true for children with special educational needs.

References

Anderson-Inman, L., Paine, S. C., & Deutchman, L. (1984). Neatness counts: Effects of direct instruction and self-monitoring on the transfer of neat-paper skills to nontraining settings. *Analysis and Intervention in Developmental Disabilities, 4,* 137–155.

Armstrong, S. W., & Frith, G. H. (1984). *Practical self-monitoring for classroom use: An introductory text.* Springfield, Ill.: Charles Thomas.

Ballard, K. D., & Glynn, T. (1975). Behavioral self-management in story writing with elementary school children. *Journal of Applied Behavior Analysis, 8,* 387–398.

Barton, E. J., & Ascione, F. R. (1984). Direct observation. In T. H. Ollendick & M. Hersen (Eds.), *Child behavior assessment* (pp. 166–194). Elmsford, N.Y.: Pergamon Press.

Bellack, A. S., Rozensky, R., & Schwartz, J. A. (1974). A comparison of two forms of self-monitoring in a behavioral weight control program. *Behavior Therapy, 5,* 523–530.

Bolstad, O. D., & Johnson, S. M. (1972). Self-regulation in the modification of disruptive classroom behavior. *Journal of Applied Behavior Analysis, 5,* 443–454.

Broden, M., Hall, R. V., & Mitts, B. (1971). The effect of self-recording on the classroom behavior of two 8th grade students. *Journal of Applied Behavior Analysis, 4,* 191–199.

Cavior, N., & Marabotto, C. M. (1976). Monitoring verbal behaviors in a dyadic interaction: Valence of target behaviors, type, timing, and reactivity to monitoring. *Journal of Consulting and Clinical Psychology, 44,* 68–76.

Christie, D. J., Hiss, M., & Lozanoff, B. (1984). Modification of inattentive classroom behavior: Hyperactive children's use of self-recording with teacher guidance. *Behavior Modification, 8,* 391–406.

Ciminero, A. R., Nelson, R. O., & Lipinski, D. P. (1977). Self-monitoring procedures. In A. R. Ciminero, K. S. Calhoun, & H. E. Adams (Eds.), *Handbook of behavioral assessment* (pp. 195–232). New York: John Wiley & Sons.

Drabman, R. S., Spitalnik, R., & O'Leary, K. D. (1973). Teaching of self-control to disruptive children. *Jounral of Abnormal Psychology, 82,* 10–16.

Epstein, L. H., Miller, P. M., & Webster, J. S. (1976). The effects of reinforcing concurrent behavior on self-monitoring. *Behavior Therapy, 7,* 89–95.

Epstein, L. H., Webster, J. S., & Miller, P. M. (1975). Accuracy and controlling effects of self-monitoring as a function of concurrent responding and reinforcement. *Behavior Therapy, 6,* 654–666.

Fixsen, D. L., Phillips, E. L., & Wolf, M. M. (1972). Achievement place: The reliability of self-reporting and peer-reporting and their effects on behavior. *Journal of Applied Behavior Analysis, 5,* 19–30.

Fleece, L., & Jolly, P. (1983). Self-monitoring: Experimental controls in a practical group comparison design. *Behavioral Engineering, 8,* 65–68.

Flowers, J. B. (1972). Behavior modification of cheating in an elementary school student: A brief note. *Behavior Therapy, 3,* 311–312.

Frederiksen, L. W., Epstein, L. H., & Kosevsky, B. P. (1975). Reliability and controlling effects of three procedures for self-monitoring smoking. *Psychological Record, 25,* 255–264.

Frith, G. H., & Armstrong, S. W. (1985). Self-monitoring for behavior disordered students. *Teaching Exceptional Children, 18,* 144–148.

Glynn, E. L., & Thomas. J. D. (1974). Effect of cueing on self-control of classroom behavior. *Journal of Applied Behavior Analysis, 7,* 299–306.

Gottman, J. M., & McFall, R. M. (1972). Self-monitoring effects in a program for potential high school dropouts: A time-series analysis. *Journal of Consulting and Clinical Psychology, 39,* 275–281.

Hallahan, D. P., Lloyd, J. W., Kneedler, R. D., & Marshall, K. G. (1982). A comparison of the effects of self versus teacher-assessment of on-task behavior. *Behavior Therapy, 13,* 715–723.

Hallahan, D. P., Lloyd, J., Kosiewicz, M. M., Kauffman, J. M., & Graves, A. W. (1979). Self-monitoring of attention as a treatment for learning disabled boys' off-task behavior. *Learning Disability Quarterly, 2*(3), 24–32.

Hallahan, D. P., Marshall, K. J., & Lloyd, J. W. (1981). Self-recording during group instruction: Effects on attention to task. *Learning Disability Quarterly, 4,* 407–413.

Hayes, S. C., & Cavior, N. (1977). Multiple tracking and the reactivity of self-monitoring: I. Negative behaviors. *Behavior Therapy, 8,* 819–831.

Heins, E. D., Lloyd, J. W., & Hallahan, D. P. (1986). Cued and noncued self-recording of attention to task. *Behavior Modification, 10,* 235–254.

Holman, J., & Baer, D. M. (1979). Facilitating generalization of on-task behavior through self-monitoring of academic tasks. *Journal of Autism and Developmental Disorders, 9,* 429–446.

Horner, R. H., & Brigham, T. A. (1979). The effects of self-management procedures on the study behavior of two retarded children. *Education and Training of the Mentally Retarded, 14,* 18–24.

Howell, K. W., Rueda, R., & Rutherford, R. B. (1983). A procedure for teaching self-recording to moderately retarded students. *Psychology in the Schools, 20,* 202–209.

Hundert, J., & Bucher, B. (1978). Pupils' self-scored arithmetic performance: A practical procedure for maintaining accuracy. *Journal of Applied Behavior Analysis, 11,* 304.

Johnson, S. M., & Bolstad, O. D. (1973). Methodological issues in naturalistic observation: Some problems and solutions for field research. In L. A. Hamerlynck, L. C. Handy, & E. J. Mash (Eds.), *Behavior change: Methodology, concepts, and practice* (pp 7–67). Champaign, Ill.: Research Press.

Kanfer, F. H. (1970. Self-monitoring: Methodological limitations and clinical applications. *Journal of Consulting and Clinical Psychology, 35,* 143–152.

Kanfer, F. H. (1977). The many faces of self-control. In R. B. Stuart (Ed.), *Behavioral self-management: Strategies, techniques, and outcomes.* New York: Brunner/Mazel.

Kazdin, A. E. (1974). Self-monitoring and behavior change. In M. J. Mahoney & C. E. Thoresen (Eds.), *Self-control: Power to the person* (pp. 218–246). Monterey, Calif.: Brooks/Cole.

Kelly, W. J., Salzberg, C. L., Levy, S. M., Warrenteltz, R. B., Adams, T. W., Crouse, T. R., & Beegle, G. P.

(1983). The effects of role-playing and self-monitoring on the generalization of vocational social skills by behaviorally disordered adolescents. *Behavioral Disorders*, 9, 27–35.

Keogh, B. K., & Hall, R. J. (1984). Cognitive training with learning-disabled pupils. In A. W. Meyers & W. E. Craighead (Eds.), *Cognitive behavior therapy with children* (pp. 163–191). New York: Plenum Press.

Kiburz, C. S., Miller, S. R., & Morrow, L. W. (1984). Structured learning using self-monitoring to promote maintenance and generalization of social skills across settings for a behaviorally disordered adolescent. *Behavioral Disorders*, 10, 47–55.

Knapczyk, D. R., & Livingston, G. (1973). Self-recording and student teacher supervision: Varibles within a token economy structure. *Journal of Applied Behavior Analysis*, 6, 481–486.

Kneedler, R. D., & Hallahan, D. P. (1981). Self-monitoring of on-task behavior with learning disabled children: Current studies and directions. *Exceptional Education Quarterly*, 2, 73–81.

Komaki, J., & Dore-Boyce, K. (1978). Self-recording: Its effects on individuals high and low in motivation. *Behavior Therapy*, 9, 65–72.

Kubany, E. S., & Sloggett, B. B. (1973). Coding procedures for teachers. *Journal of Applied Behavior Analysis*, 6, 339–344.

Kunzelmann, H. D. (Ed.). (1970). *Precision teaching*. Seattle, Wash.: Special Child Publications.

Lipinski, D. P., Black, J. L., Nelson, R. O., & Ciminero, A. R. (1975). The influence of motivational variables on the reactivity and reliability of self-recording. *Journal of Consulting and Clinical Psychology*, 43, 637–646.

Lipinski, D. P., & Nelson, R. O. (1974). The reactivity and unreliability of self-recording. *Journal of Consulting and Clinical Psychology*, 42, 118–123.

Litrownik, A. J., & Freitas, J. L. (1980). Self-monitoring in moderately retarded adolescents: Reactivity and accuracy as a function of valence. *Behavior Therapy*, 11, 245–258.

Litrownik, A., Freitas, J., & Franzini, L. (1978). Self-regulation in mentally retarded children: Assessment and training of self-monitoring skills. *American Journal of Mental Deficiency*, 82, 499–506.

Lloyd, J. W., Hallahan, D. P., Kosiewicz, M. M., & Kneedler, R. D. (1982). Reactive effects of self-assessment and self-recording on attention to task and academic productivity. *Learning Disability Quarterly*, 5, 216–227.

Lyman, R. D., Rickard, H. C., & Elder, I. R. (1975). Contingency management of self-reported cleaning behavior. *Journal of Abnormal Child Psychology*, 3, 155–162.

Mace, F. C., & Kratochwill, T. R. (1985). Theories of reactivity in self-monitoring: A comparison of cognitive-behavioral and operant models. *Behavior Modification*, 9, 323–344.

Mahoney, M. J., Moore, B. S., Wade, T. C., & Moura, N. G. M. (1973). The effects of continuous and intermittent self-monitoring on academic behavior. *Journal of Consulting and Clinical Psychology*, 41, 65–69.

McConnell, S., Biglan, A., & Severson, H. H. (1984). Adolescents' compliance with self-monitoring and physiological assessment of smoking in natural environments. *Journal of Behavioral Medicine*, 7, 115–122.

McFall, R. M. (1970). Effects of self-monitoring on normal smoking behavior. *Journal of Consulting and Clinical Psychology*, 35, 135–142.

McFall, R. M. (1977). Parameters of self-monitoring. In R. B. Stuart (Ed.), *Behavioral self-management: Strategies, techniques, and outcomes* (pp. 196–214). New York: Brunner/Mazel.

McFall, R. M., & Hammen, C. L. (1971). Motivation, structure, and self-monitoring: The role of nonspecific factors in smoking reduction. *Journal of Consulting and Clinical Psychology*, 37, 80–86.

McLaughlin, T. F. (1984). A comparison of self-recording and self-recording plus consequences of on-task and assignment completion. *Contemporary Education Psychology*, 9, 185–192.

McLaughlin, T. F., Burgess, N., & Sackville-West, L. (1982). Effects of self-recording and self-recording + matching on academic performance. *Child Behavior Therapy*, 3(2/3), 17–27.

McLaughlin, T. F., & Truhlicka, M. (1983). Effects on academic performance of self-recording and self-recording and matching with behaviorally disordered students: A replication. *Behavioral Engineering*, 8, 69–74.

Nelson, R. O. (1977). Assessment and therapeutic functions of self-monitoring. In M. Hersen, R. M. Eisler, & P. M. Miller (Eds.), *Progress in behavior modification* (Vol. 5, pp. 263–308). New York: Academic Press.

Nelson, R. O., Hay, L. R., Devany, J., & Koslow-Green, L. (1980). The reactivity and accuracy of children's self-monitoring: Three experiments. *Child Behavior Therapy, 2*(3), 1–24.

Nelson, R. O., Hay, L. R., Hay, W. M., & Carstens, C. B. (1977). The reactivity and accuracy of teachers' self-monitoring of positive and negative classroom verbalizations. *Behavior Therapy, 8,* 972–985.

Nelson, R. O., & Hayes, S. C. (1981). Theoretical explanations of reactivity in self-monitoring. *Behavior Modification, 5,* 3–14.

Nelson, R. O., Lipinski, D. P., & Black, J. L. (1975). The effects of expectancy on the reactivity of self-recording. *Behavior Therapy, 6,* 337–349.

Nelson, R. O., Lipinski, D. P., & Black, J. L. (1976). The relative reactivity of external observations and self-monitoring. *Behavior Therapy, 7,* 314–321.

Nelson, R. O., Lipinski, D. P., & Boykin, R. A. (1978). The effects of self-recorders' training and the obtrusiveness of the self-monitoring device on the accuracy and reactivity of self-monitoring. *Behavior Therapy, 9,* 200–208.

O'Leary, S. G., & Dubey, D. R. (1979). Applications of self-control procedures by children: A review. *Journal of Applied Behavior Analysis, 12,* 449–465.

Ollendick, T. H. (1981). Self-monitoring and self-administered overcorrection: The modification of nervous tics in children. *Behavior Modification, 5,* 75–84.

Peacock, R., Lyman, R. D., & Rickard, H. C. (1978). Correspondence between self-report and observer-report as a function of task difficulty. *Behavior Therapy, 9,* 578–583.

Peterson, G. L., House, A. E., & Alford, H. F. (1975). *Self-monitoring: Accuracy and reactivity in a patient's recording of three clinically targeted behaviors.* Paper read at the Southeastern Psychological Association, Atlanta.

Piersel, W. C. (1980). *Self-recording: Applications to elementary school academic and behavior problems.* Paper presented at the annual meeting of the American Education Research Association, April, at Boston.

Piersel, W. C. (1985). Self observation and completion of school assignments: The influence of a physical recording device and expectancy characteristics. *Psychology in the Schools, 22,* 331–336.

Piersel, W. C., & Kratochwill, T. R. (1979). Self-observation and behavior change: Application to academic and adjustment problems through behavioral consultation. *Journal of School Psychology, 17,* 151–161.

Rachlin, H. (1974). Self-control. *Behaviorism, 2,* 94–107.

Roberts, R. N., & Nelson, R. O. (1981). The effects of self-monitoring on children's classroom behavior. *Child Behavior Therapy, 3,* 105–120.

Robertson, S. J., Simon, S. J., Pachman, J. S., & Drabman, R. S. (1979). Self-control and generalization procedures in a classroom of disruptive retarded children. *Child Behavior Therapy, 1,* 347–362.

Rooney, K. J., Hallahan, D. P., & Lloyd, J. W. (1984). Self-recording of attention by learning disabled students in the regular classroom. *Journal of Learning Disabilities, 17,* 360–364.

Rozensky, R. H. (1974). The effect of timing of self-monitoring behavior on reducing cigarette consumption. *Journal of Behavior Therapy and Experimental Psychiatry, 5,* 301–303.

Sagotsky, G., Patterson, G. J., & Lepper, M. R. (1978). Training children's self-control: A field experiment in self-monitoring and goal setting in the classroom. *Journal of Experimental Child Psychology, 25,* 242–253.

Santogrossi, D. A. (1974). *Self-reinforcement and external monitoring of performance on an academic task.* Paper presented at the 5th Annual Conference on Applied Behavior Analysis in Education, October, at Kansas City, Kansas.

Santogrossi, D. A., O'Leary, K. D., Romanczyk, R. G., & Kaufman, K. F. (1973). Self-evaluation by adolescents in a psychiatric hospital school token program. *Journal of Applied Behavior Analysis, 6,* 277–287.

Schloss, P. J., Thompson, C. K., Gajar, A. H., & Schloss, C. N. (1985). Influence of self–monitoring on heterosexual conservational behaviors of head trauma youth. *Applied Research in Mental Retardation, 6,* 269–282.

Schunk, D. H. (1982). Progress self-monitoring: Effects on children's self-efficacy and achievement. *Journal of Experimental Education, 51,* 89–93.

Seymour, F. W., & Stokes, T. F. (1976). Self-recording in training girls to increase work and evoke staff praise in an institution for offenders. *Journal of Applied Behavior Analysis, 9,* 41–54.

Shapiro, E. S. (1984). Self-monitoring procedures. In T. H. Ollendick & M. Hersen (Eds.), *Child behavioral assessment: Principles and procedures.* Elmsford, N.Y.: Pergamon Press.

Shapiro, E. S., & Ackerman, A. (1983). Increasing productivity rates in adult mentally retarded clients: The failure of self-monitoring. *Applied Research in Mental Retardation, 4,* 163–181.

Shapiro, E. S., & Klein, R. D. (1980). Self-management of classroom behavior with retarded/disturbed children. *Behavior Modification, 4,* 83–97.

Shapiro, E. S., McGonigle, J. J., & Ollendick, T. H. (1980). An analysis of self-assessment and self-reinforcement in a self-managed token economy with mentally retarded children. *Applied Research in Mental Retardation, 1,* 227–240.

Spates, C. R., & Kanfer, F. H. (1977). Self-monitoring, self-evaluation, and self-reinforcement in children's learning: A test of a multistage of self-regulation model. *Behavior Therapy, 8,* 9–16.

Studwell, P. & Moxley, R. (1984). Self-recording in kindergarten: A study in naturalistic evaluation. *Psychology in the Schools, 21,* 450-456.

Sugai, G., & Rowe, P. (1984). The effect of self-recording on out-of-seat behavior of an EMR student. *Education and Training of the Mentally Retarded, 19,* 23–28.

Turkewitz, H., O'Leary, K. D., & Ironsmith, M. (1975). Generalization and maintenance of appropriate behavior through self-control. *Journal of Consulting and Clinical Psychology, 43,* 577–583.

Watson, D. L., & Tharp, R. G. (1972). *Self-directed behavior: Self-modification for personal adjustment.* Monterey, Calif.: Brooks/Cole.

Wood, R., & Flynn, J. M. (1978). A self-evaluation token system versus an external evaluation token system alone in a residential setting with predelinquent youths. *Journal of Applied Behavior Analysis, 11,* 503–512.

Workman, E. A., Helton, G. B., & Watson, P. J. (1982). Self-monitoring effects in a four-year-old child: An ecological behavior analysis. *Journal of School Psychology, 20,* 57–64.

Zegiob, L., Klukas, N., & Junginger, J. (1978). Reactivity of self-monitoring procedures with retarded adolescents. *American Journal of Mental Deficiency, 83,* 156–163.

CHAPTER 7

Analogue Assessment: Evaluating Academic Abilities

MARIBETH GETTINGER

University of Wisconsin–Madison

INTRODUCTION

The assessment of academic abilities is a multifaceted problem faced by psychologists and educators alike. In most schools there is an expectation that standardized achievement tests are used to evaluate children's academic skills, in part because of legislative requirements for special education evaluations. This expectation for standardized testing is held by most professionals working with children experiencing academic skill deficits (Goh, Teslow, & Fuller, 1981).

In recent years, however, the use of standardized tests for assessing academic skills has come under frequent criticism. There are several shortcomings in the use of standardized achievement tests for instructional planning. Standardized tests may be useful for indicating areas of difficulty, but they often do not provide the necessary information upon which educational strategies can be based. Although formal tests are appropriate for gaining a normative perspective on children's academic abilities, they typically do not have great instructional utility in program planning (Zigmond & Silverman, 1984). For many children, standardized testing instruments may not be appropriate for instructional programming because the test items are not closely related to actual classroom activities. Furthermore, performance generated in a standardized testing situation may not be similar to performance that occurs in the classroom. For example, many diagnosticians have been faced with the problem of evaluating children who test as though they have mastered an academic skill, but cannot demonstrate mastery of that skill in the classroom. As Smith (1980) points out, the information-processing demands placed on a child during formal testing may differ markedly from classroom demands. She cites the example of a third-grade boy who was referred for spelling problems and given the spelling subtest of the Peabody Individual Achievement Test (PIAT)

(Dunn & Markwardt, 1970). He obtained a grade-equivalent score of 3.5, indicating grade-level performance in spelling. In class, however, the child consistently failed weekly spelling tests, and his spelling on exams and compositions was extremely poor. An analysis of the test format revealed that the PIAT spelling subtest measures *recognition* (the child determines which of four stimulus words is spelled correctly) whereas classroom activities required *production* (the child generates correct spellings in writing activities). In this instance, the achievement test sampled one set of spelling skills whereas the teacher and spelling program used in his classroom stressed a different set of skills. According to Leinhardt and Seewald (1981), diagnosis should be content specific; it should incorporate information that is actually taught in a child's educational setting. The frequent lack of correspondence between what is taught and what is tested raises some concern over the validity of standarized achievement test results. For example, the degree of matching between words taught in a child's reading series and words included on a standardized reading test can clearly affect the child's resulting test score (Jenkins & Pany, 1978).

The norm-referenced aspect of many standardized tests has also been criticized. Concern is often raised about the comparison of individual children with a normative group. Tests may be used with children who differ from the standardization sample on a number of salient characteristics (race, socioeconomic status, ability level), thus rendering the normative comparisons inappropriate. Furthermore, comparison with a normative group often supersedes an individualized orientation to assessment (Keogh, 1973). For example, students of similar age and cognitive ability may be achieving poorly for very different reasons that may not be evident in their standardized test performance. Diagnosticians must consider how a learner's own perceptual, cognitive, and learning strategies interact with specific task characteristics and affect the acquisition and retention of academic skills. One final criticism of standardized achievement tests is that most tests assess how children differ from one another on several attributes without regard for the environment in which they are expected to learn. Eaves and McLaughlin (1977) contend that an appropriate assessment of academic skill problems can occur only after the child's instructional environment has been evaluated. To ensure the most appropriate instruction, assessment practices must yield information concerning students' strengths and weaknesses in actual teaching and learning environments. Educators and psychologists need an assessment procedure that will generate useful recommendations for assisting children with academic skill deficits. Traditional standardized testing procedures have generally failed in meeting this need for relevant instructional diagnostic information.

An alternate approach for academic skill assessment that circumvents many of the problems inherent in standardized achievement testing and facilitates the attainment of more useful diagnostic information is a behavioral assessment approach. The use of behavioral assessment procedures in schools has grown out of the application of applied behavior analysis to education as well as an increased emphasis on individual differences among learners. Behavioral assessment techniques, in contrast to traditional testing procedures, place an emphasis on the direct measurement of children's behavior in those situations in which the behavior occurs. A behavioral approach to assessment considers both observable learner attributes and situational determinants of behavior. It is concerned with the relationship between behavior and specific environmental contexts and, therefore, attempts to sample behavioral as well as environmental variables. Lovitt (1967) parallels this distinction between a test-based versus a behavioral assessment of academic abilities to the difference between a topographic versus a functional analysis of behavior. According to Lovitt, an evaluation of academic skills that simply describes a child's error rate on standardized test materials represents a topographic analysis and is characteristic of a test-based evaluation. In contrast, an evaluation that not only describes the child's performance, but also details the environmental contingencies in effect during assessment is a functional analysis and is characteristic of evaluations based on behavioral assessment methods.

A behavioral perspective of an academic skills assessment recognizes that children's learning behavior and abilities are a function of how their individual characteristics interact with specific task components and with aspects of the environment in which they are expected to perform. Therefore, a major objective of behavioral assessment is to evaluate the learner, task, and setting variables that lead to or interfere with academic skill acquisition. Examples of the individual learner characteristics that might be evaluated include task persistence, organizational strategies, error patterns, kinds of stimuli attended to, or speed of performing; task and setting variables might include level of difficulty of material, type and clarity of instructions, reinforcers, performance objectives, or content of material.

The use of behavioral assessment methods for evaluating school-based problems is becoming more widespread. The behavioral assessment procedures addressed in this volume have been used with considerable success in school and nonschool settings for evaluating social and emotional behaviors in children (Mash & Terdal, 1982; Ollendick & Hersen, 1984). However, less attention has been given to the use of behavioral assessment in the evaluation of academic skills (Alessi & Kaye, 1983; Kratochwill, 1982). The purpose of this chapter is to describe and evaluate one type of behavioral approach that is appropriate for the assessment of academic abilities and learning behaviors in school settings. This assessment procedure, referred to an *analogue assessment*, requires the child to respond to stimuli that simulate those found in the natural classroom environment.

This chapter first addresses the characteristics, underlying assumptions, and advantages and limitations of analogue measurement in general, as well as analogue assessment of academic abilities in particular. Specific types of analogue academic assessment procedures are then described, and methods are exemplified for several academic skill areas. Research that evaluates the validity and reliability of analogue measures is presented, and areas warranting further research efforts are outlined. Finally, a case analysis illustrating the development and implementation of analogue assessment procedures for evaluating academic skills is presented.

CHARACTERISTICS AND ASSUMPTIONS OF
ANALOGUE ASSESSMENT PROCEDURES

The direct observation and monitoring of children's learning in the classroom are valid approaches for gathering information about academic abilities. Observation of children's academic skills can take place in natural settings (the regular or special education classroom) as well as structured settings (simulated learning situations). Bersoff (1973) noted that optimal performance demonstrated in an individual assessment situation may not necessarily reflect performance in the natural environment. However, there are several limitations to the direct observation of children in the classroom (Cunningham, 1982; Hartmann & Wood, 1982). There may be situations when it is necessary to remove children from their classrooms in order to assess aspects of academic skills that are not possible to evaluate under natural conditions. Because it is often difficult and impractical to assess skills in the regular classroom, diagnosticians increasingly have used analogue assessment procedures.

Structured or analogue assessments are designed to provide controlled situations in which the behaviors of interest are likely to occur (Haynes, 1978; McReynolds & DeVoge, 1977; Nay, 1977). Using analogue assessment procedures, an evaluation of a child's academic skills is made under conditions similar to the learning environment in which the skills are taught. Thus, analogue assessment provides an evaluation of the child's learning and academic skills within an environmental context that simulates classroom learning, including similar instructional materials, teaching strategies or reinforcement contingencies. Because the child is asked to respond to learning situations or curriculum-related materials that are analogous to those found in the classroom, the use of analogue assessment enables the diagnostician to observe directly the learning behaviors of interest. Analogue assessment utilizes a "movement-by-movement" analysis of the child's learning behavior rather than a standardized test that bears only an indirect relationship to actual classroom learning (Scandura, 1977). Because all data are generated under simulated teaching and learning conditions, analogue assessment strategies yield diagnostic information that has a high degree of instructional utility (Dickinson, 1980).

McFall (1977) and Nay (1977) offer two different categorizations of analogue assessment procedures; each has relevance for describing measures of academic abilities. McFall (1977) groups analogue procedures into four types according to the particular dimension of the natural environment that is simulated. In the first category, subject analogues, the target subjects are considered to be equivalent to analogous subjects to whom the assessment results are generalized. In treatment analogues, brief simplified interventions are equivalent to analogous but more complex and extensive treatment procedures. Diagnostic or trial teaching (discussed later in this chapter) is one example of a treatment analogue for academic skill assessment. For situational analogues, structured or controlled assessment situations are equivalent to the natural environments they simulate. Most academic skill assessments are situational analogues: children respond to learning situations that simulate those found in their classrooms, or they demonstrate skill mastery on curriculum-based materials. Finally, in response analogues, one response is considered to be equivalent to analogous responses to which the results are generalized. For example, an inaccurate response or error pattern on a specific set of addition problems suggests that a similar error pattern would occur for addition problems of the same type.

Nay (1977) categorizes analogue procedures according to the method of presentation of the analogue situations and the manner or mode in which the subjects respond. Paper-and-pencil analogues require respondents to indicate how they would respond to a stimulus situation that is presented in written form. Audiotape analogues present stimulus situations in an auditory format, and videotape analogues present situations in both auditory and visual form. Neither audiotape nor videotape presentations require the examiner to be present. Taped recordings of the responses made to each analogue situation can be scored at a later time by the diagnostician. The most common type of analogue method for assessment of academic abilities, according to Nay's (1977) categorization, is an enactment analogue. Rather than presenting the learning stimulus or situation in a written or recorded form, the enactment analogue requires the child to interact with relevant stimuli (people, objects, learning materials) that are typically present in the classroom. The examiner brings these relevant stimuli to the assessment setting so that the child's responses to them can be monitored. Because the diagnostician is interested in how the child responds to classroom learning situations, the stimuli in the analogue situation must approximate those found in the classroom if a valid respresentation of the child's learning behavior and academic skills is to be obtained. Thus, careful observations of the classroom should be conducted initially to assist the examiner in the construction of appropriate analogue situations.

Several assumptions underlie the use of analogue assessment procedures for evaluating academic skills (Haynes, 1978). Assessment for instructional planning (i.e., helping a teacher decide what and how to teach) is central to an analogue assessment approach. Hence, analogue assessment necessitates the selection of instructional, relevant behaviors to be measured. Howell, Kaplan, and O'Connell (1979) stress that the more directly assessment procedures measure what is being taught, the more likely they are to have instructional utility. Herein lies the basic rationale and justification for analogue assessment of academic skills.

A major assumption of analogue assessment is that the closer the evaluation situation approximates the typical learning environment, the more reliable and valid the information that is obtained. The ultimate goal of analogue assessment is to evaluate behavior or skills in those learning situations that are of primary concern. Therefore, performance is evaluated under typical classroom conditions and on actual classroom materials that are both easy and difficult for the student. In addition, it is assumed that the behavior of children in an analogue learning situation is similar to or predicts their learning behavior in the classroom. For academic skills, this assumption has rarely been tested directly. Therefore, the extent to which knowledge gained about a child's academic skills and learning behaviors can be generalized to classroom learning is one area in which additional research is needed (as discussed later in this chapter).

Shapiro and Lentz (1985) summarize these assumptions and underscore their importance for behavioral assessment of academic skills. First, they state that assessment should reflect as closely as possible an evaluation of academic skills in the natural environment (which, in this case, is the classroom learning environment). Second, assessment should be based on the curriculum actually used to teach the child the academic skills of concern. Third, the results of academic skill assessment should provide recommendations for intervention in the regular classroom. Fourth, measures chosen for the assessment of academic skills should be empirically validated. Finally, assessment should incorporate an evaluation of performance, as well as skill deficits, of environmental as well as learner characteristics.

ADVANTAGES AND LIMITATIONS OF ANALOGUE ASSESSMENT

Compared with observation in the natural environment, analogue assessment offers several distinct advantages. First, it permits an evaluation of behaviors that are not possible to monitor in natural settings. Second, analogue observation can increase observation efficiency, particularly with behaviors that occur infrequently or are difficult to observe in the natural environment. Unlike naturalistic observation procedures, analogue methods involve the direct observation of behaviors in situations or environments other than natural ones. The main objective of observing academic skills in analogue settings is to increase the examiner's control over the assessment procedure and, consequently, to enhance the utlity of the information obtained. Analogue procedures may help simplify complex problems because of the degree of control that can be exercised. Finally, analogue procedures enable diagnosticians to achieve their goal of determining the conditions under which a child can acquire and retain academic skills. Because analogue procedures simulate teaching situations, they afford the examiner the opportunity to observe, modify, and evaluate systematically the effects of specific contingencies, teaching strategies, or task components on children's skill acquisition and retention. For example, observation of learning performance and academic skill mastery in simulated, controlled teaching situations might reveal that children's difficulties are a function of exposure to ineffective instructional techniques, an inappropriate sequence of study, an inability to work successfully under timed conditions, difficulty following or understanding task directions, or ineffective reinforcement contingencies. This type of diagnostic information may not be possible to obtain from uncontrolled observations of children's performance in the natural settings, the classroom.

Analogue assessment procedures also offer many advantages over traditional psychoeducational assessment practices. The major advantage is that a diagnostician can systematically record the child's behavior in response to relevant classroom stimuli, making this less artificial than traditional assessment approaches. This difference between traditional testing practices and analogue assessment has been conceptualized in a number of ways. One conceptualization is based on the distinction between evaluation and diagnosis (Hunter, 1979). Evaluation, which is most often associated with standardized testing, yields information that enables the examiner to categorize, label, or place the child's performance on a continuum from success to failure. Diagnosis, the objective of analogue skill assessment, is essential for effective teaching. The purpose of diagnosis is not to categorize, but to suggest interventions to improve achievement.

Poplin and Gray (1982) offer another conceptualization of the difference between standardized tests and analogue measures of academic abilities. They categorize learning and evaluation activities as either natural or synthetic. This categorization reflects the distinction between standardized tests and analogue measures. For example, if a teaching objective states that a student should use appropriate punctuation marks at the ends of sentences, and the assessment activity to evaluate punctuation skills requires the student to circle errors in contrived sentences, then the assessment is synthetic. According to Poplin and Gray, standardized testing typically uses synthetic activities to measure academic abilities. The advantage of synthetic activities is that assessment is uniform across students and settings. The disadvantage is that they do not provide the opportunity to observe mastery of a given skill in a real-life situation. In contrast, diagnosticians conduct natural assessments by observing the student performing the activity required for demonstrating mastery of the objective. In the above example, a natural assessment activity might involve evaluating the child's use of punctuation in spontaneous writing. Analogue assessment typically uses natural rather than synthetic activities to measure academic skills. According to Poplin and Gray, the most obvious advantage of natural activities is that they allow for evaluation of academic skills in the natural context in which students must learn and demonstrate skill mastery. The main disadvantage is that the products of such assessment are individual rather than uniform or normative.

Tidwell (1980) identified several additional advantages of alternate methods of academic skill assessment, such as analogue assessment, over traditional test-based assessment practices. The most important advantage is what she calls "instructional payoffs." Information derived from analogue measures can be educationally significant for school professionals who must recommend and implement instructional decisions for children. Unlike standardized tests, analogue measures can be structured to tap a specific skill dimension at a particular grade level under conditions that conform to the typical instructional characteristics (curricular emphasis, teaching style, etc.). Tidwell also cites the potential consultation orientation and facilitation of communication with parents regarding assessment data as additional advantages over traditional testing and evaluation. Analogue procedures are further characterized by their ability to be tailored to the needs of specific assessment situations. Thus, an additional advantage is their flexibility.

Because of these relative strengths, there are several reasons to prefer analogue measures over formal assessment procedures for the assessment of academic abilities. However, it is also important to consider some of the limitations of analogue assessment. One practical limitation is that analogue procedures may be more difficult to design and implement. It has been argued that analogue procedures are time-consuming and require knowledge of academic skills beyond what is necessary to score and interpret standardized tests. This argument, however, is countered by the fact that much of the information needed to develop analogue assessment measures is available from teachers, curricular materials, or special education staff; diagnosticians may consult these resources to learn about instructional approaches. Therefore, analogue assessment may actually serve to enhance communication and consultation among various professionals.

The fact that analogue procedures are typically not standardized represents another major limitation. Aside from curricular validity, the psychometric properties of analogue measures are less established. Some experts argue that, by relying on analogue measures for academic skill assessment, examiners sacrifice the documented technical properties of standardized measures. One validity issue relates to making decisions about a child's educational program based on data derived from analogue measures used in an individualized situation. In analogue assessment, diagnosticians are encouraged to define all environmental variables that influence learning and to vary these systematically in a structured situation to ascertain what influences the measured behavior. Although such control and consistency are characteristic of effective teaching procedures (Rosenshine, 1981), it is often difficult to achieve an equivalent degree of structure in the natural classroom environment. Thus, a major disadvantage is that the analogue setting never perfectly duplicates the natural setting, therefore raising the issue of questionable validity. A related problem is the possibility of limited generalizability. In other words, the learning and academic skills in an analogue learning situation may not be relevant for or predict learning in the natural classroom setting. This is due, in part, to the impossibility of presenting certain classroom stimuli (such as teacher, peers, classroom size and arrangement).

Reliability is another potential limitation to the use of analogue procedures for assessing academic abilities. Empirical data are available concerning the reliability of curriculum-based measures (Deno, 1985; Fuchs, Deno, & Marston, 1983); however, for many other analogue methods, reliability information is lacking. Although analogue assessment is particularly valuable because it yields instructionally relevant data, unknown reliability poses a significant drawback to its use (Zigmond & Silverman, 1984). One potential source of unreliable data is that examiners typically vary considerably in their skills in developing and interpreting analogue measures. Optimistically, however, developments in educational research and evaluation dealing with naturalistic inquiry (Bogdan & Taylor, 1975; Guba, 1978) may lead to improved, more reliable procedures for observing, documenting, and interpreting students' behavior on analogue measures.

Finally, perhaps the most serious limitation of analogue measurement of academic skills is that users of analogue procedures may fail to distinguish teaching from testing and may not use the data obtained from analogue measures to improve instruction. Research on analogue measures does *not* support the use of the measurement procedures to teach skills (Deno & Mirkin, 1977). As Deno, Mirkin, and Chiang (1982) state, "to assume [that analogue measures represent actual teaching practices] . . . is to act as if . . . taking a patient's temperature is an effective approach to reducing a fever. Just as medical practice has developed procedures for obtaining 'vital sign' data as a basis for evaluating physical health, the attempt here is to develop efficient procedures for monitoring educational well-being" (p. 44).

TYPES OF ANALOGUE PROCEDURES FOR ASSESSING ACADEMIC ABILITIES

In recent years, diagnosticians have turned to analogue measures to gain more valuable information during assessment and to circumvent some of the problems associated with traditional standardized testing. Despite the growing popularity of analogue measures, few efforts have been made to formalize these methods for assessing academic skills. Although analogue strategies have evolved from several diverse orientations, they do share some common characteristics. First, analogue measures are designed to provide teachers with relevant information regarding instructional and remedial planning. Second, they place a heavy emphasis on how children learn and how they can profit from instructional modifications. Third, analogue assessment takes environmental factors into consideration in evaluating academic performance.

A variety of analogue assessment strategies can be used to obtain information about what to teach and how to teach academic skills. Smith (1983) identifies several diagnostic procedures that are considered analogue measures. These include diagnostic teaching, task analysis, error analysis, modified assessment, curriculum-based assessment, work sampling, and diagnosing instruction, each of which is summarized in Table 7-1 and is discussed in greater detail in the following sections. All of these procedures address the how-to-teach question directly. Furthermore, analogue methods facilitate the monitoring of student progress and skill acquisition; therefore, they typically serve as measures for both preintervention assessment and the evaluation of intervention effectiveness. Despite their diagnostic and instructional utility, inferences derived from the procedures described below must be tested in actual classroom instruction before incorporating them as part of a child's remedial program.

TABLE 7-1 Types of Analogue Procedures for Assessing Academic Abilities

Procedure	Description	References
Diagnostic teaching	Simulated instruction that evaluates effectiveness of remedial strategies and identifies conditions under which skills are acquired.	Bryant (1966) Fowler (1980) Guerin & Maier (1983) Hutson & Niles (1974) Ozer & Richardson (1974)
Task analysis	Focuses on child's level of skills in relation to instructional objective by breaking down tasks into component skills and assessing mastery of these skills.	Howell, Kaplan, & O'Connell (1979) Resnick, Wang, & Kaplan (1973) Zigmond, Vallecorsa, & Silverman (1983)
Error analysis	Identification of item types that are consistently failed/passed and formulation of tentative hypotheses about child's deficits/abilities.	Algozzine, Siders, & Beattie (1983) Beattie & Algozzine (1982) Berman & Friederwitzer (1981) Engelhardt (1982)
Modified testing	Techniques to alter or expand standardized testing procedures (modality, language, time) to determine why a student erred in responding.	Feuerstein (1979) Hargrove & Poteet (1984) Smith (1980) West (1977)
Curriculum-based assessment	Procedure for determining instructional needs on the basis of evaluating continuous performance on existing course content and curriculum.	Deno (1985) Deno, Mirkin, & Chiang (1982) Gickling (1981) Marston, Mirkin, & Deno (1984)
Work sampling	Systematic evaluation of samples of work (writing samples, tests, completed workbook pages) that reflect the student's learning problems/strengths.	Cramer (1982) Dixon (1977) Pikulski (1974) Semb (1972)
Diagnosing instruction	Procedure to determine aspects of instruction that are inadequate in meeting individual needs and to recommend modifications in instruction.	Bleismer (1972) Duffey & Fedner (1979) Engelmann, Granzin, & Severson (1979)
Computer-assisted assessment	Use of microcomputers to present academic tasks, monitor responses, and score, interpret, and analyze errors on task performance.	Bright (1984) Hasselbring & Crossland (1981) Hasselbring & Gray (1985) Wedman & Stefanich (1984)

Diagnostic Teaching

Diagnostic or trial teaching is an analogue assessment strategy that addresses the issue of how to teach academic skills most directly (Salvia & Ysseldyke, 1981; Smith, 1980). Assessment from a diagnostic teaching perspective focuses on the identification of effective instructional strategies for individual children. One objective of diagnostic teaching is to determine the conditions under which a child can acquire and demonstrate academic skills. This is accomplished by hypothesizing where the interference in the child's performance exists, determining how the child learns best, and then modifying the task accordingly in analogue situations.

Trial teaching is brief, intensive, simulated classroom instruction that attempts to try out and evaluate the effectiveness of particular remedial techniques. Using a diagnostic teaching procedure, a variety of instructional techniques, such as varying teaching materials, methods of presentation, or types of feedback, may be systematically implemented and evaluated in a simulated teaching-learning situation. Diagnostic teaching extends beyond the administration of standardized tests and informal measures. It encompasses an evaluation of the student's progress during intervention in that the diagnostician continues to collect assessment information while teaching the student. The utility of diagnostic teaching rests on the examiner's interpretation of how the child learns and an analysis of the nature of the child's performance.

Another objective of diagnostic teaching is to obtain information about children's academic content needs for instructional purposes. Diagnostic teaching strategies are designed to yield information regarding how children learn curriculum-related material and how the curriculum may be modified to enhance skill acquisition. Several writers have advocated the importance of teaching curriculum-related material as part of academic skills assessment (e.g., Bryant, 1966; Hutson & Niles, 1974). In sum, an emphasis on trial teaching has the advantage of evaluating actual learning behaviors and providing the opportunity to explore the effects of instructional variables on students' learning. After a period of diagnostic teaching, the examiner is able to address instructional factors that influence skill acquisition and can facilitate the planning of individualized instruction.

According to Hunter (1979), trial teaching can be used to obtain diagnostic information in three areas. First, the diagnostician is able to determine where new learning should begin in a curriculum and whether the level of curricular material matches the student's skill level. Second, the way in which students learn may be diagnosed to allow for an accommodation for their individual learning styles. Assessment of learning styles through diagnostic teaching is typically based on four considerations: (1) how the student acquires information or skills during the miniteaching situation, (2) how the student demonstrates learning, (3) which learning environment offers the greatest potential for the student's achievement, and (4) which aspects of the student's characteristic learning effort (persistence, motivation, work habits, etc.) affect performance. Finally, the examiner is able to ascertain which instructional or environmental factors are critical for student achievement (e.g., the number of times the student should practice a learned skill, what motivates a student). Barsch (1965) delineated six factors in instruction that can be readjusted or modified by the examiner in an analogue trial teaching situation. These are space (physical setting), time (amount of time allocated or spent learning), multiplicity (number of items or the size of the instructional unit), difficulty level of material, language of learning tasks and directions, and interpersonal relationship variables.

A number of assessment strategies have emerged in recent years that are categorized as diagnostic teaching approaches. For all strategies, assessment information about the student's learning can be obtained through short teaching lessons. Typically, after giving a standardized test the examiner learns more about the student by developing short lessons that teach the apparent deficit skills and then observing the student's performance and reactions to these. In trial teaching, the diagnostician teaches the student the necessary skills to solve items that were missed on standardized tests or novel items from the student's curriculum that are similar to those missed on tests. For example, Ancevich and Payne (1961) supplemented their traditional assessment battery with a minilearning experiment that investigated children's ability to learn sight words through different modalities. Myers and Hammill (1969) recommended teaching words to children using different teaching strategies during assessment. Hutson and Niles (1974) described a "dynamic evaluation" of children's learning by incorporating short sessions of trial teaching during academic skill assessment. Ozer and his associates (Ozer & Dworkin, 1974; Ozer & Richardson, 1972, 1974) developed an evaluation protocol called the Child Development Observation (CDO) form that simulates the process of learning during a fifteen-minute period in order to gauge the potential of different strategies to facilitate learning.

Bryant (1966) developed a procedure called "trial remediation for sight words" that involves teaching fifteen to twenty sight words in small units of five words each. Each five-word unit is taught using a different instructional approach. For example, for one unit the student is instructed to trace each word after it is presented; for another unit the student writes each word after its presentation; for another unit the student is instructed to repeat the word out loud and try to image the word in his or her mind. The number of trials needed to reach a criterion of two consecutive pronunciations is the measure of acquisition; the number of words read correctly at the end of the trial remediation session is the measure of retention. Acquisition and retention measures for the various instructional techniques are compared, and recommendations for sight word instruction are derived from these comparisons.

Finally, Guerin and Maier (1983) described another diagnostic teaching approach that consists of visual, phonics, visual-motor, and kinesthetic trial lessons for students at first- through third-grade reading levels. Other trial lesson techniques are also described by Guerin and Maier for older students at higher reading levels. These types of procedures indicate how students read and comprehend best.

As with most analogue measures, there are some limitations in the use of diagnostic teaching procedures for assessing academic skills. First, because trial teaching procedures are highly structured, children's new learning must be evaluated against the teaching methods used in their regular classroom. For example, Smith (1980) cites a case in which a fourth-grade girl with spelling problems was evaluated with trial teaching using direct instruction procedures. Trial teaching revealed no difficulty in learning phonic and nonphonic words or in generalizing spelling forms to novel words. When these findings were shared with the child's teachers, it was discovered that spelling was not taught directly in the child's class. Thus, for this child, trial teaching assessment strategies did not reveal a spelling problem because the diagnostician failed to consider the classroom instruction to which the girl was typically exposed.

A number of researchers (Bracht, 1970; Eaves & McLaughlin, 1977; Ewing & Brecht, 1977; Smead, 1977; Ysseldyke & Sabatino, 1973) have reviewed results from studies designed to relate assessment data derived from diagnostic teaching to differential instructional programming. In general, empirical support for the efficacy of trial teaching is inconsistent, in part because most research efforts have been plagued with methodological problems and inadequate designs. Consequently, Ewing and Brecht (1977) stress that instructional programs designed to improve academic skill development resulting from diagnostic teaching should be viewed cautiously and monitored carefully. As they state, "learners experiencing academic difficulties can least afford unvalidated . . . activities masquerading as warranted instructional strategy" (p. 326).

Task Analysis

A task analytic approach to analogue assessment stresses the evaluation of academic skills based on the child's observed performance on learning tasks, representing a hierarchical sequence of subskills within an academic area such as reading or math. The underlying philosophy of this approach is that children fail a task because they lack subordinate competencies or the knowledge essential for the completion of that task. Task analysis procedures break down complex instructional goals into component subskills and assess mastery of these subskills (Bijou, 1970; Resnick, Wang, & Kaplan, 1973; Smith, 1980). In this way, a child can be located on a hierarchy of component skills for a given task, and subsequent skills to be taught can be identified. Unlike diagnostic teaching, which helps to identify instructional strategies, analogue measures based on task analysis identify deficits or missing competencies in a learning sequence and, therefore, are useful in directing instruction toward particular skills.

Howell *et al.* (1979) describe a task analytic assessment model that follows a continuous cycle of fact-finding, task analyzing, hypothesizing, and validating until the academic skills in question have been thoroughly evaluated and the problem is diagnosed. The purpose of the initial fact-finding phase is to identify areas of concern. The procedure advocated by Howell *et al.* is to observe children's performances on academic tasks they are failing, either in an analogue or natural classroom setting. The objective in this phase is to specify what children do (or do not do) while performing the task. The second phase in task analysis requires the examiner to isolate subtasks necessary to complete the task successfully and to generate possible causes of the performance deficit. The next phase is to formulate hypotheses regarding the subtasks for which the child's competency is in doubt. The cycle is complete when a second analogue assessment begins. In this phase the examiner tests the validity of each assumed cause using probes that represent each subtest. Validation of assumed causes has educational utility because it tells a teacher what to teach. Howell *et al.* stress that academic skill assessment is not complete until an attempted intervention is found to be successful, either in an analogue or natural instructional setting.

The informal task analysis procedures suggested in the Howell *et al.* model are used to construct hierarchical structures in various academic content areas of school curriculum. These hypothesized instructional sequences are then used in the development of analogue academic tasks to assess mastery of particular subskills. This approach is limited, however, in that the scope and sequence of item domains are not empirically derived. In recent years, mathematical techniques have been developed that are capable of representing learning structures empirically. These techniques have led to the development of a method of evaluating academic abilities termed path-referenced assessment (Bergan, 1981). Path-referenced assessment is subsumed under analogue measurement inasmuch as information is obtained about children's development and progress in relation to an empirically validated learning sequence that parallels instruction in a content area such as language, math, reading, or science. This procedure enables the diagnostician to identify the student's specific skill deficiencies or "position" within an ordered learning sequence as well as the appropriate "path" of instruction needed to ensure mastery of the task. In addition to the utilization of empirically validated structures, path-referenced assessment has the advantage of yielding information explaining the magnitude of effects that mastery of subordinate subskills will have on achieving mastery of the superordinate task. Thus, programming decisions may be linked directly to information about a child's current status in the sequence (e.g., "John does not recognize vowel sounds") as well as projected future achievement (e.g., "The probability of children learning to read phonetically is fifty times greater for children who recognize vowel sounds than for children who have not mastered vowel sound recognition").

Content Analysis and Error Analysis

The goal of content analysis is to identify the types of items that are consistently failed or passed on academic tasks and to form tentative hypotheses about the nature of the child's abilities (Algozzine, Siders, & Beattie, 1982). For example, if a diagnostician analyzed a boy's performance on the mathematics subtest of the

PIAT and noted that he missed all items that involved addition, the content area of addition would be identified as a hypothesized source of difficulty. Subsequently, an analogue situation would be set up during which addition items taken from the student's actual math curriculum would be administered. The diagnostician may then engage in a product analysis that is prompted by consistent error patterns. Product analysis is an examination of how the student arrives at an outcome. It is an analysis of the product or answers as well as the processes or methods a student employs to arrive at those answers. For example, this student may demonstrate adequate knowledge and application of basic skills of addition, but has difficulty with place value.

Error analysis is particularly advantageous for instructional planning because it is often difficult to translate standardized test scores into meaningful instructional objectives. For example, a 3.2 grade equivalent score on the reading recognition subtest of the PIAT in itself does not indicate specifically what should be taught. An analysis of the reading recognition items on the PIAT indicates that several word patterns are present within the words that are tested. However, the number of words selected to represent various patterns is limited. Although it is possible to analyze the type of errors a child makes in this small sample of reading behavior, the examiner can form only tentative hypotheses regarding the nature of the child's reading problem. However, an analysis of the words that were read incorrectly may provide information for educational planning beyond that provided by global test scores. To facilitate this process, a more detailed analysis of word attack skills is warranted.

In sum, a diagnostic process for evaluating word reading skills based on error analysis incorporates the following steps: First, a formal measure of reading recognition is administered, scored, and interpreted in relation to its designated use. Second, errors within the actual set of words are recorded and identified as particular word types. Third, reading performance on specific word types is obtained and errors are again noted. Finally, all errors are analyzed and teaching activities are designed based on the results of error analysis. A similar process can be applied for evaluating other academic skills as well.

Modified Testing

Modified testing techniques are analogue activities selected by the diagnostician to determine why a student responded in a particular way on standardized test items. Such techniques are similar to Feuerstein's (1979) use of dynamic assessment. Using Feuerstein's approach, a student is presented with a problem and then given the training necessary to solve it. This assessment process focuses on the degree to which the student learns in the analogue teaching situation (i.e., the amount of teaching necessary and the extent to which the student can apply what has been learned to novel items). Hargrove and Poteet (1984) describe several dimensions along which standardized testing may be modified by the examiner in order to obtain information regarding how to teach. Such learning task dimensions include modality (input and output characteristics of the test items), language complexity (level of abstraction, amount of information), and time allocated. It is the discrepancy between initial test performance and performance after modifications that indicates which competencies a child has if the task is matched to his or her preferred strategies. Subsequently, trial teaching items and observing the degree of generalization of skills to similar items yield information on what and how a child can learn.

One specific type of modified assessment is testing-the-limits. This technique is used to determine the consistency of errors noted on standardized test protocols. Using this approach, high frequency error types are identified, and items that are representative of these errors are readministered. With additional modifications or prompting during the readministration of items, the diagnostician can determine the malleability of the error, that is, whether the error can be eradicated with minimal additional cues from the teacher.

Several cautions regarding the use of modified assessment techniques should be acknowledged. First, responses to modifications should be considered only after the standardized administration and scoring have been followed. Modifications are appropriately used only if the examiner has observed a consistent pattern of responding; modifications of all items and components is not practical. Finally, in order to gain the most useful diagnostic information, the items selected for further assessment should be classified according to their common characteristics.

Curriculum-based Assessment

In selecting measures to incorporate in analogue situations, it is important to use materials that are directly related to the curriculum. Curriculum-based assessment was developed on the basis of this need for diagnosticians to analyze and use curriculum materials. Gickling (1981) defines curriculum-based assessment as "a procedure for determining the instructional needs of a student based upon the student's ongoing performance within the existing course content" (p. 4). The focus in this assessment method is on the curriculum that is being used to teach students; this curriculum serves as the content of assessment tasks. Curriculum-based assessment includes direct observation and simulation of the learning environment, an analysis of the processes used to complete tasks, and a controlled arrangement of tasks in order of difficulty. It provides a way of matching student ability to instruction (Thompson, Gickling, & Havertape, 1983). According to Gickling and Thompson (1985), instructional tasks for academic skill assessment should be developed according to three components: (1) the type of task (drill versus reading), (2) the nature and number of items in the task (knowns versus unknowns), and (3) the student's level of performance (instructional versus independent versus frustration).

Deno and Mirkin (1977) identified effective curriculum-based measures called skill probes that have been shown to be valid and reliable indexes of academic skill knowledge. Skill probes are timed assessments derived from the curriculum that the child has been expected to learn in school. For example, for reading, measures of oral reading rate and comprehension may be used as probes; for spelling, correct and incorrect words from spelling lists dictated in paragraphs may be used. Shapiro and Lentz (1985) also recommend the use of end-of-book tests in math and other curriculum-based measures as skill probes.

Several researchers have recently documented that it is possible to standardize curriculum-based procedures to establish local norms for the comparison of individual children (Deno, 1985; Germann & Tindall, 1985; Peterson, Heistad, Peterson, & Reynolds, 1985). For example, Germann and Tindall (1985) provide an account of establishing a curriculum-based assessment model in five rural schools. Their data indicate that by standardizing student performance measures in basic academic skills, school systems have a practical way of determining eligibility for special education services.

Curriculum-based assessment can also provide useful data for planning remediation. A basic assumption underlying curriculum-based assessment is that learning proceeds best when children experience a high rate of success interspersed with acceptable levels of challenge. Thus, assessment determines children's levels of functioning in the curriculum as well as the nature of their deficits, and intervention involves choosing, preparing, or adapting materials to match their performance. The goal of curriculum-based assessment is to gain control over the variability of curriculum materials by determining how effectively a learner functions with that curriculum and to modify the pace, sequence, amount, mode of presentation, or difficulty level to match the learner's functioning.

Work Sampling

Semb (1972) described a work sampling, work simulation process for academic skill assessment. Using a work sampling procedure, the examiner asks the child's teacher to provide both completed and uncompleted work samples that best reflect the child's learning problem. The uncompleted work should be extensive enough to provide sufficient opportunity to observe the child's academic skills and related behaviors under simulated conditions. The uncompleted work samples should also be designed to reflect the teacher's estimate of the child's independent learning level, instructional level, and frustration level on each learning activity. The teacher also provides information about how the learning activities are presented to the student in class and the criteria for successful completion of the tasks. This information enables the examiner to simulate the real work demands of the classroom during assessment sessions.

This type of work sampling procedure has many advantages. First, it allows the examiner to assess academic skills that are closely related to the actual skill demands of the classroom. Second, the examiner is able to compare two samples of the child's work—one sample that was completed under regular classroom conditions, the other completed in an optimal one-on-one setting. Such comparisons may help clarify whether skill deficits are causing the problem or whether environmental factors within the classroom are contributing to the child's difficulties. Third, this process encourages teachers to do a more careful task analysis of children's learning problems. Issues such as how learning tasks are assigned in class, what skills are needed for task completion and the sequencing of those skills, and the teacher's criteria for successful performance are elucidated. Finally, closely simulating regular academic work makes for a more realistic setting when evaluating the child's mediational processes related to task completion, such as the kinds of self-statements and problem-solving strategies the child uses when approaching and completing an academic task.

Diagnosing Instruction

Traditional procedures used to diagnose children's learning and academic skill deficits are limited because they typically do not assess the instruction the learner receives; they assess only the learner. Traditional academic skill assessment usually occurs outside the instructional context in which learning occurs. Engelmann, Granzin, and Severson (1979) argue that accurate conclusions about the child can be reached only after an adequate diagnosis of instruction has been made. Failure to consider instruction as a variable results in few, if any, implications for teaching. For a remedial suggestion to follow from diagnosis, the diagnosis must inform teachers about what they can do to improve learner performance. Engelmann *et al.* describe a model for diagnosing instruction that attempts to determine aspects of instruction that are inadequate, to ascertain precisely how they are inadequate, and to recommend what must be done to correct their inadequacy. Their model involves two critical steps: (1) observing and interpreting the instruction the learner receives according to the "minimum-knowledge assumption," and (2) providing a "maximum-knowledge test." The minimum-knowledge assumption identifies the least possible knowledge the learner needs in order to perform as he or she does. The test of maximum knowledge structures the situation so that the learner cannot use the simplest mechanism or least possible knowledge.

To illustrate the application of these two steps, Engelmann *et al.* present the example of a preschool girl who is being taught basic number counting skills in the following way. A teacher places a domino in front of the child and states how many dots there are. If the child has a domino with a matching number of dots, she places it on the table. The child in this case places a domino on the table for every trial, regardless of the accuracy. She is praised by the teacher for every response that happens to be appropriate. In this example, the minimum knowledge the learner must possess to perform in the observed manner is to put a domino on the table every time the teacher presents one. She does not have to count the dots on the dominoes or comprehend the concept of matching. A maximum-knowledge test must evaluate the child's knowledge of matching numbers and dots in such a way that the simple mechanism of placing dominoes on the table for every trial cannot lead to successful performance. An example would be to place a row of dominoes on the table and have the child place her domino next to the one with the same number of dots. Suggestions for remediation follow directly from the learner's performance on the maximum-knowledge test. If she fails the test, a recommendation is made that she should work on tasks or activities that account for passing the test, which, in this case, would be number concept and matching.

Computer-based Analogue Assessment

The advent of the microcomputer has precipitated considerable growth in classroom utilization of computer technology for both instructional and assessment purposes. Although the primary use of microcomputers in academic assessment has been with the administration of standardized instruments, they can also be valuable in conjunction with analogue measures. Microcomputers can assist diagnosticians in constructing, administering, and evaluating performance on analogue tasks (Salend & Salend, 1985). Through the use of computerized interactive testing, the quality of analogue assessment can be greatly enhanced while reducing the time and effort required for implementation. For example, when programmed appropriately, microcomputers can present the student with academic tasks, monitor student responses, score, interpret, and summarize performance. Hasselbring and Gray (1985) describe several existing computer programs that can be used interactively to assess reading, spelling, and math skills. These programs have been successful in saving examiner time, facilitating the observation of children's behavior during analogue learning situations, and providing specific diagnostic information.

Video disc technology and other hardware innovations also make possible the construction of analogue tasks that correspond closely to real learning situations. Such simulations are clearly less cumbersome and less expensive to administer and score than paper forms. Computer simulations can be used in several different ways for a variety of assessment purposes, including the evaluation of academic skills and problem-solving abilities. With simulations it is possible to present realistic settings with which students can interact. Wedman and Stefanich (1984), for example, describe several procedures for conducting computer-based evaluations of concept and problem-solving strategy learning.

In instances where students exhibit difficulties on computerized analogue tasks, it is necessary to specify the pattern of errors and develop an appropriate instructional plan to remediate the hypothesized deficit. The necessity for individual interviews or the examination and identification of consistent error patterns makes error analysis time-consuming for most diagnosticians. One way to facilitate this process is through the use of microcomputer technology. Microcomputers not only indicate correct and incorrect responses on analogue tasks, they can also be programmed to perform diagnostic error analysis. For example, Bright (1984) describes the use of microcomputers for conducting an error analysis of students' performance on analogue mathematics tasks.

One example of an interactive spelling assessment program is the Computerized Diagnostic Spelling Test (CDST) (Hasselbring & Crossland, 1981). The CDST is a computerized version of the Kottmeyer Diagnostic Spelling Test (1970). In this program, the computer simulates a dictation spelling test. As the student types each word, the microcomputer scores the response, identifies the error type, and stores this information. The computer then provides a listing of the number of correct and incorrect words, the misspelled words along with correct spellings, and the nature of the errors (short vowels, doubling, etc.). Wilson and Fox (1982) describe a similar computer-administered interactive testing procedure for evaluating receptive language skills.

The use of microcomputers has several inherent benefits. First, students can independently complete the task. This saves time for the examiner and allows students to perform analogue tasks on their own without the potential pressure of having an examiner wait for them to complete the task. Second, the computer eliminates the need for students to respond in writing. The variety of ways in which students can interface with computers decreases problems because of difficulties in the response mode. Third, a microcomputer is generally appealing to students. For example, teacher feedback and reinforcement have been shown to promote motivation during regular classroom instruction. Thus microcomputers can be programmed to deliver these to students in a way that simulates what they receive in their classes. The branching capabilities of microcomputers can also help foster motivation by preventing frustration over persistent failure, again, similar to what typically occurs in the classroom.

Before diagnosticians proceed with unreserved acceptance of microcomputers for analogue assessment, however, there are several issues that need to be investigated empirically. It is possible, for example, that student performance may be affected by the medium and its particular cognitive demands. The format of the task, including presentation and response modes, appearance, and spatical organization, can affect performance. For example, Varnhagen and Gerber (1984) found that third-grade students took longer to respond and made more errors on a computerized version of a dictation spelling test than on a handwritten version. They concluded that the increased response key search time induced by the use of the microcomputer interfered with the cognitive processes and academic abilities being assessed. Therefore, students must be completely comfortable with running the computer and using the assessment programs. Finally, although computers have the potential of enhancing the analogue assessment of academic abilities, their usefulness will not be fully realized unless programs are developed and carefully evaluated before implementation.

ANALOGUE MEASURES FOR ASSESSING ACADEMIC SKILLS

Analogue measures have been developed and used by researchers and practitioners for assessing academic abilities among school children. The following sections describe methods that have been recommended and, in some instances, empirically validated for evaluating reading, language, writing, and mathematics, and cognitive strategy abilities of handicapped and nonhandicapped learners. A detailed description of each method is beyond the scope of this chapter; therefore, only an overview of procedures is presented. The intent is to provide examples of analogue methods and to illustrate the range of procedures and skills subsumed under analogue assessment.

Reading

Reading difficulties are considered to be a major factor distinguishing children who fail from those who succeed in school. Given the importance of reading for school achievement and the variety of approaches for teaching reading, the assessment of skills and evaluation of effective instruction are critical for informative diagnosis of a child's reading ability. Analogue measures have been used to evaluate reading in these areas: word recognition, passage comprehension, and content area reading.

To conduct analogue assessments in oral reading, several types of information must be available. The first is a hierarchy of word types that the child is unable to decode. Second the diagnostician must know what items from the hierarchy have already been tested with a formal reading measure. Third, the examiner must have available sets of word lists for each type of word tested. Finally, the examiner needs a teaching strategy by which new skills may be taught once the nature of those skills is identified. Deno, Mirkin, and Chiang (1982) developed curriculum-based analogue measures of reading performance for elementary school children (learning disabled and regular education students) from grades one through five. These measures included the following: (1) words in isolation (60 words selected from Harris-Jacobson (1972) *Basic Elementary Reading Vocabularies*); (2) words in context (120 underlined words in passages selected from three different basal reading series); (3) oral reading (300-word passages selected from basal reading series); (4) cloze comprehension (300-word passages selected from basal reading series with every fifth word deleted); and (5) word meaning (60 underlined words in passages selected from basal reading series). Deno *et al.* (1982) conducted three concurrent validity studies to examine the relationship between these five analogue measures and standardized reading tests, the Stanford Diagnostic Reading Test (Karlsen, Madden, & Gardner, 1977) and Woodcock Reading Mastery Test (Woodcock, 1973). Correlational analyses provided evidence for the criterion validity of the analogue measures. Correlations between the two types of measures (analogue and standardized) in terms of the accuracy rate ranged from .60 for comprehension to .91 for word recognition measures. Thus, simple analogue measures of oral reading provide a valid index of students' reading proficiency as measured by standardized tests. Deno *et al.* (1982) also found that correct performance on analogue measures is a more valid measure of reading proficiency than number of errors, that sufficiently valid data on oral reading can be obtained by sampling reading behavior for one minute, and, finally, that the difficulty level of reading material selected for analogue reading tasks does not appear to affect the validity of the obtained data.

Analogue assessment of reading comprehension is based on observing students' responses in reading situations. Diagnosticians can assess a student's comprehension through interviews concerning what they have read. In this procedure, the child retells a passage, and the examiner follows up with probing questions to have the child clarify his or her understanding. This allows children to describe what they understood and how they related to their understanding. No constraints are placed on the reader's responses, as is the case with standardized reading comprehension tests. Moore (1983) states that "personal comprehension" is also measured by these procedures. Personal comprehension denotes outcomes that are unique according to the idiosyncratic nature and style of each individual and that occur when readers set their own purposes and integrate their own experiences with the reading material.

Pikulski (1974) presented another analogue approach for evaluating reading comprehension skills. In this method, stories are read aloud to the student with questions of a "what next" nature interspersed throughout the session. This is a method that simulates a classroom situation in which the teacher or peers read orally. It determines whether the child is listening carefully and comprehending the material, both of which are critical skills to evaluate.

Hansell (1981) described analogue measures for diagnosing content area reading skills. The best content area assessments, according to Hansell, are analogue procedures that require students to carry out tasks similar in content and complexity to what is expected of them in school. Students' performance on these simulated tasks may suggest instructional steps that are necessary to accomplish the instructional goals. All measures are employed with textbooks or curricular material used in a particular content area. In evaluating content area reading skills, diagnostic questions might include: Does the student know the basic concepts? Can the child handle the vocabulary or must it be taught? Are the child's overall reading skills and rate equivalent to the level of the material the teacher uses?

One approach described by Hansell (1981), called the readability approach, uses readability ratings to estimate the relative difficulty level of textbooks. Several readability formulas have been developed that attempt to measure the difficulty level of a book (Dale & Chall, 1948; Fry, 1968; McGlaughlin, 1969). Using a readability rating, textbook difficulty levels are determined and compared with the student's overall reading level. In effect, this approach diagnoses the curriculum rather than the learner and enables the diagnostician to determine the degree of fit between students' reading levels and the level of difficulty of material they are expected to read. A readability approach does not provide information about how children will read a text or their familiarity with the topic presented in the text. Therefore, a skills perspective is also recommended for evaluating content area reading.

In contrast to a readability approach, the focus of the skills approach is on each student. A skills perspective enables the diagnostician to use actual textbooks to determine whether a student has the skills necessary to read them. Burmeister (1978), for example, suggests developing an inventory of fifteen questions covering a 1500- to 3000-word passage from the textbook: five questions addressing details, five focusing on main ideas, and five requiring the student to interpret and use information from the text. During the assessment session, Burmeister recommends that the diagnostician introduce the passage just as the student's regular classroom teacher typically introduces a reading activity in class (previewing, eliciting questions, etc.). Several reading specialists (Estes & Vaughan, 1978; Shepherd, 1978; Strang, 1964; Thelan, 1976) recommend using this approach to assess the skills that students must use with materials in various content areas. It enables the diagnostician to determine what a student can or cannot do in relation to a teacher's goals for a study unit.

Language

Receptive, processing, and expressive language skills can have a significant impact on a child's thinking, problem solving, and overall academic progress. Therefore, teachers and diagnosticians must carefully monitor and evaluate children's language abilities. Expressive language skills are difficult to evaluate with standardized measures because of the limited number of formal language tests that are available. Therefore, analogue measures are an alternative to standardized testing for evaluating language abilities.

The use of elicited language production in analogue situations is warranted when particular aspects of language need to be observed, when the frequency of occurrence in a natural setting such as the classroom is limited, or if standardized language tests do not afford a detailed analysis of language skills. An additional advantage is that these procedures can elicit language behavior in a short period of time. In general, analogue assessment of language skills involves constructing simulated situations that prompt the child to produce the desired language behavior.

Basic to the development of language elicitation procedures is the identification of specific contexts that prompt language and that pose a problem for the child. These contexts will differ depending on the age of the child and the purpose and type of language skills that are a problem (discussion, convergent language production, etc.). When constructed appropriately, analogue procedures can increase the efficiency and specificity of assessing language behaviors. For example, Werner, Goossens, and Green (1981) describe a puppet show procedure used to assess syntactic and semantic expression of wh- questions among young children (3 to 6 years old). In this procedure, the child and puppets (representing the teacher and peers in the classroom) take turns asking each other wh- questions (who, why, which, where, what, when) in response to pictures that represent typical classroom stimuli. Schmidt (1981) described an analogue role-play approach for eliciting and evaluating more complex linguistic structures, such as negation, and interrogation, among older children (5 to 10 years old). Role-playing situations are also appropriate for evaluating overall expressive quality and production among children older than ten. For example, simulated discussion groups or situations in which the student must make an oral presentation about a reading passage, book, or picture provide an opportunity to observe and evaluate general language expression.

Dixon (1977) described the use of language experience stories as a diagnostic tool. Language experience stories are relatively simple to obtain in a minimum amount of time and reflect the uniqueness of each child. Analysis of the dictating-recording-reading process can generate three categories of information: (1) observable behaviors (e.g., Does the child pace his or her dictation, indicating an awareness of the connection between the spoken word and printed symbol?), (2) global language usage or general productive verbal skills (e.g., Does the child use complete sentences?), and (3) refined language usage (e.g., Does the child use adverbs and adjectives appropriately?). In an attempt to validate this procedure as a way of evaluating language skills among preschoolers, Dixon correlated data derived from the dictated stories in an individualized simulated puppet play with scores obtained on a language readiness battery and the Metropolitan Readiness Test (Nurss & McGauvran, 1976). Correlations ranged from .54 to .87 for the language battery and from a .58 to .73 for the readiness test, thus supporting the validity and diagnostic value of the information derived from the language samples.

Writing

Written expression is one of the most demanding forms of language; it includes a full range of skills that are often difficult to evaluate with standardized measures. Cramer (1983) contrasts what he terms "holistic" evaluation with "analytic" evaluation of writing skills. Holistic evaluation is a method of assessing writing, typically using standardized measures, to obtain a global indication of the level and quality of writing. Analytic evaluation is a detailed analysis of each strength and weakness found in a sample of writing, typically obtained in a structured analogue situation rather than a standardized testing situation or classroom.

Researchers have investigated the writing of students in analogue situations as it is influenced by a variety of techniques. These have included methods that stimulate writing (e.g., showing pictures, providing a story title, giving a lead sentence, reading a story) or provided direct instruction for specific skills (Lovitt, 1975b). In their review of the literature, Deno, Marston, and Mirkin (1982) identified six indexes of written language that are easily obtained from samples of writing. The average length of thought units, number of words not included on a standard word list, total number of words produced, average word length, number of correctly spelled words, and correctly spelled letter sequences comprised the set of descriptors that Deno *et al.* (1982) used to evaluate written language performance in an analogue test situation. Students (7 to 12 years old) were seen individually, and each was presented with a "story starter" to complete. To evaluate the concurrent validity of this procedure, scores were correlated with performance on standardized written language tests, the Test of Written Language (Hammill & Larsen, 1978), Developmental Sentence Scoring System (Lee & Canter, 1971) and word usage subtest of the Stanford Achievement Test (Madden, Gardner, Rudman, Karlsen, & Merwin, 1973). Correlation coefficients ranged from .43 to .86 for five of the six indexes. The results of this research lend empirical support for the validity of fairly simplistic and economical measures of written language skills derived from analogue assessment procedures.

Written expression also requires a knowledge of spelling. Although there have been fewer studies in spelling than in reading, the interventions evaluated in analogue teaching situations have been more diverse than in reading. Systematic trial teaching procedures have included direct instruction (Foster & Torgesen, 1983), study strategies (Gettinger, 1985; Graham, 1983; Graham & Freeman, 1985), mastery leaning (Gettinger, Bryant, & Fayne, 1982), grouping words to be learned according to certain similarities (content, phonic generalization) or number of words (Bryant, Drabin, & Gettinger, 1981), reinforcement contingencies, and modifying the response mode (oral, written) (Lovitt, 1975b).

Mathematics

Researchers have conducted a substantial number of analogue studies concerning a wide variety of arithmetic skills and interventions, including the use of reinforcement contingencies, drill, feedback, and modeling (Lovitt, 1975b). Engelhardt (1982) suggested using children's computational errors as a basis for developing analogue tasks or diagnostic teaching strategies. According to Engelhardt, there are four categories of computational errors. These are mechanical (resulting from perceptual-motor difficulties such as misaligned symbols), careless (resulting from responding without attending to the task carefully), conceptual (resulting from incorrect concepts such as inappropriate understanding of subtraction), and procedural (resulting from inappropriate procedures such as incorrect "carrying"). When diagnosticians examine children's computational errors on standardized tests, they should consider a variety of possibilities for those errors and be aware of multiple directions for follow-up using analogue procedures. For example, careless errors may be accidental. Using instructional cues that focus attention during miniteaching sessions may remediate the errors and provide a viable recommendation for classroom teachers. As another example, a procedural error may occur because the student spends so much time on the computational aspects that he or she forgets procedural steps. In this case, diagnostic teaching should focus on training the computational steps to an automatic level.

According to Fowler (1980), a math concept may be understood by the student, but another type of error results in an incorrect response. In this situation, diagnostic teaching is helpful in eliminating the needless repetition of known concepts that do not reduce the number of errors on similar problems. For example, diagnostic teaching may reveal that a child has the multiplication algorithm, but makes errors in addition that result in incorrect responses for multiplication items. This child does not need more instruction in multiplication but might profit from learning procedures for checking his or her work (if errors are inconsistent) or reviewing addition facts (if similar errors are made on a regular basis).

Although recognition of error patterns is necessary for successful diagnosis of math problems, it is possible to assess children's math skills using other analogue procedures as well. The diagnostic process should not only investigate a child's errors but also attempt to assess areas of strength. Math is an area in which reasonable inferences about covert behaviors can be made from observing correlated overt responses. When the faulty thinking or cognitive routine cannot be identified by analyzing the error patterns, students can be asked to make their routine overt by "thinking aloud" as they solve a certain type of problem. For example, listening to the child explain how a problem is done provides valuable insight into faulty as well as accurate thinking processes and arithmetic strategies. The use of manipulative materials is another means of gathering diagnostic information. For example, Berman and Friederwitzer (1981) suggest that a diagnostician can have the student display a problem with blocks or chips and then describe his or her actions in working it through. This technique allows for observing the child's manipulation for each step of the algorithm while listening to the oral explanation, thus enabling the diagnostician to focus on two behavioral indexes of possible causes of error. Another diagnostic aid is to ask the child to show the problem as a picture and then explain the picture (Driscoll, 1979). Diagnosticians who assess thinking with analogue tasks never directly measure such cognitive activity. What they evaluate is a set of overt responses by the student to a series of tasks presented. The inferences made on the basis of overt responding are only as valid as the tasks on which they are based.

Identifying specific reasons why children have difficulty solving verbal math problems also necessitates looking at the way in which children solve problems and listening to what they say. Charles (1983) suggests that a comprehensive evaluation of problem-solving skills is impossible without observing and questioning children as they complete story problems. West (1977) recommends addressing three questions during an evaluation of problem-solving skills. The first is whether the child comprehends the content of the problem. Only by questioning children on the conditions of the problem can the examiner determine whether or not they understand. If the student does not comprehend the problem, then techniques for improving comprehension may be used in a diagnostic teaching approach. For example, the examiner may have the child read the problem aloud several times, read the problem to answer specific questions, read the problem silently while listening to a taped version, draw a picture of the problem, or recite the problem in his or her own words. The second issue is whether the child is able to translate the problem into a computational format; that is, can he or she choose the appropriate operation and set up the problem correctly? The third question is whether the child can carry out the computation that is required. By systematically questioning and completing steps for the child in a simulated instructional situation, the examiner is able to determine where the student breaks down in the problem-solving process and how the breakdown point can be circumvented or remediated. West (1977) stresses that several samples of behavior are necessary to evaluate children's problem-solving skills accurately. Furthermore, the presentation and response formats should approximate those in the regular classroom with curriculum.

The manner in which a student learns mathematics varies from student to student. Nonetheless, certain factors must be considered in the remedial process and may be evaluated in an analogue teaching situation. For example, Kennedy and Michon (1973) emphasize that children will not display a complete understanding of mathematical concepts with only a few exposures to the task. Mere repetition alone, however, will likely not be of benefit to the student. Thus, to achieve the repeated exposures needed and at the same time avoid boredom and a low attention level, game-like activities are suggested as appropriate remedial techniques. Beattie and Algozzine (1982) described several such activities that are simple to implement in a diagnostic teaching situation. These activities, much as the use of concrete objects for teaching abstract concepts like place value, provide for the assessment of math skills without the potential confounder of low attention level or motivation.

Mediational Factors

It is impossible to know the type of thinking that occurs as children perform an academic task. As described above, children's overt task-related behavior can be observed or their errors can be analyzed. However, analogue assessment can also be used to evaluate what Quirk and Worzbut (1983) call "mediational factors." Using an analogue approach, the child is exposed to a problem or learning situation and asked to respond as naturally as possible. Once the analogue task has been developed and presented, there are three approaches for having children report their ongoing mediation. The thinking aloud approach requires children to report continuously what they are thinking while engaged in the academic activity. If children are capable of doing this, it will provide the most comprehensive sample of mediational factors. However, many children beyond the age of eight have learned to inhibit vocalizations during task performance, or many of their thoughts associated with task performance are so habitual and automatic that they go unreported. Random sampling of mediation during a simulated situation is easier for most children. This procedure involves stopping the task periodically and asking children to report what they are thinking. Although there are limitations to this procedure (e.g., interruptions may interfere with task performance and mediation; when to interrupt to obtain significant information is questionable), it is a more productive technique than the thinking aloud approach. The technique that appears to work best with children is a reconstruction procedure in which the analogue situation is videotaped and children are asked to review the tape after the assessment period and so reveal their thinking.

An assessment of the student's general personal adjustment and attitudes can also be made through the use of analogue techniques. For example, during an analogue teaching situation the examiner might observe that a child will give up, refuse to work, become tense, or work on one item for a long time when the tasks become more difficult. In analogue situations, questions such as the following can often be probed: What is the student's attitude toward the learning problem? Is the student's attitude one of interest or indifference? What is the student's overall motivation for learning? How does he or she approach new material and new learning situations?

PSYCHOMETRIC PROPERTIES OF
ANALOGUE MEASURES

Analogue measures must be reliable and valid if the results are to be accepted as evidence of student achievement and as a basis for making educational decisions. Thus, both reliability and validity issues need to be addressed by diagnosticians who consider using analogue assessment procedures. Tidwell (1980) has argued that analogue measures should not be required to have the *same* psychometric qualities as formal tests; however, they should be as psychometrically defensible as the situation permits. Thus, reliability and validity are related to the consistency and accuracy with which decisions are made about instructional programming on the basis of data derived from analogue measures.

Validity means that a given measurement procedure adequately samples the criterion behaviors of interest. One critical issue related to the validity of analogue measures is generalizability, that is, the exent to which behavior observed in analogue situations generalizes or predicts behavior in the natural classroom environment. It is generally agreed that the best way to learn how individuals behave in a given situation is to observe them in that situation and see directly how they respond. Howell *et al.* (1979) stated that "the more similar a test is to the function itself, the better is the degree of validity of measurements. Thus, we test a person's typewriting ability on a typewriter; how well a person swims by his swimming performance; and how well he handles social situations by observing him in [social situations]" (p. 80). The implication is that the greater the similarity between the simulated test situation (from which one is predicting a person's behavior) and the natural situation (to which one is predicting that person's behavior), the greater the accuracy of prediction. Thus, validity ultimately relates to how similar analogue situations are to real-life classroom situations. The issue of similarity between analogue behavior and real-life behavior is a complex one because the degree of similarity varies with a number of factors, including the extent to which the child is involved in the analogue and is able to accept the situation as a real learning situation. It is evident that the behaviors children exhibit in an analogue situation necessarily come from their existing repertoire of skills, and thus tell the examiner something valid about children's academic abilities. McReynolds and DeVoge (1977) provide evidence that children draw from the same repertoire of behaviors and skills in analogue situations that they use in real-life situations. Because content validity of analogue measures is so critical to the generalizability of assessment findings, analogue situations should be constructed only after observing or interviewing target children, consulting with teachers, and examining the curriculum and typical teaching-learning environment.

Analogue measures potentially provide more valid assessments of academic skills than do standardized tests because observations occur in simulated learning contexts. Furthermore, in analogue assessment, students respond to everyday classroom tasks rather than to contrived or artificial standardized test situations. For example, a standardized test of phonics skills may assess a student's letter-sound association knowledge, but not the application of this skill in actual reading. If the desired skill is to use letter-sound knowledge in reading, then the most direct way to obtain a valid measure of this skill is to put students in a real reading situation and observe the extent to which they demonstrate the skill. Because observations occur during a simulated reading lesson, children demonstrate their skills in a way that is not confounded by common sources of error in standardized testing, such as anxiety or the imposition of time constraints. Thus, diagnosticians can achieve validity in their analogue assessments by measuring relevant academic skills objectively in a natural context and using tasks that simulate the tasks children are required to perform in school.

Researchers have systematically compared data derived from analogue measures of academic skills with data obtained from other assessment methods in order to establish the concurrent validity of analogue procedures. For example, Eaton and Lovitt (1972) compared children's performance on standardized reading achievement tests, the Wide Range Achievement Test (WRAT) (Jastak & Jastak, 1978) and Metropolitan Achievement Test (Prescott, Balow, Hogan, & Farr, 1978), with performance on five-minute samples of reading behavior that were scored for correct words, errors, and reading rate. They found that analogue measures provided more valuable and accurate information regarding placement, evaluation, and remediation than did standardized measures. For example, in one instance, WRAT scores at the start and end of a school year erroneously reflected eight years of progress in reading, and in a second case, pre- and postyear WRAT scores showed no improvement for a student who had actually progressed from a primer to a 2.2 level in the reading series that was used in his class. In another study, Lovitt and Fantasia (1980) found that data derived from an analogue assessment of reading skills correlated approximately .50 with the number of book levels passed throughout the school year by children from eight to twelve years old. For this analogue assessment procedure, children read passages at three grade levels from curricular reading series and answered questions about each passage. In addition to demonstrating the validity of this assessment procedure, Lovitt and Fantasia also reported high interrater agreement for accuracy and reading rate (81.7% to 92.3%).

Marston, Mirkin, and Deno (1984) contrasted a screening and referral procedure that used measurement of student performance on curriculum-based tasks in reading, spelling, and written expression with a traditional teacher-referral procedure. For the reading task, students read words selected randomly from the grade-appropriate Harris-Jacobson (1972) word list. Words from the Harris-Jacobson list were also used for the dictation format spelling task. Measurement of written expression consisted of providing a story starter and having students write a story composition. Students referred on the basis of this curriculum-based assessment were compared with students referred by their teachers for learning disability services on standardized measures of aptitude, achievement and social-emotional behaviors. The comparison revealed several findings that lend support for the validity and reliability of analogue, curriculum-based assessment. First, both groups were similar in aptitude and achievement measures, thus attesting to the accuracy of curriculum-based measurements in identifying appropriate referrals. Second, the gender distribution was more balanced among the curriculum-based measurement referrals than the teacher referrals. Third, the data suggested that with females, classroom behavior influenced teacher referral decisions more than curriculum-based referral decisions; teacher-referred girls were rated as having more behavior problems. This particular finding suggests that referrals for academic problems from teachers may be subject to the influence of inappropriate classroom behaviors. Finally, a greater percentage of the referrals made from curriculum-based assessments met the district criteria for learning disability (80% of the referrals) than those from teacher referrals (36%), thus suggesting that the former procedure may create more consistency in evaluations of learning disabilities. Marston *et al.* summarize their findings by stating that "curriculum-based measurement compares favorably with teacher referral. It results in referring approximately the same number of students and appears to negate the influence of biasing factors (e.g., sex, social behavior). . . . [The] measurement of student performance on curriculum tasks is a feasible and efficacious approach to assessment . . ." (p. 116). Concurrent validity of similar measurement procedures has also been established for the number of words read correctly in one minute from a basal reader (Deno, Mirkin, & Chiang, 1982), the number of words spelled correctly from dictated word lists (Deno, Mirkin, Lowry, & Kuehnle, 1980), and the number of words written in a story composition (Deno, Marston, & Mirkin, 1982).

The importance of validating analogue behavior against the criterion behavior in the natural environment depends on the goals of the assessment. If the examiner views the analogue as a probe of the child's academic skills and is not interested in making inferences about the classroom setting, validation is not as crucial. However, a frequent application of analogue assessment is the trial implementation and evaluation of interventions for academic skills. The validity of tentative conclusions and remedial suggestions based on diagnotistic teaching can be established only after the program of remediation has been tried and evaluated in the actual classroom. Thus, demonstrating that instructional programming can be accomplished as effectively on the basis of curriculum-based assessment as with standardized achievement tests provides evidence of the validity of analogue assessment. In addition, documenting a functional relationship between interventions that are derived from analogue assessment and improved classroom performance lends further support to the validity of analogue measures. In general, there are few studies that have evaluated intervention strategies based on the results of analogue assessment. Nonetheless, research does suggest that children assessed on various analogue measures change or improve in the classroom as a function of the remedial recommendations that result from the assessment (Lovitt & Fantasia, 1980; Lovitt & Hansen, 1976).

One final validity issue and potential impediment to the instructional utility of analogue assessment is the lack of normative data. For analogue assessment to be optimally useful in instructional planning, there must be norms with which the learning behaviors and academic skills of a child can be compared. The feasibility of implementing a systemwide, normative, curriculum-based approach for determining the eligibility for learning disability services has been evaluated in both public schools (Tindal, Wesson, Germann, Deno, & Mirkin, 1982) and private preschool classes (Magliocca, Rinaldi, Crew, & Kunzelmann, 1977). In general, these researchers conclude that such measurement represents a viable alternative to traditional assessment procedures, provides more instructionally relevant information, fosters improved communication between teachers and parents, and is nondiscriminatory.

An equally important issue related to analogue assessment is reliability. A measure is reliable if it yields approximately the same results consistently over time. In order to establish the consistency of analogue measurement, judgments about a child's academic skills should be based on multiple observations; that is, tasks related to a particular skill should be repeated several times (Cunningham, 1982). Reliability is a relative strength of analogue measures in comparison with standardized tests because examiners make repeated observations as students perform on several samples of academic material. In traditional test formats, examiners present a range of items within one testing period. Analogue measures may yield more reliable data than traditional tests because they provide a larger, more representative sample of behavior on relevant learning material. Zigmond, Vallecorsa, and Silverman (1983) recommend a strategy for verifying a student's errors that increases the reliability of assessment findings. They suggest that when a student exhibits an error on a standardized test, the examiner should administer a probe to verify the error type and to determine the consistency and frequency of the error on material that simulates classroom learning.

NEEDED RESEARCH AND RESEARCH STRATEGIES

Several studies have evaluated the degree of generalization between analogue situations and naturalistic settings, and most have obtained moderate correlations. Nonetheless, additional research evaluating the utility of analogue measures for assessing academic skills is needed. Future research efforts should be directed toward a comparative evaluation of the amount of information gained per unit of professional time, client time, financial expenditure, and applicability of assessment findings for instructional planning and evaluation of student progress.

Lovitt (1975a) outlined seven general areas in which research relevant to analogue assessment is needed. The first is defining behaviors or subskills that comprise academic subject areas. For example, although researchers have identified some isolated skills that constitute reading (phonemic segmentation and synthesis, letter knowledge, etc.), descriptions of behaviors that are necessary for competent reading are generally vague. Recent research on academic skills (Resnick & Ford, 1981) has also demonstrated that children approach academic tasks in different ways. Information on the behaviors and strategies children use in performing academic tasks can be helpful in constructing analogue measures and planning remediation (Carpenter, Moser, & Romberg, 1982).

A second research area relates to the sequencing of behaviors in an academic domain. Research should be conducted to determine whether there are optimal sequences for the development of academic skills. Bergan and his associates (Bergan, 1980) have validated learning sequences in areas such as reading and math. Their steps for developing empirically validated learning hierarchies include: (1) conducting a review of the literature to generate hypotheses about the hierarchical ordering of basic academic skills, (2) developing a set of analogue items reflecting hypothesized hierarchical sequences in the basic skill areas, (3) validating hypothesized hierarchical structures to establish the construct validity for the sequence, (4) determining the reliability of responses to the academic learning tasks, and (5) determining the concurrent validity of performance on academic learning tasks with respect to overall academic achievement.

The third research area Lovitt identifies relates to the most effective techniques for remediating academic skills. For example, if the ability to produce sounds for consonant blends is necessary for reading, then research should examine the effectiveness of various techniques on the acquisition of that behavior. If diagnosticians have information regarding techniques that enhance the development of particular skills, then procedures can be systematically tried and evaluated in analogue settings. Another area of needed research is in the determination of performance mastery. When conducting evaluations of learning behavior in analogue situations, examiners should be concerned not only with effecting behavioral change, but also with determining whether the change was "real," or reflected mastery performance. Two additional areas are retention and generalization research. A survey of several curriculum studies (McClurg, 1973) showed that few included a follow-up to determine the extent to which academic skills are retained. Research that determines how children should be taught to retain and generalize skills can lead to the utilization of appropriate techniques in analogue situations. The last and perhaps most critical area is what Lovitt calls "logistics research," which involves examining the extent to which data derived from structured simulated settings are valid for the natural learning environment.

Deno, Mirkin, and Chiang (1982) outline a research strategy for identifying analogue measures that provide assessment data that are both reliable and valid. This strategy was employed in several studies designed to develop and evaluate measures of academic and social skills, including spelling (Deno, Mirkin, Lowry, & Kuehnle, 1980), written expression (Deno, Marston, & Mirkin, 1982), reading (Deno, Mirkin, & Chiang, 1982), and social adjustment (Deno, Mirkin, Robinson, & Evans, 1980). The first step they recommend is to conduct a review of literature to identify behaviors and skills that represent achievement in a skill area. Second, measurement procedures for observing and recording those behaviors should be developed. Finally, data derived from these measurement procedures should be correlated with scores obtained on standardized measures that are technically adequate and exhibit acceptable psychometric qualities.

GUIDELINES FOR CONDUCTING
ANALOGUE ASSESSMENT

General guidelines for the development and utilization of analogue measures have been outlined by several researchers. Smith (1969) offered the following criteria for selecting analogue activities for the observation of children's learning and academic skills: (1) Each activity should reflect what is part of the ongoing academic program or curriculum to which the child is exposed. (2) Academic tasks should be interesting so that attitudinal or motivational problems do not mask the child's "true" ability. (3) Activities should be selected to measure specific academic skills directly. (4) Each diagnostic activity should be selected for objectivity, and during the administration attempts should be made to control possible sources of bias. Bleismer (1972) underscored the importance of evaluating academic skills in the context of a normal learning situation. He advocated greater use of evaluation techniques such as analogue measures. For example, it might be possible for a child to read a list of words on a norm-referenced test without being able to pronounce any of them in the context of passage reading. A more valid procedure for evaluating this child's reading is to observe what he or she does upon encountering unknown words in the context of reading material. Thus, the content of analogue assessment should correspond closely to the curricular program used in the student's regular classroom. Duffey and Fedner (1978) stress that when evaluating children's academic skills on curriculum-based materials and procedures, examiners should test only those skills that appear to be deficient; in addition, they should evaluate the maximum-knowledge skills and then move to easier material in the curriculum.

When short instructional interventions or modified assessment procedures are planned (such as changes in teaching methods and materials, modifications in response format or time limits, or the addition of reinforcement techniques), the behaviors targeted for measurement should be sensitive to these modifications.

Furthermore, diagnosticians should strive to maximize the representativeness of analogue situations while simultaneously striving to maximize control over the situation to insure some standardization and relevance of the assessment task.

A number of basic measurement principles can be applied to the construction and use of analogue measures that result in procedures of higher technical quality and greater utility for educational decisions. Bennett (1982) offers these suggestions for increasing the technical adequacy of analogue measures: (1) Specify the purpose of assessment. (2) Construct procedures or select learning tasks that are relevant to the specified purpose. (3) Specify dimensions on which performance will be judged. (4) Determine criteria for evaluating performance. (5) Obtain as large a sample of learning behavior as possible. Diagnosticians should recognize that a variety of reasons may exist for a child's correct or incorrect analogue task performance. It is important for an examiner to try to determine the reasons for correct and incorrect performance and to simulate the conditions under which the child performs best.

In sum, the following guidelines should be used by practitioners in developing analogue measures of academic skills. First, identify the precise behavior that should be evaluated (e.g., naming letters, writing numerals). Second, determine the mastery performance level against which the child's actual performance level will be compared. Third, arrange a simulated situation within which the identified behavior can occur and be observed (e.g., arrange a miniteaching session, develop skill probes). If diagnostic teaching or modified assessment is planned, collect baseline data, such as standardized test scores. Furthermore, throughout the assessment, observe and record the child's performance and study the error patterns. On the basis of observed behaviors and patterns of responding, select a type of teaching technique to administer during a simulated teaching session. The technique should be both natural (typical of what could happen in a regular classroom) and simple (available and easy to administer). The next section exemplifies the implementation of these guidelines.

CASE STUDY

The following case example of the evaluation of a third-grade girl's reading skills incorporates the five phases of an analogue assessment process as described by McFall (1977). The first phase is a situational analysis phase. The aim of this phase is to identify learning situations that characteristically pose problems for the target child. Suggestions of problem situations may be drawn from several sources, including interviews with classroom teachers and the child, observation of classroom learning situations, or prior assessment information. The second phase, item development, is devoted to the development of a pool of items for use in assessing the problem academic skill area. In the response enumeration phase, a sample of responses to the learning situations using curriculum-related material is obtained.

The next phase is the response evaluation phase, during which the accuracy of the responses obtained in the preceding phase is evaluated. In addition, errors are analyzed for characteristic patterns. The final phase, validation, is to determine whether the performance in the analogue situation is related to learning behavior in the actual classroom.

Karen is midway through the third grade and is currently placed in the second level of the basal reading series used in her school. She was given the Metropolitan Achievement Test at the end of the second grade and scored at the ninth percentile (1.1 grade equivalent) in reading. Her teacher reports that Karen is motivated and creative; she reads slowly and makes numerous errors in oral reading that impede comprehension. The purpose of this evaluation is to determine the factors interfering with Karen's reading ability and to recommend strategies for remediation.

The evaluation began with classroom observation during reading, an examination of the reading curriculum used in her class, and an interview with Karen's teacher to determine the nature of the reading instruction that Karen typically receives. This preliminary situational analysis phase revealed that word recognition is taught utilizing primarily a whole-word approach. A total of thirty new words taken from the stories for each week are presented on Monday, and children are instructed to practice with one other child, reading each word correctly two times. The word presentation and practice occur on Monday, stories are read aloud by children on Tuesday through Thursday, and short-answer quizzes testing factual comprehension of the stories are given on Friday. Performance on the weekly tests are recorded on a chart in front of the classroom. Karen's average performance on weekly quizzes is 60% in accuracy, compared with the class average of 85%.

Several analogue procedures were employed with Karen during four, forty-five-minute individual evaluation sessions. During the item development phase, the examiner selected short passages from the first- through third-grade level basal readers. In addition, ten words were chosen from each passage to teach as new sight words. Finally, the examiner developed a short quiz for each passage modeled after the weekly factual comprehension tests given by the classroom teacher. Thus, the analogue stimuli and tasks clearly paralleled those in the natural learning environment.

During the first session of the response enumeration phase, Karen read aloud one passage at each grade level while the examiner observed Karen's reading behavior and skills. Subsequent to this session, the response evaluation phase occurred, during which the examiner analyzed and characterized Karen's errors in oral reading and on comprehension measures. This first session yielded three diagnostic conclusions: (1) Karen's independent reading level is approximately midfirst grade, which is one year below the difficulty level of the material she is expected to read in class. (2) Over two-thirds of her oral reading errors are substitutions of visually similar words (e.g., substituting house for horse). (3) Karen's errors on comprehension measures accurately reflect her word recognition errors;

that is, although Karen misreads words in context, she is able to understand and retain what she misreads. On the basis of these preliminary conclusions, the diagnostician raised the hypothesis that weak visual discrimination skills are interfering with Karen's oral reading ability, which subsequently impedes accurate comprehension.

Sessions two and three were devoted to trial remediation of word recognition ability. First, baseline data were recorded for accuracy of reading words in isolation and in the context of passages and for comprehension following teaching and testing procedures that simulated those in the regular classrooms. Next, an equivalent number of words selected from passages of equal difficulty as baseline passages were taught with two additional remedial steps: (1) Karen wrote each word on an index card following its presentation by the examiner and used the cards to practice toward mastery (two correct pronunciations). (2) She received a brief discrimination practice in which she discriminated each new sight word from three visually similar miscue words that necessitated, in a gradual fashion, more precise visual discrimination (specifically of medial letters, which where most often confused in oral reading). Examples of miscues for the word *head* include *him, hush,* and *heed.* The purpose of these additional steps was to circumvent Karen's weak visual discrimination skills by drawing her attention to each letter in the words and providing direct discrimination practice. Whereas word reading accuracy was similar to that in the baseline condition, oral reading accuracy and comprehension improved significantly, and the proportion of substitution errors fell to 25%. Finally, session four was devoted to retention testing of the words taught during previous sessions. Retention of words taught with the additional remedial procedures increased from 60% (baseline) to 90%.

On the basis of these procedures and the resulting performance, several recommendations were offered to Karen's teacher. During the validation phase, these recommendations were implemented in the regular classroom, and Karen's oral reading and comprehension accuracy were closey monitored. First, because Karen was reading at a first-grade level, the diagnostician recommended that she be placed in the first level of the reading curriculum used in her class. Second, ten words (rather than thirty) should be presented to Karen at one time. Karen should be instructed to write each word on an index card after the teacher presents it; these cards can be stored in a card file and used for cumulative practice and review of the week's thirty new sight words. Words should continue to be practiced, the criterion being two correct pronunciations. In addition to this mastery practice, the teacher should provide brief discrimination practice after all the words have been presented. For this practice, Karen should discriminate each new sight word from visually similar miscues. Finally, Karen needed to practice reading the new words in the context of stories to enhance discrimination and retention of words in fluent reading. After four weeks of implementing these recommendations, the teacher reported that Karen's oral reading in class had improved markedly and that her accuracy on weekly comprehension quizzes was consistently around 80%.

CONCLUSIONS

Traditional, standardized assessment measures are typically used, and are often necessary, for evaluating children's academic skills. However, formal assessment should be considered only part of a total evaluation of academic skills. A comprehensive evaluation should also include analogue procedures that further probe the results of formal assessment. Observations of academic skills and learning behaviors in analogue situations should not be viewed as better than traditional, test-based methods of academic skill assessment. Rather, they should be viewed as complementary, providing diagnostic as opposed to normative information. Whereas standardized testing is a crucial first step in evaluating academic skills to determine the overall level of functioning in relation to a normative group, the use of analogue procedures enables the examiner to address more specific diagnostic questions. Behavioral observations in simulated situations are useful for instructional programming because a direct sample of learning behavior is obtained. Thus, analogue assessment of academic skills may be conceptualized as broadening the range of existing measures for gathering data relevant to instructional planning. Data derived from analogue assessment methods should not be considered in isolation, but rather interpreted in light of all currently available data.

In an analogue assessment approach, evaluation of academic skills typically begins with norm-referenced or criterion-referenced tests. The assessment then moves to probes or learning tasks developed by the examiner that tap skills and learning behaviors more directly. The goal of analogue assessment is to detect areas of learner strength and weakness in simulated learning situations and to deduce a child's instructional needs. Analogue measures attempt to verify, probe, or discard initial conclusions based on more formal, standardized measures.

Elliott and Piersal (1982) describe an assessment paradigm that attempts to link assessment to intervention by integrating standardized testing with analogue measures. Their model incorporates many components of analogue measurement in terms of both the content and process of evaluation. The content of assessment, according to their model, goes beyond standardized testing to include observation, informal academic skill measures, and curriculum-based tests or probes. The process of assessment is described as being an experimental one. In effect, the examiner functions as a researcher who collects information concerning a student's learning, generates hypotheses about the nature of the learning problem, and, finally, tests these hypotheses. Thus, evaluation and diagnosis are a continuous process of hypothesis raising and hypothesis testing activities, utilizing both standardized testing and analogue measures.

Smith (1980) also advocates a combination of standardized tests and analogue measures. In her model, standardized tests provide a global estimate of a child's level of skill functioning and sample a broad range of skills on particular academic tasks. As such, they offer suggestions for further assessment. Criterion-referenced measures may yield more specific information about discrete capabilities, but, unlike analogue measures, they do not provide information about how to teach. Competencies and deficits are analyzed to formulate hypotheses regarding the way in which task components interact with learner characteristics. The end of this assessment process involves testing hypotheses through diagnostic teaching, setting or task modifications, or curriculum-based assessment. Smith described an evaluation format used at the Syracuse University Psychoeducational Teaching Laboratory that incorporates this assessment sequence combining standardized test procedures with analogue measures. The evaluation procedure she describes is based on a systems approach developed by Eaves and McLaughlin (1977). According to Eaves and McLaughlin, analogue assessment is characterized by (1) the use of direct behavioral data, (2) the narrowing of possible areas and strategies for intervention, and (3) the use of simulated and optimal learning environments as the primary setting for data collection. In Smith's model, assessment begins with the most global methods of standardized testing and structured interviews in order to narrow the choice of subsequent measurement techniques and content areas.

According to Guerin and Maier (1983), diagnosticians should move from defining "exceptional children" to defining "exceptional situations within the school." Their suggestion takes into account that the learning environment is a critical consideration in evaluating learning and academic skills. This view implies that examiners should go beyond collecting traditional, test-based assessment data by focusing on variables in the learning environment, such as materials, settings, and teaching styles. One way to conduct this type of assessment is through the use of analogue measures that simulate or create as many of these variables as possible. Given the limited utility of traditional assessment for academic skill diagnosis and remedial planning, the analogue approaches addressed in this chapter clearly merit consideration and implementation in schools.

Notes

The author wishes to express her appreciation to Trevor Cory Brown for his cooperation in the preparation of an earlier draft of this manuscript and to Karen Kraemer for the typing of this chapter.

References

Alessi, G. J., & Kaye, K. H. (1983). *Behavior assessment for school psychologists.* Kent, Ohio: National Association of School Psychologists.

Algozzine, B., Siders, J., & Beattie, J. (1982). Using assessment information to plan reading instructional programs: Error analysis and word-attack skills. *Reading Improvement, 19,* 156–163.

Ancevich, S. S., & Payne, R. W. (1961). The investigation and treatment of a reading disability in a child of normal intelligence. *Journal of Clinical Psychology, 11,* 416–420.

Barsch, R. H. (1965). *A movigenic curriculum* (Bulletin No. 25). Madison, Wisc.: Department of Public Instruction, Bureau for the Handicapped.

Beattie, J., & Algozzine, B. (1982). Testing for teaching. *Arithmetic Teacher, 30,* 47–51.

Bennett, R. E. (1982). Cautions for the use of informal measures in the educational assessment of exceptional children. *Journal of Learning Disabilities, 15,* 337–339.

Bergan, J. R. (1980). The structural analysis of behavior: An alternative to the learning hierarchy model. *Review of Educational Research, 50,* 225–246.

Bergan, J. R. (1981). Path-referenced assessment in school psychology. In T. R. Kratochwill (Ed.), *Advances in school psychology* (Vol. I, pp. 255–280). Hillsdale, N.J.: Lawrence Erlbaum Associates.

Berman, B., & Friederwitzer, F. J. (1981). A diagnostic prescriptive approach to remediation of regrouping errors. *Elementary School Journal, 82,* 109–115.

Bersoff, D. N. (1973). Silk purses into sow's ears, the decline of psychological testing and a suggestion for its redemption. *American Psychologist, 28,* 892–898.

Bijou, S. W. (1970). What psychology has to offer education—now. *Journal of Applied Behavior Analysis, 3,* 65–71.

Bleismer, E. (1972). Informal teacher testing in reading. *Reading Teacher, 28,* 268–272.

Bogdan, R., & Taylor, S J. (1975). *Introduction to quantitative research methods.* New York: John Wiley & Sons.

Bracht, G. H. (1970). Exprimental factors related to aptitude-treatment interactions. *Review of Educational Research, 40,* 627–645.

Bright, G. W. (1984). computer diagnosis of errors. *School Science and Mathematics, 84,* 208–219.

Bryant, N. D. (1966). Clinical inadequacies with learning disorders—the missing clinical educator. In J. Hellmuth (Ed.), *Learning disorders* (Vol. 2, pp. 28–46). Seattle, Wash.: Special Child Publications.

Bryant, N. D., Drabin, I., & Gettinger, M. (1981). Effects of varying unit size on spelling achievement in learning disabled children. *Journal of Learning Disabilities, 13,* 83–86.

Burmeister, L. E. (1978). *Reading strategies for middle and secondary school teachers* (2d ed.). Reading, Mass.: Addison-Wesley.

Carpenter, T. P., Moser, J. M., & Rombert, T. A. (1982). *Addition and subtraction: A cognitive perspective.* Hillsdale, J.J.: Lawrence Erlbaum Associates.

Charles, R. I. (1983). Evaluation and problem solving. *Arithmetic Teacher, 54,* 6–7.

Cramer, R. L. (1983). Informal approaches to evaluating children's writing. In J. J. Pikulski & T. Shanahan (Eds.), *Approaches to the informal evaluation of reading* (pp. 80–94). Newark, Del.: International Reading Association.

Cunningham, P. (1982). Diagnosis by observation. In J. J. Pikulski & T. Shanahan (Eds.), *Approaches to the informal evaluation of reading* (pp. 12–22). Newark, Del.: International Reading Association.

Dale, E., & Chall, J. S. (1948). A formula for predicting readability. *Educational Research Bulletin, 27,* 11–54.

Deno, S. L. (1985). Curriculum-based measurement: The emerging alternative. *Exceptional Children, 52,* 219–232.

Deno, S. L., Marston, D., & Mirkin, P. (1982). Valid measurement procedures for continuous evaluation of written expression. *Exceptional Children, 48,* 368–371.

Deno, S. L., & Mirkin, P. K. (1977). *Data based program modification: A manual.* Reston, Va.: Council for Exceptional Children.

Deno. S. L., Mirkin, P. K., & Chiang, B. (1982). Identifying valid measures of reading. *Exceptional Children, 49,* 36–45.

Deno. S. L., Mirkin, P. K., Lowry, L., & Kuehnle, K. (1980). *Relationships among simple measures of spelling and performance on standardized achievement tests* (Research Report No. 21). Minneapolis, Minn.: University of Minnesota, Institute for Research on Learning Disabilities.

Deno, S. L., Mirkin, P. K., Robinson, S., & Evans, P. (1980). *Relationships among classroom observations of social adjustment and sociometric rating scales* (Research Report No. 24). Minneapolis, Minn.: University of Minnesota, Institute for Research on Learning Disabilities.

Dickinson, D. J. (1980). The direct assessment: An alternative to psychometric testing. *Journal of Learning Disabilities, 13,* 472–476.

Dixon, C. N. (1977). Language experience stories as a diagnostic tool. *Language Arts, 54,* 501–505.

Driscoll, M. J. (1979). Diagnosis: Taking the mathematical pulse. *Focus on Learning Problems in Mathematics, 1,* 31–33.

Duffey, J. B., & Fedner, M. L. (1978). Educational diagnosis with instructional use. *Exceptional Children, 45,* 246–251.

Dunn, L., & Markwardt, F. (1970). *Peabody Individual Achievement Test.* Circle Pines, Minn.: American Guidance Service.

Eaton, M., & Lovitt, T. (1972). Achievement tests vs. direct and daily measurement. In G. Semb (Ed.), *Behavior analysis and education* (pp. 78–86). Lawrence, Kans.: University of Kansas.

Eaves, R. C., & McLaughlin, P. (1977). A systems approach for the assessment of the child and his environment: Getting back to basics. *Journal of Special Education, 11,* 99–111.

Elliott, S. N., & Piersel, W. C. (1982). Direct assessment of reading skills: An approach which links assessment to intervention. *School Psychology Review, 11,* 267–280.

Engelhardt, J. M. (1982). Using computational errors in diagnostic teaching. *Arithmetic Teacher, 29,* 16–19.

Engelmann, S., Granzin, A., & Severson, H. (1979). Diagnosing instruction. *Journal of Special Education, 13,* 355–364.

Estes, T. H., & Vaughan, J. L. (1978). *Reading and learning in the content classroom: Diagnostic and instructional strategies.* Boston: Allyn & Bacon.

Ewing, N., & Brecht, R. (1977). Diagnostic/prescriptive instruction: A reconsideration of some issues. *Journal of Special Education, 11,* 323–327.

Feuerstein, R. (1979). *The dynamic assessment of retarded performers: The learning potential assessment device, theory, instruments and techniques.* Baltimore, Md.: University Park Press.

Foster, K., & Torgesen, J. (1983). The effects of direct instruction on the spelling performance of two subgroups of learning disabled students. *Learning Disability Quarterly, 6,* 252–257.

Fowler, M. A. (1980). Diagnostic teaching for elementary school mathematics. *Arithmetic Teacher, 27,* 34–37.

Fry, E. A. (1968). A readability formula that saves time. *Journal of Reading, 11,* 513–516.

Fuchs, L. S., Deno, S. L., & Marston, D. (1983). Improving the reliability of curriculum-based measures of academic skills for psychoeducational decision making. *Diagnostique, 8,* 135–149.

Germann, G., & Tindal, G. (1985). An application of curriculum-based assessment: The use of direct and repeated measurement. *Exceptional Children, 52,* 244–265.

Gettinger, M. (1985). Effects of teacher-directed versus student-directed instruction and cues versus no cues for improving spelling performance. *Journal of Applied Behavior Analysis, 18,* 167–171.

Gettinger, M., Bryant, D., & Fayne, H. (1982). Designing spelling instruction for learning-disabled children: An emphasis on unit size, distributed practice, and training for transfer. *Journal of Special Education, 16,* 439–448.

Gickling, E. E. (1981). Curriculum-based assessment. In J. A. Tucker (Ed.), *Non-test-based assessment: A training module* (pp. 3–8). Minneapolis, Minn.: National School Psychology Inservice Training Network, University of Minnesota.

Gickling, E. E., & Thompson, V. P. (1985). A personal view of curriculum-based assessment. *Exceptional Children, 52,* 205–218.

Goh, D. S., Teslow, C. J., & Fuller, G. B. (1981). The practices of psychological assessment among school psychologists. *Professional Psychology, 12,* 699–706.

Graham, S. (1983). Effective spelling instruction. *Elementary School Journal, 83,* 560–568.

Graham, S., & Freeman, S. (1985). Strategy training and teacher- vs. student-controlled study conditions: Effects on LD students' spelling performance. *Learning Disability Quarterly, 8,* 267–274.

Guba, E. G. (1978). *Toward a methodology of naturalistic inquiry in educational evaluation* (CSE Monograph Series in Evaluation, No. 8). Los Angeles: UCLA Graduate School of Education, Center for the Study of Education.

Guerin, G. R., & Maier, A. S. (1983). *Informal assessment in education.* Palo Alto, Calif.: Mayfield.

Hammill, D. D. (1971). Evaluating children for instructional purposes. *Academic Therapy, 6,* 119–131.

Hammill, D. D., & Larsen, S. C. (1978). *The test of written language.* Austin, Tex.: Pro-Ed.

Hansell, T. S. (1981). Four methods of diagnosis for content area reading. *Journal of Reading, 24,* 696–700.

Hargrove, L. J., & Poteet, J. A. (1984). *Assessment in special education: The education evaluation.* Englewood Cliffs, N.J.: Prentice-Hall.

Harris, A. J., & Jacobson, M. D. (1972). *Basic elementary reading vocabularies.* New York: Macmillan.

Hartmann, D. P., & Wood, D. D. (1982). Observational methods. In A. S. Bellack, M. Hersen, & A. E. Kazdin (Eds.), *International handbook of behavior modification and therapy* (pp. 109–138). New York: Plenum Press.

Hasselbring, T. S., & Crossland, C. L. (1981). Using microcomputers for diagnosing spelling problems in learning-handicapped children. *Educational Technology, 21*(4), 37–39.

Hasselbring, T. S., & Gray, J. T. (1985). Using the microcomputer for assisting in teacher decision-making. *Peabody Journal of Education, 62,* 87–102.

Haynes, S. N. (1978). *Principles of behavioral assessment.* New York: Gardner Press.

Howell, K. W., Kaplan, J. S., & O'Connell, C. Y. (1979). *Evaluating exceptional children: A task analysis approach.* Columbus, Ohio: Charles E. Merrill.

Hunter, M. (1979). Diagnostic teaching. *Elementary School Journal, 80,* 41–46.

Hutson, B. A., & Niles, J. A. (1974). Trial teaching: The missing link. *Psychology in the Schools, 11,* 188–191.

Jastak, J., & Jastak, S. (1978). *Wide Range Achievement Test.* Wilmington, Del.: Jastak Associates.

Jenkins, J. R., & Pany, D. (1978). Standardized achievement tests: How useful for special education? *Exceptional Children, 7,* 448–453.

Karlsen, B., Madden, R., & Gardner, E. (1977). *Stanford Diagnostic Reading Test.* New York: Harcourt Brace Jovanovich.

Kennedy, L. M., & Michon, R. L. (1973). *Games for individualizing mathematics learning.* Columbus, Ohio: Charles E. Merrill.

Keogh, B. K. (1973). Early detection of learning problems—questions, cautions, guidelines. *Academic Therapy, 9,* 187–191.

Kottmeyer, W. (1970). *Teacher's guide for remedial reading.* New York: McGraw-Hill.

Kratochwill, T. R. (1982). Advances in behavioral assessment. In C. R. Reynolds & T. B. Gutkin (Eds.), *The handbook of school psychology* (pp. 314–350). New York: John Wiley & Sons.

Lee, L. L., & Canter, S. M. (1971). Developmental sentence scoring. *Journal of Speech and Hearing Disorders, 36,* 335–340.

Leinhardt, G., & Seewald, A. (1981). Overlap: What's tested, what's taught. *Journal of Educational Measurement, 18,* 85–96.

Lovitt, T. C. (1967). Assessment of children with learning disabilities. *Exceptional Children, 34,* 233–239.

Lovitt, T. C. (1975a). Applied behavior analysis and learning disabilities. Part I: Characteristics of ABA, general recommendations, and methodological limitations. *Journal of Learning Disabilities, 8,* 432–443.

Lovitt, T. C. (1975b). Applied behavior analysis and learning disabilities. Part II: Specific research recommendations and suggestions for practitioners. *Journal of Learning Disabilities, 8,* 504–518.

Lovitt, T. C., & Fantasia, K. (1980). Two approaches to reading program evaluation: A standardized test and direct assessment. *Learning Disability Quarterly, 3,* 77–87.

Lovitt, T. C., & Hansen, C. (1976). The use of contingent skipping and drilling to improve oral reading and comprehension. *Journal of Learning Disabilities, 9,* 481–487.

Madden, R., Gardner, E. F., Rudman, H. C., Karlsen, B., & Merwin, J. C. (1973). *Stanford Achievement Test.* New York: Harcourt Brace Jovanovich.

Magliocca, L. A., Rinaldi, R. T., Crew, J., & Kunzelmann, H. P. (1977). Early identification of handicapped children through a frequency sampling technique. *Exceptional Children, 44,* 414–420.

Marston, D., Mirkin, P., & Deno, S. (1984). Curriculum-based measurement: An alternative to traditional screening, referral, and identification. *Journal of Special Education, 18,* 109–117.

Mash, E., & Terdal, L. (1982). *Behavioral assessment of childhood disorders.* New York: Guilford Press.

McClurg, J. F. (1973). To teach loving. *Educational Leadership, 31,* 14–17.

McFall, R. M. (1977). Analogue methods in behavioral assessment: Issues and prospects. In J. D. Cone and R. P. Hawkins (Eds.), *Behavioral assessment: New directions* (pp. 152–177). New York: Brunner/Mazel.

McGlaughlin, G. H. (1969). SMOG grading—a new readability formula. *Journal of Reading, 12,* 639–646.

McReynolds, P., & DeVoge, S. (1977). Use of improvisational techniques in assessment. In P. McReynolds (Ed.), *Advances in psychological assessment* (Vol. 4, pp. 246–294). San Francisco: Jossey-Bass.

Moore, D. W. (1983). A case for naturalistic assessment of reading comprehension. *Language Arts, 60,* 957–969.

Myers, P., & Hammill, D. (1969). *Methods for learning disorders.* New York: John Wiley & Sons.

Nay, W. R. (1977). Analogue measures. In A. R. Ciminero, K. S. Calhoun, & H. E. Adams (Eds.), *Handbook of behavioral assessment* (pp. 233–277). New York: John Wiley & Sons.

Nurss, J., & McGauvran, M. (1976). *Metropolitan Readiness Test.* New York: Harcourt Brace Jovanovich.

Ollendick, T. H., & Hersen, M. (1984). *Child behavioral assessment: Principles and procedures.* Elmsford, N.Y.: Pergamon Press.

Ozer, M. N., & Dworkin, S. (1974). Assessment of children with learning problems: An in-service teacher training program. *Journal of Learning Disabilities, 7,* 539–544.

Ozer, M. N., & Richardson, H. B. (1972). Diagnostic evaluation of children with learning problems: A communication process. *Childhood Education, 48,* 244–247.

Ozer, M. N., & Richardson, H. B. (1974). Diagnostic evaluation of children with learning problems: A process approach. *Journal of Learning Disabilities, 7,* 88–92.

Peterson, J., Heistad, D., Peterson, D., & Reynolds, M. (1985). Montevideo Individualized Prescriptive Instructional Management System. *Exceptional Children, 52,* 239–243.

Pikulski, J. J. (1974). Critical review: Informal reading inventories. *Reading Teacher, 28,* 141–151.

Poplin, M., & Gray, R. (1982). A conceptual framework for assessment of curriculum and student progress. In J. J. Neisworth (Ed.), *Assessment in special education* (pp. 53–64). Rockville, Md.: Aspen.

Prescott, G., Balow, I., Hogan, T., & Farr, R. (1978). *Metropolitan Achievement Tests.* New York: Psychological Corporation.

Quirk, J. P., & Worzbut, J. C. (1983). *The assessment of behavior problem children: A systematic behavioral approach.* Springfield Ill.: Charles Thomas.

Resnick, L. D., & Ford, W. W. (1981). *The psychology of mathematics for instruction.* Hillsdale, N.J.: Lawrence Erlbaum Associates.

Resnick. L. D., Wang, M. C., & Kaplan, J. (1973). Task analysis in curriculum. *Journal of Applied Behavior Analysis, 6,* 679–710.

Rosenshine, R. V. (1981). Academic engaged time, content covered, and direct instruction. *Journal of Education, 3,* 38–66.

Rude, R. T., & Oehlkers, W. J. (1984). *Helping students with reading problems.* Englewood Cliffs, N.J.: Prentice-Hall.

Salend, S. J., & Salend, S. M. (1985). Implications of using microcomputers in classroom testing. *Journal of Learning Disabilities, 18,* 51–53.

Salvia, J., & Ysseldyke, J. E. (1981). *Assessment in special and remedial education* (2d ed.). Boston: Houghton Mifflin.

Scandura, J. M. (1977). Structural approach to instructional problems. *American Psychologist, 32,* 33–53.

Schmidt, S. (1981). Eliciting negative structures through role-playing. In J. F. Miller (Ed.), *Assessing language production in children: Experimental procedures* (pp. 148–151). Baltimore, Md.: University Park Press.

Semb, G. (1972). *Behavior analysis and education.* Lawrence, Kans.: University of Kansas.

Shapiro, E. S., & Lentz, F. E. (1985). Assessing academic behavior: A behavioral approach. *School Psychology Review, 14,* 325–338.

Shepherd, D. L. (1978). *Comprehensive high school readiness methods* (2d ed.). Columbus, Ohio: Charles E. Merrill.

Smead, V. (1977). Ability training and task analysis in diagnostic/prescriptive teaching. *Journal of Special Education, 11,* 113–125.

Smith, C. R. (1980). Assessment alternatives: Non-standardized procedures. *School Psychology Review, 9,* 46–56.

Smith, C. R. (1983). *Learning disabilities: The interaction of learner, task, and setting.* Boston: Little, Brown.

Smith, R. M. (1969). Collecting diagnostic data in the classroom. *Teaching Exceptional Children, 1,* 128–133.

Strang, R. (1964). *Diagnostic teaching of reading.* New York: McGraw-Hill.

Thelan, J. (1976). *Improving reading in science.* Newark, Del.: International Reading Association.

Thompson, V. P., Gickling, E. E., & Havertape, J. F. (1983). The effects of medication and curriculum on task-related behaviors of attention deficit disordered and low achieving peers. *Monograph in behavior disorders: Severe behavior disorders of children and youth* (pp. 34–48). Reston, Va.: Council for Children with Behavior Disorders.

Tidwell, R. (1980). Informal assessment to modify the role and image of the school psychologist. *Psychology in the Schools, 17,* 210–215.

Tindal, G., Wesson, C., Germann, G., Deno, S., Mirkin, P. (1982). *A data-based special educational delivery system: The Pine County Model* (Monograph No. 19). Minneapolis, Minn.: University of Minnesota, Institute for Research on Learning Disabilities.

Varnhagen, S., & Gerber, M. M. (1984). Use of microcomputers for spelling assessment: Reasons to be cautious. *Learning Disability Quarterly, 7,* 266–270.

Wedman, J. F., & Stefanich, G. P. (1984). Guidelines for computer-based testing of student learning of concepts, principles, and procedures. *Educational Technology, 24,* 23–28.

Werner, S., Goossens, C. C., & Green, E. E. (1981). Eliciting wh- questions: Puppet show procedure. In J. F. Miller (Ed.), *Assessing language production in children: Experimental procedures* (pp. 141–142). Baltimore, Md.: University Park Press.

West, T. A. (1977). Rx for verbal problems: A diagnostic-prescriptive approach. *Arithmetic Teacher, 25,* 57–58.

Wilson, M. S., & Fox, B. J. (1982). Computer-administered bilingual language assessment and intervention. *Exceptional Children, 49,* 145–148.

Woodcock, R. (1973). *Woodcock Reading Mastery Test.* Circle Pines, Minn.: American Guidance Service.

Ysseldyke, J. E., & Sabatino, D. A. (1973). Toward validation of the diagnostic-prescriptive model. *Academic Therapy, 8,* 415–422.

Zigmond, N., & Silverman, R. (1984). Informal assessment for program planning and evaluation in special education. *Educational Psychologist, 19,* 163–171.

Zigmond, N., Vallecorsa, A., & Silverman, R. (1983). *Assessment for instructional planning in special education.* Englewood Cliffs, N.J.: Prentice-Hall.

CHAPTER 8

Analogue Assessment: Methods for Assessing Emotional and Behavioral Problems

EDWARD S. SHAPIRO
Lehigh University

THOMAS R. KRATOCHWILL
University of Wisconsin–Madison

INTRODUCTION

Psychologists are often faced with referrals for various behavioral and emotional problems that occur in the school setting. Although direct observation within the natural setting probably provides the most ecologically valid data for behavioral assessment (Cone 1978), certain types of behavior problems do not easily lend themselves to direct observation.

Some behavior problems tend to occur only in specific situations. For example, a child with limited social skills can only show this deficiency when a situation arises on the playground that requires social interaction. Many classroom instructional situations explicitly prohibit social interaction, and thus direct observation for social skills problems conducted during this period may not reveal any significant difficulties.

Related to this problem is the accessibility of observers to the target child in settings where the problem is likely to occur. Taking the social skills example, it may be possible to observe directly the child's problem during a recess or lunchroom period. Yet, if the problems are occurring in the hallways between classes, on the school bus, or on the street corner waiting for the bus, it may be difficult or even impossible to have observers present during these periods.

Likewise, certain problems may occur only in the child's home or community. For example, a child may demonstrate problems only in compliance to parental requests when the child is at home and his or her mother makes the request. Placing observers into these settings may again be a problem.

Another problem with direct observation is the cost associated with the assessment of low frequency behaviors. Although a child may have a significant social skills problem, opportunities to observe the behavior may only occur once or twice a day. It would be economically prohibitive to have individuals observe a child to record behavior that occurs at such a low rate.

Beyond economic concerns, certain types of behavioral problems result in infrequent opportunities for the behavior to occur in the natural setting. For example, problems such as fears and anxiety that may be related to certain private events may be unlikely to occur since the children themselves will actively avoid contact with the feared stimulus. Thus, the observer might never have an actual opportunity to view the child's response to the fearful stimulus or event.

Certain types of "behavioral" events are unobservable. Assessment of cognitive processes through self-report is often the only method available in individual behavioral assessment (Cone, 1978; Nelson & Hayes, 1979).

Given that direct observation of behavior within the natural setting is not always possible or feasible, the use of analogue assessment procedures have often been employed in the behavioral assessment of certain types of behavioral and emotional problems. Detailed descriptions and definitions of analogue assessment are provided in Chapter 7 by Gettinger and Chapter 9 by Prout and Ferber in this volume. In brief, an analogue assessment involves conducting observations of behavior under conditions that simulate the situation in which the behavior actually occurs. Although all analogue measures require inferences between performance on the measure and behavior in the natural setting, analogue measures differ in the degree to which they simulate behavior under natural conditions. For example, where some measures require actual behavioral responses (e.g., role-play tests), other are strictly paper-and-pencil measures.

Cone (1978) conceptualized the methods of behavioral assessment along a continuum from direct to indirect measures (see Chapter 1 of this volume). The closer an assessment measure comes to evaluating the actual behavior to be changed within the setting or conditions in which it occurs, the more the measure falls towards the direct end of the continuum. Included among direct measures by Cone (1978) are any form of direct observation including self-monitoring. In contrast, measures that require an individual to assess behaviors using retrospective reporting (such as informant report and interviews), are considered as indirect measures.

Analogue assessment is considered a direct assessment method since it requires the observation of behavior during its actual occurrence. However, because the conditions under which the behavior occurs are simulated, analogue assessment is less direct than observation within the naturalistic setting.

Cone (1978) identifies two types of analogue measures: free behavior and role-playing. Free behavior analogues involve the observation of behavior as it occurs but within a simulated setting such as a laboratory, clinic waiting room, or other contrived setting. In contrast, role-playing analogues are situations in which the individual is told to act as if they were in the described situation. The behavioral response of the individual is then observed.

Analogue measures offer several advantages that address the problems of using direct observation in natural settings. The reader is again referred to detailed discussions in chapters by Gettinger, and Prout and Ferber in this volume. In brief, analogue measures provide a technique for using direct observation methodologies, increase the opportunities to observe behaviors that occur at a low rate, and offer an economical way to conduct observations of behaviors that are less likely to occur under natural conditions.

Despite these advantages, analogue measures have several serious limitations. Perhaps the most salient is the degree to which these measures relate to behavioral occurrences under natural conditions. Given the extent to which behavior is situationally specific (Mash & Terdal, 1981; Nelson & Hayes, 1979), creating simulated environments in which the behavior is supposed to occur may actually be creating conditions that never really occur in the real world.

In this chapter, the use of analogue measures is presented for assessing avoidance behavior, compliance, social skills, problem solving, and other areas of cognitive-behavioral skills. For each of these areas, only those strategies that have received some empirical evaluation are examined, and only strategies that require some type of motor response by the individual being assessed are examined in detail. Paper-and-pencil analogues (Nay, 1979) are briefly mentioned but not discussed extensively since many of these measures are more accurately considered informant reports and are discussed by Edelbrock (this volume) and Shapiro (1987).

AVOIDANCE BEHAVIOR

Despite the long-standing interest and investigation of childhood fears and anxiety (e.g., Jersild & Holmes, 1935; Lapouse & Monk, 1959; MacFarlane, Allen, & Hozik, 1954), development of assessment and intervention strategies for these problems is a rather recent phenomenon (Barrios & Shigetomi, 1985; Morris & Kratochwill, 1983). In particular, the recognition of the potential relationship between anxiety problems in children related to surgical, dental, and other health treatment, and later health problems (Karoly, 1982; Melamed, 1979), suggests the importance of preventative treatment for possibly transient childhood fears and anxieties (Cowen, 1982; Gelfand & Hartmann, 1977).

The assessment of avoidance problems in general is problematic. First, these problems are often related to private events that are accessible only through verbal self-report. When the child is presented with a feared stimulus, an examiner can only ask him or her to tell how fearful they are. Clearly, potential bias with this type of data collection is evident.

Second, probably the most effective coping mechanism for dealing with fears is to learn those behaviors that lead to contact with the feared stimulus. Any attempt to make a direct observation of the individual's reaction to contact with the feared stimulus in the natural setting becomes extremely difficult.

With children, the problems in assessing fears and anxiety become even greater. Often, children cannot reliably assess their own response, and, therefore, verbal self-report is rendered meaningless. Like adult avoidance problems, children learn effective coping mechanisms to prevent them from making contact with the feared stimulus. Direct observation under natural conditions again becomes an unlikely assessment procedure.

Three types of analogue measures have been used in the assessment of avoidance behavior. Behavioral avoidance tests, the most direct form of the assessment of avoidance, places the individual into a simulated condition in which they come into contact with the feared stimulus. The individual's behaviors are objectively recorded on some specified variables. Self-report measures are a second type of indirect, paper-and-pencil analogues. These measures typically require the individual to report a degree of fear to specific stimuli on some predetermined rating scale. Finally, informant reports, paper-and-pencil measures completed by significant others (usually parents or teachers), are also used to assess childhood anxieties.

Behavioral Avoidance Tests

The Behavioral Avoidance Test (BAT) is considered the primary method of behavioral assessment of avoidance problems. The procedure places the individual into controlled contact with the feared stimulus while observations are made of various behaviors. Although the exact technique differs across studies, the procedure usually involves an experimenter instructing the subject to perform each step of a graded hierarchy that brings the subject closer and closer to the feared stimulus. The subject's compliance in performing each step is recorded along with other variables such as self-rating of anxiety levels, facial expressions, and number and type of verbalizations. A passive BAT has been employed in which the individual remains stationary and the feared stimulus is brought closer to the individual (e.g., Murphy & Bootzin, 1973). Table 8-1 provides an example of a BAT hierarchy used by Morris (1976) in assessing the fear of entering a swimming pool.

It is important to recognize that the BAT does not represent a single, standardized technique, but rather a general strategy for assessing avoidance behavior. Barrios and Shigetomi (1985) provide a comprehensive review of the use of BATs for assessing children's fears. They noted that the nonstandardized nature of BATs may present a significant disadvantage in drawing effective conclusions regarding their value in the assessment of children. For example, the number of steps in the hierarchy range from one (Evans & Harmon, 1981) to eighty-five (Ultee, Griffioen, & Schellekens, 1982). Across studies examining fears of similar objects (small animals), the hierarchy ranged from one step (Evans & Harmon, 1981) to twenty-nine steps (Ritter, 1968). Morris and Kratochwill (1983) point out that while the number of steps in hierarchies is not in itself problematic, evidence that subdivid-

TABLE 8-1   Hierarchy for Children Afraid to Enter a Swimming Pool

1. Let's begin by walking into the pool room to the white marker (one-quarter of the way to the pool).
2. Walk to the yellow marker on the floor (half of the way).
3. Walk to the red marker on the floor (three-quarters of the way).
4. Walk to the green marker by the edge of the pool.
5. Sit down right there (by the edge of the pool).
6. Let's see you put your feet in the water, while I slowly count to 9. 1 . . . 2 . . . 3
7. . . . 4 . . . 5 . . . 6
8. . . . 7 . . . 8 . . . 9
9. Get up and walk into the water to the red marker and stay there until I count to 6. 1 . . . 2 . . . 3
10. . . . 4 . . . 5 . . . 6
11. Walk to the green marker (halfway down ramp) and stay there until I count to 6. 1 . . . 2 . . . 3
12. . . . 4 . . . 5 . . . 6
13. Walk to the yellow marker (bottom of ramp: 2'6" deep) and stay there until I count to 9. You can hold onto the edge. 1 . . . 2 . . . 3
14. . . . 4 . . . 5 . . . 6
15. . . . 7 . . . 8 . . . 9
16. Let's see if you can stand there without holding on (only if person held on in previous step).
17. Walk out to the red marker (3' from edge) and then come back to me.
18. Splash some water on yourself; hold on to the edge if you like.
19. Do that without holding on (only if person held on in previous step).
20. Splash some water on your face; you may hold on to the edge if you like.
21. Do that without holding on (only if person held on in previous step).
22. Squat down and blow some bubbles in the water. You can hold on if you like.
23. Blow bubbles without holding on (only if person held on in previous step).
24. Put you whole face in the water. You may hold on if you like.
25. Do that again without holding on (only if person held on in previous step).
26. Put your whole body under water. You can hold on if you like.
27. Do that again without holding on (only if person held on in previous step).
28. Walk out in the water up to your chin (if pool depth permits).
29. Hold onto the kickboard and put your face in the water.
30. Hold onto the kickboard and take one foot off the ground.
31. Hold onto the kickboard and take both feet off the ground.
32. Put your face in the water again and take your feet off the bottom.
33. Let's go down to the deep end of the pool. Sit on the edge and put your feet in the water.
34. O.K. Now climb down the ladder.
35. Now hold onto the edge right here by the green marker.
36. While still holding on, put your whole body under water.
37. Hold onto the kickboard.
38. While still holding on put your face in the water.
39. Do that again, but now put your whole head under water.
40. O.K. Now climb out of the pool and come over to the blue marker. Jump in the water right here (at pool depth of 3'6" or 5' depending on person's height).

Source: R. J. Morris, *Behavior Modification with Children: A Systematic Guide.* (Cambridge, Mass.: Winthrop, 1976.) Reprinted with permission.

ing a fear hierarchy into smaller steps may produce increased approach behavior (e.g., Nawas, 1971) makes comparative conclusions across studies questionable.

Another problem related to the lack of standardization is the potential effect that instructions may have on the outcome of BATs. Some BATs may provide more information to subjects (e.g., "The dog will not bite you"). Some clinicians who use BATs instruct children to "do your best," which may again alter the degree of approach behavior (Kelley, 1976). Further, children may be allowed to terminate the BAT, a factor that may influence performance.

BATs may also vary in the way in which the procedure is presented to a child. Some studies employ both verbal and modeled instructions. Barrios, Hartmann, and Shigetomi (1981) note that the use of models in the adult phobic literature suggest that this may facilitate approach behavior (Bernstein & Nietzel, 1973).

Another issue related to the use of BATs is the part that demand characteristics may play in performance. Although few studies have been conducted with children, Kelley (1976) suggests that simply instructions such as "try as hard as you can" influence approach behavior.

Psychometrically, BATs have not been subjected to rigorous examination. Barrios and Shigetomi (1985) present an excellent summary of the reliability and validity data available on twenty-one studies using BATs in assessing children's avoidance behavior. Of these studies, data reported on reliability and validity were primarily obtained through visual inspection of the results rather than any technically sound strategy.

One of the most significant disadvantages of the BAT is its specific analogue characteristics. The degree to which a child's response under the controlled and relatively safe environment of the laboratory is similar to the same stimulus under more natural conditions is rarely examined. This weakness in external validity, common across all analogue measures, clearly suggests the need for other types of assessment procedures.

Despite potential problems with BATs, these measures offer several advantages. The very nature of avoidance problems makes their assessment in natural settings very difficult. Opportunities for the direct observation of a child approaching a feared stimulus are obviously infrequent. By using a BAT, such opportunities can be created under controlled conditions.

Investigators have also begun to observe more than a single dimension (i.e., number of steps successfully completed) of behavior during a BAT. For example, some investigators have recorded multiple responses such as stiffness, eye contact, speech disturbance, latency to approach, and cumulative contact time (e.g., Esveldt-Dawson, Wisner, Unis, Matson, & Kazdin, 1982; Evans & Harmon, 1981; Milos & Reiss, 1982; Ultee *et al.*, 1982). Likewise, Van Hasselt, Hersen, Bellack, Rosenblum, and Lamparski (1979) collected measures across assessment domains (motoric, cognitive, and physiological) during the administration of the BAT.

Another important advantage of the BAT is its potential link to intervention. Similar to other analogue assessment measures, the BAT often serves to structure the treatment strategies, and therefore can become a measure sensitive to behavior change across time.

Observational Rating Scales

Although not always conducted in a contrived or analogue setting, observational rating scales have been developed to assess certain types of avoidance behavior that can not readily be assessed through a BAT. Barrios *et al.*, (1981), Barrios and Shigetomi (1984), and Morris and Kratochwill (1983) provide extensive discussions of these measures.

The basic strategy employed in this type of assessment involves using a predefined observation code when observing a child coming into contact with the feared stimulus. This technique can be used both within the natural setting (such as an actual visit to the dentist, [Melamed, Hawes, Heiby, & Glick, 1975]) or in a contrived setting (such as performing tasks in the presence or absence of mother when assessing separation anxiety in preschoolers [Glennon & Weisz, 1978]).

Overall, Barrios and Shigetomi (1985) report that many of these observational scales have acceptable reliability and reasonable content and construct validity. Although some of the observational instruments require extensive training, many involve parents and teachers as observers and are easy to learn.

Self-Report

A large number of self-report and informant-report measures for assessing avoidance problems in children have appeared in the literature (see Morris & Kratochwill, 1983, and Barrios *et al.*, 1981 for detailed disucussion). Although considered indirect rather than analogue assessment measures by Cone (1978), these measures are conceptualized by Nay (1979) as paper-and-pencil analogues.

Two self-report measures representative of most of these assessment instruments are the Fear Survey Schedule for children—Revised (Ollendick, 1983) and the Fear Thermometer (Kelley, 1976). The Fear Survey Schedule for Children—Revised is a revision of a scale developed by Scherer and Nakamura (1968). The child is asked to report on a three-point scale (none, some, a lot) the degree to which they are afraid of each of eighty items. Included on the scale are items such as "sharp objects," "getting lost," and "riding on a train." Normative data for children and adolescents has been reported for this measure and it appears to have acceptable reliability and validity (Ollendick, 1983; Ollendick, Matson, & Helsel, 1985).

The Fear Thermometer is an assessment method in which the child is asked to provide a rating of the degree to which they felt anxious. Kelley (1976), in adapting a version used with adults (Walk, 1956), had children identify their fear levels by selecting a specific color that corresponded to a facial representation of how he or she felt during a specific situation. The method appears to have adequate reliability and validity (Glennon & Weisz, 1978), although the frequency of its use in the literature is rather sparse. In general, the use of a Fear Thermometer may have significant clinical utility in helping children quantify internal physiological states.

Summary and Conclusions

The assessment of avoidance behavior in children presents several problems. The questionable validity of self-report necessitates the use of some form of direct observation. Although the use of the BAT appears promising, there are several issues that need to be addressed in research. In particular, the failure to develop standardized formats for hierarchy development and instruction make the current status of the psychometric properties of BATs somewhat of a mystery. Perhaps even more critical is the relationship between BAT behavior and behavior under natural conditions. Finally, while the link between assessment and treatment in using the BAT is clear, the generalization of improvement during BAT assessments and changes in the natural setting has rarely been investigated.

Despite the potential limitations of the BAT, the technique appears to be one of the most useful analogue assessment strategies available. Considering the difficulties and potential expense of assessing avoidance behavior under natural conditions, the usefulness of the BAT becomes clear. Perhaps future research should be aimed at developing a more systematic observational code to be used during administration of a BAT. Such a code might be based on research that has identified the most critical and salient variables related to reductions of avoidance behavior in children. Further, consistent use of behavioral assessment across modalities similar to Van Hasselt *et al.* (1979), is recommended strongly.

COMPLIANCE

Parental compliance is often a significant problem linked to a number of behavior problems in children (Forehand, 1977). Indeed, Forehand and King (1977) found that children referred by a clinic may exhibit noncompliance on 57% to 80% of the opportunities for compliance. Research has demonstrated that there is a clear relationship between the way parents issue commands for compliance and the child's response (e.g., Green, Forehand, & McMahon, 1979).

The assessment of compliance in the natural setting may be problematic. Frequencies with which opportunities for compliance occur may vary. Noncompliance may occur only in the presence of a mother or other situationally specific variables. As such, direct observation of the problem in those settings may be costly and difficult. Day and Roberts (1983) have developed an analogue measure that is designed specifically to assess child compliance to parental instructions.

The Compliance Test

As a direct observation procedure, the Compliance Test is a measure performed as a clinic analogue to examine the probability of child compliance to parental instruction. The parent and child are brought to a room with four sets of specifically designated toys (animals, cars, blocks, and dolls), three containers (box, house, and bus), and distractor toys. Parents are provided with a "bug-in-the-ear" device used to prompt the parent behind a one-way observation window.

Following a warm-up period, children are told by their parents that they are going to be asked to do things and that it is important for them to do them right away. The parent then issues the specific instruction. Thirty standardized instructions are presented at approximately fifteen-second intervals. All commands are in the form of, Put this (animal/car/block/doll) in the (box/house/bus). After each command, a tape recorder is started for a five-second interval, during which the observer records child behavior. The observer then rewinds the tape and prompts the next instruction.

Child behavior is recorded as compliant if a continuous motor response within the five-second period results in the child grasping the designated toy. All other behavior is defined as noncompliant. A compliance ratio is calculated by dividing the number of compliant responses by the number of instructions issued per assessment (30).

The Compliance Test was developed specifically to evaluate the compliance training program of Forehand and McMahon (1981). The test is designed to be used with children between two and seven years old and is not aimed for use with infants or elementary school children (Roberts, in press). Agreement ratios across studies have been consistently high, ranging from 97.4% to 99.1% (e.g., Day & Roberts, 1983; Roberts; 1982). One week, test-retest coefficients were .73 across a subset of unpublished clinic referrals and nonclinic volunteers (Roberts, in press). The test was found to be extremely homogeneous (KR-20 = .99). The measure has also been found to be responsive to various treatment intervention programs (Roberts, 1982, 1984a, 1984b; Roberts, Hatzenbuehler, & Bean, 1981).

One of the significant advantages of the Compliance Test is its standardized nature. The procedures can be easily replicated and behavioral observation is straightforward. Unfortunately, the measure currently has several characteristics that should be considered when it is used.

First, the age range appropriate for the test is rather restricted. Children older than seven are often referred for similar problems of noncompliance. As clearly stated by Roberts (in press), this measure is not appropriate for those individuals.

Second, although the measure is sensitive to changes in compliance training, the external validity of the measure may be limited. The types of compliance tasks (Put the toy in the house) are somewhat different than the types of tasks required in a home or school (Get dressed and brush your teeth before breakfast). Research is needed that addresses the degree to which this analogue measure (like other analogue measures), effectively assesses the behavior in the natural setting.

Third, there is a need to examine the situational events that surround compliance. For example, a child may show highly compliant behavior to his mother but not to his preschool teacher. Although it seems that the measure can be generalized to adults beside his mother, research is needed to demonstrate that such changes do not alter compliance ratios.

Fourth, the Compliance Test has only been employed using one-way observation mirrors in a laboratory type of setting. The degree that the measure can be used in a more clinical context has not been investigated. The necessity of the bug-in-the-ear device may limit the feasibility of using the measure in nonresearch settings.

Despite the limitations of the Compliance Test, Day and Roberts (1983) have offered an interesting methodology for future development. In particular, the extension of their assessment strategy to older children and different types of compliance problems (e.g., following teacher directions, completion of assignments) is needed. The generalization of the results of any adaptation of the compliance test methodology to nonanalogue situations must be evaluated.

SOCIAL SKILLS

Much attention in the literature has been given to the problem of social skills in children. Indeed, many books (e.g., Cartledge & Milburn, 1986), training programs (e.g., Goldstein, Sprafkin, Gershaw, & Klein, 1980; Hazel, Bragg-Schumaker, Sherman, & Sheldon-Wildgen, 1981) and journal articles (*School Psychology Review*, 1984 [13] entire issue) have addressed various aspects of assessment and intervention for children's social skills.

Assessment of social skills has involved both direct observation in the natural setting as well as analogue methods. Problems similar to both compliance and avoidance behavior in terms of opportunities to observe the behavior, expense of direct observation, and situational specificity of the problem behavior, make assessment of social skills within the natural setting somewhat difficult. As alternatives to direct observation in the natural setting, analogue assessment procedures such as role-play tests, contrived situation tests, self-report measures, and peer assessment have all been employed.

Role-Play Tests

In a role-play test, an individual is presented with a specific interpersonal situation and told to respond as if the situation were actually occurring. The response of the targeted individual is observed and recorded according to some predetermined set of behaviors. Situations presented to the individual will often be based upon those types of social interactions typically found to be a problem. For example, some role-play tests may present scenes involving accepting criticism from peers, or giving compliments.

As with BATs, role-play tests are a general assessment strategy rather than a specific, standardized technique. Although the method of presentation within a role-play test might be consistent, the types, number, and content of scenes presented would vary across role-play tests. The behaviors targeted for observation may be different across assessments.

The typical format of role-play tests is similar across studies. After instructions are presented, a specific interpersonal scene is described to the child. A prompt is provided and the child is instructed to respond. For example, if one were assessing the skill of helping, the following scene might be used:

> Narrator: "Imagine you are with a group of children. One of the children is having trouble learning to play a new game. He says, "I'm having trouble with this game!"
>
> Child's Response: _____

After the child's response, the next scene is presented. Typically, the role-play test is administered in a setting removed from the natural setting and under controlled conditions.

The behaviors chosen for observation have often been based on the results of studies from the adult literature (e.g., Eisler, Miller, & Hersen, 1973) that have identified specific verbal and nonverbal behaviors considered components of socially skilled behavior. Included among these behaviors are eye contact, smiles, duration of reply, number of words, latency of response, affect, speech disturbances, gestures, compliance, requests for new behavior, regard, positive behavior, and appreciation. Each of these response categories has been defined objectively (Van Hasselt, Hersen, Whitehill, & Bellack, 1979).

Bornstein, Bellack, and Hersen (1977) developed a prototype role-play test for children, the Behavioral Assertiveness Test for Children (BAT-C). The test included a set of twenty-four scenes encompassing varying types of child-to-child interpersonal situations. Each scene was scored on a set of eleven variables. The specific method for developing scenes was not identified by Bornstein *et al.* (1977). A full description of the scenes and the scoring procedures is provided in Michelson, Sugai, Wood, and Kazdin (1983). A revision of the BAT-C is described by Ollendick, Hart, and Francis (1985) using an extended interchange beyond the child's initial response. Table 8-2 provides a subset of scenes from the BAT-C.

Many variations of the BAT-C have appeared in the literature. In some cases, scene development was more objective and based upon informant ratings (e.g., Reardon, Hersen, Bellack, & Foley, 1979). Others have used fewer scenes than the BAT-C (e.g., Beck, Forehand, Neeper, & Baskin (1982), and other studies have employed more than a single child response to a scene (e.g., Van Hasselt, Hersen, & Bellack, 1981). Some studies have also employed prolonged interchanges (1 minute) to scenes (Van Hasselt, *et al.*, 1981; Van Hasselt, Hersen, & Kazdin, 1985). Finally, LaGreca and Santogrossi (1980) used a single situation (making friends with a new child at school) and a single rating (0 to 10) as a role-play test.

Gaffney and McFall (1981) provided an excellent example of an empirically based role-play measure. The Problem Inventory for Adolescent Girls (PIAG) was

TABLE 8-2 Role-Play Scenes for the Behavioral Assertiveness Test for Children

1. *Narrator:* Imagine you're sitting with a boy in class. You tell a story. He thinks it's good and so do you. He says:
   Prompt: "That was a neat story."
2. *Narrator:* Pretend that you're watching your favorite TV program. Your friend comes over and turns on something you don't like and he says:
   Prompt: "I'm going to watch this instead."
3. *Narrator:* You draw a picture in art class and the boy next to you says:
   Prompt: "Wow, that's really great."
4. *Narrator:* You're reading a comic during recess. Pretty soon another kid takes the comic and says:
   Prompt: "I want to read it by myself."
5. *Narrator:* Pretend you're racing one of the guys and you beat him. He says:
   Prompt: "Gee, you're really fast."
6. *Narrator:* Imagine it's your turn to play the video game. Your friend leaves it on the table for you. But someone else gets there first and says:
   Prompt: "I'm taking this."
7. *Narrator:* Imagine you're playing ball with some of your friends and you've made a good catch. One of your friends says:
   Prompt: "Hey _____, that was a good play."
8. *Narrator:* Pretend that you're standing near the TV. Suddenly your brother or sister comes by and pushes you and says:
   Prompt: "Get out of my way."
9. *Narrator:* You've been working really hard on a project that's coming up. One of the boys says to you:
   Prompt: "That's a really neat project you did."
10. *Narrator:* Someone else makes a mistake and blames it on you. He says:
    Prompt: "You're the one who did it."
11. *Narrator:* Imagine you're getting dressed to go on a special outing. Your friend says:
    Prompt: "_____, you look very nice today."
12. *Narrator:* Your friend is teasing you. He keeps calling you names. You're getting tired of it. He says:
    Prompt: "What's the matter? Can't you take a joke?"
13. *Narrator:* Imagine you just finished decorating your room with posters and other stuff. A friend says to you:
    Prompt: "Wow, _____, you really did a good job."
14. *Narrator:* You forgot something you were supposed to bring and someone says:
    Prompt: "You're so dumb! You'd forget your head if it weren't screwed on!"

Source: From L. Michelson, D. P. Sugai, R. P. Wood, & A. E. Kazdin, *Social Skills Assessment and Training with Children: An Empirically Based Handbook* (New York: Plenum Press, 1983).

developed based on the behavioral analytic model suggested by Goldfried and D'Zurilla (1969). After conducting a situational analysis using structured interviews with many individuals such as parents, teachers, counselors, community leaders, and delinquent and nondelinquent youth, a total of seventy-eight situations were identified as potential problems for adolescent girls. An item was written for each situation that required the subject to state how she would solve the problem. These items were administered to both delinquent girls and nondelinquent girls and boys. The nondelinquent sample was obtained by asking all students in two ninth-grade and tenth-grade classes to nominate the six boys and girls in their class who they considered the most competent. Those with the highest number of nominations were administered the seventy-eight-item scale.

Responses to the items from all individuals were scored by judges on a five-point scale regarding the competence of the response. The final inventory was determined by an examination of the internal consistency among the four raters on each item. The final scale consisted of fifty-two items. The final rater's manual also included explicit criteria and examples for each point of the five-point rating scale.

After the scale was complete, it was administered to twenty-nine delinquent and nondelinquent girls. A discriminant function analysis found that the scale accurately classified 85% of the subjects.

Many studies have examined the concurrent validity of role-play tests with other measures of social skills. Michelson, DiLorenzo, Calpin, and Ollendick (1982) investigated the situational determinants of the BAT-C with seriously disturbed children. Results suggested that negative scenes elicited different responses than positive scenes. These findings, however, were not consistent across component skills assessed.

Van Hasselt *et al.* (1981) examined the interrelation of role-play tests with observations in a natural setting, peer assessment, and teacher ratings. Results showed role-play tests to have limited correspondence to either teacher assessment or assessment of interactions within a more naturalistic setting. Similar results were found by Williamson, Moody, Granberry, Lethermon, and Blouin (1983).

Beck, Forehand, Neeper, and Baskin (1982) compared role-play tests with more naturalistic assessment. Subjects in their study were asked to wait in a room where a confederate subject was playing a game. Observations of the four-minute interaction were made and scored on various component social skills. Results showed that the children in the role-play situations displayed significantly more responses than in the naturalistic observation.

Ollendick *et al.* (1985) examined the relation between adult and child judges of social skills. Children were videotaped while performing a role-play test (BAT-C) and later scored for component social skills. These tapes were then judged by peers on a five-point scale (How much would you like this child to be your friend). Results suggest that, while response components may be used by adult judges in differentiating socially skilled and unskilled children, peers infrequently rely on such components in their decisions. Children appeared to be responding more to likability than assertiveness.

Hughes and Hall (1985) used a role-play test with videotaped scenes to investigate the predictive validity of these measures in discriminating emotionally disturbed from nondisturbed boys. Results of their study suggested that the role-play test accurately classified 91% of the nonemotionally disturbed boys but only 65% of the disturbed boys. Although the use of videotaped scenes with a standard scoring protocol appears to be a significant improvement in methodology, the failure of the role-play test to classify accurately 35% of the emotionally disturbed boys may be a problem.

Overall, the use of role-play tests has several limitations. Perhaps the most salient is the questionable generalization of these measures with behavior in naturalistic settings. Indeed, studies with adults also substantiate the somewhat poor external validity of role-play tests (Bellack, Hersen, & Lamparski, 1979; Bellack, Hersen, & Turner, 1978; McNamara & Blumen, 1982). Given the extent to which demand characteristics, situational specificity, and other events affect social interaction, these results should not be surprising (Bellack, 1979). For example, Kazdin, Esveldt-Dawson, and Matson (1983) showed that children's behavior in a role-play test of social skills could be easily manipulated by instructional set. Telling a student to "fake good" or "fake bad" significantly influenced the observed behavior on the measure. What is perhaps more of a problem, however, is that studies that demonstrate changes in social skill using role-play measures may seriously lack social validity. Children's behavior during the role-play may bear little relation to behavior changes considered either important or relevant for improving interpersonal skills. Indeed, few studies have found strong relations between changes in role-play assessments of social skills and peer assessments (see Hobbs, Walle, & Hammersly, 1984, for an exception).

Despite this serious limitation of role-play tests, the measures do have several advantages. First, the measures offer flexibility in the choice of interpersonal situations that can be assessed. This allows the examiner to match the type of scene with the actual type of behavioral problem experienced by the subject. If one employs an empirical approach to selecting scenes used in the role-play test, one may be able to produce more accurate situations that more closely approximate the problem as it occurs in the natural environment.

Second, because the format for role-play tests are standardized, control can be exerted on persons and environmental contingencies allowing a more precise form of measurement. Repeated use of the measure across time offers a more accurate assessment of behavior change.

Third, measurement of component skills such as eye contact, speech duration, and length of responses, offers a more precise evaluation of skills that should be affected by training programs. Although global rating scales are at times redundant to component scores (e.g., Van Hasselt *et al.*, 1981), changes on these component skills may suggest specific areas of change that accounts for changes in global rating scores.

Other advantages of role-play tests are their ease of administration and relatively small cost. The measures can be employed with little training and involve only a small amount of time. However, the primary limitation of these measures in external validity may make them questionable to use alone. One analogue measure that has attempted to respond to the issue of generalization are contrived situation tests.

Contrived Situation Tests

A contrived situation test differs from a role-play test in that an attempt is made to obtain data under more naturalistic conditions. Instead of instructing a subject to act "as if" he or she were in the situation described, the target individual is unobtrusively observed while responding to the prompt of a confederate when a specific social situation occurs. In other words, confederates create opportunities for social skills to occur within the natural environment.

Wood, Michelson, and Flynn (1978) described the Children's Behavioral Scenario (CBS) measure designed to assess assertiveness in children. The CBS is administered in an interview format with a confederate adult. Embedded in the interview are specific prompts designed to assess identified social skills. The child's performance is observed and scored on such behaviors as greeting others, making requests, giving and receiving praise, giving compliments, expressing empathy and feelings, refusing unreasonable requests, and initiating and terminating conversations. Assessed skills can be modified to reflect the skills of interest for a specific child. Both the scripts and scoring criteria are fully described in Michelson *et al.*, (1983). In the only study using this measure, Wood *et al.*, (1978) reported significant but moderate correlations among self-report, teacher report, and the CBS.

Shapiro, Stover, and Ifkovits (1983), and Shapiro, Gilbert, Friedman, and Steiner (1985) developed the Contrived Test of Social Skills (CTSS). This measure was employed for assessing social skills in a classroom setting. Scenes were developed based upon teacher interviews within broad areas of social skills, such as giving compliments, responding to criticism, or giving help. Each scene was presented in an unobtrusive manner during a period of independent work. The teacher instructed a peer to prompt the target child for a specific behavior related to social skills. For example, in one scene designed to assess giving compliments, a child was told to show a spelling test marked with a star to a peer and say, "Look at my spelling test." The target child was then observed directly by the teacher or an observer sitting in the classroom and scored for specific predefined social skills. Neither the confederate child nor the target child realized that the assessment was contrived. A series of scenes like this were presented across a specific time span (e.g., 30 minutes) to obtain a rating of social skills.

In the Shapiro *et al.* (1983, 1985) studies, the relations between the CTSS, role-play assessment, and teacher report on paper-and-pencil measures was examined. Results of the studies found significant and moderately strong correlations between role-play and the CTSS measures. These results must be considered quite tentative given certain methodological difficulties with these studies. Additional research is needed to examine the degree to which a contrived test of social skills more accurately portrays behavior under naturally occurring conditions. Although it would appear logical that such measures would be closer approximations to actual behavior than role-play tests, empirical documentation to support this assertion is needed.

Self-Report and Informant Report Measures

A large number of self-report and informant report measures have been developed for the assessment of social skills. Indeed, almost all training packages include checklists and rating scales that can be used to evaluate behavior prior, during, and after intervention. These measures can be considered paper-and-pencil analogues (Nay, 1979) and usually require a rater to simply check or rate on some Likert type scale, the degree to which specific social skills are evident.

A recent addition to paper-and-pencil measures to assess social skills is a series of measures still under development by Gresham and Elliott. The Social Skills Rating Scales (SSRS) consist of a set of three instruments, each containing items that examine a child's social skills. The measures are completed by the child, a teacher, and a parent, and are designed to be used in an integrative fashion as screening measures and to assist the decision to select appropriate targets for intervention. Unlike other measures, the SSRS assess the individual's social competencies rather than deficiencies. The measures provide information about acceptability as well as frequency of each behavior.

Clark, Gresham, and Elliott (1985) reported on the results of the teacher version of the SSRS, known as the TROSS (Teacher Rating of Social Skills). A factor analysis of the measure yielded four factors: academic performance, social initiation, cooperation, and peer reinforcement. Concurrent validity as assessed with a measure of academic performance and the Walker Problem Behavior Identification Checklist appear to be adequate. The scale also appeared to discriminate effectively between mildly handicapped and nonhandicapped children (Gresham, Elliott, & Black, 1987a). Additionally, the factor structure was replicated with a somewhat different population (Gresham, Elliott, & Black, 1987b). Normatization of the scales on a national sample as well as full development of the parent and self-report scale are under construction.

Although these types of self-report and informant report measures require the rating of a series of specific behaviors, an attempt to incorporate situational specificity in behavioral responding is notably absent. There have been a few scales developed for assessing social skills that consider this aspect of behavioral responding.

Wood, Michelson, and Flynn (1978) developed the Children's Behavioral Assertiveness Scale (CABS), a self-report measure designed to assess assertive and nonassertive behavior in children. The scale consists of twenty-seven items each describing a situation. Items attempt to assess assertiveness in a variety of content areas such as giving and receiving compliments, making requests, and initiating conversations. For each item, five alternative responses are provided and the child is instructed to select the response most like what he or she would do. Respondents choose two responses for each item; one response if the someone in the scene described was another child and one response if the someone was another adult. Items are scored along a dimension from very passive to very aggressive. The scale results in three scores: passive, aggressive, and overall assertiveness. Thus, the scale provides data on both the severity and directionality of the child's social skills problems. Michelson *et al.* (1983) provide full descriptions of the scale along with items and scoring criteria. A parallel version (TRCABS) designed to be completed by teachers has been developed and is also described in Michelson *et al.* (1983).

Wood *et al.* (1978) and Michelson, Andrasik, Vucelic, and Coleman (1981) have found moderate correlations between the CABS and TRCABS across 149 fourth graders in Florida. Michelson and Wood (1982) showed the CABS to have adequate test-retest reliability across a four-week period.

Another measure that appears to be a paper-and-pencil analogue measure for assessing social skills in children is the Children's Action Tendency Scale (CATS) (Deluty, 1979). The scale has a somewhat interesting format because children are presented with a series of scenes and a set of three forced choice responses. For example, one item from the scale is as follows:

> You and a friend are playing in your house. Your friend makes a big mess, but your parents blame you and punish you. What would you do?
> a. Ask my friend to help me clean up the mess. *or*
> b. Refuse to talk to or listen to my parents the next day.
>
> a. Clean up the mess. *or*
> b. Ask my friend to help me clean up the mess.
>
> a. Refuse to talk to or listen to my parents the next day. *or*
> b. Clean up the mess.

Children are instructed to choose one of the two alternatives for each set of item choices. The format of the test was designed to evaluate aggressiveness, assertiveness, and submissiveness. The scale was also developed based on the behavior-analytic framework of Goldfried and D'Zurilla (1969).

Studies examining the factor structure of the CATS as well as interrelationships with other self- and informant report measures have found the CATS subscales to have moderate and significant correlations to social desirability and self-esteem (Deluty, 1979). Deluty (1984) found the CATS to have significant correlations with a behavior checklist and direct observation of forty-five children in regular third-, fourth-, and fifth-grade classrooms.

Although both the CABS and CATS have potential use in the assessment of social skills, there has been relatively limited research conducted with these measures. Indeed, studies are needed that examine whether these measures are sensitive to behavior change. Further, other than Deluty's (1984) study, the relation of the CATS and CABS to behavior in the natural setting are unknown.

Peer Assessment

One final form of social skills assessment that is also a type of analogue assessment is peer assessments. Three types of peer assessment have appeared in the literature—peer nominations, peer ranking, and peer ratings. A detailed discussion of these measures is beyond the scope of this chapter and so they will only be examined briefly. Interested readers should see Kane and Lawler (1978) and Hops and Lewin (1984).

Peer nominations ask children to choose a limited number of peers on specific dimensions. For example, a child may be asked to list the three students he or she would most like to sit next to during lunch, or the three students he or she would least like to play with. For younger children, a picture format is employed and students then point to pictures of the nominated individual (McCandless & Marshall, 1957). The number of total nominations across the population sampled represents the child's score on the measure.

Although nominations are the easiest type of peer assessment measure to administer and score, they are rather a problem. Students who receive few positive nominations may not necessarily be disliked. It is entirely possible that failure to be nominated is a function of the presence of a few popular children who are nominated by all. Children may fail to be nominated because they were simply not considered by their peers.

Peer ratings require a child to provide a rating for all peers on a particular dimension. For example, children may be asked to rate on a scale of one to five how much they would like to play with each class member (Hymel & Asher, 1977). Ratings can be accompanied by visual prompts, such as faces ranging from smiles to frowns, to help children assign numeric ratings (Singleton & Asher, 1977).

The advantage of this method is that it provides data on every child, thus eliminating the problem of a child being forgotten by classmates. The most significant problem is the time of administration, which can be lengthy depending on the number of children and the number of dimensions rated.

Peer rankings are also employed. This procedure requires children to rank in order all children in a class on a particular dimension. It is similar to peer ratings in that ranks are obtained on all children in the class. The measure is difficult to interpret, however, and is a problem when used for statistical manipulation.

Although the use of peer assessment has been widespread in the literature on social skills, the measures have not always been useful for identifying targets for treatment and showing sensitivity to change following treatment. Peer assessment measures tell us little about why a child is disliked, only that they have lower status in relationship to peers (Michelson *et al.*, 1983). Although some have shown peer assessment to correlate with social competence (e.g., Greenwood, Walker, Todd, & Hops, 1977), others have found little relation between peer assessment and observational indexes of social interacion (Gottman, 1977; Gottman, Gonso, & Rasmussen, 1975).

Despite the limitations of peer assessment, these measures appear to be a potential screening device for identifying children who may require additional assessment. Given the relative ease of the administration of these measures, as well as their inherent social validity, peer assessment appears to be an important component of social skills assessment.

INTERPERSONAL PROBLEM SOLVING

Analogue assessment has played a particularly important role in the assessment of children's and adolescent's problem-solving behavior. Often, children with emotional and behavioral disorders display difficulties in deciding successfully upon and enacting solutions to common interpersonal problems. In an extensive and ongoing research program, Spivack, Shure, and their colleagues have identified specific components of interpersonal problem solving (Spivack, Platt, & Shure, 1976; Spivack & Shure, 1974). According to Spivack and Shure (1974), interpersonal problem-solving skills are defined as a set of cognitive variables that act as mediators of adjustment. These skills are:

1. Problem sensitivity—awareness of problems and ability to consider what went wrong in any interpersonal interaction.
2. Alternative solution thinking—ability to generate a wide range of potential solutions.
3. Means-ends thinking—ability to articulate step-by-step means to the solution.
4. Consequential thinking—tendency to consider consequences of social acts in terms of self as well as others, and to generate alternative consequences to any act.
5. Causal thinking—recognition that how one feels and acts may have been influenced by (and, in turn many influence) how others feel and act.

Clearly, the measures derived to assess these skills must be analogue. Given the unobservable nature of cognitive variables, assessment techniques evaluating these skills must rely on verbal or written output. Typically, these measures present a series of situations and ask for a written or verbal response that is scored for specific aspects of problem solving.

Preschool Interpersonal Problem-Solving Test (PIPS)

The PIPS is one measure developed by Spivack and Shure (1974) to assess alternative solution thinking. This form of problem solving has been found to be the most consistent predictor of adjustment in young (4 to 5 years old) children (Spivack, Platt, & Shure, 1976). Children who are four to five years old are verbally presented with two sets of problem situations (with accompanying pictures). In the first problem (peers), the child is shown a situation in which one child wants to play with a toy that is being played with by another child. The child being assessed is asked to identify (verbally) a possible solution to the problem. After one possible solution is given, pictures of new toys and child characters are presented (a total of 7). In the other problem situation (authority), five items are shown in which the child in the story has done something wrong to make its mother angry. In both cases, a standard inquiry is employed allowing the child to generate as many possible solutions to the problems. The total number of relevant solutions to both problem situations provides the child's score on the PIPS.

Extensive research on the use of the PIPS has been reported by Spivack and Shure (1974). Overall, interrater agreement for numbers of solutions were found to be excellent (97%, peer; 95% authority). Test-retest reliability (one-week), however, was not found to be very high ($r = .72$ and $.59$ in two different samples) (Spivack *et al.*, 1976). Studies that have used the PIPS as pre/post measures of training alternative solutions thinking have found that the measure reflected improvement in problem-solving scores (Spivack & Shure, 1974).

Means-Ends Problem-Solving Test (MEPS) and Children's MEPS

Spivack, *et al.* (1976) have identified means-ends thinking as critical cognitive skills related to adjustment from middle childhood through adolescence and into adulthood. Specifically, the ability to articulate step-by-step means to solving problems, is viewed as a higher order process relative to alternative solution thinking that is assessed in the PIPS.

The MEPS (for adults) is a story completion technique in which the individual is presented with the beginning and end of a situation and is asked to "fill in the middle." Stories are scored for number of: (1) relevant means; (2) irrelevant means; (3) no means; (4) enumerations of means; (5) obstacles; and (6) time references. Ten stories presented have successful outcomes and involve themes such as getting to know a beautiful girl, successfully stealing a diamond, getting along with one's boss, and finding a lost watch. For adolescents, the test is shortened to three or four stories, with problems such as making friends, dating, or dealing with peers.

The MEPS for children (10 to 12 years old), contains six themes involving getting even with a child who said something nasty, being new in a neighborhood and making friends, stealing a diamond from a store window, averting mother's anger for braking her favorite flower pot, earning money to buy mother a birthday present, and becoming the owner of a desired sportscar. The total number of means, obstacles, and time references is used as the score on the test.

Butler and Meichenbaum (1981) have raised a number of important issues about the PIPS and MEPS. They noted that the two tests are somewhat different in the instructional set provided for the subject. Where the PIPS is more like a standardized interview, the MEPS are storytelling exercises that do not attempt to induce any type of problem-solving set to the subject. The PIPS may be seen as an attempt to assess ability where the MEPS assesses typical performance. Butler and Meichenbaum (1981) suggest that the MEPS might become a more effective measure of problem-solving abilities if subjects were instructed specifically to tell how they would solve a problem, rather than the storytelling type of response used in the measure.

Perhaps even more important is whether the format of the MEPS has any relation to the behavior that would occur in a real-life situation. The overreliance on verbal reports suggests that the test may actually be assessing an individual's level of verbal abilities rather than problem-solving skills. In response to this concern, Spivack and his colleagues have consistently found that scores on these measures are related to adjustment with IQ scores statistically accounted for or controlled in the design. Still, as Butler and Meichenbaum (1981) note, the degree to which verbal skills affect test performance is not clear.

Other aspects of the PIPS and MEPS require critical examination. For example, the test stimuli used appear to be, in some cases, relatively artificial situations not commonly encountered by children. In particular, items like stealing a diamond, becoming the owner of a sportscar, or breaking mother's favorite flower vase, may lack content validity. Finally, questions have been raised about scoring procedures, test-retest reliability, the correlational nature of many of the studies on interpersonal problem solving, use of known groups in discriminant function analyses, and the choice of criterion variables in validity studies (Butler & Meichenbaum, 1981).

Other Measures of Problem Solving

The Purdue Elementary Problem-Solving Inventory (PEPSI) was designed to assess problem-solving skills in disadvantaged elementary school children (Feldhusen & Houtz, 1975). Items were developed to represent twelve component skills that may underlie efficient problem solving. These skills are: (1) sensing a problem exists; (2) defining problems; (3) clarifying goals; (4) asking questions; (5) guessing causes; (6) judging if more information is needed; (7) noticing relevant details; (8) using familiar objects in unfamiliar ways; (9) seeing implications; (10) solving single solution problems; (11) solving multiple solution problems; and (12) verifying solutions. The test consists of forty-nine items showing experiences of inner-city children between grades two and six. Each item is presented with an accompanying slide and audiotape to minimize the academic skills required to take the test. Responses to the items are provided in a multiple-choice format.

Little research has actually been conducted with the measure. Feldhusen, Houtz, and Ringenbach (1972), reported a KR-20 reliability coefficient of .79 but no test-retest reliability. The relation of this measure to any behavioral index of adjustment is unknown at present.

Overall, despite a format that appears useful with elementary school-age children, insufficient research has been conducted with the PEPSI to suggest that it may be a valuable measure. Its sensitivity to behavior change has not been investigated.

Spivack *et al.* (1976) have developed the What Happens Next Game (WHNG) to assess consequential thinking in young children and adults. In children, the measure presents two interpersonal situations using a format identical to the PIPS (grabbing a toy from a peer and taking something from an adult without asking). Inquiry is made to elicit responses to the question. "What might happen next in the story?" Responses are scored for number of consequences identified in the stories. Results of a study reported by Spivack *et al.* (1976) found significant changes pre- and posttreatment on the WHNG after children were given training in consequential thinking.

A few researchers have tried to respond to the consistent criticism of all problem-solving measures. For example, McClure, Chinsky, and Larsen (1978) developed the Friendship Club Interaction measure. This measure involved children in a contest with specific rules: (1) all six team members must agree on the best answer to the question; (2) all six members must help answer the question; and (3) all six members must be club officers. Embedded in the contest were additional interpersonal problems: (4) there are only five chairs for six subjects; (5) there are only five officer cards for six subjects; and (6) they must distribute officer titles. Responses were scored for enumeration of solutions and the effectiveness of those solutions. Results of their study found that children receiving problem-solving training showed significantly higher FCI scores than nontreatment controls.

Summary and Conclusions

There appears to be little question that effective problem solving and successful emotional adjustment are related. Unfortunately, many of the assessment methodologies that have been developed to evaluate the results of training problem solving have questionable psychometric characteristics. Given the analogue nature of these measures, it is surprising how few studies have attempted to examine the relation between results on the analogue assessment and the direct observation of interpersonal problem solving. Based on the research involving social skills assessment, there are probably, at best, only marginal relations between the analogue and an in vivo measure. Indeed, Butler and Meichenbaum (1981) suggest that the research perspective in assessing problem solving should be focused on the observable behavior of individuals and not their verbal reports. They suggest that researchers concentrate efforts on examining the problem-solving behavior of *competent* individuals to provide data on the behaviors that differentiate competent from incompetent problem solvers.

One difficulty with the work of Spivack and his colleagues is the tendency to view problem-solving skills as discrete and autonomous cognitive abilities that mediate behavior. Other researchers have concentrated their efforts on examining the degree to which an individual is knowledgeable of the variables that affect efficient use of problem-solving skills (e.g., Flavell & Wellman, 1977; Meichenbaum & Asarnow, 1979; Sternberg, 1979). An investigation of these metacognitive variables suggests that one may need not to train specific skills but to increase the confidence or perceived ability to solve interpersonal problems. The work of Bandura in self-efficacy (Bandura, 1977) is an excellent example of how such metacognitive variables may influence actual performance.

COGNITIVE PROCESSES

Closely related to interpersonal problem solving are a number of other cognitive processes that may have underlying relations to observed child behavior. In the assessment of children's behavior, for example, it may be important to understand how a child interprets reward. Indeed, a child's perception and interpretation of contingencies may be determining factors in behavior change. Likewise, treatment programs such as self-instruction training (Meichenbaum & Goodman, 1971), or stress-inoculation training (Meichenbaum, 1985), are designed to alter cognitions. This requires the development of measures to assess cognitive change. Similar to other measures discussed in this chapter, only the outcome of cognitive change is observable. As such, analogue assessment is used exclusively in the evaluation of cognitive processes.

Social Cognition

An extensive literature has emerged in developing an understanding of what children actually know about social and interpersonal situations and how they come to know it. Included within the processes of social cognition are matching affective states, imitating motor behavior, making inferences about others from available cues, and role-taking or perspective-taking (Selman, 1976). Of these skills, there has been a substantial development of measures designed to assess role-taking in particular, and social understanding in general. Readers interested in additional approaches to social cognition should consult sources such as Kohlberg, (1958), Flavell, Botkin, Fry, Wright, and Jarvis (1968), Garvey and Hogan (1973), and Chandler, Greenspan, and Barenboim (1973).

The Chandler Bystander Cartoons (Chandler, 1973) measure requires a child to tell a series of stories based on a cartoon sequence. During the initial story, the child is instructed to pay attention to what the main character is thinking and feeling in the story. After the initial story, the child is asked to retell the story from the point of view of a bystander who arrives later in the story and is unaware of what happened in the story's beginning. The child's responses are scored based on the degree of information reported in the bystander's story that was only available from the child's original story.

Limited data have been reported on the psychometric properties of the measure. Interrater reliabilities have been reported between .78 and .96, with test-retest correlations (2 to 4 weeks) of .80 (Kurdek, 1977). Inconsistent results have been reported examining the interrelationships of this measure with other role-taking tests. The measure does appear sensitive to training effects, as reported in a series of studies (e.g., Chandler, 1973; Chandler *et al.*, 1974).

Kendall, Pellegrini, and Urbain (1981) note that the failure of the measure to have concurrent validity with other role-taking measures suggests that the Bystander Cartoons may assess only a restricted range of perspective-taking abilities. In particular, the format of the measure suggests that it may be vulnerable to ceiling and floor effects since a child can attain perfectly correct or incorrect responses if he or she realizes that the bystander is actually unaware of what has happened in the story.

The Feffer Role-taking Task (RTT) (Feffer, 1959) measure presents a series of pictures similar to the Thematic Apperception Test depicting interpersonal situations. After the child tells an initial story about the picture, he or she is requested to retell the story from the point of view of each character. Responses are scored based on the degree that the child's story remains consistent and both perspectives (initial and modified) are integrated.

Interrater reliabilities on the measure are reported as between .80 and .90 (e.g., Chaplin & Keller, 1974; Feffer, 1959). Test-retest correlations were reported as .60 by Kurdek (1978). Kendall *et al.*, (1981) note that few studies have investigated performance of the RTT with clinical populations and training studies demonstrating any sensitivity of the RTT to intervention strategies are lacking.

Borke's Interpersonal Awareness Measure, Borke (1971, 1973) developed a measure of interpersonal awareness, rather than perspective-taking. First, the child's ability to discriminate between emotional states is established by showing children a series of pictures. The child is then told a story in which the main character engages in behavior likely to arouse a particular emotion (i.e., eating a favorite snack, getting lost in the woods at night). After selecting the picture showing best how the child in the story feels, a series of eight stories involving peer interaction are presented. The child is asked to identify the feeling of the character in response to specific actions (i.e., sharing cards, pushing him off a bike). Responses are scored simply as correct or incorrect against a preestablished criterion.

Borke (1971, 1973) reported that the task can be performed by three-year-olds. By four and one-half to five years old, most children master the task. Kendall *et al.*, (1981) reported that, although Borke's measure may provide some indication of developing abilities in identifying affect in preschool children, its relationship to behavior is unclear.

The Affective Situations Test (AST) was developed by Feshbach and Feshbach (1969) and attempts to measure more complex skills than identifying emotions alone. In this measure, the child is presented with a series of slides depicting elementary school children in one of four different affect arousing situations (happiness, sadness, fear, and anger). After each slide sequence, the child is asked, "How do you feel?" Responses are scored as empathic if there is a match between the child's affective state and the affect described in the picture.

Studies investigating this measure have reported that identifying the affect of the stimulus character may not be related to identifying one's own affective state (Feshbach & Roe, 1968). Despite these findings, Kendall *et al.* (1981) point out that there is a need for measures that assess more realistically affective states. They note that "it is difficult to comprehend why a mature ten-year-old would feel sad along with a cartoon character who loses a toy and even more difficult to accept such a response, should it occur, as mature empathy" (p. 237).

Selman's Measure of Interpersonal Awareness (IA), Selman (1980) developed an open-ended format, presented as a semistructured interview designed to assess general interpersonal awareness in children. An interpersonal dilemma is presented with standard inquiry about individuals (e.g., how do people get to be the way they are, how do people change), peer groups (e.g., how are peer groups formed), and conceptions about peer group relations (e.g., what makes a cohesive group). Each response is scored by comparing them with examples of reasoning at five hypothetical stages of development.

Data suggest that Selman's IA measure relates broadly to behavioral adjustment. Kendall *et al.* (1981) report that studies with the measure have found that clinic children show significant deficits in interpersonal awareness in relation to matched controls. In comparison with teacher ratings, the IA was found to have no relations to problem behavior, but consistent and positive relationships to behavioral competence. Kendall *et al.* (1981) point out that the measure may be somewhat biased toward the use of the probing interview and that may tend to inflate what children actually do when confronted with real-life problems.

Children's Attributions

Although there has been substantial research on adult attributional style (e.g., Metalsky & Abramson, 1981), there have been few studies on attributional styles of children. Yet, the degree to which a child attributes their behavior to luck, fate, or personal competence may play a significant role in the child's ability to change.

Perhaps one of the most frequently researched attributional styles is Rotter's (1966) locus of control. According to Rotter (1966), an individual can be distributed along a continuum according to the degree to which they view environmental events as under their control. Those who tend to have an external locus of control attribute behavioral effort to forces outside their control. In contrast, those with an internal locus of control tend to view their behavior as the result of their own personal competence and skills.

For school-age children, the Nowicki-Strickland Internal-External Scale for Children (Nowicki & Strickland, 1973) is the most frequently employed. The scale is designed to measure locus of control in a generalized fashion and not specific to any one situation. The measure is completed as a self-report with children responding Yes or No to each item. Test-retest reliabilities reported for the scale range from .63 to .71, with internal consistency ranging from .63 to .81 (Nowicki & Strickland, 1973).

Measures used to assess attributional styles other than locus of control have been developed along the same methodological format but have not had the same research development as the Nowicki-Strickland. Typically, investigators develop a series of vignettes used to tap certain attributional styles that they are examining. Often, these measures lack any psychometric characteristics and results of studies cannot easily be compared. Indeed, Kendall *et al.*, (1981) report that there really is no one attributional test.

Problem-Solving Style

Another type of cognitive process that affects children's behavior is their approach to solving nonsocial problems. Most often, the process assessed is the impulsive-reflective dimension (Kagan, 1966).

The matching Familiar Figures Test (MFF), developed by Kagan (1966) to assess cognitive tempo, presents a child with twelve match-to-sample items that require difficult discriminations. The child's latency to the first response and total response errors are recorded. Children whose scores are above the median error score and below the median latency score are identified as impulsive (too fast and inaccurate).

Test-retest data reported by Messer (1976) range from .58 to .96 for latencies and .34 to .80 for errors. Norms have been developed and reported by (Salkind, 1979). Although some studies show relations of conceptual tempo to behavioral correlates, the literature is problematic and it is unclear to what degree the MFF is related to adjustment (e.g., Block, Block, & Harrington, 1974, 1975). Kendall *et al.,* (1981) state that the MFF has some major problems both methodological and conceptual. However, the MFF has shown to be sensitive as an outcome measure in a number of intervention programs (e.g., Kendall & Finch, 1976, 1978).

Although originally developed to measure intelligence (Porteus, 1933), the Porteus Maze Test has been employed as a measure of the cognitive processes of planning ability, foresight, and impulsivity. Riddle and Roberts (1974, 1977) reported reliabilities (test-retest, alternate form) from .43 to .97. Despite some studies to the contrary, Riddle and Roberts (1977) reported that the Porteus does not validly discriminate between delinquent and nondelinquent groups. The test has been used to evaluate behavioral treatment for impulsive children with some success (e.g., Douglas, Parry, Marton, & Garson, 1976; Kendall & Wilcox, 1980).

GENERAL CONCLUSIONS

Regardless of the type of problem being assessed, it is clear that analogue measures have a consistent set of problems that limit their interpretation. Despite many of the measures having adequate internal validity, almost all measures suffer from limited external validity. Few of the analogue measures described have been compared with behavior as it occurs in the natural setting. Those studies that have made such comparisons have often found only moderate or slight relations between performance on the analogue assessment and the direct observation of behavior. Given that the reason for using the analogue assessment device was to create a simulation of the natural environment, failure to find strong relations between analogue and direct observation is most problematic.

Another important problem with analogue measures relates to the types of behaviors being assessed with these measures. Very often, the behavior assessed itself is not observable. This is particularly true of assessment strategies evaluating cognitive processes and problem solving. Given that we cannot directly observe these processes, we must rely on verbal self-report as our modality of assessment. Unfortunately, there is a potential bias of self-report making such assessment methods suspect (Mash & Terdal, 1981).

Some analogue assessment also suffers from a lack of standardization.

Procedures used across studies may vary, making comparison of results across investigations very difficult (e.g., for an assessment using BATs). Further, even when similar methods of presenting items are used (such as in role-play tests), the content of the items may differ.

Besides the differing content of analogue measures assessing similar behavior, the responses chosen for observation may also vary. Indeed, the assessment of social skills, for example, may involve the evaluation of many components that may not be identical across studies.

Related to this problem is the social validity of the behavior chosen for observation. One may raise serious questions about how the specific social skills components or interpersonal problem-solving styles were chosen for assessment.

An additional problem with analogue assessment is the potential influence of demand upon the performance of children and adolescents. It is very possible that the responses children make are more a reflection of what they *think* the experimenter wants them to do than it is indicative of their actual behavior. Further, their responses may often be performance of what they think they *should* do rather than what they really do in the situation presented.

Finally, a problem facing the clinician in using an analogue assessment measure is accessibility to these instruments. Many measures are unpublished and may or may not be obtainable from the author or secondary sources.

Despite the serious limitations of analogue assessment measures, the continued use of such measures in combination with more direct assessment measures can be recommended. Many of the behaviors assessed through analogue assessment strategies cannot be readily evaluated using direct observation. In particular, the assessment of cognitive processes can only be obtained using analogue assessment. Providing an assessment from a multimodal perspective remains critical to effective behavioral assessment and assessment of the cognitive modality is one important component of the evaluation process.

Future research on analogue assessment strategies needs to focus upon ways to make the assessment methods more closely relate to actual behavior in natural settings. The degree to which this objective can be accomplished will indicate the future usefulness of analogue assessment in the evaluation of emotional and behavior problems of children and adolescents.

References

Bandura, A. (1977). Self-efficacy: Toward a unifying theory of behavioral change. *Psychological Review, 84*, 191–215.

Barrios, B. A., Hartmann, D. P., & Shigetomi, C. (1981). Fears and anxieties in children. In E. J. Mash & L. G. Terdal (Eds.), *Behavioral assessment of childhood disorders* (pp. 259–304). New York: Guilford Press.

Barrios, B. A., & Shigetomi, C. C. (1985). Assessment of children's fears: A critical review. In T. R. Kratochwill (Ed.), *Advances in school psychology* (Vol. IV, pp. 80–132). Hillsdale, N.J.: Lawrence Erlbaum Associates.

Beck, S., Forehand, R., Neeper, R., & Baskin, C. H. (1982). A comparison of two analogue strategies for assessing children's social skills. *Journal of Consulting and Clinical Psychology, 50,* 596–597.

Bellack, A. S. (1979). A critical appraisal of strategies for assessing social skill. *Behavioral Assessment, 1,* 157–176.

Bellack, A. S., Hersen, M., & Lamparski, D. (1979). Role-play tests for assessing social skills. Are they valid? Are they useful? *Journal of Consulting and Clinical Psychology, 47,* 335–342.

Bellack, A. S., Hersen, M., & Turner, S. M. (1978). Role-play for assessing social skills: Are they valid? *Behavior Therapy, 9,* 448–461.

Bernstein, D. A., & Nietzel, M. T. (1973). Procedural variations in behavioral avoidance tests. *Journal of Consulting and Clinical Psychology, 41,* 164–174.

Block, J., Block, J. H., & Harrington, D. M. (1974). Some misgivings about the Matching Familiar Figures Test as a measure of reflection-impulsivity. *Developmental Psychology, 10,* 611–632.

Block, J., Block, J. H., & Harrington, D. M. (1975). Comment on the Kagan-Messer reply. *Developmental Psychology, 11,* 249–252.

Borke, H. (1971). Interpersonal perception of young children: Egocentrism or empathy? *Developmental Psychology, 5,* 263–269.

Borke, H. (1973). The development of empathy in Chinese and American children between three and six years of age: A cross-cultural study. *Developmental Psychology, 9,* 102–108.

Bornstein, M. R., Bellack, A. S., & Hersen, M. (1977). Social-skills training for unassertive children: A multiple-baseline analysis. *Journal of Applied Behavior Analysis, 10,* 183–195.

Butler, L., & Meichenbaum, D. (1981). The assessment of interpersonal problem-solving skills. In P. C. Kendall & S. D. Hollon (Eds.), *Assessment strategies for cognitive-behavioral interventions* (pp. 197–225). New York: Academic Press.

Cartledge, G., & Milburn, J. F. (1986). *Teaching social skills to children* (2d ed.). Elmsford, N.Y.: Pergamon Press.

Chandler, M. (1973). Egocentrism and antisocial behavior: The assessment and training of social perspective-taking skills. *Developmental Psychology, 9,* 326–332.

Chandler, M., Greenspan, S., & Barenboim. C. (1974). Judgments of intentionality in response to videotaped and verbally presented moral dilemmas: The medium is the message. *Child Development, 43,* 315–320.

Chaplin, M. V., & Keller, H. R. (1974). Decentering and social interaction. *Journal of Genetic Psychology, 124,* 269–275.

Clark, L., Gresham, F. M., & Elliott, S. N. (1985). Development and validation of a social skills assessment measure: The TROSS-C. *Journal of Psychoeducational Assessment, 4,* 347–356.

Cone, J. D. (1978). The behavioral assessment grid (BAG): A conceptual framework and taxonomy. *Behavior Therapy, 8,* 411–426.

Cowen, E. L. (1982). Primary prevention research: Barriers, needs, and opportunities. *Journal of Primary Prevention, 2,* 131–137.

Day, D. E., & Roberts, M. W. (1983). An analysis of the physical punishment component of a parent training program. *Journal of Abnormal Child Psychology, 11,* 141–152.

Deluty, R. H. (1979). Children's Action Tendency Scale: A self-report measure of aggressiveness, assertiveness, and submissiveness in children. *Journal of Consulting and Clinical Psychology, 47,* 1061–1071.

Deluty, R. H. (1984). Behavioral validation of the Children's Action Tendency Scale. *Journal of Behavioral Assessment, 6,* 115–130.

Douglas, V. I., Parry, P., Marton, P., & Garson, C. (1976). Assessment of a cognitive training program for hyperactive children. *Journal of Abnormal Child Psychology. 4,* 389–410.

Eisler, R. M., Miller, P. M., & Hersen, M. (1973). Components of assertive behavior. *Journal of Clinical Psychology, 29,* 295–299.

Esveldt-Dawson, K., Wisner, K. L., Unis, A. S., Matson, J. L., & Kazdin, A. E. (1982). Treatment of phobias in a hospitalized child. *Journal of Behavior Therapy and Experimental Psychiatry, 13,* 77–83.

Evans, P. D., & Harmon, G. (1981). Children's self-initiated approach to spiders. *Behaviour Research and Therapy, 19,* 543–546.

Feffer, M. (1959). The cognitive implications of role taking behavior. *Journal of Personality, 27,* 152–168.

Feldhusen, J., & Houtz, J. (1975). Problem solving and the concrete-abstract dimension. *Gifted Child Quarterly, 19,* 122–129.

Feldhusen, J., Houtz, J., & Ringenbach, S. (1972). The Purdue Elementary Problem-Solving Inventory. *Psychological Reports, 3,* 891–901.

Feshbach, N., & Feshbach, S. (1969). The relationship between empathy and aggression in two age groups. *Developmental Psychology, 1,* 102–107.

Feshbach, N., & Roe, K. (1968). Empathy in six- and seven-year-olds. *Child Development, 39,* 133–145.

Flavell, J., Botkin, P., Fry, C., Wright, J., & Jarvis, P. (1968). *The development of role-taking and communication skills in children.* New York: John Wiley & Sons.

Flavell, J. H., & Wellman, H. M. (1977). Metamemory. In R. V. Kail & J. W. Hagen (Eds.), *Perspectives on the development of memory and cognition* (pp. 3-33). Hillsdale, N.J.: Lawrence Erlbaum Associates.

Forehand, R. (1977). Child noncompliance to parental requests: Behavioral analysis and treatment. In M. Hersen, R. M. Miller, & P. M. Miller (Eds.), *Progress in behavior modification* (Vol. 5, pp. 111–147). New York: Academic Press.

Forehand, R., & King, H. E. (1977). Noncompliant children: Effects of parent training on behavior and attitude change. *Behavior Modification, 1,* 93–108.

Forehand, R. M., & McMahon, R. J. (1981). *Helping the noncompliant child: A clinician's guide to parent training.* New York: Guilford Press.

Gaffney, L. R., & McFall, R. M. (1981). A comparison of social skills in delinquent and nondelinquent adolescent girls using a behavioral role-playing inventory. *Journal of Consulting and Clinical Psychology, 49,* 959–967.

Garvey, C., & Hogan, R. (1973). Social speech and social interactions: Egocentrism revisited. *Child Development, 44,* 562–568.

Gelfand, D. M., & Hartmann, D. P. (1977). The prevention of childhood behavior disorders. In B. Lahey & A. E. Kazdin (Eds.), *Advances in child clinical psychology* (Vol. 1, pp. 362–395). New York: Plenum Press.

Glennon, B., & Weisz, J. R. (1978). An observational approach to the assessment of anxiety in young children. *Journal of Consulting and Clinical Psychology, 46,* 1246–1257.

Goldfried, M. R., & D'Zurilla, T. J. (1969). A behavioral-analytic model for assessing competence. In C. D. Speilberger (Ed.), *Current topics in clinical and community psychology,* (Vol. 1, pp. 151–166). New York: Academic Press.

Goldstein, A. P., Sprafkin, R. P., Gershaw, N. J., & Klein, P. (1980). *Skillstreaming the adolescent.* Champaign, Ill.: Research Press.

Gottman, J. M. (1977). Toward a definition of social isolation in children. *Child Development, 48,* 513–517.

Gottman, J. M., Gonso, J., & Rasmussen, B. (1975). Social interaction, social competence, and friendship in children. *Child Development, 46,* 709–718.

Green, K. D., Forehand, R., & McMahon, R. K. (1979). Parental manipulation of compliance and noncompliance in normal and deviant children. *Behavior Modification, 3,* 245–266.

Greenwood, C. R., Walker, H. M., Todd, N. M., & Hops, H. (1977). *Normative and descriptive analysis of preschool free play social interactions* (Report No. 26). Eugene, Oreg.: University of Oregon Press.

Gresham, F. M., Elliott, S. N., & Black, F. L. (1987a). Factor structure replication and bias investigation of the Teacher Rating of Social Skills. *Journal of School Psychology, 25,* 81–92.

Gresham, F. M., Elliott, S. N., & Black, F. L. (1987b). Teacher-rated social skills of mainstreamed mildly handicapped and nonhandicapped children. *School Psychology Review, 16,* 78–88.

Hazel, J. S., Bragg-Schumaker, J., Sherman, J. A., & Sheldon-Wildgen, J. (1981). *Asset: A social skills program for adolescents.* Champaign, Ill.: Research Press.

Hobbs, S. A., Walle, D. L., & Hammersly, G. A. (1984). Assessing chldren's social skills: Validation of the Behavioral Assertiveness Test for Children (BAT-C). *Journal of Behavioral Assessment, 6*, 29–35.

Hops, H., & Lewin, L. (1984). Peer sociometric forms. In T. H. Ollendick & M. Hersen (Eds.), *Child behavioral assessment: Principles and procedures* (pp. 124–147). Elmsford, N.Y.: Pergamon Press.

Hughes, J. N., & Hall, D. M. (1985). Performance of disturbed and nondisturbed boys on a role play test of social competence. *Behavioral Disorders, 11*, 24–29.

Hymel, S., Asher, S. R. (1977). *Assessment and training of isolated children's social skills.* Paper presented at the Biennial Meeting of the Society for Research in Child Development, New Orleans, Louisiana.

Jersild, A. T., & Holmes, F. N. (1935). Methods of overcoming children's fears. *Journal of Psychology, 1*, 75–104.

Kagan, J. (1966). Reflection-impulsivity: The generality and dynamics of conceptual tempo. *Journal of Educational Psychology, 71*, 17–24.

Kane, J. S., & Lawler, E. E. III. (1978). Methods of peer assessment. *Psychological Bulletin, 85*, 555–586.

Karoly, P. (1982). Cognitive assessment in behavioral medicine. *Clinical Psychology Review, 2*, 421–434.

Kazdin, A. E., Esveldt-Dawson, K., & Matson, J. L. (1983). The effects of instructional set on social skills performance among psychiatric inpatient children. *Behavior Therapy, 14*, 413–423.

Kelley, C. K. (1976). Play desensitization of fear of darkness in preschool children. *Behaviour Research and Therapy, 14*, 79–81.

Kendall, P. C., & Finch, A. J., Jr. (1976). A cognitive-behavioral treatment for impulse control. A case study, *Journal of Consulting and Clinical Psychology, 44*, 852–857.

Kendall, P. C., & Finch, A. J., Jr. (1978). A cognitive-behavioral treatment for impulsivity. A group comparison study. *Journal of Consulting and Clinical Psychology, 46*, 110–118.

Kendall, P. C., Pellegrini, D. S., & Urbain, E. S. (1981). Approaches to assessment for cognitive-behavioral interventions with children. In P. C. Kendall & S. C. Hollon (Eds.), *Assessment strategies for cognitive-behavioral interventions* (pp. 227–285). New York: Academic Press.

Kendall, P. C., & Wilcox, L. E. (1980). Cognitive-behavioral treatment for impulsivity: Concrete versus conceptual training with non-self controlled problem children. *Journal of Consulting and Clinical Psychology, 48*, 80–91.

Kohlberg, L. (1958). *The development of modes of moral thinking and choice in the years ten to sixteen.* Unpublished doctoral dissertation, University of Chicago.

Kurdek, L. A. (1977). Structural components and intellectual correlates of cognitive perspective taking in first–through fourth-grade children. *Child Development, 48*, 1503–1511.

LaGreca, A. M., & Santogrossi, D. A. (1980). Social skills training with elementary school students: A behavioral group approach. *Journal of Consulting and Clinical Psychology, 48*, 220–227.

Lapouse, R., & Monk, M. A. (1959). Fears and worries in a representative sample of children. *American Journal of Orthopsychiatry, 29*, 803–818.

MacFarlane, J. W., Allen, L., & Hozik, M. P. (1954). *A developmental study of the behavior problems of normal children between twenty-one months and fourteen years.* Berkeley: University of California Press.

Mash, E. J., & Terdal, L. G. (Eds.). (1981). *Behavioral assessment of childhood disorders.* New York: Guilford Press.

McCandless, B. R., & Marshall, H. R. (1957). A picture sociometric technique for preschool children and its relation to teacher judgments of friendship. *Child Development, 28*, 139–148.

McClure, L. F., Chinsky, J. M., & Larsen, S. W. (1978). Enhancing social problem-solving performance in an elementary school setting. *Journal of Educational Psychology, 70*, 504–513.

McNamara, J. R., & Blumen, C. A. (1982). Role-playing to assess social competence: Ecological validity considerations. *Behavior Modification, 6*, 519–549.

Meichenbaum, D. (1985). *Stress inoculation training.* Elmsford, N.Y.: Pergamon Press.

Meichenbaum, D., & Asarnow, J. (1979). Cognitive-behavior modification and metacognitive development: Implications for the classroom. In P. C. Kendall & S. C. Hollon (Eds.), *Cognitive-behavioral interventions: Theory, research, and procedures* (pp. 11–35). New York: Academic Press.

Meichenbaum, D., & Goodman, J. (1971). Training impulsive children to talk to themselves: A means of developing self-control. *Journal of Abnormal Psychology, 77*, 115–126.

Melamed, B. G. (1979). Behavioral approaches to fear in dental settings. In M. Hersen, R. Eisler, & P. M. Miller (Eds.), *Progress in behavior modification* (Vol. 7, pp. 171–203). New York: Academic Press.

Melamed, B. G., Hawes, R., Heiby, E., & Glick, J. (1975). The use of film modeling to reduce uncooperative behavior of children during dental treatment. *Journal of Dental Research, 53*, 797–801.

Messer, S. B. (1976). Reflection-impulsivity: A review. *Psychological Bulletin, 83*, 1026–1052.

Metalsky, G. I., & Abramson, L. Y. (1981). Attributional styles: Toward a framework for conceptualization and assessment. In P. C. Kendall & S. C. Hollon (Eds.), *Assessment strategies for cognitive-behavioral interventions* (pp. 13–58). New York: Academic Press.

Michelson, L., Andrasik, F., Vucelic, J., & Coleman, D. (1981). Temporal stability and internal reliability of measures of children's social skills. *Psychological Reports, 48*, 678.

Michelson, L., DiLorenzo, T., Calpin, J., & Ollendick, T. H. (1982). Situational determinants of the BAT-C. *Behavior Therapy, 13*, 724–734.

Michelson, L., Sugai, D. P., Wood, R. P., & Kazdin, A. E. (1983). *Social skills assessment and training with children: An empirically based handbook.* New York: Plenum Press.

Michelson, L., & Wood, R. (1982). Development and psychometric properties of the Children's Assertive Behavior Scale. *Journal of Behavioral Assessment, 4*, 3–14.

Milos, M. E., & Reiss, S. (1982). Effects of three play conditions on separation anxiety in young children. *Journal of Consulting and Clinical Psychology, 50*, 389–395.

Morris, R. J. (1976). *Behavior modification with children: A systematic guide.* Cambridge, Mass.: Winthrop.

Morris, R. J., & Kratochwill, T. R. (1983). *Treating children's fears and phobias: A behavioral approach.* Elmsford, N. Y.: Pergamon Press.

Murphy, C. M., & Bootzin, R. R. (1973). Active and passive participation in the contact desensitization of snake fear in children. *Behavior Therapy, 4*, 203–211.

Navas, M. M. (1971). Standardized scheduled desensitization: Some unstable results and an improved program. *Behaviour Research and Therapy, 9*, 35–38.

Nay, W. R. (1979). *Multimethod clinical assessment.* New York: Gardner.

Nelson, R. O., & Hayes, S. C. (1979). The nature of behavioral assessment: A commentary. *Journal of Applied Behavior Analysis, 12*, 491–500.

Nowicki, S., & Strickland, B. R. (1973). A locus of control scale for children. *Journal of Consulting and Clinical Psychology, 40*, 148–154.

Ollendick, T. H. (1983). Reliability and validity of the revised Fear Survey Schedule for Children (FSSC-R). *Behaviour Research and Therapy, 21*, 685–692.

Ollendick, T. H., Hart, K. J., & Francis, G. (1985). Social validation of the revised Behavioral Assertiveness Test for Children (BAT-CR). *Child & Family Behavior Therapy, 7*, 17–33.

Ollendick, T. H., Matson, J. L., & Helsel, W. J. (1985). Fears in children and adolescents: Normative data. *Behaviour Research and Therapy, 23*, 465–467.

Porteus, S. D. (1933). *The maze test and mental differences.* Vineland, N.J.: Smith.

Reardon, R. C., Hersen, M., Bellack, A. S., & Foley, J. M. (1979). Measuring social skill in grade school boys. *Journal of Behavioral Assessment, 1*, 87–105.

Riddle, M., & Roberts, A. H. (1974). *The Porteus Mazes: A critical evaluation.* Unpublished manuscript, Department of Psychiatry, University of Minnesota: Report number PR-74-3.

Riddle, M., & Roberts, A. H. (1977). Delinquency, delay of gratification recidivism, and the Porteus Maze Tests. *Psychological Bulletin, 84*, 417–425.

Ritter, B. (1968). The group treatment of children's snake phobias using vicarious and contact desensitization procedures. *Behaviour Research and Therapy, 6*, 1–6.

Roberts, M. W. (1982). The effects of warned versus unwarned time-out procedures on child noncompliance. *Child & Family Behavior Therapy, 4*, 37–53.

Roberts, M. W. (1984a). An attempt to reduce time-out resistance in young children. *Behavior Therapy, 15*, 210–216.

Roberts, M. W. (1984b). Resistance to time-out: Some normative data. *Behavioral Assessment, 4,* 237–246.

Roberts, M. W. (in press). The compliance test. In M. Hersen & A. S. Bellack (Eds.), *The dictionary of behavioral assessment,* New York: Pergamon .

Roberts, M. W., Hatzenbuehler, L. C., & Bean, A. W. (1981). The effects of differential attention and time-out on child noncompliance. *Behavior Therapy, 12,* 93–99.

Rotter, J. B. (1966). Generalized expectancies for internal versus external control of reinforcement. *Psychological Monographs, 30* (Whole No. 1).

Salkind, N. J. (1979). *The development of norms for the Matching Familiar Figures test.* Manuscript available from the author, Bailey Hall, University of Kansas, Lawrence, Kans. 66045.

Scherer, M. W., & Nakamura, C. Y. (1968). A Fear Survey Schedule for Children (FSS-FC): A factor analytic comparison with manifest anxiety (CMAS). *Behaviour Research and Therapy, 6,* 173–182.

Selman, R. L. (1976). The development of social-cognitive understanding. In T. Lickona (Ed.), *Moral development and behavior: Theory, research, and social issues.* New York: Holt, Rinehart, & Winston.

Selman, R. L. (1980). *The growth of interpersonal understanding: Development and clinical analyses.* New York: Academic Press.

Shapiro, E. S. (1987). *Behavioral assessment in school psychology.* Hillsdale, N.J.: Lawrence Erlbaum Associates.

Shapiro, E. S., Gilbert, D., Friedman, J., & Steiner, S. (1985). *Concurrent validity of role-play and contrived tests in assessing social skills in disruptive adolescents.* Paper presented at the annual meeting of the Association for the Advancement of Behavior Therapy, November, at Houston, Texas.

Shapiro, E. S., Stover, J. E., & Ifkovits, G. A. (1983). *Predictive and concurrent validity of role-play and naturalistic assessment of social skills in kindergarten children.* Paper presented at the annual meeting of the Association for the Advancement of Behavior Therapy, November, at Washington, D.C.

Singleton, L. C., & Asher, S. R. (1977). Peer preferences and social interaction among third-grade children in an integrated school district. *Journal of Educational Psychology, 69,* 330–336.

Spivack, G., Platt, J., & Shure, M. B. (1976). *The problem-solving approach to adjustment.* San Francisco: Jossey-Bass.

Spivack, G., & Shure, M. B. (1974). *Social adjustment of young children.* San Francisco: Jossey-Bass.

Sternberg, R. J. (1979). *New views on IQ's: A silent revolution of the 70's* (Technical report no. 17). Office of Naval Research, Arlington, Va.

Ultee, C. A., Griffioen, D., & Schellekens, J. (1982). The reduction of anxiety in children: A comparison of the effects of 'systematic desensitization in vivo'. *Behaviour Research and Therapy, 20,* 61–67.

Van Hasselt, V. B., Hersen, M., & Bellack, A. S. (1981). The validity of role-play tests for assessing social skills in children. *Behavior Therapy, 12,* 202–216.

Van Hasselt, V. B., Hersen, M., Bellack, A. S., Rosenblum, N. D., & Lamparski, D. (1979). Tripartite assessment of the effects of systematic desensitization in a multi-phobic child: An experimental analysis. *Journal of Behavior Therapy and Experimental Psychiatry, 10,* 51–55.

Van Hasselt, V. B., Hersen, M., & Kazdin, A. E. (1985). Assessment of social skills in visually handicapped adolescents. *Behaviour Research and Therapy, 23,* 53–63.

Van Hasselt, V. B., Hersen, M., Whitehill, M. B., & Bellack, A. S. (1979). Social skill assessment and training for children: An evaluative review. *Behaviour Research and Therapy, 17,* 413–437.

Walk, R. D. (1956). Self-ratings of fear in a fear-invoking situation. *Journal of Abnormal and Social Psychology, 52,* 171–178.

Williamson, D. A., Moody, S. C., Granberry, S. W., Lethermon, V. R., & Blouin, D. C. (1983). Criterion-related validity of a role-play social skills test for children. *Behavior Therapy, 14,* 466–481.

Wood, R., Michelson, L., & Flynn, J. (1978). *Assessment of assertive behavior in elementary school children.* Paper presented at the annual meeting of the Association for Advancement of Behavior Therapy, November, at Chicago, Ill.

CHAPTER 9

Analogue Assessment: Traditional Personality Assessment Measures in Behavioral Assessment

H. THOMPSON PROUT
State University of New York–Albany

SUSAN M. FERBER
Schalmont (N.Y.) Central Schools

INTRODUCTION

The assessment of children's and adolescents' emotional and behavioral problems remains a task that varies a great deal with the orientation of the professional. Assessment can range from use of projective techniques with a focus on "unconscious" variables that supposedly manifest in behavior problems, to approaches that emphasize direct observation (e.g., see Chapter 3 of this volume) of behaviors considered excessive, deficient, or inappropriate for the situation. Needless to say, these different approaches produce quite different descriptions of individuals, are apt to yield different diagnostic classifications, and are likely to result in different intervention or treatment plans.

The purpose of this chapter is to describe and discuss issues related to the use of traditional personality assessment measures of children's and adolescents' emotional and behavioral functioning in the context of conducting a behavioral assessment. Specifically, this chapter focuses on the role of projective techniques within a behavioral assessment framework. It is proposed that certain projective techniques can be used within this framework and can help pinpoint or target areas for intervention. It must be emphasized that the role of projectives is viewed in a much more limited manner than it would be in a more traditional view of assessment. A discussion on general issues related to the use of projectives is followed by an examination of several specific techniques and their utility in behavioral assessment. Several brief case examples support this chapter's viewpoint.

ANALOGUE METHODS: A DEFINITION

An analogue method of assessment is an indirect measure of how an individual might behave in a real-life situation; that is, it is a measure that assesses behavior in a simulated or hypothetical situation or task to predict the individual's behavior in the real environment. Thus, an analogue measure always involves a degree of inference—actual behavior in the natural environment is not being assessed. The assessor who uses analogue measures assumes that there is some similarity between the behavior and responses in the analogue situation and how the person behaves and responds in the environment.

McFall (1977) has described four types of analogue methods that have been used by psychologists in clinical research on assessment and treatment. The first is the *subject* analogue, which is typified by its use of nonclinical populations to study the effectiveness of various treatment strategies. A counseling outcome study using nonreferred high school students is an example of the subject analogue procedure. It is hypothesized that the treatment effectiveness shown with non-referred students will have relevance for referred students. The second is the *treatment* analogue in which a more complex intervention strategy is done in a brief and simplified manner to help understand the components of the total intervention process. This is also often done within a subject analogue framework. An example of a treatment analogue is the study of the effects of brief relaxation exercises in isolation from a total anxiety reduction intervention. The third type of analogue is the *situational* analogue, in which naturalistic behaviors are evaluated under more controlled or structured conditions. Role-playing certain social situations in a group counseling format is a situational analogue. Finally, there is the *response* analogue, in which a response to a stimulus is viewed as equivalent to responses in the environment. Response analogues are typified by the range of testing instruments traditionally employed by psychologists. An emotional response to a projective stimulus is viewed as analogous to the response to the real-life situation.

This chapter focuses on the response or "testing" types of analogues. These analogue procedures can be broken down further in terms of the type of stimulus and the type of expected response. This distinction might be useful in selecting the most appropriate assessment procedure to use with a specific child or adolescent. For example, a verbal child might respond well to techniques that require verbal responses (e.g., a thematic technique). Conversely, a child who is less verbal might respond better to a drawing technique that requires minimal verbal description. The following stimulus/response combinations represent the various analogue assessment procedures available.

1. Visual stimulus and verbal response. The child or adolescent is presented some type of visual stimulus that requires asking the child to describe what he or she sees, to respond to a series of specific questions, or to describe how they would respond to the situation in the stimulus situation. Techniques in this area include inkblot procedures (e.g., Rorschach and Holtzman), thematic tests (Thematic Apperception Test, Children's Apperception Test, Roberts Apperception Test, School Apperception Test, Tasks of Emotional Development), and use of videotaped situations with verbal responses.

2. Verbal stimulus and verbal response. The child or adolescent is given either an oral or written stimulus with an oral or written response. Older children and those with adequate writing abilities will usually respond better to tasks that require a written response. Techniques in this area include the mutual storytelling techniques, the Three Wishes technique, and a variety of incomplete sentence techniques. The incomplete sentence approaches can be administered in either oral or written format.

3. Verbal stimulus and motoric response. The child or adolescent is given the task of drawing something specified by the assessor. Draw-a-Man, self-drawings, House-Tree-Person, and family drawings are examples of this type of technique. A slight variation that actually is a verbal stimulus, and motoric and verbal response technique are Kinetic Drawings—family and school—that require both production of a drawing and verbal labeling of the drawing with response to inquiry.

4. Verbal, behavioral, and visual stimulus, and behavioral response. These situations usually involve some type of verbal description of a situation with situational props (i.e., visual stimuli), while others engage in behavior appropriate to the situation described verbally. The behavioral response also includes verbal behavior. The wide variety of role-playing techniques typify this area. A group counseling situation in which the group leader describes a classroom situation, the leader role-plays the teacher while other group members play student roles, and the counseling room is set up like a classroom is an example of this technique. The child who is the focus of the assessment would act out how he or she would respond in the situation and to the behavior of the others.

Since this entire volume is devoted to the topic of assessment, which has traditionally emphasized the direct assessment of behavior, the question of the relevance of inferential analogue methods for behavioral assessment is obvious. In other words, why use indirect methods of assessment? McFall (1977) has addressed this issue by analyzing the research on this subject. Increased experimental control, avoidance of certain ethical problems, systematic examination of clinical techniques, and greater convenience, economy, and efficiency are advantages of analogue research. The greatest disadvantage is the degree to which research findings interface with real-life situations. Do analogue research findings generalize to clinical practice? The analogue situation is invariably contrived and artificial to some extent.

In a similar way, the clinical use of analogues has advantages and disadvantages. The obvious disadvantage involves predicting behavior in the natural environment. Does a response to a thematic picture of a child interacting with his or her parents correspond to the child's actual response in a similar, real-life situation? We feel that the analogue assessment methods can offer several advantages in a comprehensive, multifaceted approach. Some of the reasons for using analogue methods include:

1. Many of the questions that could be answered using analogue measures could also be answered through direct interview of self-report techniques (see chapters by Witt *et al.*, and Edelbrock, both this volume) with a child or adolescent. However, this approach is not without problems (Palmer, 1970) and some children may deny or be reluctant to discuss certain topics when queried directly. The indirect analogue approach may be less threatening and the child may reveal information that he or she would not discuss during direct questioning. For example, a child may deny or refuse to discuss problems at home, yet may provide information about family functioning through responses to family-oriented thematics or a family drawing.
2. The analogue approach uses a variety of modalities for data collection. Thus, this approach may be useful for certain types of children. As mentioned above, the less verbal child may respond well to a behavioral or drawing response format.
3. The analogue approach allows an assessment of the environment not always accessible to the assessor. In some cases, parental and family issues may be difficult or impossible to assess directly. The use of thematic tests and family drawings still allow some assessment of family issues and problems.
4. Similarly, an analogue assessment can be cost-effective because it allows an assessment of many different environments within a relatively short time span. For example, several thematic procedures and incomplete sentence procedures address issues related to parents, siblings, peers, and school within the same format. Techniques requiring only a few minutes can address a multitude of environmental problems and situations.
5. Finally, and perhaps most importantly, analogue measures can produce information that provides the bases of hypotheses to be assessed in more depth and through more direct means. For example, analogue assessment indicating peer problems might be followed by a structured observation focusing on peer interactions. Thus, analogue assessment can help plan other types of assessment.

A PERSPECTIVE ON ASSESSMENT

The views on analogue assessment in this chapter are offered within a broader perspective of the purposes and functions of assessment. These views include a hypothesis testing model of personality and behavioral assessment, a situationally based view of children's and adolescents' problems, adherence to a multimodal assessment model, use of several assessment techniques (i.e., multimethod), and the need to tie assessment findings to intervention.

The hypothesis testing model of assessment can be viewed as an inferential process that occurs throughout assessment and into the conducting of intervention programs. Any assessment procedure that uses inference should be viewed as leading to hypotheses, not absolute diagnoses. In fact, virtually all types of psychological and behavioral assessment involve some level of inference. Goldman, Stein, and Guerry (1983) have stated: "The entire diagnostic process is concerned with hypothesis formation, hypothesis testing, and the integration of information which leads to further hypothesis formation" (p. 121). The analogue approach, in particular, may be most valuable in this latter function of leading to further hypothesis formation. This hypothesis testing model ultimately leads to a degree of acceptance for some hypotheses, and the rejection of others. The analogue approach should not be used as the primary base for this type of decision—it would be unwise to reject a hypothesis based on a child's or adolescent's responses to projective.

The situational or psychosituational (Bersoff & Grieger, 1971) view of personality has been popularized by Mischel (1968, 1973) in his reconceptualization of a social learning view of personality. This view emphasizes a link between behavior and environment that states that behavior should be assessed under the conditions in which it occurs. The context of the behavior is seen as more important than personality traits or underlying psychological drives or internal states. In the assessment of children, this most often involves an examination of behavior across a variety of settings—the family and school context in particular.

The multimodal view of assessment and intervention is the approach developed by Lazarus (1976) and applied with children by Keat (1979). This model views psychological problems within seven interactive modalities that are assessed or evaluated in order to pinpoint the components of a problem and to target the most efficacious point at which to intervene. Lazarus (1976) has called this model the "BASIC ID.":

Behavior—overt behavior of the person
Affective—feelings, emotion
Sensation—motor, visual, sensory reactions
Imagery—imagination, fantasy
Cognition—thoughts

Interpersonal—relationships with others
Drugs-Diet—health, nutrition, medical factors

This model implies that all these modalities could potentially be evaluated in an assessment of an emotional problem. For example, anxiety problems could have behavioral (withdrawal), affective (fear), sensation (sweating), imagery (nightmares), cognitive (irrational beliefs), interpersonal (family problems), and diet (too much caffeine) components. For some of these modalities, direct methods of assessment may not yield enough information to understand the problem fully. Projective stimuli may elicit information useful in developing hypotheses about irrational thought patterns or affective responses. In a similar vein to Lazarus's approach, a multimethod approach (Gresham & Elliott, 1984; Nay, 1979; Ollendick & Hersen, 1984) to assessment is advocated. This view also emphasizes comprehensive behavioral assessment using multiple methods to assess a problem.

The final perspective on assessment involves the need to tie the assessment of emotional problems to the development of intervention or treatment plans. The notion that the primary purpose of emotional assessment is to label or diagnose is rejected—diagnostic labels are only useful if they lead to more efficacious treatment and intervention. Palmer's (1970) views are consistent with this perspective: "the essential purpose of a psychological assessment is to determine the nature and extent of the disturbance in order to select and formulate the mode(s) of behavioral change" (p. 5).

PROJECTIVE TECHNIQUES

Projective techniques have a long and controversial history in professional psychology. Some professionals rely heavily on projective assessment while some, particularly behaviorists, view projectives as worthless, and, in many cases, harmful in the types of conclusions that are drawn from projective data. Undoubtedly, many practitioners fall between these two extreme positions. In fact, in a recent survey of school psychologists and trainers (Prout, 1983), 73% of the practitioner respondents indicated that they use projective techniques in their assessments of children referred with concerns about social-emotional functioning. Projective techniques were ranked third behind behavioral observation and clinical interview techniques in terms of importance in assessing social-emotional problems, but ahead of the use of behavior rating scales and objective tests. Further, over 50% of the practitioners reported at least "frequently using" the following projective techniques: human figure drawings (83%), incomplete sentence blanks (73%), emotional indicators on the Bender-Gestalt (72%), House-Tree-Person (62%), and Kinetic Family Drawings (61%). Other projectives were used less frequently, but still had their adherents: Thematic Apperception Test (47%), Children's Apperception Test (31%), and Roschach (28%). Similarly, 64% of training program directors indicated their programs currently give at least some emphasis to projective assessment. According to the program directors, clinical training is provided for the following techniques: human figure drawing (77% of programs), emotional indicators for the Bender-Gestalt (74%), Thematic Apperception Test (63%), incomplete sentence blanks (64%), House-Tree-Person (60%), Children's Apperception Test (56%), Kinetic Family Drawings (54%), and the Rorschach (38%). Although Prout (1983) noted that projectives are not now the most favored approaches to assessment and that there appears to have been a shift to more behaviorally oriented approaches, it is obvious that projectives are still widely used and given emphasis in training programs. Thus, despite all the criticisms, projective assessment seems to have persevered and is viewed as having some value in the assessment of social-emotional functioning.

The Traditional View

The primary rationale for projective techniques has historically been rooted in Freudian analytic and psychodynamic approaches to understanding the unconscious (Lindzey, 1961). This thinking assumes that the most significant aspects of personality and the resultant manifested behavior are not observable to the clinician and in most cases beyond the awareness of the individual. Thus, the individual cannot describe or report on these personality variables in a direct fashion (Sundberg, 1977). Hidden sexual and aggressive drives and urges are viewed as the forces behind most observed behavior. The actual behavior displayed and the situation or conditions under which the behavior occurs are not considered as important within this perspective. Further, these internal drives are viewed as generalized across situations and as relatively enduring personality characteristics. Projective techniques produce data that are indirect measures or assessments of these internal states. A number of characteristics are common to this traditional view of projective techniques (Sundberg, 1977):

1. Projective assessment uses a sign approach to clinical interpretation. Responses to projective stimuli are seen as a sign of underlying personality structures and dynamics. Behavioral techniques, in contrast, treat data as samples of behavior.
2. Projective techniques rely on the Freudian assumption of psychic determinism. This assumption posits that all behavior is internally and psychologically determined—no behavior is random, accidental, or situationally determined. Further, there are hidden motives behind all behavior. Behavior is overdetermined in that it is a reflection of a total enduring personality pattern.
3. The distinction between primary and secondary processes of thinking is relevant to projective interpretation. Primary process is the thinking that we are born with and that is largely illogical and dominated by the search for gratification and relief from tension—the Pleasure Principle. Secondary process is conscious thinking that helps us adapt to reality, and is verbal, logical, and relatively unemotional. Some projectives, notably the Rorschach, assume that the ambiguous stimuli lessens the reality controls and thus allow access to primary process thinking. Thus, a goal of traditional

assessment is the attainment of some insight into this primary process thought.
4. The concept of projection is obviously a key to this perspective. Projection, a general phenomenon that occurs in day-to-day routine functioning, refers to the view that a person's perceptions, interpretations of reality, and outward behavior are all a reflection of these inner forces, urges, and drives. The individual's private views are projected onto the stimuli presented to him or her. The projective hypothesis, in particular, assumes that these private views will be seen in responses to unstructured or ambiguous stimuli.

Anastasi (1982) describes the major distinguishing feature of projective techniques is the "assignment of a relatively unstructured task, i.e., a task that permits an almost unlimited variety of possible response" (p. 564). Brief, general instructions paired with vague or ambiguous test stimuli allow access to the person's fantasy and private world.

AN ALTERNATIVE VIEW

The conceptual base for an alternative view of projectives is most closely associated with Lazarus's (1976, 1981) multimodal theory of behavior and personality, discussed briefly above. Lazarus posits that learning plays a major role in the development and resolution of emotional problems. The many processes and concepts related to classical conditioning, operant conditioning, modeling, imitation, and vicarious learning are clearly important variables in examining behavior. However, Lazarus (1981) feels that restricting assessment to the "triad" of classical, operant, and modeling and vicarious conceptualizations may obscure important factors in emotional problems. He states: "Thus *private events* [thoughts, feelings, images, and sensations] must be added to the pool of basic concepts" (p. 36). Lazarus, while viewing these covert events as important, does not emphasize "unconscious" variables in his theory. Thus, private events there are not the same as private events in more dynamically oriented theories. Idiosyncratic uses of language, semantics, problem-solving abilities, expectancies, goals, and performance standards as well as the effects of beliefs, values, and attitudes on overt behavior must be considered. Lazarus accepts Bandura's (1978) principle of reciprocal determinism that includes the view that behavior is not totally determined by external, overt stimuli, but is also influenced by a person's thoughts about the stimuli. Lazarus also views these psychological processes as interactive with the need to integrate these various conceptualizations selectively into intervention programs.

Theoretically, from an assessment standpoint, the recognition of various interactive modalities leads to comprehensive coverage that addresses several aspects of a problem, hopefully so that an essential feature of a problem will not go undetected. Further, Lazarus (1981) places considerable value on unique, idiographic data, feeling that one bit of information may be valuable in planning an intervention, even though it may not be strictly empirically verifiable. Here, Lazarus adopts the view of Erickson (1953) that "the nature and character of a single finding can often be more informative and valuable than a voluminous aggregate of data whose meaning is dependent upon statistical manipulation" (p. 68). Thus, data gathered from projective tests may be useful if they lead to further hypotheses, targeted assessment, or intervention plans.

Another aspect of an alternative view of projective techniques is that it is erroneous to group all techniques together and to criticize or invalidate all techniques because of problems relating to one technique. In a similar vein to the classification of analogue techniques offered earlier in this chapter, Lindzey (1959, 1961) has categorized projective techniques. His categorization includes association techniques in which the subject responds to a stimulus with the first thoughts, images, words, or perceptions that come to mind (e.g., Rorschach, word association), construction techniques in which the individual is given the task to produce a story or drawing (e.g., thematic procedures, family drawings), completion techniques in which the subject must finish a partially complete stimulus (sentence completion), choice or ordering techniques, which involve a selection among alternatives according to some ranking instructions (e.g., self-report measures that allow the selection of the best personal descriptor), and expressive techniques, which focus on the manner or style in which a person behaves while engaged in some activity (e.g., assessment using role-playing situations). Given this wide range of techniques available, it is erroneous to criticize the sentence completion technique because of problems with projective techniques in general. The sentence completion technique, for example, has very little in common with the Rorschach. There has been a tendency to treat projective techniques as a homogeneous group of procedures, when, in actuality, it is a very heterogeneous collection of assessment strategies. Thus, the merits and utilization of individual techniques should be considered separately—there is no easy way to generalize across techniques.

Following are a few alternative conceptualizations to the traditional view of projectives. The term projective is used here and throughout the remainder of the chapter, even though the term may be a misnomer in conjunction with this alternative view. These views place these techniques more closely in the realm of a behavioral assessment perspective.

1. Projective techniques, themselves, are essentially atheoretical. The presentation of an ambiguous picture or the request of a child to draw his or her family all engaged in an activity are tasks that are not tied to any particular theoretical framework. Interpretation, however, is a highly theoretical activity. A child's response of *my mother* to a sentence completion item, *I hate* _____ can be interpreted either psychoanalytically or behaviorally. Adherents of either of these diverse viewpoints would likely interpret and attend to a statement of this nature, yet the interpretations

may vary widely. Thus, many of the criticisms of projectives may lie at the interpretation stage and not with the techniques as vehicles for data collection.

2. Projective techniques are not tests and they should not be used for differential diagnosis. Validity data on projective instruments' ability to make meaningful distinctions between clinical groups are meager at best (reliability and validity issues are discussed later). Thus, the potential for these instruments to contribute significantly to diagnostic and educational classification decisions is minimal. Traditional ways of scoring these techniques are unlikely to yield information relevant to treatment and intervention.

3. "Useful" projective techniques provide data relevant to situational and cross-situational aspects of a problem or disorder. This data does not assume a trait or underlying drive as a major variable in personality and behavioral functioning. There is minimal emphasis on unconscious motivations, urges, private views of the world, and so on.

4. Projective techniques should be viewed in the context of structured or semistructured interviews. The use of family drawings or thematic approaches displaying certain social situations should be viewed as an opportunity to interview the child about those specific situations. Ample utilization of inquiry and follow-up questioning about the child's responses is advocated. Similarly, the use of standardized scoring systems that promote a "test" view of the techniques is not generally recommended. Thus, it is permissible to deviate from standardized administration procedures to pursue a line of inquiry with a child or adolescent. The techniques, above all else, are simply a procedure to gather more information about an individual's problems or concerns.

5. With children, in particular, projective techniques allow an assessment of concerns that may not be as easily accessible through direct interview. When a child readily cooperates with direct interview, the assessment should focus on interview strategies. However, with some less verbal children or some children who do not respond well to direct questioning, the indirect methods of projective assessment may produce useful information or facilitate discussion of the child's concerns. Children who are unwilling to talk about family concerns, after the completion of a family drawing, may relate details of functioning within their family. Similarly, some adolescents who reveal few concerns in an interview, may detail a variety of problems on a sentence completion task.

6 The primary useful information gathered in projective assessment lies in the cognitive, social perception, and affective domains consistent with the domains dictated in Lazarus's model (1976, 1981). With the increasing popularity of cognitively based therapy approaches, the tapping of cognitive variables through projective assessment is particularly helpful. A child can describe what he or she might be thinking in relation to a social

situation portrayed in a thematic picture—an adolescent views a picture of a school situation in which the student is thinking about failing a test and the resulting "awful" consequences. Similarly, a child's perceptions and affective reactions in social situations may be revealed. For example, a child who draws a school picture in which he or she is shown feeling sad because the teacher is yelling might have a generally negative social perception of the school situation.

7. Data produced in projective assessment yield information that can lead directly to intervention strategies. As in the example above, an adolescent with certain cognitions about failing a test and the consequences of that might respond to cognitive change strategies. Information gathered with projective techniques that does *not* yield educational recommendations, suggestions for foci for intervention, or assessment hypotheses to be addressed through other means should be discarded. At this point, however, projective measures used in this manner do not provide empirically reliable and valid data collection systems to monitor progress in a behavioral or therapeutic intervention. Again, their primary value lies in pinpointing target concerns, developing hypotheses, and facilitating the development of other modes of assessing specific concerns.

Levels of Inference

As mentioned previously, virtually all methods of psychological assessment involve some degree of inference. Obviously, the behavioral perspective would support instruments that involve minimal or low levels of inference. Projective techniques can lend themselves to a wide range of inferential interpretation.

Low Inference

Projective assessment data that allow direct interpretation involve minimal levels of inference. It is inferred that from the response the behavior occurs, in some fashion, in the child's environment. The child is responding to *my* school, *my* family, or an *I* statement. Further, what is revealed in the response is taken at its face value and there is no hypothesizing about other variables. For example, in the case of a child who produces a family drawing in which his or her parents are portrayed arguing and fighting, a low inference interpretation is plausible. One would infer that the child is at least concerned about what he or she perceives as occurring in the home. Further, one could hypothesize that parental disagreement does occur at home and that more assessment might be indicated in this area. Sentence completion techniques also allow direct interpretation because of their use of stems that reflect real-life issues. "At school . . .", "My mother . . .", "I feel . . . ," all directly personalize the item for the child or adolescent and involve minimal projection. One other case where low levels of inference are involved is the situation in which the child or adolescent is describing the actions of a character in a stimulus situation and stops referring to the central figure as *him* or *her*, but rather *I* or *me*. This can occur with thematic tests when the child begins relating how he or she would respond in the situation and stops talking about the little boy or little girl in the story or picture.

Moderate Inference

At the moderate level of inference, the child or adolescent is projecting onto a hypothetical person and dealing with hypothetical situations. At this level, the child does not personalize his or her responses. The child is not saying this happens in *my* family or at *my* school or with *my* friends. Rather, the child is responding to the situation and relating what the little boy or little girl in the story or picture is doing, thinking, feeling, etc. Still, the interpretation of the child's responses is relatively direct—there is not a search for hidden meaning in the child's responses. For example, for a child who continually describes conflict in the home of the child in the story, one would hypothesize that this also might be a concern of the child being assessed. Similarly, for a child who provides descriptions of a child not having friends in response to thematic pictures of children interacting, one might hypothesize problems in the area of peer relationships. The child's responses are treated at face value as in the low inference situations, but interpretation is more tentative since the child does not personalize the responses.

High Inference

High levels of inference rely heavily on symbolic and analytic interpretation to make inferences about underlying or unconscious motives, drives, and so on. This level of interpretation is most often associated with psychodynamic theory. The particular aspect of a visual stimuli that the child responds to (e.g., specific parts of an inkblot), specific objects included in drawings or stories, and styles of responding may be interpreted to have some underlying meaning. For example, in family drawings, the inclusion of stars, the sun, trains, snakes, refrigerators, lamps have all been hypothesized to represent some underlying psychological need or motive. These characteristics of drawings are viewed as symbols of the underlying psychological process. This type of interpretation is not advocated here—it is particularly inconsistent with the behavioral perspective.

Issues in Reliability and Validity

The issues related to the psychometric validity and reliability of projective techniques have been studied extensively. There have been literally thousands of studies across the wide variety of techniques that fall into the projective category. There is no real way to summarize these findings in a concise manner. In fact, Maloney and Ward (1976) have commented: "The wide variety and scope of projective techniques make an [research] evaluation of them extremely complex. A comprehensive review of research literature in this area would cover several volumes" (p. 363). Thus, it is extremely difficult to offer generalizations that apply to all types of techniques. Nonetheless, it is clear from the literature that projective techniques in general do not stand up well under psychometric scrutiny. Further, a large majority of studies in this area of research are methodologically or procedurally flawed, thus yielding a confusing and inconclusive research base (Anastasi, 1982). Maloney and Ward (1976) have attempted to offer a few generalizations about research in this area. They feel that standardization of scoring and administration procedures as well as normative data are "insufficient from a psychometric point of view" (p. 364) and describe the studies of reliability and validity as producing "consistently negative psychometric results" (p. 370). Anastasi (1982) notes that most validity studies of projectives have produced very low or nonsignificant correlations with criterion variables. Further, the critical variables, when there have been moderately positive results, appear to be a function of the particular clinician with an examinee, that is, the examiner rather than the technique is the key variable.

The most extensive critical reviews of the use of projectives in differential diagnosis with children have been offered by Gittelman (Gittelman, 1980; Gittelman-Klein, 1978). Gittelman notes that the results of child and adult projective research studies have been treated as interchangeable. She feels that this is an erroneous assumption and that whatever validity has been found in adult studies does not necessarily generalize to child populations. In fact, it is quite likely that disturbed children and disturbed adults present rather different psychopathology and diagnostic data. Gittelman's reviews focus largely on the Rorschach, human figure drawing, draw-a-person, the Bender-Gestalt, the Thematic Apperception Test, and the Children's Apperception Test. At a general level, Gittelman finds that many studies were flawed from a methodology standpoint, specifically very few were using a blind analysis of diagnostic data and there was a tendency for studies not to control for IQ and other developmental variables. She finds virtually no data to suggest the projectives were useful in assessing aggression and self-esteem, two variables frequently mentioned in the theoretical descriptions of these instruments. Similarly, data did not support several other variables that were hypothesized to be found in projective response patterns. Similar results were found in studies that attempted to distinguish between "normal" and "clinical" samples, and that attempted to discriminate between different diagnostic classifications. The studies reviewed tended to rely on group data with some studies indicating differences between different clinical groups. However, despite group mean differences in some cases, there was no support for efficacious discrimination, that is, useful "hit" rates in terms of diagnosis. Further, Gittelman concludes that research on the various types of reliability is flawed and inconclusive.

Needless to say, Gittelman's (1978, 1980) reviews are rather damning and pessimistic about the role of projective assessment with children. Her concluding comments in the 1978 review perhaps sum up her view of the area:

> The current status of projective tests in children can be summarized succinctly: sometimes they tell us poorly something we already know.

Resources in the mental health field are limited. On the basis of empirical data, it is clear that the use of projective testing in children does not deserve a high priority.

Has the horse [research on and use of projective tests with children] been finished off? Not quite. He refuses to die, but hardly even places in the money. A cautious gambler would not bet on him. The status of the research is reminiscent of the joke about the gambler who, returning from the track, was asked how he had done. He replied, "I broke even, and boy did I need it!" (pp. 160, 162)

Gittelman's reviews are indeed impressive and offer strong arguments against the use of projectives with children. However, within the context presented in this chapter, some of her criticisms are not relevant. First, the alternative view offered here does not emphasize differential diagnosis nor does it advocate the use of projectives as the major data source for an assessment of social-emotional functioning. Secondly, the tests reviewed by Gittelman are ones that do not fit with the alternative view of projectives offered here (see the next section of this chapter). Finally, Gittelman may have been somewhat overzealous in her attempt to resolve the issue of the "uselessness" of projectives with children. French, Graves, and Levitt (1983) note that Gittelman may have been somewhat selective in her review of studies by selecting primarily those that supported her point of view.

In general, it is difficult to disagree with these assessments of the psychometric properties of projectives when used in the traditional manner. However, the framework for using projectives offered above in some ways negates the need to establish validity and reliability in the traditional sense. The alternative view proposes treating the data in a similar fashion as interview data, advocates the use of direct, face value interpretation with external clinical validation of hypotheses, and argues against the use of standard scoring systems. One or two responses may lead to the development of clinical hypotheses that are later tested through other means of data collection. These "clinically significant" responses would be unlikely to show up in a psychometric analysis of scoring procedures. Consider the incomplete sentence response *school and all the teachers* to the item *I hate _____* and assume that this is the only reference the child makes about school. It is unlikely this response would be detected in any standard scoring system, yet it would be foolish to ignore the response and not follow up with the child. Thus, the standard procedures that have been the focus of research and validation studies may be somewhat irrelevant to how projective data is used clinically. This may be related to the fact that projectives continue to be used frequently, as discussed above, despite the consistently discouraging empirical results.

The suggested alternative use of projective tests calls for a somewhat different perspective in addressing issues of reliability and validity in future research. As mentioned, differential diagnosis and classification are not, and should not be, goals of this type of assessment. The primary goals of projective testing, as discussed here, focus on developing hypotheses and pinpointing targets as monitoring devices for interventions, and are not well established or empirically verified. Future research may yield better ways to quantify this data so that it may be used in this manner.

Related to the issue of hypothesis testing and pinpointing target concerns, it may be best to view projective tests as psychological problem screening devices, with data produced leading to testing of specific hypotheses. As the multimodal view addresses several modalities, projective tests can quickly address several issues to help organize more comprehensive assessment. For example, assume that a series of thematic cards addressed a variety of issues confronted by an adolescent—parents, siblings, peer relationships—and that the system yielded hypotheses about these particular issues. To assess the validity of these measures as psychological problem screening devices, one could simply look at the "hit" rate and "miss" rate for these hypotheses, that is, the percentage of hypotheses confirmed (or denied) through other, more detailed and specific assessment procedures. What represents an acceptable "hit" rate is somewhat subjective depending on the variables assessed and the type of decisions being made. This is influenced by the importance of the decisions, the base rate for hypothesis testing and development without the use of the screening procedure (i.e., incremental validity), and the type of actions taken as a result of the data (Allen & Yen, 1970). Ultimately, the incremental validity issue may determine the utility of using projective tests in this way. If the test results confirm hypotheses that would have otherwise not been tested (i.e., undetected) through other behavioral assessment procedures, then these strategies may have use in comprehensive assessment approaches. The statistics produced would be a "hit" rate or percentage of confirmed hypotheses not addressed through other means. Again, what represents an acceptable "hit" rate is very subjective. As Lazarus (1981) posits, one could argue that the more idiosyncratic hypotheses or bits of data need not occur frequently to be valuable; thus, a relatively low hit rate may still suggest utility for psychological problem screening purposes. The case studies that follow provide examples of uses of these more idiosyncratic hypotheses.

The second area of needed research for the suggested approach to using projective tests focuses on the more traditional views of reliability and validity as addressed in more psychometrically based test development. The issue of reliability (i.e., essentially internal consistency issues), since it affects validity, needs to be addressed first in the future development of scoring systems for projective tests. Currently, systems for analyzing data from projective tests generally yield too few categories, have differing numbers of responses, provide dichotomous scoring systems (i.e., present or absent), and have other characteristics that prevent the establishment of adequate reliability (Obrzut & Boliek, 1986). Further, the systems still rest on projection and the related theoretical assumptions. Nunally (1967) discusses a number of ways of increasing reliability including adding more items, using statistically based item analysis, and employing scaled (vs. dichotomous) response formats. Current scoring systems have been developed that essentially ignore these basic principles of test development—it is not surprising that psychometric properties of these instruments are disappointing. Virtually all projectives have not employed test development approaches often seen in objective inventories and behavior rating scales.

Consider the psychological construct of depression as it might be measured in a twenty-card series of thematic pictures. With an open-ended format, the child would generally be scored only for depression when she or he specifically mentioned that the child in the story felt sad or depressed. Thus, the system might yield a small, dichotomously scored quantification of the construct since depression would not be specifically addressed on each card. An alternative might be a more structured inquiry in which the child is specifically asked whether the child in the story felt happy (e.g., score = 0), neither happy nor sad (score = 1), a little sad (score = 2), or very sad (score = 3) at the end of the story. Thus, a twenty-item scale of depression with a scaled scoring system would result. This would be similar to some of the popular objective self-report measures, but adds the dimension of the visual stimulus in the child's responses. This may be more concrete and easier to understand for some children than paper-and-pencil tasks. Further, standard item analysis techniques might be used to further refine such a scale. This approach necessitates the refinement and modification of current scoring systems for projective tests. If adequate internal consistency reliability can first be established, then more standard criterion validity studies could be conducted. If projective tests can establish themselves as more psychometrically reliable and valid instruments, they might then have potential value as tools to monitor affective variables in intervention and treatment programs. Obviously, projective tests need considerable research before being useful in this manner.

This view may be seen as an attempt to rationalize the poor psychometric properties of projective tests. Admittedly, this does place current usage of these techniques somewhat in the realm of clinical intuition. It must be emphasized, again, that a very cautious, nondifferential diagnostic use of these techniques is advocated. They are a data collection tool and, in most cases, should not be the sole or primary assessment approach. The alternative view, however, is currently without empirical verification. Studies, perhaps different from the standard validity and reliability methodology, are needed to investigate whether projectives used in a different way actually do lead to better and more efficacious formulation of clinical hypotheses and to more specifically targeted assessments to test their hypotheses.

AN EVALUATION OF TECHNIQUES WITHIN THE BEHAVIORAL PERSPECTIVE

An alternative view of projective techniques provides a framework for using these techniques within an overall behavioral perspective. Obviously, this "alternative" view of projectives suggests that some techniques have no place within this perspective. The rationale for not including several of the more popular techniques within our "alternative" view follows.

The Rorschach and the Holtzman Inkblot Test procedures provide no situational data to assist in understanding a problem or disorder. Direct interpretation with an emphasis on high levels of inference is not feasible. Further, these techniques purport to be tests and useful in differential diagnosis. In general, they do not directly produce responses related to cognitive, social perception, or affective functioning. They do not provide a format for more detailed interview or inquiry about issues related to the person's real-life situation or environment. Data produced does not directly lead to pinpointing problems for treatment or intervention.

Thematic Apperception Test (TAT) and Children's Apperception Test (CAT) thematic procedures do meet several of our criteria. There is some assessment of cognitive, social perception, and affective variables, and it is possible to utilize extended inquiry. However, the TAT and CAT have traditionally emphasized high levels of inference. Most important, though, is that the situations depicted in the stimulus materials are not typical of realistic situations faced by a child or adolescent. The TAT usually uses adult figures in their stimulus situations, and most of the situations are rather bizarre depictions of life situations. The CAT uses animals as the characters in the pictures, perhaps a bit too removed from real-life situations.

Bender-Gestalt (emotional indicators) drawing technique, requiring the copying of geometric designs, also fails to provide situational, affective, cognitive, or social perception information, and does not provide a format for interviewing the child about any situational issues. Interpretation is based largely on the style and qualitative aspects of the child's responses, involving a high level of inference. At best, it provides a task in which to observe the child's behavioral response to a semistructured task.

Draw-a-Man and House-Tree-Person drawing techniques come closer to meeting our general criteria than do some techniques, yet they still yield minimal situational data. Given more situationally relevant instructions, these techniques may have some value. For example, asking a child to draw a picture of him- or herself at school or of how he or she feels in a specific situation would yield more information than the more general noncontextual instructions. If these techniques are used they should be employed to facilitate interviews with the child and to personalize the response. Without this, one is left with interpretation using highly inferential approaches.

The techniques that fit more closely with the alternative view are discussed below. It is important to note that the emphasis is on the aspects of these techniques that match our alternative view. In most cases, this involves the abandonment of the recommended scoring and analysis procedures, as well as the interpretative guidelines offered by the technique developers. The first three techniques discussed are thematic and generally involve moderate levels of inference—the child is telling a story about the character in the picture and not describing his or her own reactions to the situation. If the child does personalize the story (e.g., "I did . . ." or "My father . . ."), then the response is treated as a more direct or lower level of inference. The other techniques discussed, sentence completion techniques and family and school drawings, generally involve lower levels of inference—the child is responding specifically to his or her personal situation.

The Tasks of Emotional Development (TED) (Cohen & Weil, 1971, 1975) is a thematic instrument that is based on a series of photographs that are slightly differentiated for use by boys and girls and according to age (6 to 11 years old and 12 to 18 years old). Children respond to the pictures by telling a story. The adolescent series includes an additional card depicting a possible dating situation. The photographs in each series represent specific tasks of emotional development that the authors hypothesize occur during the maturation of all children. The thirteen tasks depicted are (Cohen & Weil, 1975, p. 2):

1. Socialization within the peer group.
2. Establishment of trust in people.
3. Acceptance and control of aggressive feelings toward peers.
4. Establishment of positive attitudes toward academic learning.
5. Establishment of a conscience with respect to the property of others.
6. Separation from the mother figure.
7. Identification with the same-sex parent.
8. Acceptance of siblings.
9. Acceptance of limits from adults.
10. Acceptance of affection between parents (resolution of Oedipal conflict).
11. Establishment of positive attitudes towards orderliness and cleanliness (the ability to control drives).
12. Establishment of a positive self-concept.
13. Establishment of positive heterosexual socialization.

According to Cohen and Weil (1975), the purpose of the test is to provide a means to assess the emotional and social adjustment of children. Purportedly, the stories the children relate in response to the pictures will provide a clinician with the basis for assessing and interpreting personality development within an Ericksonian model (French, Graves, & Levitt, 1983). Objective rating scales have been included for each task that allows a child's or adolescent's story to be rated from most to least mature. Children's story responses are further rated on perception, outcome, affect, motivation, and spontaneity (Ammons & Ammons, 1972). According to the authors, the inclusion of rating criteria makes the instrument more useful for less experienced professionals and enhances its use for research purposes.

Specific directions for administration in the manual provide the child with guidelines for the information that could be included in the story (e.g., what's happening in the picture, what are the people doing, what are they thinking and feeling, how does the story end). The clinician is encouraged to use probes so that the responses can accurately be scored. Examples of probes for the rating dimensions are provided in the instruction manual. Unfortunately, the manual provides virtually no information on the interpretation of the scores in the dimensions with the emphasis on interpretation in a clinical, analytic, and dynamic framework.

The TED has not received positive reviews, particularly with respect to test development methodology (Levitt, 1975; Wise, 1975). Ammons and Ammons (1972) note that despite relatively adequate size of normative groups (over 1000 well distributed across sex and socioeconomic levels plus clinic samples), interpretation is impossible because of a lack of validity and reliability data. French, Graves, and Levitt (1983) have also faulted the TED for a lack of validity data.

Overall, the TED is a thematic device much in the vein of traditional, analytically oriented instruments. Interpretation and scoring criteria are virtually nonexistent as are clear, concise descriptions or psychometric properties. The inclusion of scoring criteria is essentially invalidated because of these deficiencies. Further, on a subjective level, the photographs seem outdated, and some children may have difficulty relating to them.

Despite these problems with the TED, the situations depicted in the photographs do correspond to many real-life situations. The themes described by the authors do not necessarily have to be followed—most behaviorally oriented assessors would not deal with Oedipal conflict as a variable. Yet, the card dealing with parental affection may still add a dimension to an assessment. Because of this, the TED may have some value as a component in an overall behavioral assessment of a child. Many of the modalities described by Lazarus (1976) (discussed earlier in this chapter) can be addressed in a thematic instrument of this nature. Information about situationally specific behavior, affect, and cognitions can be addressed—for example, what did the person do, how did he or she feel, what was he or she thinking. A child who consistently describes outcomes involving anger (she's mad at the other kids because they were mean to her) and aggression (they got in a fight) may be exhibiting his or her ability to describe a logical story with a positive outcome, and this may help sort out whether the child knows expected appropriate behavior in different situations. The thoughts a child attributes to individuals in his or her stories may be useful in selecting specific cognitions to target in intervention. These data would then be used in conjunction with naturalistic observation, interviews, and behavior ratings to generate hypotheses or further define other data. The stimulus material might also be used during intervention to facilitate a child's discussion of specific situations.

The uses noted above will generally apply to the other thematics discussed here. As has been mentioned several times, data from the TED (or other single instrument or technique) should not be used in isolation from other data to plan interventions. Further, its value in educational placement decisions (e.g., a diagnosis of emotional disturbance) is minimal. It is largely a technique to be used as a supplement to other procedures.

The Roberts Apperception Test for Children (RATC) (McArthur & Roberts, 1982) is also a thematic procedure that is designed to evaluate children's perceptions of interpersonal situations, facilitate an understanding of the child's personality development, and assist in clinical treatment (McArthur & Roberts, 1982). The test is comprised of twenty-seven total cards (eleven with male and female versions) with sixteen of the drawings used routinely to depict "common situations, conflicts, and stressors in children's lives" (p. 1).

The premise behind the RATC is similar to other thematic tests—the child's responses to ambiguous drawings will provide insight into his or her thoughts, conflicts, and coping strategies (McArthur & Roberts, 1982). The drawings depict situations involving family confrontation, maternal support, school attitude, parental affection, racial interaction, child support and aggression, dependency and anxiety, family conference, physical aggression, sibling rivalry, fear, parental conflict, aggression release, limit setting, sexuality, and parental support. The test is further scored on scales measuring adaptive and maladaptive functioning. There are also three clinical indicators of severe problems (atypical response, maladaptive outcome, and refusal).

As in other thematic procedures, the child is directed to tell a story about the picture—what is happening, what led up to it, what is being talked about, how it ends, what are people feeling. Limited inquiries focus on these same areas. McArthur and Roberts (1982) advocate a fairly standard and rigid administration procedure. Specific scoring procedures and protocols are available and are relatively easy to use, taking about twenty-five to thirty minutes (Friedrich, 1984). The scoring procedure and the inclusion of interpretive guidelines based on deviations in scaled scores and variations within scales makes the RATC somewhat different than other thematic procedures (McArthur & Roberts, 1982, Sines, 1985).

According to Sines (1985) and Friedrich (1984), the RATC is unique in its attempt to combine projective assessment with objective, quantitative measurement. The standardization sample, which was compiled over several years, is described as a cross section of 200 lower-, middle-, and upper-income, "well-adjusted" children in California. However, no actual socioeconomic data delineation was reported (Friedrich, 1984).

The psychometric data reported in the RATC manual are comprised primarily of four unpublished studies. The first compared 200 clinic with 200 nonclinic children, with the results indicating no significant differences on scales of aggression, anxiety, and depression, factors that usually discriminate between these groups (Sines, 1985). Friedrich (1984) notes, however, some positive correlations with behavior rating data and that acceptable levels of interrater and split-half reliabilities have been reported.

In general, the RATC does possess some characteristics not found in other thematic procedures—well-described scoring, administration, and interpretative procedures in addition to normative, reliability, and validity data. Although considerably more data are needed, particularly in the area of research independent from the test developers, Friedrich (1984) feels that the test holds an "undetermined amount of promise" (p. 548). Sines (1985), however, feels that the RATC does not address current issues and trends in personality assessment. Despite the

RATC's being more comprehensive than other thematic procedures, the lack of conclusive research data does not yet support the RATC as a valid measure from a psychometric standpoint.

The use of the RATC in behavioral assessment is similar to that of the TED. It is viewed as a supplemental data collection technique to address situations portrayed in the RATC stimulus cards. One advantage of the RATC is that the drawings are less distracting than the outdated TED photographs, and the somewhat more ambiguous stimulus materials may promote more varied response patterns. A disadvantage (if one adheres closely to the recommended administration and inquiry guidelines) is that there is little room for using the cards to facilitate more in-depth interviewing around certain topics. The view presented in this chapter is that it would be permissible to use extended inquiry to further examine social perception, cognitive, interpersonal, and affective variables related to the situations depicted in the drawings. Perhaps with further research, the RATC will prove to be more useful as a clinical psychometric tool. At this point, its value is in the informal, alternative way of using projective data in conjunction with other data.

The School Apperception Method (SAM) (Solomon & Starr, 1968) is also a thematic procedure in which the child responds to drawings and pictures. As with many thematic procedures, it is psychodynamic in its theoretical base. However, the SAM differs from other thematic techniques in that it is entirely school-related and was developed largely to assist school psychologists in understanding the behavior of children in school and to facilitate the development of more relevant recommendations for school personnel. The twenty-two drawings all involve school situations such as lunch in the cafeteria and various classroom scenes. Twelve of the drawings are intended for routine administration, with ten additional cards intended for supplemental or special theme assessment. The recommended range in age is kindergarten through ninth grade (Soloman & Starr, 1968).

The authors of the SAM feel that the test stimuli are situationally relevant to understanding the behavior of problem children in school. Further, the specific stimuli assure associations oriented around schools and that they will generate hypotheses that will assist in developing classroom management strategies. They feel that this data used in hypothesis generation would not otherwise be available (Solomon & Starr, 1968).

Administration directions are similar to other thematic approaches; the child is told that these are some pictures about school and is directed to make up a story including what the people are doing, thinking, feeling, and so on. Frequent questions and inquiries are recommended, although no specific questions are suggested. Rather than a scoring procedure, the authors recommend a "framework for analysis" that includes the following (Soloman & Starr, 1968):

1. Formal qualities: reaction time, manner of expression, length and complexity of story.

2. Attitudes toward the teacher and other authorities.
3. Attitudes toward schoolmates.
4. Attitudes toward academic activity.
5. Aggression.
6. Frustration.
7. Anxiety and defense mechanisms.
8. Home and school.
9. Punishment.

There are no empirical data to support this framework, nor does the manual report any other type of validity, reliability, or normative data. There have apparently been no empirical studies on the SAM.

Reviews of the SAM by Reitz (1972) and Sundberg (1972) were critical of the SAM because of the lack of any empirical base and the lack of any scoring procedures in the manual. Reitz (1972) questions the validity of the authors' assumption that data produced in this method will be any more useful than that of any other thematic procedure. At the time of these reviews, both indicated the need for considerable research, and that the use of the SAM by school psychologists should not supplant other, more accepted techniques such as interview and observation.

The SAM could in no way be construed as a psychometric instrument. The method of use described negates its use in this manner without even considering the apparent total lack of empirical data. Further, the authors' claims that this school-based data would not otherwise be available is also unsubstantiated. Nonetheless, the SAM could be used in a manner similar to that described for the TED and the RATC—assessing affective, social perception, and cognitive variables, and in conjunction with other assessment techniques. There are likely to be certain children with certain presenting problems to whom the SAM will add meaningful information. The SAM also has the advantage of providing school-focused stimuli. However, for many of the situations depicted in the drawings and their hypothesized foci, there are likely to be more direct means of assessment. Further, since one of the advantages of using an analogue approach is to obtain information about situations and settings not accessible to the psychologist, the school psychologist's base *in* the schools may diminish the value of the SAM. The SAM may actually be of more value to the clinician outside the school who wants to address school issues in an assessment.

Sentence Completion Techniques

Sentence completion techniques are considered to be a semistructured form of a projective measure. The procedure involves having the child read and complete sentence stems (e.g., My mother is _____). Theoretically, the free association involved with the sentence stem will provide insight into the child's thoughts and feelings. Since the material presented in the sentence stem is more structured and obvious, the child is thought to have more conscious control over his or her responses (Goldman, Stein, & Guerry, 1983; Watson, 1978). In terms of traditional, analytic use of projectives, this raises the issue of its usefulness in identifying underlying personality dynamics (Watson, 1978). Behaviorists may see this as an asset.

There are a wide variety of sentence completion forms available. The Forer Structured Sentence Completion Test and the Rotter Incomplete Sentence Blank are two of the most commonly used instruments. Most of the tests for children range in length from twenty-five to sixty stems, and require that the child be able to read and write. Typically, the stems cover a range of child or adolescent concerns including parents, brothers or sisters, school, peers, the opposite sex, perceptions, interpersonal relationships, and self-concept issues. Techniques are available for elementary school-age and up. Sentence completion tests are among the least researched and reviewed of the major projective approaches (Goldman, Stein, & Guerry, 1983; Hart, Kehle, & Davies, 1983). In fact Goldman, Stein, and Guerry (1983) note that no "good data on standardization or various forms of reliability and validity appear readily available" (p. 236). According to Watson (1978), however, the techniques are considered a flexible clinical tool that do provide the option of several scoring systems, and do present validity and reliability data as good as any of the other projective techniques. Although the sentence completion tests appear to be more structured and somewhat less analytic in nature, they seem to encounter many of the same problems inherent in other projectives: lack of adequate normative, reliability, and validity data, and vague or inconcise interpretative guidelines.

Within a behavioral perspective, sentence completion techniques are used in much the same way as thematic approaches. These techniques, however, are more structured and involve lower levels of inference. This may produce less ambiguous and more easily and directly interpretable information. French, Graves, and Levitt (1983) note children's responses in these techniques may serve as a springboard for more in-depth interviews around specific concerns. For children and adolescents who can handle reading and writing tasks, these techniques offer the advantage of relatively quick and easy coverage of a variety of situations. In fact, many of the stems lend themselves to assessing variables within the multi-modal framework.

The Kinetic Drawing System (Knoff & Prout, 1985) brings together the Kinetic Family Drawing (K-F-D) (Burns & Kaufman, 1970, 1972) and the Kinetic School Drawing (K-S-D) (Prout & Phillips, 1974) as a way of addressing children's perceptions of both home and school settings. These drawing techniques ask the child to draw a picture of him- or herself in both settings *and* that all the characters included in the drawings should be doing something. The K-F-D includes the direction to draw "everyone in your family" and the K-S-D directs the child to "draw yourself, your teacher, and a friend or two" (Knoff & Prout, 1985, p. 4). Thus, the drawings address the setting, people, and behaviors and relationships in the setting. The approach can be used with children as young as age five and there is no specific older age limit, although it is rarely used beyond early to middle adolescence.

After the child completes the drawings, with the assistance of the assessor, the child labels each drawing by naming the individuals he or she drew and by describing their actions. At this point, ample inquiry is suggested. This has the effect of treating the completed and labeled drawing as thematic or serving as the focus of an interview. Inquiry can address behaviors, antecedents and consequences, feelings, cognitions, interpersonal relationships, and so on. Interpretative guidelines offer both analytic, behavioral, and empirically based suggestions for interpretation. A scoring system is available, but this is essentially a checklist of different characteristics that could be addressed in analysis, and has minimal empirical validation.

A number of studies have separately examined the K-F-D and the K-S-D. In general, the K-F-D has shown adequate interrater reliability, but relatively low test-retest reliability. Validity studies have been mixed with some studies finding differences between clinical groups, and others finding no discriminants. Few studies have addressed the K-S-D, but the overall results are similarly inconclusive. Prout and Celmer (1984) found several K-S-D variables correlated with school achievement, suggesting the drawing is globally related to school performance. A few studies have reported normative data for different groups that were included in the research, but formal norms do not exist. In general, however, neither technique offers adequate data from a psychometric standpoint.

As with the other techniques discussed, a variety of aspects of the multimodal assessment perspective can be addressed. This technique may be particularly useful in getting information on how younger and less verbal children view their two most important behavioral settings—home and school. Perhaps more than the drawings themselves, the inquiry and interview that follows the completion of the drawings may be most useful in a comprehensive assessment.

Summary

The instruments presented above are viewed as having some value within a behavioral assessment perspective. However, there are a number of deficiencies in the techniques that prevent them from being tools used as the major focus of an assessment. In general, they are unsound from a traditional psychometric standpoint, the scoring systems are inadequate, and the analytic theory that underlies their recommended interpretations is questionable. Thus, the use of these instruments as tests and in differential diagnosis and educational placement decision making is discouraged. The positive side is that, when used in conjunction with other techniques, they may contribute clinically meaningful information about affective, behavioral, cognitive, and social perception variables. Responses to these techniques may also serve as a springboard for more in-depth interviews with a child about different concerns as well as assist the assessor in developing and testing other clinical hypotheses.

CASE EXAMPLES

Because these techniques represent somewhat diverse approaches, it is unlikely that several of these instruments would be used on a single case. Three brief case examples are presented below (not comprehensive case studies) that demonstrate the use of thematic, sentence completion, and kinetic drawing techniques. The cases presented here provide examples of where projective tests have proven useful in particular situations. Again, current psychometric research literature on these techniques does not suggest that this is necessarily a generalized experience; these case studies may represent somewhat isolated cases of "clinical" validity.

Thematic Technique

Todd was a six-year-old first-grade student who was referred for evaluation by his classroom teacher. Her primary concerns were Todd's withdrawn behavior and lack of interaction with his classmates or herself. In the teacher interview, Todd was described as an academically capable student who completed all his assignments, but who participated minimally in class activities and became upset when called upon. Classroom observation indicated that Todd was generally attentive to tasks, able to complete written work, and follow directions. However, he appeared to be alone most of the day, not initiating contact with peers or the teacher, and responding passively to peer-initiated interaction (e.g., not talking back or simply following their activity). His responses to the teacher were either to cry or to verbalize minimally.

Todd's behavior during an interview was similar to that observed in the classroom with minimal interactions and one- to three-word responses to most questions. Although he didn't cry, his eye contact was minimal and he kept his hands in his lap the entire time. After two more sessions, which largely involved playing games, he was administered the Roberts Apperception Test for Children (RATC). He responded consistently to pictures with statements about the child not being liked and not having friends. He expressed feelings of sadness and fear of being laughed at. When asked what the children in the drawings could do to be liked, he responded, "Nothing." Further discussion of his responses to the cards seemed to indicate that Todd lacked the skills to play and talk with others. He was afraid of making a mistake and being laughed at. This information, in addition to other data, suggested a child with significant social skill deficits. The scenes depicted in the RATC picture were helpful in obtaining information about Todd's skills, thoughts, and feelings that were not obtained through observation or teacher report. A behavioral program to teach Todd specific peer interaction skills was developed, along with a program for reinforcement in the classroom for classroom participation.

Sentence Completion

Marcia, a thirteen-year-old seventh-grade student, was referred for evaluation by her guidance counselor. Referral concerns involved a rapid, continual drop in grades from the sixth grade, belligerent classroom behavior, truancy, and a hostile attitude towards her teachers, particularly male teachers.

An interview with Marcia's mother indicated no changes in the family living situation or any recent family crisis. Marcia resided with her mother, stepfather, and two younger siblings. This family situation had been stable for five years, and Marcia had no contact with her natural father for over seven years. According to Marcia's mother, Marcia viewed her stepfather as her biological parent. Teacher reports and behavioral ratings consistently indicated problems with acting out and aggressive behaviors, and with poor academic performance. Marcia was described as generally resistant and negative in class. If ignored, Marcia would become more disruptive and, seemingly, enjoyed removal from class. Classroom observations were consistent with these reports, with a higher frequency of negative behaviors occurring with male teachers and on Mondays and Fridays.

An initial interview with Marcia yielded minimal information other than factual data (e.g., number of people in her family, grade placement) and several I don't know responses. At the beginning of the second interview, Marcia was given a sentence completion task and asked to complete it with the first thoughts that came into her mind. Several of Marcia's responses were negative statements about her stepfather (e.g., "I wish my stepfather was dead"; "My father treats me too grown up") and about men (e.g., "Teachers are O.K. if they're girls"). There were also statements about the future (e.g., "I most want to leave home") and peers (e.g., "My friends aren't like me anymore"). Further questioning of Marcia about her responses led to her revealing that her stepfather had sexually abused her during the summer when her mother had been away on vacation. This information was used to make a referral for specialized counseling services and a social service intervention that eventually resulted in the stepfather's removal from the home.

Kinetic Drawings

Jason, a nine-year-old third grader, was referred by his classroom teacher because of behavioral and peer problems in the classroom, and after his mother had related concerns about Jason's reactions to the recent separation of his parents. During an interview, Jason's mother stated that she had noticed increased bickering and fighting with a younger sister and that Jason generally appeared sullen. His mother was also concerned about Jason's inability or unwillingness to ask questions or express any feelings about the separation, describing him as "bottled up."

In an initial interview, Jason was cooperative but denied any problems at home or school. "Everything's O.K.," was a typical response, and a variety of questions yielded vague and unelaborated answers. Following the interview, Jason was asked to produce a Kinetic Family Drawing (K-F-D). Initially, he had some difficulty deciding who to include in the drawing since his father was no longer living at home. He eventually completed a drawing that depicted the family in relatively normal activities that reflected the family situation before the marital conflict and separation. Intensive inquiries and interviews stemming from the drawing revealed a number of misconceptions Jason had about the family problems as well as more explicit details of his affective reactions. This provided a format to clear up the misconceptions and lay the base for a more affectively oriented intervention that followed.

Jason also completed a Kinetic School Drawing (K-S-D) in which he again initially hestitated before beginning the drawing. In response to the direction that he include a friend or two in the drawing, he stated that he really didn't have too many friends at school. He eventually drew himself isolated from his classmates and in an activity that got him in trouble with the teacher. Again, extended inquiries and interviews based on the drawing were employed. This yielded information about Jason's primary mode of getting attention in class was to engage in negative behavior. This was later confirmed with more specific classroom observation and an interview with the teacher, providing the foundation for a behavioral program in which Jason was taught positive behaviors that elicited positive attention from his peers and teacher.

CONCLUSION

The analogue method of assessment provides a number of options for assessing the behavioral and emotional problems of children and adolescents. Projective assessment techniques used in the traditional manner, however, appear essentially without an empirical base. In addition to being theoretically inconsistent with behavioral assessment, their scoring procedures, normative data, and validity and reliability data are inadequate. An alternative view of projective assessment is more consistent with the behavioral perspective, but is also currently without empirical support. Nonetheless, these analogue methods can be used cautiously in behavioral assessment to produce clinically useful data. This data should be used for hypothesis generation and supplemental to and in conjunction with other data collection procedures. Analogue approaches should not be the sole or primary focus in the assessment of social-emotional problems and should not be used in differential diagnosis, formal, classification, and educational placement decision making.

References

Allen, M. J., & Yen, W. M. (1979). *Introduction to measurement theory*. Monterey, Calif.: Brooks/Cole.
Ammons, C. H., & Ammons, R. B. (1972). Review of The Tasks of Emotional Development Test. *Psychological Reports, 31,* 679.

Anastasi, A. (1982). *Psychological Testing* (5th ed.). New York: Macmillan.

Bandura, A. (1978). The self-system in reciprocal determinism. *American Psychologist, 33,* 344-358.

Bersoff, D. N., & Grieger, R. M. (1971). An interview model for the psychosituational assessment of children's behavior. *American Journal of Orthopsychiatry, 41,* 483-493.

Burns, R. C., & Kaufman, S. H. (1970). *Kinetic Family Drawings (K-F-D).* New York: Brunner/Mazel.

Burns, R. C., & Kaufman, S. H. (1972). *Actions, styles, and symbols in Kinetic Family Drawings (K-F-D): An interpretative manual.* New York: Brunner/ Mazel.

Cohen, H., & Weil, G. R. (1971). *Tasks of emotional development: A projective test for children and adolescents.* Brookline, Mass.: T.E.D. Associates.

Cohen, H., & Weil, G. R. (1975). *Tasks of emotional development: A projective test for children and adolescents* (2d ed.). Brookline, Mass.: T.E.D. Associates.

Erickson, M. H. (1953). Therapy of a psychosomatic headache. *Journal of Clinical and Experimental Hypnosis, 1,* 2-6.

French, J., Graves, P. A., & Levitt, E. E. (1983). Objective and projective testing of children. In C. E. Walker & M. C. Roberts (Eds.), *Handbook of clinical child psychology* (pp. 209-247). New York: John Wiley & Sons.

Friedrich, W. N. (1984). Review of the Roberts Apperception Test for children. In D. J. Keyser & R. C. Sweetland (Eds.), *Test critiques* (Vol. 1, pp. 543-548). Kansas City, Mo.: Test Corporation of America.

Gittelman, R. (1980). The role of psychological tests for differential diagnosis in child psychiatry. *Journal of the American Academy of Child Psychiatry, 19,* 413-438.

Gittelman-Klein, R. (1978). Validity of projective tests for psychodiagnosis in children. In R. L. Spitzer & D. F. Klein (Eds.), *Critical issues in psychiatric diagnosis* (pp. 144-166). New York: Raven Press.

Goldman, J., Stein, C. L., Guerry, S. (1983). *Psychological methods of child assessment.* New York: Brunner/Mazel.

Gresham, F. M., & Elliott, S. N. (1984). Assessment and classification of children's social skills: A review of methods and issues. *School Psychology Review, 13,* 292-301.

Hart, D. H., Kehle, T. J., & Davies, M. V. (1983). Effectiveness of sentence completion techniques: A review of the Hart Sentence Completion Test for Children. *School Psychology Review, 12,* 428-434.

Keat, D. B. (1979). *Multimodal therapy with children.* Elmsford, N.Y.: Pergamon Press.

Knoff, H. M., & Prout, H. T. (1985). *Kinetic drawing system for family and school: A handbook.* Los Angeles: Western Psychological Services.

Lazarus, A. A. (1976). *Multimodal behavior therapy.* New York: Springer.

Lazarus, A. A. (1981). *The practice of multimodal therapy.* New York: McGraw-Hill.

Levitt, E. E. (1975). Review of the Tasks of Emotional Development Test. *Professional Psychology, 6,* 101-102.

Lindzey, G. (1959). On the classification of projective techniques. *Psychological Bulletin, 56,* 158-168.

Lindzey, G. (1961). *Projective techniques and cross-cultural research.* New York: Appleton-Century-Crofts.

Maloney, M. P., & Ward, M. P. (1976). *Psychological assessment: A conceptual approach.* New York: Oxford University Press.

McArthur, D. S., & Roberts, G. E. (1982). *Roberts Apperception Test for Children: A manual.* Los Angeles: Western Psychological Services.

McFall, R. M. (1977). Analogue methods in behavioral assessment: Issues and prospects. In J. D. Cone & R. P. Hawkins (Eds.), *Behavioral assessment: New directions in clinical psychology* (pp. 152-177). New York: Brunner/Mazel.

Mischel, W. (1968). *Personality and assessment.* New York: John Wiley & Sons.

Mischel, W. (1973). Toward a cognitive social learning reconceptualization of personality. *Psychological Review, 80,* 252-283.

Nay, W. R. (1979). *Multimethod clinical assessment.* New York: Gardner Press.

Nunnally, J. C. (1967). *Psychometric theory.* New York: McGraw-Hill.

Obrzut, J. E., & Boliek, C. A. (1986). Thematic approaches to personality assessment with children and adolescents. In H. M. Knoff (Ed.), *The assessment of child and adolescent personality* (pp. 173–198). New York: Guilford Press.

Ollendick. T. H., & Hersen, M. (1984). *Child behavioral assessment of children.* New York: John Wiley & Sons.

Palmer, J. O. (1970). *The psychological assessment of children.* New York: John Wiley & Sons.

Prout, H. T. (1983). School psychologists and social-emotional assessment techniques: Patterns in training and use. *School Psychology Review, 12,* 377–384.

Prout, H. T., & Celmer, D. S. (1984). School drawings and academic achievement: A validity study of the Kinetic School Drawing technique. *Psychology in the Schools, 21,* 176–180.

Prout, H. T., & Phillips, P. D. (1974). A clinical note: The Kinetic School Drawing. *Psychology in the Schools, 11,* 303–306.

Reitz, W. E. (1972). Review of the School Apperception Method. In O. K. Buros (Ed.), *The seventh mental measurements yearbook* (pp. 613–614). Highland Park, N.J.: Gryphon Press.

Sines, J. O. (1985). Review of the Roberts Apperception Test for Children. In J. V. Mitchell (Ed.), *The ninth mental measurements yearbook* (pp. 1289–1291). Lincoln, Neb.: The University of Nebraska, the Buros Institute of Mental Measurements.

Soloman, I. L., & Starr, B. D. (1968). *School apperception method.* New York: Springer.

Sundberg, N. D. (1972). Review of the School Apperception Method. In O. K. Buros (Ed.), *The seventh mental measurements yearbook* (pp. 614–615). Highland Park, N.J.: Gryphon Press.

Sundberg, N. D. (1977). *Assessment of persons.* Englewood Cliffs, N.J.: Prentice-Hall.

Watson, R. I. (1978). The sentence completion method. In B. B. Wolman (Ed.), *Clinical diagnosis of mental disorders: A handbook* (pp. 255–280). New York: Plenum Press.

Wise, A. J. (1975). Review of the Tasks of Emotional Development Test. *Professional Psychology, 6,* 102–103.

CHAPTER 10

Informant Reports

CRAIG EDELBROCK
University of Massachusetts Medical School

INTRODUCTION

Reports by informants play an important role in the assessment of behavior problems and competencies. Almost all phases of work with disturbed children, including referral, initial assessment, diagnostic and placement decisions, treatment monitoring, and outcome evaluation, involve information from adults such as parents and teachers. These informants are not expert observers of children's emotional and behavioral functioning, and the data they provide is neither precise nor perfectly reliable and valid. Nevertheless, the assessment of child psychopathology depends heavily on adults' cumulative impressions of children's functioning in naturalistic settings such as home and school.

Numerous behavioral checklists and rating scales have been developed to capture parents' and teachers' perceptions of children's emotional and behavioral functioning. These measures have many advantages over informal methods of obtaining information. First, they provide a standard inventory of descriptors to be rated, which provides a data language for communicating about a given child. Standardizing *what questions are asked* reduces variability in the information obtained and ensures that particular target phenomena will be covered. This permits one to make more direct comparisons among children and to determine how they are different or similar in reported behaviors. Second, checklists and rating scales provide an operation means for rating the presence, frequency, and severity of specific behaviors and for rating global attributes. Standardizing *how questions are asked* reduces the subjectivity inherent in such judgments and boosts reliability.

Checklists and rating scales have several other advantages. Compared with other assessment procedures, such as psychological testing, direct observation, and clinical interviewing, rating instruments are simple, fast, and economical in terms of both cost and professional time. They are also more amenable to large-scale assessment efforts, including epidemiological studies, screening efforts, and program evaluations. Rating scales can yield a wealth of information that is directly relevant to many clinical and research questions. They also yield quantitative indexes of child functioning that are useful for plotting stability and change in reported behaviors over time and in response to interventions. Rating scales with age-graded norms also provide a means of determining whether reported behaviors are appropriate or deviant in relation to normal peers.

The goal of this chapter is to review the use of checklists and rating scales as means of obtaining information on child functioning from informants such as parents and teachers. The major assumptions and limitations of this assessment approach are outlined first. The general rationale and method underlying the development and use of a rating scale are discussed. A few specific measures are reviewed and guidelines for choosing a rating scale are then offered. Finally, applications of rating scales in school settings are outlined and illustrated by a case example.

ASSUMPTIONS AND LIMITATIONS

The use of parent and teacher ratings to assess child behavior depends on many assumptions. As Cairns and Green (1979) have pointed out, it is assumed that the rater understands the construct being rated and knows which observable behaviors pertain to that construct. It is further assumed that there is universal agreement regarding the reference points for scaling such ratings. Moreover, the informant must be able to extract a cumulative impression of the target construct from the stream of everyday life activities. There is considerable variability in the degree to which these assumptions are fulfilled.

There are many risks of measurement error at virtually all phases of the rating process. Informants may have different interpretations of an item such as hyperactivity, for example, and they may regard different observable behaviors as pertaining to that item. Slippage also arises from how reference points, such as not at all, just a little, pretty much, and very much, are interpreted and used when making ratings.

Informants also differ in the type and amount of exposure they have to the target child and in their ability to make accurate ratings based on their experience. Since children's behaviors vary across time, settings, and situations, differences among reports by different informants are expected. Moreover, the characteristics of the informants themselves are likely to influence their reports to some degree. Recent studies, for example, have shown that mothers who describe themselves as depressed report more problem behaviors in their children (see Brody & Forehand, 1986; Friedlander, Weiss, & Traylor, 1986). This suggests that depression may bias adult perceptions of child problem behavior, resulting in inflated ratings. Of course, it is also possible that maternal depression is associated with an actual increase in child problem behaviors. Whatever the explanation, it is clear that adults' ratings of child behaviors reflect both true child behaviors and diverse and complex aspects of the informant.

GENERAL RATIONALE AND METHOD

Many child behavior rating scales have been developed and they differ in many ways. However, the construction of most rating scales has followed similar steps. First, a list of items covering child abilities, behaviors, or characteristics is generated. Procedures for obtaining ratings of the presence, frequency, or severity of each item are also developed. Ratings on a large sample of children are then collected. Scales reflecting different domains, dimensions, or syndromes are constructed and scoring procedures are developed. These scales can then be standardized on normative samples and can be evaluated psychometrically. This may sound simple enough, but major issues arise at virtually every step in the development process.

Target Phenomena

First of all, what should be assessed? Most rating scales are not linked to any theory of maladaptive behavior that would dictate what to assess. The target phenomena are usually selected on just a rational basis. The focus may be broad (e.g., child psychopathology, behavioral functioning, maladjustment, social competence) or narrow (e.g., hyperactivity, depression, aggression). Even if the conceptual focus of the measure is clear, it is still necessary to develop specific items. Untrained informants such as parents and teachers cannot be expected to make complex clinical inferences regarding underlying psychological constructs. They require items that refer to fairly overt, easily observable events, behaviors, or characteristics. Items are often culled from existing literature in the area of interest or from previously developed measures. Sometimes, the items are derived from more primary sources such as case records of disturbed children, unstructured reports by teachers, etc. Items may also be pretested for clarity, acceptability, comprehension, and relevance by obtaining feedback from parents, teachers, or child mental health professionals.

Response Scaling

After the item pool has been developed, one must select a means of recording responses. What aspect of the target phenomena should be rated? Presence? Frequency? Duration? Severity? Obviously, response formats can vary widely and range from dichotomous alternatives (e.g., Yes/No; True/False; Present/Absent) to quantitative gradations (e.g., Not at all; Rarely; Sometimes; Often; Always). Most child behavior rating scales do not attempt to obtain precise information regarding the specific frequency or intensity of target behaviors. For example, parents are generally not asked to report exactly how many temper tantrums their child has had in a particular period of time, but rather to make a global rating (e.g., None; A few; A lot). Informant reports are recognized as being fairly crude and attempts to be overly precise in the rating format tend to decrease rather than increase reliability and validity. As a general rule, it is better to obtain crude data that are relatively robust, rather than precise data that are untrustworthy.

Time Frame

What time frame should be used? Again there is no correct answer; it depends upon the focus and purpose of the measure. Typical time frames are usually from one day to several months. Rating scales that cover long time spans depend more on the assumption that the informant can extract a cumulative impression of the target phenomena from many observations and interactions with the child. Surprisingly, many rating scales do not specify a time frame for making ratings. This is a major methodological shortcoming. Without specific guidelines, informants may base their ratings on different time frames, thus adding to measurement error and reducing the comparability of data across subjects.

Scale Construction

With most rating scales, the interest is not just in the specific items, but in broader patterns, domains, dimensions, or syndromes. The rating of specific items is usually combined into summary scores. Moreover, multidimensional measures comprising several different scales are superior to unidimensional ones. But how are scales developed and how are summary scores obtained? Some measures are scored according to rational or a priori scales reflecting traditional clinical constructs such as "hyperactivity" or "anxiety." However, empirical evaluations often show that such a priori scales are not internally consistent. Their items are not highly correlated with one another, suggesting that they do not tap a uniform domain. The validity of a priori scales is obviously limited if they fail to reflect the natural patterning of the target phenomena.

As an alternative approach, scales can be constructed empirically using statistical procedures such as factor analysis. Factor analysis is a multivariate statistical procedure that summarizes correlations among many variables in terms of a few underlying dimensions or factors. Each factor comprises a set of salient items that are highly correlated with the underlying dimension (and with each other). The salient items from each factor can be used to construct a scale comprising a homogeneous set of closely related items. Unlike the a priori scales, factor-based scales are virtually guaranteed to be internally consistent and to reflect the natural patterning of the data.

Factor Analysis

There are many technical problems and issues related to the use of factor analysis to develop scales (see also Edelbrock, 1986). For one, it is possible to obtain factors that do not reflect any familiar domain, syndrome, or dimension. Some factors are very difficult to interpret. An unusual subgrouping of items, despite their appearing to be a confusing conglomeration, may still be valid and useful. However, the possibility remains that it is a statistical artifact. Second, there are many different types of factor analysis, and different methods can yield different results when applied to the same data. Moreover, each step in the factoring procedure entails many methodological alternatives. Some of the complexities of factor analysis can be illustrated by considering some rather basic questions.

First, how many factors are there? One might expect that there would be a simple, straightforward, and standard procedure for determining the number of factors. Unfortunately there is not. Some analysts use *eigenvalues* to determine the number of factors. An eigenvalue is a measure of how much variance is accounted for by a factor. An eigenvalue of 1.00, for example, reflects the average variance of one item, an eigenvalue of 2.00 reflects the average variance of two items, and so on. Intuitively, a factor that accounts for less variance than a single item (eigenvalue < 1.00) is not worth much. One might just as well score each item individually. For that reason, many researchers retain only those factors having eigenvalues greater than 1.00. This is the most common rule for determining the number of factors.

Factors are extracted from the correlation matrix in the order of the amount of variance they explain. The first factor is the largest, accounts for the most variance, and therefore has the highest eigenvalue. This is followed by successively smaller factors with smaller and smaller eigenvalues. In most factor analysis the first few factors account for the greatest proportion of variance. These are often followed by many factors with eigenvalues just slightly higher than 1.00. Why retain many factors that are just marginally better than single items? Why not focus on the major factors that account for the most variance? Cattel's (1966) *scree test* was developed to do just that. Rather than considering the absolute magnitude of the eigenvalues, the scree test considers their relative magnitude. Using the scree test, one examines the factors in order of extraction and finds the point where there is a relatively large drop in eigenvalues. Only factors above that point are retained. This is obviously a more conservative rule. Despite the appeal of the scree test, it is a fairly subjective procedure. The researcher simply inspects a plot of eigenvalues and chooses a breakpoint. Sometimes there is an obvious breakpoint corresponding to a large drop in eigenvalues. However, other times the curve is fairly smooth and the choice of breakpoint is difficult and arbitrary. To complicate matters further, some researchers do not use eigenvalues at all to determine the number of factors. They might select the number of factors on rational or theoretical grounds (e.g., Kohn & Rosman, 1972), or they might specify that a factor must have a minimum number of items with loadings exceeding some cutoff (e.g., Achenbach & Edelbrock, 1983).

After determining the number of factors, one must still determine which items comprise which factors. Factor analytic methods are designed to yield simple structure. That is, the method should yield a parsimonious set of relatively independent factors, each factor should comprise a distinct subset of highly loaded items, and each item should load highly on few factors. Unfortunately, simple structure is an ideal that is rarely obtained in the real world. Usually, factors are not perfectly independent, they comprise some items with low to moderate loadings, and some items may load highly on numerous factors.

There is no consensus regarding statistical criteria for simple structure, and different factoring procedures try to achieve simple structure in different ways. The initial factor matrix can be transformed in different ways to approximate simple structure. Different types of transformations are called rotations. Some types of rotations are aimed at constructing perfectly independent factors. The Varimax rotation, for example, is designed to yield uncorrelated (orthogonal) factors. Oblique rotations, such as Equamax, Quartimax, and Quartimin, in contrast, permit correlations between factors.

After obtaining a factor solution, the researcher often wants to translate each factor into a scale comprised of a subset of highly loaded or salient items. The factoring results themselves do not reveal which items are salient for which factors. Rather, the loadings of each item on each factor are listed. Several problems must be solved in order to translate these results into scales.

First, a minimum loading must be selected for identifying salient items. For each factor, items having loadings above that cutoff point are retained for the scale, whereas those having loadings at or below the cutoff point are discarded. The choice is somewhat arbitrary, but minimum loadings in the range of .25 to .40 are commonly used. Generally speaking, higher minimum loadings yield more homogeneous scales than lower minimum loadings. However, as the minimum loading increases, fewer and fewer items will be retained. If the minimum loading is too high, the resulting scale will be comprised of too few items. Conversely, if the minimum loading is too low, the resulting scale will be comprised of many items, but many will be only weakly related to the underlying factor.

Second, it is common to find items having high loadings on two or more factors. This occurs because each factor accounts for only a portion of the total variance of an item and different factors may account for different variance components. Items that load highly on two or more factors have been treated in different ways. In some studies, such items have been retained on all scales in which they exceed the minimum loading. After all, a given behavior may be relevant to different syndromes or dimensions. Poor peer relations, for example, might be related to either shyness or aggression. In other studies, such items have been discarded completely or have been retained only on the factor on which they load most highly. This is thought to result in purer and more independent scales.

In summary, factor analysis is a commonly used method of constructing scales from checklists and rating scales, but it entails many technical and methodological problems and issues. Despite the broad range of alternative factoring procedures, most researchers have opted for principal components or principal factor analysis with Varimax rotation. In the area of parent and teacher ratings of child behavior, for example, these factoring procedures have been used almost exclusively (see Achenbach & Edelbrock, 1978, 1984 for reviews). Nevertheless, criteria for determining the number of factors have varied widely, as have the criteria for determining salient items and for translating factors into scales.

Scoring

After determining which items will comprise a given scale, scoring procedures must be developed for translating raw item responses into summary scores. Numerical values are first assigned to each response alternative. For example, for True or False ratings, a response of True might be assigned a value of one, and a response of False might be assigned a value of zero. Adding these values for each item scored on the scale yields a summary score for the scale, which in this case reflects the total number of scale items reported as true. The situation is more complex when dealing with multistep scales reflecting a combination of presence, frequency, and severity. Response alternatives such as not at all, a little, and a lot, for example, might be assigned various numerical values. For example, values of 0, 1, and 2 might be assigned to not at all, a little, and a lot, respectively. This decision is somewhat arbitrary, but it has many implications. For one, the response a lot is given twice as much weight as the response a little, even though it does not necessarily reflect twice as much frequency or severity. The scaling of responses is obviously crude and the numerical values assigned to responses might not accurately reflect the target phenomena. For a given item and informant, for example, a rating of a lot may reflect five times the frequency or severity as a rating of a little, but the former response would still be given only twice as much weight as the latter.

Another question that often arises is whether items should be differentially weighted when computing summary scores. For example, more salient items might be given more weight than less salient items. The assumption here is that emphasizing the core items results in a better summary index. This may sound like a compelling argument, but most authorities do not favor differential weighting of items. The major difficulty is in determining the weights themselves. What criteria should be used to determine item weights? Factor loadings have been used, but this has many shortcomings. For instance, factor scores can be obtained by multiplying the raw score for each item by its loading, then totaling these products. Not only is this procedure extremely complicated and cumbersome, but the contribution of the few highly loaded salient items is often washed out by the cumulative contribution of the many low loading items. In other words, a little bit of signal is obscured by lots of noise. Alternatively, if one uses a minimum loading to define only salient items, the range of loadings will be limited and the net effect of weighting each salient item by its loading will be minimal.

There is a more fundamental problem with differentially weighting items. Because the weights themselves are often poorly estimated and are unreliable, summary scores based on weighted items are rarely better than those based on equal weights (see Wainer, 1976). In terms of predictive and discriminative power, scores based on equal weights perform as well as or better than scores based on differential weights. Moreover, scores based on equal weights are more robust—they hold up better over time and across samples—than weighted scores.

In sum, to obtain summary scores for scales comprised of subsets of items, each response alternative can be assigned a numerical value. The values can be added across all items scored for the scale yielding a raw scale score. Differentially weighting items within a scale is not advisable because the weights are difficult to determine. Furthermore, scores based on weighted items perform no better than scores based on equally weighted items.

Standardization

Raw scale scores have limited utility. They can be used to test for differences between criterion groups and to plot change over time. However, raw scores have little intrinsic meaning and they are difficult to interpret. The meaning and value of raw scores can be greatly enhanced by standardization. The purpose of standardization is to locate a given score on a continuum in relation to some reference group. One can then determine if the scores are typical, high, or low, compared with the reference group. A second purpose of standardization is to metrify the raw data, that is, to translate raw scores on different scales into a common metric. Two key questions arise when constructing norms: What is the appropriate reference group? What form should standardization take?

The appropriate reference group is usually taken to be a representative sample of children of the same general age. Random sampling of school or community populations is presumed to yield samples reflecting the general population (see Goyette, Conners, & Ulrich, 1978; Miller, 1972). Of course, a representative sample is likely to include a certain proportion of subjects known to be deviant on the characteristic being measured, which can contaminate the norms to some degree. To avoid this problem, a normative sample can be constructed that includes subjects considered "normal" according to some criterion (e.g., Achenbach & Edelbrock, 1983). The criteria for defining what is normal vary, but the basic principle is to obtain a sample of the healthy population.

In the simplest form, standardization is comprised of a measure of central tendency (i.e., median or mean) and a measure of variability (i.e., range or standard deviation) of raw scores. In more complex schemes, data from normative samples have been used to transform raw scale scores into standard scores. For example, raw scores for each scale can be converted into z-scores (mean $= 0$, standard deviation $= 1.00$) or T-scores (mean $= 50$, sd $= 10$). Standard scores can be constructed in different ways. The most common procedure is to construct deviation scores, which are based on deviation from the normative mean as measured in standard deviation units. This works well when the raw score distribution is nearly normal in shape. When the distribution of raw scores is highly skewed, as is the case in most measures of psychopathology, deviation scores are less appropriate. In nonnormal distributions, the standard deviation is a poor measure of variability around the mean and it is highly influenced by outliers. Moreover, in skewed data, deviation scores do not correspond to percentile ranks dictated by the normal curve. For these reasons, normalized T-scores are often used when raw score distributions are highly skewed. Normalized T-scores are based on percentile ranks, not deviations from the mean. Percentile rank is a good index of relative standing in skewed data and it is not influenced by outliers.

Norms also vary in quality and usefulness. Few behavior rating scales have been standardized in adequate normative samples and no standardization efforts to date have approached the rigor of intelligence and achievement test norms. Norms for some measures are based on small, haphazard, and potentially biased samples that are poorly representative of any general child population. Also, given the large differences usually found between boys and girls and between children differing in age, it is generally advisable to stratify norms by sex and age, but this is not always done (see Edelbrock, 1984).

HISTORICAL PERSPECTIVE

Many checklists and rating scales have been developed in the past twenty-five years. The "first generation" of checklists and rating scales (e.g., Conners, 1969, 1970; Miller, 1967, 1972; Peterson, 1961; Ross, Lacey, & Parton, 1965; Rutter, 1967; Walker, 1970) were relatively crude by current standards. Most of these measures were somewhat limited in scope and coverage of items, were developed on small or haphazard samples, or were poorly standardized or not standardized at all. They have been followed by a "second generation" of measures that are superior in many ways. The newer measures comprise a broader and more comprehensive pool of items, employ newer rating formats and procedures, have been developed on larger and more representative samples, and have been more adequately standardized. The more recently developed measures are also geared more to current diagnostic constructs and criteria than their predecessors.

Clinical and research attention in the last ten years has focused on a handful of second generation measures having undergone extensive development. Unfortunately, a recent survey of school psychologists (Goh & Fuller, 1983) indicated that the most widely used rating scales in school settings are informal, nonstandardized ones. Moreover, when more formally developed rating scales are employed, they tend to be first-generation measures. Second-generation measures, despite their conceptual and methodological advantages, have not been widely used in the schools.

OVERVIEW OF MEASURES

The focus of this review is on three second-generation measures that have been widely researched in the past ten years. Each of these measures taps a broad range of emotional and behavioral problems and is therefore useful in diverse clinical and research applications. Two of these measures represent revisions of first generation measures: the Revised Behavior Problem Checklist (Quay & Peterson, 1983) and Conners' Revised Parent and Teacher Rating Scales (Goyette, Conners, & Ulrich, 1978). Although the original versions will be reviewed briefly, the more recent revisions are recommended for clinical and research applications. The third measure, the Child Behavior Checklist and Profile (Achenbach & Edelbrock, 1983), is a new second-generation measure. Several other measures, including some focused on particular areas, will also be discussed.

This review is obviously selective. It covers primarily second-generation parent and teacher rating scales focused on children's emotional and behavioral functioning. Hoge (1983) has recently provided a broader review of teacher ratings of pupil aptitude, behavior, and achievement. For more comprehensive discussions of behavior problem scales, see the recent reviews by Barkley (1986) and McMahon (1984) and the excellent book *Behavioral Assessment of Childhood Disorders* (Mash & Terdal, 1981).

The Behavior Problem Checklist

The Behavior Problem Checklist (BPC) represents one of the first efforts to standardize an informant's ratings of children's emotional and behavioral functioning. The original version contained fifty-eight items referring to fairly overt, observable behaviors (e.g., has temper tantrums, says no one likes him or her, impulsive) that were commonly reported in child guidance center case histories. Each item is rated on a 0-1-2 response scale corresponding to not a problem, a mild problem, and a severe problem, respectively. No time frame for making ratings is given. Peterson (1961) administered the BPC to teachers of 831 children attending regular school classes in kindergarten through the sixth grade. Separate factor analysis for each grade revealed two behavioral syndromes that were labeled Personality Problem and Conduct Problem. The Personality Problem syndrome consisted of inwardly directed behaviors such as feelings of inferiority, social withdrawal, and anxiety, whereas the Conduct Problem syndrome consisted of outwardly directed behaviors such as arguing, fighting, disobedience, and disruptiveness.

These two syndromes have emerged in analyses of parent, teacher, and mental health worker ratings, and in studies of diverse child populations, such as normal seventh and eighth graders (Quay & Quay, 1965), disturbed children (Quay, Morse, & Cutler, 1966), and preadolescent delinquents (Quay, 1966). Overall, these studies suggest that the dichotomy between Personality Problem and Conduct Problem syndromes have broad generalization to a wide range of measures, informants, and child populations. Some analyses of the BPC have yielded a third factor comprised of behaviors such as preoccupation, short attention span, and distractibility (see Quay, 1979 for a review). This factor was originally labeled Immaturity, but has been reinterpreted as reflecting primarily attention problems.

The BPC has undergone many minor revisions and over the years some items have been added or reworded based on research findings. The BPC has been used in more than 100 published studies and has proven to have adequate reliability and validity as an index of child problem behavior (see Quay, 1977). The BPC has also been used for very diverse purposes including epidemiological surveys, screening and early identification efforts, prevention programs, treatment research, and program evaluation.

Prompted by the widespread use of the BPC, Quay and Peterson undertook a major revision of the measure in 1979. The item pool was expanded to 150 items to strengthen scales having few items and to test for the existence of other syndromes, particularly anxiety, psychotic behavior, and overactivity. Factor analysis of four separate clinical samples of children revealed six major behavioral syndromes: Conduct Disorder, Socialized Aggression, Attention Problem-Immaturity, Anxiety-Withdrawal, Psychotic Behavior, and Motor Excess (Quay & Peterson, 1983, 1984). Sample items from these six scales of the Revised Behavior Problem Checklist (RBPC) are listed in Table 10-1. The number of items has been trimmed to eighty-nine by eliminating items not scored on any scale.

As shown in Table 10-1, the RBPC yields greater resolution of the broadband Conduct Problem syndrome into more circumscribed narrow-band syndromes. Specifically, items that comprised the previous Conduct Problem syndrome have been split into four distinct syndromes: Conduct Disorder, Socialized Aggression, Attention Problems-Immaturity, and Motor Excess. The new Attention Problems-Immaturity syndrome resembles the Immaturity syndrome derived from some previous BPC analyses. The new Anxiety-Withdrawal syndrome is very similar to the previous Personality Problem syndrome, but the new Psychotic Behavior syndrome had no counterpart in previous BPC analyses (primarily because such items were lacking in the orginal BPC).

Norms for the RBPC scales, in the form of means and standard deviations, are available for teacher ratings and parent ratings of nonclinical samples of children. Comparison can also be made with scores obtained by special populations including inpatient and outpatient clinic attendees, special education students, gifted students, and institutionalized delinquents.

The RBPC is a relatively new rating scale, so there is little data regarding its reliability and validity. However, there is every reason to expect that it will perform psychometrically as well as its predecessor. Initial analyses (see Quay, 1983; Quay & Peterson, 1983, 1984) have shown that the RBPC scales have high internal consistency (mean = .83). Interteacher reliability has been high for the Conduct Disorder scale (.85) and the Socialized Aggression scale (.75), but has been somewhat lower for the remaining four scales (mean = .55). Mother-father agreement has averaged .73 for the six RBPC scales. Two-month test-retest reliabilities have ranged from .49 to .83.

The validity of the RBPC is supported by several lines of evidence. First of all, clinically referred children have been found to score significantly higher on all six

TABLE 10-1 Sample Items from the Six Scales of the Revised Behavior Problem Checklist (RBPC)

Conduct Disorder
    Disruptive, annoys and bothers others
    Fights
    Impertinent, talks back
    Blames others, denies own mistakes

Socialized Aggression
    Stays out late at night
    Loyal to delinquent friends
    Has "bad" companions, ones who are always in some kind of trouble
    Admires and seeks to associate with "rougher" peers

Attention Problems—Immaturity
    Short attention span, poor concentration
    Distractible, easily diverted from the task at hand
    Sluggish, slow moving, lethargic
    Has trouble following directions

Anxiety—Withdrawal
    Self-conscious, easily embarrassed
    Feels inferior
    Lacks self-confidence
    Generally fearful, anxious

Psychotic Behavior
    Repetitive speech
    Expresses strange, farfetched ideas
    Expresses delusions
    Parrots others' speech

Motor Excess
    Restless
    Tense
    Hyperactive
    Squirms, fidgets

scales than nonreferred "normal" children (see Quay, 1983). Second, scores on the RBPC scales have been found to discriminate significantly between diagnostic subgroups of disturbed children (Quay & Peterson, 1983). Third, RBPC scores have been found to correlate significantly with both peer nominations and behavioral observations. For example, scores on the Conduct Disorder scale correlated positively with observational ratings of aggression and negatively with observational ratings of cooperation (see Quay & Peterson, 1983). Lastly, RBPC scores have been found to correlate negatively with measures of intellectual ability and academic achievement.

In summary, the original BPC represented one of the first efforts to obtain standard reports of children's behavioral functioning from informants such as parents and teachers. The BPC has been widely used for both clinical and research purposes and its reliability and validity are supported by a large body of findings. The Revised BPC yields a more finely grained assessment of behavioral syndromes and early research on it suggests that it will be useful as the original version.

Conners's Rating Scales

The rating scales developed by Conners (1969, 1970, 1973) have been widely used in research, particularly in the area of childhood hyperactivity. These rating scales have undergone various revisions and have been under some factor analysis many times, both by Conners and by other investigators. Conners and his colleagues have also revised and restandardized these measures (Goyette, Conners, & Ulrich, 1978). Several different versions of the questionnaires, scales, and norms are available. Furthermore, some versions have variations in item wording or have completely different items and therefore cannot be scored according to existing scales and norms. This situation has caused considerable confusion among users and integration of research findings across studies is almost impossible. It is extremely important, therefore, to identify which version of Conners's scales one is using and to determine which sets of scales and norms should be used in scoring.

Conners's original teacher rating scale (Conners, 1969) had thirty-nine items covering primarily overt behavior problems (e.g., excitable, defiant, inattentive). Each item is rated on a four-step scale corresponding to not at all present, just a little present, quite a bit present, and very much present. Five behavioral syndromes were derived through factor analysis: Aggressive Conduct Disorder, Daydreaming-Inattentive, Anxious-Fearful, Hyperactivity, and Sociable-Cooperative (Conners, 1969). Scores on these factor-based scales were sensitive to the effects of drug treatment of hyperactivity and, among the placebo group, were highly reliable over a one-month retesting interval (average $r = .84$).

At least four other sets of factor-based scales and norms for the thirty-nine-item teacher rating scale have been published by others (Glow, 1979; Thorley, 1983; Trites, Blouin, & Laprade, 1982; Werry, Sprague & Cohen, 1975). In a manual, Conners (undated) has recommended the use of six scales derived by Trites *et al.* (1979) from data on a very large sample of Canadian children. These scales have been labeled Hyperactivity, Conduct Problem, Emotional Overindulgent, Anxious-Passive, Asocial, and Daydream-Attendance Problem. Norms for each scale, broken down by age and sex, have been published by Trites *et al.* (1982) and have been reprinted in the manual. Unfortunately, these norms are drawn from one Canadian city, which limits their generalization.

Conners and his colleagues have also completed a major revision and restandardization of the original teacher rating scale (Goyette, Conners, & Ulrich, 1978). The Revised Teacher Rating Scale is comprised of only twenty-eight items and is scored on three factor-based scales: Conduct Problem, Hyperactivity, and Inattentive Passive. Norms, in the form of means and standard deviations based on 373 randomly selected school children, have also been published (See Goyette, Conners, & Ulrich, 1978).

The original parent rating scale had seventy-three items that were rated on the same four-step scale as the teacher measure. Factor analysis of parent ratings yielded five syndromes: Aggressive Conduct Disorder, Anxious-Inhibited, Antisocial Reaction, Enuresis, and Psychosomatic Problems. Scores on these scales discriminated well between referred and nonreferred children, supporting the validity of the measure. Moreover, scores on two scales, Aggressive Conduct Disorder and Anxious-Inhibited, were found to discriminate significantly between conduct disordered and neurotic subgroups of disturbed children.

Conners and Blouin (1980) reanalyzed the original data (Conners, 1970) and derived eight new factors: Conduct Disorder, Fearful-Anxious, Restless-Disorganized, Learning Problem-Immature, Psychosomatic, Obsessional, Antisocial, and Hyperactive-Immature. Means and standard deviations based on 683 children ages six through fourteen are available, but have not been broken down by age and sex.

Conners' Parent Rating Scale has also been revised and restandardized (Goyette, Conners, & Ulrich, 1978). The parent measure was shortened to forty-eight items and six new scales were derived through factor analysis. These scales were given the summary labels Conduct Problems I (e.g., destructive, fighting), Learning Problem, Psychosomatic, Impulsive-Hyperactive, Conduct Problems II (e.g., arguing, disobedience), and Anxiety. Norms for each scale have been reported separately for boys and girls ages three to five, six to eight, nine to eleven, twelve to fourteen, and fifteen to seventeen.

Conners (1973) has also developed a brief questionnaire, sometimes called the "Hyperkinesis Index." The main asset of this ten-item scale is brevity. It is so easy to complete that it can be administered repeatedly in order to plot changes in reported behavior over time and in response to interventions. Unfortunately, there are several versions of this measure in circulation, each with unique item content and wording (see Ullmann, Sleator, & Sprague, 1985). In addition, the Revised Parent and Teacher Rating Scales (Goyette, Conners, & Ulrich, 1978) can be scored on a ten-item Hyperkinesis Index, but there are some differences between the parent and teacher versions and neither version corresponds to the previous Abbreviated Questionnaires (Abbott Labs, 1972; Conners, 1973). This situation is so complex and confusing that some have recommended that Conners's scales simply be abandoned in favor of newer measures (Ullmann, Sleator, & Sprague, 1985). Another alternative might be to use the ten-item scales (and norms) published by Goyette, Conners, and Ulrich (1978) and to assiduously avoid comparisons with any and all findings based on previous versions.

There is a considerable body of research supporting the reliability and validity of Conners's rating scales, but the findings obviously depend on the specific version used and on which scales and norms were employed in scoring. Generally speaking, short-term test-retest reliabilities for parent and teacher ratings have ranged from .7 to .9, whereas interrater (mother-father, teacher-teacher) reliability has ranged from .5 to .7 (Conners, 1969, 1973; Edelbrock, Greenbaum, & Conover, 1985; Glow, 1979; Goyette, Conners, & Ulrich, 1978). One year stability has ranged from .3 to .5 for teachers' ratings and from .4 to .7 for parents' ratings (Glow, Glow,

& Rump, 1982). Parent-teacher agreement has ranged between .3 and .5 for scales having similar content (Glow, 1979; Goyette, Conners, & Ulrich, 1978).

'The validity of Conners's scales is supported by (1) highly significant correlations with many other measures of child behavior and psychopathology, (2) the ability to discriminate well between normal and hyperactive children, (3) significant discrimination between diagnostic subgroups of children, and (4) proven sensitivity to drug effects in double-blind treatment trials (see Barkley, 1977, 1981, 1986; Conners, undated; Edelbrock & Rancurello, 1985; for reviews).

In summary, Conners's ratings scales have been widely used in research on child psychopathology and they have adequate reliability and validity for diverse clinical and research applications. However, different versions of the parent and teacher scales exist and several different sets of scales and norms have been published. Care must be exercised when selecting one of Conners's scales for use, when scoring and interpreting the data, and when comparing results with previous findings. Conners has recommended that if the thirty-nine-item teacher rating scale is used, it should be scored according to the scales and norms developed by Trites *et al.* (1982). Goyette, Conners, and Ulrich (1978) have provided the appropriate scales and norms for the revised parent rating scale (forty-eight items) and the revised teacher rating scale (twenty-eight items). The original parent rating scale should be scored according to the scales derived by Conners and Blouin (1980). Norms are available for these scales (see Conners, undated), but they are limited to children aged six through fourteen and are not broken down by sex. There are many versions of the ten-item Abbreviated Questionnaire (Hyperkinesis Index) so users must be extra cautious about misinterpretations arising from incorrect norms and invalid comparisons with previous findings based on different versions. Moreover, the validity and usefulness of both the ten-item and the thirty-nine-item teacher rating scales have recently been questioned (Ullmann, Sleator, & Sprague, 1985).

The Child Behavior Checklist

The parent and teacher versions of the Child Behavior Checklist (CBCL) have been designed to tap a broad range of children's behavior problems and adaptive competencies (Achenbach, 1978; Achenbach & Edelbrock, 1979; Edelbrock & Achenbach, 1984). The CBCL, designed to be completed by parents, includes twenty social competence items covering school performance, social relations, and amount and quality of participation in hobbies, activities, and sports, and 118 items covering specific behavior problems (e.g., argues, cries, temper tantrums, steals). Behavior problem items are rated on a 0-1-2 scale, corresponding to not true, somewhat or sometimes true, and very or often true, respectively. Parents are instructed to use a six-month baseline for reporting their children's behavior.

The parent CBCL is scored on the Child Behavior Profile, which is comprised of three a priori social competence scales labeled Activities, Social, and School, and behavior problem scales derived through factor analysis of CBCLs completed on large samples of clinically referred children. To account for age and sex differences in the prevalence and patterning of reported behaviors, Profiles have been developed and standardized separately for boys and girls ages four to five, six to eleven, and twelve to sixteen. Norms for each scoring Profile have been constructed from CBCLs completed by 1300 randomly selected nonreferred children age four through sixteen (see Achenbach & Edelbrock, 1981, 1983).

Table 10-2 lists the behavior problem scales derived for each age and sex group. As shown in this table, from eight to nine behavioral syndromes were derived for each group. Several syndromes are similar enough across groups to warrant the same summary labels (e.g., Aggressive, Delinquent, Somatic Complaints). Some syndromes are specific to boys (e.g., Uncommunicative) or girls (e.g., Cruel), whereas other syndromes are specific to younger children (e.g., Depressed) or older adolescents (e.g., Immature). In other words, the six sex and age editions of the Profile comprise both common syndromes and syndromes specific to one sex or developmental period.

Table 10-2 also lists which narrow-band behavior problem syndromes for each sex and age group align with broad band groupings. Second-order factor analysis, which involves analyzing the correlations among scores on the narrow-band syndromes, revealed two broadband groups, labeled Internalizing and Externalizing. The Internalizing syndrome is comprised of behaviors such as anxiety, withdrawal, and depression, whereas the Externalizing syndrome encompasses behaviors such as aggression, delinquency, and hyperactivity. Thus, Internalizing and Externalizing correspond to the global Personality Problem and Conduct Problem syndromes derived from the Behavior Problem Checklist (see Achenbach, 1966; Quay & Peterson, 1983). The Child Behavior Profile is one of the few measures that permits simultaneous scoring of both narrow-band and broadband behavior problem syndromes.

The teacher version of the Child Behavior Checklist and Profile have also been completed recently (Achenbach & Edelbrock, 1986; Edelbrock & Achenbach, 1984). The teacher checklist is similar in content and format to the parent CBCL, but there are some differences. The competence section of the teacher version is focused more on school placement, classroom behavior, and academic performance than on general social functioning. The behavior problem section overlaps about 80% with the parent version, but items that are inappropriate for teachers (e.g., nightmares, bedwetting, relations with siblings) were replaced with items more relevant to school settings (e.g., difficultly following directions, disrupts class, messy work).

The teacher Checklist is scored on profiles that include a priori school performance and adaptive functioning scales and behavior problem scales derived through a factor analysis of Checklists completed on large samples of clinically referred children. Separate scoring profiles have been developed and standardized for boys and girls ages six to eleven and twelve to sixteen. Norms have been constructed from Checklists completed on 1100 randomly selected children attending regular school classes (see Achenbach & Edelbrock, 1986).

TABLE 10-2 Syndromes Derived from the Child Behavior Checklist

Group	Internalizing Syndromes	Mixed Syndromes	Externalizing Syndromes
Boys age 4–5	1. Social Withdrawal 2. Depressed 3. Immature 4. Somatic Complaints	5. Sex problems	6. Schizoid 7. Aggressive 8. Delinquent
Boys age 6–11	1. Schizoid or Anxious 2. Depressed 3. Uncommunicative 4. Obsessive-Compulsive 5. Somatic Complaints	6. Social Withdrawal	7. Hyperactive 8. Aggressive 9. Delinquent
Boys age 12–16	1. Somatic Complaints 2. Schizoid 3. Uncommunicative 4. Immature 5. Obsessive-Compulsive	6. Hostile Withdrawal	7. Delinquent 8. Aggressive 9. Hyperactive
Girls age 4–5	1. Somatic Complaints 2. Depressed 3. Schizoid or Anxious 4. Social Withdrawal	5. Obese	6. Aggressive 7. Sex Problems 8. Hyperactive
Girls age 6–11	1. Depressed 2. Social Withdrawal 3. Somatic Withdrawal 4. Schizoid-Obsessive		5. Hyperactive 6. Sex Problems 7. Delinquent 8. Aggressive
Girls age 12–16	1. Anxious-Obsessive 2. Somatic Complaints 3. Schizoid 4. Depressed Withdrawal	5. Immature-Hyperactive	6. Delinquent 7. Aggressive 8. Cruel

Table 10-3 lists the behavior problem scales of the teacher profile for each sex and age group. Several syndromes were similar enough to those derived from parents' reports to warrant the same summary labels (e.g., Aggressive, Delinquent, Social Withdrawal). As with the parent CBCL and Profile, some syndromes derived from teachers' ratings were common across sex and age groups, whereas others were specific to one sex or age group. Also, second-order factor analysis revealed higher-order groupings of scales resembling the dichotomy between Internalizing and Externalizing found previously (see Table 10-3).

One-week test-retest reliabilities for the behavior problem scales have averaged .89, whereas two- and four-month stabilities have averaged .77 and .64, respectively. Validity of the teacher Checklist and Profile is supported by highly significant correlations with observational ratings of children's classroom behavior, and other measures of child problem behavior; and by the ability to discriminate significantly between clinically referred and nonreferred children, diagnostic subgroups of disturbed children, and pupils in regular versus special education classes (Edelbrock & Achenbach, 1984; Edelbrock, Costello, & Kessler, 1984; Edelbrock,

TABLE 10-3 Syndromes Derived from the Teacher Version of the Child Behavior Checklist

Group	Internalizing Syndromes	Mixed Syndromes	Externalizing Syndromes
Boys age 6–11	1. Anxious 2. Social Withdrawal	3. Unpopular 4. Self-destructive 5. Obsessive-Compulsive	6. Inattentive 7. Nervous-Overactive 8. Aggressive
Boys age 12–16	1. Social Withdrawal 2. Anxious	3. Unpopular 4. Obsessive-Compulsive 5. Immature 6. Self-destructive	7. Inattentive 8. Aggressive
Girls age 6–11	1. Anxious 2. Social Withdrawal	3. Depressed 4. Unpopular 5. Self-destructive	6. Inattentive 7. Nervous-Overactive 8. Aggressive
Girls age 12–16	1. Anxious 2. Social Withdrawal	3. Depressed 4. Immature 5. Self-destructive	6. Inattentive 7. Unpopular 8. Delinquent 9. Aggressive

Greenbaum, & Conover, 1985; Harris, King, Reifler, & Rosenberg, 1984; Kazdin, Esveldt-Dawson, & Loar, 1983; Reed & Edelbrock, 1983).

Other Measures

This review has concentrated on three measures that are widely used, cover diverse child behaviors, and are designed for a broad range in age. Several other measures deserve mention. Some are omnibus measures of child behavior that have been less widely used, but still have distinct assets. Others are more narrowly focused on particular domains of child behavior or on a particular age group.

The Preschool Behavior Questionnaire

The Preschool Behavior Questionnaire (PBQ) (Behar, 1977; Behar & String-field, 1974) is one of the few measures designed for children as young as three years old. It is designed to be completed by teachers or teacher aids and includes thirty items, each rated on a 0-1-2 scale corresponding to doesn't apply, applies sometimes, and certainly applies, respectively. The PBQ is scored on three factor-based scales labeled Hostile-Aggressive, Anxious, and Hyperactive-Distractible. A total behavior problem score can also be computed as a general index of maladjustment. PBQ scores have been found to have adequate reliability and to discriminate significantly between normal and disturbed preschoolers. Scores on the Hyperactive-Distractible scale have been useful in identifying very young hyperactive children (see Campbell et al., 1982).

Eyberg's Child Behavior Inventory

The Eyberg Child Behavior Inventory (ECBI) is a thirty-six-item parent rating scale focused primarily on childhood conduct problems (Eyberg & Ross, 1978). The ECBI employs a unique type of response scaling. Parents indicate whether or not each behavior is a problem by circling either yes or no. Each item is then rated on a 1 (never) to 7 (always) frequency scale. The ECBI yields a problem score, which is simply the number of behavior problem items present, and an intensity score, which is the sum of frequency ratings (range: 36 to 252). Three-week test-retest reliability has been reported as .86 for the intensity score and .88 for the problem score (Robinson, Eyberg, & Ross, 1980). Mother-father agreement has averaged .79 (Eyberg & Robinson, 1983). Adequate normative standardization has not been done, but data on 102 pediatric referrals are available as a comparison group (Eyberg & Robinson, 1983). In terms of validity, ECBI scores discriminate significantly between normal and conduct problem children; correlate significantly with observational assessment of parent-child interactions; and are sensitive to the effects of parent training in child behavior management skills (Eyberg & Robinson, 1983; Eyberg & Ross, 1978; Robinson & Eyberg, 1981).

Brief Hyperactivity Scales

Several brief scales have been developed to assess childhood hyperactivity (see Edelbrock & Rancurello, 1985 for a review). Two measures have been designed to tap DSM-III criteria for Attention Deficit Disorder with Hyperactivity (ADDH). Ozawa and Michael (1983) developed a fifteen-item teacher rating scale in which each item is rated from 1 (never) to 5 (always). It yields a nine-item impulsivity score and a six-item distractibility score, as well as a composite score. The SNAP Rating Scale (see Atkins, Pelham, & Licht, 1985; Johnston, Pelham & Murphy, 1985) is a literal translation of DSM-III criteria into a rating scale that uses the four-step response format of Conners's measures. The SNAP rating scale has been used in research to identify children with ADDH (see Johnston *et al.*, 1985).

Loney and Milich (1981) used Conners's teacher ratings scale as the basis for a new ten-item scale that taps independent dimensions of aggression and hyperactivity. Using chart ratings of clinically referred children as a criterion, five items were selected that correlated primarily with aggression, and five items were selected that correlated primarily with inattention and overactivity. The measure has been used to differentiate among three diagnostic subtypes: pure aggressive, pure hyperactive, and mixed aggressive and hyperactive (see Langhorne & Loney, 1979; Loney, Langhorne, & Paternite, 1978).

Several other brief hyperactivity scales deserve mention. The Werry-Weiss-Peters Activity scale is a thirty-one-item scale focused more narrowly on restless and fidgety behavior (see Routh, Schroeder, & O'Tauma, 1974). Davids (1971) has developed a seven-item hyperactivity scale designed to be completed by either parents or teachers. Spring and his colleagues have developed a thirty-three-item

Hyperactivity Rating Scale designed to be completed by teachers (Spring, Blunden, Greenberg, & Yellin, 1977). Lastly, Ullmann and her colleagues have developed a brief teacher rating scale focused on attention deficits that has considerable promise as a research tool (Ullmann, Sleator, & Sprague, 1985).

Home and School Situations Questionnaires

Barkley (1981) has developed two unique measures that assess the situations in which child problem behaviors occur. The Home Situations Questionnaire (HSQ) lists sixteen situations at home (e.g., while watching TV, when playing alone, when going to bed) and asks whether any behavior problems occur during these times. Parents indicate either yes or no to each item, and if yes is indicated they rate the severity of the problem on a 1 (mild) to 9 (severe) scale. The School Situations Questionnaire (SSQ) is similar in format, but situations at school are listed (e.g., during lectures, during individual desk work, at recess). Preliminary analyses suggest that these measures are useful when the situational contingencies of problem behavior are of interest (see Barkley & Edelbrock, 1987).

GUIDELINES FOR CHOOSING RATING SCALES

It is difficult and perhaps inadvisable to make blanket recommendations regarding specific rating scales. The range of possible settings, informants, child populations, assessment purposes, time constraints, and available resources is too great to permit the formulation of simple rules for choosing an informant report measure. However, some simple conceptual, practical, and technical guidelines can be offered.

A basic conceptual consideration is whether the measure suits the application. There obviously must be a good match between the measure and the purpose of the assessment. For example, a measure may be too narrowly focused for purposes such as initial assessment of general referrals. Alternatively, it may be too broad for an evaluation of an intervention aimed at modifying specific behaviors.

Practical considerations will also help narrow the range of choices considerably. The measure must be appropriate for the age range of the subjects as well as the particular informant that will be used (i.e., parent or teacher). The response burden of the measure should also be considered. Teachers may balk at having to fill out an extremely long rating scale on every child in their classes, but may cooperate in completing a brief screening measure. The financial costs of the assessment materials themselves should not be overlooked. Time requirements, both for completion and scoring, may be a limiting factor in certain large-scale applications.

Several technical aspects of how the measure has been developed and standardized have been discussed in the previous section on rationale and method (see also Edelbrock, 1983). Briefly, the specific items, materials, and rating procedures should be carefully inspected. Some measures contain items that are simply inappropriate or irrelevant. Rating scales also differ in level of analysis: some are focused on global attributes, whereas others are comprised of extremely molecular items. Response scaling also varies considerably. In general, dichotomous response scaling (e.g., Yes/No, True/False, Present/Absent) is less useful than polychotomous scaling (e.g., not true, somewhat true, very true). On the other hand, complex response formats that require precise estimates of frequency, duration, or severity are less useful with untrained raters such as parents and teachers. The number and type of scales for scoring item responses should also be considered. In general, multidimensional assessments are superior to unidimensional ones (depending on the purpose of the assessment) and empirically derived scales are superior to scales developed a priori. The availability of norms is also essential and the type and quality of normative standardization should be carefully considered (see Edelbrock, 1984).

Lastly, the psychometric performance of the measure should be weighed. Adequate test-retest and interrater reliability should be provided by the developer. By definition, all factor-based scales have high internal consistency, but that does not guarantee high reliability. Most measures demonstrate short-term (one week to one month) test-retest reliabilities of $r = .80$ or better. Interrater reliability occurs largely because there is a base of similar experiences with the target child. Mothers and fathers have fairly similar exposure to their children's behaviors and their ratings tend to be highly correlated with one another ($r = .70$ or better). On the other hand, parents and teachers observe and interact with children in very different situations and settings, so their ratings tend to correlate only moderately with one another ($r = .30 - .40$). No measure is ever proven valid for all applications, but evidence supporting validity should also be supplied.

APPLICATIONS IN SCHOOL-BASED ASSESSMENTS

The applications of informant report measures in school-based assessment are similar to those in clinical settings. Edelbrock and Rancurello (1985) have recently outlined several roles rating scales can play in clinical work. First, they are directly relevant to initial evaluations of referred children. The goal in an initial assessment is often to obtain a broad overview of the child's emotional and behavioral functioning, including the identification of salient problems and competencies. Omnibus rating scales, such as the Child Behavior Checklist and Revised Behavior Problem Checklist, are well suited to initial evaluations of general referrals. Such assessments can help determine if the child is in fact behaviorally deviant and whether further action is warranted.

Rating scales are also relevant to the diagnosis and classification of disturbed children. Edelbrock (1986) has outlined ways in which behavioral ratings can be used to group subjects into categories. A variety of procedures is available for classifying subjects according to the severity and patterning of scores on behavioral dimensions. Only a few measures, such as the SNAP rating scale, have been designed to tap diagnostic criteria per se. Most do not attempt precise assessment of specific diagnostic criteria, such as those offered in the *Diagnostic and Statistical Manual of Mental Disorders* (DSM) (American Psychiatric Association, 1980). However, most rating scales tap diagnostically relevant aspects of children's emotional and behavioral functioning. Moreover, scores on many empirically derived dimensions of child behavior have been shown to discriminate between diagnostic subgroups of disturbed children, so their role as part of a more comprehensive diagnostic workup seems well justified. No one would recommend basing clinical diagnoses on a single assessment instrument, but informants' reports are crucial to the differential diagnosis of many child psychiatric disorders. The DSM (APA, 1980, pp. 41–45), for example, recommends that teachers' reports of the child's behavior be considered when diagnosing Attention Deficit Disorder (hyperactivity). Unfortunately, the DSM does not say how such information should be obtained. Rating scales provide one solution to this dilemma.

Reports and ratings from parents and teachers are also crucial when making treatment and placement decisions. Standardized rating scales can help determine the type and degree of behavioral deviance in relation to normal peers, and if the child is in need of special treatment or school placement. They can also quantify the degree of deviance in several areas, which may facilitate the selection and prioritization of treatment goals.

The quantitative information derived from parent and teacher ratings is also useful in treatment monitoring and evaluation. Rating scales, especially the brief ones, can be readministered periodically to monitor changes in the child's behavior and to determine if treatment goals are being met. Some rating scales, such as those developed by Conners, have been shown to be sensitive to treatment effects. Rating scales have also been widely used in research on child psychopathology: as descriptive and classification tools in epidemiological surveys, as a means of selecting homogeneous samples of disturbed children, and as dependent variables in studies of the etiology, development, treatment responsiveness, and outcome of variations and deviations in child behavior (see Barkley, 1986; Edelbrock & Rancurello, 1985, for examples).

Several administrative and research applications seem particularly relevant to schools (see also Achenbach & Edelbrock, 1986). First, if a given rating scale is used as part of a core evaluation of all referrals within a school, a database will develop that can be mined in numerous ways. Such a database, for example, could be used to establish more explicit and operational criteria for referral and placement. By documenting the types and degree of behavioral deviations among children who are already placed in special classes or programs, one can study the implicit criteria at work in such placement decisions. Guidelines can be developed for determining how similar a newly referred child is to those already judged appropriate for a particular program or placement.

Another important research goal is to determine which interventions are helpful with which particular types of children. Longitudinal follow ups can reveal which types of children benefit from which types of educational mental health services—and, alternatively, which types do not benefit. This information can be used to develop a more prescriptive system for an optimum match of children to the services and placements they receive, and it can spur the development of innovative programs for types of children who have uniformly poor outcomes. Lastly, many pupils referred for evaluation have poor academic achievement. Behavioral disturbances may stem from underlying cognitive impairments. For children with normal cognitive abilities, however, emotional and behavioral problems may cause or contribute to their poor academic performance. Problems of inattention and hyperactivity, for instance, are highly incompatible with good academic performance.

CASE EXAMPLE

The use of parent and teacher rating scales can be illustrated by a case example of an eight-year-old boy named Billy. Rating scales were used, in conjunction with several other assessment methods, in several phases of Billy's initial evaluation, treatment, and outcome assessment.

During the third month of the second grade, Billy was referred to a school psychologist for evaluation. The teacher's primary complaint was that he was "aggressive," "disruptive," "restless," and "not learning." Billy's academic progress in first grade had been slightly below average, but he had been falling farther behind in reading and math since starting the second grade. Billy's parents had met with his teacher shortly after school began because they were concerned about his slow progress in the past year. They felt that he was "immature" and that he would "grow out" of his behavioral problems soon.

Billy was tested with the WISC-R and obtained a Performance IQ of 102 and a Verbal IQ of 109 (Full Scale IQ was 105). Further psychological testing did not show any significant delays or deficits in speech, language, perception, or memory. This suggested to his school psychologist that behavioral problems may be causing his poor academic performance. Results from the Peabody Individual Achievement Test revealed that he was in fact lagging behind his peers in both reading and math achievement.

The teacher's version of the Child Behavior Checklist was used to assess Billy's behavior. The behavior problem portion of the scored teacher profile as shown in Figure 10-1. For boys ages six to eleven, the teacher profile is comprised of eight behavior problem scales: Anxious, Social Withdrawal, Unpopular, Self-Destructive, Obsessive-Compulsive, Inattentive, Nervous-Overactive, and Aggressive. The first two scales correlate positively with one another and form a broadband Internalizing grouping, whereas the last three scales form a broadband Externalizing grouping (see Figure 10-1). The behavior problem scales are ordered from left to right on the profile according to their loadings on the broadband dichotomy between Internalizing and Externalizing. The Anxious scale, for example, is the most highly loading Internalizing scale, followed by Social Withdrawal, and so on. Conversely, Aggressive is the most highly loading Externalizing scale, followed by

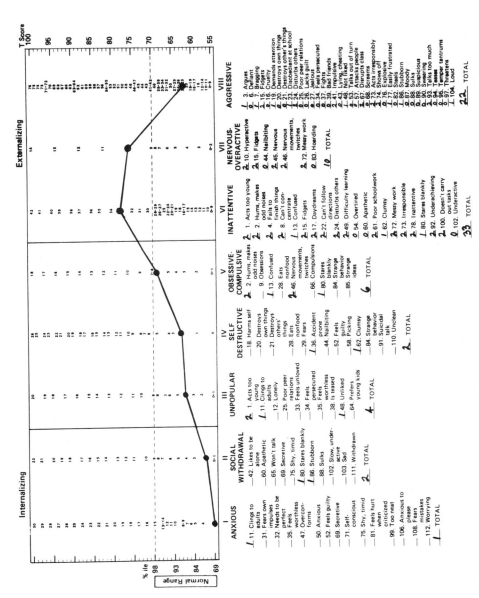

FIGURE 10-1. Sample Teacher Profile for an Eight-Year-Old Boy

374

Nervous-Overactive, Inattentive, and so on. The three scales in the middle of the profile had moderate loadings on both the Internalizing and Externalizing factors and therefore represent mixed scales.

Items scored on each scale are shown in Figure 10-1, as are the teacher's response to each item. As discussed previously, each item is rated by the teacher on a 0-1-2 scale, corresponding to not true, somewhat or sometimes true, and very or often true, respectively. A raw score for each scale is computed by adding the 0, 1, or 2 for each item on the scale. For example, only one item (11. Clings to adults) was rated a 1 on the Anxious scale, so the raw score for that scale is 1. Raw scores for each scale are converted to standardized T-scores by entering them in the graphic display above the scale. For example, a raw score of 1 for the Anxious scale corresponds to a T-score of 55, a raw score of 2 for the Social Withdrawal scale corresponds to a T-score of 57, and so on. T-scores, which range from 55 to 100, correspond to percentiles obtained by 300 randomly selected boys ages six to eleven (see Edelbrock & Achenbach, 1984). A "perfectly normal" boy would obtain a T-score of 55 on each scale, which corresponds to at or below the 69th percentile, as shown on the left side of the profile. A T-score of 60, which is one standard deviation above the mean, corresponds to the 84th percentile, and so on. Two standard deviations above the mean obtained by the normative sample is taken as the upper limit of the "normal range" of scores, as indicated on the scored profile. This corresponds to a T-score of 70 (the 98th percentile obtained by the normative sample of boys ages six to eleven. Scores at or below T = 70 are interpreted as within the normal range of variation, whereas scores greater than T = 70 represent clinically significant behavior problems.

As shown in Figure 10-1, Billy obtained scores well within the normal range on scales I through V, suggesting no significant problems in the areas of anxiety, social withdrawal, peer acceptance, suicidal and self-destructive behavior, or obsessions—compulsions. However, he scored well outside the normal range on scales VI and VII, suggesting clinically significant problems of inattention and overactivity. As shown by the items his teacher rated as being very or often true, Billy was described as having severe problems in concentrating, following directions, finishing his work, carrying out assigned tasks, learning, and working up to his potential. He was also reported to act too young for his age, make odd noises in class, daydream, disturb other pupils, and act irresponsibly. The items on the Nervous-Overactive scale also suggest that Billy is extremely restless, tense, fidgety, and overactive in class. Surprisingly, Billy's score on the Aggressive scale was within the normal range. The initial referring complaints involved aggressiveness, but this was not borne out by the teacher profile. Billy was not overtly aggressive, but was mildly disobedient and impulsive, and often disrupted the class by clowning and showing off.

An in-depth interview with his teacher revealed that Billy's disruptiveness stemmed from his becoming bored and distracted during class. Instead of listening and following directions, Billy was often fidgety and restless in his chair, he dropped things on the floor, and he got out of his seat repeatedly. He tended to distract other children in the class and was prone to acting up and clowning when others were watching him. To help identify the situations in which Billy acted up, his teacher completed Barkley's (1981) School Situations Questionnaire. The results revealed that he was pretty well behaved in most school situations, but tended to be a problem during lectures to the class. This was particularly irritating to his teacher because he made it more difficult for other children to concentrate on what was being said.

The parent version of the Child Behavior Checklist was completed by Billy's mother. All scores on the Child Behavior Profile were within the normal range. Few behaviors related to inattention and overactivity were reported, but Billy was described as mildy oppositional (stubborn temper tantrums, disobedient, uncooperative). Billy's mother reiterated her conviction that these were signs of "immaturity" and that he would soon grow out of these problems. As a further test, the school psychologist asked Billy's mother to make him complete one hour of reading and math homework, which was obtained from his teacher and sent home with him. Billy's mother called the next day and said she was very surprised how difficult it was for Billy to sit still, to concentrate on the homework assignment, to follow directions, and to complete the task. He was constantly fidgeting in his chair, he got up many times, and he was easily distracted by the slightest noises in the room. These problems were also obvious when the school psychologist observed Billy in his classroom over the next few days.

Billy's teacher suggested placement in a special class for behaviorally disordered children at the same school, but the school psychologist recommended against it. According to the teacher's own report, Billy was not as severely disturbed as children in that class. On the average, children in the behavior disorders class had much higher scores than Billy on the Inattentive and Nervous-Overactive scales and they had very high scores on the Aggressive scale, which made them behaviorally very different from Billy. The decision was made that Billy was not severely disturbed enough to warrant special class placement.

Billy's teacher agreed to try to manage his behavior in her regular class and met with the school psychologist to work out a behavioral program designed to reduce his disruptiveness and increase his academic performance. The school psychologist suggested a token economy wherein Billy would earn points for on-task behavior and completing his assignments. However, the teacher felt it was too difficult to implement such a program for one child in a regular class. They agreed to try two things. First, the teacher set time limits for Billy to complete specific assignments. Billy was given a quota of work to be done during a specific time period that was timed. Second, each day Billy's teacher completed a Daily Report Card in which she rated his performance in four areas (participation, class work, homework, and social interaction) for each class period during the school day (see Barkley, 1983, p. 108). The Daily Report Card was sent home with Billy each day. Billy's mother met with the school psychologist and agreed to use the Daily Report Card as a means of determining rewards and privileges for Billy at home. These interventions were tried for one month and some slight improvements were seen.

Billy seemed less disruptive to class discipline and he sometimes worked hard at his desk. However, the major problems of distractibility, short attention span, and fidgety behavior persisted and even seemed a little worse.

Since Billy's scores on the teacher version of the Child Behavior Profile closely resembled those of children diagnosed as having Attention Deficit Disorder (Edelbrock, Costello, & Kessler, 1984), the school psychologist recommended that he be evaluated by his pediatrician. Based on a more comprehensive medical and psychiatric evaluation, his pediatrician felt that he would benefit from a trial of stimulant medication to reduce his inattention and distractibility. To monitor treatment effects, the pediatrician asked Billy's teacher to complete Conners's ten-item Abbreviated Teacher Questionnaire at the end of each week during the four-week drug trial. Billy's teacher was also told that some days Billy would be on the medication, and other days he would be on a placebo, so improvements in his behavior might fluctuate. Scores on Conners's measure during the drug trial are shown in Figure 10-2.

During the first week on medication, Billy's teacher noticed a big improvement in his behavior. He seemed less fidgety and restless and was better able to listen, follow directions, and concentrate. Few problems were reported on Conners's measure so his score was rather low (see Figure 10-2). During the second week, he seemed to be back to his old self and his score was very high. However, during the third and fourth weeks he was very well behaved in class and his scores were very low. The teacher even wrote on the form that he was doing very well in class and that he seemed to be learning more.

As it turned out, during the first week Billy was taking a low dose of the medication, which resulted in some improvements. He was on the placebo during the second week, so it was not surprising that his teacher noticed more problems. During the third and fourth weeks, Billy was taking a moderate dose of the drug, which resulted in substantial improvement.

On the basis of this placebo-controlled trial, Billy's pediatrician decided to keep him on the moderate dose for the rest of the school year. His teacher reported that he was doing much better in class, and was much more able to listen, concentrate, follow directions, and complete his work without being distracted. Two months after the initial evaluation, the teacher Checklist was completed again. All scores were within the normal range. However, his teacher reported that he was still prone to act up and clown occasionally in front of others, especially during lectures. He was doing much better in reading, but his math skills still lagged behind the rest of the class. A simple program was developed in which Billy earned one point for each hour in class that he did not act up and clown around. When he earned enough points, the entire class got a reward, which resulted in encouragement from some of his friends. This seemed to help so the program was continued for six weeks. Billy also began spending fifty minutes a day in a resource room receiving special math tutoring.

This case example illustrates several uses of informant reports during several phases of a school psychologist's job. The initial referring complaints from the

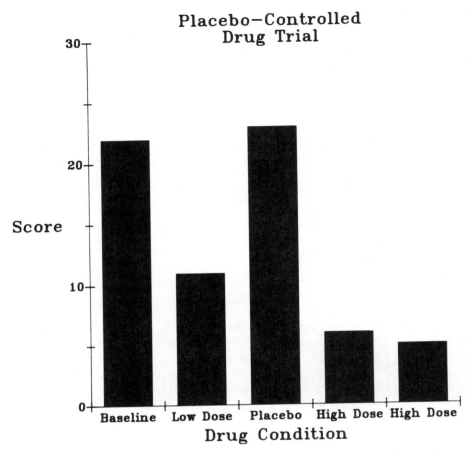

FIGURE 10-2. Scores on the Conners Abbreviated Teacher Questionnaire during a Four-Week Placebo-Controlled Drug Trial

teacher, for example, were sketchy and somewhat misleading. Obtaining a standardized report helped specify the perceived problem, identify major areas of behavioral deviation, and quantify the severity of the deviation. The use of a questionnaire focused on situations helped identify the specific settings and circumstances that seemed to trigger the problem behaviors. Obtaining both parent and teacher reports proved useful despite the fact that the two informants did not agree about the nature of Billy's problem. It seemed clear, for example, that Billy's attention problems emerged primarily at school and not at home. However, when his mother watched him trying to work on reading and math problems, she could see the problems noted by his teacher.

Placement in a behavior disorders class also seemed inadvisable since Billy was not as severely inattentive and overactive as many children already in that class and he did not manifest the overt aggression seen in many of those children. Standardized teacher's ratings also proved diagnostically useful. The brief teacher rating scale was also very useful in monitoring treatment effects. The full teacher measure was also readministered later in the school year to evaluate outcome and to see whether other problems remained after the primary treatment objectives had been accomplished. It is important to note also that informant ratings were not the sole means of assessing Billy's behavior, ability, and potential. They were part of a much broader multimethod assessment that included psychological testing, interviewing, and direct observation.

SUMMARY AND CONCLUSIONS

The assessment of child psychopathology depends heavily on reports and ratings by adults. Despite progress in other areas, such as self-reports and direct observations, adults' cumulative impressions of children's behavioral functioning are crucial and continue to play a central role in clinical and research efforts pertaining to children. Informant reports are certainly crude and fallible indexes of children's behavior, abilities, and competencies, but several instruments designed to capture parents' and teachers' perceptions have acceptable reliability and validity. These measures have the additional advantages of being relatively inexpensive and efficient in terms of time and professional resources.

Checklists and rating scales designed for parents and teachers differ in many ways, and conceptual, practical, and psychometric considerations are important in choosing an instrument for a particular application. The available measures have a broad range of clinical applications, including initial evaluation, diagnosis and classification, treatment selection and monitoring, outcome evaluation, and professional training. The research and administrative applications of checklists and rating scales are also broad. Such measures can be applied to a number of important tasks in the area of school mental health, particularly when used as part of a broader multimethod assessment of child psychopathology.

Acknowledgments

Preparation of this chapter was supported in part by NIMH grant #MH37372 and by a Faculty Scholar's Award from the William T. Grant Foundation.

References

Abbott Labs. (1972). *Teacher's questionnaire*. Chicago: Author.
Achenbach, T. M. (1966). The classification of children's psychiatric symptoms: A factor-analytic study. *Psychological Monographs, 80*, (7, Whole No. 615).

Achenbach, T. M. (1978). The Child Behavior Profile: I. Boys aged 6–11. *Journal of Consulting and Clinical Psychology, 46,* 478–488.

Achenbach, T. M., & Edelbrock, C. S. (1978). The classification of child psychopathology: A review and analysis of empirical efforts. *Psychological Bulletin, 85,* 1275–1301.

Achenbach, T. M., & Edelbrock, C. S. (1979). The Child Behavior Profile: II. Boys aged 12–16 and girls aged 6–11 and 12–16. *Journal of Consulting and Clinical Psychology, 47,* 223–233.

Achenbach, T. M., & Edelbrock, C. S. (1981). Behavior problems and competencies reported by parents of normal and disturbed children aged 4 through 16. *Monographs of the Society for Research in Child Development, 46* (1, Serial No. 188).

Achenbach, T. M., & Edelbrock, C. S. (1983). *Manual for the Child Behavior Checklist and Revised Child Behavior Profile.* Burlington, Vt.: Author.

Achenbach, T. M., & Edelbrock, C. S. (1984). Psychopathology of childhood. *Annual Review of Psychology, 35,* 227–256.

Achenbach, T. M., & Edelbrock, C. S. (1986). *Manual for the teacher version of the Child Behavior Checklist and Profile.* Burlington, Vt.: Author.

American Psychiatric Association. (1980). *Diagnostic and statistical manual of mental disorders* (3d ed.). Washington, D.C.: Author.

Atkins, M. S., Pelham, W. E., & Licht, M. H. (1985). A comparison of objective classroom measures and teacher ratings of Attention Deficit Disorder. *Journal of Abnormal Child Psychology, 13,* 155–168.

Barkley, R. (1977). A review of stimulant drug research with hyperactive children. *Journal of Child Psychology and Psychiatry, 18,* 137–165.

Barkley, R. (1981). *Hyperactive children: A handbook for diagnosis and treatment.* New York: Guilford Press.

Barkley, R. (1983). Hyperactivity. In R. J. Morris & T. R. Kractochwill (Eds.), *The practice of child therapy.* Elmsford, N.Y.: Pergamon Press.

Barkley, R. (1986). A review of child behavior rating scales and checklists for use in research on child psychopathology. In M. Rutter, A. H. Tuma, & I. Lann (Eds.), *Assessment and diagnosis in child and adolescent psychopathology.* New York: Guilford Press.

Barkley, R., & Edelbrock, C. S. (1987). Assessing situational variations in children's problem behavior: The Home and School Situations Questionnaires. *Advances in Behavioral Assessment of Children and Families, 4,* 157–176.

Behar, L. (1977). The Preschool Behavior Questionnaire. *Journal of Abnormal Child Psychology, 5,* 265–275.

Behar, L. B., & Stringfield, S. (1974). A behavior rating scale for the preschool child. *Developmental Psychology, 10,* 601–610.

Brody, G., & Forehand, R. (1986). Maternal perceptions of child maladjustment as a function of the combined influence of child behavior and maternal depression. *Journal of Consulting and Clinical Psychology, 54,* 237–240.

Cairns, R. B., & Green, J. A. (1979). How to assess personality and social patterns: Observations or ratings? In R. B. Cairns (Ed.), *The analysis of social interactions* (pp. 209–226). Hillsdale, N.J.: Lawrence Erlbaum Associates.

Campbell, S. B., Szumowski, E. K., Ewing, L. J., Gluck, D. S., & Breaux, A. M. (1982). Multidimensional assessment of parent-identified behavior problem toddlers. *Journal of Abnormal Child Psychology, 10,* 569–592.

Cattell, R. B. (1966). The scree test for number of factors. *Multivariate Behavioral Research, 1,* 245–276.

Conners, C. K. (Undated). *The Conners Rating Scales: Instruments for the assessment of childhood psychpathology.* Unpublished manual.

Conners, C. K. (1969). A teacher rating scale for use in drug studies with children. *American Journal of Psychiatry, 126,* 884–888.

Conners, C. K. (1970). Symptom patterns in hyperkinetic, neurotic, and normal children. *Child Development, 4,* 667–682.

Conners, C. K. (1973). Rating scales for use in drug studies with children. *Psychopharmacology Bulletin*, (special issue), 24–84.

Conners, C. K., & Blouin, A. G. (1980). Hyperkinetic syndrome and psychopathology in children. Paper presented at the anuual meetings of the American Psychological Association, Montreal, Canada.

Davids, A. (1971). An objective instrument for assessing hyperkinesis in children. *Journal of Learning Disabilities*, 4, 499–501.

Edelbrock, C. (1983). Problems and issues in using rating scales to assess child personality and psychopathology. *School Psychology Review*, 12, 293–299.

Edelbrock, C. (1984). Developmental considerations. In T. H. Ollendick & M. Hersen (Eds.), *Child behavioral assessment: Principles and procedures* (pp. 20–37). Elmsford, N.Y.: Pergamon Press.

Edelbrock, C. (1986). Diagnosis and classification. In S. Elliott (Ed.), *Handbook of behavior therapy in education*. New York: Plenum Press.

Edelbrock, C., & Achenbach, T. M. (1984). The teacher version of the Child Behavior Profile: I. Boys aged 6–11. *Journal of Consulting and Clinical Psychology*, 52, 207–217.

Edelbrock, C., & Achenbach, T. M. (1985). The teacher version of the Child Behavior Profile: II. Boys aged 12–16 and girls aged 6–11 and 12–16. Unpublished manuscript.

Edelbrock, C., Costello, A. J., & Kessler, M. K. (1984). Empirical corroboration of Attention Deficit Disorder. *Journal of the American Academy of Child Psychiatry*, 23, 285–290.

Edelbrock, C., Greenbaum, R., & Conover, N. C. (1985). Reliability and concurrent relations between the teacher version of the Child Behavior Profile and Conners' Revised Teacher Rating Scale. *Journal of Abnormal Child Psychology*, 13, 295–304.

Edelbrock, C., & Rancurello, M. (1985). Childhood hyperactivity: An overview of rating scales and their applications. *Clinical Psychology Review*, 5, 429–445.

Eyberg, S. M., & Robinson, E. A. (1983). Conduct problem behavior: Standardization of a behavior rating scale with adolescents. *Journal of Clinical Child Psychology*, 12, 347–354.

Eyberg, S. M., & Ross, A. W. (1978). Assessment of child behavior problems: The validation of a new inventory. *Journal of Clinical Child Psychology*, 7, 113–116.

Friedlander, S., Weiss, D. S., & Traylor, J. (1986). Assessing the influence of maternal depression on the validity of the Child Behavior Checklist. *Journal of Abnormal Child Psychology*, 14, 123–133.

Glow, R. A. (1979). Cross-validity and normative data on the Conners Parent and Teacher Rating Scales. In K. Gadow & J. Loney (Eds.), *Psychosocial aspects of drug treatment for hyperactivity*. Boulder, Colo.: Westeview Press.

Glow, R. A., Glow, P. H., & Rump, E. E. (1982). The stability of child behavior disorders: A one-year test-retest study of the Adelaide versions of the Conners teacher and parent rating scales. *Journal of Abnormal Child Psychology*, 10, 33–60.

Goh, G. B., & Fuller, D. S. (1983). Current practices in the assessment of personality and behavior by school psychologists. *School Psychology Review*, 12, 240–243.

Goyette, C. H., Conners, C. K., & Ulrich, R. (1978). Normative data on Revised Conners Parent and Teacher Rating Scales. *Journal of Abnormal Child Psychology*, 6, 221–236.

Harris, J. C., King, S. L., Reifler, J. P., & Rosenberg, L. A. (1984). Emotional and learning disorders in 6–12-year-old boys attending special schools. *Journal of the American Academy of Child Psychiatry*, 23, 431–437.

Hoge, R. D. (1983). Psychometric properties of teacher-judgment measures of pupil aptitudes, classroom behaviors, and achievement levels. *Journal of Special Education*, 17, 401–429.

Johnston, C., Pelham, W. E., & Murphy, H. A. (1985). Peer relationships in ADDH and normal children: A developmental analysis of peer and teacher ratings. *Journal of Abnormal Child Psychology*, 13, 89–100.

Kazdin, A. E., Esveldt-Dawson, K., & Loar, L. (1983). Correspondence of teacher ratings and direct observations of classroom behavior of psychiatric inpatient children. *Journal of Abnormal Child Psychology*, 11, 549–564.

Kohn, M., & Rosman, B. L. (1972). A social competence scale and symptom checklist for the preschool child. *Developmental Psychology, 6,* 430–444.

Langhorne, J. E., & Loney, J. (1979). A four-fold model for subgrouping the Hyperkinetic/MBD syndrome. *Child Psychiatry and Human Development, 9,* 153–159.

Loney, J., Langhorne, J. E., & Paternite, C. E. (1978). An empirical basis for subgrouping the hyperkinetic/minimal brain dysfunction syndrome. *Journal of Abnormal Psychology, 87,* 431–441.

Loney, J., & Milich, R. S. (1981). Hyperactivity, inattention, and aggression in clinical practice. *Advances in Developmental and Behavioral Pediatrics, 2,* 113–147.

Mash, E. J., & Terdal, L. (1981). Behavioral assessment of childhood disorders. New York: Guilford Press.

McMahon, R. J. (1984). Behavioral checklists and rating scales. In T. H. Ollendick & M. Hersen (Eds.), *Child behavioral assessment: Principles and procedures* (pp. 80–105). Elmsford, N.Y.: Pergamon Press.

Miller, L. C. (1967). Louisville Behavior Check List for males 6–12. *Psychological Reports, 21,* 885–896.

Miller, L. C. (1972). School behavior checklist: An inventory of deviant behavior for elementary school children. *Journal of Consulting and Clinical Psychology, 38,* 134–144.

Ozawa, J. P., & Michael, W. B. (1983). The concurrent validity of a behavior rating scale for assessing Attention Deficit Disorder in learning disabled children. *Educational and Psychological Measurement, 43,* 623–632.

Peterson, D. R. (1961). Behavior problems of middle childhood. *Journal of Consulting Psychology, 25,* 205–209.

Quay, H. C. (1966). Personality patterns in pre-adolescent delinquent boys. *Educational and Psychological Measurement, 26,* 99–110.

Quay, H. C. (1977). Measuring dimensions of deviant behavior: The Behavior Problem Checklist. *Journal of Abnormal Child Psychology, 5,* 277–287.

Quay, H. C. (1979). Classification. In H. Quay & J. Werry (Eds.), *Psychopathological disorders of childhood.* New York: John Wiley & Sons.

Quay, H. C. (1983). A dimensional approach to behavior disorder: The Revised Behavior Problem Checklist. *School Psychology Review, 12,* 244–249.

Quay, H. C., Morse, W. C., & Cultler, R. L. (1966). Personality patterns of pupils in special classes for the emotionally disturbed. *Exceptional Children, 32,* 297–301.

Quay, H. C., & Peterson, D. (1983). *Manual for the Revised Behavior Problem Checklist.* Coral Gables, Fla.: Author.

Quay, H. C., & Peterson, D. (1984). *Appendix I: Manual for the Revised Behavior Problem Checklist.* Coral Gables, Fla.: Author.

Quay, H. C., & Quay, L. C. (1965). Behavior problems in early adolescence. *Child Development, 36,* 215–220.

Reed, M. L., & Edelbrock, C. (1983). Reliability and validity of the Direct Observation Form of the Child Behavior Checklist. *Journal of Abnormal Child Psychology, 11,* 521–530.

Robinson, E. A., & Eyberg, S. M. (1981). The dyadic parent-child interaction coding system: Standardization and validation. *Journal of Consulting and Clinical Psychology, 49,* 245–250.

Robinson, E. A., Eyberg, S. M., Ross, A. W. (1980). The standardization of an inventory of child problem behaviors. *Journal of Clinical Child Psychology, 9,* 22–28.

Ross, A. O., Lacey, H. M., & Parton, D. A. (1965). The development of a behavior checklist for boys. *Child Development, 36,* 1013–1027.

Routh, D. K., Schroeder, C. S., & O'Tauma, L. (1974). Development of activity level in children. *Developmental Psychology, 10,* 163–168.

Rutter, M. (1967). A children's behavior questionnaire for completion by teachers: Preliminary findings. *Journal of Child Psychology and Psychiatry, 8,* 1–11.

Spring, C., Blunden, D., Greenberg, L. M., & Yellin, A. M. (1977). Validity and norms of a hyperactivity rating scale. *Exceptional Children, 11,* 313–321.

Thorley, G. (1983). Data on Conners Teacher Rating Scale in a British population. *Behavioral Assessment, 5,* 1–10.

Trites, R. L., Blouin, A. G., & Laprade, K. (1982). Factor analysis of the Conners Teacher Rating Scale based on a large normative sample. *Journal of Consulting and Clinical Psychology, 50,* 615–623.

Ullmann, R. K., Sleator, E. K., & Sprague, R. L. (1985). A change of mind: The Conners Abbreviated Rating Scales reconsidered. *Journal of Abnormal Child Psychology, 13,* 553–566.

Wainer, H. (1976). Estimating coefficients in linear models: It don't make no nevermind. *Psychological Bulletin, 83,* 213–217.

Walker, H. M. (1970). Walker Problem Behavior Identification Checklist (manual). Los Angeles: Western Psychological Services.

Werry, J. S., Sprague, R. L., & Cohen, M. N. (1975). Conners Teacher Rating Scale for use in drug studies with children: An empirical study. *Journal of Abnormal Child Psychology, 3,* 217–229.

CHAPTER 11

Child Self-Report: Interviewing Techniques and Rating Scales

JOSEPH C. WITT
TIMOTHY A. CAVELL
ROBERT W. HEFFER
MICHAEL P. CAREY
Louisiana State University

BRIAN K. MARTENS
Syracuse University

Man can embody Truth but he cannot know it. —Yeats

INTRODUCTION

The remnant influences of Watson's elementism and other functionalist scientific traditions are still quite apparent in the conceptualization and conduct of behavioral assessment. Among other things, this tradition calls for a molecular rather than a molar level of analysis, a reliance on the observable and measurable aspects of behavior, and, above all, an insistence on *objective* data that have been reliably obtained. The focus of this chapter is data that have been obtained through self-report. Such data are, by definition, based upon the *perceptions* and *interpretations* of the person providing the information. Thus, such data must be considered unobservable (i.e., not directly so by the evaluator) and subjective as opposed to objective. So why and how do chapters pertaining to self-report methodology end up with increasing frequency in textbooks devoted to behavioral assessment?

One simple answer is that self-report, particularly the unstructured interview, is one of the most, if not the most, frequently used of all assessment methods. The obvious reason for this high frequency of use is that self-report—that is, the perceptions of children, however colored and biased—have apparently provided valuable information. Even the most hard-nosed of behaviorists may question children concerning reinforcement preferences. There has always been a recognition that self-report data were biased (Cone & Hawkins, 1977), but psychologists have sought to understand this bias and interpret it within the context of other information obtained in a multimethod assessment. In recent years a considerable amount of data have been collected that supports the need for and importance of self-report methods. Developmental psychologists, for example, are helping us understand ways in which self-report data are biased as a function of cognitive development (Clarke-Stewart, Friedman, & Koch, 1985). Other researchers have established the importance of children's perceptions about behavioral treatments as potent predictors of treatment efficacy (Elliott, 1986). In addition, the technology of eliciting self-report information has improved so that information can be more reliably and validly obtained. Thus, in the past, self-report data have been routinely collected because "clinical judgment" suggested such data were useful. However, an emerging empirical data base describes the extent to which children can accurately report on their own behavior and events in their environment and the importance of obtaining such information. In addition, there exists a burgeoning array of instruments and methods for collecting self-report data. The purpose of this chapter is to describe the use and value of self-report measures within the context of a multimethod functional analysis of behavior. More specifically, this chapter has the following goals: (1) to establish a need and rationale for using self-report measures within a comprehensive assessment, (2) to review major issues pertaining to accuracy and validity of self-report data, (3) to provide a context and process for selecting, using, and evaluating various interview formats, and (4) to provide a context and a process for selecting, using, and evaluating self-report rating scales. In the course of accomplishing these goals, the authors provide the reader with an overview of available self-report instruments, methods for deciding which are the best for specific purposes, and our evaluation of some of the more widely known and better instruments.

ADVANTAGES AND CONTRIBUTIONS OF SELF-REPORT DATA TO THE FUNCTIONAL ANALYSIS OF BEHAVIOR

This section develops a rationale and need for using self-report measures within the context of a multimethod assessment. The need to incorporate self-report measures is derived primarily from the unique and important contributions of self-report data in understanding and treating children with learning and adjustment problems. These contributions include: (1) the capacity to obtain information that is not available through methods of assessment, and (2) the relationship between child self-report and treatment outcome.

Self-Report methods yield information not available through methods of assessment. Any given method of assessment is used because it provides information that is considered essential, and because the information is not redundant with the findings of other methods. Thus, unless we are concerned with the validity of a given test of intelligence, only one intelligence test will be administered to a particular child. Similarly, self-report assessment exists because it provides specific types of data that are not available using other methods. In this section we consider the unique contribution of self-report data.

Self-report allows for both direct and indirect information to be obtained. When considering the type of information obtained through self-report methods, most of the data elicited can be classified as indirect. That is, the data consist of the child's *reports* about actual events. If the psychologist could have observed the event on which the child is reporting, then he or she would have direct, rather than indirect, information about the event. The preponderance of the information reviewed in this chapter pertains to indirect data that have been obtained through self-report. However, within the self-report arena, the interview allows for the collection of not only indirect but also direct data about the child's functioning. That is, as the child is reporting about perceptions of events, he or she is also exhibiting a variety of cognitive and interpersonal skills that can be observed directly

Through the direct observation of interpersonal interactions it is possible to obtain information about a wide variety of domains including social skills (e.g., courtesy, social initiations skills, ability to maintain a conversation, eye contact, mannerisms), cognitive abilities (e.g., type and quality of information recalled, processes and strategies utilized to recall information), and activity level in a one-on-one situation (e.g., attention span, motor movements). The collection of this type of information emphasizes the importance of not only what the child has to say but *how* he or she says it. The situation has an analogy in the assessment of reading in which two children may have the same grade equivalent score on a test of reading comprehension. However, one child approached each reading passage very slowly and exhibited contortions of face and body while reading and the other child sailed fluidly through each passage with confidence. The content produced by each child was the same but the process was much different. Both process and content have implications for intervention, and, therefore, are important to include within a comprehensive assessment framework.

Self-report format, especially interviewing, allows more flexibility. The interview provides an opportunity to obtain information that is impossible or difficult to acquire by any other means of assessment. The most obvious aspect of this uniqueness is the control that an interviewer has in determining what will be assessed, how much will be assessed, and how the questions will be phrased. In most other forms of behavioral assessment, the assessor is either at the mercy of the environment to produce a situation which will yield valuable information—as is the case in naturalistic observation—or must rely on structured rating scales which may not be flexible or comprehensive enough to yield the desired information. (Note: Analog assessment situations provide another alternative but are used infrequently in school settings because of logistical problems with such procedures.) With the interview, the assessor may control the type of question asked and the amount of information elicited about a particular subject. If the child does not respond, the assessor can wait. If the child avoids the question asked by saying something irrelevant, the assessor can redirect the question. If the child appears to be lying, the assessor can probe further. If the child has difficulty responding because of social skill deficits, the assessor can try allowing the child a variety of response formats to determine the manner in which the child responds best.

Ideally, the interview situation will be similar to that of computerized adaptive testing in mathematics. With adaptive testing, the computer begins with some general questions and proceeds quickly through a wide range of skills until a weakness is located. Once identified as a general weaknes, the computer then zeros in and presents a number of math problems that identify some specific weaknesses. Similarly, the interview can allow an assessor to identify general and specific weaknesses. For example, an assessor may note that a child has very little to say and makes poor eye contact. The assessor can then determine if this is true with respect to every conversational subject or if the child seems more socially skilled when discussing television programs versus school work.

The flexibility of the unstructured interview in particular allows for an examination of a wider array of problems. It is not uncommon, for example, that a child will be referred for one problem when another, more fundamental, problem is the real issue. For example, in an actual case, a junior high school boy was referred for poor work performance and a refusal to attend school. The parents and school authorities considered the problem to be a lack of motivation on the part of the student. However, after several interviews with the child it was learned that he was being sexually molested by a teacher. An objective functional analysis of this situation might have resulted in measurement of the classroom and the task properties which maintained this behavior and led to the implementation of a behavior management program to increase school attendance and improve assignment completion. The flexibility to cover a wide range of topics and some degree of clinical insight were required to learn the true antecedent of the behavior observed.

Information about certain problems is obtained more validly through self-report methods. Childhood behavioral disorders can be conceptualized as either externalizing or internalizing (Achenbach, 1978). Externalizing disorders, in which children act out, disrupt classrooms, and engage in a variety of other inappropriate behaviors can be reliably assessed by observing what the child *does* or asking parents and teachers to report on what the child has done. For internalizing disorders, such as problems with fear, depression, anxiety, and self-evaluation, the literature suggests that self-report may be the method of choice for assessment (Garber, 1984).

Although information obtained through self-report is undeniably biased, it is also "correct" in an important sense. A child may have developed belief and attributional systems that are definitely and decidedly wrong according to all societal or objective standards. At some level, however, we must come to understand and work with this belief system if treatment is to be successful. For example, if a child has problems in school, and he attributes the problems to his teacher or to a disease in his brain, he may be less likely to put forth the effort required for successful intervention to occur. Even though the problem is one of a lack of effort on the part of the child, one must deal at some level with the child's perception of the situation. Self-report provides a means to understand the child's perception of the problem.

An example of an actual case will help to illustrate this problem further. In this case, an adolescent was hospitalized in a psychiatric facility because he thought he was God and this, of course, influenced his interactions with other people who did not share his perception. The boy underwent a relatively standard behavioral treatment procedure whereby inappropriate statements (i.e., those referring to himself as God) were put on an extinction schedule. This consisted of, among other things, people in the adolescent's environment physically turning away from him when he began talking about himself as God. When he was behaving appropriately, others would make eye contact with him and interact in a very positive manner. As expected, the rate of inappropriate behavior reduced in frequency and, after about two weeks, disappeared altogether. As the patient was about to be dismissed from the hospital, one of the psychologists said to him, "You have really improved here. When you came into the hospital you actually thought you were God and now you don't think that way anymore do you?" The patient replied, "Oh yes I do think I'm God but no one wants to talk with me about it!" In other words, the individual's belief system was unaltered but his behavior had become much more appropriate. A radical behaviorist would suggest that if behavior is appropriate, then one's work as an interventionist is complete. However, given the belief system of this individual, what are the chances that his behavior would generalize in other settings? One only need review the research on generalization and maintenance of behavioral interventions to know that one must begin conceptualizing problems differently (Rutherford & Nelson, in press) and this should include some assessment of individuals' self-reported belief systems.

Relationship Between Child Self-Report and Intervention Efficacy

Evidence is accumulating that a child's perception of the treatment that is applied to him or her is an important predictor of intervention efficacy (Turco, Elliott, & Witt, 1985; Witt & Elliott, 1985). For example, Kirigin, Braukmann, Atwater, & Wolf (1982) in their assessment of the Achievement Place program found that target youths' own evaluations of satisfaction with the program were more highly correlated with a reduction in criminal and other offenses than were evaluations by others involved with the development and implementation of the program. It is noteworthy that parent satisfaction with the program showed almost no correlation with treatment efficacy. This study provides evidence that children's satisfaction with and acceptance of a treatment may be different from, and possibly more useful than, similar evaluations by adult mediators (parents and teachers). In another investigation, De Charms (1976) found school-based interventions that elicited student opinions resulted in lower drop-out rates and higher student achievement than did similar programs in which student opinion was ignored. The interested reader is referred to McMahon and Forehand (1983) Turco, *et al.* (1985), or Elliott (1986) for comprehensive reviews of this literature.

Research of this type has two major implications for assessment through self-report: (1) self-report can be viewed as the initial step in the intervention process and is therefore important from the standpoint of developing rapport and allowing the child to feel involved in the assessment and intervention process, and (2) information collected by questioning the child about treatment preferences can be used to design interventions that are more acceptable to the child, while still remaining effective.

First, one must assume that intervention efficacy is an important outcome for most assessment activities. Within this context, assessment and intervention blend together and assessment can even be conceptualized as the beginning of treatment. Thus, the development of rapport and other relationship enhancing aspects of the unstructured interview in particular may influence intervention effectiveness. The mere act of questioning a child about his or her attitudes and opinions, therefore, may create the perception that the assessor is interested in the child's welfare and may increase the degree to which the child feels involved in and committed to a treatment program. To the extent that such perceptions are created by the assessment process, intervention activities are more likely to be successful.

In addition to influencing the perceptions of the child being assessed, the *actual information obtained* can be used to design treatments that are more acceptable to the child. Information about reinforcement preferences, peer involvement, parent involvement, timing and length of treatment, and even type of treatment can be obtained through interviews and rating scales. If this information is used during treatment planning, there is a greater probability that treatment will be effective.

THREATS TO THE RELIABILITY AND VALIDITY OF SELF-REPORT DATA

Although behaviorists in general are suspicious of *any* type of self-report data, there are special concerns about such information obtained from children. Children remember and distort information in systematic ways as a function of their age and cognitive ability (Clarke-Stewart, Friedman, & Koch, 1985). In the last few years a considerable amount of data has accumulated in relation to a child's ability to respond to interviews and self-report rating scales. In the following sections we will describe the major threats to obtaining reliable and valid data from children using self-report measures. Suggestions also are made on how to elicit information from children in a more reliable and valid manner.

Developmental Issues

In obtaining self-report data from children it is important to consider a child's capacity to interpret and understand the questions posed and his or her ability to respond. These abilities are influenced by the child's cognitive, especially social cognitive, level of development. According to Bierman (1983), many of the reports pertaining to the notorious invalidity of child self-report data area at least partially attributable to the assessor's ignorance of developmental issues.

> Young children will simply not respond to standard interview procedures. Unschooled in proper interviewee behaviors, they must be won over, cajoled, and supported through sessions by an energetic and engaging clinician. To the extent that the interviewer relies on open-ended questions and standard probes, he or she is likely to elicit only blanket refusals to talk or vague, tangential, disorganized, and brief answers. Young children are able to describe their thoughts and feelings, but they require specialized interview techniques to do so. Moreover, characteristics of conceptual organization and information processing associated with cognitive and linguistic development result in a phenomenological world for the young child that is qualitatively different from the adult's world. Clinicians who are unfamiliar with the thought processes associated with various developmental levels are likely to find children's reasoning exceedingly difficult to follow or comprehend. To conduct effective child interviews, clinicians must both acquire an understanding of the characteristics of developing social-cognitive processes, and they must make some major adjustments in their interviewing techniques and strategies. (Bierman, 1983, pp. 218–219)

Although this passage is directed toward the unstructured interview, it should be obvious that the thought processes that affect interviews also affect other self-report techniques. The social cognitive processes most relevant to our discussion here pertain a child's knowledge and development in two primary areas: (1) *person perception processes* and (2) *social roles and interpersonal relationships* (Bierman, 1983). A third developmental issue to be discussed is the extent to which training can after a child's ability to perceive and interpret information.

Person Perception Processess

The study of person perception processes is an area that has to do with the degree to which children are capable of taking in, processing, and then using information about other people. To begin with, major developmental changes occur in the initial taking in or perception of information about other people. Typically, children under the age of seven who are asked to describe other people will focus on the physical characteristics of those people, particularly observable behavior and will be able to recall only a few disjointed pieces of information (Bierman, 1983; Livesley & Bromley, 1973).

Children differ not only in terms of their initial perceptions, but there are also marked age differences in how children process and use the information which has been perceived. Developmental changes have been noted in the labels children use to describe what they have observed about other people. Younger children typically use a very narrow range of descriptors for evaluating others. In the area of human emotion, for example, older children and adults make distinctions between emotions such as love, anger, sadness, fear, and rage, but young children are able to interpret human emotion with respect only to a few simple dimensions such as happy or sad (Borke, 1973; Saltz, Dunin-Markiewicz, & Rourke, 1975). As children mature, they begin to use a wider variety of descriptors when evaluating others and these descriptors are increasingly abstract and inferential (Barenboim, 1977; Peevers & Secord, 1973).

Not only do young children differentiate only a few dimensions of human functioning, their thinking tends to polarize and become all-or-nothing with respect to a single dimension (Bierman, 1983; Ervin & Foster, 1960; Livesley & Bromley, 1973). As in the above example, young children who observe information that is ambiguous or seemingly inconsistent (e.g., observations of a mother who engages in both loving and punishing behaviors) tend to categorize the person in an all-or-nothing manner (i.e., as either good or bad, happy or sad, etc.). In an experiment conducted by Gollin (1958), children were shown a movie in which a person engaged in two "good" acts and two "bad" acts and were asked to describe the character in the movie. Six-year-old children tended to describe the character in black-and-white terms. If the person was described as good, the children in the experiment tended to ignore or even deny information that was contrary to their evaluation. By the age of ten, children in Gollin's study were able to incorporate and to reconcile both the good and bad acts observed and, by early adolescence, were able to see the good and bad acts as manifestations of a common abstract theme.

Young children also characterize their own behavior in similarly simplistic terms. Thus it is not uncommon for children who are considered to be very well behaved to refer to themselves as "bad" because of one minor incident in which they behaved inappropriately. They also tend to categorize their likes and dislikes in all-or-nothing terms. For example, a child indicates that he "hates" school. When it is pointed out to him that on many occasions he has said he enjoyed his teacher, the things they do at school, and all the children with whom he plays, he replies that he "hates naps." Such a child makes the love/hate decision based upon only one piece of information even though this piece of information is inconsistent with nearly all the other information available. The same child may "love" school the next day because he has changed his focus to some other aspect of the school environment. This feature of child development is often disconcerting to parents who become alarmed when a child indicates he hates school, himself, or his parents. As children grow older, their judgments of other people and themselves become more stable because those judgments are based upon more information about both settings and people. As this skill develops, children are able to make predictions about how a person will behave in the future or how they themselves will react in a certain situation.

A unique summary of research in relation to person perception processes has been provided by Shantz (1981):

If one were to view the "child as a psychologist" who subscribes to certain positions or theories, the developmental changes, broadly put, suggest the following: prior to seven or eight years of age, the child conceives of persons largely as a demographer-and-behaviorist, defining the person in terms of his/her environmental circumstances and observable behavior; during middle childhood, persons are conceived more as a trait personality theorist would, ascribing unqualified constancies to persons; and by the onset of adolescence, a more "interactionist" position emerges in which people and their behavior are often seen as a joint function of personal characteristics and situational factors." (p. 28)

The interested reader is referred to Bierman (1983), Shantz (1981)), and Clarke-Stewart *et al.* (1985) for additional elaboration on this line of research.

Social Roles and Interpersonal Relationships

As we develop, we form increasingly complex attitudes and expectations about how individuals in various social roles should respond (Maccoby, 1959). The roles of playmate, father, policeman, friend, and teacher are examples of social roles about which one forms attitudes and expectations. Obviously one's expectations of, for example, what a father should be and what we can expect from his change and become more complex as we grow older.

Within the domain of social roles, developmental trends are similar to those observed in person perception processes. Young children typically notice and respond to a limited number of domains or dimensions of interpersonal relationships and within a particular domain they tend to oversimplify and to interpret what they see in an all-or-nothing manner (Selman, 1980). For example, Moore, Cooper, and Brickland (cited by Bierman, 1983) discovered that preschool children considered a mother as someone who took care of children. If a mother did not take care of her children, then she could not be a mother. Similarly, a father was someone who fixed the car, and if a mother fixed the car then she could not be a mother, she must be a father. As children grow older they learn that some mothers fix the car and some fathers prepare meals and they begin to develop a broader, more abstract, conceptualization of what it means to be a mother or a father.

The evolution in the meaning of friendship offers another example of the development of an important social role. For the preschool child, a friend is simply someone with whom to play (Bierman, 1983). Children in elementary school indicate that liking, helping, and sharing are essential aspects of friendship (Bigelow, 1977). As children reach adolescence their expectations for the social role of friend call for the establishment of a relationship with another person based on mutual trust, loyalty, and the sharing of personal intimacies (Bierman, 1983).

Understanding the development of social role expectations is an important aspect of making sense out of child self-report data. The interpretation of a child's response to a question depends upon how the child is likely to interpret the question and the child's view of social roles and interpersonal relationships. The next section elaborates on the extent to which developmental processes are capable of being altered given specific training or an alteration in task demands.

The Effects of Training and Alteration of Task Demands

Piaget (1965) and other stage theorists have argued that children develop in a relatively rigid and unalterable series of stages from incompetent child to competent adult. A preoperational chilld, for example, was presumed unable to accomplish certain types of reasoning tasks and this inability would persist, despite external attempts to quicken the child's development, until the child was biologically and psychologically "ready" to progress to the next stage. Over the past fifteen years, however, stage theories have been called into question because of studies demonstrating the progression from stage to stage can be accelerated by external training and the ease with which a child can demonstrate knowledge associated with a particular stage has been shown to vary as a function of task demands (Gelman & Baillargeon, 1983).

Developmental researchers have established that children are capable of reasoning at a much higher level than Piaget and other theorists hypothesized (Murray, 1978), that children can be induced through training to perform reasoning tasks for which they are not yet "ready" (Gelman & Baillargeon, 1983), and that attainment of cognitive competence commensurate with a particular stage is not an all-or-nothing proposition but tends to be task specific (Cooper, Leitner, & Moore, 1981, cited by Gelman & Baillargeon, 1983). A study by Koslowski (1980) is illustrative of this research. The experiment involved presenting three- and four-year-old children with a traditional seriation task using ten sticks, and an abbreviated version of that task involving only four sticks. To demonstrate seriation, children must perform seriation in the same direction, must insert additional items in an already established series, and must be able to correct an erroneous series completed by someone else. Koslowski (1980) found that, for children who demonstrated no seriation ability on the traditional task, 75% could construct a systematic series using the abbreviated task, 81% could insert sticks into an already existing series, and 100% could correct errors in a series constructed by someone else.

Unfortunately research on children's self-report lags far behind research on children's cognitive development. However, it is possible to make some cautious implications of this research for conducting assessment through self-report. The major implications re that children are probably capable of producing better and more accurate self-report data than was originally thought. Furthermore, the burden for extracting this information is upon the assessor. Modification of task demands or training children in how to report what they know may produce information that is more abundant and useful than has previously been the case. Evaluating the effects of such modifications is an area that is clearly in need of good research.

Other Threats to Reliability and Validity

In addition to the many developmental considerations that may have an impact on the quality of self-report data, there is a wide array of other factors that can influence reliability and validity. Most of these potential sources of error (e.g., scoring errors, "test" length, social desirability, etc.) have been discussed at length by other writers (Cronbach, 1970) because these problems also pose difficulties for a wide range of assessment methodologies other than self-report. Little would be gained from a discussion here of these general influences. Instead, a brief discussion of some of the more important considerations having special relevance to self-report methodology follows.

Self-report methods for collecting assessment information are expected to possess the same fundamental psychometric properties (e.g., reliability and validity) as any other assessment tool or test. Each of the major self-report methods (i.e., the unstructured interview, the structured interview, and the self-report rating scale) has somewhat different problems in the areas of reliability and validity. With the unstructured interview, for example, the first problem in determining reliability is deciding upon a method for assessing reliability. Consider, for example, two school psychologists who are each instructed to "interview" a child. Not only are they likely to cover different topics, but they may also interpret and summarize interview information in different ways. Which is the more reliable interview of different problem areas to be identified? Also, what procedures should be followed in quantifying interview information so that reliablity coefficients can be computed? With traditional tests, it is possible to correlate total scores in a test-retest manner or to examine internal consistency. But with interviews, what numbers do you plug into the formulas to determine reliability?

According to Cone (1977), assessment must be concerned with the degree to which assessment information can be generalized. Cone has specified six universes of generalization: scorer, item, time, setting, method, and dimension. When compared with traditional tests, the problems in generalization for behavioral interviews are enormous. One example will illustrate this. If one is to assess the test-retest reliability of an unstructured interview, one has a number of sources of possible variation. There may be variation between interviewing styles between the two occasions (either between interviewers or within the same interviewer) resulting in different questions (i.e., items) being asked. There may be differences in the manner in which the interviewee's responses are interpreted and scored because of differences between interviewers or even within the same interviewer. Of course there may be time and setting differences between the two interviews. Quite obviously, there may be differences in the interviewee's status and perceptions from one setting to another. All of these factors reduce the reliability of the interview.

Several structured interviews have been developed (Paget, 1984) that require the interviewer to ask a series of specific questions, the responses to which are scored objectively. Typically, these structured interviews yield both global land specific scores pertaining to specific types of problems. It is possible to apply classical psychometric measures to assess the reliability of these measures. It does not require too great an inference to suggest that structured interviews are more reliable than unstructured interviews, although this has not been tested empirically. Because of its structure, however, the structured interview may miss critical problems or pose questions in such a way that it is misunderstood by children. With unstructured interviews, the interviewer has complete freedom in selecting the types of questions that will be asked and the meaning that will be attached to each of the responses. Typically, the reliability of unstructured interviews has been assessed by comparing the accuracy and consistency of some global inference or some classification statement. For example, after interviewing someone, the interviewer might be asked to list the problems detected in the interview and to make an inference about a diagnosis or the stimulus conditions that are maintaining the problem behaviors. The accuracy of these statements is then compared as a measure of reliability.

In one of the few studies assessing the reliability of unstructured interviews, Hay, Hay, Angle, and Nelson (1979) achieved a high degree of consistency concerning the overall number of problems specified in interviews but failed to achieve good reliability concerning the specific nature of the problems identified. Given that behavioral assessment is concerned more with the conditions maintaining a problem than with a simple listing of problems, the lack of reliability data in this area is a serious limitation to the behavioral interview.

The validity of self-report methods can be placed in perspective by asking a common question: "Do you believe everything everyone tells you?" Most of the data pertaining to validity has come from studies on the accuracy of parent and teacher reports of child behavior. Although it is risky to generalize results from studies on adults to children, such studies do serve as a guide to problems one might reasonably expect with children, especially since reliability land validity problems with children are likely to be more pronounced. Yarrow, Cambell, and Burton (1970) collected data that suggest that parents are horribly inaccurate reporters of their children's development and behavior. Parent recall, in particular, appears to be influenced by social desirability and perceptions advanced by the lay press about how children should behave and develop. In a study of behavioral contracting for truancy, Schnelle (1974) asked parents to monitor school attendance for four weeks. These data were compared with actual records of school attendance and there was a complete lack of relationship between the records and parent report. Some caution in interpreting these results is required because of the extremely low educational level of the parents involved in the study.

The data regarding the interview are not completely dismal. Herjanic, Herjanic, Brown, and Wheatt (1975) interviewed both parents and children using the same relatively structured interview format. Results indicated that parents and children agreed more than 80% of the time. Correspondence between parents and children was even higher when only factual questions were anlayzed.

Perhaps the most surprising aspect of the literature regarding self-report measures for children is the paucity of good research on widely used assessment techniques. There is very little known about the accuracy and validity of self-reports and even less about the precise effects of the variables that affect the quality of the data obtained. Obviously, self-report measures will continue to be used because for certain purposes there is no adequate replacement. Children will continue to identify problems and there will be continued assesment of children's perceptions of problems. Whether these perceptions mesh with reality is a separate and independent question.

The sections following will present an elaboration of the issues surrounding reliability and validity in the context of a discussion of each of the three major types of self-report methods. Before leaving the area of threats to reliability and validity, however, it is appropriate to offer some suggestions for improving the quality of self-report data.

Improving Children's Responses to Self-Report Measures: Methods of Decreasing Problems of Reliability and Validity

The research described above has suggested that children perceive, respond, and interpret events in their environment differently depending upon the developmental level at which they are functioning. Assessors who ignore the developmental level of the child in first asking, then interpreting questions will introduce an unwanted source of error into their assessment data. To the extent that this error can be minimized, child self-report data can be considered more reliable and valid. The following section describes the implications of developmental research for the collection of child self-report data. More specifically, three methods are looked at for enhancing the quality and quantity of data obtained from children: (1) modification of stimulus complexity, (2) modification of response complexity, and (3) providing the child with appropriate expectations.

Modification of Stimulus Complexity

A major task of the assessor wanting to obtain valid self-report data from children is to *enable* the child to respond as fully and completely as the child's cognitive development and language facility will permit. This enabling process often takes the form of asking open-ended questions (Cormier & Cormier, 1979). Virtually every graduate student in psychology has been trained and encouraged in the use of open-ended questions as a standard interview technique. This has been true for individuals working with both adults and children as Kanfer, Eyberg, and Krahn (1983) suggest.

> Asking open-ended questions leads to more information per question, and minimizes the possibility that the inteviewer will lead the child to conclusions that are the interviewer's rather than the child's. They are especially useful in opening up new areas of discussion and facilitate spontaneous, continued conversation. (p. 188)

Despite almost universal support in the psychological literature for the use of open-ended questions, from a developmental perspective such recommendations are illustrative of the lore surrounding self-report methodology that has shown a singular insensitivity to cognitive and language differences in children as a function of age. Contrary to popular belief, the open-ended question may stifle the amount of responding on the part of the child and restrict the number of topics about which useful information can be obtained. This discussion of stimulus complexity began by identifying problems with open-ended questions. Their use seems to be ingrained in assessors everywhere and there is a need to counter this oversaturation of learning. The use of open-ended questions is appropriate if, and only if, they *enable* children to provide information that is not obtained more appropriately through other means. The open-ended question can be very useful with older children and adults, but assessors may have to be somewhat more flexible in presenting questions to young children.

Stimulus complexity can be reduced in several ways. To begin with, the assessor must consider the level and complexity of the language used to pose questions and the format, written or oral, in which the stimuli are presented. This dilemma is illustrated by considering a common problem faced by behaviorally oriented assessors: what is the determination of reinforcer preferences? Most children would have difficulty understanding, "What kinds of activities are reinforcing to you?" and may respond better to, "What sort of things do you like to do?" (Kanfer, *et al.*, 1983). The complexity of the question might be further reduced by having the child respond to a series of questions such as: "Do you like _____ ?" It is also possible to use either a written (i.e., present the child witrh a list of possible reinforcers), oral (i.e., orally list a number of possible reinforcers) or visual (i.e., actually show the child various potential reinforcers) format in determining reinforcer preferences, depending upon the child's reading level, verbal fluency, and other factors.

Bierman (1983) has suggested that direct questions may arouse anxiety and produce resistance in some children. For example, an assessor may want to know why a young girl remains on one side of the playground and refuses to play with other children during recess. Asking the child a direct question about this behavior may not be very useful, because a situation that is producing anxiety may cause additional anxiety if the child is asked to talk about it. As an alternative to asking about this problem directly, Bierman (1983) has offered two alternatives. First, it may be possible to use concrete objects, such as dolls, so the child might talk about the dolls instead of herself. In this case, the assessor might present the child with three dolls, two of whom go off to play and one of whom stays behind. The child could then be questioned about the reason one stayed behind and did not want to play with the others. Another indirect method suggested by both Bierman (1983) and Yarrow (1960) involves the assesor posing the question in the following manner: "A kid I know told me that he hardly ever plays with others at school and he wishes he had more friends. Do you ever feel that way?" In this manner the assessor can either ask the child to provide reasons why "another" child may behave this way or, as in the example, indicate only that other children have this problem as a means to get information about the target child's belief system.

To the behaviorist, indirect techniques such as those described above come dangerously close to projective techniques. Bierman (1983) points out, however, that there are marked differences in the intent of the procedures. From a behavioral perspective, the intent is to enable the child to provide information that he or she might have difficulty providing using other means; and from the perspective of projective assessment, the goal is to use the child's verbalizations as projections of inner feelings, drives and impulses.

Modification of Response Complexity

In addition to modifications in the manner in which questions are asked, there are a number of options available for the modification of the way in which the questions are answered. On the dimension of complexity an oral response to an open-ended question about an abstract concept (e.g., anger, fear, etc.) is very difficult for many children. Responding to questions can be simplified in several ways, the most common of which include: (1) allowing the child to respond orally to a limited number of predefined options (e.g., providing a child with three possible reponses to a question and requiring that the child select the best response), (2) allowing the child to respond to a limited number of predefined written options (e.g., some self-report rating scales require that children indicate the extent to which they agree or disagree with particular written statements), and (3) allowing the child to respond by selecting a concrete representation of his or her response (e.g., an assessor may have a child point to the one picture from an array of pictures that most accurately describes the child's response to the question).

From a behavioral perspective, simplification of the response requirements for children (e.g., allowing them to point to pictures) can be viewed as a means of prompting or shaping responses. The following interview from Bierman (1983) describes the use of pictures of happy, sad, and angry faces as simple response options and illustrates shaping and prompting processes with a relatively nonverbal child whose only previous response to questions had been, "I don't know."

T: How would you feel if you got to stay in the place where you live now?
B: (He points to a sad face.)
T: How would you feel if you could live with your mom?
B: (He points to happy, and then circles happy with a felt pen.)
T: How did you feel when you had to leave your mom's?
B: (He points to sad.)
T: How come you had to leave?"
B: Cause they were fighting.
T: How did you feel when your mom and dad were fighting?
B: (Points to angry.) Really mad.

T: What Happened?
B: Nothing . . . I don't know . . . I ran away.
T: It must have been scary.
B: It was.
(Bierman, 1983, p. 236)

The pictures appeared to serve as a prompt, and gradually the length and quality of the child's verbalizations increased. The use of concrete objects, such as pictures, appears to be particularly enabling for young children to describe abstract concepts.

It almost goes without saying that, when using self-report rating scales, it is important to ensure that children are capable of reading and understanding the stimuli. For example, Gorsuch, Henighan, and Barnard (1972) examined the realiability of Bailer's locus of control scale as a function of verbal comprehension ability. In this experiment the locus of control scale and a measure of verbal ability were read aloud to a group of children. Although the test manual for the Bialer locus of control scale reports an internal consistency reliabiity of .89 for the total scale, the findings of Gorsuch *et al.* suggested the reliability of the scale was nowhere close to that for children of low verbal ability. In fact, when children were grouped according to verbal ability, the correlation between each group's verbal ability score and locus of control reliability was .95. Also, there was a positive correlation between locus of control scores and verbal ability, which prompted Gorsuch *et al.* to conclude:

> The positive correlation may have been a function of the unreliability of the low-verbal ability children's scores instead of being a true relationship. Naturally, if the locus of control scales have a spurious correlation with verbal ability, *they will also have spurious correlations with all variables which normally correlate with verbal ability.* This would be dangerous indeed. (Italics in the original, p. 588)

Two important implications can be derived from this study. First, the capacity of a child to comprehend the demands of the task has an obvious effect on reliability, and consequently, validity. Second, scales that report reliability coefficients for the total scale across age groups may yield reliabilities that are much lower for specific age and ability groups.

It is not uncommon for assessment specialists who obtain invalid data from young children to, in essence, blame the child and fail to consider the possibility that the way in which the child was assessed had anything to do with the invalidity of the data obtained: For example, Edelbrock, Costello, Dulcan, Kalas, and Conover (1985) in their investigation of the Diagnostic Interview Schedule for Children concluded:

> If a test-retest reliability of .70 is used as a criterion, children aged 10 and older are reliable reporters in many symptom areas. Applying the same standard to children aged 6-9 suggests they are not reliable in reporting on their own symptoms, except for

fears. This suggests that highly structured interviews with children below age 10 should be interpreted cautiously. Adequate reliability was obtained only for fears, and that does not insure the validity of the child's report. (pp. 272–273)

We do not question that data from children under ten be "interpreted cautiously," but the general tone of the statement implies that the problem is with the children and not the instrument. Such logic is roughly equivalent to administering an intelligence test in English to someone who speaks only French, and concluding that the person had grave difficulties in many areas.

Providing Appropriate Expectations

Children, particularly young children, have usually had very little experience with the assessment process. Often they do not know what to expect and they frequently do not know their role in the interaction. According to Bierman (1983), "In general, children do not expect and are not prepared merely to sit down with an adult and discuss themselves or the events and feelings that are important to them" (p. 240). It may therefore be worthwhile to provide children with some structure and expectation about their role. In addition, the motivational properties of the setting should be optimized.

With respect to expectations, it is appropriate to begin by telling the child the purpose of the assessment process, why it has occured, and what will be the likely outcome. In this regard, some individuals tell the child that they will be "playing some games" that the child should find interesting. The authors disagree with this because it sets an inappropriate expectation for the child. To the child, playing games may imply that optimal performance or being truthful is not required. At the other extreme is Bersoff (1976), who has suggested children might be told they are to be evaluated and, depending on how they do, they might be classified as retarded or as having some other problem and placed in special education for several years. In between these extremes is the goal of providing a child with realistic expectations of what to expect and how to respond so that the child is appropriately motivated without being overly fearful of the process. The literature on training children successfully in cognitive tasks, as discussed previously, provides an optimistic outlook in terms of providing children with proper expectations and perhaps the skills to respond more accurately when evaluated with self-report instruments.

THE UNSTRUCTURED CHILD INTERVIEW

The unstructured interview as a means of collecting self-report data has enjoyed a long history as one of the most frequently used assessment strategies. (Burke & DeMers, 1979; Haynes & Jensen, 1979). Although far more attention has been devoted to interviewing adults than children (Yarrow, 1960), the unstructured child interview can be a valuable assessment tool if the interview *process* takes into account the child's level of cognitive and social-cognitive development, and the interview *content* is considered in relation to other information obtained during assessment (e.g., cumulative record review, naturalistic observation, parent and teacher report, test data).

This section begins with a discussion of issues pertaining to the reliability and validity of the unstructured child interview as an assessment instrument. Next, a conceptual model is presented for interviewing children that focuses upon three domains: (1) how the interviewer goes about soliciting information; (2) how the child repsponds during the interview situation; and (3) what areas are addressed in questioning (Burke & DeMers, 1979). The first two domains are involved in the process of interviewing and allow for direct observation of child behavior. In contrast, the third domain is concerned with the content of interviewing and results in collection of indirect information (e.g., self-report) about the child's behavior in other settings. Following discussion of the conceptual model for conducting unstructured child interviews, specific process issues are presented that relate to the behavior of both the interviewer and the interviewee. The section concludes with a listing of content areas typically addressed in interviews with children.

Psychometric Properties of the Unstructured Child Interview

Despite widespread use of the unstructured child interview, there have been few investigations into its psychometric adequacy as an assessment device (Herjanic, *et al.* 1975). Burke and DeMers (1979) described the situation well by noting that "the same characteristics which make the assessment interview so widely used (e.g., its flexibility, spontaneity, and ease of administration) are also the interview's greatest liabilities when the psychometric qualities of reliability and validity are considered" (p.51). Given the paucity of research focusing directly upon interviews with children, much of the following discussion is based upon findings in the child development literature, investigations using structured interview formats, and studies with adult populations. However, the issues raised are common to all interview situations, and the discussion is believed to have direct implications for assessing the reliability and validity of unstructured interviews with children.

Reliability

Reliability of the unstructured child interview may be ascertained through a comparison of statements made during the interview situation (i.e., internal consistency), a comparison of information obtained on separate occasions (i.e., testretest), or a comparison of information obtained by different interviewers (i.e., interrater). Investigations conducted to date have focused on the latter two forms of reliability, and findings have suggested that inconsistencies in interviewer rather than interviewee behaviors may make greater contributions to interview unreliability.

In a study conducted by Hay, Hay, Angle and Nelson (1979), interviews conducted by four individuals with the same client were audiotaped, and interviewers dictated a summary following each interaction. Results indicated that the interviewer did not differ in the number of problem areas identified. In contrast, specific problem content, number of queries made in each area, and information included in the dictated summaries showed significant inconsistencies across interviewers. Since client report was relatively consistent across interview situations as determined by ratings of audiotapes, Hay *et al.* concluded that interviewer characteristics such as training emphasis, question pool, and inaccurate recording of client responses were important contributors to unreliability.

Other considerations in the reliability of information obtained during the unstructured child interview include accuracy of recall and attentiveness to the interviewer's questions (Burke & DeMers, 1979). As in any self-report measure, reliability may be reduced because children simply forget information that is relevant to interviewer questioning. Moreover, the extent to which children are engaged in competing activities, such as play, is likely to reduce their attention to interviewer questions and thereby further contribute to the inaccuracy of self-report.

Validity

The issues discussed above concerning the reliability of unstructured child interviews are also critical to the validity of information obtained. Additional considerations in the validity of child interview data include the relation of child reports to information obtained by other assessment strategies (e.g., concurrent validity), the extent to which interview questions cover appropriate topics (i.e., content validity), and the effect of children's perceptions on subsequent treatment decisions (i.e., treatment validity). Only issues related to concurrent and content validity are presented here because discussion of the relationship between treatment efficacy and children's self-report has been presented earlier.

Information concerning the concurrent validity of unstructured child interviews is sparse. In the literature concerning interviews with adult populations, self-report has been shown to correlate significantly with other measures of behavior such as blood pressure (Kleinman, Goldman, Snow, & Korol, 1977) and responses to questionnaires; Wincze, Hoon, & Hoon, 1978). Although inconclusive, these data suggest that rejection of the unstructured child interview out-of-hand (without some scrutiny) as a valid assessment tool is unwarranted and, at the very least, suggest the need for an additional investigation of its psychometric properties.

The content validity of unstructured child interviews is related to the number and type of questions asked, their topical focus, and structure (Haynes & Jensen, 1979). In terms of the assessment process, the content validity of *any* instrument employed must be considered in relation to the initiating problem or referring concern. Thus, although a variety of topic areas may be appropriate for questioning children, information obtained during the interview is likely to be valid in content to the extent that problem areas, their controlling factors, and potential treatment strategies are identified (Burke & DeMers, 1979). Since children often have difficulty responding to open-ended questions or questions calling for evaluative or answers of high inference, the content validity of unstructured interviews is also a function of question format and difficulty of response requirements.

A Conceptual Model for the Unstructured Child Interview

Particularly with children, the process of interviewing and the content areas in which responses are elicited are interdependent, (Burke & DeMers, 1979) and use of unstructured interview formats to obtain accurate representations of children's behavior can be likened to the use of an expensive, manually operated camera to obtain high quality pictures. Although the topic of the picture is up to the discretion of the photographer, the extent to which that topic is accurately captured on film is a function of how the picture is taken. Specifically, consideration of such issues as film speed, length of exposure, lighting, and angle are important determinants of the extent to which the resulting picture can be held as an accurate and useful representation of its referent in front of the lens. Similarly, when inteviewing children by using an unstructured format, the reliability and validity of information obtained (i.e., content) is largely a function of how the interview is conducted (i.e., process). Specifically, information obtained during the interview on various topic areas is likely to be "of higher resolution" if the interviewer provides the child with proper expectations for the interview situation, uses stimulus conditions that maximize the child's ability to respond, and tailors questions to the child's level of cognitive and social-cognitive functioning (Bierman, 1983).

The interdependence of interview process and content suggests that use of a step-down strategy as a heuristic technique in guiding interviewer behavior may help to enable the interviewer to integrate direct observational and indirect self-report information obtained during the interview situation. An example of one such step-down procedure might involve starting at a given level of question generality or stimulus complexity, and systematically altering this to provide increasing structure for interviewee responses. By monitoring characteristics of the responses given in relation to different levels of stimulus complexity, task requirements can be regulated to maximize the child's information output given his or her level of cognitive development. Once an optimum level of stimulus complexity has been determined, the interviewer might use this information when approaching subsequent content areas, thereby helping the child to respond as completely as possible. The use of this or a similar sequential strategy appears to have some support in the child development literature. Specifically, Selman, (1980) found that children exhibiting emotional difficulties showed less mature reasoning in their conceptions of self and interpersonal relationships than control children. In addition, Bierman (1983) noted that children show less mature reasoning (e.g., black-and-white logic, use of global descriptors) when interviewed concerning areas of emotional stress.

Process Issues: Behaviors of the Interviewer

Introducing the Interview

As discussed spreviously, it is important to provide children with proper expectations of their role and the role of the interviewer at the outset of the interview. In identifying the role of the interviewer, it may be useful to identify the purpose of the visit as well as activities in which the interviewer will engage during the interview session. For example, by describing oneself as a helper, or someone who wants to know more about the child to help him or her do better in school, the interviewer may reduce anxiety in children who appear uneasy or apprehensive about the upcoming interaction. Similarly, if a child is told the interviewer will be writing down what the child says to help the interviewer remember it later, the child may be less likely to inquire about what the inteviewer is doing during actual questioning or to be distracted by note-taking activities.

Since children are not typically prepared to engage in lengthy discussions with adults concerning their perceptions or behavior (Bierman, 1983), identifying what is expected of the child during the interview session can also be helpful in reducing apprehension, while at the same time help to establish a response set for upcoming questions. For example, indicating to the child that the interviewer would like them to "be a good helper" by telling as much as he or she can when asked a question may be a useful strategy in reducing the need for follow-up questioning as the interview progresses.

Structuring the Questions

When structuring the questions to which children will respond, degree of stimulus complexity, use of prompts (i.e., verbal, written, physical), and use of praise are important parameters in tailoring the interview process to the child's level of cognitive and social-cognitive development. Issues in the determination of stimulus complexity include the vocabularly level employed by the interviewer, the amount of information provided in each question, the extent to which questions require abstract or high inference answers versus factual recall, and the use of questions that employ open-ended versus multiple choice formats.

Children may be successfully prompted to give additional or more detailed information by rephrasing a question to make it less ambiguous or to highlight essential dimensions, by utilizing concrete referents (e.g., having the child use a textbook to show problems which are most or least difficult), or by writing important components of a question on paper and employing a forced choice format. For example, a child may be asked to rank the names of adults in order of whom they would like to spend time.

Finally, praising children for detailed, apparently honest answers to interview questions not only allows for direct observation of the effectiveness of this type of social reward, but helps the interviewer maintain control over children's nonverbal behavior in the interview setting. Related to the use of praise, setting behavioral limits (e.g., asking the child to remain seated during the interview) and making requests (e.g., asking the child to close the door or to hand the interviewer a toy) are additional means of enhancing the amount and type of direct observational information that can be obtained during the interview while again helping to control child behavior through redirection.

Process Issues: Behaviors of the Child

Social Appropriateness

Careful observation of the extent to which the child is cooperative and courteous or demonstrates socially appropriate behaviors, such as establishing and maintaining eye contact or proximity to the interviewer, can provide valuable information concerning the level of social skill development and situational specificity of reported behavior problems. For example, if a child is reported to be noncompliant and aggressive toward adults at home but is cooperative and helpful during the interview, such information may provide partial support for characterizing the inappropriate behavior as a performance rather than a skill deficit.

Level of Activity

Observation of a child's general activity level, including posture, movement, gesturing, and time on-task (e.g., time spent maintaining eye contact with the interviewer and answering questions), can also provide useful information for a comparison of behavior across settings. These observations can be helpful in tailoring treatment and instructional strategies to the child's rate of activity or length of attention span.

Speech

Although not typically a direct focus of interview assessment (with the exception of children referred for articulation or language dysfunctions), the manner in which children speak can nevertheless serve as a useful marker of cognitive functioning or of the presence of emotionally laden issues. Perhaps the most obvious characteristics of children's speech are expressive vocabulary and production. Thus, if a child who has been quite expressive in answering questions suddenly shifts to one- and two-word responses when a certain topic is reached, anxiety associated with that area may be indicated.

Additional speech characteristics worthy of monitoring include volume, rate, and response latency. For example, if a child consistently initiates an incomplete or incorrect response to questioning before the question is completed, the use of a cognitive modeling strategy (e.g., stop-wait-answer) may be a useful consideration as a component of treatment if similar observations are obtained in other situations.

Response Organization

In addition to the amount of information produced in children's responses and characteristics of their speech, aspects of response organization, such as temporal sequencing of reported events, logic, extent of the detail of and the level of differentiation, and unidimensionality, may also provide data relating to cognitive functioning or developmental level. Consideration of the extent to which information obtained during the interview is internally consistent may serve as an additional index of reliability. For example, a child may report having "a lot of friends" but be unable to name more than one, or later complain that no one likes him or her. Such internal inconsistencies may be due to pervasive limits in cognitive or developmental skills, or failure of the child to function as a reliable self-reporter on a specific area. In either case, additional information may be needed to resolve the discrepancy.

Content Issues

One reason for the attractiveness of the unstructured child interview as an assessment strategy is the freedom that this format provides in addressing topic areas inaccessible by other more structured procedures. Because of the idiographic nature of learning and adjustment problems in children, it would be difficult to identify all possible areas which could be potentially covered in a child interview. For example, Haynes and Jensen (1979) identified several content areas and functions of unstructured interviews, including information about client concerns, factors maintaining problem behaviors, history of referral concerns, procedures and goals of treatment, and treatment outcome.

This section concludes, therefore, with a listing of general content areas and specific topics (see Table 11-1) that are typically assessed in interviews with children. Although not a comprehensive listing, Table 11-1 is representative of information derived from several sources in both the behavior therapy and clinical child literature (Bierman, 1983; Herjanic, *et al.*, 1975).

STRUCTURED INTERVIEWS

A recent trend in research involving child psychopathology and psychiatry has been the emergence of structured interview schedules. Several forces have converged to produce this trend. Structured interview schedules for use with *adults* have been adopted by many researchers and are now commonly used methods of

TABLE 11-1 Content Areas Typically Addressed in Interview with Children

General Area	Specific Topics
Demographic information	Age/grade
	Address
	Number in family
	Names of teachers
Academic performance	Difficulty in academic subjects
	Difficulty in specific activities (e.g., remembering addition facts)
	Description of current curricula
	Favorite and least favorite subject areas
	Earned grades
	Use of compensatory strategies
	Study habits
Classroom behavior	Classroom rules and teacher expectations
	Consequences (rewards/punishers)
	Desired material or activity reinforcers
Peer relations	Number and names of friends
	Playtime activities
	Resolution of disputes
	Desired qualities
	Sexual relations
Interests	Spare time activities
	Preferred television programs
	Employment
	Career aspirations
	Participation in sports/clubs
Relations with parents and other adults	Parental expectations
	Shared interests
	Contacts with the authorities
	Responsibilities at home
Treatment preferences	Perceptions of treatment procedures
	Importance of goals
	Reinforcement choices
Other referral concerns	

assigning patients to homogeneous diagnostic groups. Low reliability associated with unstructured interviews prompted researchers to structure interview formats so that variance due to differences in interviewer behavior was minimized (Endicott & Spitzer, 1978). Also, diagnostic criteria set forth in DSM-III (APA, 1980), designed to be less descriptive and more definitional than previous classificatory schemes, are more easily transformed to a structured interview format. As a result, current interview schedules are thought to be affected less by errors resulting from ambiguous diagnostic criteria.

The downward extension of adult structured interviews to child and adolescent populations was an inevitable response to the trend in adult psychopathology and psychiatry (e.g., Puig-Antich, Blau, Marx, Greenhill, & Chambers, 1978). Also, as can be seen in DSM-III, the classification of childhood disorders has expanded in scope and specificity. Because broadly based categories used in DSM-II have given way to a more detailed psychiatric taxonomy, structured interview formats have been proposed as important aids to making reliable diagnostic discriminations.

Other factors contributing to the development and use of structured interview techniques include the increasing realization that child self-report data are not inherently unreliable and invalid (Herjanic et al., 1975; Edelbrock, et al., 1985). In fact, for certain symptoms and behaviors, children may be the most accurate source of information on certain symptoms and behaviors. Many problem behaviors are not exhibited in the presence of adults, are not reported to adults, or do not produce consequences that are immediately obvious to adults. Occasionally, given adequate incentives and suitable cognitive and language capabilities, children may report important behaviors occurring outside the purview of parents and teachers (e.g., stealing), or complain of cognitions and emotions that do not have overt, behavioral concomitants (e.g., worrying, guilt). For the most part, however, this does not seem to occur. Accumulated research evidence would suggest that with certain types of disorders (e.g., internalizing) information gained from children or adolescents often deserves greater weight than that provided by parents or teachers (Bierman, 1983). Of course, in the event a child denies covert problems or is too young to understand and describe complex emotional and cognitive disruptions, structured interview data will also be inadequate.

Currently, structured interviews developed for us with child and adolescent populations are used primarily to assign patients to homogenous research groups. Other applications have included epidemiological studies of childhood psychopathology and investigations into the reliability and validity of child self-report. Diagnostic classification of children according to DSM-III criteria is seldom a priority for school psychologists, however. Traditional concerns of school psychologists—evaluation, placement, and habilitation of cases involving mental retardation, specific learning disorders, and emotional and behavioral disorders—usually do not rely on DSM-III diagnoses. Furthermore, previous reviews of current child structured interviews have questioned their utility when used on an individual, case by case basis (Costello, in press; Paget, 1984).

Nevertheless, Paget (1984), in her review of child structured interviews, identifies several, potential benefits to school psychologists using this mode of assessment. Structured interviews (1) enhance the systematic and objective collection of child interview data, (2) allow for comparisons across interviewers and time, (3) allow for comparisons of children's interpersonal functioning within a standardized interview format, and (4) ensure that a broad range of symptoms are assessed.

Reviewing information concerning the strengths and weaknesses of these instruments is justified whether or not current interviews are adopted for use. Researchers are very likely to continue to use structured interviews in attempting to understand and treat problem behavior in children. An informed perspective, therefore, is important for evaluating studies using these instruments. Secondly, studies involving structured interviews have served to enhance knowledge of the accuracy and value of child self-report. Finally, school psychologists interested in developing structured interviews more appropriate for use in school settings might benefit from research involving current diagnostic interview schedules.

In this section we review five structured interviews developed for use with children and adolescents. Accompanying the discussion of these instruments are two tables. Table 11-2 presents descriptive information such as the age range of potential respondents, time required for administration, type and amount of training required of interviewers, information yielded by each instrument (e.g., symptom scores, diagnoses), and the methods used to produce diagnoses from interview data (e.g., computerized algorithms versus clinical judgment). Other aspects included in Table 11-2 are administration format, interview structure, and response codes. Administration format refers to the various components of the interview, the use of skip functions which can economize interview time, and the need for concurrent parent interviews. Interview structure, borrowing from Burke and DeMers (1979), refers to (1) whether questions are to be asked verbatim (i.e., structured) or whether interviewers have some latitude in phrasing and ordering questions (i.e., semistructured); and (2) whether questions are almost exclusively closed (e.g., yes or no) or are open-ended questions commonly used. Response codes refer to the specific manner in which the child's verbal responses are quantified. For these instruments, response codes range from simple present or absent dichotomies to nine-point severity scales.

Table 11-3 presents more technical aspects of the five interview schedules. Structured interviews, because of their standardized format and quantification of information, are more amenable to psychometric evaluation than unstructured interviews. Included in Table 11-3 are summaries of available reliability data and information regarding validational studies. Normative data are not yet available for any of the five currently reviewed interview schedules. Reliability data are presented separately for individual items or symptoms, interview subscales, and diagnoses. In addition, distinction is made between interrater reliability and test-retest reliability. As used here, the former refers to agreement between raters viewing the same interview session (either in person or through videotape), and the latter is based on concordance over two separate interview sessions using identical or different interviewers. Information from the limited number of available validation studies includes sample sizes and validation criteria; evaluative statements regarding the instruments' validity are found in the text. Generally speaking, conclusions regarding the validity of structured child interviews are limited by the paucity of psychometric studies conducted.

It should also be noted that data regarding agreement between child and parent interviews should be viewed as reflective of the instruments' validity and not their reliability (c.f., Herjanic *et al.*, 1975). Questions regarding the significance of discrepancies between child and parent interview information are illustrative of the problems associated with choosing appropriate validity criteria for diagnostic interviews. In the case of differences in parent and child report, one may conclude (1) parent report is completely inaccurate, (2) child report is completely inaccurate, (3) children and parents can provide accurate reports on a common subset of

TABLE 11-2 Descriptive Characteristics of Child Structured Interviews

Instrument Name	Ages	Time	Raters/ Training	Interview Structure	Response Codes	Skip Function	Parent Interview	Diagnostic Process	Scores Produced	Interview Format
DICA	6–17	60–90 mins.	lay/ minimal	structured/ close questions	Yes/No	yes	optional	computer algorithms available	symptom scores; total symptom score; diagnoses	joint parent-child interview; child interview; behavior ratings
K-SADS	6–17	45–120 mins.	clinician/ extensive	semistructured/ open-ended questions common	6- & 7-pt. scales	yes	required	clinical judgment	symptoms; subscales; diagnoses	parent interview; child interview; behavior and global ratings
ISC	8–17	45–90 mins.	clinician/ extensive	semistructured/ open-ended questions common	4- & 9-pt. scales	minimal	required	clinical judgment	symptom scores; mental status; behavioral & clinical ratings; diagnoses	parent interview; child interview; ratings; diagnostic addenda
DISC	6–17	50–60 mins.	lay/ minimal	structured/ close questions	3-pt. scales	yes	optional	computer algorithms	symptom scores; symptom subscales; total symptom score; diagnoses	child interview
CAS	7–16	60 mins.	clinician/ minimal	structured/ open-ended questions common	Yes, No, Ambiguous, N/A, NR	minimal	optional	standardized/ manual approach	content scores; symptom complexes; total symptom score; diagnoses	child interview; behavior ratings

interview items only, or, (4) children and parents give accurate accounts concerning different aspects of a child's functioning. Previous research examining specific areas of parent and child agreement and disagreement suggests both (3) and (4) above are correct (Chambers *et al.*, 1985; Herjanic *et al.*, 1975; Herjanic & Reich, 1982; Kovacs, 1983b; Reich, Herjanic, Welner, & Gandhy, 1982). Parents and children can agree on certain, obvious phenomena (e.g., number of siblings, previous hospitalizations), but depending on the symptoms in question, differential weights should perhaps be given to parent and child reports. Therefore, using parent-report to validate child interview information is hardly sufficient.

Problems regarding appropriate validity criteria are not insurmountable, however. For example, subjects with different diagnoses have been followed and differences in the course of their adjustments have supported the construct validity of diagnoses derived from structured interviews (Kovacs, Feinberg, Crouse-Noval, Paulaukas, & Finkelstein, 1984). Also, diagnoses produced from interviews with adolescents have been compared with diagnoses based on all other information available, including child and parent interviews, teacher reports, and school records (Storber, Green & Carlson, 1981b). Unfortunately, in this particular study, a structured interview designed for use with adults was applied to a sample of adolescents. Similar studies are needed which utilize currently available child instruments.

Diagnostic Interview for Children and Adolescents (DICA)

The current version of the DICA is derived from previous forms developed by Herjanic and her associates at Washington University. The DICA is a highly structured inteview schedule which can be administered by lay interviewers after only minimal training. The exact wording of questions is specified and questions are designed to elicit simple yes or no responses. A parallel version of the DICA for parents is also available and is typically given by a different interviewer simultaneously with the child interview. A joint parent-child interview, also highly structured, is conducted prior to the separate parent and child sessions. The child interview is organized by diagnostic categories and is followed by a brief rating scale whereby interviewers can rate observable interview behavior. A potential problem with the DICA is its fairly direct style of questioning, especially in light of recommendations made previously in this chapter regarding ways to minimize anxiety arousing probes (e.g., Some children are known to do *x*. Do you ever do *x* ?).

Very little reliability data exist for the DICA and that reported has been presented in terms of percentage of agreement, a method of calculating reliability that does not control chance agreement and is thus susceptible to inflated values (Bartko & Carpenter, 1976). An average interrater agreement of 84% has been reported for earlier versions of the DICA. Test-retest reliability (same raters) over two to three month intervals ranged from 80% to 95% (average = 89%) (Herjanic *et al.*, 1975).

TABLE 11-3 Technical Characteristics of Child Structured Interviews

Instrument	Interrater Reliability	Test-Retest Reliability	Validity Studies
DICA	*Symptoms*: average = 84%	*Symptoms*: 80%–95% average = 89% (2–3 month interval)	1. Herjanic *et al.* (1975) *Sample*: 50 clinic referrals; *Criteria*: agreement with parent interview 2. Herjanic & Campbell (1977) *Sample*: 50 pediatric referrals, 50 psychiatric referrals; *Criteria*: group membership 3. Herjanic & Reich (1982) *Sample*: 257 psychiatric referrals, 50 pediatric referrals; *Criteria*: agreement with parent interview 4. Reich *et al.* (1982) *Sample*: Same as study #3; *Criteria*: agreement with parent interview
K-SADS	*Symptoms/ Subscales* (combined) .65–.96 (ICC) average =.89	*Symptoms*: .09–.89 (ICC) average = .54 *Subscales*: .41–.81 (r) average = .68 *Diagnoses* .24–.70 (kappa) average = .53 (1–3 day interval)	1. Puig-Antich *et al.* (1979) *Sample*: 13 prepubertal depressed children; *Criteria*: response to imipramine 2. Puig-Antich *et al.* (1979) *Sample*: 4 prepubertal depressed children; *Criteria*: cortisol; hyposecretion 3. Chambers *et al.* (1985) *Sample*: 52 clinic referrals; *Criteria*: agreement with parent interview 4. Gershon *et al.* (1985) *Sample*: 29 children of bipolar depressed parents, 37 children of controls; *Criteria*: incidence of affective disorder
ISC	*Symptoms*: .64–1.0 (ICC) average = .89	None reported	1. Kovacs (1983a) *Sample*: 75 psychiatric referrals; *Criteria*: agreement with parent interview 2. Kovacs *et al.* I (1984) *Sample*: 114 psychiatric referrals; *Criteria*: course of disorder for depressive and nondepressive diagnostic groups 3. Kovacs *et al.* II (1984) *Sample*: 95 followed from study #2; *Criteria*: risk for subsequent depressive episode
DISC	*Symptoms*: .94–1.0 (r) average = .98	*Symptoms*: .28–.78 (ICC) average = .62 *Diagnoses*: .21–.47 (kappa) average = .34 (mdn = 9 day interval)	1. Costello *et al.* (1985) *Sample*: 40 psychiatric referrals, 40 pediatric referrals; *Criteria*: a) group membership b) Child Behavior Checklist (CBCL) 2. Shekim *et al.* (1985) *Sample*: 114 nine-year-olds from rural community; *Criteria*: a) agreement with parent interview, b) comparison with previous prevalence data 3. Lewis *et al.* (1985) *Sample*: 612 youths selected randomly; *Criteria*: negative reactions to DISC interview session

TABLE 11-3 (*Continued*)

Instrument	Interrater Reliability	Test-Retest Reliability	Validity Studies
CAS	*Symptoms*: .47–.61 (range of M Kappa's over four raters) *Subscales*: Total Score, $r = .90$: Content Areas, .59–.84 (r) average $= .72$ Symptom Areas, .44–.82 (r) average $= .67$	None reported	1. Hodges *et al.* (1982) *Sample*: 18 psychiatric inpatients, 32 psychiatric outpatients, 37 controls; *Criteria*: a) CBCL, b) STAIC, c) CDI 2. Hodges *et al.* (1985) *Sample*: 67 w/ behavior disorder, 30 recurrent abdominal pain 42 healthy controls, *Criteria*: group membership 3. Hodges *et al.* (in press) *Sample*: 29 clinic referrals; *Criteria*: a) K-SADS, b) agreement with parent interview

Validity data pertinent to the DICA consist primarily of concordance with parent interviews (Herjanic & Reich, 1982; Reich *et al.*, 1982). Given the problems associated with parent interviews as criteria, little can be said about the validity of the DICA. Researchers interested in what aspects of functioning or which diagnoses exhibit the greatest degree of parent-child disagreement may find these studies informative. The only other published validity study, based on an earlier version of the DICA, found pediatric clinic referrals and matched psychiatric referrals differed with respect to the total number of symptoms reported (Herjanic & Campbell, 1977).

Schedule for Affective Disorders and Schizophrenia for School-age Children (Kiddie-SADS)

The schedule for Affective Disorders and Schizophrenia for School-age Children (K-SADS), developed by Puig-Antich and Chambers, is a downward extension of the *Schedule for Affective Disorders and Schizophrenia* (SADS) used with adults (Endicott and Spitzer, 1978). Despite its name, the K-SADS is a broadly construed instrument designed to assess a variety of diagnostic problems. As it is typically used, adminsitration of the K-SADS includes an informal parent interview focusing on presenting problems and treatment history, a semistructured parent interview, an informal interview with the child, and finally, a semistructured child interview. Ultimately, clinician summary ratings are made from information obtained from both informants and these ratings are used to determine diagnosis. Child interview questions are grouped according to affective, anxiety, conduct, and psychotic symptomatology and are followed by a clinician rating scale consisting of sixteen observational items. To interview both informants requires two to three hours.

The K-SADS is intended for use by experienced clinicians familiar with DSM-III criteria and who receive specific training in use of the interview schedule. In one study, seven clinicians were trained by the developers of the K-SADS but three of these "were judged after the training period to not be able to perform the semistruc-tured interview adequately" (Chambers *et al.*, 1985, p. 697). Though this may bode well for the rigors of diagnostic classification in that study, it raises questions about the generalizability of the K-SADS when used by other researchers or clinicians.

Limited interrater reliability data concerning the K-SADS are available but it appears that raters are able to achieve adequate agreement. For example, intraclass correlation coefficients (ICCs) were reported to average .89 across depressive symp-toms. Internal consistency (alpha coefficients) of symptom subscales have also been reported and range from .25 (somatization) to .86 (conduct disorder) with most above .65. Information concerning the homogeneity of interview subscales is unique among child interviews to the K-SADS. Test-retest reliability (1) for individual symptoms ranged from .09 to .89 (ICC's) and averaged .54; (2) for subscales ranged from .41 to .81 (product moment correlations) and averaged .68; and (3) for diag-noses, kappa coefficients, which control for chance agreement, ranged from .24 (anxiety disorder) to .70 (nonmajor depressive disorders) and averaged .53 (Chambers *et al.*, 1985).

Validity data in support of the K-SADS are limited. Two studies have been conducted in which the K-SADS was used to identify depressed prepubertal chil-dren. In one study, six of thirteen depressed subjects responded to imipramine treatment (Pluig-Antich *et al.*, 1979) whereas another study found two of four subjects demonstrated cortisol hyposecretion, itself an equivocal neuroendocrine marker of depressive abnormality (Puig-Antich, Chambers, Halpern, Hanlon, & Sachar, 1979). Other studies involving the K-SADS looked at parent-child agree-ment (Chambers *et al.*, 1985) and compared the prevalance of affective disorders in the offspring of bipolar affective disorder patients and controls (Gershon, *et al.*, 1985). The latter study found no group differences in the prevalance of affective disorders when the K-SADS was used for assessment.

Interview Schedule for Children (ISC)

The Interview Schedule for Children (ISC) was developed by Kovacs for use in a childhood depression research project. Similar to the K-SADS, the ISC is adminis-tered to children and adolescents after parallel interviews are conducted with parents. Following a brief, informal discussion of current problems and their dura-tion, the semistructured ISC proceeds with questions regarding core (primarily affective) symptomatology, collateral behaviors if indicated (e.g., queries concerning suicidal behavior), and mental status. Following the interview, observed behavioral ratings and clinical ratings are made. If needed, additional items are available in separate addenda according to diagnostic classification. The ISC is a highly flexible interview schedule. Therefore, experienced clinicians are recommended as inter-viewers. Completion of both child and parent interviews can require two to four hours (Kovacs, 1983b, Kovacs *et al.*, 1984).

Several features of the ISC reflect an appreciation by its developer for the nuances of obtaining useful child-report information. Because of the instrument's flexibility, inteviewers are allowed to use alternative methods of eliciting responses from children. For example, interviewers are instructed in the use of the child's drawings or hand gestures in place of verbal responses when dealing with very young or shy and uncomfortable children. Also, questions are worded simply and briefly and are often preceded by enabling statements (e.g., "When kids are angry, sometimes they . . ."). Finally, *double check* questions are used throughout the ISC in order to ascertain children's understanding of what is asked and the degree of consistency in their responding.

Test-retest reliability data on the ISC are not available. Interrater reliability for individual items has been shown to be adequate: ICC's ranged from .64 to 1.00 across core symptoms and averaged .89 (Kovacs, 1983b). Evidence for the validity of the ISC rests primarily with follow-up studies conducted on psychiatric clinic referrals. Kovacs and her colleagues (Kovacs, Feinberg, Crouse-Novak, Paulauskas, & Finkelstein, 1984; Kovacs, *et al.*, 1984) have examined the differential courses of children diagnosed through the ISC as Major Depressive Disorder (MDD), Dysthymic Disorder (DD), and Adjustment Disorder with Depressed Mood (ADDM). They have found important differences in rates of recovery and future risk of subsequent episodes of MDD among the three groups. Additional research into the psychometric properties of the ISC is needed, however, before other researchers can use it confidently.

Diagnostic Interview Schedule for Children (DISC)

The Diagnostic Interview Schedule for Children (DISC) is a highly structured child interview developed by Costello and his associates for use in large scale epidemiological studies. Interview questions are read verbatim and for most items the child is asked to respond in one of three ways—Yes, No, and Somewhat (or Sometimes). Because of its structure, lay interviewers receiving minimal training are capable of giving the DISC and, in fact, have been found to perform as well as trained clinicians (Costello, Edelbrock, & Costello, 1985). The DISC yields diagnostic classifications, a total symptom score, behavior and conduct and affective and neurotic symptom subscale scores, and individual symptom scores.

As with the ISC, the DISC has features which are designed to enhance the quality of information derived from child respondents. Questions are short and often are broken into smaller, manageable components, follow-up questions ensure that previous probes were correctly understood, and items that may be somewhat threatening are softened by suggestions that other children may feel or behave similarly.

An average (product moment) correlation of .98 (range = .84 to 1.00) was found when interrater reliability of DISC symptom scores was assessed (Costello, in press). Extensive test-retest reliability data on the DISC also exist. Given average intervals of nine days, interviews by different raters yielded ICCs for symptom scores ranging from .28 to .78 with an average of .62. Stability of DISC scores was greater for behavior and conduct (average ICC = .75) than for affective and neurotic (average

ICC = .59) symptoms and for fourteen to eighteen year olds (average ICC = .71) than for ten to thirteen year olds (average ICC = .60) and six to nine year olds (average ICC = .43) (Edelbrock *et al.*, 1985). Across all ages, test-retest reliability for DSM-III diagnostic classifications is reported to range from .21 to .41 (kappas) and average .34 (Costello, in press).

As the newest structure interview for children, the DISC as only recently been subjected to tests of its validity. Costello *et al.* (1985) found psychiatric referrals (ages 7 to 11) received greater total symptom scores and more psychiatric diagnoses than matched pediatric referrals when both were assessed with the DISC. Correlations between DISC total symptom scores and the Child Behavior Checklist (CBCL); (Achenback & Edelbrock, 1983) were disappointingly low, however (*r* = .29 for pediatric referrals; *r* = .14 for psychiatric referrals). The DISC has also been used to assess prevalance of attention deficit disorder (ADD) in a sample of nine-year-old children living in a rural community (Shekim *et al.*, 1985). When compared with the parent version of the DISC (DISC-P), the child interview indentified fewer ADD children. Also, many discrepancies between the DISC and DISC-P were found when additional diagnoses assigned to ADD children were examined. One interesting apsect of an interview's validity which has been examined for the DISC is the reaction of children to its administration. Lewis, Gorsky, Cohen, and Hartmark (1985) found negligible ill effects occurring among children who were interviewed via the DISC.

When use with children below age twelve and when used independently of the DISC-P, DISC appears questionable in its validity. When combined with parent data, however, the DISC has been shown to classify psychiatric and pediatric referrals efficiently (Costello *et al.*, 1985).

Child Assessment Schedule (CAS)

The Child Assessment Schedule (CAS) has been described as a semistructured child interview that is suitable for both clinical and research purposes (Hodges, Kline, Stern, Cytryn, & McKnew, 1982). In actuality, the CAS is rather structured with respect to the flexibility allowed interviewers, though many items are open-ended. Questions are organized by content areas as opposed to diagnoses, and are said to flow naturally from familiar topics, such as school, to more threatening subjects, such as fears and acting out behaviors. Questions concerning though disorders are asked only if indicated. Because of the freqeuent use of open-ended questions and the schedule's topical organization, children are said to experience the interview as an informal discussion, especially when administered by experienced clinicians.

Questions pertaining to the onset and duration of various symptoms are contained in a later section and are asked only if a symptom report was positive. At the conclusion of the interview, interviewers complete a fifty-nine-item observation rating scale. Recent supplements to the CAS include questions which expand its use to adolescent populations and a parallel version for parents, the P-CAS. Accompanying most CAS items are minimal criteria which must be met if a symptom is to be coded as present. Five response codes are available: Yes, No, Ambiguous, Not Applicable, and No Response. The CAS yields a total symptom score, scores based on content areas and symptom complexes, and various DSM-III diagnoses.

Interrater reliability data has been calculated for individual items from the CAS (.47 to .61, range of mean kappas among four raters), CAS total score ($r = .90$), content area scores (r's $= .59$ to .84, average $r = .72$), and symptom complexes (r's $= .44$ to .82, average $r = .67$) (Hodges *et al.*, 1982). Interrater reliability for diagnostic classifications and stability coefficients associated with CAS scores have not been reported.

Of the five interview schedules reviewed here, the CAS has associated with it the most extensive body of validity information. CAS total symptom scores, as well as most of the content and symptom subscale scores, were found to discrimate between child psychiatric referrals and normal controls (Hodges *et al.*, 1982). CAS total scores also correlated .53 with number of problems and .57 with severity of problems reported by parents on the CBCL. In addition, CAS Overanxious symptom subscale scores correlated .54 with scores from the State-Trait Anxiety Inventory for Children (STAIC) (Spielberger, 1973), while Depression symptom scores correlated .53 with Child Depression Inventory (CDI) (Kovacs, 1983) scores. Total symptom scores from the CAS have also been found to differ for behavior disordered children compared with children with recurrent abdominal pain and healthy controls (Hodges, Kline, Barbero, & Woodruff, 1985). Finally, a recent study by Hodges and her colleagues (Hodges, McKnew, Burbach, & Roebuch, in press) found poor concordance between child versions of the CAS and the K-SADS when administered by lay interviewers. Good agreement was found, however, between the CAS and the K-SADS when based on parent interview only or a combination of parent and child interviews. This is the first study to compare results from two different structured child interviews when used to assess the same sample of subjects.

SELF-REPORT RATING SCALES

Only recently have behaviorally oriented psychologists come to recognize the significance of including child self-report in the assessment process (Garber, 1984; Mash & Terdal, 1981; Ollendick & Hersen, 1984). As a result, child self-report rating scales were not routinely included in a behavioral assessment of childhood disorders. Although problems do exist in using self-ratings with children (e.g., unreliability because of limited linquistic and cognitive development), such objective data are more conducive to empirical analyses (e.g., reliability and validity studies) than informally collected interview data. Self-report rating scales should appeal, therefore, to an assessor interested in a scientific approach to measuring overt and covert behavior in children.

This section briefly discusses assessment issues that pertain to self-rating instruments, and provides an overview of some of the more psychometrically sound and frequently used self-rating measures available for use with children and adolescents. A substantial portion of this section is devoted to a reference table in which descriptive and evaluative infomation regarding various self-rating scales is presented.

Assessment Issues

As noted earlier in this chapter, child self-ratings have long been suspect because of their lack of agreement with ratings by others and with observed behavior (Finch & Rogers, 1984; Ollendick & Meador, 1984). However, some researchers have reported a high degree of correspondence between children's self-ratings and parent ratings of certain childhood behavior problems, such as fears (Bondy, Sheslow, & Garcia, 1985). What may account for such divergent findings regarding the accuracy and value of child self-ratings?

If the behavior of responding to a self-rating scale is broken down into discrete skills, the complexity of such a response becomes readily apparent. First, a child must be able to attend to and understand written and verbal instructions regarding completion of the measure. Second, an understanding of the instructions must be generalized accurately to the actual test stimuli. In addition, a child must have the capacity to negotiate the grammar, vocabulary, units, and anchors of the items and to choose the response appropriate for him or her. The outcome of such a choice may be influenced by a variety of variables (e.g., impulse control; written, receptive, and expressive language skills; experience with responding to written materials; ability to interpret properly units and anchors of the scales for each item). Given the number of levels at which the process of responding to a self-rating instrument may go awry, it is not surprising to find some instruments produce inadequate reliability coefficients. In addition, some researchers have reported convergence of self-ratings with other measurement methods, whereas other researchers have found discrepancies between other assessment procedures and child self-ratings.

Rather than merely wringing one's hands in frustration at this glitch in the child behavioral assessment universe (i.e., the occasional unreliability of child self-ratings and the lack of convergent validity with other assessment methods), the resourceful psychologist will view the situation as an opportunity for effective problem solving. The modification of stimulus and response complexity, as discussed earlier in this chapter, are especially relevant to creatively and systematically solving some of the difficulties in assessing behavior problems through child self-rating instruments. For example, care should be given to select test stimuli (i.e., written statements or questions) appropriate for the age and skill level of the target population. Reading and comprehending written material demands development of selective attention, encoding skills, and memory organization, among other requisite skills (Byrd & Gholson, 1984). Deficits in any of these reading skill areas may adversely affect a child's ability to respond to self-ratings. Recall Gorsuch, Henighan, and Barnard (1972) found a clear relationship between children's verbal ability and the reliability of a self-report locus of control scale. They interpreted their findings by citing evidence that suggested lower ability children responded randomly because they failed to understand the scale items. The authors agree with Gorsuch et al. (1972) that "a scale needs to be reliable for all children with whom it is used" (p. 579). Developers of child self-rating instruments should specify age and reading levels for which their scales are appropriate, and assessors should systematically determine whether or not a given child can read and comprehend the written stimuli presented in a particular scale.

In addition to modifying stimulus complexity, a developer of child self-ratings should consider matching the response complexity with the developmental level of children for whom the scale is targeted. For example, many self-ratings developed for adults require the informant to endorse a response using a five-, seven-, or nine-point scale. Given data from the developmental literature regarding acquisition of cognitive skills (e.g., seriation, continuous quantities), it is possible that children, especially younger children, fail to understand scales with five or more units (Inhelder & Piaget, 1964; Inhelder, Sinclair, & Bovet, 1974). Although few empirical studies exist that have directly investigated appropriate scale units and anchors for children of various ages, some psychologists recommend using three-point scales with symbolic anchors (e.g., smiling, neutral, & frowning faces) for children in third grade and below (Turco, Elliott, & Witt, 1985). The issue of developmentally appropriate scale units and anchors for child self-ratings clearly is fertile ground for research.

An evaluation and description of selected self-ratings follows. The criteria used to determine whether an instrument would be included are the psychometric properties (i.e., reliability and validity) of the measure. Thus, only those measures that reported data on the psychometric properties are included in this review. Child self-ratings designed for screening global behavior problems and measures of personality constructs are covered first. A discussion of instruments designed to assess specific problems are then presented. Although very general comments concerning these instruments are all that are found in the text, much more specific information is contained in Tables 11-4 and 11-5.

Behavior Checklists and Personality Inventories

Multidimensional behavioral checklists and personality self-report inventories allow the assessor to obtain information regarding a child's or adolescent's personal perspective on a number of variables simultaneously. Data obtained from these multidimensional instruments can be compared with information obtained from other informants (e.g., parents, teachers, peers, other professionals), thus providing the assessor with a more complete representation of the child's problems. However, as seen in Table 11-4, the area of self-report behavior checklists, and particularly personality inventories for children, have received relatively little empirical evaluation. Moreover, the length and theoretical orientation underlying the development of these measures often inhibit their use by behaviorally oriented school psychologists.

TABLE 11-4 Self-Report Behavioral Checklists and Personality Inventories

Content Areas	Response Format	Age Range	Subscales	Reliability	Validity	Comments
Behavior checklists Child Behavior Checklist (CBCL) Youth Form Achenbach & Edelbrock, 1983	120 items not true/very true	11–18 years	not available	Test-Retest .69 over six month period	Limited data is available on the CBCL youth form at this time. Convergent validity has been demonstrated between the youth CBCL total score and CBCL's completed by the mother and clinician for a sample of thirty 12–17-year-olds seen at a community mental health center.	Currently, the youth form of the CBCL has not been systematically evaluated in terms of its validity and reliability. Therefore, its use is recommended for research purposes.
Behavior Rating Profile (BRP) Self-report form from Brown & Hammill, 1978	60 items 3 scales 20 items per scale true/false	6–13 years	Peer; Home; School	Internal Consistency range .74-.87;	Concurrent validity of BRP with other behavior rating scales (RBPCL), Walker, Vineland Social Maturity Scale across 3 groups of behaviorally handicapped youths: inpatient psychiatric patients, public school emotionally disturbed, learning disabled students. Convergent validity with BRP as rated by parent and teacher. BRP distinguishes psychiatrically disturbed from nondisturbed youths.	BRP has a large ($n = 1326$) representative standardization sample. Use of alternate informants faciliates interpretation. Recommend its use for clinical and research purposes. BRP available from author.

Personality inventories

Instrument	Items	Age	Scales/Scores	Reliability	Validity	Comments
Millon Adolescent Personality Inventory (MAPI) Millon, Green & Meagher, 1982	150 items true/false	13–19 years	Introversion; Inhibited; Cooperative; Sociable; Confident; Forceful; Respectful; Sensitive	Internal Consistency range .67–83; Test-Retest range .69–82 over 5-mo; .55–68 over 1-yr.	MAPI has been evaluated in relation to other personality measures (e.g., 16PF, California Personality Inventory, Edwards Personal Preference Survey). MAPI also has been factor analyzed.	MAPI has large ($n = 2157$) representative standardization sample and is easily scored. Computer scoring and reports are available. MAPI provides a descriptive profile of the adolescents thoughts and feelings. Recommend its use as a research tool assessing personality.
Minnesota Multiphasic Personality Inventory (MMPI) Adolescent Norms Hathaway & Monachesi, 1963	550 items true/false alternate form: 168 items	14–18 years	Questions; Correction; Faking-Good; Faking-Bad; Hypochondriasis; Depression; Hysteria; Psychopathic Deviate; Masculinity-Femininity; Paranoia; Psychothenia; Schizophrenia; Hypomania	Test-Retest range .32–56 over 3-year interval	MMPI has extensive concurrent and predictive validity with adolescents. The shortened form (168) has been used frequently with adolescents although this scale diminishes its validity and reliability.	MMPI has long administration time. Extensive normative data are available on the MMPI. Recommend MMPI (168) as a research tool assessing broad categories of personality.
Children's Personality Questionnaire (CPQ) Porter & Cattell, 1979.	two forms 140 items per form;	8–12 years	14 dichotomous scores (e.g., dull vs. bright; sober vs. enthusiastic)	Alternate Form range .20–29 Test-Retest range .28–87 over 1-wk	Numerous validity studies have been conducted assessing low and high achievers, delinquents, and personality disorders in children.	Extensive normative data are available; however no information is given concerning the demographic variables. Manual is available from author; however, it does not effectively facilitate interpretation. Not recommended for clinical use in schools due to inconsistent reliability, and difficulty with manual.

TABLE 11-5 Characteristics of Behavior-Specific Self-Report Instruments Used with Children and Adolescents

Content Areas	Response Format	Age Range	Subscales	Reliability	Validity	Comments
Anxiety						
Revised Children's Manifest Anxiety Scale (R-CMAS) Reynolds & Richmond (1978)	37 items; True/False	6-17 years	Lie; Worry; Physiological; Concentration; Total Anxiety	Internal Consistency range .78–.83. Test-Retest range .68 9-month interval .98 3-week interval.	Concurrent validity with STAIC; Convergent validity with Walker Problem Behavior Checklist; Coefficents of Congruence of .96–.99 between gender and ethnic groups; No relation to State anxiety.	R-CMAS is easily scored; has a large ($N = 4200$) standardization sample; applicable to wide age range. Recommend its use as a measure of general anxiety.
State-Trait Anxiety Inventory for Children (STAIC) Spielberger (1973)	40 Items; 20 State, 20 Trait 3-point scale	9-12 years;	State Anxiety; Trait Anxiety	Internal Consistency range .78–.87. Test-Retest median .68 for Trait and .39 for State over six week interval.	Concurrent validity with R-CMAS, GASC, California Achievement Test, and teacher assigned grades STAIC scores. Scores on State version change in response to stressful situations.	STAIC has been used extensively cross-culturally. Preliminary normative data are available for fourth through sixth graders from Florida. Bibliography for STAIC available from C. D. Spielberger.
State-Trait Anxiety Inventory (STAI) Spielberger (1983)	40 Items: 20 State, 20 Trait items 3-point scale	above age 13	State Anxiety; Trait Anxiety	Internal Consistency range .86–.90. Test Retest range median .73 for Trait over 30 days and .48 for State.	Concurrent validity with Beck Depression Inventory, and Children's Depression Adjective Checklist scores of adolescent psychiatric inpatients; stable factor structure.	STAI has been employed in over 2000 studies; however, few studies have been conducted with youths. Limited norms ($n = 424$) for high school students. Utility limited to research purposes for youths.

Instrument	Format	Age	Content	Reliability	Validity	Comments
General Anxiety Scale for Children (GASC) Sarason *et al.* (1960)	45 Items Yes/No	Grades 1–9	General Anxiety; Lie Scale	Test-Retest range .64–.79 over a four-month interval, dependent on type of administrator.	Concurrent validity coefficients with test anxiety, achievement, and IQ. Zero order correlations with lie scale of CMAS.	GASC has been infrequently employed. Not recommended for use in schools other than as a measure of general anxiety, may be useful as a research instrument.
Test Anxiety Scale for Children (TASC) Sarason *et al.* (1960)	30 Items Yes/No	Grades 1–9	Not applicable	Internal Consistency range .82–.89. Test-Retest range .65–.82 2-mo.; .55–.78 4-mo.	Same validity coefficients as with the General Anxiety Scale for Children.	TASC has little normative, reliability, and validity data. Use should be limited to research studies on test anxiety.
Fears Fear Survey Schedule for Children (FSS-FC) Scherer & Nakamura (1968)	80 Items 5-point scale from none to very much	9–12 years	Failure; Major and Minor fears; Medical; Death; Dark; Home-School; Miscellaneous Fears	Internal Consistency .94 using Spearman-Brown formula. Test-Retest range .63–.83 depending on gender and grade of child.	Concurrent validity with Children's Manifest Anxiety Scale. Factor analysis indicated eight fear content areas. Convergent validity with mother's report of children's fears.	FSS-FC is a checklist of childhood fears. Normative data consist of sample of 99 children. Items drawn from adult fear survey schedules and professional familiar with childhood fears. Not recommended for use in schools, although may be useful as a research tool.
Children's Fear Survey Schedule (CFSS) Ryall & Dietiker (1979)	48 items 3-point scale: not afraid to very afraid	4–12 years	not applicable	Test-Retest range .79–.91 over a one week period with K-6th graders.	CFSS was able to distinguish 24 outpatient children from 24 nonreferred public school children matched on age, sex, and grade.	The CFSS is appropriate for a wide range in age and is briefer than other available fear surveys. CFSS items were developed by asking children what others their age were afraid of as well as what they feared. Little normative data. Not recommended for clinical use.

TABLE 11-5 (*Continued*)

Content Areas	Response Format	Age Range	Subscales	Reliability	Validity	Comments
Fear Survey Schedule for Children-Revised (FSSC-R) Ollendick (1983)	80 items 3-point scale: none to a lot	8–18 years	Failure and Criticism; Unknown; Injury and Small Animals; Danger and Death; Medical Fears	Internal Consistency range .92–.95. Test-Retest range .81–.89 over one week, .55–.62 over a three month period.	Concurrent validity with trait anxiety, self-concept, and locus of control. Factor analyses indicated five factors similar to FSSC. FSSC-R distinguished a matched control group from a clinical group of school-phobic youths.	The CFSS-R is appropriate for a wide range in age and has been validated extensively. Scaling of the FSSC-R was constructed taking into account developmental and cognitive level of normal, clinical, and mentally retarded children. Recommend use as a research tool and clinical use although caution should be used in its interpretation.
Depression Children's Depression Inventory (CDI) Kovacs & Beck (1977)	27 items choose best sentence	8–17 years	not applicable	Internal Consistency range .70–.89. Test-Retest .51 two week, .74–.77 three weeks, .43 one month .41–.69 one year.	The CDI has been evaluated in many validation studies. Concurrent validity has been established with social skills, dysphoric mood, problem solving, academic achievement, overt behavior, anxiety, stress, life events, etc. Some evidence of convergent validity has been obtained with parental report. Factor analyses have indicated the CDI is multidimensional. The CDI has been able to distinguish depressed/nondepressed youths and is sensitive	Extensive normative data are available for the CDI with school, medical, inpatient, and outpatient psychiatric populations. The CDI is a downward extension of the BDI and appears to be more appropriate for children and early adolescents. Recommend its use for research purposes and as a screening device for depression with young children. Measure is available from author.

| Beck Depression Inventory (BDI) Beck et al. (1961) | 21 items choose best sentence | 12 years and above | not applicable | Internal Consistency range .79–.90. Test-Retest .69 over 5-day period with inpatient youths, .75 over 6-wk period. | The BDI has been used extensively with normal and referred adolescents. Concurrent validity has been obtained with other depression measures, assertion, dysphoric mood, anxiety, problem solving, academic achievement, self-esteem, locus of control, life events, etc. The BDI also is able to distinguish depressed from nondepressed adolescents and is sensitive to treatment effects for depression. | The BDI is one of the most widely used measures of depression in adolescents. Tentative screening cut scores for depression have been established. However, normative data are easily accessible and are scattered over several investigations. Recommend its continued use for research and as a screening device for depression in adolescence. |
| Center for Epidemiological Studies of Childhood Depression (CES-DC) Weissman et al. (1980) | 20 items 4-point scale: none to a lot | 6 years and above | not applicable | Internal Consistency range .77–.86 with inpatient youths. Test-Retest range .12–.69 over a 2-wk interval. | The CES-DC has been used infrequently by researchers. Concurrent validity is limited to a modest correlation with the CDI and distinguishing children of high and low risk of depression. Also, the CES-DC has obtained equivocal results concerning its ability to distinguish clinically depressed from nondepressed youths. | Normative data on the CES-DC is currently lacking. Also, since the CES-DC has extremely low test-retest reliability with children it should be used with extreme caution. Not recommended for general clinical use, although may be useful as a research tool. |

TABLE 11-5 (Continued)

Content Areas	Response Format	Age Range	Subscales	Reliability	Validity	Comments
Reynolds Adolescent Depression Scale (RADS) Reynolds (1985)	30 items 4-point scale	12–17 years	not applicable	Internal Consistency range .91–.96. Split-half of .91. Test-Retest .80 over 6-wks, .79 over 3-months, .63 over 1-year.	The RADS has been extensively validated. Concurrent validity has been established with other depression measures, self-esteem, loneliness, anxiety, stressful life events, etc. Moreover, convergence validity has been obtained between the RADS and a semistructured interview of depression. Further, the RADS has been shown to be sensitive to treatment effects.	Extensive normative data are available on the RADS ($n = 8000$) with adolescents. The RADS, like the BDI, is easy to administer and score. Moreover, the RADS appears to be a reliable and valid measure of depression. Recommended for research and clinical use in schools.
Depression Self Rating Scale (DSRS) Birleson (1981)	18 items 3-point scale	6–13 years	not applicable	Internal Consistency range .73–.86. Split half range .61–.67. Test-Retest .80 duration unspecified.	The DSRS has preliminary concurrent validation with the CDI. Also, convergent validity has been reported with a semistructured interview of depression. The DSRS has some support for its ability to distinguish depressed and nondepressed children.	Currently, little normative data are available on the DSRS ($n = 73$). Moreover, the DSRS is in need of additional reliability and validity data. As such, the use of the DSRS is not recommended at this time by school psychologists.

Reinforcement/Activity Schedules					
Children's Reinforcement Survey Schedule (CRSS) Cautela (1967, 1977)	2 forms each 25 items. 3rd form 75 items dislike/like very much	Grades K-3 use 1st form; grades 4-6 use 75 item form	not applicable	Test-Retest range .48-.72 with a group of 141 elementary school children. Males responses less stable than females.	CRSS has been used primarily to identify reinforcing stimuli and their associated valences.	CRSS has not been evaluated extensively from a psychometric perspective. The CRSS is available from the author. Since there are few reinforcement scales available, the CRSS is recommended with caution as an idiographic survey of young children's reinforcing stimuli.
Adolescent Activity Checklist (AAC) Carey, Kelley, Buss, & Scott (1986)	100 items rated for frequency and valence; 50 pleasant, 50 unpleasant items	Grades 7-12	Pleasant Events, Unpleasant Events	Internal Consistency range .94-.95. Homogeneity median .48 for pleasant events; .53 for unpleasant events.	Criterion-related validity with self-ratings of depressive behaviors. No significant differences in age, grade, race, or socioeconomic status.	Normative data are currently available for 300 adolescents. AAC was developed by asking adolescents & professionals to report pleasant and unpleasant activities. Due to limited validity and normative data, recommend its use for research purposes.
Major Life Events Junior High Life Experiences Survey (JHLES) Swearingen & Cohen (1985)	39 items 7-point scale	Grades 7-8	not applicable	No reliability data available.	Initial concurrent validity has been established with the STAIC, BDI. Gender differences were found on the JHLES with males scoring lower than females on the number of negative and uncontrollable events and negative impact ratings.	Items on the JHLES were obtained from previous life events measures and pilot testing with youths. JHLES has been used in only one study. No reliability reported. Not recommended for general use.

TABLE 11-5 (Continued)

Content Areas	Response Format	Age Range	Subscales	Reliability	Validity	Comments
Life Event Record (LER) Coddington (1972)	30–42 items dependent on age	Grades K–12; 4 forms	not applicable	not reported	Concurrent validity with rating of health status, problem solving, depression, locus of control, accident frequency, and other related constructs.	Major limitations of LER are its reliance on weighted unit scores, does not adequately sample child and adolescent life events, scores not reflective of positive or negative impact of items, and lack of data on its reliability. Strength is its extensive norm group ($n = 3526$). Recommend its use for research and clinical uses (with caution).
Life Events Checklist (LEC) Johnson & McCutcheon (1980)	44 items rate frequency; valence; and impact	10–17 years	not applicable	Test-Retest range .62–.72 over a 2-wk interval.	Concurrent validity of LEC with BDI, locus of control, trait anxiety, reports of school days missed, and health problems. No relation was found between social desirability and LEC scores.	Major limitation is the lack of a suitable standardization sample. Items on the LEC were generated from the Life Experiences Survey Johnson & Sarason (1979) and adolescents. Strengths include its assessment of valence, frequency, and impact along with initial reliability data. Recommend its use for research purposes and clinically as a idiographic profile of major life events.

Self Evaluation

Instrument	Items/Format	Age/Grades	Subscales	Reliability	Validity	Comments
Self-Esteem Inventory (SEI) Coopersmith (1967)	58 items Like me/Unlike me	8–15 years	General Self; Home-Parents; School-Academic; Social Self-Peers; Lie (School Form)	Internal Consistency range .80–.92. Test-Retest range: .88 5-wk. interval; .64 12-mo. interval; .42–.70 3-yr. interval.	Concurrent validity with SPPC; Convergent validity with PHSC, other measures of self-concept, & measures of social desirability. Factor analyses have yielded 5–9 factors somewhat related to School Form subscales.	Large standardization sample ($n = 1748$); easily scored. School, School Short, & Adult Forms. Manual available from publisher Recommend its use based on data from 100+ studies.
Self-Perception Profile for Children (SPPC) Harter (1983)	36 items structured alternative format	Grades 3–7	Scholastic Competence: Social Acceptance; Athletic Competence; Physical Appearance; Conduct/Behavior; Self-Worth	Internal Consistency for subscales range .72–.87. Test-Retest range .70–.87 3-mo. interval; .69–.80 9 mo. interval.	Concurrent validity with SEI. Factor analysis indicated 5 factors, thus supporting subscale structure. Grade & gender differences found for some subscales.	Revision of Perceived Competence Scale for Children based on sample of 748 children. Scored on 4-point scale (most to least adequate self-judgement). Abbreviated teacher form. Manual available from author. Recommend its use as research instrument.
Self-Observation Scales (SOS) Stenner & Katzenmeyer (1979)	50–72 items across forms yes/no	Grades K–12	Self-Acceptance; Self-Security; Social Maturity; School Affiliation; Teacher Affiliation; Peer Affiliation; Social Confidence; Self-Assertion	Internal Consistency for forms K-6 grades range .65–.85. Test-Retest range .73–.91 1-wk. interval.	Validity studies reported only for K-3 & 4-6 grade forms. SOS scores distinguished between groups of teacher-rated "socially insecure," "aggressive," & "very healthy" children. Factor analyses used to derive subscales for each form.	K-3, 4-6, 7-9 & 10-12 grade forms, computer scoring, standardized national norms, & manual available from publisher. K-3 grade form administered verbally and items answered by marking happy/sad faces. Scores for each subscale; no total score. Incomplete & difficult to interpret validity studies. Recommend its use as research & clinical (limited) instrument.

TABLE 11-5 (Continued)

Content Areas	Response Format	Age Range	Subscales	Reliability	Validity	Comments
Piers-Harris Self-Concept Scale (PHSC) Piers & Harris (1964)	80 items yes/no	Grades 4–12	Behavior; School & Intellectual Status; Phyiscal Appearance & Attributes; Anxiety; Popularity; Satisfaction; Happiness cluster scores	Internal Consistency for total score range .88–90; for cluster scores range .73–81. Test-Retest range .42–96.	Convergent validity with SEI & other measures of self-concept. Factor analyses have inconsistently supported structure of cluster scores. PHSC has distinguished between racial, age, & clinical groups in numerous studies.	Standardization sample ($n = 1183$) from one school district in Pennsylvania. Computer scoring & manual available from publisher. Response Bias & Inconsistency Indexes provided. Recommend use of total score for research & clinical purposes based on numerous studies since development of PHSC.
Offer Self-Image Questionnaire for Adolescents (OSIQ) Offer, Ostrov, & Howard (1981)	130 items 6-point scale; describes me very well/does not describe me at all	13–19 years	12 subscales within 5 categories. Psychological Self, Sexual Self, Social Self, Familial Self, Coping Self, Total	Internal Consistency range .30–91. Test-Retest range .49–81.	Concurrent validity with measures of self-concept, "mental health," & "adjustment." Many studies have found OSIQ discriminates between age, gender, & clinical/normal groups.	Parent rating form. Manual, computer scoring, newsletter, & forms available from author. Revised 1985. Authors report OSIQ's use with over 20,000 from 14+ countries. Despite widespread use, inadequate psychometric data & length of OSIQ limit its clinical value.

Social Behavior

Instrument	Description	Grades	Scores	Reliability	Validity	Comments
Children's Self-Efficacy for Peer Interaction Scale (CSPI) Wheeler & Ladd (1982)	22 items 4-point scale; !HARD/ !EASY	Grades 3–5	Total score; Conflict & Nonconflict factors	Internal consistency range .73–.85. Test-Retest range .80–90 2-wk. interval.	Concurrent validity with PHSC subscales (General, Social, Physical), peer ratings & sociometrics, & teacher ratings of social self-efficacy. Two factors obtained (Conflict & Nonconflict situations).	Developed from sample (n = 245) 3–5 graders. Higher scores (range = 22–88) = perceptions of greater efficacy. Manual & forms available from author. Recommended for research.
Children's Action Tendency Scale (CATS) Deluty (1979)	39 items 3 paired comparison alternatives	Grades 3–6	Total, Aggressiveness, Submissiveness & Assertiveness scores	Internal consistency range .63-77. Test-Retest range .48–57 4-mo. interval.	Concurrent validity of subscale scores with respective peer & teacher ratings. Assertiveness & Aggressiveness scores correlated with peer report of behavioral adjustment, sociometric of popularity & PHSC, depending on gender, in expected directions.	Forms & norms (n = 600+) available from author. Deleting items 3, 12, & 13 improves validity. Format may be difficult for children. Recommended for research.
Children's Assertive Behavior Scale (CABS) Michaelson & Wood (1982)	27 items 5-point scale passive/ assertive/ aggressive responses	Grades 4–6	Total assertive behavior, Passive & Aggressive scores	Internal consistency range .77–.80. Test-Retest range .66–86 4-wk. interval.	Concurrent validity with behavioral observations & peer, parent & teacher ratings of social skill. Convergent validity with measures of social competence. Factor analyses revealed homogeneous factor structure. Discriminated trained and untrained in social skills.	Developed using sample of 319 4–6 graders. Reading level & response format socially validated in pilot work. Scored −2/ +2. Scrambled continuum of passive/ assertive/aggressive responses-child chooses usual response. Available from author. Recommended for research & (limited) clinical uses.

TABLE 11-5 (Continued)

Content Areas	Response Format	Age Range	Subscales	Reliability	Validity	Comments
Children's Inventory of Anger (CIA) Nelson & Finch (1973)	71 items 4-point scale; "I don't care" to "I'm furious" faces	Grades 4-8	6 factor scores	Internal consistency .96. Test-Retest .82 3-mo. interval.	Concurrent validity with peer & "blind" staff ratings of anger control problems in hospitalized (psychiatric) children. Modestly correlated with acting out factor of Walker Problem Behavior Checklist (teacher rating). Factor analysis yielded 6 factors reflecting sources of anger.	Manual, forms, & normative data available from author. Exemplary use of developmentally appropriate scale anchors (faces). Large samples ($n = 376 - 1000$) used to develop CIA. Grade 4 reading level. Recommended for research due to length & need for more validation studies.
Matson Evaluation of Social Skills with Youngsters (MESSY) Matson et al. (1983)	62 items 5-point scale; not at all to very much	4–18 years	5 factors	Internal consistency range .80–.95. Test-Retest ? 2-wk. interval.	Factor analyses yielded 5 factors related to appropriateness of social behavior. Low correlation with structured child interview. Not correlated with behavioral role-playing, sociometrics, or teacher ratings of popularity, social skills, & social adjustment. Gender, grade level, & handicapped/nonhandicapped group differences found with some MESSY factors.	Teacher & Self-Rating forms available from author. Developed using large ($n = 422$) sample & samples of visual & hearing handicapped children. Recommended for research due to length & sparse concurrent validity.

Instrument	Items/format	Age	Factors/subscales	Reliability	Validity	Comments
Locus of Control Nowicki-Strickland Locus of Control Scale for Children (CNS-IE) Nowicki & Strickland (1973)	40 items yes/no	Grades 3–12	3–9 factors found across studies	Interval consistency range .63–.81 (split-half method). Test-Retest range .63–.71 6-wk. interval.	Concurrent validity with 2 other locus of control measures. Internal control correlated with academic achievement & PHSC for males. Factor analyses yielded 3–9 factors.	Large standardization sample (n = 1017). Higher scores = more external control. Grade 5 reading level; 2 short forms (grades 3–6 & 7–12); form for 4–8 years using cartoon drawings & appropriate vocabulary. Global, not specific, assessment. Recommended for clinical & research. Available from author.
Children's Locus of Control Scale (CLCS) Bialer (1961)	23 items yes/no	6–14 years	Total score	Split-half coefficient range .49–.87. Test-Retest range .84 7-day interval; .68 2–3 wk. interval.	Convergent validity with CNS-IE, but not other locus of control measures. Correlated with intelligence & delay of gratification measures & response to cues of success/failure.	Developed using small samples of mentally retarded (17–28 years) & normal (grades 1–3) subjects. Higher scores = more internal control. Alternate (reverse) form. As with CNS-IE, internal control tends to increase with age. Not recommended. Available from author.
Multidimensional Measure of Children's Perceptions of Control (CPC) Connell (1980)	48 items 4-point scale; very true/not at all true	8–14 years	Source of control; Competency domain; Outcome; Realm of reference	Item-total correlation range .28–.89. No test-retest.	Higher external scores of epileptic children relative to diabetic & healthy peers. Unknown control in academic domain related to school achievement.	Standardization sample (n = 521) data, forms, & manual available from author. 3 sources of control assessed: Internal, Powerful Others, & Unknown. 4 competency domains: cognitive, social, physical, & general. Parallel forms. Due to insufficient psychometric properties, recommended for research.

433

TABLE 11-5 (Continued)

Content Areas	Response Format	Age Range	Subscales	Reliability	Validity	Comments
Attitudes Toward School Estes Attitude Scales (EAS) Estes & Johnstone (1974)	15 items in each area 3- and 5-point scales	Grades 2-12	English, mathematics, reading, science, social studies	Internal consistency range .76-.93 (3-6 grades), .76-.88 (7-12 grades). No test-retest.	Convergent validity with peer & teacher ratings & (for 7-12 grades) grades, achievement scores & extracurricular, course related activities. Factor analyses supported subscale structure.	Large standardization sample ($n = 1815$). Easily scored. Developmentally appropriate scales (3-point for grades 2-6; 5-point for grades 7-12). Available from publisher. Lack of test-retest is problematic. Recommend for research & (limited) clinical uses.
Pupil Behavior Rating Scale (PBRS) Lambert et al. (1979)	70 items happy/sad scale (K-3); 24 items 4-point scale (4-7)	Grades K-7	6 scores (if used in PBRS battery)	Internal consistency range .78-.89 (K-3); .86-.88 (4-7). Test-Retest .52-.72 unspecified interval.	Concurrent validity with adjustment ratings by 3 clinicians. Good short- & long-term (7 years) predictive validity (behavior problems, academic functioning).	Forms for grades K-3 (boys/girls) & 4-7. Battery (teacher, peer & self-ratings) & manual available from publisher. Classroom adaptation, interpersonal behavior, total, teacher & peer rating scores. Picture items for K-3 grades. Recommend for research & clinical uses.

Instrument	Items/Format	Grade	Scores	Reliability	Validity	Comments
Minnesota School Attitude Survey (MSAS) Ahlgren (1983)	Variable # of items 3-, 4-, and 5-point scales	Grades 1-12	21 cluster & 3 summary scores	Internal consistency & Test-Retest inaccurately reported.	Face validity only.	Forms for grades 1-3 (smiling/neutral/frowning face anchors; read to student) & 4-7 (grade 3 reading level). Manual, computer scoring, & forms available from author. Not recommended due to insufficient psychometric properties.
Toward School Inventory (ATSI) Meir & McDaniel (1974)	45 items 5-point scale; agree/disagree	Grades 4-6	School Work, Teacher & General School	Internal consistency .94. Test-Retest .85 1 wk. interval.	Convergent validity with peer & teacher ratings of attitudes towards school.	Large standardization sample ($n = 1000+$) from Louisiana, Ohio, & Indiana. Available from author. Not recommended due to lack of validation studies.

One measure that has been used frequently is the Behavior Rating Profile (BRP), (Brown & Hammill, 1978). As seen in Table 11-4, the BRP is a relatively short instrument that assesses the child's situation-specific behavior (i.e., home, school, peers) as opposed to global personality variables. Although further validation is required on the BRP, its attention to the situational specificity of the child's behavior may assist the assessor in treatment planning. Another promising measure is the Child Behavior Checklist-Youth Form (CBCL) (Achenback & Edelbrock, 1983). Because it is in its preliminary stages of development, it is recommended only for research purposes.

Several self-report personality inventories are also available for use with children and adolescents. For instance, one of the more established measurers is the Millon Adolescent Personality Inventory (MAPI) (Millon, Green, & Meager, 1982). The MAPI was developed in accordance with Millon's personality theory, which postulates eight styles of personality functioning. These eight personality styles are based on two dimensions that form a 4×2 matrix. The first dimension relates to the adolescent's pursuit of positive reinforcement and the avoidance of emotional pain and distress; the second dimension represents the coping behaviors that are used to maximize reinforcement and minimize pain or discomfort (Millon, 1969). Two strengths of the MAPI are that the items have been written at the sixth-grade level and the manual is comprehensive. However, the MAPI has several limitations, including its reliance on Millon's relatively unproven theory, the lack of an adequate description of the scoring system in the manual (thus requiring computer scoring), and, finally, factor analyses of the MAPI have not confirmed the underlying structure of the inventory.

Two additional personality inventories include the Minnesota Multiphasic Personality Inventory (MMPI) (Hathaway & Monachesi, 1963) and the Children's Personality Questionnaire (CPQ) (Porter & Cattell, 1979). The MMPI was orginally developed for use with adults, adolescent norms having been developed later (Marks, Seeman, & Haller, 1974). The MMPI has been used extensively with adolescents; however, its length and scoring time have severely restricted its utility, particularly in a school setting. The CPQ was developed for young children and was derived from the adult personality inventory developed by Cattell. The CPQ is easily scored; however, it has a lengthy administration time and the manual is overly jargonistic. The MMPI and CPQ are not recommended for general clinical use by school psychologists.

Self-Ratings of Specific Behavior Problems

Behavior-specific measures are more focused than global checklists and include more contextual information (Mash & Terdal, 1981). Behavior-specific self-ratings typically measure cognitive controlling stimuli from the child's perspective (Evans & Nelson, 1977; Statts, 1972) and often are incorporated into an assessment when one or more distinct behavior problems are identified through more global measures (e.g., behavior checklists). These measures are best employed to fine-tune an assessment, to screen for particular behavior problems, and to evaluate the outcome or ongoing effects of intervention. Child and adolescent self-rating instruments have been designed to measure a variety of content domains, including attitudes, perceptions, and behaviors as shown in Table 11-5.

Anxiety and Fears

Anxiety-based behaviors are frequently encountered in school settings (e.g., somatic complaints, school refusal, test anxiety). Standardized measures of anxiety and fears are useful in identifying fear evoking situations and anxious behaviors, thus facilitating the development of an effective treatment plan. As seen in Table 11-5, a number of self-report instruments are available to assess anxiety and fears. One of the most widely used instruments of general anxiety is the Revised-Children's Manifest Anxiety Scale (R-CMAS) (Reynolds & Richmond, 1985), a revision of the Children's Manifest Anxiety Scale (CMAS)(Castaneda, McCandless, & Palermo, 1956). The original scale was revised in order to reduce the difficulty of the vocabulary and thus make the scale appropriate to a wider range of ages (i.e., grades 1 through 12). The R-CMAS is easily administered and scored. In line with Cone's (1978) behavioral assessment grid, the R-CMAS subscales facilitate the assessment of the two modes of anxiety: physiological and cognitive. The Lie scale included with the R-CMAS serves as an added check on the accuracy of the information reported by the student. As with several other measures of anxiety, the R-CMAS lacks situation specificity. However, as seen in Table 11-5, the R-CMAS appears to be a reliable and valid measure of general anxiety.

Two other frequently used scales are the State-Trait Anxiety Inventory for Children (STAIC) (Spielberger, 1973) and the State-Trait Anxiety Inventory (STAI) (Spielberger, 1983). Both measures have been developed with considerable methodological rigor. In general, the STAIC is a downward extension of the STAI. However, the STAIC should not be considered as a parallel form of the STAI since the two scales correlate only moderately in adolescents and have distinctive factor structures (Faulstich & Carey, 1985). One unique feature of these two instruments is the incorporation of a state and trait scale. The state form is particularly useful for assessing situation-specific behaviors. For instance, the state form could be used as an outcome measure of anxious behaviors associated with test taking. As with the R-CMAS, the STAI and STAIC have been subjected to considerable empirical evaluation, but are recommended for research uses.

Two additional anxiety scales are the General Anxiety Scale for Children (GASC) and the Test Anxiety Scale for Children (TASC), which were both developed by Sarason, Davidson, Lighthall, Waite, and Ruebush (1960). Both scales are lacking data pertaining to their reliability and validity. Therefore, the use of GASC and TASC is recommended only for research purposes.

Several instruments are also available that assess childhood and adolescent fears. Three of the most frequently used instruments include the Fear Survey Schedule for Children (FSS-FC) (Scherer & Nakamura, 1968), Children's Fear

Survey Schedule (CFSS) (Ryall & Dietiker, 1979) and the Fear Survey Schedule for Children-Revised (FSSC-R) (Ollendick, 1983).

The FSS-FC was developed by asking professionals and school personnel the extent to which children were fearful of various stimuli, and combining that information with items from the Wolpe-Lang Scale. However, the FSS-FC had a narrow range in age and seemingly did not take into account the developmental and cognitive limitations of young children. The FSS-FC lacked data concerning its reliability, validity, and normative data prior to the development of the FSSC-R (Bondy, *et al.*, 1985). The FSS-FC was later revised by Ollendick (1983) to take the aforementioned weakness into account and also to provide reliability and validity data on the FSSC-R (Ollendick, 1983; Ollendick, Matson, & Helsel, 1985). Therefore, the FSSC-R is a considerable improvement over the FSS-FC. However, a large representative normative sample on the FSSC-R is still needed. A third measure, the CFSS, was developed in 1979 by asking children ages four to twelve to report frequently feared stimuli. This assured a sampling of a larger domain than with the previously mentioned instruments. As with the FSS-FC, the CFSS has a restricted age range, has not been adequately evaluated in terms of its reliability and validity, and a representative normative sample has not been reported. Thus, all three fear survey schedules have identified problems; however, the FSSC-R has received the most systematic empirical evaluation and has the widest range in age of the available surveys.

Depression

Recently, considerable attention has been focused on the assessment of depressive behaviors in children and adolescents (Kazdin & Petti, 1982). In part, this increase is due to the relation of depression to suicidal behavior in children and adolescents. Researchers have also found modest relationships between depression and poor academic achievement. Moreover, recent data have suggested a poor long term prognosis for those youths who first experience a depressive disorder during childhood (Kovacs, Feinberg, Crouse-Novak, Palauskas, & Finkelstein, 1984; Kovacs, Feinberg, Crouse-Novak, Palauskas, Pollack, & Finkelstein, 1984; Eastgate & Gilmour, 1984). Therefore, Reynolds (1985a) has advocated the need for school psychologists to be proficient in the assessment and identification of depression.

One method for assessing depression is the use of self-report instruments. Self-report instruments are particularly well suited to the assessment of depression because students' subjective distress may not be apparent to parents or teachers (Reynolds, Anderson, & Bartell, 1985; Saylor, Finch, Spirito, & Bennett, 1984). A number of instruments are currently available to assess depression in children and adolescents; however, few have been subjected to empirical evaluation.

One of the most widely used and validated self-report instruments of depression in childhood is the Children's Depression Inventory (CDI) (Kovacs & Beck, 1977). Generally, the CDI measures depressive affect, oppositional behavior, and self-depreciation (Carey, Faulstich, Gresham, Ruggiero, & Enyart, in press). An evaluation of the CDI's readability has indicated that it can be read by children as young as first grade (Kazdin & Petti, 1982). As seen in Table 11-5, the CDI's reliability and validity have been extensively studied (Carey *et al.*, in press; Kovacs, 1983; Saylor *et al.*, 1984; Smuker, Craighead, Craighead, & Green, 1986). Moreover, the CDI has extensive normative data (Finch, Saylor, & Edwards, 1985; Smucker *et al.*, 1986) and is sensitive to treatment effects (Butler, Freidman, & Cole, 1980; Stark, Reynolds, & Kaslow, in press). At present, the CDI appears to be the most appropriate self-report instrument for assessing depression in children. Two other instruments have been frequently used with adolescents, specifically, the Beck Depression Inventory (BDI) (Beck, Ward, Mendelson, Mock, & Erbaugh, 1961) and the Reynolds Adolescent Depression Scale (RADS) (Reynolds, 1985b). The BDI was originally developed to be used with adults; however, a number of investigations have indicated the BDI is also a reliable and valid measure with adolescents (Chiles, Miller, & Cox, 1980; Kaplan, Hong, & Weinhold, 1984; Strober, Green, & Carlson, 1981a; Teri, 1982a, 1982b). In contrast, the RADS was specifically developed for assessing depression in adolescents. Like the BDI, the RADS has been subjected to rigorous empirical evaluation and appears to be a reliable and valid measure of the severity of adolescent depression (Reynolds, 1985b, in press; Reynolds *et al.*, 1985). Moreover, the RADS has the added advantage of extensive normative data by gender and grade. Both the BDI and RADS demonstrated they are sensitive to treatment outcome (Reynolds & Coats, in press).

Two other measures that have been used with children and adolescents are the Center for Epidemiological Studies of Childhood Depression (CES-DC) (Weissman, Orvaschel, & Padian, 1980) and the Depression Self-Rating Scale (DSRS) (Birleson, 1981). Currently, the DSRS has received favorable results concerning reliability; however, only limited validation and normative data are available (Birleson, 1981). The CES-DC has received unfavorable results concerning its test-retest reliability and criterion-related validity with children (Faulstich, Carey, Ruggiero, Enyart, & Gresham, in press). Therefore, neither the CES-DC nor the DSRS can be recommended for general clinical practice by school psychologists, although they may be useful research tools.

Reinforcement and Activity and Major Life Events

Few instruments exist that quantify reinforcers and routine activities of children and adolescents (see Table 11-5). Two measures that quantify reinforcers and activities are the Children's Reinforcement Survey Schedule (CRSS) (Cautela & Kastenbaum, 1967) and the Adolescent Activity Checklist (AAC) (Carey, Kelley, Buss, & Scott, 1986). These scales may be useful for identifying reinforcers or target behaviors (e.g., specific aversive events). The CDSS was modified from the Reinforcement Survey Schedule (Cautela, 1977) for adults and consists of three lists of reinforcers specific to age. The CRSS, as with other measures in Cautela's (1977) booklet of behavior analysis forms, has not been systematically evaluated. Therefore, the CRSS has a limited use. The AAC is an activity checklist that was empirically developed to quantify pleasant and unpleasant events frequently experienced by adolescents. One useful aspect of the AAC is that it allows the adolescent to rate the pleasantness or unpleasantness of each event and frequency of occurrence. Thus, idiographic lists of frequently occurring pleasant and unpleasant events can be generated for the adolescent to self-monitor. Both the CRSS and AAC need further validation before they can be recommended for general use in the schools. However, the AAC may be a useful tool for assessing behaviors associated with adolescent depression.

Whereas the aforementioned scales measure discrete reinforcers and frequently occurring pleasant or unpleasant events, several scales have been developed for assessing major life events (see Table 11-5). Such scales have frequently been used to quantify the level of stress an individual has experienced over an extended time interval. Moreover, major life events schedules may assist the assessor to develop a thorough learning history. Three of the most frequently used schedules include: the Junior High Life Experiences Survey (JHLES) (Swearingen & Cohen, 1985); the Life Event Record (LER) (Coddington, 1972) and the Life Events Checklist (LEC) (Johnson & McCutcheon, 1980).

The JHLES is a new instrument that was constructed by borrowing items from existing scales and conducting a small pilot study with youths. Currently, the instrument developers have yet to report data on its reliability. Furthermore, limited validity data have been reported. The LER is the most frequently used major life events schedule with children and adolescents. Although the LER has a substantial normative sample its reliance on outdated weighted unit scores limits its current utility. In contrast to the JHLES and LER, the LEC has reported results concerning its temporal stability. Moreover, the LEC has demonstrated concurrent validity with a variety of related behaviors and constructs (Brand & Johnson, 1982; Johnson, 1982); (see Table 11-5). However, limited normative data is available at present on the LEC. In summary, the JHLES is not recommended for general use, whereas the LER and LEC are recommended for research purposes and cautious clinical use.

Self-Evaluation

A plethora of research has centered on a construct alternately labeled self-concept, self-worth, self-esteem, self-perception, self-image, and self-evaluation. Typically, the choice of a label for this construct is a function of one's theoretical orientation and views regarding the etiological course of normal and problem behavior. Common to all definitions of this construct, however, is the concept of a judgment, perception, and attitude about one's own abilities to function in society. The authors refer to this construct as self-evaluation and define it as self-appraisal of competence in specific skill domains related to cognitive, affective, and interpersonal efficacy (Karoly, 1981; Kendall & Braswell, 1985).

Table 11-5 describes five self-rating instruments designed to assess self-evaluation in children and adolescents. The Self-Esteem Inventory (SEI) (Coopersmith, 1967) is designed "to measure evaluative attitudes toward the self in social, academic, family, and personal areas of experience" (Coopersmith, 1984). The SEI School Form consists of fifty items related to antecedents, consequences, and correlates of self-esteem, provides eight Lie Scale items, and offers four subscale scores. A twenty-five-item School Short Form is available as an alternative to the School Form. A total score correlation of .86 was found between these two alternative forms. In addition, an Adult Form, appropriate for persons over fifteen, has recently been developed. As shown in Table 11-5, the SEI is recommended as a reliable and valid measure of self-evaluation in children.

Two other generally reliable self-evaluation scales are the Self-Perception Profile for Children (SPPC) (Harter, 1983) and the Self-Observation Scales (SOS) (Stenner & Katzenmeyer, 1979). The SPPC, a recent revision of the Perceived Competence Scale for Children (Harter, 1982), yields subscale scores representing six competency or skill domains. Respondents complete a form entitled "What I am Like" by marking "really true for me" or "sort of true for me" on one of two alternate statements for each item. For example, item number eleven requires a choice between "Some kids usually do the *right* thing but other kids often *don't* do the right thing." This response format may be difficult for some children to understand (Davis, Gresham, & Carey, 1985), and, therefore, limits the utility of the SPPC.

The SOS provides analytically derived subscale score factors that differ for each of four forms (i.e., Grades K to 3, 4 to 6, 7 to 9, & 10 to 12). Reading level and response format vary across forms and are age appropriate. For example, the Kindergarten through third grade form is administered verbally to the child, who responds by marking the nose of a happy or sad face. In spite of exemplary attention to developmental issues in constructing the SOS, its clinical use is limited because of a paucity of validity studies and restricted circulation of information (i.e., descriptive reports are available only through the National Testing Service).

The two remaining measures of self-evaluation listed in Table 11-5, the Piers-Harris Self-Concept Scale (PHSC) (Piers & Harris, 1969) and the Offer Self-Image Questionnaire for Adolescents (OSIQ) (Offer & Howard, 1972) have enjoyed wide-spread use. The PHSC, or "The Way I Feel About Myself," was written at a third-grade reading level and provides an overall self-concept score or a profile of six cluster scores. However, factor analytic research has inconsistently supported the structure of PHSC cluster scores. The recently revised manual (Piers, 1984) reports two new scores—the Response Bias Index, which assesses negative response sets or acquiescence, and the Inconsistency Index, which identifies random response patterns to facilitate judgments regarding the veracity of a child's report on the PHSC. Many investigations of the reliability and validity of the PHSC support use of the overall self-concept score for research and clinical purposes.

The OSIQ has undergone several revisions and has been translated into many languages for international distribution (Offer, Ostrov, & Howard, 1981; Wisniewski, 1985; Young, 1984). An OSIQ parent rating form is currently available and a newsletter, describing recent developments with the OSIQ, is published several times a year. Although the OSIQ is a well-promulgated instrument, inadequate psychometric properties (e.g., some reports of poor reliability) and length (i.e., 130 items) limit its practical utility.

Social Behavior

Behavioral assessment of social behavior in children and adolescents typically has relied on information culled from sociometric measures, ratings-by-others, behavioral role-play tests, and naturalistic observations. Within the past decade, however, child self-ratings of interpersonal behaviors have been added to the school psychologist's assessment armamentarium. Each of the social behavior measures presented in Table 11-5 has the same basic goal: to measure a child's perspective on his or her social competence. Most authors agree that identification of cognitive and overt behaviors related to social relations is critical to a conceptualization of social competence (Eisenberg & Harris, 1984). The authors endorse Gresham's (1986) conceptualization of social competence as being comprised of adaptive behavior and social skills. In this definition, social skills refer to interpersonal behaviors, self-related cognitions, and task-related behaviors (e.g., attending behavior, following directions). Each of the social behavior self-ratings described below attempt to measure various aspects of social competence in children (e.g., self-efficacy, assertiveness). Although some of these self-ratings show potential, most are not recommended currently for general clinical use due to a need for further validatiion.

The Children's Self-Efficacy for Peer Interaction Scale (CSPI) was developed to measure a child's self-report of "ability to enact prosocial verbal persuasive skills in specific peer situations" (Wheeler & Ladd, 1982, p. 796). The CSPI total self-efficacy score is derived by summing scores across twenty-two items, which are divided into conflict and nonconflict social situations. The CSPI is firmly grounded in the literature regarding children's social cognitions and, with additional validation, may become a useful tool for school psychologists.

Two measures purported to assess a child's self-perception of aggressive, assertive, and submissive or passive behaviors are the Children's Action Tendency Scale (CATS) (Deluty, 1979, 1981), and the Children's Assertive Behavior Scale (CABS) (Michelson & Wood, 1982). The CATS was developed following the behavioral analytic model described by Goldfried and D'Zurilla (1969). Informants read an item in which a social conflict situation is presented and then choose a response from three pairs of alternatives representing all possible pairs of submissive, assertive, and aggressive responses. Although the test author believes such a response format avoids providing respondents with the opportunity to give only socially desirable answers, it may tax the comprehension skills of children for whom the CATS is targeted (i.e., 3rd through 6th graders).

In contrast, the CABS presents social situations requiring assertive behaviors (e.g., initiating conversations, making requests), followed by five possible answers that vary along a scrambled continuum of very passive, passive, assertive, aggressive, and very aggressive responses. The respondent is instructed to choose the response most like the one he or she usually would give in a given situation. This response format appears easier to complete than the paired comparison alternatives employed in the CATS. Although Hobbs and Walle (1985) present results suggestive of the validity of the CABS, further validation is warranted before we can whole-heartedly recommend the CABS for general clinical use.

A shining example of sensitivity to developmental issues in the construction of self-ratings for children is the Children's Inventory of Anger (CIA) (Nelson & Finch, 1978). Reading specialists were consulted to ensure the CIA was written at a fourth-grade reading level and, drawing from pilot work that suggested impulsive or aggressive children tend to have less well-developed verbal skills (Stein, Finch, Hooke, Montgomery, & Nelson, 1975), symbolic anchors were used in the four-point rating scale for each item. These symbolic anchors ranged from a smiling, nonchalant face labeled "I don't care. That situation doesn't even bother me" to an intensely angry face, described as "I can't stand that! I'm furious!" Informants use these symbolic anchors to respond to seventy-one anger provoking situations, derived from interviews with normal and emotionally disturbed childen regarding what makes them angry. The CIA appears to be a promising instrument for assessing anger in children, although its clinical utility is hindered by its length and by a need for more studies investigating its validity.

The Matson Evaluation of Social Skills with Youngsters (MESSY) (Matson, Rotatori, & Helsel, 1983) was developed as a measure of social behavior excesses and deficits in children. Factor analyses indicate five factors have been found to underlie the sixty-two items self-report form (Appropriate Social Skills, Inappropriate Assertiveness, Impulsive/Recalcitrant, Overconfident, and Jealousy/Withdrawal). Matson and his colleagues are to be commended for constructing the MESSY based on a behavioral conceptualization of social skills, and for adapting the MESSY for use with handicapped children (Matson, Macklin, & Helsel, 1985; Matson, Heinze, Helsel, Kapperman, & Rotator, 1986). However, the authors cannot yet recommend the MESSY for clinical purposes, because of its length and an insufficient demonstration of convergent validity with other measures of social behavior.

Locus of Control

The construct labeled locus of control of reinforcement alludes to one's perception of the degree of influence he or she exerts over the outcome of events. Rotter (1966) described an internal and external continuum in which internal locus of control refers to a belief that reinforcers are completely within one's power and external locus of control refers to a perception that reinforcers are determined by factors outside one's influence. Provided in Table 11-5 are three instruments intended to measure children's attributions of control over environmental events. Although direct assessment of locus of control has little clinical value per se, locus of control has been studied as a moderator variable and as a predictor of treatment outcome (Finch & Rogers, 1984).

Two of the earliest measures constructed to assess generalized locus of control in children and adolescents are the Nowicki-Strickland Locus of Control Scale for Children (CNS-IE) (Nowicki & Strickland, 1973) and the Children's Locus of Control Scale (CLCS) (Bialer, 1961). The CLCS was developed using small samples of mentally retarded and normal children and is administered verbally. Gozali and Bialer (1968) designed an alternate form of the CLCS in which the positively and negatively keyed items were reversed. A correlation of .67 was found between the two CLCS forms, leading the authors to discount potential effects of a response set on CLCS scores. Although the CLCS has been found to correlate significantly with the CNS-IE (Bialer, 1961), Bachrach and Peterson (1976) reported the CLCS did not correlate significantly with two other measures of locus of control in a sample of twenty-five first to third graders. In spite of its widespread use the CLCS can not be recommended over the psychometrically superior CNS-IE.

The CNS-IE was written at a fifth-grade reading level and constructed based on data from a large standardization sample of third to twelfth graders. For grades three and four, oral administration is recommended. CNS-IE items are intended to assess attribution of control in multiple situations (e.g., belief in chance influencing interpersonal relations, school achievment). Two CNS-IE short forms are available: (1) a twenty-item primary form for third to sixth graders, and (2) a twenty-one-item secondary form for seventh to twelfth graders. Nowicki and Duke (1974) developed a downward extension of the CNS-IE, the Preschool and Primary NS-IE (PPNS-IE), which is appropriate for children four to eight years old. The thirty-four items of the PPNS-IE are worded at a four-year-old level and are illustrated using cartoon drawings. Although the PPNS-IE is appealing because of the consideration for developmental issues that entered into its construction, its clinical use cannot be recommended currently due to psychometric inadequacies (Herzbergen, Linney, Seidman, & Rappaport, 1979). However, extensive empirical analyses support clinical and research use of the CNS-IE as a measure of generalized locus of control in children (Finch & Rogers, 1984).

In contrast to the CNS-IE and the CLCS, which are measures of general locus of control, the Multidimensional Measure of Children's Perceptions of Control (CPC) (Connell, 1980) assesses children's attributions of control over success and failure outcomes across three competency domains (social, physical, and academic) and one general domain. The CPC, or "Why Things Happen" scale, also assesses three sources of control (Internal, Powerful Others, and Unknown), as well as beliefs regarding why the child succeeds or fails (i.e., personal realm of reference). An attractive feature of the CPC is the manner in which it taps children's situation specific perspectives on control. The CPC's psychometric inadequacies, however, preclude its present use other than as a research instrument.

Attitudes Toward School

A multitude of instruments designed to assess students' attitudes toward various facets of the school environment are available to school psychologists

(Johnson, 1976; Mitchell, 1985). Rating scales developed to assess students' sentiments toward different areas of school life include the Scale of Reading Attitude Based on Behavior (Rowell, 1972), the Index of Student Perception of Teacher Reinforcement (Davison, 1972), the Attitudes Toward Riding the Bus Scale (Barker, 1966), and the Attitude Toward Cheating Scale (Sherrill, Salisbury, Horowitz, & Friedman, 1971). Rather than presenting an exhaustive review of such diverse rating scales, the authors will focus on instruments which assess students' opinions toward school in a general manner. Listed in Table 11-5 are four self-ratings used to obtain students' attitudes toward general classroom and interpersonal experiences at school.

The Estes Attitude Scales (EAS) (Estes & Johnstone, 1974) surveys elementary and secondary students' impressions of various school subjects. The elementary (i.e., grades 2 to 6) form requires students to indicate on a three-point scale their agreement or disagreement with positively and negatively valenced statements regarding basic school subjects. Reading, mathematics, and science subscale scores are obtained from the elementary form. The secondary (i.e., grades 7 to 12) form uses a five-point scale and yields English, reading, mathematics, science, and social studies subscale scores. The EAS may be administered as a complete battery or specific subscales may be given separately. Pilot work validated the age appropriateness of the reading level for each form. Item analyses were employed to select the most discriminating items and factor analyses were used to support the subscale structure of the EAS. Although the EAS appears to have been constructed empirically with proper attention to developmental issues, the authors failed to report test-retest reliabilities for EAS scores. Considering the lack of data on the stability of EAS scores, we cautiously recommend the EAS for research and limited clinical purposes.

Another student attitude rating scale is the Pupil Behavior Rating Scale (PBRS) (Lambert, Hartsough, & Bowert, 1979), which is known also as A Process for the Assessment of Effective Student Functioning. The PBRS is a battery of teacher, peer, and self-rating scales developed to identify children at risk for school-related problems due to psychological (e.g., depression) or social (e.g., peer rejection) constraints. The Picture Game, the PBRS self-rating scale for Kindergarten through third grade, has separate forms for girls and boys, and consists of seventy pictures portraying a child in situations at home, at school, with peers, and alone. Students respond to these pictures with happy or sad ratings. The form for grades four to seven, entitled The School Play-II, requires a student to report choices he or she believes their teacher and their peers would make for positive, neutral, or negative roles in a given play. The School Play-II is used in conjunction with a peer nomination form, The School Play-I. At-risk status is determined by noting the students receiving the five highest percentages of nominations for roles involving negative behaviors. Students with the highest scores among their classmates on two of the three PBRS rating scales (i.e., teacher, peer, and self-report) are deemed at-risk for problems in school.

Test-retest reliabilities were not reported for the most recent version of the

PBRS self-rating scale. In addition, the authors believe the indirect measurement method utilized in the PBRS (i.e., reporting choice of roles in a play) is inferior to a more direct method such as asking a child to report how he or she usually behaves in a particular situation. However, all three PBRS rating scales were shown to predict behavior problems and academic functioning over a seven year period. Given the predictive validity of the PBRS and its exemplary use of a multiple source approach to assessment, the authors recommend it as a screening measure for potential behavioral and academic problems in Kindergarten through seventh grade school children.

The remaining two student attitude scales listed in Table 11-5 are the Minnesota School Attitude Survey (MSAS) (Ahlgren, 1983) and the Attitude Toward School Inventory (ATSI) (Meir & McDaniel, 1974). The MSAS assesses students' opinions regarding aspects of the school setting such as academic subjects, peers, school personnel, methods of instruction, stress, motivation, and self-evaluation. Although the MSAS seems to have been designed with consideration for developmental issues (e.g., age appropriate reading level and response format), insufficient reliability and validity data preclude our endorsement for its use at present. Like the MSAS, the ATSI surveys students' general sentiments toward school (i.e., teacher, school work, and school in general). Also similar to the MSAS, the ATSI cannot currently be recommended due to an absence of research establishing its concurrent validity.

References

Achenbach, T. M. (1978). The Child Behavior Profile: I. Boys aged 6 through 11. *Journal of Consulting and Clinical Psychology, 46,* 478–488.

Achenbach, T. M., & Edelbrock, C. S. (1985). *Manual for the Revised Child Behavior Checklist and Profile.* Burlington, Vt.: University Associates in Psychiatry.

Ahlgren, A. (1983). *Minnesota School Attitude Survey.* Chicago: Science Research Associates.

American Psychiatric Association (1980). Diagnostic and statistical manual of mental disorders (3d ed.). Washington, D.C.: Author.

Asarnow, J., & Carlson, G. A. (1985). Depression Self-Rating Scale: Utility with child psychiatric inpatients. *Journal of Consulting and Clinical Psychology, 53,* 491–499.

Bachrach, P., & Peterson, R. A. (1976). Test-retest reliability and interrelation among three other laws of control measures for children. *Perceptual and Motor Skills, 43,* 260–262.

Barenboim, C. (1977). Developmental changes in the interpersonal cognitive system from middle childhood to adolescence. *Child Development, 38,* 1467–1474.

Barker, D. G. (1966). Measurement of attitudes toward riding the school bus. *Psychology in the School, 3,* 278–281.

Barrios, B. A., Hartmann, D. P., & Shigetomi, C. (1982). Fears and anxieties in children. In E. J. Mash & L. G. Terdal (Eds.), *Behavioral assessment of childhood disorders.* New York: Guilford Press.

Bartko, J. J., & Carpenter, W. T. (1976). On the methods and theory of reliability. *The Journal of Nervous and Mental Disease, 163,* 307–317.

Beck, A. T., Ward, C., Mendelson, M., Mock, J., & Erbaugh, J. (1961). An inventory for measuring depression. *Archives of General Psychiatry, 4,* 53–63.

Bersoff, D. (1976). *Legal issues in school psychology.* Paper presented at the annual meeting of the Arizona Association of School Psychologists at Phoenix, Arizona.

Bialer, I. (1961). Conceptualization of success and failure in mentally retarded and normal children. *Journal of Personality, 29,* 303–320.

Bierman, K. L. (1983). Cognitive development and clinical interviews with children. In B. Lahey & A. E. Kazdin (Eds.), *Advances in clinical child psychology* (Vol. 6, pp. 217–250). New York: Plenum Press.

Bigelow, B. J. (1977). Children's friendship expectations: A cognitive-developmental study. *Child Development, 48,* 246–253.

Birleson, P. (1981). The validity of depressive disorder in childhood and the development of a self-rating scale: A research report. *Journal of Child Psychology and Psychiatry & Allied Disciplines, 22,* 73–88.

Bondy, A., Sheslow, D., & Garcia, L. T. (1985). An investigation of children's fears and their mother's fears. *Journal of Psychopathology and Behavioral Assessment, 7,* 1–12.

Borke, H. (1973). The development of empathy in Chinese and American children between three and six years of age: A cross-cultural study. *Developmental Psychology, 9,* 102–108.

Brand, A. H., & Johnson, J. H. (1982). Note on reliability of the Life Events Checklist. *Psychological Reports, 50,* 1274.

Brown, L. L., & Hammill, D. D. (1978). *The Behavior Rating Profile: An ecological approach to behavioral assessment.* Austin, Tex.: Pro-Ed.

Burke, J. P., & DeMers (1979). A paradigm for evaluating assessment interviewing techniques. *Psychology in the Schools, 16,* 51–60.

Butler, L., Miezitis, S., Freidman, R., & Cole, E. (1980). The effect of two school-based intervention programs on depressive symptoms in preadolescents. *American Educational Research Journal, 17,* 111–119.

Byrd, D. M., & Gholson, B. (1984). A cognitive-developmental model of reading. In B. Gholson & T. L. Rosenthal (Eds.), *Applications of cognitive-developmental theory* (pp. 21–48). New York: Academic Press.

Carey, M. P., Faulstich, M. E., Gresham, F. M., Ruggiero, L. J. & Enyart, P. (in press). The Children's Depression Inventory: Construct and discriminant validity across clinical and normal populations. *Journal of Consulting and Clinical Psychology.*

Carey, M. P., Kelley, M. L., Buss, R. R., & Scott, O. (1986). Relationship of activity to depression in adolescents: Development of the Adolescent Activity Checklist. *Journal of Consulting and Clinical Psychology, 54,* 320–322.

Castaneda, A., McCandless, B. R., & Palermo, D. S. (1956). The children's form of the manifest anxiety scale. *Child Development, 27,* 317–326.

Cautela, J. R. (1977). *Behavior analysis forms for clinical intervention.* Champaign, Ill.: Research Press.

Cautela, J. R., & Kastenbaum, R. (1967). A reinforcement survey for use in therapy. *Psychological Reports, 20,* 1115–1130.

Chambers, W. J., Puig-Antich, J., Hirsch, M., Paez, P., Ambrosini, P. J., Tabrizi, M. A., & Davies, M. (1985). The assessment of affective disorders in children and adolescents by semistructured interview. *Archives of General Psychiatry, 42,* 696–702.

Chiles, A., Miller, M. L., & Cox, G. B. (1980). Depression in an adolescent delinquent population. *Archives of General Psychiatry, 37,* 1179–1184.

Clarke-Stewart, A., Friedman, S., & Koch, J. (1985). *Child Development: A topical approach.* New York: John Wiley & Sons.

Coddington, R. D. (1972). The significance of life events as etiologic factors in the diseases of children: I-A Survey of professional workers. *Journal of Psychosomatic Research, 16,* 205–213.

Cone, J. D. (1977). The relevance of reliability and validity for behavioral assessment. *Behavior Therapy, 8,* 411–426.

Cone, J. D. (1978). The behavioral assessment grid (BAG): A conceptual framework and taxonomy. *Behavior Therapy, 9,* 882–888.

Cone, J. D., & Hawkins, R. P. (1977). *Behavioral assessment.* New York: Brunner/Mazel.

Connell, J. P. (1980). A *multidimensional measure of children's perceptions of control: Manual*. Unpublished manuscript, University of Denver, Psychology Dept., Denver, Colo.

Coopersmith, S. (1967). *The antecedents of self-esteem* (pp. 3-10). Palo Alto, Calif.: Consulting Psychologists Press.

Coopersmith, S. (1984). *Self-Esteem Inventories*. Palo Alto, Calif.: Consulting Psychologists Press.

Cormier, W. H. & Cormier, L. S. (1979). *Interviewing strategies for helpers*. Monterey, Calif.: Brooks/Cole.

Costello, E. J., Edelbrock, C. S., & Costello, A. J. (1985). Validity of the NIMH diagnostic interview schedule for children: A comparison between psychiatric and pediatric referrals. *Journal of Abnormal and Child Psychology, 13*, 579-595.

Cronbach, L. J. (1970). *Essentials of psychological testing* (3d ed.). New York: Harper & Row.

Davis, C. J., Gresham, F. M., & Carey, M. P. (1985). The relationship between social competence and self-esteem. Unpublished raw data.

Davison, D. C. (1972). Perceived reward value of teacher reinforcement and attitude toward teacher: An application of Newcomb's Balance Theory. *Journal of Educational Psychology, 63*, 418-422.

De Charms, R. (1976). *Enhancing motivation*. New York: Irvington.

Deluty, R. H. (1979). Children's Action Tendency Scale: A self-report measure of aggressiveness, assertiveness, and submissiveness in children. *Journal of Consulting and Clinical Psychology, 41*, 1061-1071.

Deluty, R. H. (1981). Alternative thinking ability of aggressive, assertive, and submissive children. *Cognitive Therapy and Research, 5*, 309-312.

Eastgate, J., & Gilmour, L. (1984). Long-term outcome of depressed children: A follow-up study. *Developmental Medicine and Child Neurology, 26*, 68-72.

Edlebrock, C., Costello, A. J., Dulcan, M. K., Kalas, R., & Conover, N. C. (1985). *Child Development, 56*, 265-275.

Edelbrock, C., Costello, A. J., Kalas, R., Dulcan, M. K., & Conover, N. C. (1985). Age differences in the reliability of the psychiatric interview of the child. *Child Development, 56*, 265-275.

Eisenberg, N., & Harris, J. D. (1984). Social competence: A developmental perspective. *School Psychology Review, 8*, 267-277.

Elliott, S. N. (1986). Children's ratings of the acceptability of classroom interventions for misbehavior: Findings and methodological considerations. *Journal of School Psychology, 24*, 23-35.

Endicott, J., & Spitzer, R. L. (1978). A diagnostic interview: The Schedule for Affective Disorders and Schizophrenia. *Archives of General Psychiatry, 35*, 837-844.

Ervin, S. M., & Foster, G. (1960). The development of meaning in children's descriptive terms. *Journal of Abnormal and Social Psychology, 61*, 271-275.

Estes, T. H., & Johnstone, J. P. (1974). Assessing attitudes toward reading: A validation study. In *Twenty-third yearbook of the National Reading Conference* (pp. 219-223).

Evans, I. M., & Nelson, R. O. (1977). Assessment of child behavior problems. In A. R. Ciminero, K. S. Calhoun, & H. E. Adams (Eds.), *Handbook of behavioral assessment* (pp. 603-680). New York: John Wiley & Sons.

Faulstich, M. E., Carey, M. P., Ruggiero, L., Enyart, P., & Gresham, F. M. (1986). Assessment of depression in childhood and adolescence: An evaluation of the Center for Epidemiological Studies Scale for children. *American Journal of Psychiatry, 143*, 1024-1027.

Faulstich, M. E. & Carey, M. P. (1985). Assessment of anxiety in adolescents: Psychometric comparison of Spielberger's Trait Anxiety Inventories for children (STAIC) and adults (STAI). Submitted for publication.

Finch, A. J., Jr., & Rogers, T. R. (1984). Self-report instruments. In T. H. Ollendick & M. Herson (Eds.), *Child behavioral assessment: Principles and procedures*. (pp. 106-123). Elmsford, N.Y.: Pergamon Press.

Finch, A. J., Saylor, C. F., & Edwards, G. L. (1985). Children's Depression Inventory: Sex and grade norms for normal children. *Journal of Consulting and Clinical Psychology, 42*, 424-425.

Garber, J. (1984). Classification of childhood psychopathology: A developmental perspective. *Child Development, 55,* 30–48.

Gelman, R., & Baillageon, R. (1983). A review of some Piagetian concepts. In P. H. Mussen (Ed.), *Armichael's manual of child psychology* (pp. 167–230). New York: John Wiley & Sons.

Gershon, E. S., McKnew, D., Cytryn, L., Hamovit, J., Schreiner, J., Hibbs, E., & Pellegrini, D. (1985). Diagnoses in school-age children of bipolar affective disorder patients and normal controls. *Journal of Affective Disorders, 8,* 283–291.

Goldfried, M., & D'Zurilla, T. J. (1969). A behavioral-analytic model in assessment and research. In C. D. Spielberger (Eds.), *Current topics in clinical and community psychology* (Vol. 1, pp. 151–196). New York: Academic Press.

Gollin, E. S. (1958). Organizational characteristics of social judgements: A developmental investigation. *Journal of Personality, 26,* 139–154.

Gorsuch, R. L., Henighan, R. P., & Barnard, C. (1972). Locus of control: An example of dangers in using children's scales with children. *Child Development, 43,* 579–590.

Gozali, J., & Bialer, I. (1968). Children's locus of control scale: Independence from response set bias among retardates. *American Journal of Mental Deficiency, 72,* 622–625.

Gresham, F. M. (1986). Conceptual and definitional issues in the assessment of children's social skills: Implications for classification and training. *Journal of Clinical Child Psychology, 15,* 3–15.

Harter, S. (1982). The Perceived Competence Scale for Children. *Child Development, 53,* 87–97.

Harter, S. (1983). *Supplementary description of the Self-Perception Profile for Children—Revision of the Perceived Competence Scale for Children.* Unpublished manuscript, University of Denver, Psychology Dept., Denver, Colorado.

Hathaway, S. R., & Monachesi, E. D. (1963). *Adolescent personality and behavior: MMPI patterns of normal delinquent, dropout, and other outcomes.* Minneapolis: University of Minnesota Press.

Hay, W. M., Hay, L. R., Angle, H. V., & Nelson, R. O. (1979). The reliability of problem identification in the behavioral interview. *Behavioral Assessment, 1,* 107–118.

Haynes, S. N., & Jensen, B. J. (1979). The interview as a behavioral assessment instrument. *Behavioral Assessment, 1,* 97–106.

Herjanic, B., & Campbell, W. (1977). Differentiating psychiatrically disturbed children on the basis of a structured interview. *Journal of Abnormal Child Psychology, 5,* 127–134.

Herganic, B., Herjanic, M., Brown, F., & Wheatt, T. (1975). Are children reliable reporters? *Journal of Abnormal Child Psychology, 3,* 41–48.

Herjanic, B., & Reich, W. (1982). Development of a structured psychiatric interview for children: Agreement between child and parent on individual symptoms. *Journal of Abnormal Child Psychology, 10,* 307–323.

Herzbergen, S. D., Linney, J. A., Seidman, E., & Rappaport, T. (1979). Preschool and primary locus of control scale: Is it ready for use? *Developmental Psychology, 15,* 320–324.

Hobbs, S. A., & Walle, D. L. (1985). Validation of the Children's Assertive Behavior Scale. *Journal of Psychopathology and Behavioral Assessment, 1,* 145–153.

Hodges, K., Kline, J. J., Barbero, G., & Woodruff, C. (1985). Anxiety in children with recurrent abdominal pain and their parents. *Psychometrics, 26,* 859–866.

Hodges, K., Kline, J., Stern, L., Cytryn, L., & McKnew, D. (1982). The development of a child assessment interview for research and clinical use. *Journal of Abnormal Child Psychology, 10,* 173–189.

Hodges, K., McKnew, D., Burbach, D. F., & Roebuck, L. (in press). Diagnostic concordance between two structured child interviews using lay examiners: The Child Assessment Schedule and Kiddie-SADS. *Journal of the American Academy of Child Psychiatry.*

Inhelder, B., & Piaget, J. (1964). *The early growth of logic in the child.* New York: W. W. Norton.

Inhelder, B., Sinclair, H., & Bovet, M. (1974). *Learning and the development of cognition.* Cambridge, Mass.: Harvard University Press.

Johnson, J. H. (1982). Life events as stressors in childhood and adolescence. In B. B. Lahey & A. E. Kazdin (Eds.), *Advances in clinical child psychology,* (Vol. 4). New York: Plenum Press.

Johnson, J. H., & McCutcheon, S. (1980). Assessing life stress in older children and adolescents: Preliminary findings with the Life Events Checklist. In I. G. Sarason & C. D. Speilberger (Eds.), *Stress and anxiety* (Vol. 7). Washington, D. C.: Hemisphere.

Johnson, O. G. (1976). *Tests and measurements in child development: Handbook II* (Vols. 1 & 2). San Francisco: Jossey-Bass.

Kanfer, R., Eyberg, S. M., & Krahn, G. L. (1983). Interviewing strategies in child assessment. In C. E. Walker & M. C. Roberts (Eds.), *Handbook of clinical child psychology* (pp. 95–108). New York: John Wiley & Son.

Kaplan, S. L., Hong, G. E., & Weinhold, C. (1984). Epidemiology of depressive symptomatology in adolescents. *Journal of the American Academy of Child Psychiatry, 23,* 91–98.

Karoly, P. (1981). Self-management problems in children. In E. J. Mash & L. G. Terdal (Eds.), *Behavioral assessment of childhood disorders* (pp. 79–126). New York: Guilford Press.

Kazdin, A. E., & Petti, T. A. (1982). Self-report and interview measures of childhood and adolescent depression. *Journal of Child Psychology and Psychiatry, 23,* 437–457.

Kendall, P. C., & Braswell, L. (1985). *Cognitive-behavioral therapy for impulsive children.* New York: Guilford Press.

Kirigin, K. A., Braukmann, C. J., Atwater, J. D,. & Wolf, M. M. (1982). An evaluation of teaching-family (achievement place) group homes for juvenile offenders. *Journal of Applied Behavior Analysis, 15,* 1–16.

Kleinman, K. M., Goldman, H., Snow, M. Y., & Korol, B. (1977). Relationship between essential hypertension and cognitive functioning: II. Effects of biofeedback training generalize to non-laboratory environment. *Psychophysiology 1977,* Mar, *14*(2), 192–197.

Koslowski, B. (1980). Quantitative and qualitative changes in the development of seriation. *Merrill-Palmer Quarterly, 26,* 391–405.

Kovacs, M. (1978). *Children's Depression Inventory (CDI).* Unpublished manuscript, University of Pittsburgh, Pittsburgh, Pennsylvania.

Kovacs, M. (1983a). *The interview schedule for children.* Unpublished manuscript, University of Pittsburgh, School of Medicine, Pittsburgh, Pennsylvania.

Kovacs, M. (1983b). The Children's Depression Inventory: A self-rated depression scale for school-aged youngsters. Unpublished manuscript.

Kovacs, M., & Beck, A. T. (1977). An empirical-clinical approach toward a definition of childhood depression. In J. G. Shulterbrandt & A. Raskin (Eds.), *Depression in childhood: Diagnosis, treatment, and conceptual models.* (pp. 1–25). New York: Raven Press.

Kovacs, M., Feinberg, T. L., Crouse-Novak, M. A., Paulaukas, S. L., & Finkelstein, R. (1984). Depressive disorders in childhood: I. A longitudinal prospective study of characteristics and recovery. *Archives of General Psychiatry, 41,* 229–237.

Kovacs, M., Feinberg, T. L., Crouse-Novak, M. A., Paulauskas, S. L., Pollack, M., & Finkelstein, R. (1984). Depressive disorders in childhood: II. A longitudinal study of risk for a subsequent major depression. *Archives of General Psychiatry, 41,* 643–649.

Lambert, N. M., Hartsough, C. S., & Bower, E. M. (1979). *A process for the assessment of effective student functioning.* Monterey, Calif. Publishers Test Service.

Lewis, S. A., Gorsky, A., Cohen, P., & Hartmark, C. (1985). The reactions of youth to diagnostic interviews. *Journal of the American Academy of Child Psychiatry, 24,* 750–755.

Livesley, W. J., & Bromley, D. B. (1973). *Person perception in childhood and adolescence.* London: John Wiley & Sons.

Maccoby, E. E. (1959). Role-taking in childhood and its consequences for social learning. *Child Development, 30,* 239–252.

Marks, P. A., Seeman, W., & Haller, D. L. (1974). *The actuarial use of the MMPI with adolescents and adults.* Baltimore: Williams & Wilkins.

Mash, E. J., & Terdal, L. G. (1981). Behavioral assessment of childhood disturbance. In E. J. Mash & L. G. Terdal (Eds.), *Behavioral assessment of childhood disorders* (pp. 3–76). New York: Guilford Press.

Matson, J. L., Heinze, A., Helsel, W. J., Kapperman, G., & Rotatori, A. F. (1986). Assessing social behaviors in the visually handicapped: The Matson Evaluation of Social Skills with Youngsters (MESSY). *Journal of Clinical Child Psychology, 15,* 78–87.

Matson, J. L., Macklin, G. F., & Helsel, W. J. (1985). Psychometric properties of the Matson Evaluation of Social Skills with Youngsters with emotional problems and self-concept in deaf children. *Journal of Behavior Therapy and Experimental Psychiatry, 16,* 117–123.

Matson, J. L., Rotatori, A. F., & Helsel, W. J. (1983). Development of a rating scale to measure social skills in children: The Matson Evaluation of Social Skills with Youngsters (MESSY). *Behavior Research and Therapy, 21,* 335–340.

McMahon, R. J., & Forehand, R. L. (1983). Consumer satisfaction in behavioral treatment of children: Types, issues, and recommendations. *Behavior Therapy, 14,* 209–225.

Meir, R. S., & McDaniel, E. (1974). A measure of attitude toward school. *Educational and Psychological Measurement, 34,* 997–998.

Michelson, L., & Wood, R. (1982). Development and psychometric properties of the Children's Assertive Behavior Scale. *Journal of Behavioral Assessment, 4,* 3–13.

Millon, T. (1969). *Modern psychopathology.* Philadelphia: Saunders.

Millon, T., Green, C. J., & Meager, R. B. (1982). *Millon Adolescent Personality Inventory Manual.* Minneapolis: National Computer Systems.

Mitchell, J. V. (1985). *The ninth mental measurements yearbook* (Vols. 1 & 2). Lincoln, Neb. University of Nebraska Press.

Murray, F. B. (1978). Teaching strategies and conservation training. In A. M. Lesgold, J. W. Pellegrino, S. D. Fekkema, & R. Glaser (Eds.). *Cognitive psychology and instruction* (Vol. 1, pp. 268–307). New York: Plenum Press.

Nelson, W. M, III, & Finch, A. J., Jr. (1978). *The Children's Inventory of Anger.* Unpublished manuscript, Xavier University, Psychology Dept. Cincinnati, Oh.

Nowicki, S., & Duke, M. P. (1974). A preschool and primary internal-external control scale. *Developmental Psychology, 10,* 874–880.

Nowicki, S., & Strickland, B. R. (1973). A locus of control scale for children. *Journal of Consulting and Clinical Psychology, 40,* 148–154.

Offer, D., & Howard, K. I. (1972). An empirical analysis of the Offer Self-Image Questionnaire for Adolescents. *Archives of General Psychiatry, 27,* 744–746.

Offer, D., Ostrov, E., & Howard, K. I. (1981). *The Offer Self-Image Questionnaire for Adolescents: A manual.* Chicago: Michael Reese Hospital.

Ollendick, T. H. (1983). Reliability and validity of the Revised Fear Survey for Children (FSSC-R). *Behavioral Research and Therapy, 21,* 685–692.

Ollendick, T.H., & Hersen, M. (1984). An overview of child behavioral assessment. In. T.H. Ollendick & M. Hersen (Eds.), *Child behavioral assessment: Principles and procedures* (pp. 3–19). Elmsford, N.Y.: Pergamon Press.

Ollendick, T. H., Matson, J. L., & Helsel, W. J. (1985). Fears in visually impaired and normally sighted youths. *Behavioral Research and Therapy, 23,* 375–378.

Ollendick, T. H., & Meador, A. E. (1984). Behavioral assessment of children. In G. Goldstein & M. Hersen (Eds.), *Handbook of psychological assessment* (pp. 351–368). Elmsford, N. Y.: Pergamon Press.

Paget, K. D. (1984). The structured assessment interview: A psychometric review. *Journal of School Psychology, 22,* 415–427.

Peevers, B. H., & Secord, P. F. (1973). Developmental changes in attribution of descriptive concepts to persons. *Journal of Personality and Social Psychology, 27,* 120–128.

Piaget, J. (1965). *The moral judgment of the child.* New York: Free Press.

Piers, E. V. (1977). *The Piers-Harris Self-Concept Scale: Research monograph number one.* Nashville, Tenn.: Counselor Recordings and Tests.

Piers, E. V. (1984). *A manual for The Piers-Harris Children's Self-Concept Scale.* Los Angeles: Western Psychological Services.

Piers, E. V., & Harris, D. B. (1964). *A manual for the Piers-Harris Self-Concept Scale.* Nashville, Tenn.: Counselor Recordings and Tests.

Porter, R. B., & Cattell, R. B. (1979). *What you do and what you think.* Institute for Personality and Ability Testing.

Puig-Antich, J., Blau, S., Marx, N., Greenhill, L. L., & Chambers, W. (1978). Prepubertal major depressive disorder: A pilot study. *Journal of the American Academy of Child Psychiatry, 17,* 695–707.

Puig-Antich, J., Chambers, W., Halpern, F., Hanlon, C., & Sachar, E. J. (1979). Cortisol hyposecretion in prepubertal depressive illness: A preliminary study. *Psychoneuroendocrinology, 4,* 191–197.

Puig-Antich, J., Perel, J. M., Lupatkin, W., Chambers, W. J., Shea, C., Tabrizi, M. A., & Stiller, R. L. (1979). Plasma levels of imipramine (IMI) and desmethylimipramine (DMI) and clinical response in prepubertal major depressive disorder: A preliminary report. *American Academy of Child Psychiatry,* 616–627.

Reich, W., Herjanic, B., Welner, Z., & Gandhy, P. R. (1982). Development of a structured psychiatric interview for children: Agreement on diagnosis comparing child and parent interviews. *Journal of Abnormal Child Psychology, 10,* 325–336.

Reynolds, C. R., & Richmond, B. O. (1978). What I think and feel: A revised measure of children's manifest anxiety. *Journal of Abnormal Child Psychology, 6,* 271–280.

Reynolds, C. R., & Richmond, B. O. (1985). Revised Children's Manifest Anxiety Scale (RCMAS). Los Angeles: Western Psychological Services.

Reynolds, W. M. (1985a). Depression in childhood and adolescence: Diagnosis, assessment, intervention strategies, and research. In T. R. Kratochwill (ed.), *Advances in school psychology* (Vol. 4). Hillsdale, N. J., Lawrence Erlbaum Associates.

Reynolds, W. M. (1985b). Development and validation of a scale to measure depression in adolescents. Paper presented at the Annual Meeting of the Society for Personality Assessment, at Berkeley, California.

Reynolds, W. M., Anderson, G., & Bartell, N. (1985). Measuring depression in children: A multimethod assessment investigation. *Journal of Abnormal Child Psychology, 13,* 513–526.

Reynolds, W. M., & Coats, K. I. (in press). A comparison of cognitive-behavioral therapy and relaxation training for the treatment of depression in adolescents. *Journal of Consulting and Clinical Psychology.*

Rotter, J. E. (1966). Generalized expectancies for internal versus external control of reinforcement. *Psychological Monographs, 80,* (1, Whole No. 609).

Rowell, C. G. (1972). An attitude scale for reading. *The Reading Teacher, 25,* 442–447.

Rutherford, R., & Nelson, J. (in press). Generalization and maintenance of treatment effects. In J. C. Witt, S. N. Elliott, & F. M. Gresham (Eds.), *Handbook of behavior therapy in education.* New York: Plenum press.

Ryall, M. R., & Dietiker, K. E. (1979). Reliability and clinical validity of the Children's Fear Survey Schedule. *Journal of Behavioral Therapy and Experimental Psychiatry, 10,* 303–309.

Saltz, E., Dunin-Markiewicz, A., & Rourke, D. (1975). The development of natural language concepts, II: Developmental changes in attribute structure. *Child Development, 46,* 913–921.

Sarason, S. B., Davidson, K. S., Lighthall, F. F., Waite, R. R., & Ruebush, L. J., (1960). *Anxiety in elementary school children.* New York: John Wiley & Sons.

Saylor, C. F., Finch, A. J., Spirito, A., & Bennett, B. (1984). The Children's Depression Inventory: Systematic evaluation of psychometric properties. *Journal of Consulting and Clinical Psychology, 52,* 955–967.

Scherer, M. W., & Nakamura, C. Y. (1968). A fear survey schedule for children (FSS-FC): A factor analytic comparison with manifest anxiety (CMAS). *Behaviour Research and Therapy, 6,* 173–182.

Schnelle, J. F. (1974). A brief report on the invalidity of parent evaluations of behavior change. *Journal of Applied Behavior Analysis, 7,* 341–343.

Selman, R. L. (1980). *The growth of interpersonal understanding: Developmental and clinical analyses.* New York: Academic Press.

Shantz, C. V. (1981). Social cognition. In J. H. Flavell & E. M. Markman (Eds.), *Cognitive development,* Vol. 2 of P. H. Mussen (Ed.), *Carmichael's Manual of Child Psychology.* New York: John Wiley & Sons.

Shekim, W. O.., Kashani, J., Beck, N., Cantwell, D. P., Martin, J., Rosenberg, J., & Costello, A. (1985). The prevalence of attention deficit disorders in a rural midwestern community sample of nine-year-old children. *Journal of the American Academy of Child Psychiatry, 24,* 765-770.

Sherrill, D., Salisbury, J. L., Horowitz, B., & Friedman, S. T. (1971). Classroom cheating: Consistent attitude, perceptions, and behavior. *American Educational Research Journal, 8,* 503-510.

Smucker, M. R., Craighead, W. E., Craighead, L. W., & Green, B. J. (1986). Normative and reliability data for the Children's Depression Inventory. *Journal of Abnormal Child Psychology, 14,* 25-39.

Spielberger, C. D. (1973). *Manual for the state-trait anxiety inventory for children.* Palo Alto, Calif.: Consulting Psychologists Press.

Spielberger, C. D. (1983). *Manual for the state-trait anxiety inventory* (rev. ed.). Palo Alto, Calif.: Consulting Psychologists Press.

Staats, A. W. (1972). Language behavior therapy: A derivative of social behaviorism. *Behavior Therapy, 3,* 165-192.

Stark, K. D., Reynolds, W. M., & Kaslow, N. J. (in press). A comparison of the relative efficacy of self-control and behavior therapy for the reduction of depression in children. *Journal of Abnormal Child Psychology.*

Stein, A. B., Finch, A. J., Jr., Hooke, J. F., Montgomery, L. E., & Nelson, W. M., III. (1975). Cognitive tempo and the mode of representation in emotionally disturbed children and normal children. *Journal of Psychology, 90,* 197-201.

Stenner, A. J., & Katzenmeyer, W. G. (1979). *Self-observation scales: Technical manual and user's guide.* Durham, N. C.: NTS Research Corporation.

Strober, M., Green, J., & Carlson, G. A. (1981a). Utility of the Beck Depression Inventory with psychiatrically hospitalized adolescents. *Journal of Consulting and Clinical Psychology, 49,* 482-483.

Strober, M., Green J., & Carlson, G. A. (1981b). Reliability of psychiaric diagnosis in hospitalized adolescents. *Archives of General Psychiatry, 38,* 141-145.

Swearingen, E. M., & Cohen, L. H. (1985). Measurement of adolescent's life events: The Junior High Life Experiences Survey. *American Journal of Community Psychology, 13,* 69-85.

Teri, L. (1982a). Depression in adolescence: Its relationship to assertion and various aspects of self-image. *Journal of Clinical Child Psychology, 11,* 101-106.

Teri, L. (1982b). The use of the Beck Depression Inventory with adolescents. *Journal of Abnormal Child Psychology, 10,* 277-284.

Turco, T. L., Elliott, S. N. & Witt, J. C. (1985). Children's involvement in treatment selection: A review of theory and analogue research on treatment acceptability. In S. Braaten, R. B. Rutherford, & W. Evans (Eds.), *Programming for adolescents with behavior disorders* (pp. 54-62), Reston, Va.: CEC.

Watson, J. B., & Rayner, P. (1920). Conditioned emotional reactions. *Jurnal of Experimental Psychology, 3,* 1-14.

Weissman, M., Orvaschel, H., Padian, N. (1980). Children's symptom and social functioning: Self-reports scales. *Journal of Nervous and Mental Disorders, 168,* 736-740.

Wheeler, V. A., & Ladd, G. W. (1982). Assessment of children's self-efficacy for social interactions with peers. *Developmental Psyhology, 18,* 795-805.

Wincze, J. P., Hoon, E. F., & Hoon, P. W. (1978). Multiple measure analysis of women experiencing low sexual arousal. *Behaviour Research & Therapy 16(1),* 43-49.

Wisniewski, S. (Ed.). (1985). *OSIQ Newsletter, 1,* (2).

Witt, J. C., & Elliott, S. N. (1985). Acceptability of classroom management strategies. In T. R. Kratochwill (Ed.), *Advances in school psychology* (pp. 251–288), Hillsdale, N.J.: Lawrence Erlbaum and Associates.

Yarrow, L. J. (1960). Interviewing children. In P. H. Mussen (Ed.), *Handbook of research methods in child development* (pp. 151–182), New York: John Wiley & Sons.

Yarrow, M. R., Cambell, J. D., & Burton, R. V. (1970). Recollections of childhood: A study of the retrospective method. *Monographs of the Society for Research in Child Development, 35,* 1–83.

Young, S. (Ed.). (1984). *OSIQ Newsletter 1,* (1).

CHAPTER 12

Behavioral Interviews with Teachers and Parents

FRANK M. GRESHAM

C. J. DAVIS

Louisiana State University

After all is said and done more is said than done. —*Anonymous*

INTRODUCTION

Psychological interviews represent one of the most frequently used assessment methods in both clinical and school settings (Haynes & Jensen, 1979; Linehan, 1977; Prout, 1983). Most assessment interviews in adult clinical psychology are conducted with individuals seeking therapeutic interventions. In contrast, school psychologists interview teachers and parents to collect information concerning children and youth referred for academic and behavior problems. Interviews with teachers and parents represent an analogue to informant reports and ratings (see Edelbrock, this volume) in that the same *source* is used to collect information and the information collected is removed in *time* and *place* from the actual occurrence of behavior. The major difference, however, between interviews and informant ratings is that interviews are a much more flexible and potentially more valuable assessment method in designing interventions.

Although interviews are used almost universally by school psychologists, they are usually applied informally and unsystematically in the assessment process. Cursory "interviews" (read conversations) between school psychologists and teachers or parents are common, but these "interviews" are usually unstructured, nonspecific, and do not result in accurate problem definition or the identification of environmental events that occasion or maintain academic or social behavior problems in school settings (Bergan, 1977; Tombari & Davis, 1979). Consequently, interviews traditionally have not been treated as a formal assessment method in

455

school or clinical child psychology. This is perplexing because decisions regarding children in the schools are often made on the basis of teachers' verbal behavior (e.g., referral for special education assessment, psychological interventions in the classroom, etc.).

There are several factors that might explain why interviews have not been considered a formal assessment method by school psychologists: (1) "subjective" reports of behavior by teachers and parents have often been regarded as suspect (Evans & Nelson, 1977; Mash & Terdal, 1981); (2) school psychological assessment has long been dominated by the use of standardized, norm-referenced tests, particularly the use of intelligence, perceptual-motor, and academic achievement tests (Goh, Telzrow, & Fuller, 1981). A final reason that interviews are not used formally and systematically is that they are not taught as such in school psychology training programs (Gresham, 1984; Kratochwill & Van Someren, 1984). Interviews are often taught as an entré to more formal assessment procedures, such as tests, rather than as formal assessment strategies in their own right.

The purpose of this chapter is to describe and discuss the use of behavioral interviews with teachers and parents. Various types of behavioral interviews will be described, however, the behavioral interview model developed by Bergan and his colleagues (Bergan, 1977; Bergan & Tombari, 1975, 1976; Brown, Kratochwill, & Bergan, 1982) are emphasized and discussed in detail. Evidence for the psychometric adequacy of behavioral interviews is reviewed, along with examples of how to translate behavioral interview data into viable interventions.

BEHAVIORAL VERSUS TRADITIONAL INTERVIEWS

Behavioral interviews can be differentiated from more traditional interview formats in relation to the assumptions underlying traditional versus behavioral assessment (Goldfried & Kent, 1972; Kratochwill, 1982; Nelson & Hayes, 1979). Behavioral interviews focus upon current environmental conditions (i.e., antecedents and consequences), view behavior as a sample of responding in specific situations, and use interview data to plan, implement, and evaluate the outcomes of intervention plans (Gresham, 1984; Haynes & Jensen, 1979; Tombari & Davis, 1979). The major characteristics of the behavioral interview are the specification and definition of target behaviors, the identification and analysis of environmental conditions surrounding target behaviors, and the use of the above information to formulate, implement, and evaluate interventions (Linehan, 1977; Morganstern, 1976).

In contrast, traditional interviews typically focus on various types of historical information that are far removed in time and place from the occurrence of target behaviors. Data obtained from traditional interviews lack specificity and do not focus upon current environmental conditions that may be maintaining problem behavior. Instead, traditional interviews are based upon the supposition that problem behaviors are a reflection of global personality states or traits. As such, information derived from traditional interviews is not particularly useful in designing interventions or evaluating the outcomes of intervention plans (Bergan, 1977; Kratochwill, 1982).

Advantages of Behavioral Interviews

Behavioral interviews have several advantages over other assessment methods in behavioral assessment (e.g., self-reports, self-monitoring, direct observations, etc.). The behavioral interview is *flexible*—both general and specific information regarding various areas of concern can be obtained. The behavioral interviewer can clarify, modify, and extend the interviewee's verbal description of behavior and situational variables (Linehan, 1977), whereas this flexibility is not possible with other behavioral assessment methods. Behavioral interviewers can thus broaden or narrow the assessment band depending upon the relevance and importance of the information to the interviewee. Other behavioral assessment methods lacking this flexibility may fail to capture the target behaviors of specific concern to teachers and parents.

A second advantage of behavioral interviews is that teachers' or parents' receptivity to intervention strategies can be assessed. Wolf (1978) has suggested that for a behavioral intervention to have *social validity* it must be judged by significant others (e.g., teachers and parents) to be acceptable. Teachers and parents who are unreceptive to certain intervention techniques are less likely to implement those procedures properly, if at all (Kazdin, 1980; Witt & Elliott, 1985). Moreover, the type of verbal behavior school consultants emit in consultation interviews with teachers predicts whether or not teachers will identify resources to be used in implementing intervention plans in classrooms (Bergan & Neumann, 1980). Behavioral interviews offer the unique opportunity to assess not only problem behaviors and their controlling variables, but also teachers' and parents' acceptability of behavioral intervention procedures.

Acceptability has been more formally assessed using self-report measures such as the Intervention Rating Profile (Witt, Elliott, & Martens, 1984) for teachers and the Treatment Evaluation Inventory (Kazdin, 1980) for parents. Behavioral interviews have the added advantage over these formal acceptability measures because interviews can assess the qualitative aspects of teacher or parent acceptability of proposed interventions and can adjust aspects of the plan to make it more acceptable.

A third advantage of behavioral interviews is that irrational beliefs or unrealistic expectations that teachers or parents have about children can often be detected. Forman and Forman (1978) identified several irrational beliefs that teachers typically express concerning the expected behaviors of children in classrooms. In addition, parents often have a poor sense of what is developmentally "normal" or "atypical" for their children (Achenbach, 1982). Other behavioral assessment methods (e.g., informant ratings, direct observations, self-monitoring, etc.) are not as likely to yield information concerning beliefs, expectancies, or values adults possess regarding children's behavior. Beliefs and expectations represent important behaviors to be assessed in interviews with teachers and parents because these beliefs and expectations may have an impact upon which children are referrred, how adults interact with children, and the success of subsequent interventions for problem behaviors (Bandura, 1986).

Behavioral interviews have distinct advantages over other behavioral assessment methods. The flexibility, social validity, and qualitative aspects of interviews provide a more complete picture of the child and the environmental events that may be maintaining problem behaviors. No other behavioral assessment method offers these advantages and, as such, behavioral interviews are essential for a complete, school-based assessment.

Purposes of Behavioral Assessment

This volume covers a broad range of behavioral assessment techniques, some of which can be classified for selection or classification purposes and others that are useful for planning interventions. Hops and Greenwood (1981) indicate that the extent to which an assessment procedure yields information about specific behavioral excesses or deficits determines it usefulness as a selection or classification or an intervention related assessment procedure.

The authors use a slightly different criterion for classifying behavioral assessment methods—one that is based upon the extent to which the assessment procedure yields information for a functional analysis of behavior. In this view, the extent to which the assessment procedure provides data concerning the antecedent, sequential, and consequent conditions surrounding behavior determines its utility as a screening, classification, or intervention related assessment method. Given this criterion, informant ratings, although they provide information about specific behavioral excesses and deficits, would *not* be considered an intervention related assessment method.

Behavioral interviews would be classified as an intervention related assessment procedure because they do provide data for a functional analysis of behavior (Bergan, 1977; Bergan & Tombari, 1975). Although behavioral interviews are considered an indirect behavioral assessment method (i.e., the data produced are removed in time and place from the actual occurrence of behavior), they can be classified primarily as an intervention assessment method because of their functional analysis potential. It could be argued that behavioral interviews might be classified as both screening and intervention methods. However, screening and subsequent classification decisions typically are not made on the basis of interview data alone and are usually supported by informant ratings.

It should be emphasized that behavioral interviews must yield information about behaviors, the setting or settings in which behavior occurs, and intervention plans to be considered an intervention related behavioral assessment method. This is discussed more fully in a subsequent section of this chapter on the use of behavioral consultation interviews.

A Behavioral Assessment Model: Kanfer and Grimm's System

Kanfer and Grimm (1977) have proposed a useful system of classifying behavioral assessment data obtained from behavioral interviews. The value of the Kanfer and Grimm system is that it allows not only for a specification of behavioral excesses and deficits, but also for a functional analysis of these excesses and deficits for intervention purposes. Table 12-1 presents an outline of the Kanfer and Grimm (1977) behavioral analysis system.

Readers should note that the Kanfer and Grimm categories are organized around the nature of the behavior problem (e.g., skills deficits, lack of knowledge, etc.), excesses in emotional arousal responses that inhibit appropriate behaviors (e.g., conditioned anxiety), inappropriate consequent control (e.g., noncontigent reinforcement, lack of reinforcement, etc.), and problems in antecedent or stimulus control (e.g., lack of opportunity, cues for behavior, etc.). In sum, the Kanfer and Grimm system provides a useful conceptual organizer for conducting behavioral interviews that will yield functional analysis data. Although this system was developed for use in clinical settings, it is directly applicable for use in school settings in the conduct of behavioral interviews with teachers and parents.

Summary

Behavioral interviews may be conceptualized as an indirect form of assessment because the data obtained from interviews are based upon retrospective judgments or reports of the occurrence of behavior. In this sense, interview data are not considered as "pure" as direct observation data, which are collected at the time and place of actual behavioral occurrences. Behavioral observations, however, are limited by the availability of reliable observers, the low and inconsistent rates of certain behaviors, and the physical impossibility of having continuously available observers to record behavior in school and home settings. As such, school psychologists must rely upon the reports of qualified informants to provide information on the occurrence of behavior. The "indirectness" of behavioral interviews is a necessary evil, but it can also be a blessing in disguise because data are more easily and cheaply obtainable, and interviewees can describe target behaviors that are of greatest concern.

Perhaps the greatest advantage of behavioral interviews is their potential for a functional analysis of behavior, which leads directly to the design and implementation of interventions for problem behaviors. Interviewers who do not know how to conduct functional analyses of behavior are at a loss when using interviews because of the paucity of useful information for intervention purposes derived from such interviews. Thus, it becomes imperative that interviewers become skilled in the applied analysis of behavior in order to derive maximum benefit from behavioral interview data.

Behavioral interviews necessarily focus upon different content areas when the

TABLE 12-1 Classification of Data Obtained in Behavioral Interviews

I. Behavioral Deficits
   A. Inadequate base of knowledge for guiding behavior
   B. Failure to engage an acceptable social behaviors because of skills deficits
   C. Inability to supplement or counter immediate environmental influences and regulate one's behavior through self-directing response
   D. Deficiencies is self-reinforcement for performance
   E. Deficits in monitoring one's own behavior
   F. Inability to alter response in conflict situations
   G. Limited behavior repertoire due to restricted range of reinforcers
   H. Deficits in cognitive or motor behavior necessary to meet the demands of daily living

II. Behavioral Excesses
   A. Conditioned inappropriate anxiety to object or events
   B. Excessive self-observational activity

III. Problems in Environmental Stimulus Control
   A. Affective response to stimulus objects or events leading to subjective distress or unacceptable behavior
   B. Failure to offer support or opportunities for behaviors appropriate in a different milieu
   C. Failure to meet environmental demands or responsibilities arising from inefficient organization of time

IV. Inappropriate Self-Generated Stimulus Control
   A. Self-description serving as cues for behavior leading to negative outcomes
   B. Verbal and symbolic activity serving to cue inappropriate behavior
   C. Faulty labeling of internal cues

V. Inappropriate contingency arrangement
   A. Failure of the environment to support appropriate behavior
   B. Environmental maintenance of undesirable behavior
   C. Excessive use of positive reinforcement for desirable behaviors
   D. Delivery of reinforcement independent of responding

Adapted from F. H. Kanfer & L. G. Grimm (1977). Behavioral analysis: Selecting target behavior in the interview. *Behavior Modification, 1*, 7–28.

interviewees are teachers rather than parents. For example, content areas for teacher interviews include instructional methods, classroom management procedures, and school and classroom environmental factors that may influence occurrences of behavior. In contrast, parent interviews might focus upon child discipline methods, marital status problems, and home and community factors that might occasion problem behaviors. Information obtained from teacher and parent interviews represents a useful means of multiply operationalizing children's behavior and in determining the situational specificity or cross-situational generality of problem behaviors (Gresham, 1985). Conducting interviews with parents is one way to assess the existence of problem behaviors in nonschool settings. If problem behaviors occur only at school and not the home setting, there is a strong possibility that the problem behaviors are less severe and situation specific (Gresham, 1982a).

BEHAVIORAL CONSULTATION INTERVIEWS

Consultation has been a major function of school psychologists since the inception of school psychology as a professional discipline (Bardon, 1968; Tindall, 1979). The major goal of school-based consultation is to provide educators with knowledge of and assistance in the application of psychological principles to ameliorate academic and social behavior problems in school settings. Behavioral psychologists use interviews to collect information regarding a precise definition of target behaviors, and to conduct functional analyses of those conditions surrounding these behaviors. In the behavioral assessment of school-based problems, interviews are typically conducted with three information sources: teachers, parents, and the referred child (Gresham, 1982a). Each information source yields potentially useful information concerning those behaviors perceived as disturbing in particular environments (e.g., school, home, etc.).

The best-known system for conducting behavioral consultation interviews was developed by Bergan and colleagues (Bergan, 1977; Bergan & Neumann, 1980; Bergan & Tombari, 1975, 1976: Tombari & Bergan, 1978. Behavioral consultation represents a problem-solving model that is designed to assist consultees (e.g., teachers, parents, etc.) in defining the referral problems they have in dealing with children and youth, formulating intervention plans to solve these problems, and in evaluating the outcomes of intervention plans (Bergan, 1977). Another useful interview format has been presented by Alessi and Kaye (1983); however, because of the lack of empirical research using this format, the behavioral consultation model of Bergan (1977) is presented here. Interested readers may also wish to consult the interview formats presented by Kanfer and Saslow (1969), Holland (1970), and Goldfried and Sprafkin (1974). In addition, the chapter by Gross (1984) on behavioral interviewing provides useful information for practitioners working in clinical settings.

Behavioral consultation consists of four stages: (1) Problem Identification, (2) Problem Analysis, (3) Plan Implementation, and (4) Problem Evaluation. Movement through these four stages is effected by the use of three interviews: (a) Problem Identification Interview, (b) Problem Analysis Interview, and (c) Problem Evaluation Interview. These are discussed in detail later in this section. Before embarking on a comprehensive description of each interview, this section discusses a system for classifying and using verbal behavior in consultation interveiws to achieve the goals of behavioral consultation.

Verbal Behavior in Consultation Interviews

Interviews consist of verbal interchanges between two or more persons. Information regarding problem behaviors is reported on and clarified through verbal accounts or reports of *past* occurrences (or lack of occurrences) of behavior. Behavioral assessment rests upon the assumption that behavior must be specified in operational, measurable terms before it can be changed through behavioral interventions. To elicit a specification of behavior in measurable terms, interviewers must control their verbal behavior in ways that will lead to operational definitions of behavior and the specification of environmental conditions surrounding problem behaviors. Behavioral interviews are not conversations that identify global areas of concern. Instead, behavioral interviews focus upon precise definitions of behavior, its antecedents and consequences, and intervention plans to change behavior.

An example can be used to highlight the differences between more traditional and behavioral interviews. A traditional interview question may be, "Do you think Joe is immature?" A behavioral interview question on this same topic may be, "What specific things does Joe do that make you say he is immature?" The difference in these two questions may seem to some to be insignificant, however, the effect these two questions have on the definition and implementation of problem behaviors are substantial. The first question leads to a dead-end street because it does not specify a behavior in operational terms and implies that the cause of Joe's problems must be due to some magical, underlying personality trait of immaturity. In contrast, the second question leads to specification of behavioral exemplars of immaturity and carries with it the implication that the focus of the interview will be on observable behaviors rather than unobservable personality traits.

Bergan and Tombari (1975) indicate that methods for analyzing verbal behavior in interviews have a long history in psychology (Bales, 1950; Curran, 1945; Synder, 1945). Behavioral consultation interviews differ from these earlier attempts because the verbal interchange occurs between a consultant and consultee rather than between a therapist and a client.

Bergan and Tombari (1975) developed a system for classifying verbal behavior in consultation interviews called the Consultation Analysis Record (CAR). The CAR contains four message classification categories: (1) Content, (2) Process, (3) Source, and (4) Control.

Content

The content message category captures what is said and the topics under discussion in a consultation interview. Although an unlimited range of topics might be discussed in a consultation interview, behavioral interviewers should have the larger percentage of their verbalizations in the *behavior, behavior setting, observation*, and *plan* subcategories.

The *behavior* subcategory refers to a description of overt or covert actions of the client (Bergan & Tombari, 1975). For example, the following verbalizations would be coded in the behavior subcategory: (1) What does Steve do that makes you say he's hyperactive?; (2) Give me some examples of Joe's inappropriate sexual behavior; (3) What does Ed do that leads you to say he's immature? Behavioral interviewers should have a large portion of their verbalizations in the behavior subcategory because the most important initial task in behavioral interviewing is defining behavior in operational terms (Bergan & Tombari, 1976).

The *behavior setting* subcategory refers to the antecedent, sequential, and consequent conditions surrounding behavior. This subcategory reflects verbalizations that are used to conduct a functional analysis of behavior by having the consultee identify environmental events that consistently precede and follow the target behavior. Examples of verbalizations in this subcategory include: (1) What happens just before Bud blurts out inappropriately in class?; (2) How do the other class members respond to Dan's disruptive behavior?; (3) Does Ron complete more work in the morning or afternoon?

The *observation* subcategory refers to the recording or measurement of behavior. The purpose of verbalizations in this subcategory is to devise a system for obtaining baseline rates of behavior and continuing measurement of behavior throughout the intervention phase. Examples of this subcategory are: (1) What are some ways that we could keep a record of Bob's out-of-seat behavior?; (2) Could you keep a record of Tom's math worksheets this week?; (3) I can come into your classroom this Friday and observe Jill's classroom behavior.

The *plan* subcategory includes verbalizations that describe procedures for changing problem behaviors. This subcategory can be further subdivided into two categories of *plan strategies* and *plan tactics*. A plan strategy refers to general procedures or approaches to solving problems (e.g. What are some ways we could get Tom to complete more of his math work?). Plan tactics refer to specific, concrete procedures and materials for implementing intervention plans (e.g., How could you reinforce Tom for math completion?).

The remaining content subcategories are individual characteristics, background environment, and other. Behavioral interviewers avoid the use of these subcategories because they focus on variables over which teachers, parents, and psychologists have no control. For example, the verbalization, Frank comes from a broken home, describes a background environment variable relative to Frank, however, there is nothing anyone can do to change this fact about Frank's developmental history. The verbalization, John is mentally retarded, refers to an individual characteristic of John, but it is one that cannot be changed. Given the immutable aspects of background environment and individual characteristics, behavioral interviewers eschew the use of verbalizations in these subcategories.

Process Category

The process category reflects *how* the content is discussed in behavioral interviews. The most important of these process subcategories is *specification*. Specification provides definitional or descriptive information about a particular topic or content subcategory discussed in an interview. Examples of specification verbalizations are: (1) Bob is stupid (Individual Characteristics Specification); (2) Mary hits others in class (Behavior Specification); (3) John is most disruptive just before lunch (Behavior Setting Specification). A large portion of a behavioral interviewer's and interviewee's verbalizations should be in the specification subcategory.

Two other important process subcategories are *validation* and *summar-*

ization. Validation refers to verbalizations that call for agreement (positive validation) or disagreement (negative validation) regarding some content discussed. Validation verbalizations can always be answered with a yes or no reply (e.g., Can you take baseline data on Ed's peer interactions?). Summarization verbalizations review information previously discussed in an interview. These verbalizations represent an important subcategory because they ensure that the content discussed is accurately summarized (e.g., So far we've established that Bob is out of his seat more in reading and that this usually occurs about five minutes into the lesson).

The remaining process subcategories of *evaluation* and *inference* are deemphasized in behavioral interviews because they are not particularly useful in defining behavior or in designing interventions. Evaluation verbalizations represent value judgments of some event (e.g., I like this plan; Bob is horrible; etc.). Inference verbalizations refer to predictions or probabilistic statements (e.g., This plan won't work; Do you think Sally behaves this way because she's immature?; etc.).

Source and Control Categories

The source category identifies who is talking in an interview, the consultant or the consultee. Consultants are usually school psychologists, educational diagnosticians, counselors, and other support personnel. Consultees are usually teachers or parents.

The message control category classifies verbal behavior whether it is likely to have a direct effect on the verbal behavior of the listener. Verbal behaviors that are likely to elicit a verbal response on behalf of the listener are called *elicitors.* Elicitors are similar to what Skinner (1957) refers to as *mands,* or verbal behaviors that demand a response from the environment. Elicitors typically take the form of questions (e.g., What does Linda do to show her low self-concept?) or imperatives (e.g., Tell me more about Jim's reading skills). Interviewers control the scope and content of behavioral interviews through the frequent use of elicitors (questions and imperatives). These elicitors relate mainly to the content subcategories of behaviors, behavior setting, observation, and plan using the message process subcategories of specification, validation, and summarization.

The other control subcategory is called an *emitter.* An emitter is similar to what Skinner (1957) refers to as *tacts,* which are verbal behaviors not occasioning a response from the environment. Emitters are declarative statements that can be about any of the content subcategories using any of the message process subcategories. Behavioral interviewers use few emitters in relation to their use of elicitors. In other words, interviewers must ultimately control the interview and do so by asking questions (elicitors) about the right things (behavior, behavior setting, observation, and plan) at the right time (Problem Identification, Problem Analysis, and Problem Evaluation). The following sections discuss three types of behavioral consultation interviews: (1) Problem Identification Interview, (2) Problem Analysis Interview, and (3) Problem Evaluation Interview.

PROBLEM IDENTIFICATION INTERVIEW

Problem identification is the most important stage of the behavioral consultation process because the greatest impact of consultation takes place during the problem identification phase. Problem identification sets the course for the entire consultation process and communicates to consultees what is going to be focused on and how the problem will be conceptualized (i.e., behaviorally). Several studies have demonstrated the importance of problem identification in the consultation process (see Bergan & Tombari, 1976; Curtis & Watson, 1980; Tombari & Bergan, 1978).

Using a sample of 806 children (Grades K to 3) who had been referred for psychological services, Bergan and Tombari (1976) had eleven trained behavioral consultants provide consultation services to teachers whose students were experiencing academic and behavior problems. Problem behaviors included physical assault, disruption, not following rules, academic deficits, and social skills deficits. Using a series of multiple regression analyses, Bergan and Tombari found that the single best predictor of whether or not an intervention plan would be implemented was successful *problem identification* (R = .776). In other words, over 60% of the variance in plan implementation was accounted for by simply identifying the problem to be solved during a problem identification interview. Moreover, it was also found that the effectiveness of consultants' interviewing behaviors (i.e., verbalizations mainly in the *content* subcategories of setting, behavior, observation, and plan, and the *process* subcategories of specification, summarization, and validation) had their greatest impact on the problem-solving process at the problem identification phase.

This study has significant implications for the behavioral consultant. When a consultant lacks behavioral interviewing skills, there is a high probability that problem solving in consultation will never take place. It is imperative that problems be adequately defined during consultation.

The Problem Identification Interview (PII) plays a pivotal role because it sets the state for either a *behavioral* or *medical model* perspective on the child's problem. The behavioral perspective emphasizes the role of immediate environmental events as the primary cause of the child's problem. Teachers, parents, and school psychologists can usually control or change immediate environmental events. By contrast, the medical model stresses remote environmental events and internal characteristics as determinants of behavior. Consultants and consultees have relatively little influence over these remote events.

A study by Tombari and Bergan (1978) bears out the importance of taking a behavioral perspective during problem identification. Teachers were given either behavioral cues (e.g., "When does this behavior typically occur in your classroom?") or medical model cues (e.g., "When does _____'s problem typically manifest itself?") during consultation interviews. Tombari and Bergan found that cue type (behavioral versus medical) exerted a substantial influence on teacher expectancies concerning their ability to solve the problem presented in consultation (rated on a 7-point scale of probable to improbable). Expectancies, in turn, strongly affected teachers' ability to define the problem (written definition of a child's problem categorized as behavioral or medical model). This study strongly suggests that verbalizations focusing on behavior and behavior setting are predictive of teachers' ability to define problems and lead to more positive expectations concerning their ability to solve problem behaviors.

The behavioral perspective on a problem is more likely to result in collection of baseline data and a commitment to pursue consultation through subsequent phases. The medical model, on the other hand, provides little direction for the collection of precise data related to the problem and is less likely to result in specific classroom interventions. Thus, the subsequent phases of consultation are less likely to be pursued. Failure, then, on the part of a behavioral consultant to elicit a behavioral definition of the problem during the PII will, in all probability, end the consultative relationship (Kratochwill, 1985).

Objectives for the PII

There are six objectives for the PII. Behavioral consultants must meet all six of these objectives in order to adequately define problems presented in consultation.

First, consultants must specify the problem to be solved in consultation. In other words, consultants must elicit from teachers the goals they have in mind for consultation. Objective identification of goals is brought about by the use of verbalization relating to behavior and in the content category, and by the use of specification verbalizations in the process category.

Teachers may identify several goals of consultation. For example a teacher might identify a child's daydreaming, off-task behavior, lack of completion in math, and disruptive behavior as problems. The behavioral consultant in this case may ask the teacher to rank these behavior problems from most disturbing to least disturbing. A more effective approach, however, might be to select the target behavior that would lead to the greatest amount of behavior generalization. In this case the consultant might select math completion as the target behavior because daydreaming, off-task, and disruptive behavior are all incompatible with working diligently on math assignments. Thus, by selecting math completion as the target behavior, one is likely to get four behaviors changed for the price of one.

The second objective of the PII is eliciting an objective description of target behaviors. This is related to the first objective because the consultant uses behavior specification questions (elicitors) to obtained objective, clear descriptions of child behavior. For example, a teacher might say, "What really bothers me about Jeff is his immaturity." Behavioral consultants would elicit an objective description of immaturity by asking, "What are some of the things Jeff does to show his immaturity?" As you can see, this question forces the teacher to identify specific behaviors which she or he considers immature. Getting problems defined in behavioral terms so that the consultant and the teacher can both agree on the nature of the problem leads to more effective and efficient steps toward problem solution.

A third objective of the PII is to identify the environmental conditions surrounding the target behavior. Consultants elicit from consultees descriptions of events that come before (antecedents), during (sequential), and after (consequent) the problem behavior. This is done by behavior-setting specification questions. For example, a consultant might ask, "What usually happens just before Ted gets out of his seat?" "Does Ted get out of his seat more during math than during reading?"; and "What do you do just after Ted gets out of his seat?" These three questions all relate to the conditions surrounding Ted's out-of-seat behavior (antecedent, sequential, and consequent, respectively).

The fourth objective of the PII is to have the teacher estimate the frequency, intensity, and duration of the problem behavior. The purpose of this objective is to give the consultant some notion of the severity of the problem behavior. This, in part, will determine the length of baseline data in that more severe problems (severely aggressive behaviors or school phobia) will need to be attended to more quickly thus shortening the number of baseline days.

The fifth objective is to agree on the type of data collection procedures that will be used (frequency, direct evidence, duration, etc.) and who will collect the data. Teachers should collect data if at all possible because of the time savings for the consultant and, perhaps more importantly, it gets the teacher involved in the problem-solving process. Because teachers will be collecting baseline data, it is extremely important to use the simplest recording procedure possible that will yield the most valid data. Many time there is a tradeoff between optimal and recording procedures. Practical recording procedures are frequency, duration, direct evidence, and some time sampling methods. One should remember to use the appropriate procedure with the appropriate behavior. For example, one cannot measure off-task behavior with frequency recording and one is likely to underestimate behavior rates with relatively long time sampling intervals (e.g., at the end of 10-minute intervals), particularly with high rate behaviors.

The final objective of the PII is to set a date for the next interview. The time that elapses between the PII and the next interview (Problem Analysis Interview) will depend upon the number of days the teacher will collect baseline data. This, in turn, depends upon the nature and severity of the problem behavior and the stability of baseline data. An optimal length of baseline is about five days and certainly no less than three days. Table 12-2 provides an outline of a PII provided by Witt and Elliott (1983) and Table 12-3 provides examples of interviewer behavior for the PII.

Problem Analysis Interview

Problem analysis takes place after adequate baseline data have been collected on the problem identified in the PII. The consultant's task during problem analysis is to help the teacher identify variables that could influence the solution of the problem and to assist the teacher in using those variables (manipulating them) to design a plan to change behavior.

Problem analysis has two phases: The *analysis phase*, and the *plan-design phase* (Bergan, 1977). During the analysis phase, the consultant focuses upon the

TABLE 12-2   Components of Problem Identification

I. Explanation of Problem Definition Purpose
   A. Sets tone for interview
   B. Gives overview of what is to be accomplished
   C. Focuses upon client behaviors
   D. Establishes that consultee owns the problems

II. Identification and Selection of Target Behaviors
   A. Defines behaviors in specific operational terms
   B. Establishes discrepancy between observed performance
   C. Prioritizes behaviors in terms of importance to consultee

III. Identification of Problem Frequency, Duration, and Intensity
   A. Focuses upon objective features of behavior
   B. Compares behavior rates with other clients in classroom
   C. Provides feedback to consultee regarding normal expectations for behavior of concern

IV. Identification of Conditions Under Which Behavior Occurs
   A. Specifies antecedent conditions
   B. Specifies consequent conditions
   C. Specifies sequential conditions

V. Identification of Required Level of Performance
   A. Determines consultee expectations for behavior
   B. Sets goals or objectives for terminal behavior rates
   C. Specfies time lines for meeting behavioral goals

VI. Identification of Client's Strengths
   A. Establishes if consultee recognizes any positive value in child
   B. Detects irrational ideas of consultee
   C. Identifies potential client reinforcers

VII. Identification of Behavioral Assessment Procedures
   A. Explains rationale for data collection
   B. Determines what will be recorded
   C. Determines who will record behavior
   D. Determines how behavior will be recorded
   E. Determines when and where behavior will be recorded

VIII. Identification of Consultee Effectiveness
   A. Models problem-solving skills for consultee
   B. Evaluates consultee's previous problem-solving attempts
   C. Assesses consultee's motivation for solving problems
   D. Identifies logistical problems that may interfere with intervention plan

IX. Summarizes and Identifies Methods and Times of Future Contacts
   A. Summarizes important points discussed in interview
   B. Sets time for next interview
   C. Provides means of contacting consultant and consultee regarding problem behavior, re-
      cording methods, and functional analysis of behavior

Adapted from J. C. Witt & S. N. Elliott (1983). Assessment in behavioral consultation: The initial interview. *School Psychology Review, 12,* 42–49.

TABLE 12-3 The Problem Identification Interview (PII)

I. Purpose of PII
  A. Define Problem(s) in Behavioral Terms
  B. Tentative Identification of Conditions Surrounding the Behavior: antecedent, situational, consequent
  C. Tentative Strength specification—How often or severe at present vs. acceptable level
  D. Establish Procedure for Collection of Baseline Data Sampling Plan, What, Who, How Behavior is Recorded, etc.
  E. Detection of Irrational Ideas

II. Essential Interviewing Behaviors
  A. Directional question to introduce discussion of problem; e.g., "Describe Diane's hyperactive behavior." "Let's see, you referred Johnny because of his poor self-concept, lack of progress, and rebellious behavior—which of these do you want to start with. . . ?" Describe Johnny's rebellion (self-concept or lack of progress) in the classroom.
  B. Examples of behavior question(s); e.g., "What does Charles do when he is hyperactive? What does Mary do when she is disrespectful?"
  C. Preceding Conditions Questions e.g., "What happens before Mary makes an obscene gesture to the rest of the class?" "What happens before Egbert begins to hit other children?"
  D. Situational Condition Question e.g., "When does Mary. . . ? Who is Mary with. . . ? What is Mary supposed to be doing when. . . ?"
  E. Consequent Conditions Questions e.g., "What happens after Mary. . . ?" "What do the other students do when Charles climbs on the radiator?" "What do you do when Egbert hits other children?"
  F. Frequency/Severity Questions e.g., "About how often does Patrick refuse to do his homework?" "How many times each day or week does Charles race about the room?"
  G. Tentative Definition of Goal Question e.g., "How often would Patrick have to turn in his work in order to get along OK?"
  H. Assets Question e.g., "Is there something that Mary does well?"
  I. Question About Approach to Teaching or Existing Procedures e.g., "How long are Charles and the other students doing seat work problems?" What kind of. . . ?"
  J. Summarization statement and agreement question "Let's see, the main problem is that Charles gets out of his seat and runs around the room during independent work assignments. He does this about four times each day, and . . . Is that right?"
  K. Directional statement to introduce discussion of data recording "We need some record of Sarah's completion of homework assignments—how often assignments are completed, what assignments are completed, etc. This record will help us to determine how frequently the behavior is occuring and it may give us some clues about the nature of the problem. Also the record will help us decide whether any plan we initiate is effective or not."
  L. Question about data recording and conditions "How would it be most convenient for you to keep a record of Charles' out of seat behavior?" "What would you record?" "When would you record?" "How often?"
  M. Summary statement "Let's see now, you'll record the number of times Danny hits other students in the hall—you'll record this in the morning before school and at noon, and you'll keep a record for one week."

conditions that might influence behavior. Recall from problem identification that consultants should focus upon the behavior-setting content. Behavior setting refers to the antecedent, sequential, and consequent conditions surrounding behavior. Thus, during the analysis phase, the consultant should concentrate on the conditions surrounding problem behavior to determine what may be maintaining it. During the plan design phase, consultants develop with teachers plan strategies that can be used to achieve the goals of consultation. After a general strategy has been agreed upon, specific plan tactics to be used in implementing the strategy are specified. Plan strategies and tactics will be discussed more fully in a subsequent section of this chapter.

Objectives for the PAI

There are four objectives for the PAI. All four of these objectives must be met in order to adequately analyze the conditions surrounding behavior and to design a plan to change target behaviors.

Problem validation is the first objective of the PAI. In problem validation, the consultant determines the adequacy of baseline data collected by the teacher. It may be that only one or two days of data have been collected when the consultant and the teacher agreed that six days would be collected. In this case, there would not be adequate data to confirm the existence of a problem. The consultant's response to this situation should be a request for the teacher to collect more data (e.g., "We need a few more days of baseline data before we can develop a plan for Dan's disruptive behavior"). Another situation might arise in which the teacher took only frequency data when the consultant had requested both frequency and duration data (e.g., in the case of temper tantrums). Again, the teacher should be asked for more baseline data for both frequency and duration of tantrums.

Another goal of problem validation is to determine the discrepancy between existing performance and desired performance of the child. For example assuming the baseline data are adequate, the teacher reports that a child is disruptive (talks out, hits, etc.) six times during a twenty-five-minute math lesson. The consultant should ask the teacher what he or she would regard as an acceptable number of disruptions during the math lesson. Most teachers would probably say zero disruptions are the only acceptable goal. This, of course, will vary according to the nature of the problem behavior. There are some behaviors that are simply too frequent, but the goal would not be to completely eliminate them (e.g., offering answers to questions in class, talking to peers, etc.). In summary, the goals of problem validation are twofold: (1) determining the adequacy of baseline data, and (2) determining the existence of a problem. There will be times when baseline data will be indadequate (e.g., not collected, collected improperly) or when the teacher will realize the problem is not as great as first thought. In either case, the consultant's job is to validate the existence (or nonexistence) of a problem based upon objective information (i.e., adequate baseline data).

The second objective of the PAI is to analyze the conditions surrounding the problem behavior. Psychological research indicates that there are a number of conditions that can affect behavior (Bergan, 1977). In behavioral consultation, your goal should be to identify the antecedent, sequential, and consequent conditions occurring in close temporal contiguity to the problem behavior. Thus, in problem analysis, a large number of your questions to the consultee should be in the behavior setting content category. There are a number of antecedent, sequential, and consequent conditions that serve to increase, maintain, and/or decrease behavior.

These are just a few of the many conditions that affect behavior. In consultation, teachers usually want one of two things: to decrease the frequency or magnitude of behavior, or to increase the frequency or magnitude of behavior. The consultant's job is to identify conditions in the child's immediate environment that are maintaining or are failing to maintain the target behavior(s). Once these conditions have been identified, the plan design phase of problem analysis can begin.

The third objective of the PAI is to design an intervention plan to alter the target behavior(s). There are two subgoals of plan design: development of plan strategies, and the identification of plan tactics. Plan strategies are general approaches or possible courses of action that may be adopted to effect a solution to problems in consultation. Plan strategies do not specify exactly how a technique may be applied, but rather they provide information on what general procedures might be effective (e.g., reinforcement, punishment, etc.). Examples of plan strategy verbalizations are: "You could use a reinforcement approach to increase Bill's academic behavior," Would it be possible for you to use a response cost procedure?", etc.

Plan tactics, on the other hand, refer to precise descriptions of how the general plan strategies are to be put into effect. Plan tactics include descriptions of procedures and materials to be used in implementing a consultation plan as well as specification of who is to carry out the tactic (Bergan, 1977). Consultees are much more likely to identify resources thay could use in carrying out an intervention plan if the consultant asks them rather than tells them how they could use resources. A study by Bergan and Neumann (1980) illustrates this nicely. These authors analyzed fifty problem analysis interviews recording the frequency of plan tactic questions versus plan tactic statements (i.e., the consultant telling them what to do, how to do it, and under what conditions to do it). Bergan and Neumann found that the greater the frequency of consultant plan tactic questions, the greater the frequency of consultee verbalizations about resources that could be used in implementing a plan. By the same token, the greater the frequency of consultant plan tactic statements, the less likely the consultee was able to identify resources that could be used in implementing a consultation plan. In specific terms, when consultants ask teachers how they might implement a particular procedure to solve a problem (i.e., token system, response cost, praise, etc.), the odds that they will identify a way of carrying out a procedure are fourteen times greater than if the consultant just simply told them what to do. The implication of this study is that the consultant is much more likely to achieve cooperation from teachers in carrying out a plan if they (the teachers) identify plan tactics themselves. It is unclear why this is the case, but it may have to do with teachers feeling they are an equal participant in the problem-solving process and thus more inclined to identify plan tactics. Another explanation is that teachers may enhance their sense of self-efficacy (Bandura, 1977) if they perceive themselves as competent in identifying plan tactics. Self-efficacy theory would predict that the more direct involvement teachers have in an intervention, the higher their efficacy expectations (i.e., the more they would come to believe that they had the skills to bring about behavior change).

The final objective of the PAI is to arrange a date for the next interview (Problem Evaluation Interview). The consultant should also make arrangements to monitor the implementation of the plan (e.g., "I'll drop by next week to see how things are going") and make provisions for consultee training in the application of the procedures agreed upon in consultation (e.g., "Would Thursday after school be a good day to go over with you how to conduct the restitutional overcorrection procedure?"). Table 12-4 presents an outline and objectives for the PAI.

TABLE 12-4   Outline and Examples of the PAI

I. Purpose of PAI
   A. Evaluation of the agreement of sufficiency and adequacy of baseline data
   B. Tentative functional analysis—discuss antecedent, situational, and consequent conditions
   C. Discuss and reach agreement on goal for behavior change
   D. Design an intervention plan including specification of antecedent, situational, or consequent conditions to be changed and who, what, where, and when regarding The Change
   E. Reaffirm record keeping procedure
   F. Schedule problem evaluation interview

II. Essential Interviewing Behaviors
   A. Directional statement about data and problem; "Let's look at the record on Jimmy's hitting."
   B. Summary statements regarding problem behavior and behavior setting

III. Graph Data
   A. Question or statement about strength of behavior; "It looks like Jimmy refused to do the assigned work except on Tuesday."
   B. Questions about conditions: antecedent, situational, consequent. "Did you notice anything in particular that happened just before. . . ?" "What was going on when Jimmy. . . ?" "What happened after Mary. . . ?"
   C. Summarizing statements specifying target behavior, conditions and strength; "Let's see, Mary was disrespectful by talking back, or through abusive language, on three days last week. This behavior seemed to be related to comments made by other students. We would like to eliminate this behavior and help her produce more positive comments. Is that right?"
   D. Question or statement interpreting the behavior; "Why do you think Mary is disrespectful?" or "Perhaps Mary is trying to attract attention and win status in the class by . . ."
   E. Questions about the plan; "We need to try something different. What could be done before Mary usually makes the abusive remarks?" "What could we do to change the setting which Charles gets into fights?" "How could we remove the attention from the disruptive behavior?"
   F. Summarize the plan; "Then we'll try this . . ."
   G. Statement on continuing recording procedure make an informal written agreement on the plan, data recording, etc.

PROBLEM EVALUATION INTERVIEW

Problem evaluation is the last stage of behavioral consultation and it is here that the notion of accountability assumes prominence. Problem evaluation takes place after the plan has been in effect for a reasonable period of time. Many plans appear to fail simply because they are not left in effect for adequate periods of time (Bergan, 1977). Consultants must encourage teachers and parents to give plans a chance to work before calling for what may be a premature problem evaluation.

The value of problem evaluation is that it informs the consultant and consultee about what their next steps will be in consultation. Depending on the results of the problem evaluation interview, (PEI), the participants in consultation may decide to terminate consultation, to alter the existent plan or to go back to problem identification and select new goals. Problem evaluation also serves as a feedback mechanism to both the consultant and consultee and involves the production of empirical knowledge of behavior change strategies in classroom settings. In this sense, behavioral consultation provides a blending of service to children and experimentation (Bergan, 1977). Behavioral consultation is one of the few areas in which practitioners can combine the service role with the applied research role in fulfilling their job responsibilities. Grimes (1981) presents a convincing argument, calling for more applied research by school psychologists. One of the areas that Grimes mentions for possible research activity is in the evaluation of psychological interventions. This is exactly the function of problem evaluation in behavioral consultation—demonstration of accountability and applied research.

Objectives of the PEI

There are four objectives for the PEI. The first objective is to determine whether or not the goals of consultation have been attained. Determination of goal attainment is based upon the objectives of consultation set forth in consultation and the degree to which the child's behavior approximates those objectives. For example, if the goal during problem identification was to have the child solve twenty two-digit addition problems with regrouping in five minutes with 100% accuracy; then problem evaluation would necessarily include an evaluation of the number of problems completed, rate, and accuracy. If the child completed the twenty problems in five minutes with 85% accuracy, then he or she did not attain the goal set forth in problem identification, but has perhaps moved significantly in that direction (depending upon baseline accuracy level).

Goal attainment in consultation can be conceived of in three categories: (1) goal attained, (2) goal partially attained, or (3) no progress toward goal. When the evaluation of a plan falls into one of these categories, different courses of action are suggested in consultation. When goals are attained in consultation, the participants may wish to terminate consultation or work on additional problems that the consultee deems important. If the goal is only partially attained, the consultant will usually return to problem analysis to get more information about behavior-setting conditions that may have been overlooked (antecedent, sequential, and consequent). The plan may have to be modified or changed entirely, depending upon the degree of movement toward behavioral goals. If no progress whatsoever has been made toward behavioral goals, then the consultant must return to problem analysis and maybe to problem identification. There are a number of reasons why no progress is made in consultation. These include faulty problem identification and problem analysis, unrealistic goals, and even deliberate sabotage by the consultee to ensure that the plan will not work (e.g., when the teacher knows that plan failure is the student's ticket our of his or her room to a special education class). Regardless of the reasons for no progress, it is the consultant's task to effect a reasonable solution so that the child can move toward previously established or alternative goals in consultation. This may involve a reanalysis of behavior, behavior setting, and plan, or it may involve modification of teacher beliefs, perceptions, attitudes, and expectancies regarding the child, the plan, or both (something akin to rational emotive consultation).

The second objective of the PEI is to evaluate the effectiveness of the intervention plan. This is more specific than merely evaluation goal attainment in that the consultant uses an evaluation design (typically a single case design) to determine plan effectiveness. Kratochwill (1978) has suggested that school psychologists employ single case research designs that allow for a credible form of evaluating school-based interventions. The following section presents a brief overview of single case or N=1 research designs typically used with school-based interventions. For a more in-depth discussion of these designs, see Barlow and Hersen (1984) and Kratochwill (1978).

Single Case Methodology

Much of the single case methodology has grown out of the research in behavior therapy, developmental psychology, and psychotherapy (Kratochwill, 1978). Single case research methodology has been advocated by many over large group design research (e.g., analysis of variance) because of its relative ease of implementation, its focus upon the individual, and its clarity of interpretation (e.g., detecting daily changes in individuals as a function of baseline and intervention phases). Large group research, particularly in psychotherapy, has been criticized on the grounds that it tends to obscure the effects of intervention for individuals. That is, in most psychotherapy outcome studies, some people get better, some stay the same, and some get worse. When these data are analyzed (using ANOVA procedures), the variance between groups is compared with the variance within groups and significant effects are typically observed (i.e., if the study is to be published). In ANOVA, the variance between groups is maximized (statistically) in relation to the variance within groups. Thus, one has no idea (usually) what the progress of any one individual in particular treatment is since his data are added into the group data and a mean (as well as variance) is computed. Therefore, the mean for the group is actually a mythical average since it usually does not correspond to the performance of any one person within that group (Barlow & Hersen, 1984). Given the many problems, both practical and theoretical, of large group research, the single case methodology is advocated in evaluating the outcomes of behavioral consultation.

An important consideration in any type of research is the notion of internal and external validity (Campbell & Stanley, 1963). Internal validity answers the question, "Was the intervention responsible for the changes in the target behavior?" Without internal validity, proper interpretation of the intervention plan is impossible. Suppose one implements a response cost procedure to decrease disruptive behavior in a high school student. The extent to which one can conclude that the decrease in disruptive behavior (the dependent variable) was due to the response cost procedure (the independent variable) is an indication of the internal validity of the plan. If one started with response cost and after four or five days added a time-out procedure, one could not conclude whether the change in behavior was due to response cost, time-out, or an interaction of the two. For most practical purposes in the schools, it is adequate to demonstrate that the changes in behavior are due to the plan in general. It is usually not necessary to tease out the independent contributions of each procedure (e.g., response cost, time-out, or response cost plus time-out).

External validity answers the questions, "Can I say that the plan will have similar effects on similar children with similar problems? (client generality); "Can I say that other teachers can use the same plan and obtain similar effects?" (therapist generality); "Will my plan be effective in other settings?" Thus, external validity is an indication of the extent to which one can generalize the effects of the plan across children, teachers, and settings. While important, external validity is not nearly as critical in single case research as internal validity.

Many single case research designs have been developed within the past several years. The simplest single case design is known as the *AB Design*. This design involves the collection of baseline data (A) over several points in time. Subsequent to baseline an intervention (B) is implemented and data are collected over several points in time. This allows for a comparison between baseline (A) and intervention (B). The major problem with this design is that it does not control for the possibility that an event occurring at the same time as intervention may have caused the changes in behavior. Thus, the major problem with AB designs is that they possess poor internal validity.

A much more internally valid design is the ABAB or reversal design. In this design, a baseline is established (A1), an intervention is implemented (B1), the intervention is withdrawn (A2), and the intervention is reimplemented (B2). The major advantage of the ABAB design is that it reduces the probability that extraneous events unrelated to the intervention may have produced the observed changes in behavior (i.e., the design is internally valid). The principal disadvantage of this design is that some behaviors are either not easily reversed (e.g., academic skills), or it would be unethical or impractical to reverse them (e.g., aggressive behavior, profanity, etc.).

The multiple baseline design is a design that does not require a reversal phase and is often used in school settings. Multiple baseline designs can be conducted across subjects, across behaviors, or across settings. In a multiple baseline across subjects, baseline data are taken across several children. Next, intervention is implemented for Child 1 while baseline conditions are in effect for Child 2 and Child 3. After a period of time, intervention occurs with Child 2 while data are still being taken about Child 1 (intervention data) and Child 3 (baseline data). Finally, the intervention is implemented for Child 3. Thus, intervention is implemented at three separate points in time while taking continuous data for all children. The degree to which behavior changes as a function of the intervention for each child is an indication that behavior change was produced by the intervention plan (i.e., an indication of internal validity). Multiple baselines may be conducted across behaviors (disruptiveness, aggressiveness, and out-of-seat) or across settings (several different classrooms, school versus home, etc.).

A relatively new design that is ideal for certain consultation problems is the changing criterion design. In this design, baseline data are collected for several days and a baseline average is computed. During intervention (Phase I), a criterion for performance is arbitrarily set. During each successive phase, the criterion for reinforcement is gradually raised (or lowered) until the child is performing at expected levels. Academic problems, such as math or spelling accuracy, are ideal for changing criterion designs. Suppose a child has a baseline average of 20% accuracy on math problems. During the first phase, the consultant might require 30% accuracy each day for the child to obtain reinforcement. If the child does not obtain 30% accuracy for that day, reinforcement is not administered. Succeeding phases require higher levels of accuracy (40%, 50%, 60%, etc.). This can be applied to a number of problems in which the focus is to increase rates or accuracy of academic or social behaviors. This is known as an accelerating changing criterion design.

Changing criterion designs can also be used when the focus of the intervention is to decrease problem behaviors. This is known as a decelerating changing criterion design. For example, this design might be used to decrease the number of disruptive verbal outbursts in class by the entire group. After baseline, the consultant determines that the baseline average of verbal outbursts for the class is fifteen per day. For Phase I of intervention, the consultant might award reinforcement for the class if they exhibit no more than seven verbal outbursts and so on until the frequency of verbal outbursts is zero. Decelerating changing criterion designs are amenable to the evaluation of plans that use DRL (differential reinforcement of low rates) or DRO (differential reinforcement of other behavior).

In summary, the single case design methodology allows school psychologists to evaluate the effects of intervention plans objectively, and makes it possible for them to do practical research in the schools. Most school psychologists will probably opt for the AB design because of its simplicity; however, there must be an awareness and consideration of the threats to internal and external validity with this design. An almost equally simple design that is easily applied to a variety of academic behavior problems for individuals and groups is the changing criterion design. This design is also a much more internally valid design than the AB design and should be applied more frequently by school psychologists because of its applicability to school related problems, particularly academic deficits.

The third objective of the PEI is to discuss strategies and tactics regarding the continuation, modification, or withdrawal of the plan. After the plan has been evaluated, consultees may want to leave the plan in effect, withdraw the plan immediately, or modify the plan to make it more effective or easier to monitor. The consultant's task during the postimplementation planning stage of the PEI is to advise the consultee of the possible effects of altering or withdrawing the plan. For example, if a token reinforcement plan has been in effect and is successful for one week, the consultant would want to discuss with the consultee the possibility of behavior reverting to baseline levels if the plan is suddenly withdrawn. In this case, the consultant would recommend that the original plan stay in effect slightly longer, with a gradual fading from token to social reinforcement. Ultimately, the consultant in this case would operate on a self-monitoring or self-reinforcement system.

Sometimes in problem evaluation, consultees are not satisfied with the effectiveness of the plan and wish to change the plan to make it more so. Plans are often not as effective as anticipated because of poor problem identification, poor problem analysis, or poor plan implementation (i.e., teachers apply the plan incorrectly or inconsistently). If consultees desire plan modification, it is the consultants's task to use plan strategy and plan tactic questions to have the consultee to describe how he or she will modify the plan to make it more successful. In effect, altering the original plan during problem evaluation is like conducting a second problem analysis interview because the consultant and the consultee are redesigning an intervention plan. Thus, in modifying the original plan, the same considerations of problem analysis, such as setting analysis (antecedent, sequential, and consequent), plan design, and recording procedures, are all necessary.

It is important in problem evaluation for the consultant to consider how he or she and the consultee can implement strategies to move children from external control procedures (e.g., token or point systems, time-out, overcorrection, etc.) to less stringent control procedures (e.g., self-monitoring, self-evaluation, and self-reinforcement). This process is known as fading because the consultant fades (gradually removes) the stimuli that are influencing behavior (e.g., tokens to other stimuli) that could influence behavior (e.g., peers, self, etc.). There are two major advantages to fading: (1) it requires less monitoring by the teacher when children are moved from external to self-control procedures, and (2) self-control procedures may assist in generalization across settings, behaviors, and time (Stokes & Baer, 1977).

The final objective of the PEI is to schedule additional interviews if needed or to terminate consultation. If all goals have been achieved, the consultant should formally terminate consultation. Termination should include an invitation to seek further consultation services should the need arise. Extending invitations for further service suggests a willingness on the part of the consultant to provide additional service and often prompts reticent consultees to seek services when needed (Bergan, 1977). Table 12-5 provides an outline for the PEI.

PSYCHOMETRIC CONSIDERATIONS IN
BEHAVIORAL INTERVIEWS

The requirement that behavioral assessment methods be held to the same standards of reliability and validity as more traditional assessment techniques (e.g., tests) has been stressed by many authors operating from the behavioral assessment framework (Cone, 1977, 1978, 1979; Goldfried & Linehan, 1977; Linehan, 1980). In contrast, some authors strongly maintain that traditional concepts of reliability and validity are contradictory to the assumptions and purposes of behavioral assessment (Johnston & Pennypacker, 1980; Nelson, 1983).

Arguments for Reliability and Validity

Cone (1977) has argued that the concepts of reliability and validity used in traditional assessment are applicable to behavioral assessment. The authors have

TABLE 12-5   Outline for the PEI

I. Evaluate Goal Attainment
   A. Questions about outcome "How did things go?"
   B. Questions about goal attainment "Is Charles completing his work now?" "Can we say that the goal of increasing Charles's work completion has been attained now?"

II. Evaluate Plan Effectiveness
   A. Questions regarding internal validity of plan "Would you say that the overcorrection procedure was responsible for reducing John's profane language?"
   B. Evaluate external validity of plan "Do you think this plan would have worked with another student?"

III. Conduct Postimplementation Planning
   A. Questions and Statements Regarding Plan "Perhaps we should continue the DRL program for another week."
   B. Questions and Statements Regarding Plan Modification; "You are saying that you want to discontinue the time-out procedure because it has worked so well."
   C. Questions and Statements Regarding Plan Modification; "How could we change the reinforcement procedure to make our plan more effective?" "Perhaps you could reinforce more frequently."

IV. Arrange for Subsequent Interviews or Terminate Consultation
   A. Questions and Statements Regarding Future Interviews "When can we get together again to discuss Gwen's progress under our new plan?" "We probably need to meet again next week to discuss our new plan."
   B. Statements regarding Termination of Consultation "Since our goals for Bob have been met, this will be the last time we need to meet unless you have further concerns." "If you have further problems, please feel free to call on me."

already pointed out that all behavioral assessment procedures can be ordered along a continuum, ranging from directness to indirectness. Behavioral interviews represent an indirect behavioral assessment method because they rely upon verbal reports or representations of behavior, usually retrospectively reported. It is important that information gathered in interviews be not only reliable (i.e., consistent), but also that it correspond to direct measures of beahvior (i.e., criterion-related validity). The fact that many behavioral assessment methods, such as interviews, are indirect would appear to mandate that data from interviews be validated against more direct measures of behavior (e.g., naturalistic observations). However, this rests upon the questionable assumption that direct behavioral measures are the pure standard or criterion of behavior. The direct measurement of behavior has a rather long history of measurement difficulties such as bias, drift, reactivity, and the like (see Kent & Foster, 1977).

An argument could be made that the central issue in establishing the psychometric quality of behavioral assessment data is one of content validity. Content validity refers to the extent to which the behaviors assessed represent a larger, superordinate behavioral domain or response class of interest. The extent to which behaviors actually assessed represent this behavioral domain reflects the extent to which these behaviors are content valid. Content validity also has implications for reliability in the sense that a behavioral domain cannot be content valid unless the behaviors within that domain consistently measure the domain of interest.

Historically, behavioral assessors saw no need to establish the validity of their data because the criterion behaviors were directly sampled and there was supposedly an assumption that no inferences were to be made beyond the data at hand. Linehan (1980) provides an incisive review of the relevance of content validity for behavioral assessment. Linehan (1980) convincingly argues that behavioral assessors are usually interested in making a number of inferences based upon behaviors observed in a given situation. For example, behavioral assessors sample behavior at given points in time and under certain conditions. Most behavioral assessors would be interested in generalizing these data to other times and to other situations because it is highly unlikely that behavioral assessors would be available on a continuous basis to record behavior. Thus, behavioral assessors are primarily interested in determining how well the conditions under which behavior is actually observed represent all those conditions to which one is interested in generalizing. Other authors have made similar points in comprehensive and technical discussions of behavioral interrelationships (Cone, 1979; Voeltz & Evans, 1982; Wahler, 1975).

Burns (1980) has suggested that, if the assumption in behavioral assessment that a behavioral sample measures nothing beyond itself is true, then there is no theoretical or empirical justification for using indirect behavioral assessment techniques such as interviews, ratings by others, or self-reports. This implies that behavioral assessors must always directly sample behavior in the situation of interest to remain theoretically consistent with a behavioral assessment rationale. Burns (1980) provides a comprehensive review of the literature challenging this assumption and recommends an approach for establishing the reliability and validity of behavioral assessment data called Social Behaviorism Psychometrics.

Social Behaviorism Psychometrics

Social behaviorism (Staats, 1981) and social behaviorism psychometrics (Burns, 1980) represent an approach to assessment that assumes a behavioral sample can measure something beyond itself. Strict behavioral assessment makes the assumption that a sample of a behavior in a given situation measures nothing beyond itself (Johnston & Pennypacker, 1980). Staats (1981) has argued that individuals (at birth) begin to learn "systems" of skills according to principles of learning and conditioning (i.e., cumulative-hierarchical learning). These systems are organized into basic behavioral repertoires (BBRs) that are thought to exert a causative effect upon an individual's behavior. Thus, BBRs are considered to be both an independent (causative) and a dependent (effect) variable in social behaviorism (Burns, 1980).

Staats (1981) has suggested that individuals possess three, somewhat global BBRs. (1) emotional-motivational BBR, (2) language-cognitive BBR, and (3) sensorimotor BBR. These BBRs bear a striking correspondence to the three response channels (physiological-emotional, cognitive-verbal, and overt-motoric) described by Cone (1979). Burns (1980) has indicated several implications the concept of the BBR has for assessment practice. First, the specification of a BBR leads to knowledge of the population of behaviors that constitute the BBR. For example, the behaviors of hitting others, getting out of one's seat, and throwing objects would constitute some portion of the sensorimotor BBR. Second, a specification of a BBR would help to identify the necessary learning conditions to establish a BBR as well as the importance of these learning conditions in facilitating behaviors that serve as prerequisites for the acquisition of additional skills within and across BBRs. Third, the concept of BBR provides information about how the BBR and situational variables (i.e., antecedent, sequential, and consequent conditions) jointly influence the occurrence of behavior. Finally, the assessment of one BBR can provide information regarding behavior in a nonsampled BBR because of the interrelationship between BBRs. Thus, the assumption that a behavioral sample can measure something beyond itself holds true in the context of the BBR concept. Voeltz and Evans (1982) suggest that behavior-behavior relationships create stimulus control situations in which an individual's targeted behavior is not functioning as an operant under direct environmental control, but is exhibited as a part of a variety of systems of behavioral organization (i.e., BBRs).

What are the implications of social behaviorist psychometrics for behavioral assessment, particularly behavioral interviews? First, the concept of the BBR suggests that data obtained in a behavioral interview (cognitive-verbal BBR) with a teacher or parent can provide indirect but useful information concerning children's school or home behaviors (sensorimotor BBR). This suggests that rather initially having to assess target behaviors by direct observation in the classroom or home, one can indirectly assess these behaviors through the language-cognitive

BBR of the interviewee. In a practical sense, this approach would necessarily narrow the range of target behaviors to be directly observed in naturalistic settings. A second implication that social behaviorism has for behavioral assessment is that it can assist in identifying keystone or pivotal behaviors in a response class (or BBR) that are often necessary and sufficient for a group of behaviors to occur together as a cluster or response class (Voeltz & Evans, 1982). Once these keystone behaviors have been identified, one can intervene in these responses and change all behaviors within that response class. Wahler (1975) demonstrated this phenomenon with children's behaviors in both school and home settings. Finally, the concept of the BBR provides for unification of traditional psychometric and behavioral assessment methods (Burns, 1980). The following discussion of Generalizability Theory details how this unification has been discussed for reliability and validity concerns.

There has recently been a rapprochement between behavioral assessment and psychometric concerns using concepts derived from Generalizability Theory (Cronbach, Gleser, Nanda, & Rajaratnam, 1972). Generalizability Theory maintains that the various forms of reliability and validity are simply different ways in which data from a measure can be generalized. In a restricted sense, Generalizability Theory conforms to many assumptions underlying behavioral assessment, particularly as these assumptions relate to the generalization of assessment results to data obtained in different settings, at different times, or by different observers (Gresham, 1984, 1985).

Cone (1977) has identified six universes of generalizability that are of particular interest to behavioral assessors. These are: (1) scorer, (2) item, (3) time, (4) setting, (5) method, and (6) dimension. The major value that Generalizability Theory brings to behavioral assessment is that it allows one to estimate the extent to which scores obtained under one set of conditions (e.g., scorers, times, settings, etc.) correspond (i.e., are generalizable) to scores obtained under other sets of conditions.

For example, data collected by one observer (scorer), at one point in time, in one setting, or by one method would not be generalized to other scorers, times, settings, or methods without empirical justification. Using multiple observers, collecting repeated measurements of behavior over time, assessing in a variety of settings, and using more than one assessment method (e.g., interviews, observations, ratings, etc.) not only conforms to the dictates of good behavioral assessment, but also enhances the likelihood that the data will be generalizable to other situations or conditions (i.e., the data will be reliable and valid).

Arguments Against Reliability and Validity

Several authors maintain that traditional concepts of reliability and validity are theoretically inconsistent with the purposes and assumptions of behavioral assessment (Johnston & Pennypacker, 1980; Nelson, 1983; Nelson, Hay, & Hay, 1977). For example, if behavior is assumed to be modifiable, then test-retest reliability should not be expected (Nelson *et al.*, 1977). If behavior is assumed to be situation specific, then criterion-related validity (concurrent predictive) across other situations should not be expected. If behavior varies across response channels (i.e., cognitive-verbal, overt-motoric, and physiological-emotional), then convergent validity between assessment methods should not be expected.

Nelson (1983) argues that the statistical assumptions upon which reliability and validity are based rest upon structuralism, which presupposes the existence of stable interval entities or traits. Behavioral assessment is based upon functionalism and, as such, requires a different set of procedures and different criteria to evaluate its quality.

Johnston and Pennypacker (1980) make a similar argument in their discussion of how behavioral variability is treated in the traditional psychometric versus the behavioral model. Traditional psychometric theory defines constructs into existence on the basis of variability in groups of subjects. Thus, a subject's score is only meaningful in relation to the distribution of scores of other individuals. This process of defining measured entities relatively rather than absolutely is unique to the social and behavioral sciences and is supposedly antithetical to the assumptions of behavioral assessment (Johnston & Pennypacker, 1980).

Cone (1981) has called for the use of accuracy rather than reliability or validity to evaluate the quality of behavioral assessment data. According to Cone (1981):

> It is important to note that accuracy is not fully equivalent to reliability in either traditional or behavioral uses of the latter term. Accuracy is meant to describe how faithfully a measure represents objective topographic features of a behavior of interest. (p. 59)

As such, accuracy reflects the extent to which a given measure corresponds to some incontrovertible index or standard of actual behavior. For example, if a parent endorses the item on a behavior checklist, "Destroys property," the accuracy of this rating would be established by actual physical evidence of destroyed property (a permanent by-product of behavior). The only remaining problem in establishing the accuracy of this item is to ensure that the target child was the individual responsible for the destroyed property.

It should be clear from this definition and description of accuracy that accurate measures must also be reliable. That is, there can be no correspondene between a measurement of some behavior and actual behavior unless the measurement of behavior is consistent (i.e., yields the same information). In contrast, the reverse is not true in the sense that reliable information may not necessarily be accurate. It is possible for repeated observations of some behavior to consistently (reliably) yield inaccurate information. Kent and Foster (1977) refer to this as observer drift, in which two or more observers drift away from the objective, topographic features of the behavior being observed.

Nelson and Hayes (1981) have called for the use of treatment validity to judge the quality of behavioral assessment data. Treatment validity is established when the data obtained from a behavioral assessment improves or enhances treatment outcome. Treatment validity depends on the extent to which the quality and quantity of assessment procedures contribute to the effectiveness of treatment. This is clearly a functional rather than a structural approach to validation because validity depends upon the degree to which assessment methods allow for a functional analysis of behavior and lead to effective treatment outcomes.

RESOLUTION OF PSYCHOMETRIC AND BEHAVIORAL APPROACHES

There appear to be two positions regarding how best to ensure the quality of behavioral assessment data: psychometric and behavioral. Many see these two positions as a case of "irreconcilable differences" and, as such, the field of behavioral assessment would be better served by a dissolution of the marriage between traditional psychometrics and behavioral methodology. The authors feel, however, a divorce of two approaches would represent the worst case, that of "throwing the baby out with the bath water." It would appear that many antipsychometric types (e.g., Johnston & Pennypacker, 1980; Nelson, 1983; Nelson *et al.*, 1977; Nelson & Hayes, 1981) have overlooked the issue of the purposes of assessment. There are essentially three purposes of assessment: (1) classification, (2) intervention, and (3) evaluation of intervention outcome. Clearly some assessment procedures are better for classification purposes, whereas others are preferred for planning and evaluating interventions.

When the purpose of assessment is to screen individuals and make a classification decision, it is important that the consultant's assessment procedures have the desirable psychometric properties of reliability, validity, and a normative sample against which an individual may be compared. A normative framework allows for the determination of "socially significant" behaviors and the degree to which target behaviors deviate from a normative sample of similar individuals. Kazdin (1977) and Wolf (1978) have referred to this as the social comparison method of social validation in behavioral assessment. Gresham (1986) identified behavior rating scales, behavior role-play measures, and self-report measures as being useful primarily for screening and classification purposes. Obviously, these measures do not provide very useful information from which to design or implement behavioral interventions to change target behaviors.

When the purpose of assessment is to design and implement an intervention, it is critical that the assessment procedures allow for a functional analysis of behavior. Gresham (1986) identified three behavioral assessment procedures that allow for functional analyses: (1) behavioral interviews, (2) direct observations in naturalistic environments, and (3) certain types of self-monitoring. The quality of data collected by these methods rests upon the accuracy of the functional analysis (i.e., identification of controlling variables). If the functional analysis is correct and if an intervention based upon this functional analysis is implemented with integrity, then one can conclude that the assessment data has treatment validity. That is, the assessment data leads to treatment effectiveness.

In summary, the authors feel that the field of behavioral assessment is best served by maintaining both a psychometric and a behavioral approach to ensure the quality of assessment data. One must distinguish between the purposes of assessment before applying the criteria of each approach. The following section reviews the evidence for the psychometric adequacy of behavioral interviews. The authors use traditional psychometric criteria to evaluate behavioral interviews to highlight basic measurement issues and to provide a context from which one might evaluate the treatment validity of behavioral interviews.

Reliability of Behavioral Interviews

Relatively few studies have investigated the reliability of behavioral interviews and have focused primarily upon interrater reliability (Bergan, Byrnes, & Kratochwill, 1979; Bergan & Neuman, 1980; Bergan & Tombari, 1975, 1976; Brown et al., 1982; Curtis & Watson, 1980; Hay et al., 1979; Keane et al., 1982; Perri, Richards, & Schultheis, 1977; Tombari & Bergan, 1978).

Within the behavioral consultation model, interrater reliability has been established for the task of assigning verbalizations to specific units of observation and for the task of coding verbalizations into the broad categories of content, process, and control. Bergan and Tombari (1975) had two raters code randomly selected verbalizations from consultation interviews. The raters achieved 96% agreement in assigning verbalizations to units of observation (i.e., behavior, behavior-setting, observation, specification, summarization, etc.). Interrater reliability has been established for problem identification ($r = .92$), problem analysis ($r = .94$), and problem evaluation ($r = .94$) interviews. Similar findings have been reported by others using the behavioral consultation interview strategy (Bergan et al., 1979; Bergan & Neumann, 1980; Bergan & Tombari, 1976; Brown et al. 1982; Curtis & Watson, 1980; Tombari & Bergan, 1978).

Interrater reliability has also been investigated in the clinical behavior therapy literature. Hay et al. (1979) found that interviewers agreed at fairly high levels with respect to the overall number of problems identified in behavioral interviews, but showed low levels of interobserver agreement with respect to the specific nature of problem areas. It should be noted that the Hay et al. (1979) study investigated the extent to which interviewers agreed concerning the number and nature of problems rather than the extent to which blind raters correctly assigned verbalizations to appropriate categories as in the behavioral consultation literature. The results of the Hay et al. (1979) study are discouraging because the purpose of behavioral assessment is to identify specific problem areas and to define them in operational terms so that they can be measured objectively before, during, and after intervention.

In summary, there is reasonably strong evidence to suggest that raters can agree at relatively high levels when coding behavioral interviews. Interrater reliability can also be conceptualized in terms of Generalizability Theory, in which case it would be termed scorer (or interviewer) generality. There is strong evidence for scorer generality using Bergan's (1977) Consultation Analysis Record, but little research to suggest that one can generalize across interviewers with respect to the specific nature of problems identified in behavioral interviews (Hay *et al.*, 1979).

The authors could find no published studies that have investigated the test-retest or internal consistency reliability of behavioral interviews. In terms of Generalizability Theory, there is no evidence for time or item generality in behavioral interviews. That is, it is not known if the number and nature of problems identified in a behavioral interview can be generalized across time or if the number and nature of problems in a single interview are consistent at different points in the same interview. Investigation of time and item generality in behavioral interviews is critically needed in the literature.

Validity of Behavioral Interviews

Validity can be defined as the agreement between two attempts to measure the same behavior using different methods (Campbell & Fiske, 1959). Historically, behavioral assessors were less concerned with establishing the validity of their assessment techniques because it was felt that behavior observed in naturalistic settings was, by definition, valid in and of itself (Ciminero, Calhoun, & Adams, 1977). More recently, there has been an intensified interest in establishing the validity of behavioral assessment techniques in general (Cone & Hawkins, 1977; Goldfried & Linehan, 1977; Haynes & Wilson, 1979; Linehan, 1980) and behavioral interviews in particular (Haynes & Jensen, 1979; Linehan, 1977; Morganstern, 1976). The validity or generalizability of behavioral interviews can be evaluated according to content (setting generality), criterion-related (method generality), and construct (dimension generality) validity (Gresham, 1984).

Content Validity

Content validity is extremely important in behavioral assessment. The question in content validity is how well the conditions under which a person's behavior is actually observed represent all sets of conditions to which one is interested in generalizing (Livingston, 1977). Cronbach (1971) has specified three requirements for establishing content validity of assessment techniques: (1) an adequate and unambiguous specification or definition of the universe of interest, (2) representative sampling from the universe, and (3) specification of the method of evaluating responses and combining them to form a score.

The content validity of behavioral interviews has received little empirical investigation (Haynes & Jensen, 1979). The exception to this is the work of Bergan and his colleagues using behavioral consultation interviews (Bergan, 1977; Bergan *et al.*, 1979; Bergan & Neumann, 1980; Bergan & Tombari, 1975, 1976; Brown *et al.*, 1982; Curtis & Watson, 1980; Tombari & Bergan, 1978).

The Consultation Analysis Record and its accompanying explanation (see Bergan, 1977; Bergan & Tombari, 1975) clearly define verbalizations in consultation whose purposes are to elicit from the consultee information relating to domains (universes) of behavior, behavior setting, observation, and plan. Based upon the work of Bergan and others using the behavioral consultation model, behavioral interviews appear to be relevant to the purposes of measurement, make a reliable sample the behavioral domains of interest, and yield information that has generally accepted meanings.

Criterion-related Validity

There is some evidence to suggest that behavioral interviews can be used to identify a number of target behaviors. Correlations between data obtained in behavioral interviews and a number of criteria (i.e., observed rates of behavior, expectancies of clients' or consultees' attainment of behavioral goals, etc.) is evidence for the criterion-related validity of behavioral interviews.

Significant correlations have been found between interview data and reported stress (Kleinman, Goldman, Snow, & Karol, 1977), response to treatment for alcoholism (Vogler, Weissback, Compton, & Martin, 1977), parent ratings of children's behavior (Herjanic, Herjanic, Brown, & Wheatt, 1977), and objective measures of fear (Beiman, O'Neal, Wachtel, Fruge, Johnson, & Feurerstein, 1978).

Criterion-related validity has also been established for behavioral consultation interviews (Bergan & Neumann, 1980; Bergan et al., 1979; Bergan & Tombari, 1976; Curtis & Watson, 1980; Tombari & Bergan, 1978). Using a sample of 806 children (Grades K-3) who had been referred for psychological services, Bergan and Tombari (1976) had eleven well-trained behavioral consultants provide services to these clients through their teachers (consultees). Problem behaviors included physical assault, disruption following rules, academic deficits, and social skills deficits. Using a series of multiple regression analyses, Bergan and Tombari found that the single best predictor of plan implementation was problem identification ($R = .776$). That is, over 60% of the variance in plan implementation was accounted for by simply identifying the problem to be solved during a problem identification interview. Moreover, the correlation between plan implementation and problem solution was .977. In other words, implementing a plan for problem behaviors accounted for over 95% of the variance in problem solution. It was also found that the effectiveness of consultants' interviewing behaviors had their greatest impact on the problem-solving process at the problem identification phase. Thus, when a consultant lacked behavioral interviewing skills, there was a high probability the problem solving during consultation would never take place. This study provides evidence for the predictive validity of behavioral consultation interviews.

Are behavioral interviews more predictive of a consultee's ability to define target behaviors and a consultee's expectancies concerning their ability to solve behavior problems than other interview formats? Tombari and Bergan (1978) answered these questions using a sample of sixty teachers who underwent either a behavioral or medical-model consultation interview. Teachers were given either behavioral cues (e.g., "When does this behavior typically occur in your classroom?") or medical-model cues (e.g., "When does _____'s problem typically manifest itself?") during consultation interviews. Using a path analysis, Tombari and Bergan found that cue type exerted a substantial influence on teacher expectancies concerning their ability to solve the problem (rated on a 7-point scale of probable/improbable). Expectancies, in turn, strongly affected teachers' ability to define the problem (written definition of child's problem categorized as behavioral or medical-model). These data suggest that behavioral verbalizations in consultation interviews are strongly predictive of consultee's ability to define problems and lead to more positive expectations concerning their ability to solve problem behaviors. Similar evidence for the criterion-related validity of behavioral consultation interviews has been reported by others (Bergan & Neumann, 1980; Bergan *et al.*, 1979; Curtis & Watson, 1980).

No studies could be found within the behavioral consultation literature that have investigated the relationship between consultee interview reports of behavior frequency, rate, duration, and so on and actual observed rates of behavior in classroom settings. Future research should attempt to establish the criterion-related validity of behavioral consultation interviews using observed behavior rates, teacher rating scales, self-monitored rates of behavior, and independent judges' ratings of interviewer effectiveness as criteria.

Construct Validity

Behavioral interviews also have some evidence for construct validity. In behavioral assessment, constructs are not highly abstract theoretical formulations but rather are tied to observables having clear behavioral referents within appropriate situational contents (Goldfried & Linehan, 1977).

Construct validity of a particular measure may be reflected by its ability to change as a function of a given experimental manipulation (Haynes & Jensen, 1979). Tombari and Bergan (1978) showed that cues delivered in a behavioral interview differentially affected consultees' problem definitions and expectations regarding their ability to solve behavior problems in their classrooms compared to medical model cues. Thus, this experimental manipulation (cue type) led to changes in how consultees defined problem behaviors and their expectations concerning their ability to solve problems. Bergan *et al.* (1979) showed that teachers in behavioral consultation interview conditions were more successful in using appropriate teaching skills than teachers in a medical model interview condition.

The construct validity of an assessment strategy can also be established through a discriminant validity study. Curtis and Watson (1980) found that teachers exposed to behavioral interviews by high skill consultants were better able to define problem behaviors, spent more time in describing behavior, and had a greater proportion of verbalizations based on factual rather than inferential or speculative information than consultees exposed to low skill consultants. Although the sample size was too small for a formal discriminant analysis, these data suggest that consultees' descriptions of target behaviors can be discriminated on the basis of high- versus low-skilled behavioral interviewers.

In summary, there is limited evidence for the content validity of behavioral interviews; most of the research in this area comes from the behavioral consultation camp (see Bergan, 1977). By contrast, a relatively large body of literature suggests that behavioral interviews possess criterion-related validity using somewhat global dependent measures as criteria (e.g., parent ratings of behavior, implementation of behavioral intervention plans, problem definitions, expectancies, etc.). To date, no studies have been conducted that have used naturalistically observed behavior rates, self-monitored rates of behavior, and teacher or peer ratings of behavior in classroom settings as criteria to validate behavioral interviews. Few studies have investigated the construct validity of behavioral interviews, although preliminary evidence suggests that behavioral interviews lead to more effective teaching strategies and more positive expectations concerning teachers' abilities to solve classroom behavior problems (Bergan *et al.*, 1979; Tombari & Bergan, 1978)

CONCLUSIONS

This chapter has provided a rather extensive discussion of the conceptualization and use of behavioral interviews within a behavioral assessment framework. Behavioral interviews have the advantages of flexibility, social validity, treatment validity, and the production of qualitative data not found in other behavioral assessment techniques. Behavioral interviews were classified as an indirect behavioral assessment method because the assessment data are removed in time and place from actual behavioral occurrences. Given the indirectness of behavioral interviews, one must be concerned with the accuracy of behavioral interview data. That is, does information obtained in behavioral interviews correspond to the objective, topographic features of behavior in naturalistic settings?

A classification of behavioral assessment methods based upon the purpose of assessment has been discussed as being perhaps the most useful way of classifying behavioral assessment methods. Using this perspective, any behavioral assessment method that allows for a functional analysis of behavior can be classified as an intervention-related assessment procedure. Behavioral interviews, particularly behavioral consultation interviews (PII, PAI, and PEI), clearly provide for a functional analysis of behavior. This functional analysis potential of behavioral interviews represents the most important aspect of this behavioral assessment procedure.

A crucial skill needed by behavioral interviewers is the control of their verbal behavior. Verbal behaviors emitted by behavioral interviewers must elicit from teachers and parents descriptions of behavior in operational, measurable terms as well as descriptions of the antecedent, sequential, and consequent conditions surrounding the occurrence of behavior. Bergan's (1977) CAR represents a useful means of categorizing units of verbal behavior into content, process, source, and control categories. Behavioral interviewers usually focus upon behavior, behavior setting, observation, and plan content using the verbal processes of specification, validation, and summarization. One of the most important aspects of a "good" behavioral interview is the interviewers control of the topics discussed. Interviewers control the focus and direction of the interview by the use of elicitors: verbalizations that are likely to elicit a verbal response on behalf of the listener. A "good" behavioral interview can be defined as asking questions (elicitors) about the right things (behaviors, behavior setting, observation, and plan) in the right way (specification, validation, and summarization).

This chapter focused upon the use of behavioral consultation interviews in school settings to solve academic and behavioral problems of children and youth. The PII concentrates upon specifying the problem to be solved in behavioral terms and identifying the environmental conditions surrounding problem behaviors. The PAI focuses upon the validation of behavior problems and the identification of plan strategies and plan tactics to be used in interventions. The goal of the PEI is to evaluate the effectiveness of intervention plans, primarily through the use of single case methodology.

An extremely important finding in the behavioral consultation literature has been that behavioral interviews are more predictive of teachers' ability to define target behaviors and lead to higher expectancies regarding their ability to solve behavior problems in their classrooms than traditional interviews. This finding appears to hold true for both social behavior problems (Tombari & Bergan, 1978) and academic problems (Bergan *et al.*, 1979). These findings strongly suggest that behavioral interviews are more likely to set the stage for successful problem solving with teachers and parents than traditional interviews, which focus upon internal personality traits or other nebulous individual characteristics.

This chapter discussed two approaches to establishing the quality of behavioral interview data. Evidence using the psychometric approach suggests that behavioral interviews have reasonably good evidence for interrater reliability (scorer generality), but little evidence for stability or internal consistency (item generality). Behavioral interviews also have some evidence for content, criterion-related, and construct validity; however, much additional research is required before definitive statements can be made regarding the use of behavioral interviews.

Researchers operating from the functional approach to establish the quality of behavioral assessment data argue that the assumptions underlying classical test theory are antithetical to the assumptions underlying behavioral assessment. These authors (e.g., Cone, 1981; Johnston & Pennypacker, 1980) maintain that accuracy should be the major criterion in evaluating behavioral assessment data. In order to be accurate, behavioral interview data would have to correspond to objective, topographic features of actual behavior in naturalistic settings. To date, this has not been established. Nelson and Hayes (1981) further argue that treatment validity should be used to evaluate the quality of behavioral assessment information. Treatment validity is based upon a functional rather than a structural criterion of validation. The authors argued in this chapter that these two seemingly divergent approaches to validation could be resolved by specifying the purposes of assessment. Thus, if the purpose of the behavioral interview is to screen potential clients for subsequent intervention, then the traditional psychometric criteria should be applied. In contrast, if the purpose of the behavioral interview is to conduct a functional analysis of behavior and to design an intervention plan, then the functional criterion should be applied.

Behavioral interviews are a vitally important assessment method in school psychological practice. The flexibility, utility, and quality of data produced by a competently executed behavioral interview is perhaps unrivaled by any other type of behavioral assessment procedure. One way of conceptualizing behavioral interviews within the entire behavioral assessment sequence is that the behavioral interview sets the stage for more fine-tuned, direct assessment such as naturalistic observations and self-monitoring. Behavioral interviews represent the most basic skill of behavioral assessors and in many ways predict the success or failure of an accurate functional analysis of behavior.

References

Achenbach, T. (1982). *Developmental psychopathology* (2d ed.). New York: John Wiley & Sons.

Alessi, G. J., & Kaye, J. H. (1983). *Behavior assessment for school psychologists.* Kent, Ohio: National Association of School Psychologists.

Bales, R. F. (1950). *Interaction process analysis.* Reading, Mass.: Addison-Wesley.

Bandura, A. (1977). Self-efficacy: Toward a unifying theory of behavior change. *Psychological Review,* 89, 191–215.

Bandura, A. (1986). *Social foundations of thought and action.* Englewood Cliffs, N.J.: Prentice-Hall.

Bardon, J. (1968). School psychology and the school psychologist: An approach to an old problem. *American Psychologist,* 73, 287–195.

Barlow, P. H., & Hersen, M. (1984). *Single case experimental designs: Strategies for studying behavior change.* Elmsford, N.Y.: Pergamon Press.

Beiman, J., O'Neal, P., Wachtel, P., Fruge, E., Johnson, S., & Feurerstein, M. (1978). Validation of a self-report behavioral subject selection procedure for analogue fear research. *Behavior Therapy,* 9, 169–177.

Bergan, J. (1977). *Behavioral consultation.* Columbus, Ohio: Charles E. Merrill.

Bergan, J., Brynes, I., & Kratochwill, T. (1979). Effects of behavioral and medical models of consultation on teacher expectancies and instruction of a hypothetical child. *Journal of School Psychology,* 17, 307–316.

Bergan, J., & Neumann, A. (1980). The identification of resources and constraints influencing plan design in consultation. *Journal of School Psychology,* 18, 317–323.

Bergan, J., & Tombari, M. (1975). The analysis of verbal interactions occurring during consultation. *Journal of School Psychology,* 13, 207–226.

Bergan, J., & Tombari, M. (1976). Consultant skill and efficiency and the implementation and outcomes of consultation. *Journal of School Psychology,* 14, 3–13.

Brown, D. K., Kratochwill, T. R., & Bergan, J. R. (1982). Teaching interview skills for problem identification: An analogue study. *Behavioral Assessment,* 4, 63–73.

Burns, G. L. (1980). Indirect measurement and behavioral assessment: A case for social behaviorism psychometrics. *Behavioral Assessment, 2,* 197–206.

Campbell, D. T., & Fiske, D. W. (1959). Convergent and discriminant validation by the multitrait-multimethod matrix. *Psychological Bulletin, 56,* 81–105.

Campbell, D. T., & Stanley, J. C. (1963). *Experimental and quasi-experimental designs for research.* Chicago: Rand McNally.

Ciminero, A., Calhoun, K., & Adams, H. (Eds.). (1977). *Handbook of behavioral assessments.* New York: Wiley Interscience.

Cone, J. D. (1977). The relevance of reliability and validity for behavioral assessment. *Behavior Therapy, 8,* 411–426.

Cone, J. D. (1978). The behavioral assessment grid (BAG): A conceptual framework and a taxonomy. *Behavior Therapy, 9,* 882–888.

Cone, J. D. (1979). Confounded comparisons in triple response mode assessment research. *Behavioral Assessment, 1,* 85–95.

Cone, J. D. (1981). Psychometric considerations. In M. Hersen & A. Bellack (Eds.), *Behavioral assessment: A practical handbook* (2d ed., pp. 38–68). Elmsford, N.Y.: Pergamon Press.

Cone, J. D., & Hawkins, R. P. (Eds.). (1979). *Behavioral assessment: New directions in clinical psychology.* New York: Brunner/Mazel.

Cronbach, L. (1971). Test validation. In R. L. Thorndike (Ed.), *Educational measurement.* Washington, D.C.: American Council on Education.

Cronbach, L., Gleser, G., Nanda, H., & Rajaratnam, N. (1972). *The dependability of behavioral measures.* New York: John Wiley & Sons.

Curran, C. A. (1945). *Personality factors in counseling.* New York: Grune & Stratton.

Curtis, M., & Watson, K. (1980). Changes in consultee clarification skills following consultation. *Journal of School Psychology, 18,* 210–221.

Evans, I. M., & Nelson, R. O. (1977). Assessment of child behavior problems. In A. Ciminero, K. Calhoun, & H. Adams (Eds.). *Handbook of behavioral assessment* (pp. 603–682). New York: Wiley Interscience.

Forman, S., & Forman, B. (1978). A rational-emotive therapy approach to consultation. *Psychology in the Schools, 13,* 400–406.

Goh, D., Telzrow, C., & Fuller, G. (1981). The practice of psychological assessment among school psychologists. *Professional Psychology, 12,* 696–706.

Goldfried, M., & Kent, R. (1972). Traditional versus behavioral personality assessment: A comparison of methodological and theoretical assumptions. *Psychological Bulletin, 77,* 409–422.

Goldfried, M. R., & Linehan, M. M. (1977). Basic issues in behavioral assessment. In A. Ciminero, K. Calhoun, & H. Adams (Eds.), *Handbook of behavioral assessment* (pp. 15–46). New York: Wiley Interscience.

Goldfried, M. R., & Sprafkin, J. N. (1974). *Behavioral personality assessment.* Morristown, N.J.: General Learning Press.

Gresham, F. M. (1982a). A model for the behavioral assessment of behavior disorders in children: Measurement consideration and practical application. *Journal of School Psychology, 20,* 131–143.

Gresham, F. M. (1982b). *Handbook for behavioral consultation.* Des Moines, Iowa: Iowa Department of Public Instruction.

Gresham, F. M. (1984). Behavioral interviews in school psychology: Issues in psychometric adequacy and research. *School Psychology Review, 13,* 17–25.

Gresham, F. M. (1985). Behavior disorder assessment: Conceptual, definitional, and practical considerations. *School Psychology Review, 14,* 495–509.

Gresham, F. M. (1986). Conceptual issues in the assessment of social competence in children. In P. Strain, M. Guralnick, & H. Walker (Eds.), *Children's social behavior: Development, assessment, and modification* (pp. 143–179). New York: Academic Press.

Grimes, J. (1981). Shaping the future of school psychology. *School Psychology Review, 10,* 206–231.

Gross, A. M. (1984). Behavioral interviewing. In T. H. Ollendick & M. Hersen (Eds.), *Child behavior assessment: Principles and procedures* (pp. 61–79). Elmsford, N.Y.: Pergamon Press.

Hay, W., Hay, L., Angle, H., & Nelson, R. (1979). The reliability of problem identification in the behavioral interview. *Behavioral Assessment, 1,* 107–118.

Haynes, S., & Jensen, B. (1979). The interview as a behavioral assessment instrument. *Behavioral Assessment, 1,* 97–106.

Haynes, S. N., & Wilson, C. C. (1979). *Behavioral assessment: Recent advances in methods, concepts, and applications.* San Francisco: Jossey-Bass.

Herjanic, B., Herjanic, M., Brown, G., & Wheatt, T. (1977). Are children reliable reporters? *Journal of Abnormal Child Psychology, 3,* 41–48.

Holland, C. J. (1970). An interview guide for behavioral counseling with parents. *Behavior Therapy, 1,* 70–79.

Hops, H., & Greenwood, C. (1981). Social skills deficits. In E. Mash & L. Terdal (Eds.), *Behavioral assessment of childhood disorders* (pp. 347–396). New York: Guilford Press.

Johnston, J. M., & Pennypacker, H. S. (1980). *Strategies and tactics of human behavioral research.* Hillsdale, N.J.: Lawrence Erlbaum Associates.

Kanfer, F. H., & Grimm, L. G. (1977). Behavior analysis: Selecting target behaviors in the interview. *Behavior Modification, 1,* 7–28.

Kanfer, F. H., & Saslow, G. (1969). Behavioral diagnosis. In C. M. Franks (Ed.), *Behavioral therapy: Appraisal and status.* New York: McGraw-Hill.

Kazdin, A. E. (1977). Assessing the clinical or applied importance of behavior change through social validation. *Behavior Modification, 1,* 427–451.

Kazdin, A. E. (1980). Acceptability of time-out from reinforcement procedures for disruptive child behavior. *Behavior Therapy, 11,* 329–344.

Keane, T., Black, J., Collins, F., & Vinson, M. (1982). A skills training program for teaching the behavioral interview. *Behavioral Assessment, 4,* 53–62.

Kent, R., & Foster, S. (1977). Direct observational procedures: Methodological issues in naturalistic settings. In A. Ciminero, K. Calhoun, & H. Adams (Eds.), *Handbook of behavioral assessment* (pp. 279–328). New York: Wiley Interscience.

Kleinman, K., Goldman, H., Snow, M., & Karol, B. (1977). Relationship between essential hypertension and cognitive functioning II: Effects of biofeedback training generalized to non-laboratory environment. *Psychophysiology, 14,* 192–197.

Kratochwill, T. R. (Ed.). (1978). *Single-subject research: Strategies for evaluating change.* New York: Academic Press.

Kratochwill, T. R. (1982). Advances in behavioral assessment. In C. Reynolds & T. Gutkin (Eds.), *Handbook of school psychology* (pp. 314–350). New York: John Wiley & Sons.

Kratochwill, T. R. (1985). Selection of target behaviors in behavioral consultation. *Behavioral Assessment, 7,* 49–61.

Kratochwill, T. R., & Van Someren, K. (1984). Training behavioral consultants: Issues and directions. *The Behavior Therapist, 7,* 19–22.

Linehan, M. M. (1977). Issues in behavioral interviewing. In J. Cone & R. Hawkins (Eds.), *Behavioral assessment: New directions in clinical psychology.* New York: Brunner/Mazel.

Linehan, M. M. (1980). Content validity: Its relevance to behavioral assessment. *Behavioral Assessment, 2,* 147–159.

Livingston, S. A. (1977). Psychometric techniques for criterion-referenced testing and behavioral assessment. In J. Cone & R. Hawkins (Eds.), *Behavioral Assessment: New directions in clinical psychology* (pp. 308–324). New York: Brunner/Mazel.

Mash, E. J., & Terdal, L. G. (Eds.). (1981). *Behavioral assessment of childhood disorders.* New York: Guilford Press.

Morganstern, K. P. (1976). Behavioral interviewing: The initial stages of assessment. In M. Hersen & A. Bellack (Eds.), *Behavioral assessment: A practical handbook.* Elmsford, N.Y.: Pergamon Press.

Nelson, R. O. (1983). Behavioral assessment: Past, present, and future. *Behavioral Assessment, 5,* 195–206.

Nelson, R. O., Hay, L. R., & Hay, W. M. (1977). Comments on Cone's "The relevance of reliability and validity for behavioral assessment." *Behavior Therapy, 8,* 427–420.

Nelson, R. O., & Hayes, S. (1979). Some current dimensions of behavioral assessment. *Behavioral Assessment, 1,* 1–16.

Nelson, R. O, & Hayes, S. C. (1981). Nature of behavioral assessment. In M. Hersen & A. Bellack (Eds.), *Behavioral assessment: A practical handbook* (2d ed., pp. 3–37). Elmsford, N.Y.: Pergamon Press.

Perri, M., Richards, C., & Schultheis, K. (1977). Behavioral self-control and smoking reduction: A study of self-initiated attempts to reduce smoking. *Behavior Therapy, 8,* 360–365.

Prout, H. T. (1983). School psychologists and social-emotional assessment techniques: Patterns in training and use. *School Psychology Review, 12,* 377–383.

Skinner, B. F. (1957). *Verbal behavior.* New York: Appleton-Century-Crofts.

Staats, A. W. (1981). Paradigmatic behaviorism, unifed theory construction methods, and the zeitgeist of separatism. *American Psychologist, 36,* 239–256.

Stokes, T., & Baer, D. (1977). An implicit technology of generalization. *Journal of Applied Behavior Analysis, 10,* 349–367.

Synder, W. U. (1945). An investigation of the nature of non-directive psychotherapy. *Journal of Genetic Psychology, 33,* 193–223.

Tindall, R. H. (1979). School psychology: An overview. In G. Phye & D. Reschly (Eds.), *School psychology: Perspectives and issues* (pp. 3–24). New York: Academic Press.

Tombari, M., & Bergan, J. (1978). Consultant cues and teacher verbalizations, judgments, and expectancies concerning children's adjustment problems. *Journal of School Psychology, 16,* 212–219.

Tombari, M., & Davis, R. (1979). Behavioral consultation. In G. Phye & D. Reschly (Eds.), *School psychology: Perspectives and Issues* (pp. 281–303). New York: Academic Press.

Voeltz, L. M., & Evans, I. M. (1982). The assessment of behavioral interrelationships in child behavior therapy. *Behavior Assessment, 4,* 131–165.

Vogler, R., Weissback, T., Compton, J., & Martin, G. (1977). Integrated behavior change techniques for problem drinkers in the community. *Journal of Consulting and Clinical Psychology, 45,* 267–279.

Wahler, R. G. (1975). Some structural aspects of deviant child behavior. *Journal of Applied Behavior Analysis, 8,* 27–42.

Witt, J. C., & Elliott, S. N. (1985). Acceptability of classroom intervention strategies. In T. R. Kratochwill (Ed.), *Advances in school psychology* (Vol. 4, pp. 251–280). Hillsdale, N.J.: Lawrence Erlbaum Associates.

Witt, J. C., Elliott, S. N., & Martens, B. K. (1984). Acceptability of interventions used in classrooms: The influence of teacher time, severity of behavior problem, and type of intervention. *Behavioral Disorders, 10,* 95–104.

Wolf, M. M. (1978). Social validity: The case for subjective measurement or how applied behavior analysis is finding its heart. *Journal of Applied Behavior Analysis, 11,* 203–214.

CHAPTER 13

Special Education Classification and Its Relationship to DSM-III

ESTHER SINCLAIR
STEVEN FORNESS
University of California, Los Angeles

INTRODUCTION

During the past ten years, the field of special education has undergone a great deal of change. Since the passage of Public Law 94-142 in 1975 (Federal Register, 1977), or the "Education for the Handicapped Act," much discussion has centered on the adequacy of the procedures outlined in the federal mandate for determining eligibility for special education programs (Becker, 1978; Johnson, 1981; Keogh & Margolis, 1976; Mattis, 1978).

Public Law 94-142 did not provide clear and concise guidelines or procedures for the classification of children into certain special education categories. Many states attempted to fill this gap by supplying guidelines themselves. This trend is most notable in the special education eligibility category of Serious Emotional Disturbance in which some states, such as California and Texas, are considering mandating the inclusion of certain psychiatric diagnoses as necessary requisites for determining eligibility for special education programs for the emotionally disturbed or behavior disordered (Smith, Wood, & Grimes, 1985).

As a parallel to what has been happening in special education, the field of psychiatry has also undergone many changes that center on determining adequate criteria for making psychiatric diagnoses. The development of the *Diagnostic and Statistical Manual* (Third Edition) or DSM-III as it is commonly known (American Psychiatric Association, 1980), occurred at approximately the same time as the passage of P.L. 94-142. DSM-III has currently been revised into DSM-III-R and is expected to be in use by mental health practitioners by late 1987.

494

This chapter on classification systems in special education and child psychiatry delineates a brief history of classification in the major categories in special education of learning disabilities, mental retardation, and serious emotional disturbance or behavior disorders. The historical review focuses on the inherent problems within each classification category. A discussion of psychiatric classification of childhood disorders demonstrated by DSM-III and proposed changes for DSM-III-R follows.

Research concerning the relationship between DSM-III and special education is presented with special emphasis on the interface between DSM-III and the special education category of serious emotional disturbance or behavior disorders. Despite the fact that many researchers in education advocate the use of DSM-III in diagnosing seriously emotionally disturbed children, previous research has not provided a substantive, supportive case for the concomitant use of the two classification systems (psychiatric and educational), other than to satisfy the P.L. 94-142 mandate of an interdisciplinary evaluation based on more than one criterion. Although validity taken at face value suggests that psychiatric diagnosis adds information to the clinical picture, perhaps the added information is not educationally relevant and muddles the issue of selection of appropriate educational interventions. This chapter ends with a discussion of the role of psychiatric classification in educational prescription and interventions as a separate issue from educational classification and diagnosis.

HISTORY OF CLASSIFICATION IN SPECIAL EDUCATION

Learning Disabilities

The field of learning disabilities can be historically grounded in Kirk's (1962) concept of discrepancy. He elaborated on this concept to include inter- and intraindividual measures of difference whereby interindividual measures differentiated the exceptional from the normal child along mental, physical, and social dimensions. Intraindividual measures of difference indicated the degree to which a particular child demonstrated differences in various areas of development and was represented by discrepancies in growth patterns along the same dimensions cited above.

These differences were further refined to describe exceptional groups of children with disorders in the development of language, speech, reading, and associated communication skills needed for social interaction. The educational outcome for exhibiting such inter- or intraindividual differences was the requirement of a modification of school practices in order to help the child develop to his maximum capacity.

In 1968, Kirk headed the National Advisory Committee on Handicapped Children of the United States Office of Education and presented a definition of specific learning disabilities (NACHC, 1968). This definition, which became part of Public Law 91-320 or the Learning Disabilities Act of 1969 (USOE, 1968), did not bring unification to the learning disability field. However, the most important accomplishment of the NACHC definition was the establishment of the learning disability field as a formalized category of special education. This was accomplished by providing a framework for the establishment of educational programs in the field of learning disabilities.

NACHC failed to provide a clear delineation of learning disability parameters that were functional for the purposes of educational classification as well as educational intervention. At the time, Cruickshank (1972) noted that the NACHC definition was but one of more than forty definitions that were being used as descriptors of learning disabled children.

Mercer, Forgnone, and Wolking (1976) conducted a survey and determined that 57.1% of the states were using all or part of the NACHC definition. Thus, P.L. 94-142 can be viewed, in retrospect, as a request on the part of the various states to the U.S. Office of Education to define learning disabilities more precisely. Because of the many theories circulating about the etiology of learning disabilities at the time, and because of the lack of empirical data, this was not done (Mercer, Hughes, & Mercer, 1985). For example, in November, 1976, regulations were proposed that focused on determining a discrepancy between ability and achievement by using a specific formula (USOE, 1976). However, much negative reaction to this proposal caused the formula idea to be dismissed.

The regulations for defining and identifying learning disabilities under P.L. 94-142 became part of the 1977 Federal Register. As the following definition demonstrates, the 1977 definition did not accomplish the task of defining learning disabilities more precisely than the NACHC concept of "discrepancy."

> Specific learning disability means a disorder in one or more of the basic psychological processes involved in understanding or in using language, spoken or written, which may manifest itself in an imperfect ability to listen, think, speak, read, write, spell, or to do mathematical calculations. The term includes such conditions as perceptual handicaps, brain injury, minimal brain dysfunction, dyslexia, and developmental aphasia. The term does not include children who have learning problems which are primarily the result of visual, hearing or motor handicaps, or mental retardation, or emotional disturbance, or of environmental, cultural, or economic disadvantage. (USOE, 1977, p. 65083)

Criticisms of the P.L. 94-142 definition included the argument that no level of severity was specified (McIntosh & Dunn, 1973). Bateman's (1965) discrepancy idea was not incorporated and the wording of "one or more areas" was at variance with the wording "specific." A learning disability syndrome was not established, associated conditions were not specified and, while the definition was thought of as an exclusionary one, children with other handicapping conditions could conceivably also have a special learning disability. The lack of specificity was further criticized by Hammill (1974). Myers and Hammill (1976) pointed out that when the vague terminology was removed from the definition, the definition was grossly inadequate and overly simplistic.

Dissatisfaction with the 1977 Federal Register definition was a contributing factor to the formation of the National Joint Committee of Learning Disabilities (NJCLD), which consisted of representatives from six professional organizations. Yet, the goal of the NJCLD was merely to provide a theoretical framework for the learning disabilities field rather than to specify operational criteria for the identification of individual children that were lacking in the 1977 definition. The NJCLD definition, presented in 1981, states that:

> learning disabilities is a generic term that refers to a heterogeneous group of disorders manifested by significant difficulties in the acquisition and use of listening, speaking, reading, writing, reasoning, or mathematical abilities. These disorders are intrinsic to the individual and presumed to be due to Central Nervous System dysfunction. Even though a learning disability may occur concomitantly with other handicapping conditions (e.g., sensory impairment, mental retardation, social and emotional disturbance or environmental influences (e.g., cultural differences, insufficient/inappropriate instruction, psychogenic factors), it is not the direct result of these conditions or influences. (Hammill, Leigh, McNutt, & Larsen, 1981, p. 836)

As a result, the NJCLD definition has had limited impact on state definitions. Current trends are moving in the direction of solving the problem psychometrically through the use of mathematical formulas to establish ability, expectation, and discrepancy levels (Berk, 1982; Cone & Wilson, 1982; Danielson & Bauer, 1978; Forness, Sinclair, & Guthrie, 1983; Sinclair & Alexson, 1986) and through the use of learning disability subtypes that are not only severity indexes but include measures of adaptive behavior as well (McKinney & Feagans, 1983; Strawser & Weller, 1985).

Ysseldyke and his associates at the University of Minnesota have been responsible for a large body of research in the area of learning disabilities. In a 1983 paper, they summarized their research to date and essentially concluded that they could not describe the salient characteristics of a learning disabled child after five years of work in the area (Ysseldyke, Algozzine, & Epps, 1983). They listed fourteen generalizations concerning the field of learning disorders which they felt were problematic to both educators and researchers. The critical points of their generalizations are presented below.

School placement teams make inconsistent decisions that often have little to do with the actual data collection of an individual student. There does not seem to be a defensible assessment system for determining the existence of a learning disorder. Many nonhandicapped students are declared eligible for special education services despite normal test scores and there are no reliable psychometric differences between learning disabled students and nonlearning disabled, low achieving students. They concluded that the most important decision in the assessment of any student for special education eligibility was the regular teacher's reason for referral.

The Minnesota group further stated that there are no technically adequate tests to measure the psychological processes that are presumed to underlie learning disorders. They suggested that curriculum-based measures would be a good alternative to process testing. These measures could be administered frequently by classroom teachers to evaluate the learning disabled student's response to instructional programming. Such an assessment system would aid in the implementation of classroom-based interventions and would allow for more money to be spent on teaching and instruction rather than on testing and labeling.

Thus, twenty years after Kirk's address, the field of learning disabilities has come a long way but not necessarily in the direction of a more parsimonious explanation of definitional criteria. A final suggestion was that a possible solution to the problem of definition might be found in examining these same issues in another syndrome with at least some similarity to learning disabilities.

Mental Retardation

The field of mental retardation, as it relates to special education, has had a very different history than the field of learning disabilities in terms of classification issues and criteria for eligibility for services. Mental retardation has been defined, for educational purposes, largely by a multietiological model that draws from medical, physiological, sociological, and psychometric perspectives, using nomenclature from medicine.

The official definition of Mental Retardation published by the American Association of Mental Deficiency (AAMD) has changed five times in the past twenty-five years (MacMillan, 1982). The current AAMD definition (Grossman, 1983) is as follows: "Mental retardation refers to significant subaverage general intellectual functioning resulting in or associated with impairments in adaptive behavior and manifested during the developmental period" (p. 127).

The key elements in the AAMD definition are low general intellectual functioning, problems in adaptation, and chronological age. The previous four revisions of the AAMD definition have involved change in the IQ level used to define eligibility for services, as well as the inclusion of a borderline category. Changing the IQ cutoff to 70 brought the new AAMD definitions into conformity with the laws of many states and with the international practices advocated by the World Health Organization. Previous AAMD definitions used minus one or minus two standard deviations as the criterion for the setting of the upper IQ limit. This system implied that a precise score existed below which all children were retarded and above which no child was retarded.

The most recent AAMD definition stresses the point that children should be classified according to need and not according to IQ. Chronicity and prevailing scientific models are not included in the definition. Etiological, physiological, or psychological correlates are not specified. This is perhaps partly because mental retardation is defined by certain exclusionary features.

More than forty years ago, Doll (1941) suggested that a definition of mental retardation should include six criteria covering the areas of social incompetence, mental incompetence, deficiency of development, constitutional origin, duration to adulthood, and essential incurability. Subject to controversy was his concept of mental retardation as an unchangeable condition.

The 1983 AAMD definition differs from Doll's in two ways. First, the AAMD definition makes no reference to the prognosis of the individual's future status. Second, there is no attempt to differentiate mental retardation from other disorders of childhood often associated with impaired intellectual performance such as autism or brain damage.

The P.L. 94-142 definition of mental retardation for inclusion into programs for the mentally retarded is very similar to the AAMD definition but stresses that low intellectual function must be accompanied by low measures on adaptive behavior. The federal definition states that: "mental retardation means significantly subaverage general intellectual functioning existing concurrently with deficits in adaptive behavior and manifested during the developmental period, which adversely affects the 'child's educational performance.'"

There has been much criticism of the psychometric definition of mental retardation as a given child's score on an intelligence test that undoubtedly reflects many nonintellectual factors such as measurement error, emotional factors, and motivational factors as well as the intellectual factors that the test purports to measure. Furthermore, any given IQ cutoff cannot truly discriminate between a retarded and a nonretarded individual unless the test's reliability is adequate. A further criticism of a psychometric definition of mental retardation is that it ignores the relativity of mental retardation in different environments. For example, a child with an IQ of 70 in a class where the mean IQ is 85 may not appear deviant; however, in a class with a mean IQ of 115, this child would probably be unable to compete academically.

Controversy also revolves around adequate description and measurement of adaptive behavior. Rutter (1970) points out that adaptive behavior is a most difficult characteristic to measure psychometrically because societal expectations change as a child gets older. Along the same vein as the classification of behavior that is deviant from the general population is the difficulty of finding a sociological definition of mental retardation. Normal behavior is appropriate performance according to role expectations. Mental retardation is an achieved social status in a particular social system.

As the medical, psychometric, and sociocultural parameters related to the classification of mentally retarded children in the schools have enlarged, the past two decades have been characterized by a large body of research (see Hewett & Forness, 1984; MacMillan, 1982; Mercer & Snell, 1977 for reviews), that questions the basic concept of the mentally retarded student. Before the 1960 President's Commission of Mental Retardation, there existed a rather traditional tendency to think of mental retardation as a lack of intelligent behavior and to ascribe less intelligent behavior to a lack of intelligence. As a result of work in such areas as discrimination learning, metamemory, social motivation, labeling, and behavior modification, intelligence is no longer seen as an all-encompassing, general commodity but appears to depend on a host of motivational and situational variables. These variables greatly determine whether or not a teacher elicits "intelligent" behavior from a so-called retarded child or, for that matter, from any child with learning or behavior problems.

The label of mental retardation is too general for the educational purpose of classification for special education needs. In order to create within the mentally retarded population groups of individuals who need similar treatment, one must further subclassify mental retardation into the special education categories of educable mentally retarded (IQ 50 to 70 or 75), trainable mentally retarded (IQ 30 to 50), and severely and profoundly mentally retarded (IQ below 30).

Serious Emotional Disturbance

The field of emotional disturbance and behavior disorders constitutes the special education category of serious emotional disturbance. Of the three special education fields presented, the emotional disturbance and behavior disorders category is in the greatest state of flux concerning issues of classification (Cullinan, Epstein, & Lloyd, 1981; Slenkovich, 1983; Wood, 1985; Zabel, Peterson, Smith, & White, 1981).

Public Law 94-142 incorporated Bower's (1960) definition of emotional disturbance. At present, the legal mandate for serving emotionally disturbed and behavior disordered children is unclear. Some of the lack of clarity is a result of ambiguity in the Law that suggests that, within the group of seriously emotionally disturbed children, there is a group who are socially maladjusted but not emotionally disturbed, and who are not eligible for special education. The federal definition states that:

> the term "seriously emotionally disturbed" means a condition exhibiting one or more of the following characteristics over a long period of time and to a marked degree, which adversely affects educational performance: (A) An inability to learn which cannot be explained by intellectual, sensory, or health factors; (B) An inability to build or maintain satisfactory interpersonal relationships with peers and teachers; (C) Inappropriate types of behavior or feelings under normal circumstances; (D) A general pervasive mood of unhappiness or depression; or (E) A tendency to develop physical symptoms or fears associated with personal or school problems. The term does not include children who are socially maladjusted, unless it is determined that they are seriously emotionally disturbed. (USOE, 1981, p. 3866)

That the terminology continues to be the subject of debate is evidenced by the position paper on definitional issues published by the Council for Children with Behavior Disorders (CCBD) subcommittee on terminology (Huntze, 1985). The official position of CCBD is that the term behaviorally disordered is more descriptive and useful to educators in identifying and planning appropriate placements and services for children who are handicapped by their behavior than is the term serious emotional disturbance. As the validation for this choice, they point out that the term behavior disorders is not associated exclusively with any particular theory of causation and, therefore, with any particular set of intervention techniques and, thus, might not have an exclusionary result to its use. The term is also less stigmatizing than the term serious emotional disturbance.

Historically, the classification of seriously emotionally disturbed children for special education programs has been heavily influenced by clinical diagnostic systems commonly used in medical settings (Forness & Cantwell, 1982). The most widely used clinical diagnostic system in education is DSM-III. However, for educational purposes, it seems that this system is heavily subjective (McGinnis, Kiraly, & Smith, 1985; Sinclair, Forness & Alexson, 1985).

Public Law 94-142 requires the use of multiple sources of data to determine if a student is handicapped. In terms of the evaluation of social and emotional functioning, it is clear that school personnel are having increasing contact with psychiatrists and other mental health professionals, both in face-to-face contact at individual education program (IEP) meetings, and in medical and psychiatric reports relevant to a handicapped child's schooling. Although school personnel are not likely to be engaged in making psychiatric diagnoses themselves, they may often use psychiatric diagnoses in determining eligibility for special education programs and in making a recommendation for psychiatric services (cf. Schools Should Provide Mental Health Services, 1980).

PSYCHIATRIC CLASSIFICATION SCHEMES

There is no universal consensus regarding the best way to classify psychiatric disorders of childhood (Adams, Doster, & Calhoun, 1977; Cantwell, Mattison, Russell, & Will, 1979; Garber, 1984; Quay, 1979; Spitzer, Forman, & Nee, 1979). Aside from the secondary, ancillary benefits from the use of any particular psychiatric classification system such as communication among professionals, development of scientific theory and investigation, and statistical data collection, any official psychiatric classification system must be practical and demonstrate clinical utility. Practicality and clinical utility are demonstrated by the degree to which the system is easily used in everyday practice. Ease of usage depends on the simplicity of the classification model and the extent to which the language used in the classifications are readily understood by mental health professionals, regardless of their theoretical orientation.

Classification systems of psychiatric disorders, such as the one suggested by Achenbach and Edelbrock (1983), have generally been empirically derived categorical systems whereby clinical criteria are designated for inclusion into particular diagnostic categories. Achenbach and Edelbrock (1983) employ the Child Behavior Checklist (CBCL) in determining diagnostic categories. The CBCL utilizes a 118-item checklist in a standardized format to obtain parents' and teachers' descriptions of children's behavior. The checklists have been factor-analyzed, for three age groupings and both sexes, separately for parent and teacher data. These analyses yield eight narrow band behavior problem scales. The scales are aggressive, nervous-overactive, inattentive, unpopular, self-destructive, obsessive-compulsive, anxious, and social withdrawal. Two second order factors, internalizing and externalizing, have been obtained consistently; and this reflects a distinction between fearful, inhibited, overcontrolled behavior, and aggressive, antisocial, undercontrolled behavior (see chapter 10, this volume, for a more detailed description of this measure).

DSM-III

As previously stated, DSM-III became the official psychiatric nomenclature in the United States in January of 1980. Before that, DSM-II (American Psychiatric Association, 1968), and before that, DSM-I (American Psychiatric Association, 1952), were the official systems. DSM-I offered little in the way of classification of psychiatric disorders of childhood. DSM-II contained six separate subtypes in the category of behavior disorders of childhood and adolescence. However, it was not until DSM-III that a more comprehensive classification of childhood psychopathology was provided. In the United States, the various DSMs have been used as an alternative to the mental disorders sections of the International Classification of Diseases (ICD). Clinicians and researchers in the United States felt that the ICD mental disorders sections were not adequate for their clinical and research needs (Engels, Ghadirian, & Dongier, 1983).

DSM-III differentiates the psychiatric disorders of infancy, childhood, and adolescence on the basis of the presenting essential clinical features. The system is phenomenological in that it is based on the accumulation of as much factual information as possible regarding the individual. The system is not based on etiology or a particular theoretical background. For example, a clinician with a psychoanalytical orientation would have a different view concerning the etiology of an obsessive-compulsive behavior than would a clinician with a behavioral orientation. However, adequate phenomenological classification of clinical features should allow both clinicians to agree on the presence of the obsessive-compulsive behavior even if they disagree on what etiological factors led to the behavior.

DSM-III requires that each case be assessed on five separate axes related to different types of clinical information. This multiaxial diagnosis is one of the most innovative aspects of DSM-III and a complete diagnosis requires codings on all five of the axes. The first three axes constitute the so-called official diagnosis. Axes IV and V are optional for clinicians and researchers.

On Axis I are coded all clinical psychiatric syndromes other than developmental and personality disorders. More than one syndrome may be listed and each is preceded by a five-digit number designating the code for that particular diagnosis. For instance, "312.00 Conduct Disorder, would be listed on Axis I. However, a developmental reading disorder that is strongly associated with conduct disorder in childhood might be overlooked if the clinician were not forced to look at Axis II for the presence of a developmental disorder.

An Axis II diagnosis may be designated as the principal diagnosis. In some cases, there may be no Axis I diagnosis. On either Axis I or Axis II, a diagnosis may be coded for level of diagnostic certainty, with codes for a deferred, unspecified, or atypical diagnosis. It should be noted that atypical diagnoses are used only after it has been established that the disorder cannot be classified as one of the specific subtypes of a particular syndrome.

Axis III provides the clinician with the opportunity to code any current physical disorders or conditions that are relevant to the genesis or management of the child's psychiatric problem. Essentially, any condition from the nonmental disorders sections of the ICD (ninth edition) may be coded on Axis III. For example, the management of a child with hemophilia or diabetes may be complicated by the child's tendency to manipulate parents or teachers by threatening to act in ways that may jeopardize his or her own health.

Axis IV and V are available for special clinical or research settings in which more specificity may be useful. Axis IV provides the opportunity to rate the severity of any psychosocial stressors that may be contributing to the Axis I or Axis II disorder. For example, a child who experiences a disorder after a severe stressor such as the death of a parent may have a better prognosis than might a child with the same disorder that has developed in a more favorable environment. Severity is based on the clinician's assessment of how an average person (not a particular child), with similar sociocultural values, might respond under similar circumstances. Such severity is rated on a scale of 1 to 6, no stressor to catastrophic stressor.

Axis V enables the clinician to code the highest level of adaptive functioning that the child has experienced in the past year for at least a few months. This permits the clinician to specify the baseline behavior to which the child might be expected to return upon termination of his or her current psychiatric problems. The rating of adaptive functioning is made in the three areas of social relations, functioning in a school setting, and in the use of leisure time. As with Axis IV, a specific rating scale, ranging from minimal to grossly impaired is provided.

An example of how a DSM-III-R multiaxial diagnosis might appear on a psychiatric report or medical record is given in Table 13-1.

This might represent the profile of a ten-year-old girl who is asthmatic and has had reading difficulties and some problems with hyperactive behavior since the beginning of first grade, but whose school behavior noticeably worsened a few months after her parents were divorced.

In terms of face validity, descriptive validity, and predictive validity, DSM-III is decidedly lacking (Achenbach, 1982). Interrater reliability studies have shown that experienced clinicians from different theoretical orientations and settings can agree on the presence or absence of a particular disorder or syndrome (Strober, Green, & Carlson, 1981). Thus, face validity has been established for all diagnostic classifications. Some of the disorders, such as the eating disorders and the stereo-

TABLE 13-1   DSM-III-R Multiaxial Diagnosis

Axis I:	314.01 Attention-deficit hyperactivity disorders
	296.23 Major depression single episode
Axis II:	315.00 Developmental reading disorder
Axis III:	Asthma
Axis IV:	Psychosocial stressor—divorce of parents
	Severity: 4: Severe
Axis V:	Current Global Assessment of Functioning (GAF): 51;
	Highest GAF Past Year: 64

typic movement disorders, have established descriptive validity as well. That is, these disorders have clinical features that are not commonly seen in children with other types of mental disorders or in children with no mental disorders. DSM-III has not established predictive validity whereby the differentiation of various disorders with essential clinical features would lead to predictions of differences in other areas such as natural history, biological correlates, family pattern of psychiatric illness, and response to various types of therapeutic intervention.

The establishment of descriptive and predictive validity should be a priority in the revision of DSM-III. The rationale for the inclusion of certain psychiatric disorders of children in a classification of mental disorders should be questioned if these types of validity cannot be established.

Although DSM-III has been more specific regarding the psychiatric disorders of childhood than DSM-II (Mattison *et al.*, 1979), there have been numerous criticisms (Rutter & Shaffer, 1980). The criticisms have been the impetus behind the development of DSM-III-R, which will probably be in use by 1988. For instance, studies with adult patients indicate that 25% of all psychiatrically ill adults receive a diagnosis of undiagnosed mental disorder (Williams, 1985). Although few studies have been done with children, it is likely that, as one moves down the age scale from adolescence to childhood to infancy, more children will present behavioral syndromes that do not fit into distinct classification categories because children demonstrate a more limited repertoire of behaviors than do adults.

Another limitation of DSM-III as it relates to childhood disorders is that clinicians recognize that the same behavioral symptom may have different implications depending on the age of the child. For example, school refusal in a preschool or primary school child is generally due to a separation anxiety disorder. School refusal occurring for the first time in an adolescent is usually an example of a very different clinical presentation such as a major depressive disorder. Mental health practitioners need to maintain the perspective of what is normal behavior at various developmental stages. Therefore, a more comprehensive psychiatric classification system for children should include guidelines for categorization of psychiatric disorders within a developmental framework.

For example, Harris and Ferrari (1983) focused on phobias and attentional problems in terms of what is normal about fearfulness, anxiety, and attending behaviors, and what is not. Attention is affected by age and usually improves with it. Therefore, developmental maturity would affect the normative data on what are normal deviations of attention in childhood.

Although DSM-III outlines specific diagnostic criteria for each of the psychiatric disorders, it does not describe these diagnostic criteria operationally (Spitzer & Cantwell, 1980). The criteria are specific in that DSM-III lists what criteria must be present for a particular diagnosis to be made. However, the criteria are not operational since DSM-III does not list what operations must be followed in order to make a specific diagnosis. The inclusion of specific diagnostic criteria is an improvement over the previous DSMs, which merely provided general descriptions of psychiatric disorders and did not provide specific diagnostic criteria for making diagnoses.

Each psychiatric disorder is described in terms of its essential features, associated features, age of onset, course, impairment, complications, predisposing factors, prevalence, sex ratio, familial pattern, and differential diagnosis. For some disorders, a substantial amount of information is available under each heading. For other disorders, such as the avoidant disorder, which was created for the first time in DSM-III, there may be only a brief statement under each heading that constitutes the sum total of available knowledge regarding that particular disorder.

If DSM-III were a perfect classification system, then adequate differentiation between the disorders would be possible and it would be unnecessary to make any arbitrary decisions since all children would present problems that readily fit into a specific diagnostic category.

A most interesting critique of DSM-III is that there is no definition of what constitutes a mental disorder anywhere in the manual (Kendall, 1984). The previous DSMs were also remiss in this area and provided no definition of mental disorder. A classification of mental disorders should contain an overall definition of mental disorder. Yet, this was not done because no generally accepted satisfactory definition of mental disorder could be formulated. It would seem that an adequate definition of mental disorder should be a priority in later editions.

DSM-III-R

The following is a description of the latest revision, DSM-III-R (American Psychiatric Association, 1987), which just became available at the time of writing this chapter. The authors will address the proposed changes that relate to classification of childhood disorders.

In regard to the multiaxial system of classification, a lack of conceptual basis for the distinction between Axis I and Axis II in DSM-III has been noted (Mezzich, 1980; Rutter, Shaffer, & Shepherd, 1973; Williams, 1985a, 1985b; Williams & Spitzer, 1982). Field studies by Cantwell *et al.* (1979) supported the idea that mental retardation is more reliably and appropriately diagnosed when it is on a separate axis. However, this was not done in DSM-III, perhaps to limit the number of axes. DSM-III-R, while it does not propose to create a separate axis for mental retardation, adds to Axis II mental retardation, specific developmental disorders and pervasive developmental disorders, under the rubric of developmental disorders.

As previously stated, Axis IV has been criticized for not indicating the type of stressor or how it applies to the individual child. DSM-III-R addresses one of these issues by making the distinction between acute events and enduring circumstances by recommending that clinicians note the stressor(s) as predominantly one or the other in addition to coding the severity level.

The Axis V rating in DSM-III did not consider psychological functioning. In DSM-III-R, Axis V is a new ninety-point scale that assesses psychological, social, and occupational and school functioning on a continuum ranging from good mental health to illness. Furthermore, in order to increase the value of Axis V for documenting the need for treatment and assessing prognosis, it has been proposed that both current functioning (at the time of evaluation) and highest level of functioning (for at least a few months) during the past year be coded.

Table 13-2 lists the DSM-III categories in the order in which they appear in DSM-III. The corresponding DSM-III-R categories are listed opposite their DSM-III equivalent.

It is beyond the scope of this chapter to comment systematically on all of the changes in DSM-III-R and to discuss the rationale for each proposed change. Therefore, this section highlights the changes that pertain only to disorders usually first evident in infancy, childhood, or adolescence.

Field trials based on several hundred children suggested that the diagnosis of attention deficit disorder without hyperactivity was hardly ever made (Hyler, Williams, & Spitzer, 1982). Therefore, this category was modified in the proposed changes and attention deficit, hyperactivity disorder will be grouped with conduct and oppositional disorders under the rubric of disruptive behavior disorders.

Some subdivisions of conduct disorder have been eliminated. The subtypes were judged to lack clinical usefulness and to be at odds with research findings. The revised criteria comprise a single index of symptoms selected to better describe the various manifestations of the disorder and to better identify young children with the disorder.

Avoidant disorder of childhood or adolescence was proposed for elimination since this condition has not been observed in clinical settings in the absence of another disorder. Overanxious disorder was also proposed for elimination since the revised adult category of generalized anxiety disorder was judged to be appropriate for children as well. Both were eventually retained, however.

Schizoid disorder of childhood or adolescence has been eliminated because, in clinical settings, a defect in the capacity to form social relationships has been observed only in the presence of other signs of psychopathology that suggest a pervasive developmental disorder.

The deletion of identity disorder was overruled in spite of the lack of studies or case reports since the publication of DSM-III supporting its validity.

The eating disorders have been further revised within the overall theme of

TABLE 13-2 Comparison of DSM-III and Proposed DSM-III-R Classifications of Childhood Disorders

DSM-III	*DSM-III-R*
Mental Retardation	Mental Retardation
Attention deficit disorder with hyperactivity	Attention deficit, hyperactivity disorder
Attention deficit disorder without hyperactivity	Undifferentiated attention deficit
Attention deficit disorder residual type	
Conduct disorder	Conduct disorder
undersocialized, aggressive	group type
undersocialized, nonaggressive	solitary aggressive type
socialized, aggressive	undifferentiated type
socialized, nonaggressive	Oppositional defiant disorder
atypical	
Anxiety Disorders of Childhood or Adolescence	
Separation anxiety disorder	Separation anxiety disorder
Avoidant disorder of childhood or adolescence	Avoidant disorder of childhood or adolescence
Overanxious disorder	Overanxious disorder
Other Disorders of Infancy, Childhood, or Adolescence	
Reactive attachment disorder of infancy	Reactive attachment disorder of infancy and early childhood
Schizoid disorder of childhood or adolescence	
Elective mutism	Elective mutism
Oppositional disorder	Identity disorder
Identity disorder	Stereotype/habit disorder
Eating Disorders	
Anorexia nervosa	Anorexia nervosa
Bulimia	Bulimia nervosa
Pica	Pica
Rumination disorder of infancy	Rumination disorder of infancy
Atypical eating disorder	Eating disorder NOS
Stereotyped Movement Disorders	Tic Disorders
Transient tic disorder	Transient tic disorder
	Specify: single episode or recurrent episode
Chronic motor tic disorder	Chronic motor or vocal tic disorder
Tourette's disorder	Tourette's disorder
Atypical tic disorder	Tic disorder, NOS
Atypical stereotyped movement disorder	
Other Disorders with Physical Manifestations	Speech Disorder Not Elsewhere Classified
Stuttering	Stuttering
Functional enuresis	Cluttering
Functional encopresis	Elimination Disorders:
Sleepwalking disorder	Functional encopresis
Sleep terror disorder	Functional enuresis
Pervasive Developmental Disorders	
Infantile autism	
Childhood onset pervasive developmental disorder	Autistic disorder
Atypical pervasive develomental disorder	Pervasive developmental disorder NOS

TABLE 13-2 (*Continued*)

DSM-III	DSM-III-R
Specific Developmental Disorders	Academic Skill Disorders:
Developmental reading disorder	Developmental reading disorder
Developmental arithmetic disorder	Developmental arithmetic disorder
Developmental language disorder	Developmental writing disorder
	Language and speech disorders:
	Developmental expressive language disorder
	Developmental receptive language disorder
Developmental articulation disorder	Developmental articulation disorder
Mixed specific developmental disorder	
	Motor skills disorder:
	Developmental coordination disorder
Atypical specific developmental disorder	Specific developmental disorder NOS
	Developmental disorder NOS

making these diagnoses less stringent and severe. The weight loss criterion of at least 25% of original body weight in anorexia nervosa has been found to be too restrictive. The revised criteria for bulimia specify a minimum frequency of binging episodes and have eliminated the requirement of depressed mood and self-deprecating thoughts following binges.

The tic disorders are grouped together and the criteria for each of the tic disorders have been extensively revised to reflect recent clinical and research experience that indicates that these conditions reflect varying manifestations of a single underlying disorder.

Pervasive developmental disorders are grouped together with mental retardation and specific developmental disorders. The distinction between pervasive developmental disorder and autism on the basis of age of onset in DSM-III was judged not to be valid. Therefore, these two categories have been modified in DSM-III-R with extensive revision of the criteria to constitute a more comprehensive description of the manifestations of the disorder at different ages. Developmental language disorder has been split into expressive language disorder and receptive language disorder, a distinction recognized in the DSM-III text.

INTERFACE OF PSYCHIATRY AND SPECIAL EDUCATION

It is readily apparent that the public schools and the mental health network interact extensively to serve children in special education programs with behavioral or developmental disorders (Berkovitz, 1980; Berkovitz & Sinclair, 1985; Stainback & Stainback, 1985). Yet, the different nomenclature and diagnostic criteria of the federal special education regulations and DSM-III often make effective communication between educators and mental health practitioners difficult (Sattler, 1983). Problems in reporting medical or psychiatric case findings, for example, have severely limited the relevancy of this type of clinical data in the development of school programs (Gottesman, Belmont, & Kaminer, 1975; Nichol, 1974). However, when systematic efforts are made to translate medical and psychiatric clinical findings into educationally relevant information, more successful school outcomes for behavioral disordered and developmentally disordered children appear likely (Forness & Barnes, 1981; Kellam, Branch, Agraval, & Ensminger, 1975).

Traditional psychoeducational evaluation of children with behavior and learning problems typically consists of developmental and school history, parent interview, intellectual and personality testing, teacher interview or observation of the child in the classroom, teacher rating or evaluation scales and, on increasingly frequent occasions, medical or psychiatric examination (Forness, 1983; Kazdin, 1983; Sinclair, Forness, & Alexson, 1985). However, even such a comprehensive evaluation as this has been shown to bear little direct relationship to actual classroom programming (Schenck, 1980; Sinclair, 1980; Sinclair & Alexson, 1987; Sinclair & Kheifets, 1982; Thurlow & Ysseldyke, 1982; Williams & Coleman, 1982).

Kazdin (1983) has, nonetheless, argued in favor of the inclusion of medical and psychiatric input by stating that certain educational or behavioral views of clinical disorders are unnecessarily restrictive and fail to address certain critical contextual factors of child problems that are detailed in medical and psychiatric reports. Child behavior therapists need to look at more than the elimination of certain target behaviors. Normative data as well as information regarding chronicity, onset, and severity are needed (Kazdin *et al.*, 1981).

Despite research that highlights the limitations of the interdisciplinary evaluation in relation to predicting classroom interventions (Gilliam, 1979; Gilliam & Coleman, 1981; Smith & Knoff, 1981; Turnbull, Strickland & Brantley, 1982; Yoshida, 1983; Ysseldyke, Algozzine, & Epps, 1983; Ysseldyke *et al.*, 1983), there is indeed a growing trend in special education to rely on other professional disciplines or agencies for assistance in the diagnostic process. For example, recent issues of special education journals have been substantially devoted to special symposia on the relationship of physicians to special education and interagency cooperation between public schools and health agencies (Guralnick, 1982; Martinson, 1982). Also, many studies have appeared on school children referred to clinic or hospital settings, supporting the usefulness of case information generated in these situations to school needs (Forness & Barnes, 1981; Forness, Barnes, & Mordaunt, 1983; Forness, Cronin & Lewis, 1981; Forness *et al.*, 1980; Rotberg *et al.*, 1982; Schour & Clements, 1974). Likewise, recent efforts are evident to increase communication between health or mental health professionals and schools (Forness, Sinclair, & Russell, 1984; Medway & Forman, 1980; Sandoval & Davis, 1984).

DSM-III AND SERIOUS EMOTIONAL DISTURBANCE

As previously stated, the special education category of serious emotional disturbance is currently the subject of much public debate regarding refinement and specification of guidelines for appropriate application of the label and appropriate placement of children for therapeutic educational services (Garrett & Brazil, 1979; Olsen, Algozzine, & Schmid, 1980; Raiser & Van Nagel, 1980; Wells *et al.*, 1980).

Slenkovich (1985) analyzed DSM-III against special education law and identified five definitional characteristics of the law as it applies to DSM-III diagnoses. (1) The student is so disturbed that he or she "cannot learn." (2) The student is so disturbed that he or she "cannot enter into relationships." (3) The student is so disturbed that he or she exhibits "psychotic or bizarre behavior." (4) The student is so disturbed that he or she exhibits "a heavy mood of depression." (5) The student is so disturbed that his or her symptoms must be the "outgrowth of an established emotional disturbance."

Slenkovich further argues that the criterion mentioned in the federal definition of "over a long period of time" means a minimum of six months in the case of schizophrenia and at least one year, and preferably two years, for other conditions. The criterion "to a marked degree" means "be observable" to anyone. Finally, the criterion "the condition must not constitute social maladjustment" is interpreted to mean that the child cannot be seriously emotionally disturbed if he or she is behavior disordered, conduct disordered, or antisocial unless he or she also has a diagnosed emotional condition.

The balance of Slenkovitch's is directly tied to DSM-III diagnoses. The primary thread that seems to run through this analysis is that those disorders with a major affective behavior component meet the definition (separation anxiety disorder, overanxious disorder, elective mutism, organic delusional syndrome, paranoid disorder, schizoaffective disorders, simple phobia, panic disorder, schizophrenia, and all major affective disorders). On the other hand, those disorders with a major social behavior component do not meet the definition. This work only underscores the importance of the current debate regarding the classification of serious emotional disturbance and whether the label should be changed to behavior disordered. The impact on services for emotionally disturbed and behavior disordered children would be considerably curtailed if these criteria were adopted.

In California, a recently proposed manual lists the five basic eligibility criteria now used to determine the diagnosis of serious emotional disturbance (i.e., inability to learn not due to sensory or intellectual impairments, problems in interpersonal relationships, inappropriate types of behavior or feelings under normal circumstances, pervasive depression, and physical symptoms or fears associated with school problems), and specifies the exact DSM-III diagnoses needed to determine the presence of the eligibility criteria (CASP, 1984). Note that only one of the five criteria needs to be met in order to satisfy the eligibility requirement. The apparent rationale for using DSM-III seems to be related to serious problems in reliability and validity found by both educators and psychologists in current classification systems for childhood disorders, as reviewed in other chapters of this text.

The Texas Educational Agency is examining the possibility of approving a set of classifications based on selected criteria from DSM-III to specify the type and severity of emotional disturbance (Tharinger, Laurent, & Best, 1986). In a recent questionnaire surveying Texas school psychologists' opinions on the federal seriously emotionally disturbed criteria for eligibility and DSM-III, 54% of the respondents viewed the federal criteria as inadequate and 67% viewed the inclusion of DSM-III criteria to specify type and severity of emotional disturbance as useful (Tharinger & Strocchia-Rivera, 1985).

Little empirical data is available to justify the inclusion of DSM-III psychiatric diagnoses for educational placement purposes (Bielat, Gingrich, Jensen, & Weissenburger, in press). In a series of studies examining the usefulness of psychiatric diagnosis as a predictive factor for school placement, it was found that the use of psychiatric diagnosis in conjunction with psychoeducational test data did not appreciably translate into specific educational placements any better than the use of psychoeducational test data alone (Sinclair, Forness, & Alexson, 1985; Sinclair & Alexson, 1987). A fourth study by the same researchers (Alexson & Sinclair, 1986) concluded that inpatients tended to be recommended to more restrictive or more segregated educational placements than outpatients, even when the two groups were matched for comparable psychiatric diagnoses. In other words, the study suggests that patient status has an impact on educational placement decisions disproportionate to the actual psychoeducational data. A fifth study (Sinclair & Alexson, in press) suggests that there may be a limited number of psychiatric diagnoses such as Axis II language disorders, which are predictive of placements in special education programs.

Previous research in this area also attempted to recategorize the Axis I and Axis II psychiatric diagnoses into fourteen diagnostic related groups, emphasizing the presence or absence of specific developmental disorders, that were thought to be more applicable to the task of predicting educational placements (Sinclair & Alexson, 1985). It was particularly noteworthy that in all of the case studies reviewed by these researchers (N = 350), not one psychotic or schizophrenic child was recommended to placement in a classroom for seriously emotionally disturbed children.

Although school personnel are not usually directly involved in making psychiatric diagnoses, they do have considerable contact or experience with psychiatric reports or consultation from psychiatrists and other mental health professionals, for whom these diagnoses are standard nomenclature (Johnson, McLaughlin, & Christensen, 1982). Table 13-3 presents a selected listing of the more common psychiatric disorders of children and adolescents along with the most likely special education categories for such disorders. The categories are presented in abbreviations commonly used by educators (here defined only briefly in a footnote to Table 13-3, since they are generally known and widely accepted).

Special education for children can be described by grouping programs into two general areas: special classes or schools, and mainstreaming arrangements. Special class or special school approaches are generally as follows: A residential institution for long-term custodial care, an acute psychiatric hospital for short-term

TABLE 13-3 Selected DSM-III Diagnostic Groups and Their Relationship to Special Education Diagnostic Categories

Selected DSM-III Diagnostic Group	*Special Education Diagnostic Category*
Mental Retardation	
Mild	EMR, ER
Moderate	TMR
Severe	TMR, DD
Profound	DD
Attention Deficit Disorder	
with Hyperactivity	BD, LD
without Hyperactivity	LD, BD, I
Environmental "V" Code	I
Conduct Disorder	
Aggressive	BD, I
Oppositional	BD, I
Autism	Autistic, SED, BD, SH, Aphasic
Pervasive Developmental Disorder	SED, BD, DD, SH
Specific Developmental Disorder	
Reading	LD
Arithmetic	LD
Language	Aphasia, SH, LD
Schizophrenic Disorders	SED, BD
Affective Disorders	BD, SED, LD, I

EMR = Educable Mentally Retarded
ER   = Educationally Retarded
TMR = Trainable Mentally Retarded
DD   = Developmentally Disabled
BD   = Behavior Disordered (also known as Educationally Handicapped)
LD   = Learning Disabled (also known as Educationally Handicapped)
I   = Ineligible (denotes children whose functioning in a school situation may not necessarily require special
        education or who may not be eligible for special education services under existing public laws.
Aphasic = Severe Communication Handicaps in Expressive or Receptive Language
Autistic = Early Childhood Autism
SED = Seriously Emotionally Disturbed
SH   = Speech or Language Handicapped

treatment, a special teacher to tutor the child at home on a daily basis, a residential school, a special day school, or placement in a special classroom in a regular school, either for the entire day or the better part of it. Although mainstreaming means different things to different professionals, there is some agreement that it is defined by two criteria. The mainstreamed child spends more than half the time in the regular classroom and the regular classroom teacher has the primary responsibility for the child's progress (MacMillan, Jones, & Meyers, 1976). The implication is that the child's learning handicaps or behavior problems are not so severe as to preclude their effective remediation in the regular classroom setting.

Criteria for considering whether or not to mainstream a particular child relate to such factors as the age of the child, the pervasiveness and degree of handicap, the curriculum modifications that might be needed, the child's peer relationships and social skills, the number of children in the regular classroom, teacher competency, and family resources (Forness, 1979). For more detailed descriptions of educational programs and teaching methods, the reader is referred to representative texts and research articles on the learning disabled (Bryan & Bryan, 1978; Miller & Sabatino, 1978; Sindelar & Deno, 1980) on the mildly retarded (Payne, Palloway, Smith, & Payne, 1977), on the severely and profoundly handicapped (Bender & Velletutti, 1976; Burton & Hirshoren, 1979; Sontag, 1977). A comparative description of programs for all types of handicapped children is provided by Hewett and Forness (1984) and by Kirk and Gallagher (1979).

In California, a number of class action lawsuits against various California school districts, such as *Arreola* v. *Board of Education* (1968), *Covarrubias* v. *San Diego United School District* (1971), *Diana* v. *State Board of Education* (1970), and *Larry P.* v. *Riles* (1972), have led to major changes in the policies on segregated special classes. The 1973 Riverside study on the mislabeling of minority students in classes for the educable mentally retarded resulted in massive retesting of these students, eventual decertification of an estimated 18,000 children in classes for the mildly retarded, and a limited two-year provision for transition assistance for these students upon their return to regular classrooms (MacMillan, 1982; Yoshida, MacMillan, & Meyers, 1976).

The outcome of the *Larry P.* case was to strike down the use of most IQ tests then used in California to decide diagnostic eligibility for the educable mentally retarded category of special education. This left psychologists without clear alternative measures to determine a referred student's potential against his or her functioning level because there was a lack of alternative flexible provisions in California at the time. As a result of this litigation on behalf of mildly retarded students, MacMillan, Meyers and Morrison (1980) have found that educable mentally retarded children in California's special classes now tend to be extremely disabled students with relatively little potential for mainstreaming.

It should be noted that there may be confusion between the special education designations of seriously emotionally disturbed, behavior disordered, educable mentally retarded, or learning disabled and the psychiatric use of these terms. For example, a child with an anxiety disorder might be seen by a psychiatrist as emotionally disturbed, although the child might present no serious problem in classroom management. A special educator, on the other hand, might term the same child behavior disordered rather than emotionally disturbed, since the former term frequently implies a less severe problem in classroom management (Skiba & Casey, 1985). Likewise, an attention deficit disorder may be seen as primarily a learning disability by a special education teacher, while a psychiatrist may consider it under the behavior disorder rubric. Educators in some states might still include a child with an IQ of 75 in their educable mentally retarded classification, while DSM-III no longer classifies borderline intellectual functioning (IQ 70 to 85) as a disorder but rather lists it under "conditions not attributable to a mental disorder" (p. 189).

Furthermore, a psychiatrist may be unable to diagnose a child as autistic under DSM-III unless several important distinctions can be made between the child's particular symptoms and those of other similar classifications (e.g., infantile autism or childhood onset pervasive developmental disorder). These distinctions may not be recognized as essential or necessary to the diagnosis of autism under public school definitions.

In a similar vein, a child may be diagnosed as retarded under DSM-III; but unless school personnel recognize that critical, related information is often recorded on other axes, they may fail to look for further data that are more critical to classroom placement or school management. On such occasions, school personnel may be faced with the problem of psychiatric reports or mental health consultations that are either difficult to reconcile with their own findings or lead them down unproductive diagnostic paths.

ROLE OF PSYCHIATRY IN EDUCATION

Should psychiatry and its allied mental health disciplines have a role in education? The authors believe the answer is yes but that they should not usurp the role of the school psychologist. The public schools are the only social institution in our society in a position to address the mental health needs of children on a large scale. Although attendance to other social institutions is not mandated or regulated, children must attend school. It is not necessary for children to go to church or to go to the doctor, but they must go to school between the ages of 6 and 16. Certainly, other agencies and organizations have been established to treat mental health problems. However, private mental health care is costly and community oriented clinics are usually limited to their resources and, thus, cannot effectively deal with large numbers of children.

Assuming that there *is* a role for psychiatry and its allied disciplines in education, then what should the role of the mental health practitioner be? An important role for psychiatrists, clinical psychologists, and related mental health professionals is in the provision of mental health consultation to teachers and school administrators. School psychologists are often busy in the assessment of children for special education. There are many children with primary emotional problems as well as primary learning problems in various special education programs. However, mental health issues are not only restricted to the special education population but affect the regular education population as well. There are children in regular education programs who experience transient emotional problems that are related to the environmental stresses in their lives. These emotional difficulties may affect their social and emotional functioning in the form of impaired peer relationships, impaired relationships with teachers, and loss of self-esteem. Academic achievement may be affected by the same emotional problems.

It seems that larger numbers of children are being treated with psychopharmacological agents to modify behavior that is disruptive in the classroom and detrimentally affecting their ability to learn in the classroom. Teachers need more input from psychiatrists concerning behavioral and cognitive expectations of children on medication. Furthermore, teachers are in a unique position to communicate with psychiatrists regarding behavioral and academic changes that may be affected by medication prescription.

It would seem that there is a more effective use of psychiatry and other mental health fields in school mental health intervention rather than school mental health diagnosis. Although identification of need, or diagnosis, is a necessary prerequisite to intervention, or delivery of services, overreliance on a particular diagnostic classification system such as DSM-III will undoubtedly limit needed services to children particularly in the emotionally disturbed and behavior disordered category of special education. Children in other eligibility categories of special education such as learning disabilities and mental retardation must meet prescribed guidelines that are heavily slanted toward a psychometric definition of eligibility. As previously stated, the special education category of serious emotional disturbance is in the greatest state of flux and the classification category that is looking toward psychiatry to help solve its definitional dilemma.

Special education and psychiatry as separate fields each possess a different diagnostic classification system that reflects the different treatment goals and methodologies inherent to each discipline. However, rather than being seen as testimony to the futility of interdisciplinary communication, the data presented herein should serve to remind special educators that cooperation between the two disciplines is only achieved through systematic effort in understanding each other's frame of reference.

The overall issue of the relationship between educational and psychiatric classification systems remains important. With increased participation of psychiatrists, clinical psychologists, psychiatric social workers, and others in the planning of school programs under new federal laws, there is more urgency for each profession to be familiar with the nomenclature of the other. However, it is not necessary to adopt the nomenclature of psychiatry for educational placement purposes.

Many public school districts have routinely begun to require psychiatric reports as part of their diagnostic procedures, particularly in the category of serious emotional disturbance. Whether this leads to more effective classroom programming for handicapped children remains to be seen. Previous research suggests that, with the exception of certain Axis II language disorders and specific developmental disorders, there has been little success in establishing satisfactory concordance between a particular child's DSM-III psychiatric diagnosis and the child's need for special education. DSM-III and DSM-III-R as school program classification systems have serious limitations that have not yet been resolved.

References

Achenbach, T. M. (1982). *Developmental psychopathology* (2d ed.). New York: John Wiley & Sons.

Achenbach, T. M., & Edelbrock, C. S. (1983). *Manual for the Child Behavior Checklist and Revised Child Behavior Profile.*

Adams, H. E., Doster, J. A., & Calhoun, K. S. (1977). A psychologically based system of response classification. In *Handbook of behavioral assessment* (vol. 1.) New York: John Wiley & Sons.

Alexson, J., & Sinclair, E. (1986). Psychiatric diagnosis and school placement: A comparison between inpatients and outpatients. *Child Psychiatry and Human Development, 16,* 194–205.

American Psychiatric Association (1952). *DSM-I: Diagnostic and Statistical Manual of Mental Disorders.* Washington, D.C.: American Psychiatric Association.

American Psychiatric Association (1968). *DSM-II: Diagnostic and Statistical Manual of Mental Disorders.* Washington, D.C.: American Psychiatric Association.

American Psychiatric Association (1980). *DSM-III: Diagnostic and Statistical Manual of Mental Disorders.* Washington, D.C.: American Psychiatric Association.

American Psychiatric Association (1987). *DSM-III-R: Diagnostic and Statistical Manual of Mental Disorders* (Third edition—revised). Washington, D.C.: American Psychiatric Association.

Arreola v. Board of Education (1968). Case 160-577 (Superior Court, Orange County, Calif.).

Bateman, B. (1965). An educator's view of a diagnostic approach to learning disorders. In J. Hellmuth (Ed.), *Learning disorders* (Vol. 1). Seattle, Wash.: Special Child Publications.

Becker, L. D. (1978). Learning characteristics of educationally handicapped and retarded children. *Exceptional Children, 44,* 502–511.

Bender, M., & Valletutti, P. J. (1976). *Teaching the moderately and severely handicapped: Curriculum objectives, strategies, and activities* (Vols. 1–3). Baltimore, Md.: University Park Press.

Berk, R. A. (1982). Effectiveness of discrepancy score methods for screening children with learning disabilities. *Learning Disabilities: An Interdisciplinary Journal, 1,* 11–24.

Berkovitz, I. H. (1980). School intervention: Case management and school mental health consultation. In P. Schovelar, R. Bensen, & B. H. Blinder (Eds.), *Emotional disorders of children and adolescents* (pp. 501–520). New York: Spectrum.

Berkovitz, I. H., & Sinclair, E. (1985). Teaching child psychiatrists about intervention in school systems. *Journal of Psychiatric Education, 8,* 240–245.

Bielat, B., Gingrich, D., Jensen, B., & Weissenburger, F. (in press). In F. H. Wood, C. Smith, & J. Grimes (Eds.), *Iowa model for assessment in behavioral disorders.* Des Moines, Iowa: Iowa Department of Public Instruction.

Bower, E. M. (1960). *Early identification of emotionally handicapped children in school.* Springfield, Ill.: Charles C. Thomas.

Bryan, T. H., & Bryan, J. H. (1978). *Understanding learning disabilities* (2d ed.). Sherman Oaks, Calif.: Alfred.

Burton, T. A., & Hiroshoren, A. (1979). The education of severely and profoundly retarded children: Are we sacrificing the child to the concept? *Exceptional Children, 45,* 598–602.

California Association of School Psychologists (1984). Educational and diagnostic manual for the SED student: The background and participants. *CASP Today,* September issue. pp. 1–3.

Cantwell, D. P., Mattison, R., Russell, A. T., & Will, L. A. (1979). Comparison of DSM-II and DSM-III in the diagnosis of childhood psychiatric disorders, IV: Difficulties in use, global comparison, and conclusions. *Archives of General Psychiatry, 36,* 1227–1228.

Cone, T.E., & Wilson, L. R. (1981). Quantifying a severe discrepancy: A critical analysis. *Learning Disability Quarterly, 4,* 359–371.

Covarrubias v. San Diego Unified School District (1971). Civil action 70-30d (San Diego, Calif.).

Cruickshank, W. M. (1972). Some issues facing the field of learning disability. *Journal of Learning Disabilities, 5,* 380–388.

Cullinan, D., Epstein, M. H., & Lloyd, J. (1981). School behavior problems of learning disabled and normal girls and boys. *Learning Disability Quarterly, 4,* 163–169.

Danielson, L. C., & Bauer, N. J. (1978). A formula based classification of learning disabled children: An examination of the issues. *Journal of Learning Disabilities, 11,* 163–176.

Diana v. State Board of Education (1970). Civil Action 70-37 (RFP Dist. N. Calif.).

Doll, E. A. (1941). The essentials of an inclusive concept of mental deficiency. *American Journal of Mental Deficiency, 46,* 214–219.

Engels, M., Ghadirian, A. M., & Dongier, M. (1983). DSM-III in Canada: The viewpoint of academic psychiatrists. In R. L. Spitzer, J. B. W. Williams, & A. E. Skodol (Eds.), *International perspectives on DSM-III* (pp. 135–143). Washington, D.C.: American Psychiatric Press.

Epstein, M. H., Cullinan, D., & Sabatino, D. S. (1977). State definitions of behavior disorders. *Journal of Special Education, 11,* 417–425.

Federal Register (1977). 42-163, pp. 42474–42518.

Forness, S. R. (1979). Clinical criteria for mainstreaming mildly handicapped children. *Psychology in the Schools, 16,* 508–514.

Forness, S. R. (1983). Diagnostic schooling for children or adolescents with behavior disorders. *Behavioral Disorders, 8,* 176–190.

Forness, S. R., & Barnes, T. R. (1981). School follow-up of adolescents treated in a psychiatric hospital. *Child Psychiatry and Human Development, 11,* 179–185.

Forness, S. R., Barnes, T. R., & Mordaunt, J. (1983). Brief psychiatric hospitalization: A study of its effect on special education placement. *Monographs in Behavioral Disorders, 61,* 66–75.

Forness, S. R., & Cantwell, D. P. (1982). DSM-III psychiatric diagnosis and special education categories. *Journal of Special Education, 6* 49–63.

Forness, S. R., Cronin, C., & Lewis, L. (1981). Prediction of postdischarge school adjustment from social and academic gains made during psychiatric hospitalization. *Monographs in Behavioral Disorders, 4,* 70–77.

Forness, S. R., Sinclair, E., & Guthrie, D. (1983). Learning disability discrepancy formulas: Their use in actual practice. *Learning Disability Quarterly, 6,* 107–114.

Forness, S. R., Sinclair, E., & Russell, A. T. (1984). Serving children with emotional or behavioral disorders: Implications for educational policy. *American Journal of Orthopsychiatry, 54,* 22–32.

Forness, S. R., Urbano, R., Rotberg, J., Bender, M., Gardner, R., Lynch, E., & Zemanek, D. (1980). Identifying children with school learning and behavior problems served by interdisciplinary clinics and hospitals. *Child Psychiatry and Human Development, 11,* 67–78.

Garber, J. (1984). Classification of childhood psychopathology: A developmental perspective. *Child Development, 55,* 30–48.

Garrett, J. E., & Brazil, N. (1979). Categories used for identification and education of exceptional children. *Exceptional Children, 45,* 282–292.

Gilliam, J. E. (1979). Contributions and status rankings of educational planning committee participants. *Exceptional Children, 45,* 466–468.

Gilliam, J. E., & Coleman, M. C. (1981). Who influences IEP committee decisions? *Exceptional Children, 47* 642–644.

Gottesman, R., Belmont, I., & Kaminer, J. (1975). Admission and follow-up status of reading disabled children referred to medical clinics. *Journal of Learning Disabilities, 8,* 642–650.

Grossman, H. J. (Ed.). (1983). *Manual on terminology and classification in mental retardation.* Washington, D.C.: American Association on Mental Deficiency.

Guralnick, M. J. (1982). Pediatrics, special education, and handicapped children: New relationships. *Exceptional Children, 4 8,* 294–295.

Hammill, D. D. (1974). Learning disabilities: A problem in definition. *Division for Children with Learning Disabilities Newsletter, 4,* 28–31.

Hammill, D. D., Leigh, J., McNutt, G., & Larsen, S. (1981). A new definition of learning disabilities. *Learning Disability Quarterly, 4,* 836–842.

Harris, S. L., & Ferrari, M. (1983). Developmental factors in child behavior therapy. *Behavior Therapy, 14,* 54–72.

Hewett, F., & Forness, S. R. (1984). *Education of exceptional learners* (3d ed.). Boston: Allyn & Bacon.

Hewett, F., & Taylor, F. (1980). *Emotionally disturbed child in the classroom* (2d ed.). Boston: Allyn & Bacon.

Huntze, S. L. (1985). A position paper of the Council for Children with Behavioral Disorders. *Behavioral Disorders*, 5, 167–174.

Hyler, R. E., Williams, J. B. W., & Spitzer, R. L. (1982). Reliability in the DSM-III field trials. *Archives of General Psychiatry*, 39, 1275–1278.

International Classification of Diseases (9th rev.). (1980). Washington, D.C.: U.S. Department of Health and Human Services.

Johnson, J. A. (1981). The etiology of hyperactivity. *Exceptional Children*, 47, 348–354.

Johnson, J. W., McLaughlin, J., & Christensen, M. (1982). Interagency collaboration: Driving and restraining forces. *Exceptional Children*, 48, 395–399.

Kazdin, A. E. (1983). Psychiatric diagnosis, dimensions of dysfunction, and child behavior therapy. *Behavior Therapy*, 32, 127–131.

Kazdin, A. E., Matson, J. L., & Esveldt-Dawson, K. (1981). Social skill performance among normal and psychiatric inpatient children as a function of assessment conditions. *Behaviour Research and Therapy*, 19, 145–152.

Kellam, S. G., Branch, J. B., Agraval, K. C., & Ensminger, M. E. (1975). *Mental health and going to school*. Chicago: University of Chicago Press.

Kendall, R. E. (1984). Reflections of psychiatric classification for the architects of DSM-IV and ICD-10. *Journal of Integrative Psychiatry*, 2, 43–47.

Keogh, B. K., & Margolis, J. (1976). Learn to labor and wait: Attentional problems of children with learning disabilities. *Journal of Learning Disabilities*, 9, 276–286.

Kirk, S.A. (1962). *Educating exceptional children*. Boston: Houghton Mifflin.

Kirk, S.A., & Gallagher, J. J. (1979). *Educating exceptional children* (3d ed.). Boston: Houghton Mifflin.

Larry P v. Riles (1972). USLW 2033 (US June 21).

MacMillan, D. L. (1982). *Mental retardation in school and society* (2d. ed.). Boston: Little, Brown.

MacMillan, D. L., Jones, R., & Meyers, C. E. (1976). Mainstreaming the mentally retarded: Questions, cautions, and guidelines. *Mental Retardation*, 14, 3–10.

MacMillan, D. L., Meyers, C. E., & Morrison, G. (1980). System identification of mildly mentally retarded children: Implications for interpreting and conducting research. *American Journal of Mental Deficiency*, 85, 108–115.

Martinson, M. C. (1982). Interagency services: A new era for an old idea. *Exceptional Children*, 48, 389–394.

Mattis, S. (1978). Dyslexia syndromes: A working hypothesis that works. In A. Benton & D. Pearl (eds.), *Dyslexia: An appraisal of current knowledge*. New York: Oxford University Press.

Mattison, R., Cantwell, D. P., Russell, A. T., & Will, L. (1979). A comparison of DSM-II and DSM-III in the diagnosis of childhood psychiatric disorders. *Archives of General Psychiatry*, 36, 1217–1222.

McIntosh, D., & Dunn, L. (1973). Children with major specific learning disabilities. In L. Dunn (Ed.), *Exceptional children in the schools: Special education in transition* (2d ed.). New York: Holt, Rinehart & Winston.

McGinnis, E., Kiraly, J., & Smith, C. R. (1985). The types of data used in identifying public school students as behaviorally disordered. *Behavioral Disorders*, 5, 239–246.

McKinney, J. D., & Feagans, L. (1983). Adaptive classroom behavior of learning disabled students. *Journal of Learning Disabilities*, 16, 360–367.

Medway, F. J., & Forman, S. G. (1980). Psychologist's and teacher's reaction to mental health and behavioral school consultation. *Journal of School Psychology*, 18, 338–348.

Mercer, C. D., Forgnone, C., & Wolking, W.D. (1976). Definitions of learning disabilities used in the United States. *Journal of Learning Disabilities*, 9, 376–386.

Mercer, C. D., Hughes, C., & Mercer, A. R. (1985). Learning disabilities definitions used by state education departments. *Learning Disability Quarterly*, 8, 45–54.

Mezzich, J. E. (1980). Multiaxial diagnostic systems in psychiatry. In H. I. Kaplan, A. M. Freedman, &

B. J. Saddock (Eds.), Comprehensive textbook of psychiatry (3d ed. pp. 1072–1079). Baltimore, MD.: Williams & Wilkins.

Miller, T. L., & Sabatino, D. A. (1978). An evaluation of the teacher consultant model as an approach to mainstreaming. *Exceptional Children, 45,* 86–91.

Myers, P. I., & Hammill, D. D. (1976). *Methods for learning disorders* (2d. ed.). New York: John Wiley & Sons.

National Advisory Committee on Handicapped Children (1968). *First annual report, special education for handicapped.* Washington, D.C.: U.S. Office of Education, Department of Health, Education and Welfare.

Nichol, H. (1974). Children with learning disabilities referred to psychiatrists: A follow-up study. *Journal of Learning Disabilities, 7,* 118–122.

O'Donnell, L. E. (1980). Intra-individual discrepancy in diagnosing specific learning disabilities. *Learning Disability Quarterly, 3,* 10–18.

Olsen, J. Algozzine, B., & Schmid, E. (1980). Mild, moderate, and severe EH: An empty distinction? *Behavioral Disorders, 5,* 96–101.

Payne, J. S., Palloway, E. A., Smith, J. E., & Payne, R. A. (1977). *Strategies for teaching the mentally retarded.* Columbus, Ohio: Charles E. Merrill.

Quay, H. C. (1979). Classification. In H. C. Quay & J. S. Werry (Eds.), *Psychopathological disorders of childhood* (2d ed. pp. 1–42). New York: John Wiley & Sons.

Raiser, L., & Van Nagel, C. (1980). The loopholes in Public Law 94-142. *Exceptional Children, 46,* 516–520.

Rotberg, J., Forness, S. R., Lynch, E., Gardner, T., Urbano, R., & Bender, M. (1982). Status of interagency cooperation between interdisciplinary clinics and hospitals and the public schools. *Child Psychiatry and Human Development, 12,* 1–7.

Rutter, M. (1970). Psychiatry. In J. Wortis (Ed.), *Mental retardation: An annual review* (Vol. 3). New York: Grune & Stratton.

Rutter, M., & Shaffer, D. (1980). DSM-III: A step forward or back in terms of the classification of child psychiatric disorders? *Journal of the American Academy of Child Psychiatry, 19,* 371–394.

Rutter, M., Shaffer, D., & Shepherd, M. (1973). An evaluation of the proposal for a multi-axial classification of child psychiatric disorders. *Psychological Medicine, 3,* 244–250.

Sandoval, J., & Davis, J. M. (1984). A school-based mental health consultation curriculum. *Journal of School Psychology, 22,* 31–43.

Sattler, J. M. (1983). Identifying and classifying disturbed children in the schools: Issues and procedures for school psychologists. *School Psychology Review, 4,* 384–390.

Schenck, S. J. (1980). The diagnostic/instructional link in individualized education programs. *Journal of Special Education, 14,* 337–345.

Schools should provide mental health services. BEH Proposes. (1980). *Education of the Handicapped: The Independent Bi-weekly News Service on Federal Legislation, Programs, and Funding for Special Education,* p. 1.

Schour, M., & Clemens, R. L. (1974). Rate of recommendations for children with school-related problems following interdisciplinary evaluation. *Behavioral Pediatrics, 84,* 903–907.

Sinclair, E. (1980). Relationship of psychoeducational diagnosis to educational placement. *Journal of School Psychology, 18,* 349–353.

Sinclair, E., & Alexson, J. (1985). Creating diagnostic related groups: A manageable way to deal with DSM-III: *American Journal of Orthopsychiatry, 55,* 426–433.

Sinclair, E., & Alexson, J. (1986). Learning disability discrepancy formulas: Similarities and differences among them. *Learning Disability Research, 1,* 112–118.

Sinclair, E., & Alexson, J. (1987). Factor analysis and discriminant analysis of psychoeducational report contents. *Journal of School Psychology, 24,* 363–371.

Sinclair, E., & Alexson, J. (in press). Characteristics of language disordered children in a psychiatric population. *Child Psychiatry and Human Development.*

Sinclair, E., Forness, S. R., & Alexson, J. (1985). Psychiatric diagnosis: A study of its relationship to school needs. *Journal of Special Education, 19,* 333–343.

Sinclair, E., & Kheifets, L. (1982). Use of clustering techniques in deriving psychoeducational profiles. *Contemporary Educational Psychology, 7,* 81–89.

Sindelar, R., & Deno, S. (1978). The effectiveness of resource programming. *Journal of Special Education, 12,* 17–28.

Skiba, R., & Casey, A. (1985). Interventions for behaviorally disordered students: A quantitative review and methodological critique. *Behavioral Disorders, 10,* 239–252.

Slenkovich, J. E. (1985). PL 94-142 as applied to DSM-III diagnoses: An analysis of DSM-III diagnoses vis-a-vis special education law. *Behavioral Disorders, 10,* 305–307.

Smith, C., Wood, F. H., & Grimes, J. (1985). *Issues in identification and placement of emotionally disturbed/behavior disordered students.* Report for Project on National Research Integration of Selected Issues in Education of Handicapped Children. Pittsburgh: University of Pittsburgh, Learning Research and Development Center.

Smith, C. R., & Knoff, H. M. (1981). School psychology and special education students' placement decisions: IQ still tips the scale. *Journal of Special Education, 15,* 55–64.

Sontag, E. (1977). *Educational programming for the severely and profoundly handicapped.* Reston, Va.: Council for Exceptional Children.

Spitzer, R. L., & Cantwell, D. P. (1980). The DSM-III classification of the psychiatric disorders of infancy, childhood, and adolescence. *Journal of the American Academy of Child Psychiatry, 19,* 356–370.

Spitzer, R. L., Forman, J. B. W., & Nee, J. (1979). DSM-III field trials, I: Initial interrater diagnostic reliability. *American Journal of Psychiatry, 136,* 815–817.

Stainback, W., & Stainback, S. (1985). A rationale for the merger of special and regular education. *Exceptional Children, 51,* 102–111.

Strawser, S., & Weller, C. (1985). Use of adaptive behavior and discrepancy criteria to determine learning disabilities severity subtypes. *Journal of Learning Disabilities, 18,* 205–212.

Strober, M., Green, J., & Carlson, G. (1981). The reliability of psychiatric diagnosis in hospitalized adolescents: Interrater agreement using the DSM-III. *Archives of General Psychiatry, 38,* 141–145.

Tharinger, D. J., Laurent, J., & Best, L. R. (1986). Classification of children referred for emotional and behavioral problems: A comparison of PL 94-142 SED criteria, DSM-III, and the CBCL system. *Journal of School Psychology, 24,* 111–121.

Tharinger, D., & Strocchia-Rivera, L. (1985). DSM-III in the schools: What school psychologists think. Unpublished manuscript. Austin, Tex.: Universty of Texas at Austin.

Thurlow, M. L., & Ysseldyke, J. E. (1982). Instructional planning: Information collected by school psychologists vs. information considered useful by teachers. *Journal of School Psychology, 20,* 31–40.

Turnbull, A. P., Strickland, B., & Brantley, J. Q. (1982). *Developing and implementing individualized education programs* (2d ed.). Columbus, Ohio: Charles E. Merrill.

U.S. Office of Education (1968). *First annual report of National Advisory Committee on Handicapped Children.* Washington, D.C.: U.S. Department of Health, Education, and Welfare.

U.S. Office of Education (1976). Education of handicapped children: Assistance to states: Proposed rulemaking. *Federal Register, 41,* 52404–52407.

U.S. Office of Education (1981). Education of handicapped children: Assistance to states. *Federal Register, 46,* 3866.

Wells, D., Stoller, L., Schmid, R., & Algozzine, B. (1980). Trends in definitions for emotionally handicapped or learning disabled adolescents. In R. B. Rutherford, A. Prieto, & J. E. McGlothlin (Eds.), *Severe behavior disorders of children and youth* (Vol. 3, pp. 95–105). Reston, Va.: Council for Children with Behavior Disorders.

Williams, J. B. W. (1985a). The multiaxial system of DSM-III: Where did it come from and where should it go? I. *Archives of General Psychiatry, 42,* 175–180.

Williams, J. B. W. (1985b). The multiaxial system of DSM-III: Where did it come from and where should it go? II. *Archives of General Psychiatry, 42,* 181–186.

Williams, R., & Coleman, M. (1982). A follow-up study of psychoeducational recommendations. *Journal of Learning Disabilities, 15*, 95–105.

Williams, J. B. W., & Spitzer, R. L. (1982). DSM-III forum: Focusing on DSM-III's multiaxial system. *Hospital and Community Psychiatry, 33*, 891–892.

Wood, F. (1985). Issues in the identification and placement of behaviorally disordered students. *Behavioral Disorders*, 219–228.

Yoshida, R. K. (1983). Are multidisciplinary teams worth the investment? *School Psychology Review, 12*, 137–143.

Yoshida, R. K., MacMillan, D. L., & Meyers, C. E. (1976). The decertification of minority group EMR students. In Jones (Ed.), *Mainstreaming and the minority child*, (pp. 215–233). Minneapolis, Minn.: University of Minnesota, Leadership Training Institute.

Ysseldyke, J. E., Algozzine, B., & Epps, S. (1983). A logical and empirical analysis of current practice in classifying students as handicapped. *Exceptional Children, 50*, 160–166.

Ysseldyke, J. E., Thurlow, M., Graden, J., Wesson, C., Algozzine, B., & Deno, S. (1983). Generalizations from five years of research on assessment and decision making: The University of Minnesota Institute. *Exceptional Education Quarterly, 4*, 75–93.

Zabel, R. H., Peterson, R. L., Smith, C. R., & White, M. S. (1981). Placement and reintegration information for emotionally disabled students. In F. H. Wood (Ed.), *Perspectives for a new decade*. Reston, Va.: Council for Exceptional Children.

Author Index

Italics indicate reference citation.

Subject Index